[illegible] p 439 note

EXPOSITORY LECTURES

ON THE

EPISTLE TO THE EPHESIANS.

BY THE

REV. ROBERT J. M'GHEE, A.M., M.R.I.A.

LATE MINISTER OF HAROLD'S CROSS CHURCH, DUBLIN

RECTOR OF HOLYWELL CUM NEEDINGWORTH, HUNTS.

NEW YORK:

ROBERT CARTER & BROTHERS,

No. 530 BROADWAY.

1857.

DEDICATION

TO THE

RIGHT HON. THE EARL OF RODEN, K.S.P.,

&c., &c., &c.

MY DEAR LORD,

Various are the motives which influence men in the dedication of their Works. Sometimes it is from a conviction that the Person to whom their Work is inscribed takes a warm interest in the cause in which it is written. Or, it may be, that he is eminently distinguished in knowledge and attainment on the subject of which it treats; and that, therefore, his judgment and approval are highly appreciated and prized by the Public, as well as by the Author. Or, the Writer may consider, that the sanction of a venerated name must reflect an honor on his book. Or, perhaps he may select this as a mode in which he desires to express the feelings of respect and grateful affection to a revered and distinguished friend.

These motives, which, in various degrees and modifications, may dictate other Dedications, so combine to induce me to inscribe this Work to your Lordship, that I know not to which of them, I could ascribe a preponderating influence.

To those which relate to your Lordship, I could not adequately or truly advert, without inflicting a wound on the individual whom I desire to honor.

As to those in which I am myself concerned:—While I trust I can truly say, that I desire not to seek any Patron for this work, but HIM, whose Blessed Word, it is a very weak and unworthy effort to expound—and that I desire to commit it to Him, to bless and direct its circulation, as far as, through His grace, it may conduce to the promotion of His glory, and the edification and salvation of souls—yet, I may be allowed to add, that there is not a Layman in the Church of England, on whose opinion, as to its sound and Scriptural fidelity, I should more confidently rely; and by whose approbation of it, I should feel more truly gratified and honored, than by that of ONE, to whose judgment and advice, on subjects of the gravest moment, I have felt so often and so deeply indebted—whose kindness and affection I have been permitted, for nearly half of my life, to feel as one of its greatest privileges, and best enjoyments; and in whom I have found, all that could be included in the truest, highest sense of that sacred name—A FRIEND.

These Lectures in fact, owe their existence to your Lordship—as they had never been delivered, if you had not erected the Infant School-house at Bray.

To your Lordship, then, with the sincere hope, that you may consider them true, though so inadequate to the mighty subject; and Scriptural, though alas! so very defective and unworthy—permit me to inscribe them, as an humble testimony of that grateful respect, and sincere affection, with which I am,

My Dear Lord,
Your Lordship's
Most Obliged and Faithful,
R. J. M'GHEE.

PREFACE.

THE Author would think it in some degree presumptuous to present the following Lectures to the Public without a few words of apology, or at least excuse, for their many defects and redundancies, of which he is fully conscious. He need not deprecate criticism upon them as literary compositions, from those who know the circumstances which led to their delivery and publication; but as they are now submitted to a more extended tribunal, he thinks it due to the importance of the subjects on which they treat, to account for the existence of many faults which he might be supposed to have been able by care and labor to have corrected.

Having been precluded by ill health for many years from parochial duty, although willing to work according to his ability, he undertook to deliver a weekly lecture in the Infant School-House at Bray, near which place he resided, and after proceeding through an exposition of the Epistle to the Romans, he commenced the following course:

The Lectures were delivered quite extemporaneously, without any other preparation than sincere prayer, that God would be graciously pleased to bless His own Word, plainly and simply expounded, to the instruction and edification of those who attended, and they were preserved as delivered, by a Reporter whom the Congregation assembled there, kindly employed to take them down.

Since the Author's subsequent restoration to health and engagement in official duty, time was not afforded him to prepare them however imperfectly for the press, and therefore this Work, though frequently called for, has been unavoidably delayed.

Under these circumstances the Author does not desire to incur the charge of obtruding himself on the public in general, with self-sufficient presumption as a Commentator on the Scriptures; he rather offers his book as a tribute due to those, who considering the Lectures profitable to themselves when delivered, subscribed to preserve them, and (doubtless with indulgent partiality) encouraged and urged their Publication.

These Lectures, therefore, consist of a very plain, unadorned exposition of that Apostolical Epistle, which next to those addressed to the Romans and the Hebrews, may be said to comprehend the fullest scope of Divine truth of any in the New Testament. There are not any vital doctrines which are not fully developed or implied, nor any precepts which are not enforced in the Epistle to the Ephesians, and which must not be consequently treated of, in any consistent Scriptural exposition of it. It has been the anxious desire of the Writer to adhere with the closest simplicity to the letter of the text. He can conscientiously say, that according to the best of his judgment, he has not strained a single verse or a single word to support any opinion of his own,—or of any other man,—or of any party,—nor has he attempted to force a single expression, to maintain any system derived from human authority. He has not endeavored to press the Scriptures into the principles of his exposition—but he trusts he can say with truth, that he has endeavored throughout, that the principles of the exposition should simply follow the Scriptures. He has not tried to make the Bible support the doctrines of our Church,—but he can say with honest truth, he finds the doctrines of our Church, in the plain letter of the Bible.

He does not accord with the opinion which is frequently expressed and written, that we cannot find a system in the Sacred Volume. He is fully satisfied that there is a perfect system in the Word, as well as in the Works of God; and that the laws that rule the Planets in their orbits, are not more accurately ordered in their influences and operations, than are all the plans, principles, and movements, of that mighty moral government, which is developed in the Word of Truth—all the course of that "everlasting covenant" which is "ordered in all things and sure."

It is true, that in the lofty heights and wondrous depths of the eternal Word, as in the mighty altitudes and profundities of nature, we find that we have neither instruments adequate to measure the height, nor lines to fathom the depth; and so far we must in many things await in humility and patience, the full development of those truths which we have not the means or power to comprehend—but we can advance so far in the knowledge of the system of eternal truth, that we can be sure and confident as of our existence, of the certainty of the truth we have attained; and we do not fear, in its clear and practical application, to maintain it against the sophistries of those errors that are inconsistent with, or oppose it.

We can tell the right ascension or declination of a star, though we cannot measure the angle of its orb, or calculate its distance from our sphere. We can steer with firm hearts and joyful hope, under the blessing of God, over the bosom of the deep, though we cannot fathom the depths of the abyss beneath us.

There are truths in the system of redemption, bright as the stars, yea, brighter than the orb of day; fixed as these luminaries in the firmament, and firmer than the boundaries of the fathomless ocean, on which the soul can fix its gaze with as perfect certainty, as we can see the lights that rule the day or the night, and on which it can rest with as fearless security, as we stand upon the mightiest rock that mocks the advances of the rolling billows.

Of these truths there is one which stands in the Sacred Word—the fundamental basis of Christianity.—That Christ, our glorious Redeemer, is the Alpha and Omega of man's salvation—that every sinner that shall ever enter into the gates of eternal life must enter by the righteousness and atoning blood of a crucified Saviour, through faith, and not by his own works or deservings, in whole or in part.

This sacred truth—with those that are dependent on it, and implied in it, is largely treated of in this Epistle. "Salvation to our God which sitteth upon the throne and unto the Lamb" is the theme of joy and inspired instruction to the Church on earth, as it is her song in glory. And those who tell us that there is no system in the Scriptures, but help to undermine the confidence of truth and faith, and to encourage the presumption of ignorance and error—to transfer the dependence of the heart from the unerring oracles of God, to the wavering opinions of men, varying between the extremes of sceptical latitudinarianism and drivelling superstition.

Those indeed who set up a system of their own, or of a party, or a Church, into which they endeavor to compress the revealed will and mind of God, will find no system, if they mean their own system, in the Bible. But those who through Divine Grace are enabled to cast their souls with confidence on their Master's truth, as far as it is fully revealed to them in His word, and to wait in patient humility, for clearer knowledge, on those deeper subjects, or less clearly revealed truths, or seeming inconsistencies which as yet they know not, can rejoice in the light that shines in the system of eternal truth, with as full a confidence in all its great realities, its Divine perfections, and its unerring laws, as a man can bask in the beams and warmth of the noonday sun, without knowing the laws and properties of light, or troubling himself when he hears of the spots upon the solar disc, on which learned Astronomers may please to differ and debate.

The Manna from heaven was given for food and not for chemical analysis. —"*The Living Bread that cometh down from heaven, and giveth life unto the world,*" was given to support, to nourish, and to save; and not to supply a subject for vain and speculative theories.

How satisfying is the Gospel to the soul, when the weary and heavy laden sinner comes to Christ for refuge! How sweet the green pastures of the Fields of Promise, when the soul lies down to repose and ruminate in them, beneath the watchful eye of her Shepherd!

"*I know in whom I have believed,*" is the language of the Apostle—but it may be that of every sinner who believes the Gospel of Christ, with as much confidence as it was that of St. Paul. Christ being the object of hope for both through the Spirit, is as worthy of the confidence of one, as of the other. "*The same Lord over all is rich unto all them that call upon him.*" Rom. x. 12. "*Henceforth,*" saith the Apostle, "*there is laid up for me a crown of righteousness, which the Lord the righteous Judge shall give to me in that day, and not to me only, but unto all them also that love his appearing.*" 2 Tim. iv. 8. All who with the Apostle look to Christ as "*the end of the law for righteousness to every one that believeth,*" Rom. x. 4,—all who with him trust that "*being now justified by his blood we shall be saved from wrath through him,*" Rom. v. 9, and therefore, who "*love his appearing;*" may look with joyful hope like the Apostle to a crown of righteousness.

Here is the rest of those who look for "*a kingdom which cannot be moved.*" Here the solid repose of the heart, which has Christ for its refuge and His purchased inheritance for its home. It is this alone that can enable the soul to adopt the language of the Psalmist as its joyful song—"*God is our refuge and strength, a very present help in trouble; therefore will we not fear, though the earth be removed, and though the mountains be carried into the midst of the sea, and though the waters thereof roar and be troubled, and though the mountains shake with the swelling thereof. There is a river, the streams whereof shall make glad the city of God, the holy place of the tabernacle of the most high. God is in the midst of her, therefore shall she not be moved; God shall help her, and that right early.*" Psal. xlvi. 1—5. It is this, which in that great and dreadful day when this scene of terror shall be realized at the coming of the Son of Man—when "*The kings of the earth, and the great men, and the rich men, and the chief captains, and the mighty men, and every bond-man, and every freeman shall hide themselves in the dens and in the rocks of the mountains, and shall say to the mountains and rocks, Fall on us, and hide us from the face of him that sitteth upon the throne, and from the wrath of the Lamb, for the great day of his wrath is come, and who shall be able to stand?"* Rev. vi. 15, 16, 17,—it is this that shall then enable the believer to lift up his head with joy and triumph, and to cry, "*Lo, this is our God, we have waited for him, and he will save us. This is the Lord, we have waited for him; we will be glad and rejoice in his salvation.*" Isa. xxv. 9.

This is indeed that "*hope that maketh not ashamed,*" when Christ is known as "*The Way, the Truth, and the Life,*" as the Foundation of Hope—the Source of Consolation—the Rock of Trust—when He gives peace to the conscience, and comfort to the heart,—when faith in our blessed Redeemer, brings salvation to the soul, and love to Him becomes the mainspring and motive of the conduct, making our duty our pleasure, and teaching us to feel that the service of our God, is indeed "perfect freedom."

These blessed truths, which are so fully comprehended within the scope of this Epistle, are alas! very imperfectly and unworthily treated in the Exposition. But if the Author may be permitted to express a general opinion, he would observe, that detailed expositions of the sacred Scriptures, appear to be the most useful and important religious works, that can be published or studied in the present day.

The best must be indeed defective in exposition of the fulness of truth. But if they are sincere and simple as far as they go, they may serve to guard the mind under the Divine blessing, against the pertinacious, and persevering perversities of error. Many modern works, as those of Papal and Tractarian subtlety, abundantly illustrate, how far Scripture, in detached quotations, may be pressed into the service of the grossest falsehood. And those who are not acquainted with the letter or spirit of the Bible, are in danger of being misled and perverted by them.

Those anti-Christian principles, under the guise of a strict and sanctified morality—a scrupulous observance of the ordinances and ceremonies of religion—or a mortified abandonment of the pleasures of the world, undermine the very foundations of the Christian faith, and lay the axe to the very root of all Christian morals, by totally corrupting the principle from which alone they can spring with acceptance before God. Thus really subverting morals, by the pretended interests of morality, and overturning the faith of Christ, under the pretence and semblance of religion.

There is but a step from the cell of the ascetic to the carnival of the voluptuary. It is an easy and natural transition for an emancipated mind, to pass from the adoration of a piece of paste, to the worship of the goddess of Reason—from being a posture-master in religion, to become a profligate in infidelity. It is all alike to the Prince of darkness whether he can dishonor the Majesty of God and destroy the souls of men by infidelity or superstition. Both alike reject "*the record which God hath given of his Son,*" and both alike shall perish in their ignorance and unbelief. The one makes God a liar, because it affirms He has only told part of the truth. The other makes him a liar, because it denies He has told any truth at all. But it seems to the writer that the most effectual mode of guarding against error ourselves, and opposing it in others, is to bring it to the test of God's Holy Word, not merely by comparing it with detached passages of Scripture that oppose it, but by taking a portion of Scripture, such as an Apostolical Epistle, in which the mind of God is given in its own perfect consecutive arrangement on the subject, and testing by that, any system that is opposed to it. This is a process, by which, the man who inquires after or maintains truth, will only more fully investigate, or more fearlessly sustain his Master's cause; while the opponent of truth meets at every step, principles which he cannot make to square with the falsehoods and incongruities of his scheme of error; and he will therefore shrink from the ordeal, with a conscious incapacity to endure the test to which it subjects his principles.

To follow the revealed mind of God in faithful simplicity, is necessarily to attain to truth under the guidance of the Holy Spirit, and where this is really the object of a Christian teacher, he has reason to trust that a blessing will attend his labors.

The following Lectures, the Author trusts he can truly say, were begun, continued, and ended with that object. In whatever he has failed, he desires to express regret for his inability to succeed; and for whatever measure of success has crowned his efforts, he desires to express his humble gratitude to that God, to whose grace and mercy alone he owes it; and to pray that He will abundantly bless it to promote His own glory in the salvation of men, through Jesus Christ our Lord. Amen.

PREFACE TO THE SECOND EDITION.

THE demand for this work having almost exhausted the numbers of the first volume before those of the second could issue from the press, the Author is induced to print a second edition.

Having learned from several quarters that it has pleased God to bless it to the edification and comfort of many into whose hands it has fallen, the Author can only say, that it adds another to the list of the many proofs, that God can, in His great mercy and power, work by humble and insignificant instruments. Fully conscious that to Him alone any good which it can effect is to be ascribed, he therefore desires to commit this edition to His grace and power, with an earnest prayer that as far as it is consistent with His blessed word, it may be accompanied with His Divine blessing to the souls of men, and prove to many "*a savor of life unto life.*" "*Unto him be glory in the Church, by Christ Jesus, throughout all ages, world without end. Amen.*" Eph. iii. 21.

CONTENTS.

TWENTY-FOURTH LECTURE.

EPHESIANS iii. 9, 10, 11.

TWENTY-FIFTH LECTURE.

EPHESIANS iii. 12.

TWENTY-SIXTH LECTURE.

EPHESIANS iii. 13, 14, 15, 16.

TWENTY-SEVENTH LECTURE.

EPHESIANS iii. 17, 18, 19, 20, 21.

TWENTY-EIGHTH LECTURE.

EPHESIANS iv. 1, 2

TWENTY-NINTH LECTURE.

EPHESIANS iv. 3—6.

THIRTIETH LECTURE.

EPHESIANS iv. 7—12.

THIRTY-FIRST LECTURE.

EPHESIANS iv. 12—16.

THIRTY-SECOND LECTURE.

THIRTY-THIRD LECTURE.

THIRTY-FOURTH LECTURE.

THIRTY-FIFTH LECTURE

THIRTY-SIXTH LECTURE.

THE EPISTLE

OF

PAUL THE APOSTLE, TO THE EPHESIANS.

EPHESIANS I.—1, 2, 3.

"Paul, an Apostle of Jesus Christ, by the will of God, to the saints which are at Ephesus, and to the faithful in Christ Jesus. Grace be to you and peace from God our Father and from the Lord Jesus Christ. Blessed be the God and Father of our Lord Jesus Christ who hath blessed us with all spiritual blessings in heavenly places in Christ."

THE Apostle Paul commences this Epistle in the same manner in which he commenced that to the Romans, which we have just concluded,* and as he begins all his Epistles except that to the Hebrews, by prefixing his name (as was the custom in writing in those days) instead of subscribing it at the close of the letter as we do. "PAUL AN APOSTLE OF JESUS CHRIST BY THE WILL OF GOD." You perceive he not only prefixes his name but his authority too. This is a point which few, if any of us, sufficiently consider. I do not mean that when we take up the Scriptures, we have not generally a conviction of their divine authority and inspiration; but we have not as we ought to have, that influential operative conviction which receives all that is therein contained as the pure truth of God—the whole truth; we have need to pray continually for this conviction, and the more so, because of the false opinions that are frequently not only entertained, but even expressed on the subject.

Many persons will tell you that they prefer the Gospels to the Epistles, as if they possessed some authority superior to the apostolic letters. They even profess to make from them a standard of doctrine, as it were contradistinguished from that of the Epis tles. Hence you often hear persons say, especially those who argue against salvation by grace, and quote the morality of the Scriptures, against its doctrines of redemption; "Paul expresses himself in such or such terms, but Christ says so and so—now I take the word of Christ in preference to that of Paul." Now there

* The Author had just finished a Course of Lectures on the Epistle to the Romans, similar to this, and there are so many allusions made to it in these Lectures, that it is necessary to mention the fact.

is a three-fold reason for this: First—Ignorance of the plenary inspiration of the Scriptures; that "*all Scripture is given by inspiration of God,*" 2 Tim. iii. 16; that "*Holy men of old spake as they were moved by the Holy Ghost.*" 2 Pet. i. 21. Secondly—Forgetfulness of our Lord's testimony, "*It is not ye that speak, but the Spirit of your Father which speaketh in you.*" Matt. x. 20. "*He that heareth you, heareth me, and he that despiseth you despiseth me, and he that despiseth me despiseth him that sent me.*" Luke x. 16. They do not understand or believe these and similar passages, or they would know the identity of inspiration and authority in these sacred documents; and that such a comparison between the words of Christ and His apostles, was, as it really is, a contempt of Himself of his own authority and truth.

But there is a third reason for this, viz.,—that the Epistles are more calculated to awaken the enmity of the natural mind against God than the Gospels; for although the Gospels contain much that cannot be clearly understood by these persons in a spiritual sense; still the parables, of which many are so clearly illustrative of moral truth, and the precepts of our Lord, come home at once to the natural judgment and conscience, and commend themselves to both; and therefore are not so calculated to provoke objections as the Epistles. Therefore you will find, that some persons who would substitute extracts from the Bible for the Bible itself, for the instruction of the people, are exceedingly cautious in the selections which they make from the Epistles; and are fond of quoting the passage from Peter, which they pervert, saying, that in the Epistles of Paul "*are some things hard to be understood.*" Because, as the Apostle Paul sets forth so fully salvation by grace, and holds forth the Gospel of Christ so freely, this being foolishness unto them—as "*the natural man receiveth not the things of the Spirit of God,*" 1 Cor. ii. 14; therefore such men give a preference to the Gospels, and so will often quote, and ignorantly appeal to their authority against the Apostolical Epistles. But let us remember that every word spoken by the Apostles, claims for itself the full authority of "thus saith the Lord;" because according to the words of the Lord Jesus, "*It is not they that speak but the Spirit of their Father that speaketh in them.*" Matt. x. 20.

We find then the Apostle Paul exceedingly tenacious of this authority, and always setting it forth, as if to remind the churches, that the authority with which he addressed them, was that of God; and thus, we ought to receive every word of his inspired testimony.

"TO THE SAINTS WHICH ARE AT EPHESUS, AND TO THE FAITHFUL IN CHRIST JESUS.' We considered so much at large, the persons who are included in the term "*saints*" in the Epistle to the Romans, that I shall now but briefly recall to your remembrance, that it is the Scriptural appellation of all believers in Christ. All who are justified by faith in Jesus, are also sanctified in Him, and in this sense all are alike sanctified—none more so than others—the babe in Christ is sanctified in Him, as well as the young man, the young man as well as the father. There are indeed different gifts of grace, as well as different degrees of growth in grace, in the Church of Christ, and in this sense some believers are more than others under the sanctifying influences of the Spirit of God. And this ought to be the continual object of attainment, to all the children of God. But in the sense in which all are one with Christ, as united to Him by faith, they are all sanctified in Him alike, dedi cated, set apart, consecrated in Him to God forever. In this sense their sanctification is ascribed to the salvation wrought by Christ, so saith the Apostle Paul: "*By the which will we are sanctified through the offering of the body of Jesus Christ once for all*," Heb. x. 10; and again, "*The bodies of those beasts whose blood is brought into the sanctuary by the high priest for sin are burned without the camp. Wherefore Jesus also, that he might sanctify the people with his own blood, suffered without the gate*," Heb. xiii. 11, 12. And so our blessed Lord ascribes the sanctification of his Church, in this sense, to faith in Him, in His commission to the Apostle of the Gentiles, "*to whom*" saith he "*now I send thee to open their eyes and turn them from darkness to light, and from the power of Satan unto God; that they may receive forgiveness of sins, and inheritance among them which are sanctified by faith that is in me*," Acts xxvi. 17, 18. Therefore I say, every believer in the Lord Jesus is sanctified in him, the weakest as well as the strongest—the poorest believer of this day, as much as the Apostle Paul. It is the more necessary to explain this from the gross errors that are prevalent on the subject. Many persons are in the habit of making justification only as it were an initiatory act, whereby men are brought into a state in which they *may be sanctified and saved*; and think they are not warranted to trust in Christ for salvation *till a certain purifying process takes place in them* which they call *sanctification*—a work of the Spirit separate from the salvation wrought by Christ. Nothing can be farther from the Gospel than this—this error keeps, I am satisfied, many of the children of God mourning all their days, looking for this purification in themselves which they never feel or can feel. They confound two things which are quite distinct—the sanctifying influences and power of the Spirit, which it is ever their privilege and duty to pray for—to watch for, and to receive as being the children of God; that they may serve and glorify their heavenly Father—with that work of the Spirit whereby they are quickened and brought to Christ, pardoned, washed, justified from all their sins, sanctified in Him and presented in Him to God "*without spot or wrinkle or any such thing*." The truth is equally opposed to every error, whether those that are more specious, and approach nearer the Gospel in appearance; or those by which, as in this case, the Church of Rome runs into an anti-Scriptural apostacy, canonizing, as she calls it, certain persons as saints, who are pretended to have advanced to some imaginary stage of perfection in holiness, but of whom multitudes have been characterized by devotion indeed, to her, but by ignorance of God, and enmity against His Gospel. I need not enter at length on the no less awful state of those, who profess to protest against the idolatry and superstition of Rome, but who use the very name of "SAINT" as a term of reproach and mockery, applied to those who do not fear to profess the faith, and follow the conduct of those who really are servants of Christ. Recollect then, that "*the saints and faithful brethren in* Christ" are synonymous terms for all those who truly believe in Him as the hope and refuge of their souls.

"GRACE BE TO YOU, AND PEACE FROM GOD OUR FATHER AND FROM THE LORD JESUS CHRIST."

This is the apostolical benediction with which Paul generally commences and concludes his Epistles. So we had it in the conclusion of that to the Romans on our last day. "*The grace of our Lord Jesus Christ be with you all.*" Rom. xvi. 24. Believers, then, as now, required grace continually to keep them, and enable them to stand before their God. As our bodily frames require fresh food for their daily subsistence, and without it would grow weak, languish, and die; so do we in a spiritual sense require continual supplies of heavenly refreshment. If the Israelites were obliged to go and gather the manna, morning by morning in the wilderness, so have we, my dear friends, daily need of supplies of "*the Bread of God, which is he that cometh down from heaven, and giveth life unto the world.*" John vi. 32. So should we pray continually in the language of those who heard this truth from his own lips, "*Lord, evermore give us this bread.*" v. 33. And if we "*have not*" let us remember the reason is "*because we ask not.*" Jam. iv. 2. We should use the means if we expect the end. Remember the promise, Prov. viii. 17, "*They that seek me early shall find me.*" Again—"*They that wait on the Lord shall renew their strength, they shall mount up with wings as eagles—they shall run and not be weary, they shall walk and not faint.*" Isai. xl. 31. We ought to use industry for the soul as well as for the body; for, "*The soul of the diligent shall be made fat.*" Prov. xiii. 4. This may be viewed as an apostolical prayer for the Church as well as an apostolical benediction. All require grace to keep them as well as to call them. We need daily supplies, and we receive them too, as we have just been singing in our hymn:—

"Grace turned my wandering feet,
To tread the heavenly road,
And new supplies each hour I meet,
While passing on to God."

But it is not only grace, but peace too, for which the Apostle prays for them.—True peace cannot exist without grace—and peace is the consequence of grace. The believer stands, through grace, accepted, justified by the precious blood of Jesus; the sweet apprehension of Christ by faith, brings pardon and peace to his soul; so saith the Scripture, "*being justified by faith, we have peace with God through our Lord Jesus Christ; by whom also we have access into this grace wherein we stand and rejoice in hope of the glory of God,*" Rom. v. 1, 2, they are justified by faith, and have peace—they stand in a state of grace, and rejoice in hope. Jesus "*has made peace through the blood of his cross,*" Col. i. 20, and so to know him and to enjoy the peace he has purchased through the grace that is given to them, is the subject of the apostolical prayer and benediction,—"grace be to you, and peace."

And, as then, so now it is our consolation to remember the source from whence alone grace and peace can flow. It is not from Paul, or from Apollos, or Cephas; but "*from God our Father, and the Lord Jesus Christ.*" Jehovah, the Father, the fountain, and Jehovah, the Son, the channel of all blessings. "*Jesus the same yesterday, to-day, and forever.*" Heb. xiii. 8. The Fountain of living waters, as redundant as at the creation—the Sun of Righteousness with undiminished effulgence—the Ocean unfathomable in the depths of love and mercy,—"an ocean without bottom or shore." Oh how lamentably we live below our privileges, my friends. How little we bathe in that fountain! how little we bask in that sun!—how little we ride buoyant on that ocean with our anchor cast within the veil! "Lord increase our faith."

"BLESSED BE THE GOD AND FATHER OF OUR LORD JESUS CHRIST, WHO HATH BLESSED US WITH ALL SPIRITUAL BLESSINGS IN HEAVENLY PLACES IN CHRIST."

The Apostle bursts, as it were, into a strain of praise and thanksgiving at the contemplation of their present position, and the present blessings they enjoyed through grace. He ascribes all those blessings to the source of all blessing, to Jehovah, the Father, and he calls Him, "THE GOD AND FATHER OF OUR LORD JESUS CHRIST," conveying thereby the ideas included in the amazing manifestation of His love in giving His Son to die for us, and the unity of the divine will in the salvation of all the Church of God. If it is "*a faithful saying, and worthy of all acceptation, that Christ Jesus came into the world to save sinners,*" 1st Tim. i. 15, it is no less so that "*God so loved the world that He gave His only begotten Son, that whosoever believeth in Him should not perish, but have everlasting life.*" John iii. 16. The Father cannot be separated from the Son in the whole covenant and completion of the work of Redeeming love, nor the Holy Ghost from both. The revelation of that love in the glorious person and work of Immanuel, is the revelation of the Father's character, government, and love to sinners in Jesus. "*No man knoweth the Father save the Son, and he to whomsoever the Son will reveal Him.*" Mat. xi. 27. The "*light of the knowledge of his glory*" is revealed "*in the face of Jesus Christ.*" 2 Cor. iv. 6. In the great work of salvation it may be affirmed that the unity of the divine will in the blessed persons of the Trinity is manifested through all the Sacred Volume, in the salvation of all His Church. Our Lord saith, "*All that the Father giveth me shall come to me; and him that cometh to me, I will in no wise cast out.*" And He gives as the reason, "*For I came down from Heaven, not to do mine own will but the will of Him that sent me, and this is the Father's will which hath sent me, that of all which He has given me I should lose nothing, but should raise it up again at the last day. And this is the will of Him that sent me, that every one which seeth the Son and believeth on Him, may have everlasting life, and I will raise Him up at the last day.* John vi. 37—40.

It is manifest from these words of our Lord that all His Church are the gift of His Father to Him, they shall all come to Him and He will in no wise cast them out. Again, the love by which they are given to Him by the Father, and received by Him, is immutable; it carries them on to the end, for it is the Father's will that "of all which He hath given Him He should lose nothing, but should raise it up again at the last day;" and again it is the same will which causes that "every one who seeketh the Son and believeth on Him," or, as our Lord saith in another place, "who have not seen and yet have believed," "may have everlasting life." "*The gift of God is eternal life through Jesus Christ our Lord,*" and so whosoever hath come to Christ that he may have life, whosoever has been drawn to Him as the hope and refuge of his soul, is warranted to ascribe, as the Apostle does here, the blessing of all their mercies to "the God and Father of our Lord Jesus Christ." We see the Apostle Peter uses the same language; "*Blessed be the God and Father of our Lord Jesus Christ, who according to his abundant mercy, hath begotten us again unto a lively hope, by the resurrection of Jesus Christ from the dead, to an inheritance incorruptible, &c.*, 1 Pet. i. 3, and so the song of the redeemed before the throne is "*Blessing and honor and glory and power, be unto Him that sitteth on the Throne, and unto the Lamb forever and ever.*" Rev. v. 13. We perceive here for what the Apostle ascribes this blessing to God. "WHO HATH BLESSED US WITH ALL SPIRITUAL BLESSINGS." They were blessed with them, *all things* were theirs—Christ is all and in all, and they were Christ's—as the Apostle says, 1 Cor. iii. 21–23, "*All things are yours, and ye are Christ's and Christ is God's.*" This is a truth of which believers, alas! are lamentably ignorant, and of which even those who know most, know but very little. How little are our hearts and hopes lifted up above their natural state! how heavily we drag on our spiritual life, compared with our high and holy privileges!

The Apostle, in the second chapter of this Epistle, enters more fully (as we shall see, if it pleases God to spare us,) into this subject. He contrasts the position of sinners in their natural state with that of sinners in their spiritual state—they were "*dead in trespasses and sins,*" "*children of wrath,*"—now "*quickened together with Christ—raised up together and made to sit together in heavenly places in Christ Jesus.*" Chap. ii. 1, 5, 6. The believer may ask, how can this be?—how can I feel this to be so? It is not proposed to you as an object of feeling but of faith—God speaks it—Jehovah declares it to be a fact, and it is firm as the foundations of eternal truth. We considered this subject at length, in reading the 6th of Romans, and it will come more at large than in this verse, under our consideration in the 2nd chapter, but you recollect what the testimony of the Holy Spirit is in the 6th of Romans—"*We are buried with him by baptism into death, that like as Christ was raised from the dead by the glory of the Father, even so we also should walk in newness of life*"—again, "*Reckon yourselves to be dead indeed unto sin, but alive unto God, through Jesus Christ our Lord,*" verses 4, 11,—again in Colossians, ii. 12, "*Buried with him in baptism, wherein also ye are risen with him through the faith of the operation of God, who hath raised him from the dead,*"—again, in chap. iii. 3, 4, "*ye are dead and your life is hid with Christ in God. When Christ who is our life shall appear, then shall ye also appear with him in glory.*" Their actual state of spiritual life and union with Christ is the subject not of sense indeed, but of faith. The Lord declares it to them, for it is so seen in his eye, "*according as he hath chosen them in Christ before the foundation of the world.*" v. 4. God views all his own mighty works in progress as in completion. The architect surveys in his mind's eye the building of which he has laid but the foundation stone, as a complete and perfect structure, according to the plan and elevation he has laid down for it,—the shipwright when he lays the first beam of the keel of his vessel on the stocks, views it as complete as if it were sailing on the bosom of the deep, with every sail expanded in the breeze—and if architects and shipwrights were infallible and immortal, their works and their conceptions and plans must ever correspond. But how often do we see that they who lay the foundation may never live to raise the superstructure! how often do their structures vary from their plans, and how often do their resources fail! so that in all these senses we may say, "*this man began to build and was not able to finish.*"

But God is the omnipotent, infallible, eternal architect. When the foundations of his church were laid before the foundations of the world, it stood as perfect and finished in His view as it shall appear when the "*head stone shall be brought forth with shoutings of grace, grace unto it.*" Zech. iv. 7.—And the mind of Jehovah shall be reversed—and his plans be changed—and His resources fail—or, He Himself shall cease to exist, before one stone shall fall and perish of that building which he viewed as complete from eternity. Jesus the living head of His church is exalted at the right hand of His Father, every member of His mystical body is beheld complete and safe in Him, "*raised up together with him, and made to sit together in the heavenlies in him.*"—not one of them shall be lost—his sheep shall never perish, John x. 28. It is as true of His mystical as of His natural body, "*a bone of him shall not be broken.*" John xix. 36. Promises and means are given us here, but it is the privilege of every believer in resting on those promises, and in the use of these means, to look beyond this tabernacle, to rise above this poor world of sorrow, sin, and death, and to enter by faith into those mansions, of which his Lord spake when He said, "*I go to prepare a place for you, and if I go and prepare a place for you, I will come again and receive you unto myself, that where I am, there ye may be also.*" John xiv. 2, 3. He is made unto His people, "*wisdom and righteousness, and sanctification, and redemption.*" 1 Cor. i. 30.

"How am I to feel thus," some poor believer will say, "when I feel so deserving only of hell, so bowed down beneath this body of sin and death—struggling under the pressure of this corrupt and wicked heart—constrained continually to cry out, "*O wretched man that I am, who shall deliver me from the body of this death!*" Rom. vii. 24. Paul was constrained to cry out thus before you—but you see when he records this sad experience of his own evil heart, and the power of sin in his members—even then in the midst of his complaint of sin and of his body of flesh, he bursts forth in the exercise of faith, and while groaning he asks the question, "*who shall deliver me from the body of this death?*" Faith answers in the same breath, "*I thank God through Christ Jesus our Lord.*" Rom. vii. 25. It is our privilege and our joy to rise upon the wings of faith and hope, and to soar up to our heavenly home above the strugglings of these dying bodies: how often do we see the believer even in the depths of suffering, and in the hour of death enjoying this blessed privilege.

I had a dear friend,* a physician, who died very lately of this disease that has been so prevalent and so fatal, this influenza; and there was another dear friend of his and mine, who had the privilege of watching by his bed of death; his daughter who would else have occupied that post, lay dying of consumption at the same time; indeed it was to a devoted attendance on her, humanly speaking, that he fell a sacrifice, for when he caught the disease, he would not omit his late and early watching, nor give up till he was beyond the reach of human aid. This lady who attended him told me some circumstances of his death, which evince how a believer may rise above his earthly tabernacle, and look down on it as it were while he sees it crumbling into dust before his eyes.

The day before his death he requested his medical attendant to read for him the 23d Psalm in Buchanan's Latin translation of the Psalms; he requested him afterwards to read the same Psalm in the Bible—he repeated with great joy the 4th verse, "yea, though I walk through the valley of the shadow of death I will fear no evil, for thou art with me, thy rod and thy staff they comfort me."—When this was done he said, "As all his concerns were arranged for eternity, he would now settle his affairs for

* Dr. Samuel Robinson,—he fell asleep in Christ, January 29th, 1837.

time," accordingly he arranged his will and all temporal matters. That night about eleven o'clock, a violent fit of coughing came on, he said to his dear friend who was sitting beside him, in metaphorical language, to the use of which he was very much addicted, "That was a heavy blow from the iron mace of death—I thought I should have gone off about twelve o'clock to-night, but I see from the strength of that cough that I shall last three or four hours longer"—this was precisely the case, for at four o'clock in the morning he fell asleep. Soon after he had spoken thus he added, "Now my dear friend, you will see my hands and my feet swell, and then they will grow cold and bluish in their color, and if you will be so kind when you see this to roll a little warm flannel round them, it will alleviate the bodily suffering,—you see my hands are swelling already—then you will see the cold sweat of death breaking out on my forehead, and just wipe it off with a warm cloth—I shall then fall into a sort of stupor, but I shall not be dead for some time, and let them not touch me till I am dead."—He spoke this and gave these directions, just as deliberately as if he was giving them for another dying man, and seemed just to speak of his body as of that of another person, then, after a little time he said as it were with a sort of playful triumph, "Who would have thought that I should have won the race from Sophy after all?"—alluding to his daughter, who was so near the goal, that he had been daily expecting the termination of her race. Soon after this, he fell asleep.

Thus, is it the privilege of a believer to rise above his earthly tabernacle, and while he sees and feels it sinking into the dust of death, to behold with the eye of faith his immortal spirit risen with Christ, and to long to burst the fetters which bind him here below, and spring at once to the realms of light. It is his privilege to turn his eyes away from the shroud, the coffin, the clay, and the worm, and to behold the glorious company of his brethren around the throne, and to hear the song of the redeemed as they cast their crowns at the feet of Jesus. Death is his as well as life—his, for good and glory too. "*All things are his, whether Paul, or Apollos, or Cephas, or the world, or life, or death, or things present, or things to come, all are his, and he is Christ's, and Christ is God's.*" 1 Cor. iii. 21, 22, 23.

He is "*blessed with all spiritual blessings in heavenly places in Christ.*" Oh! consider this, believer—you *have* all things—though now for the present you do not enjoy all things. It must be so, the Holy Ghost assures us, that the premises must involve the conclusion—the reasoning on them is infallible, "*He that spared not his own Son but delivered him up for us all, how shall he not with him also freely give us all things?*" Rom. viii. 32. *How shall he not?* that is to say, it is impossible but that he must. Therefore it is our glorious privilege to look out of ourselves in the flesh, and to behold ourselves by faith safe in our blessed Lord—"*Surely shall one say in the Lord I have righteousness and strength.*" Isaiah xlv. 24—in ourselves we have neither one nor the other—all weakness and all sin—"*all our righteousnesses are as filthy rags.*" Isaiah lxiv. 6; the more we examine the fact, the more we shall feel it to be so. Bring filthy rags into the light of the sun and they will appear ten times more filthy than before, so it is with all our works—bring them into the light even of our own judgment, we must condemn them, what must they be in the light of God's holy law, when we say "*thou hast set our misdeeds before thee, our secret sins in the light of thy countenance.*" Psalm xc. 8. O how should we stand if he were to "enter into judgment" with us! but if we are looking out of sin and self to the covenant promises of our God in the everlasting Gospel, then we may "*lift up the hands that hang down and the feeble knees.*" Heb. xii. 12,—then we may say in spirit and in truth, as I fear we so often mutter over in a cold heartless form, "*O come let us sing unto the Lord, let us heartily rejoice in the strength of our salvation.*" Psalm xcv. 1.

O what would become of us without the Bible?—all peace, all joy, all consolation, all hope forever gone—it would be like blotting the sun from the firmament, the soul would be in outer darkness. Let us think of that testimony of the everlasting covenant, "*all things are yours*"—and remember this is spoken of spiritual, not of earthly blessings. Poor Lazarus was not enjoying earthly blessings when he was laid at the rich man's gate full of sores, and when the dogs were coming and licking his sores, and when he was longing for the crumbs which fell from the rich man's table—but "*he was blessed with all spiritual blessings in heavenly places in Christ*"—as one of his members "*all things were his*"—all his very trials were just his Father's means of preparing his soul to be transported in a little time by the angels into Abraham's bosom. Poor Job was not enjoying earthly blessings when his oxen and his asses, and his sheep and his camels, and his servants, and his sons, and his daughters, were all swept away from him in a day, when Satan was let loose on his possessions, and his person; and his wife, as if leagued with Satan, bid him "curse God and die." Yet read the whole of his history, and mark the Apostolic comment on it, "*ye have heard of the patience of Job, and have seen the end of the Lord, that the Lord is very pitiful and of tender mercy;*" James v. 11—ye have seen the *end* of the Lord, ye have seen how all things were working together for his own good and his Master's glory. And do you not think Job knew this when he saw "*the end of the Lord*" himself? So shall you see, O believer, when you shall see his end in all dispensations towards yourself—you shall see all trials working for your good. Then learn to "*glory in tribulation*" with Paul, and you shall feel as it is in the hymn.

"Since all that I meet
Shall work for my good,
The bitter is sweet,
The medicine is food;
Though painful at present,
'Twill cease before long,
And then, O how pleasant
The conqueror's song."

Remember then, it is the privilege of faith to look at Providences in their end, to "*look, not at the things that are seen, but at the things that are not seen.*" Yes, believer, it is your privilege to see "*all things working together for your good*"—"all things are yours," whether inward or outward crosses, all afflictions, all trials, all temptations, all difficulties, all bereavements, all your sorrows whatever they be, and sooner or later you must feel sorrows:—no child of God can be more or less without them—as an old writer remarks, "*God had one Son on earth without sin, but he never had one without sorrow*,"—but these very sorrows teach you the preciousness of a "brother born for adversity," who is the man of sympathy, and the God of love and power, and who can speak peace to the winds and waves in the heaviest storm of trouble, and cause the heaving of the sinner's bosom to sink like the sea of Galilee into a great calm.—He can give peace which all the world can neither give nor take away—

"And if such peace
While under his afflicting hand we find,
What shall it be to see him as he is,
And past the reach of all that now disturbs
The tranquil soul's repose, to contemplate
In retrospect unclouded, all the means
By which his wisdom has prepared his saints
For the vast weight of glory that remains.
Come then affliction if my Father bids,
And be my frowning friend—a friend that frowns,
Is better than a smiling enemy."

Yea, even your very sins shall be made to work together for your good—they shall "humble you, and prove you, and make you know what is in your heart," and they shall serve to develop and to enhance "the unsearchable riches of Christ."

You will not misunderstand me as if I were to say it can be good for you to sin, God forbid! but I mean that the grace and mercy of God will overrule even your sin, and so humble you under the convictions of it, as to make Christ more precious to you, and that you shall learn more and more to love him, and to hate your sin, and hate yourself, for as it is sin that sets forth the grace and love of Christ to the sinner, so it is the love, the constraining love of Christ that illustrates the evil, and aggravates the bitterness, and increases the hatred of sin.

Now consider—dwell on these two points, the position of a sinner by nature, and the position of a believer by grace, and as we are all without exception by nature, in the first, O may we be found by grace, "blessed with all spiritual blessings in heavenly places in Christ." Amen.

SECOND LECTURE.

EPHESIANS I. 4—6.

"According as he hath chosen us in him, before the foundation of the world, that we should be holy and without blame before him, in love. Having predestinated us unto the adoption of children, by Jesus Christ to himself, according to the good pleasure of his will, to the praise of the glory of his grace, wherein he hath made us accepted in the Beloved."

WE considered, the last time we met, the position which those who believe in Jesus occupy by grace, and the privileges they enjoy, namely, being "blessed with all spiritual blessings in heavenly places, in Christ." And the reason of this is stated in the 4th verse with which we commence to-day—"ACCORDING AS HE HATH CHOSEN US IN HIM, BEFORE THE FOUNDATION OF THE WORLD."

God's everlasting love is the source of all that believers enjoy in time, or shall enjoy in eternity. We entered, you recollect, at large into this subject, as we went through the 8th and 9th chapters of the Epistle to the Romans. We dwelt on the uses and abuses of the doctrine of God's predestinating love, which forms such a prominent subject of those chapters; and considered how profitable the practical view of the doctrine is to the believer; and how vain and unprofitable the speculative controversies to which it so often gives rise. It is, in fact, a portion of that "*strong meat which belongeth to those that are of full age, even those who, by reason of use, have their senses exercised to discern both good and evil.*" Heb. v. 14. When men do not understand the fundamental principles of the Gospel of Christ, every effort of their mind to comprehend the doctrine of election is vain; so that, to reason with them on the subject, is like reasoning with a man born blind on colors, or with a deaf man on harmony; while, to the practical use of this, the believer owes the whole of his hope of being brought to eternal life.

If we think that our own goodness, or our good intentions, resolutions, prayers, or anything tending to excellence or superiority in us over our fellow-sinners, was the cause why God looked in his mercy upon us, we cannot believe the Gospel; we cannot really be looking to Jesus, under a consciousness of our own guilt and vileness as lost and helpless sinners.

Again, if we think that our own goodness, or faithfulness, or profitable use of means, or the purity of our intentions, or the subjection of our will, or anything in us derived from ourselves, or our own good disposition, is to be the cause of our perseverance, and final salvation, we are equally far from the knowledge of ourselves, or of the Gospel. We cannot be really looking to and leaning on Jesus, as lost and helpless sinners—we are trusting to a source of salvation as uncertain as the weathercock, or the wind that blows it about.

Look, my dear friends, not merely to the written Word of God, but look also into your own deceitful hearts—look at the working of your wayward will, not only before you knew Christ as your refuge, but now. Look at the wandering idolatrous clinging of your earthly affections to the creature, and you will see the necessity of being chosen in Christ; you will confess that it is all "*by grace ye are saved*,"—not as righteous in yourselves, but as rebels—and this merely—"ACCORDING AS HE HATH CHOSEN US IN HIM BEFORE THE FOUNDATION OF THE WORLD." Man was seen in the whole detail of his existence, and not alone in the abstract—therefore all cavilling questions, such as, Why was man allowed to fall?—Why made liable to sin? &c., resolve themselves into the one point; Why was evil permitted to exist? to which we can give but one answer—*the fact.* Look around you, and look within you—if you are taught of God, the whole testimony of your conscience, as a voluntary, accountable, rational creature, will correspond with your Lord's revealed will. And if not, if you cavil at it, and object, then I know no other answer than that of the apostle, "*Who art thou that repliest against God?*" Rom. ix. 20. Oh, my friends when we come to appear before our God, no fallen child of Adam shall be able to throw the blame of his sin on his Creator, more than his fallen forefather was. Do you think that Adam convicted his Creator of wrong, when he replied, "*The woman whom thou gavest to be with me, she gave me of the tree, and I did eat*"?

Here my brethren, is the one simple rule: all the evil that we feel within, comes from ourselves and our enemy; and all the good that we can ever put in practice, or feel, or even desire comes solely from the free gift of God. Were we to depend on ourselves, we must perish. God does not deal with us as a creditor might deal with a broken merchant, to whom he would give a capital again, to trade with, and to try to retrieve his affairs, by his own exertions and resources. We are not pardoned by a divine decree, as it were to a certain time, and then left again to ourselves, to try if we shall walk aright, and maintain our state of salvation;—no, blessed be our God, "*We are kept by the power of God, through faith unto salvation.*" 1 Pet. i. 5. Indeed were it possible that we were all placed in a state of innocence like that of Adam, like him we should individually transgress our Master's law. Oh how much more secure the salvation of those who have Christ as their Covenant Head and Covenant Hope and who can say, "*Not by works of righteousness which we have done, but according to his mercy he saved us, by the washing of regeneration and renewing of the Holy Ghost.*" Tit. iii. 5. Who can say, "*Behold God is my salvation, I will trust and not be afraid, for the Lord Jehovah is my strength and my song he also is become my salvation.*" Isaiah xii. 2.

Yes, every child of God—every converted soul, must know that he is saved indeed by free and sovereign grace. If he confesses Jesus as the *Saviour*, he will confess him too as the *seeker* of his soul, "*He is come to seek and to save that which was lost*"—and having gone as the good Shepherd into the wilderness after the sheep, and found it, and "*laid it on his shoulders rejoicing*," he does not cast it down again to perish; no, he brings it home to his friends and neighbors,—Luke xv. 5, 6—the company of his redeemed, "*having loved his own he loveth them unto the end*," John xiii. 1. Looking unto him we have all the promises secured, for he is "*faithful and true*,"—and "*all the promises of God in him are yea, and in him amen*."

But observe to what believers are chosen in Christ, "THAT WE SHOULD BE HOLY AND WITHOUT BLAME BEFORE HIM IN LOVE, HAVING PREDESTINATED US UNTO THE ADOPTION OF CHILDREN BY JESUS CHRIST TO HIMSELF, ACCORDING TO THE GOOD PLEASURE OF HIS WILL." They are chosen, "*to be holy*"—chosen to be "*without blame before him in love*"—and mark the source of all, "HAVING PREDESTINATED US TO THE ADOPTION OF CHILDREN;" "ACCORDING TO THE GOOD PLEASURE OF HIS WILL." They are chosen to be holy, as He also is holy—so saith the Apostle Peter, "*as he who hath called you is holy, so be ye holy in all manner of conversation.*" 1 Pet. i. 15.

Here, perhaps, the believer will say, "ah! that is the very thing I feel I want; if I were holy I should be happy—but I feel myself, alas! unholy and unclean." Now, we must again observe, on this point, that there are two senses in which the term holy is to be considered.

"*Holy*" is to be considered in an *absolute* and *relative* sense, and I believe much distress of conscience arises to believers, from not having a clear Scriptural knowledge of this subject. Every believer is, and is considered as absolutely holy before God. Just as the vessels of the temple were sanctified, consecrated and set apart to the service of God—so, in this sense, is every vessel of the spiritual temple, every believer, chosen in Christ, sanctified, consecrated, dedicated to the Lord's service; he is taken from the mass of the world, that lieth in wickedness—his guilt is cancelled—sin blotted out forever; he stands washed in the precious blood, and clothed in the perfect righteousness of Immanuel, without spot or wrinkle, or any such thing. In this sense, he is absolutely and positively holy; so saith the Psalmist, "*Preserve thou my soul, for I am holy.*" Psalm lxxxvi.; though in the preceding verse he cries, "*Bow down thine ear, O Lord, hear me: for I am poor and needy;*" he mourns his sin and poverty in the same breath in which he says, "*I am holy.*" God looks not at him as he is in himself, a poor, miserable sinner; I say, in this sense God looks not on him as such, but He looks on him as a member of the risen body of his risen Lord and covenant head, Christ Jesus. So it is the believer's privilege and duty to contemplate himself also as the Apostle commands, Rom. vi. "*Likewise reckon ye also yourselves to be dead indeed unto sin, but alive unto God, through Jesus Christ our Lord.*" In this sense the sanctification of the believer is the immediate and necessary consequence of his justification. As soon as he is justified from all his offences by faith in the Lord Jesus—so soon is he considered in the eye of God as sanctified in Christ. This is the sense in which the term is used in the passages before quoted. Acts xxvi. 18, in which the Lord Jesus speaks of the "*inheritance among them that are sanctified by faith which is in him.*" So it is used in Heb. x. 10, where it is said, "*By the which will we are sanctified through the offering of the body of Jesus Christ once for all*" —and in the 14th verse, "*For by one offering he hath perfected forever them that are sanctified;*" and again the same effect is ascribed to the blood of Jesus, Heb. xiii. 12, "*Christ also, that he might sanctify the people with his own blood, suffered without the gate;*" and therefore it is, that the Spirit, by the Apostle addresses all believers as "saints," or persons who are sanctified.

I will not apologize for again quoting these passages of Scripture and calling your attention again to this subject; for I believe that whenever the Lord uses words in the Scripture, it is our profitable duty again and again to consider them; for we have daily need of the same truths to be applied as living principles to our hearts.

This great truth, which the believer ought to know and feel and live on as his high and holy privilege, is too much put out of sight, and is perhaps one cause why the Church of Christ seems to be so low at this day.

The view which God takes of His Church is that of a perfect building, not one stone wanting, and every stone perfect, and perfectly fitted in its place: as He shall behold it in eternity, so He sees it in time, and so He saw it before time began. It is the privilege of believers to know this, that they may abide with full confidence and joyful hope in Christ their covenant head—"*abide in me and I in you, as the branch cannot bear fruit of itself except it abide in the vine, no more can ye unless ye abide in me.*" John xv. 4. If the branch could speak it would say, it rejoiced that it was not independent but that it was part of the tree, that all its life and fruit were from the sap that nourish the parent stem from which it grew: so all the joy of the believer should be, that he is nothing and has nothing in himself, but that all he has and is, is derived from the Lord Jesus, his covenant head, with whom he is united; "*of him are ye in Christ Jesus, who of God is made unto us wisdom, and righteousness, and sanctification, and redemption, that according as it is written, he that glorieth let him glory in the Lord.*" 1 Cor. i. 30, 31. It is perfectly clear that the pure and positive holiness in which a believer is accounted as holy before God, is that holiness which he possesses, as being sanctified perfectly in Christ. "*For if the first fruit be holy the lump is also holy, and if the root be holy so are the branches.*" Rom. xi. 16. Therefore believers are all in the same sense called holy, "*ye are a chosen generation, a royal priesthood, a holy nation, a peculiar people,*" 1 Pet. ii. 9; therefore this is one of the grounds on which they are exhorted to practical holiness, "*put on therefore as the elect of God holy and beloved, bowels of mercies, kindness, humbleness of mind, meekness, longsuffering,*" Col. iii. 12; they are exhorted to holiness because they are holy, as the vessels of the temple ought to be used in the Lord's service, because they were consecrated to Him.

How difficult is it, in our unbelief, to realize these truths! how difficult for a poor sinner who feels the burthen of his own sin within, to believe that he is accounted holy and without spot before God!—When we take the holy law as our standard and Christ the living pattern of it as our example, how deeply must we feel as we frequently confess, that "there is no health in us"—how must we feel in the language of the Apostle, "*I know that in me, that is in my flesh, dwelleth no good thing.*" Rom. vii. 18. Therefore what need have we continually to hear the apostolic admonition, "*Put ye on the Lord Jesus Christ and make not provision for the flesh to fulfil the lusts thereof,*" Rom. xiii. 14; what need to say with Paul, (Oh! that we may say so in spirit and in truth!) "*the life which I now live in the flesh, I live by the faith of the Son of God who loved me and gave himself for me.*" Gal. ii. 20. Yes, it is in Christ alone we can stand in the presence of our God—it is in the Beloved alone we are accepted, in Him alone complete, in Him alone presented "*without spot or wrinkle or any such thing,*" Eph. v. 27; and although in this body of sin and death the believer must ever say and feel when he looks into himself, that he is blameable, and sinful and vile, yet as surely as he is looking unto Jesus, so surely is he seen in Him, and chosen in Him, as "*holy and without blame before God in love.*"

But in the other sense, the believer is not only positively holy, but he is relatively holy too, and although if you are believers you are always sensible how infinitely short you fall of the perfect standard of God's holy law, yet you are holy not only positively, as has been explained in Christ, but you are relatively holy too, that is, you are holy compared with yourselves before your conversion, and holy compared with all others who are not brought to Christ —"*if any man be in Christ he is a new creature,*" 2 Cor. v. 17; that which you once hated you now love, and that which once you loved you now hate—the holy principles, the holy word, the holy conduct, the holy companions, the holy law, which once you hated, you now love, the holy God against whom your hearts were enmity, you now adore as your reconciled God and Father. Christ is precious to you, you love His cause, his honor, and his people, and though you feel you do nothing, and desire nothing, and love nothing of all, as you ought to do, yet you will and desire to love and act as in your unconverted state you never did,—the sins, the pursuits, the pleasures, the companions in which you once delighted have not only lost their charms, but would make you miserable, and even now as they recur to your mind, or as your carnal nature would desire them, they bring guilt and pain on your conscience, and the sense of your continual sin makes you constantly learn more that Christ is precious as your Redeemer and your Refuge. It is true you cannot always feel that there is this change in your own character, the power of sin and unbelief often makes you doubt whether you can be indeed children of God—and therefore I would not refer you to evidences in yourselves for peace—I neither think it safe nor scriptural to do so; but it is very important to refer you to them for self-examination, for humiliation, to stir you up to watch and pray, that you may learn to look unto Jesus, to live *on* Him for your peace and your salvation, and *to* Him for his praise and glory, that you may learn more and more to "*mortify your members*," "*to crucify the flesh with its affections and lusts*," because God hath chosen you in Christ, that, in every sense, "*you should be holy, and without blame before him in love.*"

Yes, dear friends, we are indeed vile and miserable sinners in our best estate; and if left to ourselves, must assuredly perish; but though condemned in ourselves, yet we are delivered from condemnation in Christ—unclean, yet clean—defiled, yet without spot—"black, but comely"—lost, but saved. Oh, what wondrous paradoxes are these for the poor believer. While he feels that he deserves to be cast into hell, yet "*he is raised up and made to sit in heavenly places in Christ Jesus*," as we shall see in the next chapter. God looks not on him as the judge looks on the criminal, but as the tender father looks on the beloved child, so that his very trials are to be received as tokens of love—therefore the apostle saith—"*If ye endure chastening, God dealeth with you as with sons; for what son is he whom the Father chasteneth not? but if ye be without chastisement, whereof all are partakers, then are ye bastards, and not sons.*" Heb. xii. 7, 8. If we are "PREDESTINATED TO THE ADOPTION OF CHILDREN" trials must be the portion, in a greater or less degree, of every child of God—they must pass under the rod of the outward cross, pains, sufferings of many kinds, disappointments, difficulties, temporal losses, bereavements of those dear to them, various afflictions; or they must suffer under the pressure of the inward cross—doubts, darkness, unbelief, being left to themselves to feel their own weakness, to mourn under their own corruptions, to suffer under temptations, like Paul under the buffetings of Satan.—But mark the end, the object of their suffering under the rod—"*that they may be partakers of his holiness.*" Therefore, as this is the object for which the rod is sent, so it is the motive given of our submission to it—"*We have had fathers of our flesh, which corrected us, and we gave them reverence; shall we not much rather be in subjection unto the father of spirits, and live? for they verily for a few days chastened us after their pleasure, but he for our profit, that we might be partakers of his holiness.*" Heb. xii. 9, 10. He hath predestinated his children to be holy, and therefore he will surely make them so—the beginning is love—the end is love—so all the intermediate means are love. Therefore if we are indeed his children we are called to be holy—"*as obedient children, not fashioning yourselves according to the former lusts, in your ignorance, but as he who hath called you is holy, so be ye holy in all manner of conversation; because it is written, be ye holy, for I am holy.*" 1 Pet. i. 14, 15, 16. You are graciously adopted as children, and lovingly chastened because you are such—and why? He tells us, it is "*for our profit that we should be partakers of his holiness.*"—Heb. xii. 10.

Let us suppose a man of property to adopt the child of a beggar—to make him his heir—to bring him up as his own—to provide for all his wants—to educate, to discipline, and to fit him for the sphere in which he was to move, and the inheritance he was destined to enjoy—we should consider this an act of great kindness to that child—men would say, what a fortunate and happy child he was, and how thankfully he ought to receive the instructions, and submit to all the necessary discipline of his benefactor. But if this were kind from one fellow-sinner to another, what shall we say of the love of that God, who has called and adopted rebellious worms like us—who has pardoned us, kept us, watches over us, disciplines, instructs, corrects us, and gives us the joyful hope of an "*inheritance incorruptible and undefiled, and that fadeth not away.*" 1 Pet. i. 4.

"*Behold,*" saith the apostle, "*behold,*" as if he were pointing to some remarkable object, "*behold what manner of love the Father hath bestowed on us, that we should be called the sons of God.*" 1 John iii. 1. "HE HATH PREDESTINATED US TO THE ADOPTION OF CHILDREN BY JESUS CHRIST TO HIMSELF ACCORDING TO THE GOOD PLEASURE OF HIS WILL." Herein are all blessings—all the blessings of paternal love and paternal power—included. If the Lord of glory has predestinated us to be adopted as His own children, then He has involved in this all the blessings necessary to fit us for our inheritance—all that wisdom, love, and power can plan, can wish and execute, must belong to those who are adopted as the children of God. His own glory is involved in the salvation of those whom He adopts. It is all "TO THE PRAISE OF THE GLORY OF HIS GRACE WHEREIN HE HATH MADE US ACCEPTED IN THE BELOVED." The manifestation of God's glorious attributes is the legitimate end and scope of His dealings with man. To manifest supreme good is the righteous object of supreme goodness, and all the dealings of God with His redeemed servants, are now and shall be finally exhibited to be "TO THE PRAISE OF THE GLORY OF HIS GRACE." The fact stated in the beginning of the 4th verse, namely, that He had "*chosen them in Christ, before the foundation of world,*" is a proof that their salvation proceeded from the sovereign grace of God, and these words "*according to the good pleasure of His will,*" are but an illustration of the principle on which they were chosen in Christ. They prove that it was not from any good foreseen in them, or any other cause, but purely the good pleasure of His will, as we have in Rom. ix. 15.

16. "*He hath mercy on whom he will have mercy, and He hath compassion on whom he will have compassion, so then it is not of him that willeth, or of him that runneth, but of God that showeth mercy.*" And therefore it must be "TO THE PRAISE OF THE GLORY OF HIS GRACE;" because if it be, as indeed it is, the mere gratuitous act of His own sovereign will, it cannot be from any source, but His own gracious and unmerited bounty by which he "*passed by them while they were yet in their blood and said unto them, Live,*" Ezek. xvi. 6. Yea, they were chosen in Jesus before the world began—therefore His grace must be the theme of their everlasting praise, because it is in truth the whole cause of their being called and saved in Christ; and surely there is not one amongst us, whose eyes have been open to know the hope of the Gospel, who must not confess that Grace is the only source of that mercy. "*Who maketh thee to differ from another and what hast thou that thou didst not receive?*" The first stone of the temple is laid by Sovereign Grace, and the last that shall be laid on the summit, shall be laid with shouts of "Grace—Grace unto it." The effects of this grace are manifested to the souls of all men, in the fact that they are "*accepted in the beloved.*" You see "*He hath made us accepted.*" It is a finished work for the believer—Jesus and his work are accepted with the Father, and all his people are accepted in Him. This the Apostle adduces as the glorious exhibition of grace to sinners. 2 Cor. vi. 1. "*We beseech you*" saith he, "*that you receive not the grace of God in vain; for he saith, I have heard thee*" (*i. e. Christ*) "*in a time accepted and in the day of salvation have I succored thee; behold now is the accepted time, behold now is the day of salvation*"—that is, now is the promised time come—now is Immanuel and his glorious work accepted with the Father—now, the day of salvation proclaimed to sinners; and now, saith the Apostle here "HE HATH MADE US ACCEPTED IN THE BELOVED"—we were "PREDESTINATED TO THE ADOPTION OF CHILDREN," therefore now are adopted as children—accepted in the Beloved as children! so that to all who believe in Jesus, as the hope and refuge of their souls, this is the language of inspired truth, "*Behold what manner of love the Father hath bestowed upon us, that we should be called the sons of God, beloved now are we the sons of God.*" Hear then, these words, let us behold what manner of love it is; how great—how full—how free—how unchangeable! "*I have loved thee with an everlasting love, therefore with loving kindness have I drawn thee.*" Jer. xxxi. 3. This is His language. "Wherefore, lift up the hands that hang down," O believer! Let us pray for a more enlarged view of this love of our heavenly Father—a more simple confidence in Him—that we may have our heart's affections drawn forth to him, in filial gratitude and love; that we may be enabled to feel the force of the love, and the power of the appeal when we shall come to the passage, if we are spared to do so, in this Epistle, Chap. 5, "*Be ye therefore followers of God, as dear children; and walk in love, as Christ also hath loved us,*

and hath given himself for us an offering and a sacrifice to God, for a sweet smelling savor." O! may our hearts feel all the blessed confidence of the relationship of children, and all the power of filial, holy love; that "*we may show forth the praises of Him who hath called us out of darkness unto his marvellous light.*" 1 Pet. ii. 9. "Not only with our lips but in our lives, by giving up ourselves to His service, and by walking before Him in holiness and righteousness all the days of our life." Amen, Amen.

THIRD LECTURE.

EPHESIANS I.—7, 8.

"In whom we have redemption through his blood, the forgiveness of sins, according to the riches of his grace. Wherein he hath abounded toward us in all wisdom and prudence."

IN our last Lecture we traced the spiritual blessings of the children of God to the source from which they are all declared, in His eternal Word, to spring, that is, to His eternal purpose, His everlasting love, "*according as he hath chosen us in Him, before the foundation of the world, that we should be holy and without blame before Him in love, having predestinated us to the adoption of children, by Jesus Christ, to Himself, according to the good pleasure of His will.*"

In tracing this, we found the entire glory of our salvation, from first to last, ascribed to the Creator, and no part of it to the creature. Man's glory had been his obedience, had he been faithful; but he is a fallen rebel, and God's glory is his salvation. Nothing of merit in it belongs to man, or God would be robbed of His glory; and if we are indeed His children by adoption, we shall be brought to see this.

Can a child adopt its parents? or can it adopt those who stand towards it in the room of parents? Surely not! neither then can a sinner be truly called the adopted child of God, and adopt his Heavenly Father; the spiritual child of God is not born of himself any more than the child of an earthly parent. He is "*born not of blood, nor of the will of the flesh, nor of the will of man, but of God.*" John i. 13. So saith our blessed Lord, John, xv. 16, "*Ye have not chosen me, but I have chosen you.*" Consider this, God's people are called by sovereign grace to be a peculiar people—to be His—to "*be holy and without blame before Him in love.*" Now, instead of puzzling ourselves with the theological difficulties which man's presumption is continually suggesting on this subject, let us occupy our hearts with humbly meditating on the revealed fact; and we shall find, both as it regards the world and ourselves, that, as all things come from God, and are ordered by God, that are good; so even those things that are evil shall all be finally overruled for His glory. Yea, the very sins of this fallen guilty world shall be ultimately made subservient to that great end—the sins of the sinner, when he is cast into outer darkness, shall redound to the glory of His eternal justice, as those of the redeemed who have "*washed their robes, and made them white in the blood of the Lamb*," Rev. vii. 14, shall redound to the everlasting glory of His grace, who bore their sins "*in His own body on the tree.*" 1st Peter, ii. 24. The Apostle here reduces this to the simplicity of the Gospel, and shows the grandeur of it to be commensurate with the attributes and character of God.

If there be any here, any soul in this assembly, ignorant of the Gospel, all the peace of such an one, hollow as it is, and all his hope, vain as it is, depends on something he has done, or expects to do for himself, instead of on the redemption which is in Jesus, "IN WHOM WE HAVE REDEMPTION THROUGH HIS BLOOD." And here we are taught in what this redemption consists, "THE FORGIVENESS OF SINS." The measure of this redemption too, we see—it is "ACCORDING TO THE RICHES OF HIS GRACE," as the Psalmist says, "*with Him is plenteous redemption.*" Ps. cxxx. 7; how plenteous must that be which is commensurate with the riches of the grace of God! *Redemption*—that is, the purchasing sinners back from the bondage of sin, death, and hell, unto eternal life,—bestowing on them the forgiveness of sins, and blessing them "*with all spiritual blessings in heavenly places in Christ.*"

You perceive—it is not said, in whom we have had redemption, or, in whom we shall have redemption, but, "IN WHOM WE HAVE REDEMPTION," this is all we want to know and rest on to obtain solid peace, for "*being justified by faith, we have peace with God, through our Lord Jesus Christ.*" Rom. v. 1.

We are called here to consider the person of Him "IN WHOM WE HAVE REDEMPTION." Who is this Being, this Redeemer? He is Jehovah, "*God over all, blessed forever,*" and he is the "*man Christ Jesus,*" He is the "*child born unto us,*" the "*son given unto us,*" of whom saith the Prophet, "*His name shall be called Wonderful, Counsellor, the Mighty God, the Everlasting Father, the Prince of Peace.*" Isaiah, ix. 6. He, of whom it is written, "*He is before all things, and by Him all things consist,*" Col. i. 17. He who was "*made of a woman, made under the law, to redeem them that were under the law, that we might receive the adoption of sons.*" Gal. iv. 4, 5. In this is the "*great mystery of godliness, God was manifest in the flesh.*" 1st Tim. iii. 16.

It is evident that if it were not so, the Gospel scheme of salvation must necessarily involve idolatry. The Being who brings full redemption and forgiveness of sins to the soul—relief to the distressed conscience—peace and balm to the wounded heart, of which He is the Comfort, the Refuge, the Resting-place, the Salvation, and this too, at the expense of his own most precious blood; to Him must the affections of that heart be drawn out, in Him must they be centered. In vain had the command been given, "*Thou shalt have none other Gods but me*," if He who saith "*Come unto me all ye that labor and are heavy laden, and I will give you rest*," (Mat. xi. 28,) were not that God himself.

In this consists the blasphemy of Socinianism, which, if it admit of anything it calls atonement, robs the Being who made it of His Godhead, and therein makes him an object of idolatry. In this also consists, in part, the idolatry of the church of Rome. It applies to the Virgin Mary, and to the saints, the titles which belong to Christ alone, and so it proves thereby the idolatry which it inculcates in the sinner's heart. When it addresses, as in its books of devotion to the Virgin Mary, the titles that belong to Christ; as for example in the Rosary of the Virgin: "Refuge of Sinners, pray for us." "Comfort of the afflicted, pray for us." And as the Pope, in his encyclical letter of the year 1832, calls her, "*The whole foundation of our hope*." It is perfectly clear that that on which the heart leans as its hope, and to which it flies as its comfort and its refuge, is the object on which its affections must be centered. Therefore that apostate church gives His glory to another. But of Jesus we say: "*Behold God is my salvation; I will trust and not be afraid, for the Lord Jehovah is my strength and my song, He also is become my salvation*." Isai. xii. 2. Of Him we say: "*Be thou my strong habitation whereunto I may continually resort*." Ps. lxxi. 3. Of Him, "*In God is my salvation and my glory, the Rock of my strength and my refuge is in God. Trust in Him at all times ye people, pour out your hearts before him, God is a Refuge for us*." Psalm lxii. 7, 8.

But the manhood of our blessed Lord is no less to be borne in our minds. He who knew our nature, who "knew what was in man," saw that we needed a "merciful and faithful High Priest:" "*Such an High Priest became us, who is holy, harmless, undefiled, separate from sinners, and made higher than the heavens*." Heb. vii. 26. Yet such an one too who is "*touched with the feeling of our infirmities; who was in all points tempted like as we are, yet without sin*." Heb. iv. 15. So that if the nature of God's moral government, and the work of Christ as surety for sinners and fulfiller of the law in our stead, had not required it, yet even in compassion to our necessities "such an High Priest became us." So that when we can say to the Father of our spirits, speaking of the Son, "*Let thy hand be upon the man of thy right hand, even the son of man whom thou madest strong for thyself*." Ps. lxxx. 17. We can say with Thomas to that blessed Son of Man, though we have not seen Him, "*My Lord and my God*." How we need, then, continually to have the person of Him who hath wrought our redemption ever present with us, so St. Paul saith: "*Wherefore, holy brethren, partakers of the heavenly calling, consider the Apostle and High Priest of our profession, Christ Jesus*." Heb. iii. 1.

Then consider what he has wrought—REDEMPTION—pause and think of the fact—we require to bear this in our hearts every hour. It is not a vain, but a life-giving truth, which should be present in all its fulness in our souls continually. It is that truth which tunes, and shall tune, to all eternity, the harps of the redeemed before the Throne, "*They have washed their robes and made them white in the blood of the Lamb, therefore are they before the Throne of God, and serve him day and night in his temple.*" Rev. vii. 14, 15. Therefore they cry "*with a loud voice, saying,* 'SALVATION TO OUR GOD, *which sitteth upon the Throne, and unto the Lamb.*'" Rev. vii. 10. Then observe "WE HAVE REDEMPTION THROUGH HIS BLOOD," the blessing is spoken of in the present time, "in whom we have redemption," we have it this day, now, this moment, present salvation for present necessities, for present sins.

Consider, since last we met, how often in thought, word, and deed, have we sinned! how often have we needed this redemption! O then! what it is, if we can look unto Jesus and take up this language of faith, and say, "IN WHOM WE HAVE REDEMPTION THROUGH HIS BLOOD." If there be any here ignorant of their lost condition, trusting to some outward form, saying, "*Lord, Lord,*" while they do not his will, "*drawing near with their lips, while their hearts are far from him.*" Mat. xv. 8, who instead of enjoying present redemption, are resting in some vain system of their own, or of man's invention, thinking they cannot be authorized to look to Him, until they change their lives, and reform their habits, and who are thus trying by their vain and weary efforts to recommend themselves to the favor and mercy of God; I would say to such, alas! my poor friend and fellow sinner, all your religion consists in resolves never to be executed, and intentions never to be performed, and which, if even carried into effect would profit you nothing, and never can even help to make your peace with God. "*Can the Ethiopian change his skin, or can the leopard change his spots, so soon may you do good that are accustomed to do evil.*" Jer. xiii. 23, this is the testimony of God concerning such persons, as those who try to make themselves clean in his sight. But O! the good news of the Gospel is present salvation to sinners, a proclamation of present pardon and forgiveness through the blood of Jesus. Mark these words, "IN WHOM WE HAVE REDEMPTION THROUGH HIS BLOOD." What is that? he tells us what he means, "THE FORGIVENESS OF SINS ACCORDING TO THE RICHES OF HIS GRACE."

Have you been all your life far from God? Then hear at this moment pardon is proclaimed to you through the blood of Jesus. Are you farther than the thief on the cross? when at the first in conjunction with his fellow-thief as two evangelists inform us, reproach and blasphemy hung upon his lip, yet, when through grace touching his heart, and opening his eyes, he turned to Jesus for pardon, to him was given present redemption and salvation, "*To-day shalt thou be with me in Paradise.*" Luke xxiii. 43.

Although salvation is given to us according to our several circumstances, yet it is the same salvation to all, for though all are in different states of sin, all are alike sinners. You may be a Pharisaical sinner, perhaps, high in reputation, not only for morality, but for religion, and yet be only a whited sepulchre; the devil can transform himself into an angel of light, and so does he often clothe his servants in the same livery. Saul was high in reputation, and "*after the most straitest sect of his religion, he lived a Pharisee*," at the time when he was "*breathing out threatenings and slaughters against the disciples of the Lord*," Acts, ix. 1. when by his subsequent inspired testimony he was "*a persecutor and blasphemer, and injurious.*" 1 Tim. i. 13. When the Lord smote him to the earth, when trembling and astonished he cried out, "*Lord what wilt thou have me to do*," and when the Lord ordered him to go to Damascus, the message which He sent to him there by Ananias, was a message of present pardon and salvation, "*Arise and be baptized, and wash away thy sins.*" Acts, xxii. 16.

The Philippian jailer, a sinner of a different character, was a persecutor, and a cruel one in his trade, up to the very moment when the songs of praise of Paul and Silas from the stocks, where he had fastened them—the earthquake—the falling off of the chains from the prisoners, and the bursting open of the prison doors, startled him from his slumber, when he was about to commit the most awful murder man can perpetrate, self-murder—when his sword, all but steeped in his own blood was flung down, and he cried out trembling at the feet of Paul and Silas, "*Sirs, what must I do to be saved*," What was the answer? present salvation through the blood of Jesus, "*Believe in the Lord Jesus Christ and thou shalt be saved?*" What was the result? he embraced with gratitude and joy the present remedy—that same hour of the night "*he rejoiced, believing in God.*" Acts xvi. 31. 34.

Now you are not worse than he, nor are you better. Does not your own conscience tell you that by nature and practice you are a guilty sinner? Hear then the glad tidings, salvation is proclaimed to you through the blood of Jesus. "*Be it known unto you men and brethren, that through this man is preached unto you the forgiveness of sins, and by him all that believe are justified, from all things, from which you could not be justified by the law of Moses.*" Acts, xiii. 38, 39, that is by your own efforts, by anything that you can do, by laws, by ceremonies, by forms, ordinances or morals. O! then embrace this salvation, trust in it—rejoice in it. It is not a half redemption, it is not a sort of conditional redemption, that places you in a condition to struggle as it were for your soul's deliverance, and leaves you to complete the half done work of your salvation. O no! It is full, free, finished, and complete redemption just suited to your wants, and suited to them at this moment.

Perhaps there may be several here, too, who would be much offended if I were to ask them, "do they know the meaning of the word redemption?" who would say, "we have known it all our lives." Yet it is an important question, and it is to be feared the word is but too little understood.—Let us consider it.

Suppose any article pledged for a certain sum, and that it was redeemed; would it not revert to its owner again, and be his own, and be free? Suppose a man a prisoner, and ransomed, or redeemed by having a ransom paid for him. If the ransom were sufficient and accepted, would he not be free? Suppose an estate mortgaged and redeemed from its mortgage, would it not be free? Does not redemption in all these cases mean a complete and perfect deliverance, so that if there be not deliverance, then the term redemption cannot be applied; for the person or the thing is really not redeemed. Hear, then, O sinner, the good news of the Gospel. Here is the redemption that is in Christ. It is full, free, complete redemption. Nothing remains to be paid. The prison doors are burst open, and the captive is free; pardon, liberty, and life are in the word, O! think of it, "IN WHOM WE HAVE REDEMPTION THROUGH HIS BLOOD."

Again, consider the means of its accomplishment. Consider the price. "THROUGH HIS BLOOD." Consider if any other means had been sufficient, is it possible, think you, that Christ would have died? Would the precious blood of the Lamb of God have been poured out if any price less costly had been sufficient? If you could save your children from destruction by any other means than the peril of your life, would you risk that life unnecessarily? And surely the Father had not sent his beloved Son to die upon the cross, if other ransom could have been found for guilty man. "*If righteousness come by the law*," (that is, by anything that man can do,) "*then Christ is dead in vain.*" Gal. ii. 21. But O! what can be added of weight or value to the blood of Jesus? His blood is an all-sufficient ransom. It "*cleanseth us from all sin.*" 1 John i. 7. He has purchased sinners with His own blood, and that is price enough for their redemption.

This is the whole ground of our forgiveness, so observe how different this is from the natural expectation of the heart. How different from the miserable hope that men derive from the thought that they are not so bad as others. How different from the miserable hope they derive from the idea that they have amended their lives and reformed their habits, and are better than their former selves, and therefore trust that they are on this ground more acceptable to God. How different from any such miserable hope—if hope it can be called, which must ever be clouded by the consciousness of sin, by the feeling that, however imperfect and false the standard of attainment be which we have raised, we must fall short of our own standard, and sink beneath its level, when measured even by our own conscience. True it is indeed, that if a sinner believes the Gospel, his life will be totally changed; he will be different from those who believe it not, and different from what he was himself as an unbeliever, "*If any man be in Christ he is a new creature*," 2 Cor. v. 17, but this is the *effect* not the *cause* of his salvation ; he is changed not to be saved, but because he is saved. Salvation by grace and salvation by works, are not only distinct from, but opposed to each other, light and darkness are not more opposite. They cannot be combined, they cannot be dove-tailed together. The Scripture declares they are excluded from each other by a universal negative, "*If by grace it is no more of works, otherwise grace is no more grace, but if it be of works, it is no more of grace, otherwise work is no more work.*" Rom. xi. 4. It is impossible they can co-exist as conjoint causes of salvation, and consequently as conjoint grounds of hope. The Word of God is, "REDEMPTION THROUGH HIS BLOOD, THE FORGIVENESS OF SINS, ACCORDING TO THE RICHES OF HIS GRACE." "*Where is boasting then? It is excluded. By what law? of works? Nay: but by the law of faith.*" Rom. iii. 27. If salvation were in any degree of works, then indeed, were there some room for boasting in man ; the man who had attained it by his performance, could boast over him who had lost it by his failure. But no boaster shall ever enter into eternal life, except those who boast in Christ Jesus, as it is written, "*He that glorieth let him glory in the Lord.*" 1 Cor. i. 31.

What encouragement then is here for the heavy laden heart and conscience? What a blessing to be called by the glorious Gospel to look out of itself to Jesus? to look from the depths of its own distress, to the glory and the fulness of that redemption, which is "ACCORDING TO THE RICHES OF HIS GRACE." O! how great is this redemption? well might the Psalmist say, "*with the Lord is mercy, with Him is plenteous redemption.*" It is a redemption commensurate, not only with our sins, but with the riches of the grace of Jehovah. Hence He saith, Psalm, ciii. 11, 12, "*as the Heaven is high above the earth, so great is His mercy toward them that fear Him, as far as the east is from the west, so far hath He removed our transgressions from us.*" Heaven and earth, east and west, must meet together, before the sins of His people shall be brought against them before Him. Yea, they are not only blotted from the face of heaven like a cloud, but, they are said to be blotted even from the remembrance of the Most High, "*their sins and iniquities will I remember no more.*" Heb. x. 17. This is the redemption, the forgiveness, we need, and this is the redemption through the blood of Jesus, "WHEREIN HE HATH ABOUNDED TOWARD US," or, as in Romans, "*where sin abounded, grace did much more abound.*" Rom. v. 20.

Does this then (as men say who believe not the Gospel) afford encouragement to sin? We can only answer with the Apostle, when he proposes the same question, "*What shall we say then? Shall we continue in sin, that grace may abound? God forbid.*" Rom. vi. 1, 2.

Suppose you had been injured deeply by some dependent, that he were doomed by the law to forfeit his liberty or his life for his offence, and that, at a great personal loss and sacrifice, you were content to pardon, and to procure his deliverance, and receive him again into your family—could you ever suppose him to understand, from your clemency and kindness, that he might therefore take license to repeat his offence? No—you would consider, and justly, that you had an everlasting claim on his gratitude and his affection, you would consider it as the most atrocious aggravation of his crime, that he should ever again abuse your mercy. If we would say and think thus of our fellow-man, in reference to ourselves, how much more should the principle apply to a sinner in reference to his Redeemer! surely it were the worst state to which a fallen-creature could be reduced—the deepest mark of perdition that could be branded on his brow—that he should use the means of deliverance from his sins, which the grace of God proclaims to him, as an incentive or excuse for continuing to rebel against that God. No! the salvation of the Gospel, on the contrary, is the only means whereby we can be delivered from the love and power of sin, as well as from its condemnation; all human inventions ever have failed, and must fail, to take away the love of sin from the heart, or plant the love of God within it. Vain are all the penances, the austerities, the mortifications imposed by superstition to undermine the power of sin and to attain salvation. Self-exaltation, self-deliverance, self-redemption is the virtual scope of all such religion, and genuine holiness is therefore not only unattained, but unapproached, yea, unknown even in its principle, by those who practise them; the motive, the only allowed and acceptable motive, of moral action, cannot have a place within them—and that is LOVE TO GOD.

Let me suppose that a parent saw a child or a servant performing some labored acts of obedience, but that he had means of ascertaining that these acts were performed to attain some interested and selfish end, could he give him credit for these performances? —would he not rather consider them a subject of reproof than of reward?—must he not condemn this conduct as hypocrisy, when the motive which it seemed to affect had no place in the heart?

Such exactly is the same selfish feeling that dictates the seeming obedience of the man who expects in any degree salvation from his works—the acknowledged scope of his conduct is to serve himself—to save his soul—and therefore, on his own principle, not to serve or glorify God.

But how can we ever sufficiently appreciate the language of the Spirit by the Apostle here in this amplification, if I may so speak of this redemption. Speaking of it in reference to God, as coming from him, it is "ACCORDING TO THE RICHES OF HIS GRACE." It is the mercy, the love, the grace, not of a king, but of the King of kings. It is exhibited in the fact that "WE HAVE REDEMPTION BY HIS BLOOD,"—what "RICHES OF GRACE" in God the Father, to give His Son. The Apostle John does not attempt to describe this love, but leaves it as it is, beyond description—"*God* SO *loved the world that He gave his only begotten Son that whosoever believeth in Him should not perish, but have everlasting life.*" John iii. 16.

He "SO *loved*," but how much, who can calculate!

What "RICHES OF GRACE" in God the Son, to pour out that blood for our redemption. "*Greater love*" He saith "*hath no man than this, that a man lay down his life for his friends.*" John xv. 13. This is the utmost extent to which human love can go. But what were "THE RICHES OF HIS GRACE," who laid down His life for His enemies! "*God commendeth his love towards us, in that while we were yet sinners, Christ died for us.*" Rom. v. 8. How horrible must be that sin, which cost such a price for the redemption of those who were sold under it! How unsearchable "THE RICHES OF THAT GRACE" that paid the price!—how inestimable the value of that blood that "*cleanseth from all sin!*" The riches of this Grace shall be the Hallelujah chorus of the saints in glory forever, "*Unto Him that hath loved us, and washed us from our sins in His own blood, and hath made us kings and priests unto God and His Father, to Him be glory and dominion forever and ever. Amen.*" Rev. i. 5, 6.

Then, considered in reference to His saints, the Apostle says "WHEREIN HE HATH ABOUNDED TOWARDS US," "the RICHES OF HIS GRACE," are the unsearchable riches of the King of kings, and He hath not only given us of them, but He "HATH ABOUNDED IN THEM TOWARDS US." It is not only grace but "THE RICHES OF HIS GRACE," and then, not in a scanty measure, but in the very abounding of God to our souls. The table of the wedding feast is no niggard banquet to which He invites "*the poor, and the maimed, and the halt, and the blind.*" His language is "*Eat, O friends—drink, yea, drink abundantly, O beloved.*" Cant. v. 1. So by the Prophet—"*Hearken diligently unto me, and eat ye that which is good, and let your soul delight itself in fatness, incline your ear and come unto me; hear, and your soul shall live.*" Isai. lv. 2, 3. So the response of the soul that feeds on the banquet of His love, is that of the Psalmist, "*Because thy loving kindness is better than life, my lips shall praise thee. Thus will I bless thee while I live; I will lift up my hands in thy name. My soul shall be satisfied as with marrow and fatness; and my mouth shall praise thee with joyful lips.*" Psalm lxiii. 3, 4, 5.

This is alas! foolishness to the world—to those who know not Christ and the blessed redemption in his blood, but how different is it, in its real nature and value as it comes from God. The Apostle saith, that in this grace "HE HATH ABOUNDED TOWARDS US IN ALL WISDOM AND PRUDENCE." "All wisdom" in the plan of such amazing redemption—all "prudence" in the execution and communication of it. This is full of force and power as addressed to the Ephesians. Wisdom was professedly their great object. "*The Greeks seek after wisdom.*" 1st Cor. i. 22. "Philosophy, falsely so called," was one of the many idols of Greece, but the Apostle as if to show them where alone true wisdom was to be found, places it as it were all here. Here are the abounding riches of God's grace. Here is that which your philosophers have been seeking in vain, here is "ALL WISDOM." So he saith to the Corinthians. "*The Jews require a sign, and the Greeks seek after wisdom, but we preach Christ crucified, to the Jews a stumbling block, and to the Greeks foolishness, but unto them which are called both Jews and Greeks, Christ the power of God, and the wisdom of God.*" 1st Cor. i. 22–24. As if He had said, all wisdom is in Christ; as he does to the Colossians, "*In whom are hid all the treasures of wisdom and knowledge,*" Col. ii. 3. To attain knowledge is accounted wisdom; to attain wealth, rank, glory, which men call happiness, in even the little scanty measure in which such blessings are attainable in this passing world, these are accounted as the attainments of wisdom, though all these "*perish in the using.*" But what must that wisdom be which secures all these, and secures them for eternity! To know Christ is to attain that wisdom. If we know Him, it is of small moment that we should be ignorant of other things here, because those who know Him shall surely be with Him forever, and then shall their knowledge of all things be adequate to their glorified capacity; "*then shall I know even as also I am known.*" 1st Cor. xiii. 12. The wisest man in all other knowledge, who is ignorant of Christ, knows nothing, nothing worthy of an immortal being, soon shall "*all his thoughts perish;*" and the man who knows Christ though ignorant of all things else on earth, knows that which shall make him wise and happy through eternity.* If therefore, in reference to God, He "aboundeth towards us in all wisdom and prudence" in giving us Christ; our highest wisdom and prudence must consist in receiving this "unspeakable gift;" in endeavoring to understand and appreciate its value; this is the treasure hid in the field, which when a man hath found, he selleth all he hath to purchase it. O! may our souls enjoy the blessings of this redemption, rejoice in the riches of the grace that hath wrought it, and instructed by the wisdom wherein God hath abounded in it to our souls. May we be made "*wise unto salvation through faith that is in Christ Jesus.*" Amen.

FOURTH LECTURE.

EPHESIANS I.—9, 10.

"Having made known unto us the mystery of His will, according to His good pleasure which He hath purposed in Himself: That in the dispensation of the fulness of times He might gather together in one all things in Christ, both which are in heaven, and which are on earth; even in Him."

THE Apostle having expressed among the causes of blessing and praise to God, (verse 3,) for himself and his brethren at Ephe-

* "Si Christum discis nihil est quod altera nescis.
Si Christum nescis, nihil est quod altera discis."—HOOKER.

sus, that they were accepted and redeemed by the Lord Jesus. "*He hath made us accepted in the beloved, in whom we have redemption through His blood, the forgiveness of sins according to the riches of His grace,*" proceeds to show in these verses how they had been made partakers of this redemption—what a glorious mystery it is—and what shall be its glorious consummation.

You will perceive, on reflection, the vast importance of this, for this is one great point, on which all unenlightened men, professing Christianity, are ignorant; all such, whatsoever their shades of opinion may be, are included within the scope of two classes.

One class, (if we can call them Christians, they profess to call themselves so,) expect to be saved by their own virtues, without any reference to Christ, except, perhaps, they might admit that He was an exemplar of morals. But Christ does not come into their contemplation as the hope of their salvation.

There is another class, (and this is by far the more numerous) who believe, that there is no salvation without Christ. They will say, "we believe there is no salvation without the death of Christ; we believe it is impossible for man to be saved without his atonement." These persons will insist on redemption by Christ, as they call it, but they deceive themselves when they think that they believe in Him—and that they believe the Gospel. They believe that Christ has brought salvation within their reach, that is, put them into a condition or capacity to save themselves, but then, they say, "We must labor to make ourselves worthy of this salvation, we must labor to gain it, we must labor to recommend ourselves to the favor of Christ—we must labor, (as is their common phrase,) to perform the conditions of the Gospel Covenant which are required on our part in order to the salvation of our souls, we must be righteous before we can hope in Christ." Now, to save ourselves, without Christ, and to save ourselves in this manner by Christ are two very different principles, but they are both equally false, they both deny Jesus as the Saviour of sinners. One of them sets up a false Christ, that is, a Christ who helps sinners to save themselves; the other denies Christ, and shuts him out of their scheme altogether.

To this latter class who deny Christ, may be reduced Deists, Arians, Socinians, a great multitude of those who call themselves, as is the fashion in these days, "*Liberals*" in religion. The other class embrace all the Church of Rome, and all the Protestants who hold the principles of popery, (and we all hold the principles of popery by nature—a modification of popery is the natural religion of the heart,) and this class embraces all such Protestants, and most especially, those individuals of the Church of England, those false teachers of the present day, who are setting up a system of popery within her pale.

Now, let me entreat you to consider these questions which I propose—

Is salvation altogether by ourselves without Christ?

Or is salvation partly by Christ, and partly by ourselves?

Or is salvation by Christ alone?

The scheme of salvation must be included within these three. You must consider—you must understand the answers to these, if your souls are to be saved.

Now, salvation is not by ourselves alone, otherwise Christ cannot be a Saviour, we cannot have "*redemption through His blood.*"

Salvation is not by ourselves and by Christ, He performing one part, and we another; otherwise Christ is but half a Saviour—a helper to salvation—a helper to redemption.

Salvation is by Christ alone, and Christ is an all-sufficient Saviour, "*in whom we have redemption through His blood, the forgiveness of sins according to the riches of His grace.*"

Men who are ignorant of this, may, notwithstanding, have very strict principles of religion, they may be very pious, very devoted men, they may labor very hard for their salvation, as many do, as the Israelites of whom the Apostle testifies, "*they have a zeal of God but not according to knowledge. For they, being ignorant of God's righteousness, and going about to establish their own righteousness, have not submitted themselves unto the righteousness of God. For Christ is the end of the law for righteousness to every one that believeth.*" Rom. x. 2, 3, 4. All false religion, and all false morality, that is, morality based on false principles, may be reduced to this. So these persons who are striving to save themselves, and yet, who are lost through their ignorance and rejection of the Gospel, are described in Ecclesiastes, x. 15, "*The labor of the foolish wearieth every one of them, because he knoweth not how to go to the city.*" If you wish to see the spiritual meaning of this, you may find it in Romans, ix. 31, "*Israel which followed after the law of righteousness, hath not attained to the law of righteousness.*" Is not that marvellous? is it not a wonderful thing that the man who follows after the law of righteousness cannot attain to it? Do you think if you follow after it you must attain to it? You see it is not so. Here were men who followed after it, "*Israel, who followed after the law of righteousness, hath not attained to the law of righteousness.*" Now, "*wherefore?*" what is the reason? "*because they sought it not by faith, but, as it were, by the works of the law, for they stumbled at that stumbling stone.*" They stumbled at Christ. Take care lest he be a stone of stumbling to you—beware! O beware! Remember, the Lord's words, Mat. xxi. 44.

Now, in opposition to this, stands the knowledge of Christ, as you have it in St. John's Gospel, xvii. 3, "*This is life eternal, that they might know Thee, the only true God, and Jesus Christ whom thou hast sent.*" To know the Father and Christ is life eternal.

This brings us then to consider the meaning of these verses. You will observe in this passage—

First, they had received redemption, "*we have redemption through His blood, the forgiveness of sins.*" Then, you see the means whereby they attained to this, namely, God having made it known to them—God having revealed to them, the glorious mystery of redemption by Jesus. Look at the connection of the 7th and 8th verses, "*In whom we have redemption through His blood, the forgiveness of sins according to the riches of His grace, wherein, He hath abounded towards us in all wisdom and prudence,* HAVING MADE KNOWN UNTO US THE MYSTERY OF HIS WILL, ACCORDING TO HIS GOOD PLEASURE WHICH HE HATH PURPOSED IN HIMSELF." God made it known to them, therefore, they had received it. We have also the reason why God made it known to them "ACCORDING TO HIS GOOD PLEASURE WHICH HE PURPOSED IN HIMSELF." We have more—We have the end, the consummation of the mystery which He did make known to them, namely, "THAT IN THE DISPENSATION OF THE FULNESS OF TIMES, HE MIGHT GATHER TOGETHER IN ONE ALL THINGS IN CHRIST, BOTH WHICH ARE IN HEAVEN, AND WHICH ARE ON EARTH, EVEN IN HIM."

Now, then, let us consider here, the means whereby God brought redemption, even the forgiveness of sins, to this people—the means whereby they were made partakers of it, and whereby, alone, we can be made partakers of it. Let me entreat your attention to this, because this is a point on which so many individuals are ignorant, and so many constantly full of doubts.

Persons frequently say, "I know there is redemption for sinners in the blood of Christ, but how am I to be made partaker of this redemption?—how am I to be redeemed?" Here is the answer—God making known unto you His truth, by His word, and His Spirit teaching you to understand and to believe that word—to embrace the truth it reveals as the hope of your salvation. This is the means whereby God conveys his salvation to sinners. No man, by his natural reason, can know or understand Christ, as revealed in the Scriptures—no—not had he even seen Him and His miracles, except by the teaching of the Holy Ghost. So our Lord saith to St. Peter, in St. Matthew's Gospel, xvi. 17, on St. Peter confessing Jesus to be the Christ, "*Blessed art thou Simon Bar-Jona, for flesh and blood hath not revealed it unto thee, but my Father which is in heaven.*" So, you perceive, the Apostle Paul speaks exactly in the same language, 1st Cor. ii. 9, 10, 11, "*But as it is written, eye hath not seen, nor ear heard, neither have entered into the heart of man, the things which God hath prepared for them that love him. But God hath revealed them unto us by His Spirit; for the Spirit searcheth all things, yea, the deep things of God. For what man knoweth the things of a man, save the spirit of man that is in him?—even so, the things of God knoweth no man, but the Spirit of God.*" God must reveal His truth to the sinner's heart, before the sinner can understand or receive it. So you have it set forth in the 14th verse,—"*The natural man receiveth not the things of the Spirit of God, for they are foolishness unto him, neither can he know them because they are spiritually discerned.*" So our blessed Lord, himself, exessly promises to His Apostles, in St. John, xvi. 13, "*When He, the Spirit of truth, is come, He will guide you into all truth; for He shall not speak of Himself, but whatsoever He shall hear, that shall he speak. And He will show you things to come.*" The Apostles, though hearing the word of our Lord Himself, were only guided into truth by the Spirit; and the Spirit that taught them, alone can teach any sinner the truth as it is in Jesus. So our Lord says in verse 14,—"*He shall glorify me: for he shall receive of mine, and shall show it unto you.*" And lest you should suppose that our blessed Lord speaks here, merely of the inspiration of the Apostles, which was no doubt included in it, but lest you should suppose, that it is not equally necessary that all His people should be partakers of the divine instruction of the Holy Ghost, as to His own person, work, and offices, you will find in 1st Cor. xii. 3,—"*No man can say that Jesus is the Lord, but by the Holy Ghost.*" You may name the name of Christ, and you may set up in your own imagination, a being born of the Virgin, who has performed such and such works, who lived and died, and rose again, to whom you may apply the name of Christ, but the Christ that is revealed in the Bible, as the Saviour of guilty sinners, and the work of that Christ, you know not, and cannot know, till Christ teaches you, by His Spirit, to receive as little children, the revelation of His holy word.

Many, in these days, call this enthusiasm or fanaticism, but wide is the difference between enthusiasm or fanaticism, and the true scriptural expectation of the teaching and guidance of the blessed Spirit. Enthusiasts speak of sensible or visible impulses and revelations of the Holy Ghost, which are not found in, and will not stand the test of, God's eternal word. The Holy Spirit is discernible in His effects, and not in His operations—thus our Lord teaches, "*The wind bloweth where it listeth, and thou hearest the sound thereof, but canst not tell whence it cometh, and whither it goeth: so is every one that is born of the Spirit.*" John iii. 8. It is not the office of the Holy Spirit to give new revelations—it is enthusiasm—fanaticism, to expect them. But it is the office of the Holy Spirit to teach the sinner's heart to understand, to receive, to believe, and walk in the revelations that God has given in this blessed book. Hence God's word is the guide of those who are taught by the Spirit. Therefore, true religion studies the Bible, true religion prizes and throws open the Bible, true religion calls on man to hear our Divine Master, and to "search the Scriptures." Falsehood shrinks from the Bible, shuts up the Bible from the instruction of mankind, and deprecates the study and diffusion of the Bible. I say then, the means that are here stated to have been used by God, towards the Ephesian church, to bring them to this blessed state of redemption, were His "HAVING MADE KNOWN UNTO THEM THE MYSTERY OF HIS WILL," which He did by His word preached by the Apostle and His Holy Spirit.

Again we have here, secondly, the reason why God made it known to them. "ACCORDING TO HIS GOOD PLEASURE, WHICH

4

HE HATH PURPOSED IN HIMSELF." This part of the subject is very plain in its expression, but I shall not enter into it in this verse, because it will come under our consideration, in verse 11, if it please God, and I shall refer to it on that occasion.

We shall consider now, the glorious consummation of that mystery, which according to His good pleasure, God had revealed unto them, it is this,—"THAT IN THE DISPENSATION OF THE FULNESS OF TIMES, HE MIGHT GATHER TOGETHER, IN ONE, ALL THINGS IN CHRIST, BOTH WHICH ARE IN HEAVEN AND ON EARTH, EVEN IN HIM." The Apostle here takes a most comprehensive view of the subject of divine revelation, in which he had instructed the church at Ephesus. He had sojourned with that church for more than two years, as you may recollect, Acts xix., and in that time, the whole scope of his apostolic teaching, had been brought fully before them, as he tells the elders of Ephesus, Acts xx. 27, "*I have not shunned to declare unto you all the counsel of God.*"

He embraces then in this verse, not merely one, but many subjects, and for the sake of perspicuity, I shall divide them. He says, "IN THE DISPENSATION OF THE FULNESS OF TIMES." Observe, he does not say, the fulness of a time, speaking merely of one period, you will find him speaking of this in Galatians iv. 4. There he speaks of one epoch in the dispensations of God, that is, the first coming of Christ, "*when the fulness of the time was come, God sent forth his Son, made of a woman, &c.*" But here he speaks of a "DISPENSATION OF THE FULNESS OF TIMES," and that in this, "HE MIGHT GATHER TOGETHER ALL THINGS IN CHRIST, BOTH WHICH ARE IN HEAVEN AND ON EARTH, EVEN IN HIM." Now this is a part of the mystery of his will, as you will find on considering it; and it involves several parts, each of which is a mystery in itself, as the whole is a mystery.

The first mystery which God makes known to them is, THE MANIFESTATION OF CHRIST TO SINNERS, AND SINNERS GATHERED IN CHRIST. This is a mystery, as you will find in 1 Tim. iii. 16, "*Great is the mystery of Godliness: God was manifest in the flesh.*" This was one mystery, which, "*in the dispensation of the fulness of times,*" God made known. And, oh! what a mystery! that He whom the Heaven of Heavens cannot contain, should take upon him our flesh in the womb of a virgin—that He should be born into this world, and live and die for us, and send his ministers to proclaim this Gospel—this good news, to every creature—as, in his most blessed name, I proclaim to you as sinners this day, pardon of your sins, through the blood of "*God manifest in the flesh.*" Oh, what a mystery! that the holy God, who sees each of us—such vile sinners—who measures and fathoms what we cannot ourselves—the depths of iniquity in our hearts—that that God should proclaim to us pardon through the blood of his Son—that He should "*so love the world as to give his only begotten Son, that whosoever believeth in Him should not perish but have everlasting life.*" Here is a mystery; that such sinners as we are should be gathered—if, indeed, we shall be gathered—

out of a world of guilt and sin, snatched from hell—plucked, like brands from the burning, and brought to God, through Christ Jesus! Oh, it is a mystery—an amazing mystery! No wonder the Apostle Peter says, "*the angels desire to look into these things.*" It is this mystery of salvation into which they desire to look; for, when he says that the prophets who foretold this salvation diligently sought what it was, that the Spirit within them signified; he adds, "*unto whom it was revealed, that not unto themselves, but unto us they did minister the things which are now reported unto you by them that have preached the gospel unto you, with the Holy Ghost sent down from Heaven: which things the angels desire to look into.*"—1 Peter i. 12.

The manifestation of God in the flesh, and this, that he might die for guilty sinners, and send the Holy Ghost from Heaven to teach them "the unsearchable riches" of His love; what wonder, these were mysteries of divine and amazing grace, into which "the angels desire to look."

But there is yet another mystery which forms a part of that gathering in of all in Christ, of which the Apostle speaks in this verse. That is:—THE CLOSE AND INTIMATE UNION THAT SUBSISTS BETWEEN OUR BLESSED SAVIOUR, AND THOSE WHO BELIEVE IN HIS BLESSED NAME, AND LOOK TO HIM AS THE REFUGE OF THEIR SOULS. This is set forth as another part of the mystery, as you see in this Epistle, v. 32. St. Paul in that chapter is speaking of the union between husband and wife—he is speaking of the devoted attachment of the husband to the wife, and the dutiful subjection and affection of the wife to the husband; and having dwelt on this practically, with regard to husbands and wives, he says, "*this is a great mystery; but I speak concerning Christ and the Church.*" Oh, how wonderful the union between the Lord Jesus Christ and those who believe on his name!—As a husband is responsible for all the debts of his wife, Jesus is responsible for the sins of his people, and pays the mighty debt of every poor sinner that depends upon him—As the wife is lifted up, and taken even from the meanest rank in the world, and if the husband is on a throne, she is lifted up to the rank of her husband—if he is a king, she is a queen—so the blessed Jesus takes the poor sinner out of the depths of guilt and sin, clothes him with his own righteousness, washes him in his own blood, gathers him in his arms, carries him in his bosom, and will never leave him nor forsake him, until he raises him up to sit upon his own throne. "*He raiseth up the poor out of the dust, and lifteth the needy out of the dunghill, that he may set him with princes, even with the princes of his people.*"—Psal. cxiii. 7, 8. This is an exhaustless mystery—but this is a mystery which God had taught the Ephesian church, and thus enabled them more to rejoice in that blessed hope, that they "*had redemption through his blood, even the forgiveness of sins, according to the riches of his grace.*"

But there was another part of the mystery comprehended in that of gathering in all in Christ, *in the dispensation of the fulness of times*, and that was—THE BRINGING IN OF THE GENTILES. These had been living without God, worshipping stocks and stones, and various idols, yet now were called into the church of Christ. You know that the Apostles did not for some time believe that the Gospel should be preached to the Gentiles. You know that it was by a vision from heaven (as you find in Acts x.) that St. Peter was induced to go and obey the invitation sent to him by a Gentile, to come and declare to him the way of salvation. In this Epistle, the Apostle speaks of the calling of the Gentiles as a hidden mystery now revealed. You see the passage at length, chap. iii. from 1st to 11th verses. And, in the 3d and 4th verses, he expressly calls it "*the mystery*," and "*the mystery of Christ, which in other ages was not made known unto the sons of men, as it is now revealed unto his holy Apostles and Prophets by the Spirit, that the Gentiles should be fellow heirs, and of the same body, and partakers of his promise in Christ by the Gospel.*" Ch. iii. 5, 6. That mystery, you perceive, the Apostle says, was now revealed; and how mysterious it was that God should, for so many centuries, have separated to himself a people from the whole world—should have given to that people ordinances and laws, by which they were kept distinct in their government, their religion, their habits, their customs, their manners, from all the nations of the earth—that He should have promised to them the Messiah in their family, and should promise, as He did, the amazing blessings that are predicted to the Jews hereafter—that then the Lord should command, that all the barriers between them and the other nations of the earth, should be broken down and levelled at once, and that the same salvation which was proclaimed to the Jews, should be proclaimed to the Gentiles throughout the whole world—that the same salvation proclaimed to those who had had the "*adoption, and the glory, and the covenants, and the giving of the law, and the service of God, and the promises.*"—Rom. ix. 4; should be sent to those who were worshipping "*the image that*" they said "*fell down from Jupiter*," and shouting out in the ears of the Apostles, who had been preaching the Gospel to them, "*great is Diana of the Ephesians!*" How marvellous, that God should send his Gospel to them, and to us!

Go through the fields in this very country, look at that massive stone, supported on those rude pillars, and ask your antiquarians —what was that? They will tell you that was an altar where human victims were offered, in this land, as a sacrifice to idols. And now, is it not a marvellous and mysterious blessing, that, to the descendants of those, whose hands have reeked with the blood of human victims, the Gospel should be proclaimed as it is proclaimed now, that we should be blest as we are with the oracles of God, and that our children should be taught in the way of everlasting life! "*Great indeed is the mystery of godliness!*" and that this very thing is part of that mystery, is stated in that same verse, "*Great is the mystery of godliness, God was manifest in the flesh, justified in the Spirit, seen of Angels, preached unto the*

Gentiles, received up into glory," 1st Tim. iii. 18—this is a marvellous mystery, the preaching of salvation, pardon of sin, to a lost and guilty world, through a crucified and risen Saviour.

But there is another mystery still, which is the consummation of that here spoken of. The "GATHERING TOGETHER OF ALL THINGS IN CHRIST, BOTH WHICH ARE IN HEAVEN AND ON EARTH." This you know is not as yet fulfilled, but this includes that mystery of which the Apostle speaks in 1st Cor. xv. 51, 52.

THE MYSTERY OF THE RESURRECTION. "*Behold I show you a mystery, we shall not all sleep,*" (that is, all believers in Christ shall not be asleep when Christ comes,) "*but we shall all be changed, in a moment, in the twinkling of an eye, at the last trump, for the trumpet shall sound, and the dead shall be raised incorruptible, and we shall be changed. For this corruptible must put on incorruption, and this mortal must put on immortality.*" 1st Cor. xv. 51, 52, 53. This is a part of the mystery of which the Apostle speaks, as having been revealed to them, for this was given as the hope of the Church from that day to this present. But the mode in which "ALL THINGS IN HEAVEN," things being put for persons, that is those who have fallen asleep, and are departed to be with Christ, and "THINGS ON EARTH," that is the whole Church on the earth at His coming, whom He calls collectively, chap. iii. 15, "*the whole family in heaven and earth,*" the mode in which they shall be gathered together, completes the mystery he speaks of, and this is fully set forth by the Apostle in 1st Thess. iv., where he says, speaking of those who had fallen asleep in Jesus, 14th verse, "*if we believe that Jesus died, and rose again, even so them also which sleep in Jesus, will God bring with Him. For this we say unto you by the word of the Lord, that we which are alive and remain unto the coming of the Lord, shall not prevent them which are asleep,*" we shall not be beforehand with them, a man's being alive on the earth when Christ comes, shall not give him precedence of those who have died in the faith, of one twinkling of an eye in eternal life, or in resurrection glory, it shall not give him the precedence of all the dead that have fallen asleep in Christ, from Adam to that moment, "*For the Lord Himself shall descend from heaven, with a shout, with the voice of the Archangel, and with the trump of God, and the dead in Christ shall rise first. Then we which are alive and remain shall be caught up together with them in the clouds, to meet the Lord in the air, and so shall we ever be with the Lord.*" 1st Thess. iv. 14–17. In the same twinkling of an eye that he who is alive is changed, and fashioned like to the glorious body of Christ, in that same twinkling of an eye the dead shall be raised incorruptible, when he shall appear who said, "*let there be light and there was light.*" And as the dew-drops spangle the ground, ere they are exhaled, when the sun bursts in his glory from the morning sky; so shall his people awake from their graves, and stand in regenerated life and glory, as they rise to meet their Lord in the air. This is the consummation of that great mystery, "the gathering together of all things in Christ," of which the Apostle speaks; then shall we behold Abraham, and Isaac, and Jacob, and all the saints of old, all the Old Testament Church, and the New Testament Church, "*the whole family in heaven and earth,*" then shall we behold them all "gathered together in Christ."

And you, if you be indeed His disciples, if you be indeed washed in his precious blood, you shall be of that blessed number, who shall arise in glory to meet your God. This is that "DISPENSATION OF THE FULNESS OF TIMES," when all shall be "GATHERED TOGETHER IN CHRIST, BOTH WHICH ARE IN HEAVEN, AND WHICH ARE ON EARTH, EVEN IN HIM."

Great is this mystery then, in all its course and its consummation.

Great is the mystery of Godliness, that "*God was manifest in the flesh.*" 1st Tim. iii. 16.

Great is the mystery of this Salvation, that he should be "*wounded for our transgressions, and bruised for our iniquities, that the chastisement of our peace was upon him, and by his stripes we are healed.*" Isai. liii. 5, and that we should "*have redemption through his blood, even the forgiveness of sins, according to the riches of His grace.*"

Great is the mystery of that union, that exists between Christ and his redeemed people, that "*we are members of his body, of his flesh, and of his bones.*" Eph. v. 30.

Great is the mystery that the times of the Jewish Dispensation should be completed, and that it should be revealed, "*that the Gentiles should be fellow-heirs, and of the same body, and partakers of his promise in Christ by the Gospel.*" Eph. iii. 6.

Great is the mystery of the mighty renovation that is to pass on us in that day of resurrection glory, "*When we shall all be changed, in a moment, in the twinkling of an eye, at the last trump; for the trumpet shall sound; and the dead shall be raised incorruptible, and we shall be changed.*" 1 Cor. xv. 51, 52.

And when "*the times of the Gentiles shall be fulfilled*"—and the promised day shall come, when all these dispensations shall be past—great is that mystery, when "*He shall send His angels, and shall gather together his elect, from the four winds, from the uttermost part of the earth, to the uttermost part of heaven,*"—that "IN THE DISPENSATION OF THE FULNESS OF TIMES HE MIGHT GATHER TOGETHER IN ONE ALL THINGS IN CHRIST, BOTH WHICH ARE IN HEAVEN, AND WHICH ARE ON EARTH, EVEN IN HIM."

And now, O friends, and brethren beloved, shall we be gathered in Christ in that day? Is this "*God manifest in the flesh,*" our life and our salvation? Have we indeed "*Redemption through his blood, even the forgiveness of sins according to the riches of his grace?*"

Do we know the value of that mystical union between Christ and His church, that oneness of Head and members, by which we are called, as we had it in the 6th of Romans, to reckon ourselves dead with Christ, and risen with Him: "*dead indeed unto sin, but alive unto God through Jesus Christ our Lord.*" Rom. vi. 11.

Is the Gospel of our salvation precious to us sinners of the Gentiles? shall this dispensation of grace to the Gentiles be unto us, "*a savor of life unto life, or of death unto death?*" Are our privileges, our ordinances, our churches, our Bibles, all our blessings, are they all the means of leading us to Jesus—keeping us looking unto Jesus—strengthening us and building us up in our most holy faith, upon the Rock of ages? or had it been better for us to have perished, like our pagan forefathers, without the aggravated curse, of Christ professed in name, but in heart despised, rejected, and trodden under foot by us, in guilt, hypocrisy, ungodliness, and unbelief?

Is the glorious hope of resurrection in Christ our comfort in all our conflicts in these bodies of sin and death? Shall it be true or false of us, as the solemn words are spoken over our sleeping dust, that we are committed to the ground,* "earth to earth, ashes to ashes, dust to dust, in sure and certain hope of the resurrection to eternal life, through our Lord Jesus Christ," "*who shall change our vile body, that it may be fashioned like unto his glorious body, according to the working whereby he is able even to subdue all things unto himself.*" Phil. iii. 21. O, brethren! when the trumpet shall sound, shall we be among those "*Blessed and holy, who have part in the first resurrection*"? Rev. xx. 6. And, "IN THE DISPENSATION OF THE FULNESS OF TIMES," shall we be among those of earth or heaven that are "GATHERED TOGETHER IN CHRIST," by grace, to glory?

FIFTH LECTURE.

EPHESIANS I.—11, 12.

"In whom also we have obtained an inheritance, being predestinated according to the purpose of Him who worketh all things after the counsel of his own will: that we should be to the praise of his glory, who first trusted in Christ."

THIS world were indeed a weary pilgrimage to the believer, if he were not cheered in all his trials and sorrows by the way, with the blessed hope of eternal rest, in that which is to come. "*If in this life only,*" saith the Apostle, "*we have hope in Christ, we are*

* Service for the Burial of the Dead.

of all men most miserable."—1 Cor. xv. 19. Even here, the prospect of any future good, if it be reasonably well founded, liable, as it is, to ten thousand contingencies, still cheers and supports the heart through many intervening years of anxious expectation—as we are told, "*Jacob served seven years for Rachel; and they seemed unto him but a few days, for the love he had to her.*"—Gen. xxix. 20. And if that be so with respect to this world, in reference to the future hopes of time, how much more, when the heart is enabled to repose with a solid assurance of hope upon that blessed "*rest*" which "*remaineth for the people of God.*" This supports the believer under all trials, yea, in the most afflictive of them—"*Deep calleth unto deep at the noise of thy waterspouts, all thy waves and thy billows are gone over me,*" saith the Psalmist; but in the midst of these deep waters, faith looks up and cries —"*Why art thou cast down, O my soul? and why art thou disquieted within me? hope thou in God; for I shall yet praise him, who is the health of my countenance, and my God.*"—Ps. xlii. 7, 11. Therefore, we see, that the Apostles, inspired by the Holy Spirit, continually cherish and strengthen the hope of the believer in his blessed Lord; for in direct proportion to our faith in the promises of God, and, therefore, to our hope of attaining the blessings which those promises hold out to us, so shall we be lifted up above the things of time and sense, and be enabled to realize and live for that eternal world of glory, where we look for an incorruptible inheritance. With this view, the Apostles, you perceive, confidently dwelt on God's eternal covenant promises—as, for instance, in Hebrews vi., where the Apostle, speaking of the covenant and oath of God, says, "*that by two immutable things,*" (namely, God's covenant and oath) "*in which it was impossible for God to lie, we might have a strong consolation who have fled for refuge to lay hold upon the hope set before us, which hope we have, as an anchor of the soul, both sure and steadfast.*"—Heb. vi. 18, 19. So he prays for his brethren, Rom. xv. 13—"*Now the God of hope fill you with all joy and peace in believing, that ye may abound in hope through the power of the Holy Ghost.*" So, he exhorts the Ephesians, that they may be enabled to lift up their head in all their difficulties, to "*take the helmet of salvation.*"—Eph. vi. 17; and he explains this in 1 Thessalonians, v. 8—"*putting on the breastplate of faith and love, and for an helmet, the hope of salvation.*"

There could be no confidence of hope without a security of the inheritance for which we hope. Therefore, the glorious covenant of salvation gives that inheritance, makes it over, with everlasting security, to all the elect people of God. This hope must be built alone on Jesus. When men know not the Gospel of Jesus, they cannot understand—they oppose—they hate the doctrine of any assurance of hope; therefore, this doctrine is opposed by all the principles of the Papacy: there is no such thing as assurance of hope within the pale of Rome. How can there be, when, in the darkness of Papal error, man's salvation is made to depend on his own works? Well, indeed, may such a system of ignorance as that, shut out the security and joy of hope from the soul. So, in the same manner, this grand fundamental doctrine of consolation, is also shut out from that similar system, on which, I am sorry to have occasion to remark, but which it is necessary that the faithful minister of Christ should notice in these days—that heresy in our own church, which is another form of Popery, setting up the works of man, and the sacraments, as the ground of his trust, instead of Christ, or what is virtually the same, in conjunction with Christ. There can be no such thing as assurance of hope in such a system—impossible! it opposes and denies the Gospel. The Gospel of Christ alone—Jesus, his precious blood poured out for the guilty, his finished righteousness, wrought out for man, in which Jehovah declares, he is "well pleased," that, and that alone, affords security and joyful hope to the fallen sinner.

Now, the security of the believer's inheritance in Christ, depends upon the electing love of his God and Father, as is set forth in the passage which I have read to you. Observe:—

"IN WHOM ALSO WE HAVE OBTAINED AN INHERITANCE."—How?

"BEING PREDESTINATED ACCORDING TO THE PURPOSE OF HIM WHO WORKETH ALL THINGS AFTER THE COUNSEL OF HIS OWN WILL." Being so "predestinated," "we have obtained an inheritance."

Here you will perceive, first—they have obtained an inheritance —"*In whom we have obtained an inheritance.*"

Secondly—the cause of their having obtained it—"*being predestinated according to the purpose of him who worketh all things after the counsel of his own will.*"

And, thirdly—you see the end of their election—"*that we should be to the praise of his glory who first trusted in Christ.*" Now let us consider these things.

I. "WE HAVE OBTAINED AN INHERITANCE." This is the necessary result of their being the children of God. All believers are the children of God. So you see in St. John's Gospel i. 12, 13, "*As many as received him, to them gave he power to become the sons of God, even to them that believe on his name; which were born, not of blood, nor of the will of the flesh, nor of the will of man, but of God.*" So you have in Galatians, iii. 26, "*Ye are all the children of God by faith in Christ Jesus.*" So you perceive in Romans viii. 17, the result, "*if children then heirs; heirs of God, and joint-heirs with Christ; if so be that we suffer with him, that we may be also glorified together.*" Jehovah has no paupers in his family. They may be, indeed, and they often are, in this world, poor. "*God has chosen the poor of this world,*" we are told —but then, they are "*rich in faith, and heirs of his kingdom,*"—the children of the King inherit the kingdom. So, in this first chapter of Ephesians, (read from 3d verse) you see, the Apostle shows, that believers are God's children, and predestinated to that —"*Blessed be the God and Father of our Lord Jesus Christ, who hath blessed us with all spiritual blessings in heavenly places in Christ; according as he hath chosen us in him before the foundation of the world, that we should be holy and without blame before him in love; having predestinated us unto the adoption of children by Jesus Christ to himself, according to the good pleasure of his will, to the praise of the glory of his grace, wherein he hath made us accepted in the beloved."* Therefore, I say, if they be children of God, they must be heirs of the Lord's kingdom. They have their inheritance indeed, not in possession, but they have it in reversion; and it is not like an earthly inheritance—here is no flaw to be found in the title deeds—here no error in the settlements—here no fear of cutting off the entail—here no doubt whatever as to the certainty of the possession—there are no contingent remainders, as they call them, in God's testamentary dispensation to his people. No, "*Blessed be the God and Father of our Lord Jesus Christ,*" saith the Apostle Peter, 1st Pet. i. 3, "*which, according to his abundant mercy, hath begotten us again unto a lively hope, by the resurrection of Jesus Christ from the dead,*" mark to what he hath begotten them—verse 4, 5, "*to an inheritance incorruptible, and undefiled, and that fadeth not away, reserved in heaven for you, who are kept by the power of God through faith unto salvation.*" They are begotten to this inheritance—this inheritance is reserved by God, in heaven for them, and they are kept, by God's power, on earth for it. The mansions of Jehovah's house must be overthrown, the power of Jehovah's arm must be paralyzed, before their inheritance in these mansions can be taken from them, or before they, in this wilderness can be debarred from it. So saith the Lord Jesus Christ, in St. John's Gospel x. 27, 28, 29, 30, "*My sheep hear my voice, and I know them, and they follow me: and I give unto them eternal life; and they shall never perish, neither shall any pluck them out of my hand. My Father, which gave them me, is greater than all: and none is able to pluck them out of my Father's hand. I and my Father are one.*" Therefore are they "*kept by the power of God through faith unto salvation*"—therefore have they "OBTAINED AN INHERITANCE, BEING PREDESTINATED, ACCORDING TO THE PURPOSE OF HIM, WHO WORKETH ALL THINGS AFTER THE COUNSEL OF HIS OWN WILL.

II. The cause of their having obtained it, "BEING PREDESTINATED."

Now, we come to consider this subject, which I said we should consider in the 9th verse. There is no doctrine which is more misrepresented or more cavilled at. But there is not one more clearly laid down in the Bible, than the doctrine of God's predestinating grace and love; it is inseparably interwoven with the whole of the Gospel dispensation.

One man may say "I do not understand it"—another may say "I do not believe it"—another may say "I do not like it, or, I hate it"—but I confess, I do not see how any honest man can say, it is not plainly written in God's eternal word; and if it be plainly written there, and that you know that it is God's truth, then let me entreat you to pause and consider, with calm sobriety, that solemn truth before you speak, in the manner that too many presume to speak on the subject.

It is peculiarly hateful to the natural heart of man, because it levels all his pride and self-righteousness to the dust, it leaves him a helpless, hopeless sinner at the feet of his God, depending solelv as we must all be, on his free mercy.

I well remember, myself, the difficulty I had in my own mind on the subject. I well remember how I fought against the truth, I well remember all my own cavillings and arguments, and therefore, I desire to deal tenderly and gently while I deal faithfully with others.

It is not possible, before we clearly know and believe that we are justified alone by Christ, scripturally to understand this subject. It is the strong meat of the Gospel, it is utterly unintelligible in its true scriptural sense to those who know not, and understand not, the simple truth as it is in Jesus—they cannot comprehend anything about it; therefore, salvation by Christ is the first thing for the mind of man to be applied to. Whosoever feels his heart opposed to the doctrine of God's election, depend upon it, he does not know, with perfect scriptural clearness, the foundation on which his own soul is to be saved; therefore let me entreat you to consider carefully the point.

I do not know any human composition in which the subject is more clearly, simply, compendiously, and scripturally laid down than in the 17th Article of our church. I pray you to attend to it:—

"Predestination to life, is the everlasting purpose of God, whereby (before the foundations of the world were laid) he hath constantly decreed by his counsel, secret to us, to deliver from curse and damnation, those whom he hath chosen in Christ out of mankind, and to bring them by Christ to everlasting salvation, as vessels made to honor. Wherefore, they which be endued with so excellent a benefit of God, be called according to God's purpose by his Spirit working in due season; they through grace obey the calling; they be justified freely; they be made sons of God by adoption; they be made like the image of his only begotten Son Jesus Christ; they walk religiously in good works, and at length, by God's mercy, they attain to everlasting felicity."

This is, in plain terms, the scriptural truth on the subject. It cannot be more literally expressed than in these words. But, mark—the Article goes farther:—

"As the godly consideration of predestination, and our election in Christ is full of sweet, pleasant, and unspeakable comfort to godly persons, and such as feel in themselves the working of the Spirit of Christ, mortifying the works of the flesh, and their earthly members, and drawing up their mind to high and heavenly things; as well because it doth greatly establish and confirm their faith of eternal salvation, to be enjoyed through Christ, as because it doth fervently kindle their love towards God; so, for curious and carnal persons. lacking the spirit of Christ, to have continually before their eyes the sentence of God's predestination is a most dangerous downfall, whereby the devil doth thrust them either into desperation, or into wretchedness of most unclean living, no less perilous than desperation.

"Furthermore, we must receive God's promises in such wise, as they be generally set forth to us in holy Scripture: And in our doings that will of God is to be followed, which we have expressly declared unto us in the Word of God."

Now, let me recommend you to study that Article, if you have not studied it before, and if you read it, as a commentary on passages, where the subject is treated of in the Scriptures, you will find how truly scriptural it is.

The Article, you see, declares:—First, what the doctrine of God's word on the subject is.

Secondly, what the use of that doctrine is to the Lord's children, to those who believe the Gospel.

Then, thirdly it sets forth a most dangerous and awful abuse of the doctrine.

And lastly, it tells us how men are to receive God's promises, and to do His will, and that is plainly and simply, as God hath written and revealed them.

Now, I shall touch, briefly, on both these views of the case, on the use and abuse of the doctrine. I shall speak, first, of the abuse of it. It is very necessary to consider this, because, I have myself known persons who have strangely abused it; and I tell you where that abuse is sometimes to be found. It is sometimes to be found among young people, in pious families. Their father and mother, perhaps, have endeavored to bring them up in the nurture and admonition of the Lord—they have heard the doctrines of grace repeatedly set forth and dwelt upon, in conversations, expositions of Scripture, sermons, or books. Being in themselves unregenerated, unconverted, as all must be until the grace of God converts them, they try, from this, to satisfy themselves in their own course of sin and folly. And let my young friends, or any others, whose minds may be perverted or ignorant on this subject, consider their language.

"We are told," say they, (adopting another of our Articles,) "that man cannot turn and prepare himself, by his own natural strength and good works to faith, and calling upon God, wherefore, we have no power to do good works pleasant and acceptable to God, without the grace of God by Christ, preventing us, that we may have a good will," (that is, beginning the work in our heart, and giving to us a good will,) "and working with us when we have that good will."—Art. x. "Now, since none are to be converted except by God's grace, if I am to be saved, I must be saved, and if I am to be lost, I must be lost—if I am to be saved, I cannot destroy myself, and if I am to be lost, I cannot save myself, so I will go on in my present course, and God, in His good time, will save me, if I am to be saved, and if not, I can, I know, do nothing of myself."

I have heard that argument used—I have known persons profess to act on that principle. Therefore, you see, how wisely the 17th Article lays down the awful falsehood of such an abuse of the doctrine as this.

Let us, therefore, consider this view of the subject.—The omniscience of God the Almighty Creator, may be said, in one sense, necessarily to determine the whole course of all created beings, and all created things: I mean it predetermines it in this sense,—that, as they appear to Him—as they are seen in his omniscient eye throughout the course of time and eternity, so they must remain forever unchangeable. This you must admit, unless you deny such a thing as omniscience in the Deity. The mechanist will make a machine, whether it be a clock, a locomotive engine, or anything else you please, and when he puts it out of his hands, he knows not what may become of that machine; he knows not to what use it may be turned, to what end it may be applied, nor does he know what part will stand, nor what part will fail, or anything more as to its fate or destination, after it is delivered from his hands. But do you imagine that the eternal Creator has thus formed us in this world that we inhabit? We are not indeed machines, but rational, voluntary, responsible moral agents—formed so—conscious that we are so—and treated so accordingly by God. But do you think He has been ignorant of all the results that should follow from all the works of his own mighty hand? When He endued the beings and the things He formed with reproductive and vegetative power, do you believe that he was ignorant of all the consequences that were to follow from the exercise of all the powers with which He endued them? Nay, there is not a single leaflet that ever burst from a tree in the forest, from the creation to this hour—there is not a single blade of grass that ever grew—there is not a single grain of sand upon the shore—there is not a single insect undiscovered or undiscoverable by the human eye, or by the microscopic power of human instruments—there is not a drop of water in the ocean—not a single atom of dust in the world, or anything connected with them all, that was not known as well in the mind of the Eternal God, as any single fact is known to Him at this moment. And you must admit this to be the case, unless you deny that it is He that "clothes the lilies of the field," unless you deny that there is not a single sparrow that falls to the ground unmarked by His all-seeing eye, unless you deny that He numbers the hairs of your head, unless you deny what seems more difficult than all the rest, that He will bring the secret thoughts of every sinner's heart into judgment, and that all are noted in His eternal book. Therefore, it is wholly impossible that anything different could occur from that which was present to His omniscient mind before the foundation of the world. But now mark! there is no predestination connected with man, irrespective of man's full accountability to God, as a voluntary, rational, responsible, agent. And this is just as true in temporal, as in spiritual things.

Let me illustrate this.—Whether your immortal souls or mine shall be saved or lost is as certain in the mind of God as any other act that ever shall occur. But, again,—your life, your bodily life, its continuance, its close, the place, the mode, the moment of its termination, everything connected with your life and death is as fixed in the counsel of the living God as anything concerning your immortal souls,—and you must admit this, unless you suppose that some contingency can arise connected with you which is unknown to Almighty God. But you know that such an idea is incompatible with His divine attributes; there is no use in arguing about it, it is absurd. I suppose you to admit this, for I cannot imagine you to deny it.

Now, I suppose you tell me you are tired of life: I shall place before you a cup of wine and a cup of poison; which will you drink, that wine or that poison? It is just as fixed and as certain before you were born in the eye of God, as it shall be after it is done, which you will take. But will you dare to say, will you pretend to think, that you have not the power, the freedom, as a voluntary, rational, accountable being, of taking the one or the other? Do you pretend that you act under any irresistible constraint? Do you mean to say, that if you drink that cup of poison, you are not guilty of the crime of self-murder, and that you shall not be justly accountable at the tribunal of the holy God?

Again, let me suppose an assassin,—he has his dagger in his hand—he is watching for his victim. Now, whether that victim is to fall, by the dagger of that assassin, or not, is as clearly settled in the counsels of God, that is to say, it is as clearly known to Him as it is to you, if the deed be done. But, if that murderer plunges his dagger into the victim's heart, will you say that he is not accountable as a moral rational agent for his crime to God? Will you sit on his jury, and when the fact is proved before you, give in your verdict before God, that you think he is not fit to live in human society, but that he should fall a sacrifice to public justice, and will you venture to say, that the Judge of earth and heaven is not to pronounce sentence on him, as you and the judge on the bench will do? Will you be an assassin, and will you presume to lay your guilt on your God? You know you dare not do so. Conscience—Conscience answers your cavils against the prescience of the Omniscient God.

We will go farther—I suppose you are afflicted with a disease, —your physician says, your disease is certainly mortal unless you take a certain remedy. He says to you, "here is a specific, take this." Will you say, "Oh, if I am to die, I must die; and if I am to live, I must live; and therefore, there is no use in taking any remedy, I will not take it—my fate is fixed"? Nay, verily, you would seize the cup, and drink it with an earnest, anxious, trembling hand, and invoke a prayer, I hope, for the blessing of God on the means you use.—And then—when your immortal soul is infected with a fatal distemper—When God tells you so—when the Physician of souls holds out to you a cup of mercy—a cup of his own precious blood—a cup of healing, life-giving power, —will you dash it away, and say, "if my soul is to be saved, it shall be saved; and if it is to perish eternally, it must die"? Surely, if you dare to reason thus,—if God be in heaven, and you on earth, and if you are a rational being, your blood shall be upon your own head.—And when the Lord shall bring you into judgment, and when he shall lay the cavils of your guilty heart open to the eye of man,—the whole world must shout "Amen," when

He says, "Depart, ye cursed, into everlasting fire, prepared for the devil and his angels."

Now, let me go farther still. I said, there was not a blade of grass that ever sprang from the field, without the prescience and power of God. It was but last Sunday that we returned thanks to God, as indeed we ought to thank and bless him, for the gracious harvest he has been pleased to send us. Now, let us take a field of wheat, and I propose this question to you,—

"Do you think did that productive crop of wheat spring up by accident, or was it the gracious gift of God? Do you believe, that the harvest in this field arose as a contingency, or do you believe, that before the creation of the world, the gracious produce given by God this year, was as clearly in the all-seeing eye and mind of that God, as it was when he sent the rain upon it, and commanded His sun to shine upon it this summer?" Now, let me suppose the owner of that ground to have said:—

"Oh, here is my field to be sure—but, if it pleases God to give me a good crop He will give it to me—and if He does not please to do so, He will not—so I may sit down idle—I will neither till, nor sow, or do anything."

Do you think would not this sluggard, this idler, this daring speculator on God's providence, be justly left to starve in his indolent audacious presumption? Yea, you know he would.

Again, whether you be engaged in business, or trade, or farming, or in a profession, I hope you look unto God—I hope you know and feel, that if you are prosperous, it is God that prospers you—that it is He who sends orders into your counting houses, and customers into your shops, grants you the increase of your ground, or prosperity in your profession, and supplies you with daily food and everything that you enjoy.

Now give me leave to ask, will you say, "Oh well, if God sends me orders, I shall have them—or if he sends me customers, I shall have them—or if he sends me produce in my farm, or prosperity in my profession, I shall have them—there is no use in my doing anything; I shall have them, if I am to have them—and I shall not have them, if I am not to have them—therefore I will do nothing"?

Will you thus reason? Will you presume to give utterance to such sentiments? Will you pretend to think so? Nay, you know well, that if you did so, you would be left justly to starve. You know well, that if you are not diligent in your business, if you do not take care of your counting houses—of your shops—of your farm—if you are not diligent and laborious in your profession or calling whatever it be, you know full well, you neither could or ought to expect a blessing from God on your own indolence, your neglect, your presumption, your audacious tempting of His mighty power; you know this is true. Now you will admit, I suppose, that your temporal and spiritual affairs are alike in the hand of God. Will you then venture to reason respecting your immortal souls, as you would not reason respecting the smallest trifle in all your temporal concerns? Will you presume to say, when you neglect the means that God has been pleased to give to you in His holy word, that you are to expect any blessing for your souls, or any salvation from your God? And will you dare to charge your own neglect, your own unbelief, your own rejection of the use of means, will you dare to charge them on him? Surely, conscience must convict you. Your own conscience must make a liar of you, if you dare to charge your own crime on your Creator! You are moral agents, voluntary agents, you are responsible agents, you have to deal with a righteous, just, and holy God, and if you are to rebel against your Maker, in speculating as to your immortal souls, as you would not attempt to speculate in any temporal concern,—again, I say, your blood be upon your own head.*

Remember, it is with respect to spiritual things, as it is with respect to temporal things; that as far as man's knowledge, as far as man's view, as far as man's salvation is concerned, there is no predestination irrespective of his responsibility and conduct as a moral agent. Remember, that no impenitent unbeliever, continuing in impenitence and unbelief, is predestinated to enter into eternal life. No believer is predestinated to perish. Your business is to repent, and believe the Gospel, while it is called to-day. "*To-day if ye will hear His voice, harden not your hearts.*" Heb. iii. 7, 8.

You say, "We can do no good of ourselves. The doctrine of election, as it is written in Scripture, plainly shows that man has it not in his power to do any good to his own soul." Most true. But, while it tells you your own impotence, it tells you where to go for strength and assistance, "*Ask and it shall be given you, seek and ye shall find, knock, and it shall be opened unto you; for*

* Without attempting to enter into any abstruse or metaphysical discussion on the subject, the author would venture to suggest that, much difficulty seems to have arisen from those who vindicate this doctrine of Scripture by speaking or writing against what they call the freedom of the will. This appears to be at least an unscriptural mode of treating the subject, and gives ample ground to those who oppose it, to array against them the whole body of the Word of God, which deals with man, as it confessedly does, as a voluntary responsible agent, as he certainly is.

It is the corruption of the will, the depravity and wickedness of the heart, which aggravates, instead of excusing, the guilt of a moral agent, that appears to be charged on man throughout the scriptures, and which makes his impotence to do good rather an enhancement than a palliation of his iniquity; and this appears to be not only a Scriptural truth, but a truth constantly admitted and applied to moral evil in our ordinary parlance and our common dealing with our fellow-creatures. We say, speaking of them, "That man *cannot* speak a word of truth,—That man *cannot* keep his hands from pilfering,—That man *cannot* keep himself sober,—That fellow *cannot* speak a civil word to you, or *cannot* speak without blaspheming,—That child *cannot* treat its parents with common respect or decency."—These, and similar phrases which we habitually use, and justly apply, never are considered by us, to imply either a want of freedom of will in these persons to do right, in any sense which affects their moral accountability, or any impotence to discharge their duty, which could induce us either to excuse or extenuate their guilt; on the contrary, we use the expression "*cannot*" in a sense that implies an aggravation of their crime and an indurated impenitence of character which makes them subjects of severer judgment. When we thus deal with our fellow-creatures in their several relations of accountability to us, we surely vindicate the ways of God in all his various judgments and dealing with us. And the man who denies original sin, and the man who traces all practical evil to that source alike refuse it as a plea against accountability of their fellow-creatures to themselves *every one that asketh receiveth, and he that seeketh findeth, and to him that knocketh it shall be opened.*" Luke, xi. 9, 10. If it is written, "*No man can come to me, except my Father which hath sent me draw him,*" John, vi. 44, it is also written, "*him that cometh to me, I will in no wise cast out.*" John, vi. 37. He who saith this, invites sinners to come to Him. "*Come unto me all ye that labor, and are heavy laden and I will give you rest.*" Mat. xi. 28.

He complains of their refusal, "*ye will not come to me that ye may have life.*" John, v. 40. Ye do not choose to come to me. In willingly doing what conscience testifies we can do; there is always strength vouchsafed to those who seek it, to do what the Bible tells us we cannot do.

"*Stretch forth thine hand,*" saith Jesus. Mat. xii. 13.

The man does not say, "It is withered and I cannot." No—"*he stretched it forth and it was restored whole as the other.*" Depend on it when the Judge of heaven and earth shall come, there shall be neither metaphysics nor casuistry heard at His tribunal.

Therefore, let me address all in their respective circumstances. Those that are "dead in trespasses and sins,"—If you speak to me on the doctrine of election, and say, "Alas! I am perfectly dead, perfectly insensible, I have no regard for my soul, I am living recklessly in sin, and you cannot say I am among the elect of God." Indeed I cannot, nor is it my province to pronounce. You certainly give no evidence of being one of God's people. You are as the Apostle speaks of himself, and of this very church in their unregenerate state—"*Among whom also we all had our conversation in times past in the lusts of our flesh, fulfilling the desires of the flesh and of the mind; and were by nature the children of wrath, even as others.*"—Ephes. ii. 3. But, neither can I say, that you are not among the elect of God. When the two thieves were hung on the cross and when they joined the mob in reviling Christ, if any had asked, "Are these God's elect people?"—the answer must have been, "Alas, no, they evince that they are the children of Satan." Nevertheless, God's sovereign grace touched the heart of one of these poor sinners, and he turned to Jesus, and said, "*Lord, remember me when thou comest into thy kingdom.*" You know the answer!

Now, though you may have been a hardened rebel against God to this very day, man can neither pronounce nor know whether or not you are one of God's elect. But it is my office to address you, and it is your duty to listen, as you are—a guilty sinner; it is my office to proclaim to you in the name of Jesus, pardon and free salvation from your God. I know, if you hear me, it is God's sovereign grace, overcoming your naturally hard heart, and inclining your ear to listen, opening your heart to attend to the things that are spoken, as he opened the heart of Lydia, "*to attend unto the things that were spoken of Paul,*" Acts, xvi. 14, and as the Apostle in the passage which I have quoted, (Eph. ii. 3.) shows of himself and the Ephesians, that they had been delivered from their guilt, "*But God who is rich in mercy for his great love wherewith he loved us, even when we were dead in sins, hath quickened us together with Christ, (by grace ye are saved;) and hath raised us up together, and made us sit together in heavenly places in Christ Jesus.*" Eph. ii. 4, 5, 6. And perhaps this very subject, perhaps these very words spoken this day, may be God's blessed means of bringing the truth to your heart and conscience, and of leading you to say, "Since free salvation is proclaimed in Christ, though I cannot repent or believe myself, yet God's grace is mighty to save. O let me pray that God may bring a sinner, such as I am, to the feet of Jesus." May the Lord bring this truth to your hearts! and though "dead in trespasses and sins," to this hour, yet God can give you light and life, and salvation, in Christ Jesus, the Lord.

Now, let me address those who are very weak, and who are awakened to a sense of their own inability. A person who is "*dead in trespasses and sins,*" feels no spiritual life, nor is he conscious of spiritual death, any more than a dead body. But sinners who are awakened, begin to feel their inability to do good, they feel they are not able to will or to do, they mourn over their own sin and corruption, and each is ready to cry out, "Alas, I must be lost, I cannot be one of God's people, or I could not be such a guilty sinner as I am." Nay, my dear friend, let us rather trust, that this is "*the day of small things*" with you. God saith, "*who has despised the day of small things?*" Zech. iv. 10. As much as to say, "Surely not I." No, he does not. "*A bruised reed shall he not break, and the smoking flax shall he not quench.*" Isa. xlii. 3. And if indeed you are awakened to see, and feel your own helplessness, it is not you who have awakened yourselves, nor is it the enemy of your soul, who has awakened you. Oh, no surely, if you are awakened, it is the gift of God. "*For by grace are ye saved, through faith, and that, not of yourselves, it is the gift of God, not of works, lest any man should boast.*" Ephes. ii. 8, 9. Therefore, take courage, the sight of your own disease, should lead you to prize the blessing of the Great Physician, and Oh, remember, that you cannot be so guilty, but that Jesus is more mighty to pardon and to save.

Then, again, you who are enlightened, who are strong in the faith, I need not say to you what the blessedness of the doctrine of God's sovereign electing grace is.

Ignorant persons imagine, and speak of those who hold this doctrine thus:—(it is right to mention this error,) "Oh, these persons say, they are the elect of God! they are the good! they are the holy! they are the excellent people of the earth! but for us, poor, guilty creatures, we are lost, we have not any lot or part in the matter, these men say to us, '*come not near to me, for I am holier than thou.*'" Isai. lxv. 5. Oh, my dear friends, it is not the knowledge of his goodness, but it is a knowledge of his deep guilt and misery, that makes a believer prize the doctrine of God's electing grace. It is not because there is anything good in him, but because he feels himself so full of sin, that if he could not look to

God's sovereign grace and mercy to take him, and bring him to Zion, he knows, he would not come,—he knows, that nothing but God's grace could overcome his wicked will at first, or carry on any plans of love and mercy to his soul. And therefore, I say, you who are strong in the faith of the Lord Jesus Christ, your sin has taught you the blessing of the doctrine of election.

But again, it is said, "Oh! then, you may go on in sin, and if you are elected, you may presume on the grace of God. If God has given us his grace, we may go on and live in sin." Remember, Oh! sinner, that God's promises of election are always inseparably connected both with the use of means,* and with an appropriate faith and character, so the Apostle saith, "*We are his workmanship created in Christ Jesus unto good works, which God hath before ordained that we should walk in them*, chap. ii. 10, Again, "*If any man have not the spirit of Christ, he is none of his*," again, "*As many as are led by the spirit of God, they are the sons of God.*" Rom. viii. 9, 14. Again, while our Lord testifies, "*As the branch cannot bear fruit of itself, except it abide in the vine; no more can ye, except ye abide in me.*" So He adds the proof of the fact, "*He that abideth in me, and I in him, the same bringeth forth much fruit: for without me ye can do nothing.*" John, xv. 4, 5.

So here you see in the text, the end of their election, "THAT WE SHOULD BE TO THE PRAISE OF HIS GLORY, WHO FIRST TRUSTED IN CHRIST." That we who have been brought, as it were, the first-fruits of his grace from Jews and Gentiles,—I, a blind, self-righteous persecutor from amongst the Pharisees—you, blind idolaters from the worshippers in the temple of Diana, that "WE SHOULD BE TO THE PRAISE OF HIS GLORY"—monuments, as we are, of His sovereign grace, that we should remember "*we are not our own, but bought with a price, and should therefore glorify God with our bodies and spirits, which are God's.*" 1 Cor. vi. 19, 20. That "*we should show forth the praises of him who hath called us out of darkness into his marvellous light.*" 1 Peter ii. 9. That we should "*present our bodies a living sacrifice, holy, and acceptable unto God, which is our reasonable service.*" Rom. xii. 1. That we should "*let our light so shine before men, that they may see our good works, and glorify our Father which is in heaven.*" Mat. v. 16.

Yes, if men are chosen out of the world by the grace of God, it must be for the service of God. There could be no election to serve the devil, for that is the natural course of all. If men are

* The belief in God's purposes and promises, as connected with the use of means, is remarkably illustrated by the conduct of St. Paul in the storm, Acts, xxvii. God had promised him that "*there should be no loss of any man's life*" on board, verse 22; so he confidently asserted to the crew, to cheer their hearts. Yet though God had promised, and though he had asserted it on God's authority, still when the sailors were about to make their escape out of the vessel, "*Paul said to the centurion, and to the soldiers, Except these abide in the ship, ye cannot be saved,*" verse 31; to profess to trust in any promise of God, and to despise the use of the appointed means, is not Scriptural faith, but unscriptural presumption.

elected from this service, the only proof that can be given of it is, that they are called to the service of God. As St. Peter says, "*elect, according to the foreknowledge of God the Father, through sanctification of the Spirit, unto obedience and sprinkling of the blood of Jesus Christ.*" 1 Pet. i. 2.

Believers know and feel too deeply the bitterness of sin—the burthen of the heavy conflict—the anguish of that lusting of the flesh against the spirit, so feelingly described by the Apostle, Rom. vii. 14-24, not to know and feel that their calling is an holy calling—they feel that holiness and happiness are essentially connected together. Sin is the pleasure of the unregenerate heart, it is the grief and cross of the believer—"*we that are in this tabernacle do groan, being burthened.*" 2 Cor. v. 14. Alas! how often, O believer! has your sinful corrupt heart experienced as a bitter evil what the ignorant world imputes to you as a principle—how often has your sinful heart presumed on the Lord's grace!—how often have you provoked and grieved your Master! Yet, let me ask, did you ever do so in your life that you were not made to feel it bitterly?—did you ever *sow to the flesh, that you did not reap corruption?* Gal. vi. 8,—did you ever *sow the wind, that you did not reap the whirlwind?* Hos. viii. 7. No; if you be a believer, you have felt what the evil of sin is, you feel it continually, and you know you are not elected to go to eternal life by living in your sins,—you know that you are elected to eternal life, if you are indeed one of God's people, to serve and to glorify your Father which is in heaven. But when you feel your inward corruption, when you feel the struggling of sin in your soul—the power of those temptations that would hurry your natural heart away, and draw it on into the vortex of ruin—Oh, then you know what it is to bless God that you have a mighty hand to hold you, and to keep you safe in Jesus, that he will not leave you to perish. You know how sweet are these exceeding great and precious promises and truths—"*My sheep hear my voice, and I know them, and they follow me, and I give unto them eternal life, and they shall never perish, neither shall any pluck them out of my hand. My Father who gave them to me is greater than all, and none is able to pluck them out of my Father's hand. I and my Father are one.*" John x. 27, 28, 29. Again "*This is the Father's will, which hath sent me, that of all which he hath given me, I should lose nothing, but should raise it up again at the last day.*" John vi. 39. You know the consolation of that blessed promise—"*He hath said, I will never leave thee nor forsake thee.*" Heb. xiii. 5. You love the doctrine of election, not because you think yourself good, but because you feel what a guilty sinner you are, and that if God did not keep you, you could never keep yourself; therefore you prize that glorious truth of His word, that His people "*are kept by the power of God through faith unto salvation.*" 1 Peter i. 5.

And now, beloved friends, pray over these things, pray, that God may instruct you. Oh! beware how you tempt God. Beware how you deal with God in spiritual things, as your own natural thoughts and feelings—your own carnal interests and objects make you know and feel, you would not dare to deal with Him in temporal things.—Beware of this!

And O! prize the day of small things. Cherish every feeling of conviction, every emotion of spiritual sensibility, every whisper of an awakened conscience in your hearts, cherish every gleam of hope in Jesus—if it be genuine, it comes from the Lord God, and it shall "*shine more and more unto the perfect day.*" Prov. iv. 18. Remember our Lord's words, "*watch and pray, that ye enter not into temptation.*" Mat. xxvi. 41.

And ye who are strong in faith, pray, that your strength may be renewed day by day. True Faith builds no storehouses for "the Bread that cometh down from heaven," but lives daily on the fresh supplies it gathers from the hand of God. Pray that you may be enabled to "*glorify God in your bodies and spirits which are His,*" 1 Cor. vi. 20, and "*as he who has called you is holy, so be ye holy in all manner of conversation; because it is written, Be ye holy for I am holy.* 1 Pet. i. 14, 15. Let every promise be turned into prayer, that it may be fulfilled, and every precept, that it may be observed. Pray that, during all your course you may be enabled not to "*yield your members as instruments of unrighteousness unto sin,*" but to "*yield yourselves unto God as those who are alive from the dead, and your members as instruments of righteousness unto God.*" Thus shall you glorify your Father, and LIVE TO THE PRAISE OF HIS GLORY.

SIXTH LECTURE.

EPHESIANS I.—13, 14.

"In whom ye also trusted, after that ye heard the word of truth, the gospel of your salvation, in whom also, after that ye believed, ye were sealed with that Holy Spirit of promise, which is the earnest of our inheritance, until the redemption of the purchased possession, unto the praise of his glory."

HAVING considered how God's sovereign, predestinating grace, of which we read in the last passage, no more interferes with man's responsibility as a voluntary, moral agent, or supersedes the right use of means, or the legitimate operation of second causes in spiritual things, than the predeterminate order and succession of all things on earth, supersedes them in man's temporal concerns —having shown its use and consolation to His elect people—and that those who are called by his sovereign mercy and power, are called to glorify Him, as monuments of grace, "*to the praise of his glory.*" Let us observe, how the operations of divine grace are manifested in those who are the objects of it,—that is, how those who are the objects of divine grace are to be known. How does it appear that men "*have obtained this inheritance?*" how that they are "*predestinated according to the purpose of him who worketh all things after the counsel of his own will?*" This is evidently exhibited in the words which I have read to you, "IN WHOM YE ALSO TRUSTED, AFTER THAT YE HEARD THE WORD OF TRUTH, THE GOSPEL OF YOUR SALVATION; IN WHOM ALSO, AFTER THAT YE BELIEVED, YE WERE SEALED WITH THAT HOLY SPIRIT OF PROMISE, WHICH IS THE EARNEST OF OUR INHERITANCE, UNTIL THE REDEMPTION OF THE PURCHASED POSSESSION."

Now, you perceive here how their election to their inheritance, was manifested by the power of divine grace through the Gospel, and I would specially point out three things :—

I. —In their attention to the "Word of truth," when it was preached to them.

II.—In their believing the Gospel of their salvation and trusting in the Lord Jesus.

III.—In the operations and influences of the Spirit of God upon them.

Now, let me entreat you that in the very consideration of this subject, as applied to the Ephesians, you will endeavor to carry out its practical application to your own souls. Let us remember, that the preaching of the Word can no more convey a blessing to our souls, than it could convey a blessing to the beasts that perish, unless the Spirit of God accompanies it. I can neither derive a blessing to my own soul in reading the Bible, or in preaching; nor can you in hearing, unless God by His Spirit teaches us.

May the Spirit of the living God then accompany His Word to our hearts. May He give us those blessed gifts which come alone from Him! May the word spoken in weakness be accompanied with "*demonstration of the Spirit and of power*," 1 Cor. ii. 4, to our souls, so that it may be to us "*a time of refreshing from the presence of the Lord.*"

I.—*The power of divine grace was proved in their attention to the Word preached by the Apostle.*

The natural character of man is exhibited in this, as well as many other instances, in his utter disregard of God's Holy Word. The natural man is a "deaf adder," he stoppeth his ears—he never hears the Scriptures with attention. Men will listen to the language, indeed of the preacher; they will attend, perhaps, to his voice—to his manner—they will criticise them for you, together with the style and expression of everything he says—if you ask them their opinion of these things, they will be able to give it to you readily enough—but, ask them the meaning of the holy Word preached to them—they know nothing about it, except perhaps totally to misrepresent or pervert it. How many of you can give an account of the spiritual truths that are set before you, when you leave this or any place of worship? I dare say, you will find, if you examine yourselves, that there are but too many who cannot give any. Our blessed Lord illustrates their case, in the parable of the sower, by the seed sown on the high-way-side. "*When any one*" saith our Lord, "*heareth the word of the kingdom and understandeth it not,*" (it never reaches to his understanding nor his conscience) "*Then cometh the wicked one, and catcheth away that which was sown in his heart. This is he which receiveth seed by the way-side.*" Mat. xiii. 19.

Now, what must be the end of those who hear, and hear, and hear, and hear again, and again, and again, and again, but who are at the last as though they had never heard? Do you think, is not man responsible for this inattention? When we say, that this is your natural heart, and when we say, that nothing but divine grace can deliver you from it, do you think you are not responsible for your guilty disregard of God's Word? Your mother would have corrected you when you were a child, for inattention to your alphabet, if you would not learn your letters. Your school-master or school-mistress would punish you if you neglected your lesson. If you be a clerk, or a servant, or an apprentice, your employer would dismiss you, or cancel your indentures, if you were not attentive to your business. If you be a professional man, or if you be in business yourself, your clients and customers would forsake you, if you did not attend to your profession, or counting-house, or shop. You know, this is all right and just, and you would deal so yourself with your fellow-man. And "*shall not the judge of all the earth do right*"—Gen. xviii. 25,—in bringing you into judgment, when you neglect His blessed Word? When you neglect His expostulations—His entreaties—His warnings—His promises—His threatenings—His mercies? Shall your Creator—your Preserver—your Benefactor—your Redeemer, appeal to you, and shall you neglect and despise Him—shall you be irresponsible and unpunished? Your consciences echo the justice of that solemn question, "*How shall we escape if we neglect so great salvation?*" Heb. ii. 3.

But your consciousness of this, if you feel your own negligent and inattentive hearts—if you feel the burden of that thoughtless, wandering, distracted spirit that tells you, it is not in yourselves to direct your way, but that the gift of attention is the gift of God, this should lead you to pray with the Psalmist, "*Consider and hear me, O Lord my God, lighten mine eyes, lest I sleep the sleep of death.*" Ps. xiii. 3.—"*Teach me thy way, O Lord, and I will walk in thy truth. Unite my heart to fear thy name.*" Ps. lxxxvi. 11. And if the Lord Jesus Christ, speaking of the natural wickedness of the human heart, in St. John's Gospel, vi. 44, saith, "*No man can come to me, except my Father, which hath sent me, draw him,*"—so, remember that your prayer should be the prayer of the church, in the Canticle, i. 4, "*Draw me, we will run after thee.*" Oh! that this may be the prayer of your hearts and mine! If you feel the want, remember—the God who can supply all your wants, invites you to come and ask,—"*if any of you lack wisdom, let him ask of God, who giveth to all men liberally, and upbraideth not, and it shall be given him,"* James i. 5. "*Ask, and it shall be given you; seek, and ye shall find; knock, and it shall be opened unto you. For every one that asketh, receiveth; and he that seeketh, findeth; and to him that knocketh, it shall be opened. If a son shall ask bread of any of you that is a father, will he give him a stone? or if he ask a fish, will he for a fish give him a serpent? Or if he shall ask an egg, will he offer him a scorpion? If ye then, being evil, know how to give good gifts unto your children, how much more shall your heavenly Father give the Holy Spirit to them that ask him?*" Luke xi. 9–13, for "*the hearing ear, and the seeing eye, the Lord hath made even both of them.*" Prov. xx. 12. "*The preparations of the heart in man, and the answer of the tongue is from the Lord.*" Prov. xvi. 1. Therefore attention to God's truth is one of the first manifestations of the grace of God. Oh! then, if your heart is inclined to listen to the Word of God, if you are anxiously inquiring into divine truth, cherish, I beseech you, that spark of grace in your heart. It may be but a spark but remember, Jesus "*will not quench the smoking flax,*" Isa. xlii. 3, nay, but "*He giveth more grace,*" Jam. iv. 6. Remember that the refreshing showers that brought life to the land of Israel, were at first but a little cloud, as a man's hand in the sky. And remember, again, you have a God to come to who saith, "*Him that cometh to me I will in no wise cast out.*" John, vi. 44. Oh! cherish every desire for truth, pray for more of it, "*if so be that you have tasted that the Lord is gracious.*" 1 Pet. ii. 3.

But again, I said,—II. *Faith in the Gospel of Christ, and trust in the Lord Jesus, is the manifestation of the power of divine grace,* "IN WHOM YE ALSO TRUSTED, AFTER THAT YE HEARD THE WORD OF TRUTH, THE GOSPEL OF YOUR SALVATION." Inattention necessarily must produce unbelief. How can they believe who do not hear or consider that which is proposed to their belief? "*Faith cometh by hearing.*" Rom. x. 17. Faith, the belief of the truth, is, like attention, the gift of God. You have that principle laid down in this epistle:—ii. 8. "*By grace are ye saved, through faith, and that, not of yourselves, it is the gift of God, not of works, lest any man should boast.*" The disciples, though they had been long with their Lord, hearing His words, and marking the character of His divine power, imprinted on every act He did, and every word He uttered, yet, they were ignorant of Him, and of all the Scriptures concerning Him, till after His resurrection, when, as we read in St. Luke, xxiv. 45, "*he opened their understanding that they might understand the Scriptures.*" The Apostle Paul, speaking of the impotence of man to produce any effect on the soul by his own power, saith, 1 Cor. iii. 5, 6, 7.—"*Who then is Paul, or who is Apollos, but ministers by whom ye believed, even as the Lord gave to every man. I have planted, Apollos watered: but God gave the increase*

So then, neither is he that planteth anything, neither he that watereth, but God that giveth the increase." So God alone is to receive the praise.

Thus again, in 2nd Corinthians, he sets this clearly before us, contrasting the power of Satan over the human mind, in blinding it, with the power of God in enlightening it, iv. 3, "*If our Gospel be hid, it is hid to them that are lost.*" Now, how is it hid? ver. 4, "*in whom the god of this world hath blinded the minds of them which believe not, lest the light of the glorious gospel of Christ, who is the image of God should shine unto them.*" How then, had he and those whom he addressed been delivered from this blindness? We see, verse 6, "*But God, who commanded the light to shine out of darkness, hath shined in our hearts, to give the light of the knowledge of the glory of God in the face of Jesus Christ.*" The same power that commanded the light to shine out of darkness, the same God who said, "*let there be light, and there was light,*" alone can shed light into the heart and conscience of the sinner, alone can enable him to "*believe the record that God hath given of his Son,*" 1 John, v. 10, therefore, when the Gospel is received by faith, when the sinner embraces the hope that is set before him in that Gospel,—that, I say, is a manifestation of the power of the spirit of God, as producing that influence on the soul. So you see in 1st Thessalonians, the Apostle sets forth this, as giving to him a clear testimony of their election of God, 1 Thess. i. 4, "*knowing, brethren, beloved, your election of God.*" How did he know it? "*For our gospel came not unto you in word only, but also in power and in the Holy Ghost, and in much assurance.*" He knew that they were taught of God, because his Gospel came to them, not in word only, but in power. So, brethren, when we see the Gospel come with power to the consciences of sinners, when we see the sinner thoughtless, careless, hardened; and when we see him awakened, anxious—humbled—and brought low to the feet of Jesus—when we see him who took no interest whatever in the blessed Bible, who took no interest in prayer, no interest in instruction, when we see him searching the sacred Scriptures—when we see him calling upon his God in spirit and in truth—when we see him delighting to listen to instruction—ready to receive it as a little child—when we see him who was proud and self-righteous, counting "*all things loss for the excellency of the knowledge of Christ Jesus his Lord,*" we know, that that man must be taught of God; for this is not of nature, it is of God's gift alone.

Now, faith produces that effect which the Apostle speaks of in the text, "IN WHOM YE ALSO TRUSTED, AFTER THAT YE HEARD THE WORD OF TRUTH, THE GOSPEL OF YOUR SALVATION." Trust in Jesus is the consequence of faith in Jesus, some confound these, but there is an important distinction between them. The belief of the Gospel of Jesus may often exist and does exist in the heart of many a sinner, when that sinner is not trusting or reposing, in Christ as he ought to do—he is not casting his care on Him as he ought to do—he is not rejoicing in him as he ought to do—he has no confident assurance of hope as he ought to have. The Apostle says, "*In whom ye also trusted, after ye heard the word of truth, the Gospel of your salvation.*" The word, "*trusted,*" is supplied in our translation, but it is properly and necessarily so, being carried on as you perceive from the preceding verse, "*That we should be to the praise of his glory, who first trusted in Christ, in whom ye also* (as well as we) *trusted.*" It is the word which the sense demands. It literally signifies "hoped." When we "*believe the record that God has given of his son,*" when we know what Jesus hath done for us, it is our privilege to trust with holy confidence upon the glorious work of our blessed Master.

But, alas! how few do so! how few there are who really enjoy the confidence of hope which it is their privilege to feel!

It appears to me of moment to consider this subject more attentively; for it seems of the utmost practical importance to the peace and strength of the soul. As far as my experience of the state of believers whom I have visited, both in health and sickness, extends, I feel the importance of it more and more.

The point of view in which the subject seems to me to demand attention is this, that we should endeavor to ascertain satisfactorily to our own minds, the difference which, as I have stated, exists between the belief of the Gospel and trust in the Gospel. I have said there is an important distinction between them, and though I know there are authorities high and deservedly esteemed on the opposite side, I must reiterate the assertion; and I entreat your attentive consideration of it, for I think there is not a servant of God in the world to whom it is not, at least at some times, of vast importance to his own peace.

We shall first briefly consider what the Gospel is, and then the difference between believing it and trusting in it.

The Gospel is that good news which God proclaims to man of salvation through the Lord Jesus Christ. He proclaims that blessed Saviour as our Surety, who has paid both our debt of obedience to His holy law, and of penalty for its violation. Of obedience—"*Christ is the end of the law for righteousness, to every one that believeth.*" Rom. x. 4. "*This is his name whereby he shall be called,* THE LORD OUR RIGHTEOUSNESS." Jer. xxiii. 6. Of penalty—"*Who his own self bare our sins in his own body on the tree.*" 1 Pet. ii. 24. "*Who was delivered for our offences, and was raised again for our justification.*" Rom. iv. 25.

When our Lord gave His apostles their divine commission "*Go ye into all the world, and preach the gospel to every creature,*" He said, "*He that believeth and is baptized, shall be saved.*" Mark xvi. 15, 16. There cannot be a doubt that he suspended salvation on the belief of that Gospel.

Now the Gospel is a relative term—the belief of it necessarily involves the belief of several other truths—such as the lost state of the sinner—the impossibility of salvation by anything he can do for himself—the sins and imperfections that cleave to his best actions and intentions—in fact a full conviction that he is totally unable to fulfil the holy law of God—that "*by the deeds of the law there shall no flesh be justified in his sight, for by the law is the knowledge of sin.*" Rom. iii. 20.

Therefore, the belief of the Gospel necessarily involves the conviction that the ordinary refuges of the sinner's heart are all refuges of lies, such as the hope that his virtues will be weighed against his sins, and preponderate in his favor; or if not, that Christ will be, as it were, a make-weight, thrown into the scale to turn the balance for his salvation. His virtues—his alms—his good resolutions—his prayers—his reading the Bible—his observance of religious ordinances—his respectability and high character amongst men—all these things which formerly were combined to give him some hope of acceptance with God, and which, though he believed that Christ's merits alone could make them efficient, yet he believed as sincerely must be necessarily added to Christ's merits to save him—all these he has now ceased to trust in as giving him a shadow of hope—he has learned to "*count all things but loss for the excellency of the knowledge of Christ Jesus his Lord,*" Phil. iii. 8, and that he is not to be saved because Christ gives weight or value or acceptance to his works, and thus to his person,—but that Christ hath purchased redemption for his person,—not as being righteous, but as a lost and helpless sinner; and that thus it is his blessed privilege to transfer all hope from his own miserable efforts, to the righteousness and blood of this crucified and risen Redeemer. Thus new light and hope break in on his mind, and whether it has come by slow and imperceptible degrees, as it more frequently does, one shade of error after another vanishing before "*the Sun of Righteousness,*" as He arises on the soul, "*with healing in his wings,*" Mal. iv. 2, or whether it has come, as it sometimes does, like light to a man whose eyes are opened in the noon of day, the result is the same; the enlightened sinner has been brought to see, that all his salvation is in Christ, and not in himself, or in any other, he has been brought to understand the word of the Apostle, "*Neither is there salvation, in any other, for there is none other name under heaven, given among men whereby we must be saved,*" Acts, iv. 12, he has learned that therefore his whole obedience to the commandments of God is to be rendered, not as before, with the vain expectation of its helping to obtain forgiveness for him, but because that forgiveness has been dearly purchased and freely given through the precious blood of his Redeemer.

Thus the whole foundation of the hope of his soul—the whole principle of his moral conduct—has been totally changed, in the mind of the sinner who has been brought to repent and believe the Gospel. His hope has been transferred from himself to his Redeemer, and his obedience from a principle of the self-interested efforts of a slavish fear, to the real principle, not only of the Gospel, but of the Law,—a principle of grateful love. Well may it then indeed be said, "*Therefore if any man be in Christ he is a new creature: old things are passed away; behold, all things are become new. And all things are of God, who hath reconciled us unto himself by Jesus Christ.*" 2 Cor. v. 17, 18.

But now we come to consider the nature of that faith with which a sinner believes in Christ; and this is to be viewed as differing from that trust, from which it appears so necessary to distinguish it.

The object of faith must be the same in all who believe the Gospel—Christ is all their salvation. If they do not believe the record that God hath given of Christ, then they do not believe the Gospel. "*He that believeth not God hath made him a liar; because he believeth not the record that God gave of his Son. And this is the record, that God hath given to us eternal life, and this life is in his Son. He that hath the Son hath life; and he that hath not the Son of God hath not life.*" 1st John, v. 10, 11, 12. If men do not believe this record, then the thing which they believe is not the Gospel, but some scheme of salvation different from that propounded by God.

But although the object of faith must necessarily be the same to all the children of God, for if there be but one Gospel, making all allowance for errors not affecting vital truth, they can believe but one Gospel, and there is indeed but "*One Lord, one faith, one baptism.*" Eph. iv. 5. Yet there is no truth more certain, both from Scripture—from fact—and from the experience of every believer, than that the degree of confidence with which they trust or hope in Christ, differs in almost all persons, and in the same person, at different times. When the understanding is enlightened to know, and when the heart receives the salvation proclaimed through Christ to sinners—("*for with the heart man believeth unto righteousness,*" Rom. x. 10,)—when it receives Christ as the true and only foundation on which it rests all hope of salvation thereby excluding and rejecting every other—then the sinner believes the Gospel. But how fluctuating is the confidence of his deceitful heart in the faithfulness and truth, the power and love of Him in whom he still believes as the only refuge of his soul. It is then he begins to feel and to lament his weakness, and his want of faith. He feels so often that he wants that trust, that confidence of heart in Christ, which ought to accompany the belief of his salvation, that he fears and complains he has no faith at all.

It is this that marks one great difference in the flock of Christ, and draws forth so much, the glorious character of their tender, gracious Shepherd, for thus spake the Prophet, "*He shall feed his flock like a shepherd: he shall gather the lambs with his arm, and carry them in his bosom, and shall gently lead those that are with young.*" Isai. xl. 11. The tottering steps of him who is weak in the faith—the trembling fearfulness in their pilgrimage of many a weary heavy-laden believer in the flock of Christ—too clearly illustrate the difference between him who boldly walks, with trust and confidence in his Lord, and him whose feeble hope hangs sometimes between doubt and despair.

I have known persons whose faith was in Christ alone—jealous for His truth—fervent in His cause—full of love to His people—and devoted to His service, who have nevertheless gone heavily most of all their days, from want of trust and hope in their Lord. Surely, a large proportion of the book of Psalms appears inspired for the consolation and support of the weak and timid believer—the 77th, the 143rd, and many others, are the language of their hearts; and if for *faith* in Christ, as the salvation of the soul, you substitute *trust* in Christ for its salvation, in speaking to such—instead of strengthening their faith, and comforting their heart, you rather confirm their doubts and fears, and join the enemy in harassing and afflicting them. Trust in Christ implies a consciousness that you believe, nay more, it implies a consciousness that you believe with such implicit faith—that you repose a confidence in Him to such an extent, that you feel it consolatory to your heart. Now it is the very fact of confounding faith with the consciousness of faith; or faith with trust, which necessarily implies this, by which I have seen the mind of many both living and dying, harassed and perplexed most deeply. Many a painful hour have I sat beside the dying bed of a believer, and when I would read of Christ and all his glorious work and offices, I have heard these words:—

"Oh! yes; I know that—that is all true—but, Oh! that I could believe it—O! that I had faith—O! that I could find peace," &c. &c.

Instead of deriving their consolation from Christ, they have been seeking for consolation in themselves; and instead of being satisfied with believing in Him, they have been seeking for satisfaction, in believing that they believed. Unless they feel confidence, they cannot think they have faith. In looking to their own hearts for confidence and hope, they have been looking away from the only source from which alone either could be derived. This seems to me to be produced by the erroneous principle of confounding trust with faith, and only to be overcome by showing the difference between them.

To such a one I would say—"How vain to be looking into yourself for confidence—nay, look out of yourself unto Jesus. If Jesus is the only ground of your salvation, however weak your faith, when Jesus is its object—fear not, but rejoice. "*Let the heart of them rejoice that seek the Lord.*" Psalm cv. 4.

The fact is, that faith is generally weak; and when a believer feels his faith to be so, if his mind has been imbued with the idea that confidence or trust in Christ is the only true faith, and therefore necessary to salvation, he is discouraged and oppressed; yea, I have seen him overwhelmed by looking into his own heart for this confidence, without which he could not think himself a believer. It may be said by some that this is only contending about words, for that trust or confidence is only a stronger degree of faith—or faith in lively exercise. I am not inclined to cavil as to words, but granting this to be so, though indeed it is not—yet what havoc in the Church of Christ a man would make, who should represent strong faith as necessary to salvation! this were to frighten away the Lambs from Him who "*gathers them with his arm, and carries them in his bosom*"—this were to harass and to drive to death, instead of "*gently leading those that are with young.*" Such is not the word of Him who saith to the "weary and heavy laden," "*Come unto me, and I will give you rest.*"

How often have I seen the heart refreshed by speaking thus to those who were sinking under this oppressive error. "You are turning, my friend, into your own heart, and not to Jesus—you are looking into your own heart for confidence instead of looking unto Him in whom you may have confidence and strength—"*Look unto me and be ye saved,*" Isaiah xlv. 22, is His word. "*Look*" —even to turn the eye to Jesus as our All in faith, can bring salvation to the soul—true your faith is weak, but Jesus is mighty, and remember it is written, "*God so loved the world, that he gave his only begotten Son, that whosoever believeth in him should not perish, but have everlasting life.*" John iii. 16. Think of "*whosoever,*" surely you are included here—"*whosoever believeth,*" no matter whether his faith be strong or weak—whether confident or trembling—whether a lamb of the flock or the strongest of the flock—a Babe in Christ or a Father in Christ—if Jesus is indeed the only refuge of his soul, "*whosoever believeth shall not perish, but have everlasting life.*" The infant is as safe as the giant, when both are in the fortress—the timid child as safe as the stoutest sailor, when both are in the vessel that outrides the storm. Cheer up your heart, and look unto Jesus. The question is not, whether we are strong, but whether Jesus is our refuge—not how confidently we believe, but in whom we believe.—Therefore, "*Trust ye in the Lord forever, for in the Lord Jehovah is everlasting strength.*" Isaiah xxvi. 4.

O how often have I seen the soul refreshed and lifted out of its doubts and fears, and brought to trust and confidence, and peace, by showing that when Jesus is indeed the object of faith, the weakest believer may rejoice in Jesus. I have seen them, "*out of weakness made strong, waxing valiant in fight,*" Heb. xi. 34, triumphing over sin and death, and hell, "*in all these things more than conquerors, through him that loved them.*" Rom. viii. 37.

Though this does not strictly belong to the interpretation of this text, yet as I have drawn a distinction between *believing* and *trusting*, I think it necessary to explain it knowing its practical importance; but it is clear, as I have stated that, *faith in the Gospel of Christ, and trust, in the Lord Jesus, is the manifestation of the power of divine grace,* there can be no faith, no confidence in Christ, but by the grace and power of the Spirit of God.

But we see, III.—*The power of divine grace, and their election to their inheritance, manifested by the operations and influences of the Holy Spirit upon them.* "IN WHOM ALSO AFTER THAT YOU BELIEVED, YE WERE SEALED WITH THAT HOLY SPIRIT OF PROMISE."

It is unnecessary to remark, after what has been said on the second head of this passage, that the inward power and operation of the Holy Ghost, enlightening their hearts to understand and believe the Gospel, and to trust in the Lord Jesus, must necessarily be implied in this place. It was indispensable, not only to the commencement, but to the continuance and support of divine life in their souls.

But we are not to understand the scope and meaning of the Apostle, as limited to that power and grace of the Spirit, by which alone their minds could be enlightened to understand the Gospel; it seems here that he is speaking also of the miraculous gifts of the Spirit, which God had given them by the laying on of the hands of the Apostle, after they had received the Holy Ghost in his ordinary operations. This you will perceive by referring to Acts xix. "*It came to pass, that while Apollos was at Corinth, Paul, having passed through the upper coasts, came to Ephesus, and finding certain disciples, he said unto them, have you received the Holy Ghost, since ye believed? and they said unto him, we have not so much as heard whether there be any Holy Ghost.*" He evidently intended by this question, had they received the miraculous gifts of the Holy Ghost? but they had not understood or known anything of that, about which the Apostle spoke to them. "*And he said unto them, unto what then were ye baptized? and they said, unto John's baptism.*" Had they been baptized with the baptism of Christ's ordinance, they must have been baptized, "*in the name of the Father, and of the Son, and of the Holy Ghost,*" Mat. xxviii. 19. But these disciples at Ephesus had only embraced the testimony of John, they had not known the Gospel of Christ, until Paul visited them. "*Then said Paul, John verily baptized with the baptism of repentance, saying unto the people, that they should believe on him which should come after him, that is, on Christ Jesus. When they heard this, they were baptized in the name of the Lord Jesus, and when Paul had laid his hands upon them, the Holy Ghost came on them; and they spake with tongues and prophesied.*" Acts xix. 1–6.

You see, the Holy Spirit of whom he speaks as having sealed them, (when we look to the facts of their history,) seems to have comprehended the miraculous gifts of the Spirit, which they received by the laying on of the Apostle's hands after they believed, as we know, they must also have received his influence into their hearts before, to enable them to believe in Christ.*

* The explanation of this passage, including both ordinary and extraordinary operations of the Holy Spirit, seems strictly Scriptural to the Author, although men of high name have excluded each of them alternately from the sense of the Apostle.

One, whose authority has been long in high repute, with some who ought to be better taught, says, "In the following passage St. Paul represents the faith of the Ephesians in Christ, to have been the consequence of their having heard the Gospel preached, and the communication of the Spirit to have been subsequent to their faith." Then quoting this verse, he adds, "The order to be here noticed is this—first the hearing of the word,—secondly, belief produced by that hearing,—thirdly, the communication of the Spirit in consequence of that belief." The principle which this author intended to illustrate may be seen in a sentiment which precedes this quotation by a

These miraculous gifts, we know, have ceased. We know they are not now given, although grievous error has been recently propagated on that subject.* It does not come within the scope of my intention to-day, to enter more fully into it than to say, we know that these gifts of the Spirit are not imparted; and we may just make this one observation further, that, if miraculous gifts had always continued, they had long since ceased to appear miraculous. The end for which they were given, namely, to testify to God's truth, had ceased to be answered by them, had they continued in the church.

But there are gifts of the Spirit which are always given to the Church of Christ, as you will find by referring to 1 Cor. xii. 4, 5, 6, "*There are diversities of gifts, but the same Spirit. And there are differences of administrations, but the same Lord. And there are diversities of operations, but it is the same God that worketh all in all. But the manifestation of the Spirit is given to every man to profit withal. To one is given, by the Spirit, the word of wisdom.*"—the word of wisdom—that is not an extraordinary gift. "*If any man lack wisdom, let him ask of God who giveth to all men liberally, and upbraideth not, and it shall be given him.*"—"*To another the word of knowledge by the same Spirit,*" that is not an extraordinary gift.—"*To another faith by the same Spirit.*"—That is an ordinary gift. Then the Apostle speaks of the miraculous gifts. But these are the gifts which constitute a man a disciple of Christ,—"the word of wisdom"—being "wise unto salvation." "*For to one is given, by the Spirit,*

few pages. He says, "There is not a single passage in the New Testament which leads us to suppose, that any supernatural power was exerted over the minds of ordinary hearers, and therefore we are authorized to attribute their faith to the voluntary exercise of their reason." ! ! ! The writer of this is no more—his name is not quoted—for the author would not inflict reproach on the individual who penned this sentiment—but how many embrace these principles.

Scott, in his commentary, on the contrary, says of this passage, "This cannot, with any propriety, be explained of miraculous powers, these were not the earnest, pledge and foretaste of heaven as this seal is declared to have been; for many unsanctified persons exercised miraculous powers. But the sanctifying and comforting influences of the Holy Spirit, seal believers as the children of God and heirs of heaven:—they are the first fruits of that holy felicity, and they impress the holy image of God upon their souls."

"What Scott says of the sanctifying and comforting influences of the Holy Spirit is unquestionably true—but as to the exercise of miraculous powers by "*many* unsanctified persons," this is not so very clear. It was through the laying on of the Apostles' hands that these powers were communicated, and though they may have been committed, in some instances, to persons who were false professors, as undoubtedly many such were in the Church; yet it by no means follows, that to those who were indeed the Children of God, such gifts of the Spirit were not a source of consolation and a seal of their Sonship—although distinct from, and inferior to, the inward "joy and peace in believing" which the Spirit's testimony of Jesus alone can give to the soul. But the fact in the history of the Acts quoted in the text, does not seem to justify this limited interpretation of the passage. The author therefore quite agrees with Bloomfield, who says on this. "Considering the persons of whom it is said, we are, I think, bound to understand the extraordinary and supernatural gifts of the Spirit as well as his ordinary influences and graces, though most recent commentators take it of the latter only." The historical fact, Acts xix. 6, seems quite to preclude Scott's limitation; and it were vain to multiply quotations to prove that the opinion first cited in this note, is quite at variance with the very essence of divine truth.

* The Unknown Tongues were at this time making a great noise in London.

the word of wisdom," 1 Cor. xii. 8, (for example, when men are given to learn from the Scriptures of truth, "*which are able to make them wise unto salvation, through faith which is in Christ Jesus.*" 2 Tim. iii. 15.) "*To another the word of knowledge, by the same Spirit*," ("*this is life eternal, to know thee, the only true God and Jesus Christ whom thou hast sent.*" John xvii. 3.) "*To another faith by the same Spirit*," ("*he that believeth on the Son hath everlasting life, but he that believeth not the Son shall not see life, but the wrath of God abideth on him.*" John, iii. 36.) These are gifts which, in various proportions, are given to all who are sealed unto life eternal.

The other gifts enumerated here, "*the gifts of healing*," "*the working of miracles*," "*prophecy*," "*discerning of spirits*," "*divers kinds of tongues*," "*the interpretation of tongues*," were given by the Lord for his own wise purposes, at the time. First, at Pentecost, and afterwards, by laying on of the Apostles' hands, to manifest the divine authority of the Gospel, and to testify the truth of that doctrine which the Lord sent His apostles to preach. But these gifts and fruits of the Spirit which you see in Galatians, v. 22, these are the fruits which the Spirit always produces, though in various degrees, in the children of God, "*some thirty, some sixty, some an hundred fold*," "*the fruit of the Spirit is love, joy, peace, long suffering, gentleness, goodness, faith, meekness, temperance.*" These are manifestly the gifts of grace. These manifest the influence and operation of God's sovereign power upon the souls of those who are the subjects of them. So, the Apostle says, in 2 Cor. iii. 2–3, "*Ye are our epistle, written in our hearts, known and read of all men. Forasmuch as you are manifestly declared to be the epistle of Christ, ministered by us, written not with ink, but with the Spirit of the living God ; not in tables of stone but in fleshly tables of the heart.*" Therefore, the Apostle says, the gift of the Spirit is to them the pledge or "EARNEST OF THE INHERITANCE UNTIL THE REDEMPTION OF THE PURCHASED POSSESSION." He uses this expression in 2 Corinthians, i. 22, "*who hath also sealed us, and given us the earnest of the Spirit in our hearts*," and he uses a similar expression, again, in this Epistle, iv. 30, "*Grieve not the Holy Spirit of God, whereby ye are sealed unto the day of redemption*," he calls it an earnest and a seal. Here he says it is "THE EARNEST OF OUR INHERITANCE UNTIL THE REDEMPTION OF THE PURCHASED POSSESSION." What is the meaning of that? Was not the redemption completed by the Lord Jesus Christ, when He died on the cross? Yes. The price of our redemption was paid, but the redeemed of Christ were not then, and are not yet brought home to the glory of their inheritance. The ransom might be sent out for those poor captives of our country, for whom we all have felt and feel, such deep and painful interest,* who are now prisoners, or have been so, in a distant foreign land, in the hands of savages. The ransom might have been sent out for them, and the ransom might be paid, but

* Those who had been taken captive in the Affghan War.

still, they might be travelling in the enemy's land, and not brought home to their habitation, their family, and their rest. Such is the state of the redeemed of Christ. The ransom is paid down for them, but they are not yet come to their inheritance. If you open Romans viii. 16–23, you will see this fully set forth. The Apostle says, "*The spirit itself beareth witness with our spirit that we are the children of God, and if children, then heirs, heirs of God and joint heirs with Christ, if so be that we suffer with him, that we may be also glorified together, for I reckon that the sufferings of this present time are not worthy to be compared with the glory which shall be revealed in us.*" Believers were suffering then, so they are now, but these sufferings "*are not worthy to be compared with the glory which shall be revealed in us.*" Mark those words, "the glory which shall be revealed." It was to be revealed then, and is yet to be revealed now. But though it is not yet revealed it shall be. For consider that which follows "*for the earnest expectation of the creature,*" (i. e. *all creation,*) "*waiteth for the manifestation of the sons of God.*" That is, waiteth for a certain time, namely, the time when God's children shall be manifested to the world, that will be "*the manifestation of the sons of God.*"

The sense of this passage in Romans, had been much plainer if the original word which is translated "*creature,*" in the 19th, 20th and 21st verses had been translated "*creation,*" as it is in the 22nd verse; the same translation would have given a uniform and a clearer sense to the whole. The Apostle is describing the misery in which sin has placed this whole earth, and he represents the whole world, and all its inhabitants, as it were suffering, and groaning, and longing for deliverance.

"*For the creation was made subject to vanity,*" to its present helpless and miserable condition, in which it seems as it were, to have been formed in vain, not to answer its due end, the glory of God, or the happiness of his creatures; "*not willingly, but by reason of him who hath subjected the same,*"—not by its own choice or desire, but under the righteous sentence of Him, who has brought this judgment on it for sin; the sentence of death, the penalty of sin, to its inhabitants—the fear and dread of them to all the living creatures—and thorns, and thistles, to the very ground, for their sake. But though thus subjected now, there is a blessed hope for its deliverance. God hath subjected it to vanity, for the present, but it is still "*in hope, because the creation itself shall be delivered from the bondage of corruption, into the glorious liberty of the children of God.*" The day is at hand when all the children of God "shall be delivered from the bondage of corruption," in which they have been held, in bodies of sin and death, to the resurrection inheritance of everlasting glory; and all creation shall participate in the glorious liberty—such is the triumphal song of the Psalmist, "*Let the heavens rejoice, and let the earth be glad. Let the sea roar, and the fulness thereof, let the field be joyful, and all that is therein, then shall all the trees of the wood rejoice before the*

Lord. For he cometh, for he cometh to judge the earth, he shall judge the world with righteousness, and the people with his truth." Psalm, xcvi. 11, 12, 13. That this resurrection glory, is that of which the Apostle speaks, is perfectly clear, because, he proceeds: "*For we know, that the whole creation groaneth and travaileth in pain together until now, and not only they, but ourselves also, which have the first fruits of the Spirit, even we ourselves groan within ourselves, waiting for the adoption, to wit, the redemption of our body.*" The price is paid, for the ransom of the body and soul of the believer. The soul is delivered, all its guilt is washed away in the blood of the Lamb, and it is clothed in His spotless righteousness. But still it groans in a body of sin. The body is still subject to disease and death, the sentence must be executed on it, "*dust thou art, and unto dust shalt thou return.*" Gen. iii. 18. And we know and feel ourselves, that we are, "*through fear of death, all our lifetime subject to bondage.*" Heb. ii. 15. But the gift of the Spirit, that leads us to look to Jesus, to believe on Him, in whom we have deliverance, this is the pledge, this "THE EARNEST OF OUR INHERITANCE, UNTIL THE REDEMPTION OF THE PURCHASED POSSESSION; until that body shall be raised again in glory from its dust, "*to meet its Lord in the air,*" 1 Thess. iv. 17, until the glorious "*manifestation of the sons of God,*" for which now "*all creation groaneth and travaileth in pain.*" So too the Apostle speaks in Phil. iii. 20, 21, "*Our conversation (citizenship) is in heaven, from whence also we look for the Saviour, the Lord Jesus Christ; who shall change our vile body, that it may be fashioned like unto his glorious body, according to the working whereby he is able even to subdue all things unto himself.*"

If that blessed hope, in Jesus, is then the anchor of our soul—if all the blessed promises that are given us to hope in, "*are in him yea and in him amen.*" 2 Cor. i. 20. The Spirit that teaches you to trust in Jesus is the pledge and earnest of the fulfilment of these promises, until the day of redemption,—then in that hope you may live and die with confidence—you may lift up your head above the waves of trouble in time—you may lay down your head on your pillow of death—and the last sound that falters on your dying tongue may be "*O death where is thy sting! O grave where is thy victory!*" 1 Cor. xv. 55. Your friends may commit your body to the dust, "in sure and certain hope of the resurrection to eternal life," and the tear of sorrow may be exhaled from the eye of faith and love, as it is raised to the Sun of Righteousness, with the sweet remembrance "*Precious in the sight of the Lord is the death of his saints.*" Psalm cxvi. 15; and with the still sweeter anticipation that "*when Christ who is our life shall appear, then shall ye also appear with him in glory.*" Col. iii. 4.

"*Beloved,*" saith the Apostle John, "*now are we the Sons of God; and it doth not yet appear what we shall be, but we know that, when he shall appear, we shall be like him, for we shall see him as he is.*" 1 John, iii. 2. Then shall we bear the impress of that seal of "THE HOLY SPIRIT OF PROMISE," whereby we are "SEALED UNTO THE DAY OF REDEMPTION," for "*as we have borne the image of the earthy, we shall also bear the image of the heavenly.*" 1 Cor. xv. 19. Then shall every hope be realized, and the soul shall be satiated to all the full capacities of immortality. Such is the Psalmist's joyful anticipation when speaking of those who have their portion in this life, he saith, "*As for me,*" my portion is "*I shall behold thy face in righteousness.—I shall be satisfied when I awake with thy likeness.*" Psalm xvii. 15. How naturally one may say, might the heart burst into the Doxology, from this Psalm,—"Glory be to the Father, and to the Son, and to the Holy Ghost. As it was in the beginning, is now, and ever shall be, world without end."

Surely, then, this blessed hope and the blessed Spirit who inspires it, is the manifestation of His grace and love to thy soul. O believer! surely this is the pledge and "EARNEST OF OUR INHERITANCE, TILL THE REDEMPTION OF THE PURCHASED POSSESSION, TO THE PRAISE OF HIS GLORY," till the trumpet that heralds his glorious coming in the clouds, shall awake the sleeping forms of all his saints—shall echo through the graves, and vaults, and dens, and caves, and rocks, and mountains of the earth, yea, and the depths of the ocean; and every scattered particle of His redeemed people, that had fallen into corruption, organized in death, shall rise in incorruption, glory, power, a spiritual body, "*fashioned like unto his glorious body,*" then re-united to its happy spirit, to sin, to weep, to suffer, and to die, no more.

O! how blessed is that glorious hope!—O! how secure that unfading, undefiled and incorruptible inheritance!

Happy those who have the pledge and earnest of the Holy Spirit, teaching them to "*look for that blessed hope, and the glorious appearing of the great God, and our Saviour Jesus Christ.*" Titus ii. 13.

Well then, let us remember the earnest of the Spirit and the fruits of the Spirit,—if the Spirit is the pledge in the believer's heart, so should the power of the Spirit be manifested in the believer's life, "*Grieve not the Holy Spirit of God, whereby ye are sealed unto the day of redemption.*" iv. 3. "*Quench not the Spirit.*" Thess. v. 19. "*Walk in the Spirit, and ye shall not fulfil the lust of the flesh,*" Gal. v. 16—and remember what the fruits of the Spirit are.—Let me repeat them again,—"*love, joy, peace, long-suffering, gentleness, goodness, faith, meekness, temperance, against such there is no law.*" Gal. v. 22.

May we not close such a subject with the Apostle's prayer for the Philippians, "*This I pray, that your love may abound yet more and more, in knowledge and in all judgment; that ye may approve things that are excellent; that ye may be sincere and without offence till the day of Christ, being filled with the fruits of righteousness, which are by Jesus Christ, unto the glory and praise of God.*"—1 Phil. 9, 10, 11.

SEVENTH LECTURE.

EPHESIANS I.—15, 16, 17.

"Wherefore, I also, after I heard of your faith in the Lord Jesus, and love unto all the saints, cease not to give thanks for you, making mention of you in my prayers, that the God of our Lord Jesus Christ, the Father of glory, may give unto you the spirit of wisdom and revelation in the knowledge of him."

LET me propose this question for your consideration.—What is the greatest proof of love that a Christian can give to his brother? Certainly, in my opinion, to pray for him.

Oh, how many there are who would think themselves happy if they had, what they call, interest at court, a powerful patron to speak in their favor to the Sovereign, or to some person in authority—they would think, that if a privileged friend undertook to do so, he would be a faithful friend indeed. But, oh, how much more valuable is the friend who manifests his love to the sinner in bringing him before the notice of the King of kings!

You see this strikingly exemplified here. The Apostle having spoken, as we have seen, of the blessings that had been conveyed to his brethren at Ephesus by the Spirit—of their being called in Christ Jesus—being redeemed by His precious blood—and having received the earnest of the Spirit—proceeds to convey to them the consolatory assurance that he did not cease to give thanks for them, and to pray for them. "WHEREFORE, I ALSO, AFTER I HEARD OF YOUR FAITH IN THE LORD JESUS, AND LOVE UNTO ALL THE SAINTS, CEASE NOT TO GIVE THANKS FOR YOU, MAKING MENTION OF YOU IN MY PRAYERS," and then he tells them the subject of his prayer for them.

Why does he say, "AFTER I HEARD OF YOUR FAITH IN THE LORD JESUS, AND LOVE UNTO ALL THE SAINTS?" Had not the Apostle been with the Church at Ephesus? Was it not through his instrumentality that they were called to the knowledge of Christ? Had he not labored long among them? Certainly—Why then does he say, "*after I heard?*" He had gone to Ephesus about the year of our Lord 56, about 23 years after our blessed Lord's crucifixion. He had sent, as you read in Acts xx. for the Elders of the Church of Ephesus, to Miletus, where he gave them the charge which you read in that chapter, in the year 60,—and in the year 64 he addressed this Epistle to them. Therefore, he had been absent from them, perhaps six years, certainly five, and therefore he says, "*after I heard.*" He had tidings conveyed to him, how the Church of Ephesus stood fast in the faith,—so he says, "AFTER I HEARD OF YOUR FAITH IN THE LORD JESUS, AND LOVE UNTO ALL THE SAINTS."

Mark, let me entreat you, mark the characteristics of a Christian church, "AFTER I HEARD OF YOUR FAITH IN THE LORD JESUS, AND LOVE UNTO ALL THE SAINTS." The two cardinal points of Christianity, without these, in their true Scriptural sense, Christianity can really have no existence.

To what end had the church been founded by Paul, if that church had not held the faith of the Lord Jesus and love to His saints?

There is no such thing as an individual Christian, unless a man that has this faith in the Lord Jesus, and love unto all the saints,—How then can there be such a thing as a Christian church? It is impossible it can exist without this,—there may be an outward form, an outward semblance, but there is no real, spiritual church of Christ, except that which is composed of men that have the "*faith of the Lord Jesus, and love to all the saints.*"—Remember this.

What a blessed guard the Bible is against error! and therefore, those who set forth falsehood, like to substitute tradition or human authority, for the pure and holy word of God. Stand fast, then, brethren, by that word, for your own souls, for the souls of your children, and for the souls of your fellow-men.

How precious is the faith of the Lord Jesus Christ, "*He that believeth on the Son hath everlasting life.*"—John, iii. 36. This is the blessing of faith. "*He that believeth not the Son shall not see life, but the wrath of God abideth on him.*" John iii, 36, this is the misery of unbelief.

And if a man upon whom Paul had laid his hands, or Paul himself, (I speak on his own inspired authority,) aye, "*or an angel from heaven, preached any other Gospel than that which he preached,*" the sentence of God's word is "*let him be accursed.*" Gal. i. 8. Therefore, faith in Christ is one indispensable characteristic, of a member of Christ's Church, and love is another, true "*faith worketh by love;*" therefore, where there is no love, there is no faith; we argue from the non-existence of the effect, to the non-existence of the cause; so we perceive love is an inseparable test of faith. "*If a man say, I love God, and hateth his brother, he is a liar; for he that loveth not his brother whom he hath seen, how can he love God whom he hath not seen?*" 1 John, iv. 20, therefore, the Apostle stamps their character, when he says, "AFTER I HEARD OF YOUR FAITH IN THE LORD JESUS, AND LOVE UNTO ALL THE SAINTS." Since he gives this summary as the testimony of a true Christian church, we may observe, there can be no vital error where these really exist, and there can be no saving truth, whatever form there may be, where these have no existence.

Now what effect had this intelligence of their state on the Apostle? It filled his heart with thankfulness, and led him to pray continually for them: "I CEASE NOT TO GIVE THANKS FOR YOU, MAKING MENTION OF YOU IN MY PRAYERS."

Let us remember this for our guidance. St. Paul was led as

an apostle, to give thanks for them, he was led as a faithful teacher, to pray for them, he was inspired to record this for their instruction, and for ours, therefore this is for our guidance. We perceive, that the Apostle records the same for other churches of the saints. So we see in Phil. i. 3, 4, 5, "*I thank my God upon every remembrance of you, always in every prayer of mine for you all making request with joy, for your fellowship in the Gospel, from the first day until now.*" So we see the same thing, Col. i. 3, 4, "*We give thanks to God and the Father of our Lord Jesus Christ, praying always for you, since we heard of your faith in Christ Jesus, and of the love which ye have to all the saints. For the hope which is laid up for you in heaven, whereof ye heard before in the word of the truth of the Gospel.*" Now, why did he give thanks? he says to one church, "*for their fellowship in the Gospel,*" he says to another, "*for the hope that is laid up for them in heaven.*"

This was a continual memorial which he always retained in his own breast, and which he wished that they should bear too; a constant remembrance, that whenever any blessing had accompanied to the hearts of men, the words preached by the Apostles, it was not to them thanks was to be considered due, it was not their zeal, their talents, their gifts, their eloquence, their graces, their Apostleship that produced the effect. "No," he saith "*while one saith I am of Paul, and another, I am of Apollos, are ye not carnal? I have planted, Apollos watered, but God gave the increase.*" God must have the glory, not man, "*So neither is he that planted anything, neither he that watereth, but God that giveth the increase.*" 1 Cor. ii. 4, 6, 7.

We are continually prone to give glory to man, to give glory to one fellow sinner, or another, through whose instrumentality, God may have conveyed a blessing to our souls. There is no such thing in the Bible. In that word of truth, all the praise and glory is ascribed alone to God. So the Apostle saith in this Epistle, 1 Cor. iv. 6, 7, "*These things I have in a figure transferred to myself, and to Apollos for your sakes that you might learn in us,*" (in Apollos, though so "*mighty in the Scriptures,*" and in Paul, who was "*not a whit behind the very chiefest apostles,*") "*that ye might learn in us, not to think of men above that which is written, that no one of you be puffed up, for one against another; for who maketh thee to differ from another?*" If you have received any blessing, if your souls are enlightened, and led to the Lord Jesus Christ, "*who maketh thee to differ from another, and what hast thou that thou didst not receive?*" God gives this blessing to thy soul, and God is to have the praise and glory.

But the same Spirit that taught the Apostle to give thanks, taught him to pray for them also.

There is a most important lesson here.

Persons are too apt to say, or at least to think, when they know the Gospel of Christ, and when they are brought to rest on Him, "Oh that is enough, now I am a believer, now I am safe; and too many Ministers seem to consider that when a man is converted, he is, as it were, secure.

That is the inexperienced language of the inexperienced heart. The believer who knows himself, and who has experienced anything of the depths of sin that are in him, knows that this is no language for him.

True, the believer is privileged to know, that he that is in Christ is safe—but his security consists in being "*kept by the power of God through faith unto salvation*," he is kept through a life of *faith*, and a life of faith, is a life of *conflict*, of *watchfulness*, and *prayer*—he is safe, but it is in "*putting on the whole armor of God*," and the last piece of the panoply, as if it were the clasp that fastens and holds together all the rest, is "*Praying always with all prayer and supplication in the Spirit, and watching thereunto with all perseverance.*" Ephesians vi. 16.

Yes, it is then, first, men begin to pray. You never pray to Christ, till you are brought to Christ, you never come to the Father, till you come through Him, "*no man cometh to the Father but by me.*" John xiv. 6.

As Grace must begin the work, so Grace must carry it on, and Grace must consummate it. It is the same power that causes the harvest to ripen that causes the seed to spring from the ground, and it is the same God alone that can water the blessing of truth in the heart, that gave that blessing to the heart at first,—therefore, the Apostle says, "*I cease not to give thanks for you making mention of you in my prayers.*" And if I might give an opinion on the sad low condition in which we see the professors of the Gospel, I would say, that it arises from this—want of prayer to God. There is in the present day, much talk about religion, you hear much of what is called religious conversation in various companies, but if you attend to it, you will find it is talk about religious societies, or religious publications, or about preachers,—something of that kind, but, alas, very little about Christ, not many in religious conversation speak of the Lord Jesus, and if we ask, what is the cause of this? I think it might be answered, want of prayer, and being carnal, in the sense of the Apostle to the Corinthians, "*one saith I am of Paul, and another I am of Apollos, and I of Cephas, and I of Christ.*" Surely when men are "*puffed up for one against another*," we have cause to fear there must be want of prayer, want of communion between the soul and God.

Oh! if ministers would have a blessing in their own souls, and on their labors, they must pray. If the flock would have a blessing on the ministration of their minister to their souls, they must pray for him. Depend on it you will find a blessing from the ministration of your pastors in direct proportion as you pray to God for them, and for that blessing on their word. If you go away barren and unfed from church, if you go away unedified, and unimpressed by the Word of truth, ask yourselves, have I been praying this week, for a blessing on the word of my minister to my soul? and you may be satisfied your conscience will answer that you have not. Let me entreat you to remember this—carry this reflection home with you, and carry it with you to your knees, pray, O pray, for a blessing on our souls, and our labors; and may the Lord pour the spirit of the Apostle into our hearts, and give us hearts to pray for you.

Before we consider the prayer of the Apostle, we must remark the expression with which he introduces it. In speaking of the blessed person of the Trinity, to whom he prayed, and I would request your attention to this, he says, "MAKING MENTION OF YOU IN MY PRAYERS, THAT THE GOD OF OUR LORD JESUS CHRIST, THE FATHER OF GLORY MAY GIVE UNTO YOU," &c., as much as to say, I pray for you, brethren, continually, and to whom do I pray? I pray to "*the God of our Lord Jesus Christ, the Father of glory.*" Remember, that these words are the inspiration of the Holy Ghost, and they seem to have deep meaning in them. And what is that meaning? They seem to imply all that could be wanted to build up, and strengthen his brethren in the faith of Christ. To whom does he pray? "*To the God of our Lord Jesus Christ.*" In saying this, recollect, brethren, he prays to him who "*so loved the world that he gave his only begotten Son, that whosoever believeth in him should not perish, but have everlasting life*"—he prays to him who not only gives the Shepherd to the sheep, but who gives the sheep to the Shepherd; for, recollect the words of Jesus in St. John x., "*my sheep hear my voice, and I know them, and they follow me, and I give unto them eternal life, and they shall never perish, neither shall any pluck them out of my hand.*" Then mark, "*my Father which gave them me, is greater than all, and no man is able to pluck them out of my Father's hand. I and my Father are one.*" John x. 27, 28, 29, 30; and you remember, the Lord Jesus Christ, in St. John, xx. 17, uses that delightful expression, "*I ascend unto my Father and your Father, unto my God and your God.*" If you are looking to Jesus, if Christ is the refuge for your soul, then His Father is your Father, His God is your God. When the Apostle says, "*the God of our Lord Jesus Christ, the Father of glory,*" he speaks of Him as your God too,—and so he illustrates the character of God as the Father of our Lord Jesus Christ most beautifully by associating it with blessings and mercies in 2 Cor. i. 3, 4. "*Blessed be God, even the Father of our Lord Jesus Christ.*" Mark how he connects the Father with the Son, "*Blessed be God,*" who is this God? "*even the Father of our Lord Jesus Christ, the Father of mercies and the God of all comfort, who comforteth us in all our tribulation, that we may be able to comfort them that are in trouble, by the comfort wherewith we ourselves are comforted of God.*" See the illustration that he gives us here of God's character,—"*the Father of our Lord Jesus Christ, the Father of mercies, and the God of all comfort.*"

Out of Christ, God is not to be approached. When you come to God in your own righteousness, you are like one of those who would have approached the mountain when it shook with thunder and lightning. No matter with what offering they had come—no matter what costly sacrifices or propitiatory oblations they had brought in their hand, the command was, that they should be "*stoned or thrust through with a dart.*" Heb. xii. 20. Approach to God as you may,—come with your righteousness, come with your morality, come with your virtues, come with your good resolutions, come with your pious intentions, come *out of Christ*, and you come to the thunderbolts of God's eternal justice, and you shall perish from his presence forever.

Come to Jesus—however vile you are—however guilty—however despised by men—be you an outcast from society—with a self-convicted heart—a conscience writing bitter things against you—trembling at the thought of meeting God in judgment, as well you may,—come through Christ—come, pleading Jesus,—come, pleading Him who died for sinners,—come with the blood of the Lamb,—and to whom do you come?—"*To the Father of our Lord Jesus Christ. To the Father of mercies, and the God of all comfort,*"—you come to Him; and you come through Him, who saith, "*Him that cometh to me I will in no wise cast out.*"

But he calls him not only "*the God of our Lord Jesus Christ,*" but, "*the Father of glory.*" How is the greatest glory of God manifested to man? Suppose, you were now called upon to answer that question—Suppose a person examining children, were to say, "Children, how is God's glory most declared to man? Can you show me any text concerning it?" Some perhaps might quote "*The heavens declare the glory of God, and the firmament showeth his handy-work.*" Ps. xix. 1. Another might say, "*The whole earth is full of his glory,*" Isai. vi. 3, as we have it embodied in our beautiful hymn, "*heaven and earth are full of the majesty of thy glory.*" But the glory of God declared as it is by the firmament of heaven, is not his greatest glory for the sinner, for how is the sinner to go there? How is the sinner to meet Him who walketh among those orbs of light? How is he to meet that God who "*covereth himself with light, as with a garment, who maketh the clouds his chariot, who walketh upon the wings of the wind.*" Psal. civ. 2, 3. How is he to meet Him? The more you dress God in the glory of His majesty, the more you strike terror into the heart of the unconverted, unenlightened sinner.

Oh! no, it is not in all these things that the greatest glory of God, is exhibited to man. St. John tells us where that glory is to be found, i. 14, "*The Word was made flesh, and dwelt among us, and we beheld its glory, the glory as of the only begotten of the Father, full of grace and truth.*" The glory of the heavens, is nothing to a poor condemned criminal, the riches of earth, could give nothing to him, if they were poured out at his feet, but if a messenger came to open his prison door, with a reprieve—a pardon for him—that is a message of joy to his heart. Oh! when the sinner's eyes are opened to see the grace and truth that is in "the Word made flesh," that is indeed the glory of God, revealed to the sinner's soul. Yes! then, he rejoices, so the Apostle says in 2 Cor. iv. 6. "*God, who commanded the light to shine out of darkness, hath shined in our hearts, to give the light of the knowledge of the glory of God in the face of Jesus Christ.*" in that face that was "*marred more than any man's.*" Is. lii. 14, in that face of the "*man of sorrows and acquainted with grief,*" Is. lviii. 3, in that blessed face, that was bowed in death upon the Cross. Oh! that is glory for the guilty sinner, for, "*surely he hath borne our griefs, and carried our sorrows,*" Is. liii. 4. Surely, in the sufferings and agonies depicted in that blessed face, through that rent side, those hands, those feet, the glorious portals of pardon and mercy are opened to fallen rebels like you and me! Yes, he is "the Father of glory," revealed in His brightest glory through the crucified and risen Saviour, to those who feel their sin. So, the Apostle testifies this in Heb. i. 3, where speaking of the Lord Jesus he saith "*Who being the brightness of his glory, and the express image of his person, and upholding all things by the word of his power, when he had, by himself purged our sins, sat down on the right hand of the majesty on high.*" Oh, yes, this—this indeed is glory!

Do I address any of my dear Roman Catholic brethren? Alas! my poor friends, whose only expectation is, not glory, but the terrors of that blasphemous fable, Purgatory, listen to this message of glory,—"*When he had, by himself, purged our sins, he sat down on the right hand of the Majesty on High.*" There is a purgatory—a glorious purgatory—the blood of Jesus—an everlasting purgatory. Not one that you have to pass through, but one that the Lord of life and glory passed through, to bear your guilt and take it all away, and to open to you, not a place of punishment, but the gates of glory. Oh, think of this! May the Lord enable you to understand and know this; then you shall know,—then indeed shall you understand and see—then—"*God who commanded the light to shine out of darkness shall have shined into your hearts, to give you the light of the knowledge of the glory of God, in the face of Jesus Christ.*"

God is called the Father of Glory, as the Giver of Life in Christ Jesus, and in giving life in Christ, He gives glory,—as we have it in Psalm, lxxxiv. 11, "*the Lord God is a sun and a shield; the Lord will give grace and glory.*" And as we have been speaking of election in this chapter, you may see this strikingly set forth, in Romans, viii. 30. "*Whom he did predestinate, them he also called, and whom he called, them he also justified, and whom he justified, them he also glorified.*"

He is "*the Father of glory,*" as well as the "*Father of mercy,*" "*whom he justified, them he also glorified*"; for none shall pluck them out of the blessed hand of Him that died for them. Oh, remember this. Well indeed might the Apostle add, "*What shall we then say to these things? If God be for us, who can be against us? He that spared not his own Son, but delivered him up for us all,*"—(this blessed "*God of our Lord Jesus Christ, the*

Father of glory)—how shall he not, with him also, freely give us all things?"

The subject of the Apostle's prayer, I reserve for another Lecture, meantime* * * * * * * * * * *

EIGHTH LECTURE.

EPHESIANS I.—17, 18.

"That the God of our Lord Jesus Christ, the Father of glory, may give unto you the Spirit of wisdom and revelation in the knowledge of him; the eyes of your understanding being enlightened; that ye may know what is the hope of his calling, and what the riches of the glory of his inheritance in the saints."

WE have seen the consolation there was to be derived from the very name that the Apostle, by the Spirit, gives to the blessed person of the Trinity, to whom he addresses this prayer, "THE GOD OF OUR LORD JESUS CHRIST, THE FATHER OF GLORY," we shall now consider the words of the prayer itself.

Let us recollect that it was a prayer for the supply of the spiritual wants of the believers in the Church at Ephesus, inspired by Him who knew those wants,—and since it was not only inspired, but recorded by inspiration in the Sacred Volume, for our instruction, it is to teach us, that the same things which were needful for them, are needful also for us, and that, if the Apostle prayed for these blessings for the church at Ephesus, so we are called on to pray for them for ourselves, and for each other.

The petition commences, "THAT THE GOD OF OUR LORD JESUS CHRIST, THE FATHER OF GLORY, MAY GIVE UNTO YOU THE SPIRIT OF WISDOM AND REVELATION, IN THE KNOWLEDGE OF HIM." Now, why does he pray for this? Had they not received the spirit of wisdom and revelation, in the knowledge of Christ? Does not the Apostle say, verse 6, that they were "*accepted in the beloved;*" "*he hath made us accepted in the beloved.*" Does not he say in verse 11, "*in whom we have obtained an inheritance?*" therefore, surely, they must have known Christ, they must have been "*wise unto salvation, through faith which is in Christ Jesus,*" therefore, why does the Apostle pray, that they may have "*the spirit of wisdom and revelation in the knowledge of him,*" which it appears, they must have had already, by the fact of their being accepted in Christ?

* There were some local circumstances and subjects, with which this Lecture was concluded, not properly belonging to an exposition of the chapter, but applicable and important to those to whom it was addressed, and which are therefore omitted from this Publication.

To this we may answer. The time of the believer's conversion to God, is but the beginning of his spiritual life. The stage of infancy, is but the commencement and not the maturity of existence, wherefore, the Apostle in 1 Peter, ii. 2, addresses believers thus, "*as new born babes desire the sincere milk of the word, that ye may grow thereby.*" What is that knowledge, even of a temporal kind, in which man has not need to grow? And if we have need to grow in our knowledge, of every work of creation, even of any of the natural bodies that the Creator hath formed by His mighty hand, how much more have we need to grow in the knowledge of that God Himself? We only begin to know our own state as sinners, we only begin to know the character of Christ as a Saviour, when we are first brought to the knowledge of the Gospel. It is the long, sad experience of the corruption of our natural heart, that brings out the development of the glorious character of Christ as the Saviour, Prophet, Priest, and King of His people.

As they that are sick need a physician, and in a severe and dangerous disease, may, even in its commencement, receive great relief, and so have some experience of his skill,—yet it is in the lingering processes of long protracted illness,—it is in the long and weary suffering of days and nights of anguish, that they know experimentally the wise, judicious treatment, and that they learn to appreciate the skill of that physician, by whose care, under the divine blessing, they have been at length restored to health.

So it is with the believer. We suffer daily more and more of the inward disease of sin,—we feel more and more our need of the Great Physician. We are taught to appreciate more and more His glorious skill, and character, and power.

The holiest experience of the holiest man is but a sad experience of the pollution of His holy things, of the deceitfulness and desperate wickedness of his own heart, the fell corruption that rankles within,—and is but a proportionate experience of the patience, the long-suffering, the grace, the tenderness, the mercy, the compassion, the salvation of his God. Therefore is this blessed prayer recorded for sinners like us.

The 17th verse contains the summary of the prayer, and then the subject of the prayer is expanded to the end of the chapter. The summary is, "*That God may give unto them the spirit of wisdom and revelation in the knowledge of Christ.*"

Then the Apostle goes on to show what he means by this, what is that "*spirit of wisdom,*" what is that "*revelation in the knowledge of Christ,*" which he prays that the Spirit may give them.

It is this, "THE EYES OF YOUR UNDERSTANDING BEING ENLIGHTENED, THAT YE MAY KNOW WHAT IS THE HOPE OF HIS CALLING, AND WHAT THE RICHES OF THE GLORY OF HIS INHERITANCE IN THE SAINTS," &c. It is the office of the Spirit to glorify Christ, "*he shall glorify me; for he shall receive of mine, and shall show it unto you.*" John xvi. 14. And we see that the "*spirit of wisdom and revelation in the knowledge of him,*" as here set forth consists: First, in the enlightening of the understanding. Our understandings must be enlightened at first, by the power of God, to know Christ as our salvation, but what clouds and thick darkness still remain upon them! How continually do the murky vapors of the earth, arise and condense in this cold atmosphere around us, and hide "*in the dark and cloudy day,*" the Sun of righteousness, from the eye of faith in the believer! What need we have continually, of illumination from the Spirit of God!

We have need that the Spirit should both drive away the clouds and clear our distempered eye to see the light of our Redeemer's countenance! "THE EYES OF YOUR UNDERSTANDING BEING ENLIGHTENED," saith the Apostle. So the Old Testament saints prayed for this illumination. So David prays in Psalm, cxix. 18, "*Open thou mine eyes that I may behold wondrous things out of thy law.*" Again, "*Consider and hear me, O Lord my God: lighten mine eyes, lest I sleep the sleep of death.*" Psalm, xiii. 3. So the Apostle saith in this Epistle, v. 13, 14, speaking of light, "*Whatsoever doth make manifest is light, wherefore he saith, awake thou that sleepest, and arise from the dead, and Christ shall give thee light.*" But as the sun may shine in the firmament, and shine in vain, when the eye of man is blinded, but when his eye is open, then he discerns the light that shines around him,—so it is exactly with us,—though the Sun of Righteousness shines before us, though Jesus Christ is evidently set forth crucified among us, yet, our natural understandings are blinded, as blind as the inhabitants of a blind asylum, and we require the illumination of the Holy Spirit to open our eyes, that we may discern Christ at first as our salvation, and then we need increasing light, to behold more and more clearly the character of our Lord and Saviour. Therefore he prays, "THE EYES OF YOUR UNDERSTANDING BEING ENLIGHTENED, THAT YE MAY KNOW"—what?

First.—"WHAT IS THE HOPE OF HIS CALLING." We shall consider the several subjects of the prayer in regular succession.

"THE HOPE OF HIS CALLING." This may be taken either in the sense of the hope which God inspires into the hearts of his people, by the Spirit. Or, it might be taken for the object of hope; in either sense it is scriptural, and might be suitable in this passage; the first includes the second, for when that hope which the Spirit inspires, is given to the heart; the "*hope laid up for it in heaven,*" is the object of its anticipation. I therefore take this as being the fullest sense; as the hope to which He calls his people, that is the hope which those who are called by the Lord, are privileged to possess, and to enjoy.

God works in the mind through the medium of its natural feelings. Hope is the great, animating principle of all human conduct. Hope is the expectation of a good to be attained, founded on a belief that we can attain it. If we do not believe we can attain an object, however desirable, of course we cannot hope for it; therefore, I say, hope is the expectation of a good to be attained, founded on a belief—a persuasion, that it is attainable by us; and it is attended with joy, in exact proportion to the eagerness with which we desire the good, and the confidence with which we expect we shall attain it. But, brethren, how is this blessed principle of the immortal soul, like all its other faculties and powers, disordered and deranged! It is, alas! how

"Fallen from its high estate."

Alas! "*how is the gold become dim! how is the most fine gold changed!*" Lam. iv. 1. Instead of being fixed, as it ought to be, on its God, it is continually turned to some poor perishing object of this earth,—and therefore the hopes of men perish with the objects on which they rest, and sink, one after another, from the cradle to the grave, in sure and sad succession of disappointment, anguish, and despair.

Man is, generally speaking, more virtually disappointed in the attainment, than in the failure of his hopes, therefore the poet says:—

Hope, eager hope, th' assassin of our joy,
All present blessings treading under foot,
Is scarce a milder tyrant than despair!
With no past toils content, still planning new,
Hope turns us o'er to death alone for ease.
Possession, why more tasteless than pursuit?
Why is a wish far dearer than a crown?
That wish accomplish'd why the grave of bliss?
Because in the great future buried deep,
Beyond our plans of empire and renown,
Lies all that man with ardor should pursue;
And HE who made him bent him to the right.
NIGHT THOUGHTS.

True, when the heart is fixed on earth—man never is, he never can be satisfied—he never can realize the enjoyment that his eager hope anticipates. When he has attained the object of his hope, he feels that it has disappointed all his anxious expectations, and like a child satiated with a broken toy, he sighs and longs for something else. But "*the prize of the high calling of God in Christ Jesus.*" Phil. iii. 14, that is an object of aspiration and of hope commensurate with the capacities of an immortal being.

When "*the light of the glorious gospel of Christ,*" 2 Cor. iv. 4, breaks into the darkened heart of the sinner,—when the glorious prospect of the "*life and immortality brought to light through the Gospel,*" 2 Tim. i. 10, is presented to the eye of faith, as a blessing which he believes he can attain in Christ Jesus—then his desires ascend from earth to heaven—then a field is opened for the hope of the immortal soul, vast as its infinite ambition, and endless as its eternal existence. That hope is "THE HOPE OF HIS CALLING," a hope inspired by the Spirit, of attaining an object revealed by the Spirit. Oh, may the Spirit give us "WISDOM AND

REVELATION IN THE KNOWLEDGE OF HIM, THE EYES OF OUR UNDERSTANDING BEING ENLIGHTENED; THAT WE MAY KNOW WHAT IS THE HOPE OF HIS CALLING, AND WHAT THE RICHES OF THE GLORY OF HIS INHERITANCE IN THE SAINTS!"

Let us consider *the nature*—and then, *the hope, of this calling*.

I. There are various blessings that characterize the calling of God in Scripture. We are told it is a calling to peace—as for instance, in Colossians iii. 15, "*Let the peace of God rule in your hearts, to which also ye are called in one body.*" We are called to the peace of God. This is a new and wondrous calling for the sinner.—It is a very new feeling for him to be called to enjoy—peace with his God. The sinner, when called by the Spirit of God, asks,—Is there peace for me?—Can it be that there is peace made between such a guilty wretch as I am and God?—Is it possible that God can be at peace with me?—May I come near to God?—May I depend upon God that He will receive me?—That I may call Him my God?—Can my conscience be cleansed from all its sins?—May I indeed be satisfied that He, the Lord Jesus, has "*borne our sins in his own body on the tree?*" 1 Pet. ii. 24.—May I rest on him?—May my soul repose on His love, His faithfulness and truth?—May I lay down my head this night on my pillow, as I never laid it down before?—not afraid of death, but knowing that Jesus has made peace for me? Oh, my brethren, that is a new calling to the sinner, when he can say, yes, "*I thank God through Jesus Christ our Lord,*" Rom. vii. 25. Yes—it is a wondrous calling to be called of God through Christ Jesus!

Remember, oh, sinner! you are called to this through the Gospel. You are invited—God calls you by His ministers—He calls you by His ordinances—He calls you by His Word—He calls you by His appeals to your conscience—He calls you by His providences. You are called to-day! Now, there is nothing to bar your peace with God, for Jesus has made peace, Christ "*has made peace through the blood of his cross.*" Col. i. 20. He sends us, He sends those who preach His Gospel—those who proclaim His glorious salvation—on an embassy of love, as the Apostle says, "*As though God did beseech you by us, we pray you, in Christ's stead, be ye reconciled to God.*" 2 Cor. v. 20. The testimony of the Gospel is, "*that God was in Christ reconciling the world unto himself, not imputing their trespasses unto them,*" 2 Cor. v. 19, that is the proclamation; and the invitation of the Gospel is, "*be ye reconciled to God,*" trust in Jesus. You are called to peace. That is a blessed calling! Oh, that our ears may be opened to hear it, and that the Spirit may bring it to our hearts and consciences with power!

All those who are called to peace with God are called through peace to hope—they are called to "*inherit a blessing,*" and so to hope for their inheritance. So the Apostle Peter tells us, in his 1st Epistle, iii. 9, when he speaks of this as a rule for our conduct, he saith, "*not rendering evil for evil or railing for railing, but con-*

trariwise, blessing; knowing that you are thereunto called, that ye should inherit a blessing." You are called to inherit a blessing. The calling of the Lord Jesus Christ, is to the inheritance of a blessing. We see, very often, pompously paraded in the newspapers, the birth of some child born as the heir of so and so. But how continually the hope of the inheritance of a family is cut off! How many that have been proclaimed as sons and heirs are soon laid in the dust! How are the churchyards peopled throughout the world with those who have been called heirs to estates, and coronets, and crowns!!! The poor heir of a throne of earth,—how soon must he be cut off from his throne! or how soon his throne must totter from its foundation beneath him! The Scripture does not call the heirship to an earthly inheritance a blessing.

The Apostle does not say, you are called to inherit a blessing, because you may be born heir to some little spot of this poor world; but he says, you are called to inherit that which God calls a blessing—that of which you cannot be disappointed, that from which you cannot be cut off; for, those who are called to inherit the heavenly blessing, if they were the possessors of all this earth, when they are cut off from this, it is only calling them away from a poor, corruptible, defiled inheritance of dust below, "*to an inheritance incorruptible, undefiled, and that fadeth not away,*" 1 Pet. i. 4. For it is their happy privilege to say, "*We know that if our earthly house of this tabernacle were dissolved, we have a building of God, a house not made with hands, eternal in the heavens.*" 2 Cor. v. 1. Yes! this is the calling of God—they are called to inherit a blessing. And then, what a blessing! They are told in 1 Thes. ii. 12, that the magnitude and glory of the blessing, is to be the measure and standard of their walk and conversation, "*Ye know,*" saith the Apostle, "*how we exhorted and comforted and charged every one of you as a father doth his children, that you would walk worthy of God, who hath called you unto his kingdom and glory.*" You are called to "*inherit a blessing,*" to inherit, "*a kingdom and glory,*" the kingdom of God, and the glory of God. Our Lord saith, "*to him that overcometh will I grant to sit with me in my throne, even as I also overcame, and am set down with my Father in his throne,*" Rev. iii. 21; and again, speaking of their glory, He saith in His intercessory prayer, in St. John's Gospel, xvii. 24, "*Father, I will that they also whom thou hast given me, be with me where I am, that they may behold my glory which thou hast given me.*" That they be with Christ, and behold his glory, and partake of His glory: for they shall reign with him in glory.

Here then is the calling of the Lord Jesus Christ, so the Apostle Peter saith, in his First Epistle, v. 10, "*the God of all grace, who hath called us unto his eternal glory, by Christ Jesus,*" it is the same expression. Therefore, you see, what the nature of that calling is.

But then, brethren, there is another point connected with it. It is a sure calling. Those who a e called by the Spirit of God are never left to perish. We see in Rom. viii. 28, 30, who they are, and what is the security of their calling; take it in connection with the subject of which we have treated, in this chapter, and observe how they illustrate each other. "*Moreover whom he did predestinate, them he also called, and whom he called, them he also justified, and whom he justified, them he also glorified.*" Those who are called by His Spirit to himself, called to this blessing, called to this kingdom, and glory, they are justified, washed in the blood of the Lamb, there is no other calling, there is no other hope, there is no other means whereby sinners are brought to the kingdom, they are "*justified freely by his grace, through the redemption that is in Christ Jesus.*" "*And whom he justified, them he also glorified.*" If one were lost, that could not be true, "*whom he justified, them he also glorified,*" if it could be said, "except such an one, or such an one," then the general proposition could not be true, but "*whom he justified, them he also glorified.*" Jesus saith of His sheep, "*They shall never perish, neither shall any one pluck them out of my hand. My Father who gave them me is greater than all, and no one can pluck them out of my Father's hand. I and my Father are one.*" John x. 28, 29, 30. You see, then, brethren, the calling of God in Christ Jesus, you see what it is, you see the nature of it, you see the subjects of it, you see the certainty of it.

II.—Now, *what is the hope founded upon this?* WHAT IS THE HOPE OF HIS CALLING?

First, it is A HOPE THAT SPRINGS FROM FAITH, that is founded on the belief of the truth; and therefore, let us always remember there is no such thing as enthusiasm admitted into true religion. A man may have very enthusiastic ardent hopes, but if these hopes are not based on the solid word of God, if they are not based on faith in God's eternal truth, then, such hopes must perish forever. Therefore, it is not that your feelings be excited, or stimulated up to entertain some hope, but it is, "THE EYES OF YOUR UNDERSTANDING BEING ENLIGHTENED," remember that, "THE EYES OF YOUR UNDERSTANDING BEING ENLIGHTENED THAT YOU MAY KNOW WHAT IS THE HOPE OF HIS CALLING." It is the solid knowledge, it is the sober, clear, sound certainty of God's truth, that gives solid foundation for this hope. Remember that, therefore, the Scripture tells us in Romans, xv. 4, "*whatsoever things were written aforetime, were written for our learning, that we, through patience and comfort of the Scriptures, might have hope.*" Mark, "*through patience and comfort of the Scriptures.*" "It is written," "God hath spoken," therefore, through them we have hope. Hence you see the awful wickedness of taking God's word from the instruction of men. You see the awful guilt of taking that blessed word from the instruction of children. Because it *ought* to be the very basis, and *must* be the very basis of all sound knowledge of truth, therefore, of all firm belief of the truth, therefore, of all solid hope in the truth, and those who take it away, take away the foundation of faith and hope from the soul of man, and therefore, you may be sure, very sure, that all persons who do so, must be lamentably ignorant of the great and glorious hope that is built upon that Bible, for themselves. Their hope must be based on some superstition, or tradition, on their Church, or their priest, or on their own works, or on some other foundation of sand, not on Christ, the Rock of Ages.

Again the hope of the calling of God, in Christ Jesus, is a SOBER HOPE, drawn from the source of God's truth, it is the hope of the Gospel, and so it is called, you see in Col. i. 5, "*the hope that is laid up for you in heaven*," how did they know this? "*whereof ye heard before in the word of the truth of the Gospel.*" "You have heard," he says, of this hope, "in the word of the truth of the Gospel." Then in the 21st verse, speaking of the blessed presentation of the sinner to God, through the salvation of Jesus, he says, "*You that were sometimes alienated, and enemies in your minds by wicked works, yet now hath he reconciled, in the body of his flesh, through death, to present you holy and unblameable and unreprovable in his sight*"—Now mark, "*if ye continue in the faith grounded and settled*," that is in the belief of the truth, "*and be not moved away from the hope of the Gospel which ye have heard.*" You have heard this hope proclaimed to you in the Gospel, therefore it is yours, "*if you continue in the faith*," the belief of that Gospel, and therefore, are "*not moved from the hope of that Gospel.*" Your hope is founded on the sure belief of the promises of God, that cannot lie. So, in verse 27, he tells them the solid everlasting foundation of that hope, to all the saints, "*To whom God would make known what is the riches of the glory of this mystery among the Gentiles.*" And what is this glorious mystery? "*which is Christ in you the hope of glory.*"

What is your hope of glory? Let me say to each of you, whose eye or ear may see or hear these words, and let me, beseech you each, to ask yourselves, what is your hope of glory? If you have the hope that shall not be disappointed, if your hope is not the hope of "the hypocrite," that "shall perish," if your hope is the hope that shall not make ashamed, and true "*hope maketh not ashamed*," then, your hope, you will answer, is built on Christ. "Christ is all my hope. I am a poor lost sinner, Christ is my righteousness, Christ is my salvation, Christ is my hope, Christ is my all in all." "This is Christ in you," (that is in your heart,) "the hope of glory." This is the hope of the servants of God in Christ Jesus. Therefore, it is and it ought to be, "A LIVELY HOPE," so saith the Apostle Peter, 1st Pet. i. 3. "*Blessed be the God and Father of our Lord Jesus Christ, which, according to his abundant mercy, hath begotten us again unto a lively hope, by the resurrection of Jesus Christ from the dead, to an inheritance incorruptible and undefiled, and that fadeth not away, reserved in heaven for you.*" So it is A JOYFUL HOPE, as it is said, "*rejoicing in hope, patient in tribulation, continuing instant in prayer*, Rom. xii. 12. So, it is A HOPE FULL OF CON

SOLATION, as St. Paul says, in Heb. vi. 18, speaking of the glorious foundation of the hope of the believer, "*that by two immutable things*," (God's covenant promise, and His oath, by which His covenant was ratified,) "*by two immutable things, in which it was impossible for God to lie, we might have a strong consolation who have fled for refuge, to lay hold upon the hope set before us; which hope we have as an anchor of the soul, both sure and steadfast, and which entereth into that within the vail.*" An anchor of the soul, an anchor that holds firmly amidst all the storms and tempests of time and eternity. It is not an anchor dropped in the quick-sand, it is an anchor cast within the vail. That anchor cannot drag, it is cast in the covenant salvation of omnipotence, it is cast within the vail, "*the hope of our calling*" is held by a cable that cannot slip. Why?—because, you are "*kept by the power of God through faith unto salvation*;" therefore, it is "*an anchor of the soul, both sure and steadfast*,"—whatever storms, hurricanes, or whirlwinds may blow from the heavens,—whatever mountain billows may rise and rage from the deep,—the vessel that is moored, the soul that is secured by the blessed anchor of that hope shall outride every storm, and mount over every billow, till the voice of Him whose voice can still the winds and waves, shall call the peaceful spirit home to "the haven where it would be." Is not this a blessed hope? Is not this a glorious hope, to pray for, and to enjoy?

If the Poet might speak, as we have heard, of the vanity of earthly hope, so might he well change the mode of his lyre, when he comes to sing of this.

This Hope is earth's most estimable prize
This is man's portion, while no more than man.
Hope of all passions most befriends us here;
Passions of prouder name befriend us less;
Joy has her tears, and transport has her death.
Hope, like a cordial, innocent, tho' strong,
Man's heart at once inspirits and serenes;
Nor makes him pay his wisdom for his joys;
'T is all our present state can safely bear,
Health to the frame! and vigor to the mind!
A joy attempered! A chastized delight!
Like the fair summer's evening, mild and sweet!
T is man's full cup, his paradise below!

NIGHT THOUGHTS.

I must reserve the next passage of the prayer, "*the riches of the glory of his inheritance in the saints*," if the Lord will, for another occasion. But, Oh, let me ask you, do you not see how inspiration dictated and recorded the apostolic prayer? Do you not feel your own need of praying, that the Spirit may reveal that "*hope of his calling*" more and more to your souls? I would ask you, O believer, do not you feel your need of this, and that your understanding should be opened more and more to see this blessed hope to feel and to enjoy it more? Alas! my friends, how continually our hearts and thoughts are agitated and tossed about with the trifling concerns of time and sense!—how easily we are afflicted, how soon distressed, how rapidly cast down, how suddenly elated with some poor perishing trifle of this passing scene, how much we forget the glorious hope set before us, "*the prize of the high calling of God in Christ Jesus!*" Phil. iii. 14.—what need we have to pray, that God will enlighten the eyes of our understanding and reveal the truth, the hope, the prospect of eternal glory more fully and brightly to the eye of faith, for, Oh, brethren, if we had this hope as it is our privilege to possess it—if we rested in this hope—if we rejoiced in this hope—if we put on our head for a helmet this "*hope of salvation*,"—when we enter into the conflicts in which we have daily to contend—when we engage in the varied strugglings of our warfare here below—we should be enabled to "*fight the good fight of faith*," 1 Tim. vi. 12, we should "*quit us like men, and be strong*," 1 Cor. xvi. 13, nay, we should always be "*more than conquerors through Him that loved us*." Rom. viii. 37. Oh, remember, that it is on this animating hope that all our comfort, our happiness, our enjoyment, our service of our God depends.

Surely, then, I may well close the consideration of this part of the Apostle's prayer with a similar petition for another of the Churches in his day, which is, in itself, a beautiful amplification and illustration of the truth—"*Now the God of hope fill you with all joy and peace in believing, that you may abound in hope through the power of the Holy Ghost*."—Amen.—Rom. xv. 13.

NINTH LECTURE.

Ephesians I.—18.

"The eyes of your understanding being enlightened; that ye may know what is the hope of his calling, and what the riches of the glory of his inheritance in the saints."

Having considered the first part of the Apostle's prayer for the Church at Ephesus, we come to consider the second subject for which he prays, "*that the God of our Lord Jesus Christ, the Father of glory, may give unto them the spirit of wisdom and revelation in the knowledge of him*." Namely, "WHAT IS THE RICHES OF THE GLORY OF HIS INHERITANCE IN THE SAINTS."

There are some commentators of no small name and authority, who interpret this passage thus; what is the riches of the glory of the inheritance, which the saints are to possess in Christ Jesus, or "how gloriously rich is the inheritance which he has prepared for his saints."

Now I am sure that this is not the meaning of the passage. I feel satisfied it is not, for then the expression would be exactly the reverse of this. If such were the meaning of it, the words would be, "what is the riches of the glory of the inheritance of the saints in Him," or it might be, "what is the riches of the glory of his inheritance for the saints," that is, which He has reserved for them, or purchased for them, whereas it is, "*what is the riches of the glory of his inheritance in the saints*," the inheritance of Christ in the saints, the inheritance he has in them. It is not an inheritance merely, but a glorious inheritance, and not only a glorious inheritance, but more—mark the strength of the expression—"THE RICHES OF THE GLORY OF HIS INHERITANCE IN THE SAINTS."

Now let us ask, can this be properly applied to Christ? Can we justly assume this interpretation, which is certainly the plain meaning of the words, to be the true one? Can we scripturally adopt it?

First.—Is Christ set forth in Scripture as an heir? Yes, He is clearly set forth in Scripture as an heir. You will see that in Heb. i. 1, 2, "*God, who at sundry times and in divers manners spake in time past unto the fathers by the prophets, hath in these last days spoken unto us by his Son, whom he hath appointed heir of all things*." And again, you may see in Rom. viii. 16, 17, where the Apostle speaks of the blessed inheritance of God's children, he says, "*The Spirit itself beareth witness with our Spirit, that we are the children of God: and if children, then heirs; heirs of God, and joint heirs with Christ*."—I might quote various other passages, but these are enough.

Secondly—If Christ is an heir,—what is His inheritance? Of what is He heir? Is that revealed in Scripture?—clearly,—Ps. ii. 8. The Father Jehovah saith, addressing the Son, "*Ask of me, and I shall give thee the heathen (the nations) for thine inheritance, and the uttermost parts of the earth for thy possession*." Again, in Daniel, vii. 13, 14, you see the same truth set forth, "*I saw in the night visions, and behold, one like the Son of Man came with the clouds of heaven, and came to the Ancient of Days, and they brought him near before him. And there was given him dominion, and glory, and a kingdom, that all people, nations, and languages, should serve him. His dominion is an everlasting dominion which shall not pass away, and his kingdom that which shall not be destroyed*." Christ is appointed heir, and heir of the nations of the earth, "*that all people, nations, and languages, should serve him*."

But how is He heir? How can He be said to be an heir? Is He not Jehovah, and does He not, as God, possess all things?—Certainly! How is He then the heir?—This is the misery and ignorance of the Socinians,—the awful error into which they fall. Christ, as man, has no more than any other man in the world:—Of Christ, as man, it was as true as of any child that ever was born into the world, "*naked came he out of his mother's womb*." Job. i. 21. He possessed nothing as man; therefore, whatever he receives as man, he has, as a gift or heritage bestowed upon Him by Jehovah. All things that are said in Scripture of the Lord Jesus Christ, *as man*, are perfectly true of Him, as man;—because He is very man, "*bone of our bone, and flesh of our flesh.*" And therefore, when the Socinians object what the Scriptures say of Christ as man, they only fall into the snare, through their own blindness, for he is perfect man. But then come in His character and attributes as God, as Jehovah,—and this is their stumbling-block. Beware of that! Go out, with God's Word, in the full length and breadth of the glorious humanity of Christ,—but if you do, you must perish in your ignorance and sin, unless you go also forth with it in the glory of His Eternal Godhead, and know that He is "*over all God blessed forever.*" Rom. ix. 5. The arm of man cannot save the sinner. But we shall see more of this, in speaking of the inheritance of Christ—"THE RICHES OF THE GLORY OF HIS INHERITANCE IN THE SAINTS."

Now, the glory of Christ's kingdom, which you see portrayed in so many passages of God's Word is a moral glory—a glory far above that of all the kings of this earth. Read the description of the glory of King Solomon and his kingdom, "*when the queen of Sheba had seen all Solomon's wisdom, and the house that he had built, and the meat of his table, and the sitting of his servants, and the attendance of his ministers, and their apparel, and his cup bearers, and his ascent by which he went up unto the house of the Lord: there was no more spirit in her.*" 1 Kings x. 4, 5,—his throne of ivory and gold, and all the splendor of his court,—that is the splendor of an earthly monarch's kingdom,—but the glory of Christ's kingdom is a moral glory,—so you see in Isaiah ii. 2. "*It shall come to pass, in the last days, that the mountain of the Lord's house shall be established upon the top of the mountains, and shall be exalted above the hills, and all nations shall flow unto it,*" (you see "*all people, nations, and languages, shall serve him,*") "*and many people shall go and say, come ye, and let us go up to the mountain of the Lord, to the house of the God of Jacob, and he will teach us of his ways, and we will walk in his paths; for out of Zion shall go forth the law, and the word of the Lord from Jerusalem. And he shall judge among the nations, and shall rebuke many people; and they shall beat their swords into plow-shares, and their spears into pruning hooks, nation shall not lift up sword against nation, neither shall they learn war any more.*" verse 3, 4. It is not the glory of arms, and the pomp of war, and the shout of victory that graces the kingdom of Christ,—No, it is justice—righteousness—peace—mercy—love—filling the earth. So you have it in Isaiah xi. 4. "*With righteousness shall he judge the poor, and reprove with equity for the meek of the earth: and he shall smite the earth with the rod of his mouth, and with the breath of his lips shall he slay the wicked,*"—that is at his coming. Then we have a description of the subsequent peace of his kingdom, verse 6, "*the wolf also shall dwell with the lamb, and the leopard shall lie down with the kid; and the calf and the young lion and the fatling together; and a little child shall lead them.*" "*They shall not hurt nor destroy in all my holy mountain: for the earth shall be full of the knowledge of the Lord, as the waters cover the sea. And in that day there shall be a root of Jesse, which shall stand for an ensign of the people; to it shall the Gentiles* (that is, the nations of the earth,) *seek: and his rest shall be glorious.*" v. 9, 10.

The glory, then, of Christ's inheritance, the glory of His kingdom shall be *a moral glory*, and the greatest glory of Christ, at this time, is this, to reveal His salvation to lost and guilty sinners, and to make them fit vessels to inherit that glory with Him. Therefore, there is nothing that strengthens the faith of a believer so much as to know and understand, that the glory of the Lord Jesus Christ is as much identified, as much bound up with the salvation of His church, as that salvation is bound up in the humiliation and glory of our Lord. This helps to unfold the reason, why the Apostle prays this for the church at Ephesus.

And now, consider the value of this in application to our own state. What do we do? In our ignorance and unbelief, we are doubting and fearing, whether, as sinners, we may come to Christ for mercy. We want to qualify ourselves,—to make ourselves fit to come to Jesus. Alas! the poor inhabitants of an hospital might just as well expect to heal themselves before they applied to the physician. "*They that are whole need not a physician, but they that are sick*;" Mat. ix. 12.—and it is guilty sinners, like you and me, that need a Saviour. But I repeat, that in our ignorance and unbelief, we are keeping back from Christ, doubting, whether we may trust Him. "Can I come, can I depend on Christ? Can I believe that such sins as mine are blotted out?"

This is continually the language of unbelief in the human heart. But we ought to remember that the very glory of Christ consists in this, that He receives and pardons sinners. In Luke, xv. 2, we have an account, that the Pharisees and Scribes murmured, when the publicans and sinners drew near to hear Jesus, and this was their complaint, "*This man receiveth sinners, and eateth with them,*" and the Lord Jesus Christ, answering them, sets forth three parables—that of the man who had lost a sheep, and who "leaves the ninety and nine in the wilderness, and goeth after that which is lost," and carries it home "on his shoulders rejoicing";—the poor woman who had lost a piece of money, and searches the house until she finds it;—and the tender father who receives the prodigal son in all his tattered garments and his misery,—illustrating thereby the glory of his own character. As if when they murmured and said, "*this man receiveth sinners,*" He might answer them and say, "Assuredly, I receive sinners," "*for the Son of man is come to seek and to save that which was lost.*" Mat. xviii. 11. Instead of knowing that the glory of our Redeemer's character, consists in receiving sinners—in pardoning the guilty—in redeeming the lost—in pouring forth as the "Fountain of living waters," the tide of love, of mercy, of salvation, to guilty man—we stand doubting, and fearing, and questioning, whether we have salvation in Christ or not.

This may lead us well to comprehend the reason why the Apostle prays, "*That the God of our Lord Jesus Christ, the Father of glory, may give them the spirit of wisdom and revelation in the knowledge of him, that* THE EYES OF THEIR UNDERSTANDING BEING ENLIGHTENED, THEY MAY KNOW WHAT IS THE HOPE OF HIS CALLING, AND WHAT THE RICHES OF THE GLORY OF HIS INHERITANCE IN THE SAINTS."

The voices of the prophets declare, that the glory of Christ was to consist in the salvation of sinners. I might quote a multitude of passages to show this, but I shall only refer to a few. The Lord saith by Isaiah, xliv. 22, "*I have blotted out, as a thick cloud, thy transgressions, and as a cloud, thy sins; return unto me, for I have redeemed thee.*" Then, mark, how the prophet bursts out in the following verse, "*Sing, O ye heavens; for the Lord hath done it: shout, ye lower parts of the earth: break forth into singing, ye mountains, O forest, and every tree therein: for the Lord hath redeemed Jacob, and glorified himself in Israel.*" He hath glorified himself in their redemption, in their pardon, in their deliverance, and the prophet calls upon heaven and earth, the mountains, the hills, the forest, every tree and every leaf to praise the Lord for his redeeming love to those guilty sinners—His people.

In Isaiah xlix. 13, you see the same thing, "*Sing O heavens, and be joyful, O earth, and break forth into singing O mountains; for the Lord hath comforted his people, and will have mercy on his afflicted.*" Now look at unbelief in the following verse, "*but Zion said, the Lord hath forsaken me, and my Lord hath forgotten me.*" There is unbelief, doubting His love, doubting His mercy. What is his answer?

"*Can a woman forget her sucking child, that she should not have compassion on the son of her womb? Yea, they may forget, yet will I not forget thee.*" See how the voice of the prophets glorify the Lord God in the pardon of sin.

Let me read one or two more passages. Isaiah lx. 19, 21, where he speaks of the glory that shall dwell in His Zion, in the day of his inheritance. "*The sun shall be no more thy light by day, neither for brightness shall the moon give light unto thee, but the Lord shall be unto thee an everlasting light, and thy God thy glory. Thy sun shall no more go down, neither shall thy moon withdraw itself; for the Lord shall be thine everlasting light, and the days of thy mourning shall be ended. Thy people also shall be all righteous, they shall inherit the land forever, the branch of my planting, the work of my hands, that I may be glorified.*"

Here are some golden beams of light that shine on the treasures of "THE RICHES OF THE GLORY OF HIS INHERITANCE IN THE SAINTS."

I shall refer you but to one more prophecy, Jer. xxxiii. 8, 9, where He speaks of the glory of pardoning the sins of His rebellious Israel, when he shall call them home, "*And I will cleanse them from all their iniquity whereby they have sinned against me, and I will pardon all their iniquity whereby they have sinned, and whereby they have transgressed against me.*" And now mark, "*And it shall be to me a name of joy, a praise and an honor before all the nations of the earth, which shall hear all the good that I do unto them, and they shall fear and tremble for all the goodness, and for all the prosperity that I procure unto it.*" His grace, His mercy, His salvation shall be a praise, honor, joy, and glory to them, through all the nations of the earth.

When the Lord Jesus Christ was born, what were the first words that burst from the lips of the heavenly choir, that came to celebrate his birth? "*Suddenly there was with the angel, a multitude of the heavenly host praising God, and saying, glory to God in the highest, and on earth peace, good will toward men.*" Luke ii. 14. And the history of Christ's kingdom—the history of Christ's church from that day to this—the history of that which is really the holy Catholic church, not the Church of Rome—nor the Church of Scotland—nor the Church of England—nor any other outward church, that the eye of man has been able to discern, but of Christ's spiritual Church—that is, Christ's believing people—those who have fled to Christ for refuge—those who have embraced Christ's salvation,—they are Christ's Church and none other; then, I say, the history of them from that day to this, has been a history of the glory of Christ. Oh, what glory! when the Apostles went and preached "*repentance and remission of sins beginning at Jerusalem,*" Luke, xxiv. 47, proclaiming pardon through the blood of the Lamb, to those who had embrued their hands in that blood, see Acts, ii. 37–47. And Oh, how often, from that day to this, as each successive sinner has been brought to trust in his Redeemer, how often has the expression, "Glory be to God," broken in sincerity from his lips, as the light of pardon and peace from his Redeemer, has broken in on his poor, benighted soul! So it is continually, when a sinner is brought to know the riches of the grace of Christ—"glory be to God," is the language of his heart—this is the glory that Christ has received from all his saints to this day.

But this glory, however great, has been as yet but partially unfolded. It is yet all undeveloped to the world. It is not yet manifested—His dealings with all the members of His church are yet to be revealed. We have indeed, the history of them in some degree in the Bible. We have the history of Abraham, of Isaac and of Jacob—we have the history of many saints of the Old Testament—we have the story of Zaccheus—of the thief—we have the history of Saul—we have the record of many individuals, who were brought to Christ, we have much of their history given to us in the Word of God. But the secret dealings of God with all their souls, "*the unsearchable riches of Christ.*"—Eph. iii. 8,—

as they have abounded to each individual among them are not known, and shall not be known, till the revelation of His glory. Again eternal life is not yet known, it is a subject but of faith and hope; you believe in it, and you hope for it, but it is not yet seen. The Church of Christ hath not yet risen, "*the whole creation groaneth and travaileth in pain together until now, and not only they,* (all created beings) *but we* (believers) *ourselves, who have the first fruits of the Spirit, even we ourselves groan within ourselves, waiting for the adoption, to wit, the redemption of our body.*" Rom. viii. 22, 23. Our bodies are not yet redeemed, they must pass through the ordeal of death, they must enter into the grave, they must be subjected to that process of decay which awaits them, "dust thou art, and unto dust shalt thou return." Our present life is but animal life, animal existence—that must soon be extinguished, but that eternal life which the believer has in Christ, is as the Scripture tells us, "*hid with Christ in God.*" Col. iii. 3.—it is not yet seen or known, but it shall not be always so; for "*when Christ who is our life shall appear, then shall we also appear with him in glory.*" Col. iii. 4. Oh, what a glorious day, when those who sleep in death, in the dust of the earth shall "burst their cerements"—when all the redeemed of Christ shall break forth at the sound of the trumpet, springing in their renewed, regenerated bodies, from the earth and the depths of the sea, "*to meet their Lord in the air.*" Then shall the glory of Christ be revealed, then shall be displayed "THE RICHES OF THE GLORY OF HIS INHERITANCE IN THE SAINTS." When "*the travail of his soul*" shall encircle him with songs of everlasting joy! Oh! what a blessed day for those who know Christ, to look for, and to hope for! Then, indeed, shall be fulfilled the testimony of the Apostle, as he says in 2d Thessalonians i. 7, "*to you who are troubled, rest with us, when the Lord Jesus shall be revealed from heaven with his mighty angels.*" Then is beheld the fearful fate of the ungodly,—verses 8, 9, 10, "*in flaming fire, taking vengeance on them that know not God and that obey not the Gospel of our Lord Jesus Christ, who shall be punished with everlasting destruction from the presence of the Lord, and from the glory of his power.*" But then shall be revealed the life now hidden of His Church—then shall be revealed His own glorious majesty, and faithfulness, and truth, "*When he shall come to be glorified in his saints, and to be admired in all them that believe.*" Here is "THE RICHES OF THE GLORY OF HIS INHERITANCE IN THE SAINTS," He shall then "*come to be glorified in his saints, and admired in all them that believe.*" Then His Church shall appear the bride of His love—then His children, "*the travail of his soul,*"—then His glorious inheritance the purchase of his blood—then His royal diadem, with all the jewels of His crown of glory. And Oh, what glory shall then be manifested in Christ and his saints! What glory to that grace that has been proclaimed to sinners, as I proclaim to you this day in His most blessed name, free full, complete pardon for all your sins. Heard you not the words of that book this day, as they were read in the Church: "*Come now and let us reason together, saith the Lord, though your sins be as scarlet, they shall be as white as snow, though they be red like crimson, they shall be as wool.*" Isa. i. 18.

Oh! what glory to the grace of Christ, in pardoning the very chief of sinners. How shall Manasseh, Mary Magdalene, the Thief, and Saul, and you, and I, if we be there among them, sing! Alas! are any among you looking to any other refuge? No matter what your morals, or your amiability, or your fancied excellence may be—no matter with what self-delusion in your pride and ignorance, you may deceive yourselves, in reviewing your own character—no matter how your friends may blind you, by calling you amiable and excellent, as perhaps, relatively speaking, you may really be—before God you are a guilty sinner, and the wrath of God abideth on you as a sinner, and there is no hope, no shadow of hope or refuge, for your soul, but pardon in Christ. The glory of Christ is to have been a substitute for sinners, to fulfil the law for us, which we had broken, and to be "*the Lord our righteousness.*" He came to bear our sins on the cross, and therefore, the glory of His grace consists in pardoning sinners. O look unto him and be you saved.

But glory shall be to His justice. The sufferer, the victim of a violated Law, who acknowledges the justice of the sentence that dooms him to die, honors that justice as much as he who pronounces the sentence, and inflicts the blow. The thief on the cross, when God enlightened his eyes to see the Saviour, honored the justice of his sentence when he said, "*we indeed, justly, for we receive the due reward of our deeds, but this man hath done nothing amiss.*" Luke xxiii. 41.

But if man glorifies human justice in acquiescing in its sentence as pronounced against himself, how then, was the character of Jesus glorified, when he came to give himself a willing victim to the sentence of that eternal justice which had pronounced a doom and a curse on guilty man! Who can tell, what the sense of justice was in Jesus, when "*he steadfastly set his face to go to Jerusalem,*" Luke ix. 51,—knowing all that should befall him?

Oh! "*when he shall come to be glorified in his saints, and to be admired in all them that believe,*" then shall be proclaimed the glory of His justice when he underwent the "*agony and bloody sweat*" of Gethsemane—the mocking—the buffeting—the "*shame and spitting*" of the judgment hall—the cross of Calvary—the vinegar—the gall—the dark desertion of His Father, when, in that mysterious agony of suffering, He cried out, "*My God, my God, why hast thou forsaken me?*" Mat. xxvii. 46. Oh! then, it shall be seen by a guilty world, that He who came to be a willing victim for sinners, is the Lord of life and glory. Then, how shall the justice of Immanuel shine forth in the Judge of Heaven and earth! How shall the patient sufferer of justice shine forth in glory as the vindicated executor of justice when He shall come "*to be glorified in his saints*" in that day!

And then,—what glory to His mercy! Who shall appear among all the hosts of the Redeemed—who shall appear there, that is not a monument of grace and mercy! There shall be Manasseh, that deluged Jerusalem with blood—there, shall be Mary Magdalene—there, the persecuting Saul—there, perjured Peter—there, that blaspheming thief who was just rushing, with blasphemy on his lips, into hell, when the grace of God arrested him, and showed him, that he who hung beside him on the cross, was the Lord of grace and mercy. Oh, how shall the mercy of Christ be glorified in these, as in all His saints! Oh! yes! and believer, you can say, and I can say, if we be there, "Oh, how glorious is that mercy, that saved a wretch like me!" Yes, each individual who knows the secrets of his own heart—each who knows the guilt of his own corruption, his baseness, his ingratitude, his unbelief, his rebellion, his enmity, his crimes against his God, whether perpetrated, meditated, or desired—each who knows the vileness of his own nature, shall emulate the song of the loudest as he feels, that none should shout forth "GLORY TO CHRIST" louder than a sinner such as he.

Do not you know this, Oh believer? Yes, you do, every one of you who knows the Gospel of Christ, you know, that this is true.

Then, what glory to his faithfulness! Mark his words by the Prophet Isaiah, xlviii. 8, 9, 10, 11. "*I knew that thou wouldest deal very treacherously, and wast called a transgressor from the womb.*" How often has this been bitterly echoed by the voice of conscience! But how faithful is He to His covenant! and alas! how great our unfaithfulness! Yet He saith, "*For my name's sake will I defer mine anger, and for my praise will I refrain for thee, that I cut thee not off. Behold I have refined thee, but not with silver; I have chosen thee in the furnace of affliction. For mine own sake, even for mine own sake, will I do it; for how should my name be polluted? and I will not give my glory to another.*" Oh, how His faithfulness and patience shall be glorified in the salvation of sinners, like you and me, in that day.

His patience! How has He not borne with our manners and waywardness! Look back at your life, and see, how Christ has borne with you! See, how you have provoked Him, remember, how continually you have dared Him to His face—rushed into the jaws of temptation—fallen into them again and again—and yet, your God has not cut you off! He has pardoned you—He has given you again peace, and restored you to His mercy! How often have you had to say of your Shepherd, "*he restoreth my soul.*" Psalm xxiii. 3. Oh! when you remember this, how must you glorify the faithfulness and patience of your Saviour! And again, what glory to His power! What deliverances He hath wrought for you! How His providences have delivered you, how His power has rescued you from danger, from snares, from temptations, trials, yea, from what depths of sin, the Lord of life and power has rescued your soul! How often has His arm lifted you up from the precipice of death and hell! Oh, how must you glorify the Lord in that day!

And then, what glory to His holiness, when out of such a mass of sinners, he "*presents to himself a glorious church, not having spot or wrinkle or any such thing, but holy and without blemish.*" Ephes. v. 27.

How the character of Christ, His moral character shall be glorified! all the attributes of His divinity, and all the perfections of His humanity, shining, not only in himself but in all His redeemed saints! How they shall all be manifested, and how they shall all be glorified in that day, "*when He shall come to be glorified in the saints,*" and to display to all the worlds of heaven, earth, and hell, "THE RICHES OF THE GLORY OF HIS INHERITANCE IN THE SAINTS!" for they are His inheritance, they display His character, they manifest His grace, they exhibit His justice, mercy, truth, love, faithfulness, patience, power, they exhibit them all, they are the inheritance of Christ. His glory—the very essence of his glory is manifested and displayed in them.

How wonderful, that even the fall of the world, that the sin of man should be, in the end, overruled for good! to confer blessedness on the sinner that is redeemed, and to magnify and enhance the character and glory of his God.

Oh! believer, let us think what does this demand from us? "*Shall we continue in sin that grace may abound? God forbid.*" Rom. vi. 1. Because Christ is glorified in the pardon of sin, and in the salvation of sinners, shall we therefore sin against our God?—God forbid. No, it is the very manifestation of this love, it is the exhibition of Christ's character, as brought home to the heart and affections of man, by the power of the Holy Ghost, that draws that heart and these affections to his God. And it is thus, that even here, in the life of His people, their Lord is glorified, "*herein,*" saith He, "*is my Father glorified, that ye bear much fruit, so shall ye be my disciples.*"

Then, do you not see, what a blessed prayer, "*That the God of our Lord Jesus Christ, the Father of glory, might give unto them the spirit of wisdom and revelation in the knowledge of Him?*" Do you not perceive how inspiration shines in the petition, "*that* THE EYES OF THEIR UNDERSTANDING BEING ENLIGHTENED, THEY MAY KNOW WHAT IS THE HOPE OF HIS CALLING, AND WHAT THE RICHES OF THE GLORY OF HIS INHERITANCE IN THE SAINTS?" How is not this calculated to glorify Christ? —to make them glorify Him in their faith, their confidence, their hope in Him, their love to Him—in their life and conversation, as the disciples of the Lord—the redeemed of such a Saviour? Oh! that the Lord may grant, that these blessed results may flow to our souls from the revelation of the knowledge of Him!

Let us remember, that the Apostle preached these truths much better than we can preach them. He set these things forth by the inspiration of the Holy Ghost. Yet he does not say, my preaching shall produce such and such an effect upon you. Nay, brethren. You may say, and I trust you do, when you hear the word of

God faithfully set forth, "That is true,—that preaching is scriptural, —that testimony is faithful,—that word is sound." But then, this truth can produce no effect on you or me but by the power of the Holy Spirit. We may preach, but our own heart and life shall be all uninfluenced by the very word we teach, unless God by His Spirit brings it home to our own souls. So must it be with you. Therefore, remember, the Apostle does not say, I have preached to you, my preaching shall be effectual—my word shall take root and bring forth fruit in you. No, but he offers this petition to the Throne of Grace. He knows that even the very words of God himself, whether spoken or inspired, must be accompanied by the Holy Spirit to reach the heart of a sinner. He knows that all the glory of Immanuel's character, the riches of His grace, and the fulness of His salvation, shall shine in the firmament of God's eternal world as vainly as the sun in the firmament of heaven on those whose eyes are blind, unless "*the Father of glory shall give them the spirit of wisdom and revelation in the knowledge of him—unless* THE EYES OF THEIR UNDERSTANDING SHALL BE ENLIGHTENED, THAT THEY MAY KNOW WHAT IS THE HOPE OF HIS CALLING, AND WHAT THE RICHES OF THE GLORY OF HIS INHERITANCE IN THE SAINTS."

And now, perhaps, some poor blind sinner may have come in here to-day, to whom this is all unknown. He does not understand these words. He cannot tell what is "THE RICHES OF THE GLORY OF CHRIST'S INHERITANCE IN THE SAINTS." Well—perhaps through God's grace, the Spirit of eternal truth may bring home this word to your heart, and enable you to understand it ere you leave this Church. You may have come here as many come, because they think it is right to do so on the Sabbath-day, because they think it right, as they say, to do their duty—to go to church—to say their prayers—and to hear a Sermon, or, perhaps, as many do, they come to lounge away an hour—or thinking, it may be, that it is a very meritorious act, and shall be entered as an item to their credit in the Book of God for their salvation. Perhaps that such an one may be offended at being told, that "*all their righteousnesses are as filthy rags.*" Isa. lxiv. 6, and that all their religious observances, and all their duties can never save, or help to save their souls. Nay, I say to such a one, my friend, you are a sinner, and "*the wrath of God abideth on you.*" What are you to do? My dear fellow-sinner, the riches of the glory of Christ are set forth to you, in the proclamation of the pardon of sin to sinners. In the name of Jesus Christ of Nazareth, I proclaim to you, on the authority of God's eternal word, pardon of your sin through the blood of Him, which "*cleanseth us from all sin,*" 1 John, i. 7. You may ask, "What! do you mean to say, that what Christ has done and suffered, is enough for me to rest my soul on? May I depend on Him this day? Is there in Him full pardon for a thoughtless sinner like me?" Oh yes, "*today if you will hear His voice, harden not your heart.*" Psalm, xcv. 7, 8. Remember he said to Zaccheus the chief of the publi cans, "*This day is salvation come to this house.*" Luke xix. 9. Recollect He said to the Thief, "*To-day shalt thou be with me in paradise,*" and do not forget this glorious truth, that he who said thus, is "*Jesus Christ the same yesterday, to-day, and forever.*" Heb. xiii. 8.

Oh may He by the Spirit, enable you to receive these glad tidings, and then your salvation shall redound to the glory of Christ. Then you shall be able to say, as many a sinner like you hath said, "Ah, when I was not thinking at all about myself, about my sins, quite ignorant of my own state, and ignorant of Christ, God sent His word home to my conscience, I saw, I was a guilty sinner, and I heard for the first time in my life," (for if you have been listening to it all your days, it is not till it comes to your heart with power, that you hear it,) "I heard for the first time of forgiveness through the blood of Christ."

May the Lord enable you to see and to receive it. Then you shall be among those whose salvation shall redound to the glory of Christ—then you shall understand and participate in "THE RICHES OF THE GLORY OF HIS INHERITANCE IN THE SAINTS." Now they give Him glory, now they praise Him for his pardoning love and mercy. But Oh, what shall it be in that glorious day, when he shall have "*spoken and called the earth from the rising of the sun, to the going down thereof!*" When "*Out of Zion the perfection of beauty God hath shined!*" When "*Our God shall come and shall not keep silence, a fire shall devour before him, and it shall be very tempestuous round about him!*" When "*He shall call to the heavens from above, and to the earth, that he may judge his people.*" "*Gather my saints together unto me, those that have made a covenant with me by sacrifice!*" When "*The heavens shall declare his righteousness, for God is Judge, Himself!*" Psalm l. 1–6. What shall it be when He who "*hath been a strength to the poor, a strength to the needy in his distress, a refuge from the storm, a shadow from the heat, when the blast of the terrible ones is as a storm against the wall.*" What shall it be when "*He will swallow up death in victory; and the Lord God will wipe away tears from off all faces; and the rebuke of his people shall he take away from off all the earth; for the mouth of the Lord hath spoken it. And it shall be said in that day, Lo, this is our God; we have waited for him, and he will save us: this is the Lord; we have waited for him, we will be glad, and rejoice in his salvation.*" Isa. xxv. 4, 8, 9.

Then, and not till then, shall be the full response to the Apostle's prayer—then, and not till then, shall the Song of Moses and the Lamb echo from every voice of the assembled hosts of the Redeemed—then shall they enjoy in full possession their "*inheritance incorruptible and undefiled, and that fadeth not away*"—then shall be enjoyed in full fruition the glorious "HOPE OF HIS CALLING," and then revealed in the light of His countenance before the throne "THE RICHES OF THE GLORY OF HIS INHERITANCE IN THE SAINTS." Amen.

TENTH LECTURE.

EPHESIANS I.—19, 20, 21, 22, 23.

"And what is the exceeding greatness of his power to us-ward who believe, according to the working of his mighty power, which he wrought in Christ, when he raised him from the dead, and set him at his own right hand in the heavenly places, far above all principality, and power, and might and dominion, and every name that is named, not only in this world, but also in that which is to come: and hath put all things under his feet, and given him to be head over all things to the church, which is his body, the fulness of him that filleth all in all."

THERE are, as we have seen, three principal subjects in the Apostle's petition for the Church at Ephesus—three distinct points in which he prays the Father of glory to grant to them "*the spirit of wisdom and revelation in the knowledge of Christ, that the eyes of their understanding being enlightened they may know—*

1*st. What is the hope of his calling.*

2*d. What is the riches of the glory of his inheritance in the saints.*

3*d. What is the exceeding greatness of his power to us-ward, who believe, according to the working of his mighty power, which he wrought in Christ, when he raised him from the dead and set him at his own right hand in the heavenly places.*"

We have in this, as has been set forth, in the

First—The blessedness of the saints in the hope to which it is their high privilege to be called in Christ, "*which hope they have as an anchor of their soul, both sure and steadfast.*" Heb. vi. 19.

In the Second—The riches of the glory of Christ's inheritance in them, when He shall be crowned and glorified in all the salvation of His Redeemed—when the "*ten thousand times ten thousand and thousands of thousands shall say with a loud voice, Worthy is the Lamb that was slain to receive power and riches and wisdom and strength and honor and glory and blessing.*" Rev. v. 11, 12.

As the first refers to the hope of the saints in Christ, and the second to the glory of Christ's inheritance in them, so we have in the

Third—The glory of both Christ and His Church in their present union. He, as the risen head; they, as His members; one glorious mystic body. He as "*the head over all things to the Church, which is his body, the fulness of him that filleth all in all.*" Eph. v. 22, 23.

Having considered the two first,—the third point is for our consideration to-day, "WHAT IS THE EXCEEDING GREATNESS OF HIS

POWER TO US-WARD WHO BELIEVE, ACCORDING TO THE WORKING OF HIS MIGHTY POWER, WHICH HE WROUGHT IN CHRIST, WHEN HE RAISED HIM FROM THE DEAD."

Some commentators consider, that the Apostle means here simply the resurrection of Christ, and the blessings which God, by His power, in raising him from the dead, has conferred upon the Church. Others imagine, that it refers to the resurrection of believers, in that He will raise them, and that the Apostle means that this is "THE GREATNESS OF HIS POWER TOWARD THOSE WHO BELIEVE" that they also shall arise, "ACCORDING TO THE WORKING OF HIS MIGHTY POWER, WHICH HE WROUGHT IN CHRIST, WHEN HE RAISED HIM FROM THE DEAD."*

Most unquestionably both of these must be included in its meaning. It must include both the resurrection of Christ, and the future resurrection of believers. But, I think, there is much more than either one or both of these in this passage. It appears to me most especially to mean, *the present spiritual life which believers have in Christ Jesus, being risen with him as their risen head.*

In order to understand the passage, you must refer to the whole context, and examine it at length in the Epistle. The sentence does not appear to me to be concluded till the 10th verse of the next chapter. The Apostle does not appear to have fully given out his meaning till he gets to that verse. If we are spared to reach the 5th and 6th verses, you will see, I trust, the whole connection of the passage,—meantime, I would just remark, that the 5th and 6th verses of the 2nd chapter appear to me to be the explanation of this 19th verse. Here he prays, "*that the eyes of your understanding being enlightened, you may know* WHAT IS THE EXCEEDING GREATNESS OF HIS POWER TO US-WARD WHO BELIEVE, ACCORDING TO THE WORKING OF HIS MIGHTY POWER, WHICH HE WROUGHT IN CHRIST WHEN HE RAISED HIM FROM THE DEAD, AND SET HIM AT HIS OWN RIGHT HAND IN THE HEAVENLY PLACES." Now, in the 5th and 6th verses of the next chapter, he saith, "*he hath quickened us together with Christ,*

* The Author in referring to the opinions of commentators, in several parts of these Lectures, thinks it better to omit names and authorities. First, because it might give a controversial tone to this work, which is generally not profitable to our own souls. It is enough to be obliged to use the Word of God, controversionally with opponents, and it is the least that we may be allowed to enjoy it, spiritually and devotionally ourselves. Besides many persons are so wedded to names and authorities of men, that the very insinuation that a favorite commentator, was not right in every point, would disgust them, and not allow them to consider a passage with common patience or attention, it would be quite enough to stamp it as false, to suppose that Scott, or Henry, or Whitby, or Macknight, or Poole, or Bloomfield, or some other Commentator, was not almost infallible in their interpretation. But the author earnestly entreats others to do, as he would humbly desire to do himself—to study the Lord's word simply with prayer, comparing spiritual things, with spiritual; and thus he trusts they will find, that though in general, sound pious Commentators are right; yet there are many portions of Scripture, which God may be pleased to throw light on, to meek and humble enquirers, of which they may impart some feeble ray, to a fellow-sinner, which even the best Commentators, may perhaps have but slightly noticed; how often do we ourselves see texts of Scripture at some times in a brighter light, than we do at others.

(by grace ye are saved) and hath raised us up together, and made us sit together in heavenly places in Christ Jesus." I think, if you examine it, you will see, that the Apostle carries on the sense to these verses, and that they give the true interpretation of this. The explanation will naturally appear when we come to the passage; but, as the Apostle seems to conclude his meaning there, we shall wait and follow on the chapter in the order in which it lies before us.

You may observe, that the mind of the Apostle seems carried away, as it were, the moment the thought of Christ's resurrection is suggested to him, his soul seems lifted up from the church and things below, to follow up the Lord Jesus into his resurrection glory with the eye of faith. When he touches on the topic of Christ's resurrection, you observe, how, without a single pause, he follows the succession of thoughts that rise as light before him, to the end of the chapter, "WHICH HE WROUGHT IN CHRIST, WHEN HE RAISED HIM FROM THE DEAD, AND SET HIM AT HIS OWN RIGHT HAND IN THE HEAVENLY PLACES. FAR ABOVE ALL PRINCIPALITY, AND POWER, AND MIGHT, AND DOMINION, AND EVERY NAME THAT IS NAMED, NOT ONLY IN THIS WORLD, BUT ALSO IN THAT WHICH IS TO COME. AND HATH PUT ALL THINGS UNDER HIS FEET, AND GAVE HIM TO BE HEAD OVER ALL THINGS TO THE CHURCH, WHICH IS HIS BODY, THE FULNESS OF HIM THAT FILLETH ALL IN ALL." His soul, I say, seems carried away from things of earth, following up Christ in His glory, and expatiating on it as he goes, as if he were ascending up to the very mount of God—and bounding, as it were, from summit to summit, he proclaims the glory of Immanuel, from every elevation of His love and power. "*How beautiful upon the mountains are the feet of him that bringeth good tidings, that publisheth peace, that bringeth good tidings of good, that publisheth salvation, that saith unto Zion, thy God reigneth.*" Isa. lii. 7. It is glorious now, while He sitteth on his mediatorial throne; and what shall it be when He is on His throne as King of glory!

Let us observe, now, what various topics the Apostle touches on in succession here:—

1st. The Resurrection of Christ, "WHICH HE WROUGHT IN CHRIST WHEN HE RAISED HIM FROM THE DEAD."

Then 2d, the exaltation of Christ, "AND SET HIM ON HIS OWN RIGHT HAND IN THE HEAVENLY PLACES."

Then 3d, the Supremacy of Christ, over all powers in heaven, and earth, and hell,—"FAR ABOVE ALL PRINCIPALITY AND POWER AND MIGHT AND DOMINION AND EVERY NAME THAT IS NAMED, NOT ONLY IN THIS WORLD, BUT ALSO IN THAT WHICH IS TO COME."

Then 4th, the absolute executive rule and authority of Christ over all things in heaven and earth, "AND HATH PUT ALL THINGS UNDER HIS FEET."

Then 5th, the glorious headship of the Lord Jesus Christ to the

Church, "AND GAVE HIM TO BE HEAD OVER ALL THINGS TO THE CHURCH."

And 6th, the union of Christ with His Church, as of the head and members, "WHICH IS HIS BODY, THE FULNESS OF HIM THAT FILLETH ALL IN ALL."

We can only briefly touch upon these subjects. May the Lord, the Spirit of wisdom, life and power, be present with us, and teach us each to offer up the Apostle's prayer from our own hearts, and may the Lord give us an answer of peace. May "*the God of our Lord Jesus Christ, the Father of glory, give unto us the spirit of wisdom and revelation in the knowledge of him, the eyes of our understanding being enlightened, that we may know what is the hope of his calling, and what is the riches of the glory of his inheritance in the saints, and what is the* EXCEEDING GREATNESS OF HIS POWER TO US-WARD WHO BELIEVE, ACCORDING TO THE WORKING OF HIS MIGHTY POWER, WHICH HE WROUGHT IN CHRIST WHEN HE RAISED HIM FROM THE DEAD!"

Each of these subjects is a subject of faith, hope, and consolation to the believer. And FIRST—the Apostle speaks of "*the resurrection of the Lord Jesus Christ.*" The resurrection of Christ is the very basis of all the believer's hope. "*If Christ be not risen our faith is vain, we are yet in our sins,*" as the Apostle argues, 1 Cor. xv. 17. His resurrection is given to us in Scripture, as the proof of His Godhead, as we see in Rom. i. 4, "*declared to be the Son of God with power, according to the spirit of holiness, by the resurrection from the dead.*" It is the pledge of our salvation. It is, as it were, the presentation of a receipt in full to man, from the divine justice for all our debts; therefore, it is said "*he was delivered for our offences, and raised again for our justification.*" Rom. iv. 25, that the justification of man might be proclaimed through the finished work of Jesus, as risen from the dead. It is the earnest of our own resurrection, as the Apostle argues throughout the whole of first Corinthians, chap. xv. "*But now is Christ risen from the dead, and become the first fruits of them that slept, for since by man came death, by man came also the resurrection of the dead; for as in Adam all die, even so, in Christ, shall all be made alive.*" 20, 21, 22. And again, "*as we have borne the image of the earthy, we shall also bear the image of the heavenly.*" Again, verse 49, "*we shall not all sleep, but we shall all be changed in a moment, in the twinkling of an eye, at the last trump.*" verse 51, 52. Again, the resurrection of Christ, is, as we said, and as we shall see more fully, the present life of the believer's soul, chap. ii. 6, He "*hath raised us up together, and made us sit together in heavenly places in Christ Jesus,*" "*reckon ye also yourselves, to be dead indeed unto sin, but alive unto God, through Jesus Christ our Lord.*" Rom. vi. 2.

But the SECOND point is, *the exaltation of Christ.* If Christ were not exalted at the right hand of God, the blessing of His resurrection would be incomplete to us; we should not know where He had risen to go, or what He had risen to do. But now we know He is exalted, and that He is exalted as a Prophet, Priest, and King, on His Father's throne, and there He carries on His glorious work, in these blessed offices for those who believe on Him to life everlasting. So we have in Acts, ii. 33, "*therefore being by the right hand of God exalted, and having received of the Father, the promise of the Holy Ghost, he hath shed forth this, which ye now see and hear.*" That was the Holy Ghost. Christ had sent Him forth as the prophet of His Church, He had sent the blessed Spirit to teach them. So St. Peter by that Spirit, whose office it is to glorify Christ, testifies this at the moment, to the assembled multitude, and adds, "*For David is not ascended into the heavens, but he saith himself, the Lord said unto my Lord, sit thou on my right hand, till I make thy foes thy footstool; therefore let all the house of Israel know assuredly, that God hath made that same Jesus, whom ye have crucified both Lord and Christ,*" v. 34, 35, 36. And again, the same Apostle sets forth before the council, the office for which He is exalted, as we see in Acts, v. 30, 31, "*The God of our fathers raised up Jesus, whom ye slew and hanged on a tree, him hath God exalted with his right hand, to be a prince and a Saviour, for to give repentance to Israel, and forgiveness of sins,*" and He exercises His office as a prophet, in teaching His people by His word and by His Spirit.

Recollect that if you really learn any truth to your soul's good, it is only because He is exercising that office for you. How ought we then in hearing His word, to lift up our hearts in prayer to Him, that He will teach us by His Spirit, that He will clothe His truth with power, in the mouth of His servant who speaks, so that that word may come with a blessing to our hearts! If you receive any blessing, you must receive it through Christ by the Spirit. There is no blessing derived from man, man is a poor earthen vessel, "*We have this treasure in earthen vessels that the excellency of the power may be of God, and not of us.*" 2 Cor. iv. 7.

Remember, that as the Lord is exalted, as a Prophet, so He is exalted as a Priest, as the Apostle tells us in Heb. ix. 11, 12, "*Christ being come an High Priest of good things to come,*" (being come that He might be made an High Priest of good things to come,) "*by a greater and more perfect tabernacle, not made with hands, that is to say, not of this building, neither by the blood of goats, and calves, but by his own blood,*" (having come here as a Sin Offering, and poured out his own blood, He hath been now exalted, and) "*he entered in once into the holy place, having obtained eternal redemption for us;*" for as he says in verse 24, "*Christ is not entered into the holy places made with hands, which are the figures of the true,*" (alluding to the holy of holies in the temple,) "*but into heaven itself, now to appear in the presence of God for us,*" exalted an High Priest, on His Father's throne, to appear in the presence of God for us.

Oh, consider what "*the spirit of wisdom and revelation in the knowledge*" of Christ in this does for the sinner! What is it to you, that Christ is exalted a high priest at the right hand of God? —it is nothing—unless you come as a sinner to that high priest, to plead that precious blood before the bar of God for your salvation and peace—that atonement which Christ hath wrought—that blood which Christ poured out as a victim, and now offers as a Priest, and trust in Him, that having carried that blessed sacrifice into the presence of God for sinners, you may rest satisfied that that is enough for you,—you want no more. Consider, then, the use of this—the wondrous blessing, as the Apostle tells us in Heb. iv. 14-16, "*Seeing, then, that we have a great high priest, that is passed into the heavens, Jesus, the Son of God, let us hold fast our profession; for we have not an high priest who cannot be touched with the feeling of our infirmities, but was in all points tempted like as we are, yet without sin. Let us, therefore, come boldly to the throne of grace, that we may obtain mercy, and find grace to help in time of need.*" Here is the end of Christ being exalted a Priest at the right hand of God. And, what an unspeakable blessing it is to know Him in that character! If I address any of you, my dear Roman Catholic friends, here is the Priest for you to go to, or to send for. When you are sick, or when you feel the burden of your sins, then send for the priest,—not the priest of the Church of Rome,—nor the priest of the Church of England,—to take away your sins, or to make an offering for you,—as if a bit of paste, or bread and wine could make an offering to God for sins. Oh, no, send for the "*great high priest, who is passed into the heavens, Jesus, the Son of God,*" send for him. You need not wait for a messenger, you need not send man and horse as an express for Christ. A thought of the heart—a look of the eye is messenger enough for Jesus! "*Look unto me, and be ye saved, all ye ends of the earth!*" Isa. xlv. 22. Here, brethren, is a Priest for you. May the Lord enable us all, Protestants and Roman Catholics, to know the value of Christ as the high Priest that is gone to "*appear in the presence of God for us*"—again I repeat and mark it, "*Seeing that we have a great high priest that is passed into the heavens * * * let us come boldly unto the throne of grace, that we may obtain mercy, and find grace to help in time of need.*" How necessary it is to hold up these great truths, when men are setting forth priests and sacraments, to make their peace with God,—putting the shadow for the substance, the emblem for the thing signified! Grasp the substance, then you are sure to have the shadow. Hold the substance in the light of God's truth, the shadow is sure to follow, as it follows a form in the sun. If you hold Christ as you ought, you will surely place the proper value on the blessed ordinances which He has appointed.

But He is exalted, not only as a Prophet and Priest, but as a King,—and this brings us to the next consideration, His supremacy over all the powers of heaven and earth and hell, "FAR ABOVE ALL PRINCIPALITY AND POWER AND MIGHT AND DOMINION, AND EVERY NAME THAT IS NAMED, NOT ONLY IN THIS WORLD, BUT ALSO IN THAT WHICH IS TO COME." The angels, all the host of heaven, are commanded to worship him. So we have in Phil. ii. 9, 10, speaking of the exaltation of Christ, "*God also hath highly exalted him, and given him a name that is above every name, that at the name of Jesus every knee should bow, of things in heaven, and things in earth, and things under the earth.*" Angels, men, and devils, must bow before him, "*and that every tongue should confess that Jesus Christ is Lord, to the glory of God the Father.*" So in Heb. i. 6, "*when he bringeth in the first begotten into the world, he saith, And let all the angels of God worship him.*" Angels are to worship him, men are to worship him, so the Lord Jesus tells us, "*that all men should honor the Son, even as they honor the Father.*" John v. 23. How is that? It is, with the supreme adoration of Jehovah, "with all their heart, and mind, and soul, and strength;"—"*he that honoreth not the Son,*" thus, "*honoreth not the Father that hath sent him.*" Therefore, Ye Socinians, who pride yourselves on the knowledge of what you call the one God,—your God is an idol—he is no God at all; the thing you call God is no God, for if you honor not the Son as you honor the Father, you honor not the Father, but despise the God of the Bible. The being you worship is a god of your imagination, it is not the God that is revealed in the Bible, because the God that is revealed in the Bible is Jehovah, that God who "*was in Christ, reconciling the world to himself.*" So, the devils are called to worship Him, and they do worship Christ. You see, in St. Luke, iv. 34, when the man with the spirit of an unclean devil cried out, saying, "*what have we to do with thee, thou Jesus of Nazareth? Art thou come to destroy us?*" He adds, in the same breath, "*I know thee, who thou art, the Holy One of God.*" The devil knew Him. The devils are better theologians than the Socinian! Ask the Socinian, who Christ is?—he will tell you, He was a good man, a great man, a holy man, a great prophet, one gifted with the Spirit of God. Ask the devil, who Christ is?—the devil will tell you, "*the Holy One of God,*" as it is said in verse 41, "*And devils also came out of many, crying out and saying, thou art Christ, the Son of God.*" Oh, it is an awful faith which is not so sound as that of the devils! It is an awful faith, I say, which is not so sound even as the faith of devils! But the devil only knows Christ to tremble, for there is no salvation in Christ for the devil. But you, O Socinian, who have neither known Him or trembled at Him—you—though you are more ignorant and unbelieving than the devil—there is salvation in Christ for you! O come, look to Him to-day, with faith—with hope—nay, come to Him to-day, with confidence—look to Him to-day for mercy, for "*all manner of sin and blasphemy shall be forgiven unto men.*" Mat. xii. 31. Remember what a blasphemer Saul was, persecuting Christ,—yet remember, what mercy Jesus showed him. Look unto Jesus, and be ye saved. Come to Him, whatever you are,—whether Socinian, Deist, Infidel, Atheist,—whatever be your grade of ignorance, presumption, or blasphemy. You are a poor, guilty, condemned miserable sinner, "*the wrath of God abideth on you*,"—but the proclamation of the Gospel is, Christ is exalted, "FAR ABOVE ALL PRINCIPALITY, AND POWER, AND DOMINION, AND EVERY NAME THAT IS NAMED, NOT ONLY IN THIS WORLD, BUT ALSO IN THAT WHICH IS TO COME." And "*He is exalted to give repentance and forgiveness of sins*," Acts v. 31.—through him is "*proclaimed unto you the forgiveness of sins.*" Acts xiii. 39. Then, look unto Him, "*Repent, and believe the Gospel.*" Remember that those who "*with wicked hands had crucified and slain*" the Lord of Glory, were yet pardoned through the very blood that they had shed; (see Acts, ii. 23, 37–41) and the fountain that cleansed them from their guilt is still open for sin and uncleanness.

Sinner, think of this! And may the Lord give you "*the spirit of wisdom and revelation in the knowledge of him, that the eyes of your understanding being enlightened you may know what is the hope of his calling.*"

But the Apostle speaks, not only of the exaltation of our blessed Lord, but of his absolute power and authority, "HE HATH PUT ALL THINGS UNDER HIS FEET," so the Lord Jesus Christ tells us in St. Mat. xxviii. 18, "*all power is given unto me in heaven and in earth.*"

What a blessed thing it is then, if "*the spirit of wisdom and revelation*" is given to a believer to have knowledge of Christ in this character, to see him ruling and overruling all things,—directing,—controlling—restraining—subduing; eliciting good, even out of evil. "*Surely, the wrath of man shall praise thee, and the remainder of wrath thou shalt restrain.*" Ps. lxxvi. 10. No wrath of man shall go one step farther, than He who hath all things under His feet shall overrule it at the last, to His own praise and glory. What a blessing it is to the believer to remember, that in the midst of all the turmoils and confusion of this world, the troubles and disasters of private circumstances, and the shakings of kingdoms, there is one overruling power who watches over it all. Christ has "*all power in heaven and earth.*" Remember, believer, what He says, when He commands you not to be careful, He tells you, "*even the very hairs of your head are all numbered.*" Luke xii. 7. A single sparrow can no more fall to the ground without His permission and His providence, than a world could burst from its sphere, and leave the orbit in which He commanded it to roll, "*for all things were created by him and for him, and he is before all things and by him all things consist.*" Col. i. 16, 17—they are all held in the eye and in the hand of Christ, the Lord of Glory.

But consider now the blessedness of the next step in our Lord's exaltation, that is, *the headship of Christ to his Church.* "AND HATH PUT ALL THINGS UNDER HIS FEET, AND GIVEN HIM TO BE HEAD OVER ALL THINGS TO HIS CHURCH." This is full of solemn warning to the outward professing Church and full of solid comfort to the true believer. Let those where the candlestick is burning prize its light while they have it and fear its removal. "*Let Ephesus remember whence she is fallen and repent.*" Rev. ii. 5. "*Let Smyrna fear none of the things that she shall suffer,*" v. 10, "*Let Pergamos beware of them that hold the doctrine of Balaam.*" v. 14, "*Let Thyatira tremble at her encouragement of Jezebel,*" v. 20, "*Let Sardis be watchful and strengthen the things that remain,*" Rev. iii. 2. "*Let Philadelphia hold fast that no man take her crown,*" v. 11. "*Let Laodicea hear the counsel of her Lord, that the shame of her nakedness do not appear.*" v. 18. Let all remember that the promise is "*To him that overcometh.*" Rev. ii. 7, 11, 17, 25, iii. 5, 12, 21; and "*He that hath an ear let him hear what the Spirit saith unto the Churches.*" Rev. ii. 7, 11, 17, 29, iii. 6, 12, 22.

Believer! remember thou that all things are in the hands of our precious Lord and Master, and that all things are working together, for good to His people, because He is given "TO BE HEAD OVER ALL THINGS TO HIS CHURCH." "*All things.*" Nothing is too small for Christ to attend to—nothing too minute for the notice of His love, and the exercise of His power, who numbereth "*the hairs of our head.*" That blessed Spirit, whose office it is to glorify Christ, meant what he said, when He inspired the Apostle to testify and encourage His people, thus, "*casting all your care upon him, for he careth for you.*" 1 Pet. v. 7. Oh, that we did but feel and exercise our happy privilege! Then all our afflictions would seem to be what they really are, blessings sent to us from the hand of a Father's love. Then whatever trials might befall us, we should be enabled to say in spirit and truth, what alas, we so often repeat while our hearts belie our lips, "*thy will be done.*" However gloomy and surcharged with clouds our horizon might appear, the Sun of Righteousness, seen by the eye of faith, in the firmament beyond, would

> "Tinge our dark cloud, and turn it all to gold."

Believing that all things work together for our good, we should enjoy the solid happiness expressed in the words of the hymn—

> "Sweet in the confidence of faith,
> To trust His firm decrees;
> Sweet to lie passive in His hands,
> And know no will but His."

That we may enjoy this, let us remember, it is our privilege to do so, if we are looking to Christ, for "HE IS HEAD OVER ALL THINGS TO HIS CHURCH."

And the eye will not see a danger, into which the foot would step, or the hand would plunge—the sagacity of the head will not more readily direct the members to avoid it, than the providence and power of Him who is the Head of His Church, will foresee every evil and guard against every danger, with which a single member of His mystical body, could be threatened.

But if indeed you are in trouble and affliction, and are not looking to Christ, if you are not resting on Him who is the Hope and

Refuge of the guilty, then however afflictive or overwhelming your sorrows may seem to be, they are all of little consequence comparatively to you. Alas! what is all your sorrow, if you are under the weight of your sins? What is your grief as to temporal afflictions if you are not looking to Jesus, to deliver you from the wrath to come? Oh, leave your grief and go to Jesus, with your guilt. Saul's father forgot his anxiety for the loss of his asses, when he began to fear for his son, and you will soon forget to mourn for your sorrow, when you begin to feel, and to fear for your soul.

I remember reading once a little book, in which the author says, "I was very much bowed down with sorrow the other day; my father-in-law came unto me, 'Ah John,' said he, 'when sorrow is heavy, sin is light.'" If we feel our sin as we ought, whatever our sorrow be, it will be light, compared with our sin, and if we bring our sin to Jesus, joy for the forgiveness of sin, will soon dispel the gloom of sorrow.

The light of the Sun of Righteousness exhales the tears of grief from our eyes, as the light of the morning sun exhales the tear-drops of the night from the dewy drooping flowers. Then we understand what it is to have Christ as "THE HEAD OF ALL THINGS TO HIS CHURCH," then it is our privilege to look at every dispensation of Providence, as a dispensation of love, and to see all things working together for our good, and that therefore, no evil that is really an evil, can happen unto us.

The believer may say, how can that be? Surely, I have suffered under many evils.

Let me pause then here for one moment, believer, and let me ask you this question. Look back at all the course of your life, at all the trials and afflictions which you have ever encountered—and let me ask, did you ever encounter a trial, since you knew the Lord Jesus Christ, that the Lord did not make your trial a blessing? Did it not show you more of your sins? Did it not show you more of your own vileness? Did it not bring you nearer to the feet of Jesus? Did it not wean you more from the things of the world? Did it not make your heart ache more, over your broken cisterns? and did it not drive you from them, to the "*fountain of living waters?*" Jer. ii. 13.

I anticipate—yea, I know your answer. It is this—"Yes—He hath done all things well."

Oh, then, remember, that "*Jesus Christ is the same yesterday, to-day, and forever.*" Heb. xiii. 8,—and since you must know that all things have been working together for your good, remember that they are, and shall continue so to work—so nothing can be really evil to you, for things that are evil in themselves will be over-ruled to you for a blessing, because Jesus is "THE HEAD OVER ALL THINGS TO HIS CHURCH." Think of this, and remember the reasoning of the Apostle in the very passage, Rom. viii. 28, where he asserts that "*all things work together for good, to them that love God, to them that are the called according to his purpose*"—recollect he asks, "*Who shall lay anything to the charge of God's elect? it is God that justifieth: who is he that condemneth? it is Christ that died, yea, rather, that is risen again,"*—(you see, it is the same truth which he mentions here to the Ephesians, in teaching them to look to Jesus as a risen and exalted Saviour) "*It is Christ that died, yea, rather, that is risen again, who also maketh intercession for us.*" Then he boldly asks, "*who shall separate us from the love of Christ? shall tribulation, or distress, or persecution, or famine, or nakedness, or peril, or sword?*"—shall anything within or without?—any trouble, any want, any affliction, any evil?—"*Nay, in all these things we are more than conquerors through him that loved us; for I am persuaded, that neither death, nor life, nor angels, nor principalities, nor powers, nor things present,*" (however much they may press upon us)—"*nor things to come,*"—(however much we may fear them) "*nor height, nor depth, nor any other creature shall be able to separate us from the love of God, which is in Christ Jesus our Lord,*" Rom. viii. 33–39—Now why? because He is "GIVEN TO BE HEAD OVER ALL THINGS TO HIS CHURCH."

And the Head must die, or be cut off, before the same stream of vital sympathy and power that warms that Head shall cease to flow through every member that is vitally united to it. How frequently have his express revelations—His actual deliverances—His inward supports and consolations, strengthened the hearts of His servants, and carried them through countless trials. Observe, in the very Lesson we had this day, (Acts, xviii.,) when Paul went to Corinth—when he was in the midst of an idolatrous city, and in the midst of those who opposed and blasphemed, and who would be glad to have persecuted him or put him to death—"*Then spake the Lord to Paul in the night by a vision, be not afraid, but speak, and hold not thy peace. For I am with thee, and no man shall set on thee to hurt thee. For I have much people in this city.*" Acts, xviii. 9, 10.

So, in Acts xii., when Herod was determined to bring Peter out and slay him,—he "*delivered him to four quaternions of soldiers, to keep him,*" and put him "*sleeping between two soldiers, bound with two chains.*" v. 4–6.—But what was Herod? or, what the quaternions of soldiers? or, the chains? or, the guards? or, the prison? What were they, when the Lord Jesus was determined to deliver His servant out of their hand?—the chain was snapped in sunder—the prison doors were burst open, and he was brought out by the power of his Lord and Master, for "HE IS HEAD OVER ALL THINGS TO HIS CHURCH," and He is as much so now as He was then.

Look to Daniel, iii., when the King Nebuchadnezzar said to the three servants of the living God, when he had set up a golden image to worship in the plains of Dura, "*if ye worship not, ye shall be cast the same hour into the midst of a burning fiery furnace, and who is that God that shall deliver you out of my hand?*" And they refused, as you know, and said, "*Our God whom we serve is able to deliver us from the burning fiery furnace, and he will deliver us out of thy hand, O King.*" verses 15–17. And, you remember, Nebuchadnezzar got the strongest men in his army, and heated the furnace seven times more than it was wont to be heated, and commanded these strong men to cast these three men, bound, into the furnace. What did the heating of this furnace?—he made the furnace so hot that it slew his own soldiers, the strongest men in his army. What harm did it do the children of God?—it burned off their bonds, and Nebuchadnezzar was the first to cry out, "*Did not we cast three men, bound, into the midst of the fire? They answered and said unto the King, true, O King. He answered and said, Lo, I see four men loose walking in the midst of the fire, and they have no hurt! And the form of the fourth is like the Son of God.*" And so it was the Son of God, for "HE IS THE HEAD OVER ALL THINGS TO HIS CHURCH." And His promise is, "*When thou passest through the waters, I will be with thee, and through the rivers, they shall not overflow thee; when thou passest through the fire, thou shall not be burned; neither shall the flame kindle upon thee.*" Isai. xliii. 2. This is His promise, and remember, it is the promise of "*Jesus the same yesterday, to-day, and forever.*" Heb. xiii. 8.

Then, the last point is *the union of Christ with his church*, He "GAVE HIM TO BE HEAD OVER ALL THINGS TO THE CHURCH." But what is the church? "WHICH IS HIS BODY, THE FULNESS OF HIM THAT FILLETH ALL IN ALL." Recollect the Church of Christ is His body—those who believe His blessed Gospel—those who are leaning on His mighty arm—those who are servants of the King of kings, and Lord of lords—they are members of Christ's body, none else. His Church, is His body, a part of Himself, every member of that body is a member of Christ,—therefore all the images in the Scripture that refer to the union of Christ with His Church, refer to a real vital union between them, a union commensurate with their existence. Such a union as between the vine and its branches, vitally united. Such a union as exists between husband and wife,—one. Such a union as exists between a house and its foundation—inseparably connected together. Between the head and the members of the body. You see this in various pages of Scripture, so he says, "*he that toucheth you, toucheth the apple of his eye.*" Zech. ii. 8. What a tender member that is! So he says to Saul, Acts ix. 4, "*why persecutest thou me?*" so he says to the whole company of his redeemed, "*inasmuch as you have done it unto one of the least of these, my brethren, ye have done it unto me.*" Mat. xxv. 40. His union with His Church, as one with them, assures the full blessedness of all his power and offices, as exalted at the right hand of God, to be the Prophet, Priest and King of His people,—"*all power given to him in heaven and earth*" "HE THE HEAD OVER ALL THINGS TO HIS CHURCH."

Brethren, it is well to preach about these things, and it is well to hear of these things,—but, Oh, what are they if we do not realize them in our hearts? Pray, I beseech you, for *the spirit of wisdom and revelation in the knowledge of Christ*,—pray, that the Lord may teach you, that you may know these things experimentally, so that in life and death, you may be one with Christ, that "*neither death nor life, may be able to separate you from the love of God which is in Christ Jesus our Lord.*" Rom. viii. 39. Amen.

ELEVENTH LECTURE.

EPHESIANS II.—1, 2, 3.

"And you *hath he quickened* who were dead in trespasses and sins. Wherein, in time past ye walked according to the course of this world, according to the prince of the power of the air, the Spirit that now worketh in the children of disobedience. Among whom also we all had our conversation in times past in the lusts of our flesh, fulfilling the desires of the flesh and of the mind; and were by nature the children o wrath, even as others."

You recollect it was remarked, that the sense of this passage to the 10th verse, was to be taken in connection with the 19th verse of the preceding chapter. You recollect we have been dwelling on the Apostle's prayer, which commences at the 17th verse, "*That the God of our Lord Jesus Christ, the Father of glory, may give unto you the spirit of wisdom and revelation in the knowledge of him, the eyes of your understanding being enlightened, that ye may know what is the hope of his calling, and what the riches of the glory of his inheritance in the saints, and what is the exceeding greatness of his power to us-ward, who believe, according to the working of his mighty power, which he wrought in Christ when he raised him from the dead.*" This prayer may be considered with respect to Christ himself, and with respect to believers as united to Christ, their living and risen head.

In the last verses of the preceding chapter.—We have considered how God's power was manifested in reference to our Lord, when He raised Him from the dead. The Apostle there confines his observations to Christ, his exaltation, His glorious majesty, His mighty power, His sovereign rule over all things which are put under His feet, being given to be Head over all things to the church, and the church being His body. Now, we are to consider how this power is manifested in reference to believers, and for this purpose, the Apostle shows us two things. First.—The state of all believers, both Jews and Gentiles, by nature; and next, their state by grace. He shows their state by nature, in these first three verses; he shows their state by grace, in the subsequent part of the chapter. These two conditions, the Apostles keep continually before the mind of believers,—in fact, they are as inseparable from the real existence of spiritual life, as the necessities and the supplies of nutriment are indispensable to the being of our animal frame.

Now, the passage before us contains the first of these important truths, that is, a description of the state of Jews and Gentiles by nature, and it is in their deliverance from this, that the greatness of God's power toward them is manifested.

"AND YOU *hath he quickened,* WHO WERE DEAD IN TRESPASSES AND SINS." You perceive, on looking at the text, that the words, "*hath he quickened,*" are in Italics, therefore they are not in the original. The words that are not in the original Greek are supplied in Italics, to mark that they are inserted by our translators, for the purpose of showing, more clearly, the sense.—These words, "YOU HATH HE QUICKENED," both refer back to verse 19, of the preceding chapter, and onward to verse 5, of this chapter. The Apostle prays, verses 19, 20, that God might show them, "*What is the exceeding greatness of his power to us-ward, who believe, according to the working of his mighty power, which he wrought in Christ, when he raised him from the dead, and set him at his own right hand in the heavenly places.*" In the last three verses of the chapter the Apostle follows, as we have seen, the Lord Jesus Christ to His glorious exaltation in His offices, and now reverting to the subject of his petition in the 19th verse, he commences to show what the "*exceeding greatness of God's power, which he wrought in Christ, when he raised him from the dead,*" had been to those who believed, "*He is the head of the Church, which is his body.*" "*And you,* (members of that body,) *hath he quickened, who were dead in trespasses and sins.*" He then enlarges on their fallen condition.—Having diverged from his immediate subject, in the 21st, 22nd, and 23d verses, to dwell on the exaltation and glory of Christ; he does the same in the 2nd and 3rd verses here, to dwell on their degradation and misery as sinners, then in the 4th, 5th, and 6th verses, he resumes the subject of his prayer and shows how the power of God in raising Christ from the dead, and setting him at his right hand, had been equally manifested in raising up them. If we leave out both digressions as to Christ and to them, and read the passage without them, we shall more clearly see the Apostle's meaning:—"*That ye may know what is the hope of his calling, and what the riches of the glory of his inheritance in the saints, and what is the exceeding greatness of his power to us-ward who believe, according to the working of his mighty power, which he wrought in Christ, when he raised him from the dead, and set him at his own right hand in the heavenly places.*" Chap. i. 18, 19, 20. * * * *for you too hath he quickened, who were dead in trespasses and sins* * * * *God, who is rich in mercy, for his great love wherewith he loved us, even when we were dead in sins, hath quickened us together with Christ,* (*by grace ye are saved,*) *and hath raised us* *up together, and made us sit together in heavenly places in Christ, that in the ages to come he might show the exceeding riches of his grace in his kindness toward us through Christ Jesus.*" Chap. ii. 1, 4, 5, 6, 7. This, I think, will show the meaning of the Apostle. But we shall see this more fully in the next Lecture; and we now return to the verses immediately before us, to consider the state of those by nature who are called by Grace into the Church of Christ.

Mark the Apostle's description, "DEAD IN TRESPASSES AND SINS." Was this peculiar to the Ephesians? Nay, it is universally true, for they were only "WALKING ACCORDING TO THE COURSE OF THIS WORLD."

Again, under the dominion of Satan, "ACCORDING TO THE PRINCE OF THE POWER OF THE AIR, THE SPIRIT THAT NOW WORKETH IN THE CHILDREN OF DISOBEDIENCE." Observe in this, the subtlety of his agency, and the extent of his domination.

Again, "FULFILLING THE DESIRES OF THE FLESH AND OF THE MIND." This was their state. Then mark its fatal consequences,—the wrath of God abiding upon them—they "WERE BY NATURE THE CHILDREN OF WRATH, EVEN AS OTHERS."

Now, as surely as this is the word of truth, so certainly is it a description—God's description—of each and every one of us by nature. It is the picture which the pencil of inspiration draws of us. Look into this as into a mirror, behold your own face. Look into this sacred page for the exact delineation of yourselves, —see if you can recognize your natural character—"DEAD IN TRESPASSES AND SINS,"—dead, doubly dead.

First, in a state of utter spiritual insensibility, as insensible to all spiritual things, as a dead body to the things of time.

Secondly, in a state of condemnation, sentenced to death both in body and in soul. The curse pronounced on man's disobedience was, you see in Gen. ii. 17, "*in the day thou eatest thereof, thou shalt surely die*," now, he says, "*in the day*," therefore, death must have passed on our first parents even the very day they eat of the forbidden fruit. It was a state of spiritual death, they became utterly insensible of the real nature of God's character and of their own, their eyes were opened indeed, to see good and evil, but alas! it was a fatal vision, that arose before them, it was more than vision, it was the horrible experience of evil—blindness, darkness, sin, and misery, in their own souls! You have only to see, how instantly fallen Adam was, and into what a state of spiritual darkness and death he must have been precipitated, when he, who had conversed before with the Omniscient, Omnipresent God, ran to hide from His presence among the trees of the garden, ignorant of his Creator as one of the beasts that perish. Such is the state of death in which man is represented throughout the Scripture.—So in the 1st chap. of St. Luke, where the Gospel is spoken of as shining upon the people, it is, "*to give light to them that sit in darkness and in the shadow of death*," Luke, i. 79. And so you have in 1 Tim. v this description of a woman of the world, 6th verse, "*she that liveth in pleasure is dead while she liveth.*"

Oh, consider this, any of you who are, what you call, perhaps, "*enjoying life.*" "Let us enjoy life," persons say; let us live while we live.* That enjoyment of life, as you call it, is another name for living "*after the course of this world, and fulfilling the desires of the flesh and of the mind;*" while you are enjoying life, as you think, God marks you as dead while you live. If you saw an individual in the midst of a gay assembly, of whom a physician told you, "look at that person, in the thoughtless circle of this fashionable crowd, that man to my knowledge has got a disease of which he is insensible, but which renders it impossible he can outlive a week." Suppose you saw such an individual in the centre of such a throng, engaged in what the world would call enjoying life,—what would you think of him?—would you consider this enjoyment of life? Suppose he were to live ten days, —what difference would that make? Add another day, another, and another, after which it was impossible he could survive,—and at what day would your compassion for him cease? If you are living without God in the world, "thou art the man," death is in that body—and if you are living without God in the world death is in that soul. The sentence of death is passed upon you—it is the state of all unawakened men—it is the state of all unenlightened sinners; and while they are in this state, all spiritual truth comes to their ears, exactly as all the objects or the sounds of nature affect the tenant of the silent tomb. In vain the wintry storm howls around, in vain the thunders roll, and the lightnings flash across the grave. In vain the sun arises and declines, in vain the smiling spring revisits them, and decks with flowers the sod that is spread over their form. Darkness and light, storm and sunshine, winter and spring, to them are all alike, they never pierce the gloom to the eye, or break the silence to "the dull cold ear of death." So it is with the Gospel, so with the law, so with all the appeals of God's eternal word to man,—the sinner is "*dead in trespasses and sins,*" no threatenings, no warnings, no judgments, can awaken him, no voice of love and mercy, no message of peace and pardon, no sound of God's Almighty grace, no invitation from a dying Saviour, can reach his ear or touch his heart, he is "*dead in trespasses and sins.*" Perhaps, it is so with some —with, alas! too many of those whom I address. No matter what we preach, if God leaves you to your own corrupt and hardened heart, you go away unmoved. If you seem to attend during the few moments you are in church—if when you leave it, you make a few remarks on the solemn service, or on the sermon, it will not be on the public professions you yourself have made, nor on the awful warnings, or the gracious mercies you have heard, but perhaps it may be on the manner in which the service has been read, or the sermon has been delivered. God's judgments, God's mercies, have no effect upon you, you cast them all without

* Dum vivimus vivamus.

compunction or care behind you, and go back into the world to follow the course that is described in these verses.

It is enough for your destruction that you go on, "ACCORDING TO THE COURSE OF THIS WORLD." The very principle by which men console themselves, the very ground on which they build themselves up in their sins, and entrench themselves up in their iniquity, the very source of their satisfaction and self-complacency in their career, ought to be the ground of their apprehension, their fear, their terror of eternal judgment, and that is this,—

"Oh, sure, we only do what the whole world does,—sure we only live like the rest of the world,—every one does this,—every one says this,—everybody thinks so,—why should not we?—you would not have us to be singular,—surely the whole world cannot be wrong." Have you not often heard, perhaps used these and similar expressions? Nevertheless, what saith the Scripture, "*The whole world lieth in wickedness.*" 1 John v. 19,—or as it is more correctly interpreted by the context, "*lieth in the wicked one,*" lieth under the power of the devil, as the Greek idiom would imply, or lieth in the devil's arms, as the English would seem to interpret such a phrase—but it is a strict parallel to this passage. But did you never read of a time when the world said the same thing, and when the world found too late its awful mistake? The Lord Jesus in St. Luke xvii. 26, 27, refers us to a time when all men thought and spoke and acted just as you do. "*As it was in the days of Noe, so shall it be also in the days of the Son of Man, they did eat, they drank, they married wives, they were given in marriage, until the day that Noe entered into the ark, and the flood came and destroyed them all.*" For one hundred and twenty years did God spare the world from the time he denounced his judgment against it; and for one hundred and twenty years did Noe preach righteousness, judgment and salvation, to that guilty world that surrounded him; but they went on in their usual avocations, mocking Noah for his singularity, and strengthening each other in their wickedness, eating and drinking, buying and selling, planting and building, marrying wives and giving in marriage, till the flood came and swept them all to ruin. So again, he says, 28, 29 verses, "*Likewise also, as it was in the days of Lot, they did eat, they drank, they bought, they sold, they planted, they builded, but the same day that Lot went out of Sodom, it rained fire and brimstone from heaven and destroyed them all.*" What consolation in these fearful judgments did the world bestow on its votaries? Did those who strengthened each other in their sin, console one another under the wrath of God? Did the world afford an ark to rescue its victims as they were being engulphed in the rising flood of the deluge? or shield their devoted heads from the falling fire of Sodom?

"Oh, but then," you will say, "they had not the light that we have, they had not all the light and knowledge that is diffused among us in our day, they were not Christians, as we are; we are baptized, we are members of the Christian Church, we enjoy all these privileges, therefore we are not like them." Does Christ say so? Does the Lord Jesus afford this consolation to those who are called by his name? he says,—"*even thus*,"—as it was in the days of Noe, as it was in the days of Lot,—"*even thus shall it be in the day when the Son of Man is revealed.*" Luke xvii. 30. The outward privileges which men have enjoyed, the spiritual blessings which God has heaped upon them, shall only rise in judgment to condemn the souls of those who have made light of that Gospel of their salvation. Sodom and Gomorrah shall appear as witnesses against them—Bibles, Sacraments and ordinances, the rejected means and testimonies of salvation—like the sun shining on corruption, shall but generate in their guilty souls "*the worm that dieth not*," and call divine justice to pour down on them "*the fire that never shall be quenched.*"

The course of this world is according to the god of this world, "ACCORDING TO THE PRINCE OF THE POWER OF THE AIR, THE SPIRIT THAT NOW WORKETH IN THE CHILDREN OF DISOBEDIENCE." Now, here is another point. Men think that to say, persons are acting under the dominion of the devil is to imply, that they must be some notorious criminals. They think that persons who commit some flagrant offence, some awful crimes, and that only such as these are instigated by the devil. So our law speaks, in certain acts of parliament, and some of our legal indictments, referring to grievous offences, "Whereas, such and such a person, not having the fear of God before his eyes, but being instigated by the devil," &c. &c. That is all very true, but persons think it is only to be applied to those who are guilty of flagrant offences; and to tell them that if they are themselves living "ACCORDING TO THE COURSE OF THIS WORLD," they are under the power of the devil, would be a gross affront. But if you are not brought by grace to the cross of Christ, you are under the dominion of Satan, in the smooth, quiet discharge of what you imagine to be your regular duties, and which really are so, just as certainly, though not in the same manner, as those who commit the most flagrant offences. Do you imagine that the devil always exercises his power and presents his snares in a startling and revolting point of view? Mankind would shudder generally at flagrant crimes, and do you think their enemy presents destruction to them under this alarming aspect? Far from it. How did he bring "death into the world and all our woe?" Was it by any astounding act of daring wickedness? Was it by what seemed to man, or what men in general would even now pronounce a flagitious crime? Nay, multitudes would now consider the act a very insignificant offence. It was not an alarming sin, but the smooth promise of good that tempted Eve, "*thou shalt not surely die:*"—Nay, he said, "*in the day ye eat thereof, then your eyes shall be opened, and ye shall be as Gods, knowing good and evil.*" Gen. iii. 4, 5.

Many persons object to this very fact against the Bible, and say, "surely, the smallness of the sin is enough to show us that it cannot have entailed the dreadful consequences you speak of on mankind." You see how Satan works in the minds of men to make them believe, that that sin was but a small one.* God gave our first parents a test of obedience and of love to a holy God,—a light, a little test, so light, so little, that the very lightness of the test that God had laid on man, enhanced the guilt of man's violation of it, and aggravated the act of rebellion against his God. Satan came quoting Scripture to our Lord, and tempted him to manifest his own divinity and power; and he often comes, quoting Scripture to deceive and tempt men now. He comes, taking, as it were, the Sacraments in his hands, he tells you of them, that these are your salvation. He comes extolling the Church to the very skies, and he will tell you, too, that the Church is your salvation. He will come, and laud the ministers of Christ, and will tell you these are the successors of the Apostles, that you must bow your ear, your heart, your conscience, to their words, for they are God's appointed channels of salvation. The devil does not always come with blood and slaughter in his train, he becomes an angel of light more frequently than he appears as the Prince of darkness—he brings the rites and ceremonies and ordinances of religion. He comes with these as well as with ungovernable lusts and furious passions "TO WORK IN THE CHILDREN OF DISOBEDIENCE," to hide their own sin and misery, and to hide Christ from their eyes,—he comes not only himself like an angel of light, but he transforms his ministers into angels of light, testifying falsehood in morals and religion, and turning man from the only hope that God has given him in the Gospel. The Pharisees were as much under the power of the devil as Judas Iscariot. What said the Lord Jesus Christ to them in St. John viii.?—to those smooth hypocrites who brought their own morality and virtue and religious services to God, who thanked him they were "*not as other men, extortioners, unjust, adulterers.*" Luke xviii. 11.—and rejected the testimony of God against their souls.—Our Lord testifies they were as here described, "*dead in trespasses and sins,*" "*under the prince of the power of the air.*" Mark, how the Lord Jesus Christ addresses them, verses 44, 45, "*Ye are of your father, the devil, and the lusts of your father ye will do; he was a murderer from the beginning, and abode not in the truth, because there is no truth in him. When he speaketh of a lie, he speaketh of his own, for he is a liar and the father of it. And because I tell you the truth, ye believe me not.*"

The very reason they ought to have believed him, was the very

* It is a singular and awful fact, that in the doctrines of Popery, the very theft of an apple is specified as being but a venial sin.—Dr. Doyle in his Christian Doctrines, Coyne, 1828, chap. 8, p. 46, says:—

"A venial sin, for example, a vain word, an officious or jesting lie, which hurts nobody—the theft of a pin or an apple, is not of weight enough to break charity between man and man, much less between God and man."

And page 63, in answer to the question, "When is theft a mortal sin?" he says:—

"When the thing stolen is of considerable value, or causeth a considerable hurt to our neighbor"—as if the value of an article, and not the law and will of God were the standard of sin and duty.

reason they rejected him,—therefore he said, "*Ye are of your father, the devil, and the works of your father ye will do;*" and if the devil can persuade a sinner to reject God's truth, to disbelieve God's testimony, he has that sinner just as much in his power as if he instigated him to imbrue his hands in his brother's blood. Mark what God declares—He is "THE SPIRIT THAT NOW WORKETH IN THE CHILDREN OF DISOBEDIENCE." All who are disobedient to the Gospel of Christ, are under the power of Satan.

Now, you perceive the same testimony borne here of both by the Apostle, speaking alike of Jews and Gentiles. Observe the identity in this respect, between them in this passage. He is writing to Gentiles, to the Ephesians, who were idolaters, worshippers of the goddess Diana,—"*wherein in times past ye,*" (Ephesians,) "*walked according to the course of this world.*" And now look at verse 3, "AMONG WHOM ALSO, WE ALL HAD OUR CONVERSATION IN TIMES PAST, IN THE LUSTS OF OUR FLESH, FULFILLING THE DESIRES OF THE FLESH AND OF THE MIND, AND WERE BY NATURE THE CHILDREN OF WRATH, EVEN AS OTHERS," we Jews, were "*by nature the children of wrath,*" even as you, Gentiles. This is St. Paul's description of himself and his brethren. Let me entreat you to compare this with the description he gives of himself at the same time in Philippians iii. You will find there, Paul's description of his own character, as an unregenerate man, 4th verse, "*if any other man thinketh, that he hath whereof he might trust in the flesh, I more.*" Then he tells them what he was, "*circumcised the eighth day, of the stock of Israel, of the tribe of Benjamin, an Hebrew of the Hebrews, as touching the law a Pharisee, concerning zeal, persecuting the church, touching the righteousness which is in the law, blameless.*" Now, I pray you to observe this, he says, "*if any other man thinketh, he hath whereof he may trust in the flesh, I more;*" if he thinks he has any righteousness, any morality, any virtue, any excellence which he can bring before God, I meet that man, and I challenge him, saith Paul, I have more. Yet, what was he, at that time? See his description of himself in my text,—"WE HAD OUR CONVERSATION IN TIMES PAST, IN THE LUSTS OF OUR FLESH, FULFILLING THE DESIRES OF THE FLESH AND OF THE MIND, AND WERE BY NATURE THE CHILDREN OF WRATH, EVEN AS OTHERS." How could he be walking in the lusts of his flesh, when he was so moral and so virtuous, and so outwardly observant of religion? There is nothing more gratifying to the flesh, than the indulgence of its spiritual pride. Spiritual pride and self-righteousness, are among the most delightful enjoyments of the flesh,—and the man who will deny himself the indulgence of some lust, in order that he may look down upon his neighbor who falls into it, and say, "*stand by, I am holier than thou,*" the man who does so, indulges, perhaps, a deeper lust, in the denial of the sin on such a principle, than the other man who falls into the sin that he denies himself. There is no greater indulgence of the flesh than spiritual pride, or self-righteousness; therefore, while Paul was such a character as he describes himself to have been, in Philip. iii., he was also such a character as he describes himself here to have been, in Ephesians ii. While he was selected by the chief priests, as the most pious, devoted, and admirable engine of their persecution of the church, he was, as he tells us, "*a persecutor and blasphemer, not meet to be called an apostle*," (even after he had been chosen one,) "*because he persecuted the church of God.*" 1st Cor. xv. 9—therefore, the being under the power of Satan, and "FULFILLING THE DESIRES OF THE FLESH AND OF THE MIND," is not at all confined, you see, to open criminals and profligates, but just as much applies, in the sight of God, though not in that of man, to every sinner on the face of this earth, who knows not his own guilty character, and flies not to the refuge that God has proclaimed through Christ. This is a picture of man, and if we do not know it to be a picture of our own character, we do not take our character from the Bible, therefore let me entreat you to "*judge yourselves that ye be not judged of the Lord.*" Let us be assured that God will not pronounce one judgment on man now in His word, and another judgment when He comes in His glory. Nay, He expressly testifies, "*The word that I have spoken, the same shall judge you in the last day.*" John xii. 48.—that Word which He has given to us to be a "*lamp unto our feet, and a light unto our path,*" testifies to us what we are, and such as the Bible describes us to be, such shall we be found when God shall come to sit in judgment on us. If it were not so, you know, God as a Judge must contradict God as a Law-giver. God in His Word and sentence spoken when He shall come in His glorious majesty, to judge the quick and dead, must contradict God in His inspired truth which He has given to lead our souls from death to life. This, you know, must be impossible, therefore, if we do not take our character from the Bible, we are blind; but these verses in this passage are the testimony of God as to our real state and character by nature—and not ours alone, but that of the whole human race, there is no exception; therefore the conclusion is of necessity the consequence of our sin, we are "BY NATURE CHILDREN OF WRATH, EVEN AS OTHERS,"—those who are children of grace, being called by the blessed Gospel of Christ, had been by nature children of wrath. "*The wages of sin is death.*" Rom. vi. 23—and they had incurred the penalty, "*Cursed is every one that continueth not in all things which are written in the book of the law to do them.*" Gal. iii. 10.

But what must be the actual state of man as under sentence of the wrath of God? Who can justly appreciate the misery of his condition? How is it, that the announcement of the awful fact, has no effect on our hearts? that the most trifling inconvenience that could occur to annoy us, would excite us more than the revelation of God's eternal judgment against our souls? This very fact demonstrates the truth that men are "*dead in trespasses and sins.*"

Announce to a man who believes himself possessed of an enormous capital, that bankruptcy and beggary await him.—Tell a prisoner who hopes for certain deliverance, that the sentence of death is passed on him, and he may expect the summons of the executioner.—Inform a man who thinks he has got but a slight disease, that it is the symptom of a fatal plague, and advise him to prepare for death.—Thunder at a man's door, and shout that the house is on fire, and bid him escape for his life, and surely nothing but that men had sunk in death before these tidings reached their ears, could prevent their being suitably affected by them. But men can hear of the judgments and the wrath of God, as though they heard them not; such announcements are like those of the destruction of Sodom by Lot, "*He seemed as one that mocked unto his sons in law.*" Gen. xix. 14, or like the language of unbelieving Israel to the prophet, when he proclaimed the fearful judgments to come, "*Ah, Lord God! they say of me, doth he not speak parables.*" Ezek. xx. 49.

Yet what is it to be a child of wrath? It is to turn every blessing that this earth can give, into aggravated misery. The happier we see a man the more exalted in station, the more renowned by fame, the more endowed with wealth, the more miserable is his lot, when precipitated from them all to everlasting ruin. Belshazzar was more to be commiserated and contemned, than the poorest beggar within the city of Babylon, when the hand of fire came forth to write his doom upon the wall; the louder he had laughed—the more triumphantly he had "*praised the gods of gold, and of silver, of brass, of iron, of wood, and of stone,*" Dan. v. 4—the deeper draughts of luscious wine, that he and all his court had quaffed from the golden vessels of Jehovah's temple—the deadlier was the livid paleness of his face, the loosening of his joints, and the smiting of his knees, when the fatal characters of death and judgment were traced before his eyes. What profit in the vast domains of wealth, when the trumpet of eternal judgment shall awake their haughty owners from the death of trespasses and sins? When they shall call, but call in vain, upon those lofty mountains, of which, in their pride of heart, they had boasted as their own, to fall on them, and cover them, and hide them from the wrath of that God, whom they have dishonored and despised?

Oh! what is a miserable sinner, while he is a child of wrath—and such are you who hear, if you have not fled from the wrath to come.*

My subject closes here. The Apostle is speaking but of human guilt and condemnation, and I am not called to speak of the de-

* The writer, in publishing these Expository Lectures, ought perhaps to apologize for a digression from the text such as is presented in the remainder of this Lecture—but he hopes that his object in reference to those to whom they were addressed as hearers may excuse him likewise to those who read them. It may be true of some who shall read this Lecture, as of some who heard it, that perhaps it is the last treatise on religion that may ever reach their eye—and surely it is needful to the reader as to the hearer that if he is awakened to a sense of sin, he may, at the same time, read the message of salvation—and if he is led to feel the extent and danger of his disease, that he may also, through mercy, see the skill and power of the Great Physician.

liverance until I shall next address you, but I dare not wait until then; who can tell what a day, much less a week, may bring forth; I may never be allowed to speak, nor you to hear again—I know not but some sinner may have come to hear this day, who even until this hour has been "*dead in trespasses and sins.*" I know not but that even now his heart may be awakened to feel his want and misery, and that even now his spirit cries within his breast, "*What shall I do to be saved?*" I dare not leave such sinner comfortless, perhaps, this very day, the Lord saith to him as to Zaccheus, "*this day I must abide at thy house,*" Luke xix. 5; perhaps like Zaccheus, this day his soul may receive him joyfully.

The Lord Jesus never sent any away empty, who came to seek His mercy. Yea "*Thou O Lord hast not forsaken them that seek thee.*" Psalm, ix. 10. Perhaps then this day that some one who hears this description of the state of sinners, may be taught to feel the weight and burden of his sin, and now listens with a very heavy heart.—Yes, if you believe the testimony of God, concerning your own state as a sinner, your heart must be sad and heavy indeed. But the Gospel of Jesus is intended to come to lift the load off the weary and heavy-laden heart of man, and therefore, if there be any of you here who say—

"Alas! that is my case, Ah! yes, that is a description of me! I feel I have been just such a sinner as is mentioned here, '*dead in trespasses and sins,*' oh, how hard, how callous, how insensible, my heart has been! How have I slighted God's mercies! made light of and neglected His blessed Gospel!—how often has it sounded in my ears, and my heart has been as hard as the nether mill-stone! Yes, I have indeed been 'WALKING ACCORDING TO THE COURSE OF THIS WORLD,' 'FULFILLING THE DESIRES OF THE FLESH AND OF THE MIND!' The devil has led me away captive at his will! I have turned a deaf ear to God. Yes, this is a description of me,—my God, this is a true description of me!"

Well my friend and fellow-sinner! the glad tidings of salvation are the same to you that Saul rejoiced in, when they reached his ears, and when, from having been a persecutor and blasphemer, he arose, went forth, "*and preached Christ in the synagogues.*" Acts, ix. Remember the invitation of your blessed Redeemer "*Come unto me all ye that labor and are heavy laden and I will give you rest.*" Mat. xi. 28. No matter how heavy is the load that presses on your heart—how long you have been "WALKING IN THE COURSE OF THIS WORLD, FULFILLING THE DESIRES OF THE FLESH AND OF THE MIND," or how long the enemy of your soul has had you under his power, Jesus is the mighty God, and stronger than the world, the flesh and the devil! As sure as you are taught by Him to feel your state of misery and sin this day, so surely He is loosing the chain of Satan from your neck, and you shall see that Christ is anointed to "*preach deliverance to the captives.*" Isa. lxi. 1, and Luke iv. 18. His word is "*look unto me, and be ye saved,*" Isa. xlv. 22, "*the Lord hath laid on him the iniquity of us all,*" Isa. liii. 6, "*He bare our sins in his own body on the tree,*" 1st Pet. ii. 24. All the Church of Christ have felt their load of sin like you, and it was through the riches of the salvation of Christ that they have been delivered, and enabled "*to rejoice in the hope of the glory of God.*" Why should *you* not rejoice? Christ is "*the same yesterday, to-day, and forever.*" Heb. xiii. 8. It may be you are a poor backslider—what does He say? "*Return ye backsliding children, and I will heal your backslidings.*" Answer then, with those to whom He spoke, "*Behold, we come unto thee, for thou art the Lord our God.*" Jer. iii. 22. You have destroyed yourselves, it is true, but He saith, "*O Israel, thou hast destroyed thyself, but in me is thy help.*" Hosea xiii. 9. Yes, God hath "*laid help on one that is mighty.*" Psalm lxxxix. 19. Wherefore, "*lift up the hands that hang down, and the feeble knees,*" Heb. xii. 12, lift up your burdened heart and look unto Jesus, and let your soul rejoice in "*the unsearchable riches of Christ.*" Eph. iii. 8.

"*Be it known unto you, men and brethren, that through this man is preached unto you the forgiveness of sins, and by him all that believe are justified from all things, from which you could not be justified by the law of Moses.*"—Acts xiii. 38, 39. "*Who shall lay anything to the charge of God's elect? It is God that justifieth. Who is he that condemneth? It is Christ that died, yea, rather, that is risen again, who is even at the right hand of God; who also maketh intercession for us.*" Rom. viii. 33, 34. Good news, good tidings of great joy!

No doubt, with all your ignorance and sin you have flattered yourself that you were righteous, and perhaps the Lord has left you to see how guilty you are—left you to follow the devices and desires of your own heart—left you to sink in your own misery and wretchedness, in order that He may show you the more, how glorious a Saviour He is to deliver you from the depths of sin and sorrow. Lift up your eyes then, and look unto Jesus. Here you are, to-day, within the reach of His mercy—He has sent His glorious Gospel, inviting you to come to Him, and do you think he will cast you out? Oh, no, "*him that cometh to me I will in nowise cast out.*" John vi. 37. Go not then away with a heavy heart, go away, casting all your burthen on the Lord, and the more guilty and self-condemned you are, rejoice the more in hearing the glad tidings of pardon and salvation. Do you not remember the two debtors? "*one owed five hundred pence, and the other fifty,*"—remember, when they are both forgiven, which will love him most? Then, if you feel you have much to be forgiven, rejoice much in the glorious pardon that is in Christ Jesus for your soul.

Yet, O Lord Jesus, who can speak of thy mercy! who can tell of thy righteousness! who of the depths of the fountain of thy blood! who of thy long-suffering, thy patience, thy tenderness, thy grace, thy compassion! How have we "*made thee to serve with our sins, and wearied thee with our iniquities!"* Yet thy glorious Gospel is, "*I, even I, am he that blotteth out thy transgressions for mine own sake, and will not remember thy sins.*" Isa. xliii. 24, 25. Oh! the depths of the riches of his grace! Angels and archangels, and those who know Him better, even guilty sinners, redeemed by His precious blood, never through eternity can tell His love! May God the Spirit write it on our hearts, and make it manifest in our lives that "*The love of Christ constraineth us, because we thus judge, that if one died for all, then were all dead: and that he died for all, that they which live should not henceforth live unto themselves, but unto him who died for them and rose again.*" 2 Cor. v. 14, 15.—Amen.

TWELFTH LECTURE.

EPHESIANS II.—4, 5, 6.

"But God, who is rich in mercy, for his great love wherewith he loved us, Even when we were dead in sins, hath quickened us together with Christ, (by grace ye are saved;) And hath raised us up together, and made us sit together in heavenly *places* in Christ Jesus."

THESE verses, as we have seen, explain the latter clause of the Apostle's prayer, in the 19th and 20th verses of the preceding chapter, He is praying, that God would reveal to the saints at Ephesus, "*what is the exceeding greatness of his power to us-ward, who believe, according to the working of his mighty power, which he wrought in Christ, when he raised him from the dead.*" I suggested that this did not mean the mere pledge or assurance of their resurrection, that they were to rise, as certainly as Christ had risen, but that it meant the present power and glory of the resurrection of the Lord Jesus Christ, as given now to those who believe His Gospel.

In these verses the Apostle explains this, he shows what was "*the exceeding greatness of God's power towards those who believe which he wrought in Christ, when he raised him from the dead.*" In the preceding part of this chapter, we see the state of the idolatrous Gentiles, and of the Jews, we see them involved in the same common ruin by nature, and the passage shows the difference between their state as believers, and as unbelievers. The three former verses show their state as unbelievers, by nature; the three latter show their state as believers by grace. Their state as unbelievers, was that of "*death in trespasses and sins,*" they were walking "*according to the course of this world,*" they were under the power of Satan, they were "*fulfilling the desires of the flesh and of the mind, and they were by nature the children of wrath, even as others."* That was their condition as dead in trespasses and sins.

Now, what is their condition as believers by grace? what has Christ done? They were by nature dead in sin, Christ, in their place, died for sin. Christ was reckoned dead in sin for them, and they are reckoned dead for sin in Christ. So the Apostle explains in Romans vi., where he shows that those who believe are dead with Christ and adds, verse 7, "*he that is dead, is freed from sin.*"

Christ who owed nothing, becomes their heavenly surety, makes himself a debtor for them, and fully pays their debt. They who owed that mighty debt which they could never pay, are cleared of their debt through the payment of their Redeemer.

Christ "*who knew no sin was made sin,*" treated as a criminal, and bears the penalty for them. They, the real criminals are delivered from the penalty due to their crimes, and treated as righteous through Him who hath borne it for them.

Christ was actually raised from the dead for them. The Surety leaves the prison, having discharged the debt, and is exalted to glory, they are reckoned as raised from the dead with Him, their debt being paid in Him, and by Him, and they are exalted to glory too.

Christ, the spotless Son of God, was degraded, punished, slain as a vile malefactor, before God and men, for them. They, the children of the devil, and of wrath, vile malefactors before God and men, were thus rescued from the penalty of all their crimes, received, honored, rewarded, exalted as the spotless sons of God, in Christ their Lord.

Thus Christ was one with them, bearing all their sin and penalty, their guilt and degradation, judgment, curse and death,—they are reckoned one with Christ, receiving all His merits, His righteousness, and His reward, His honor, dignity and everlasting life and glory. "*Who his ownself bare our sins in his own body on the tree, that we, being dead unto sins, should live unto righteousness: by whose stripes ye were healed.*" 2 Pet. ii. 24. *For he hath made him to be sin for us, who knew no sin; that we might be made the righteousness of God in him.*" 2 Cor. v. 21—"*Oh, the depths of the riches, both of the wisdom and knowledge of God!*" Rom. xi. 33. If you do not understand this, you do not know the very foundation of a sinner's hope, you do not know the only spot on which you have to rest for salvation in time or eternity. If you do understand it, then you can comprehend something of the meaning of these verses, "GOD, WHO IS RICH IN MERCY, FOR HIS GREAT LOVE WHEREWITH HE LOVED US, EVEN WHEN WE WERE DEAD IN SINS, HATH QUICKENED US TOGETHER WITH CHRIST." Well might the Apostle pray that God would reveal to them "*what was the exceeding greatness of his power towards them who believe which he wrought in Christ, when he raised him from the dead, and set him at his own right hand in the heavenly places.*" If we ask what was the meaning of that?

what was the exceeding greatness of God's power towards them that believe, which He wrought in Christ, when he raised him from the dead? the answer is in these verses, that, as He raised Him from the dead, so He raised them up together with Him. Mark the plain words—"GOD, WHO IS RICH IN MERCY, FOR HIS GREAT LOVE WHEREWITH HE LOVED US, EVEN WHEN WE WERE DEAD IN SINS, HATH QUICKENED US TOGETHER WITH CHRIST, AND HATH RAISED US UP TOGETHER, AND MADE US SIT TOGETHER IN HEAVENLY PLACES IN CHRIST JESUS,"—now refer to 19th and 20th verses of the preceding chapter,—"*according to the working of his mighty power, which he wrought in Christ, when he raised him from the dead, and set him at his own right hand in the heavenly places.*" Now to those who understand the original, the terms will be still more explicit and clear,—"*he raised him from the dead,*" or "having raised,"—εγειρας. "*hath raised us up together,*"—συνεγειρε. "*set him at his own right hand,*"—εκαθισεν. "*hath made us sit together in heavenly places,*"—συνεκαθισεν. "*raised him up,*" "*raised us up together with him,*" "*set him at his right hand*" in glory, set believers along with him at his right hand in glory. Language cannot more explicitly set forth ideas.

Let us now consider the passage more particularly. It points out

I.—*The cause of salvation.*

II.—*The means of salvation.*

III.—*The effects of salvation.*

The effects of salvation are but partially set forth, viz., in reference to the believer's privileges; the Apostle shows them fully out afterwards, as well in reference to his duties as his privileges, which, if the Lord permit, we shall consider hereafter.

I.—THE CAUSE OF SALVATION.

What is the cause why any sinner is saved? How is this to be answered from the Bible? The answer most unquestionably is—God's rich, free, sovereign grace. There is no other source of salvation to guilty man. So the Apostle says here, as in other places, "GOD, WHO IS RICH IN MERCY, FOR HIS GREAT LOVE, WHEREWITH HE LOVED US, EVEN WHEN WE WERE DEAD IN SINS, HATH QUICKENED US TOGETHER WITH CHRIST." There is no moving cause, no moving power in man to save himself. A dead body cannot walk. A dead soul cannot move itself.

This is set forth in the Scripture as the only cause of salvation being given, or proclaimed to men in general—so we have in St. John's Gospel, iii. 16, "*God so loved the world, that he gave his only begotten Son, that whosoever believeth in him should not perish, but have everlasting life,*" and so in his 1st Epistle, iv. 10, "*herein is love, not that we loved God,*" (for, "*the carnal mind is enmity against God,*" Rom. viii. 7,) "*but that he loved us, and sent his Son to be the propitiation for our sins.*" And so with respect to the salvation of each individual sinner, while the proclamation of God's mercy is made to every man to whom the Gospel is preached; if any man receive the proclamation of that mercy, it comes of God's free and sovereign grace, to the soul of that sinner. So we hear from the Prophet Jeremiah, xxxi. 3, "*I have loved thee with an everlasting love, therefore with loving kindness have I drawn thee,*" and our Lord applies the same expression to every sinner. "*No man can come to me, except the Father which hath sent me draw him.*" John, vi. 44. And so the Apostle St. Peter says, in his 1st epistle i.—3, "*Blessed be the God and Father of our Lord Jesus Christ, which, according to his abundant mercy, hath begotten us again unto a lively hope, by the resurrection of Jesus Christ from the dead,*" and St. James illustrates this again, "*Of his own will begat he us with the word of truth.*" James i.—18. And so we had it in this epistle, i. 3, 4, "*Blessed be the God and Father of our Lord Jesus Christ, who hath blessed us with all spiritual blessings, in heavenly places in Christ, according as he hath chosen us in him before the foundation of the world, that we should be holy and without blame before him in love.*"

Man's condition, we have seen, is that of death in sin, and all who are taught by the Spirit of God, to know their own heart, know and feel, that not only in the first instance, when their eyes were enlightened to see the truth, but that now, every day, every moment, it is alike true of them, "*no man hath quickened his own soul.*" They know that as at the first they were "*called out of darkness into his marvellous light,*" 1 Pet. ii. 9, because "*God who commanded the light to shine out of darkness, had shined into their hearts to give the light of the knowledge of the glory of God, in the face of Jesus Christ.*" 2 Cor. iv. 6; so they are still indebted to the same Almighty power that first kindled the light of faith and love to keep it alive in their souls.

There is nothing to attract love in a dead, corrupting carcase,—and there is nothing to attract God's love in a dead, corrupting soul. An old woman, once speaking on this subject, made a very just and pertinent remark, "I am sure," said she, "if God did not see something in me to love before I was born, he never saw anything since." Most true, and there is not one of us who knows his own heart, who does not know that this is true, as applied to our own case. Can you ever remember anything that God has ever seen in you to recommend you to His favor? Look back—retrace your whole existence—go back to your childhood, remember the iniquities of your youth,—come to your present time of life, whatever it be,—and answer in your own conscience. Do you ever remember a time when, if even your fellow-men had seen the workings of your heart, and all that was within you, from the deceitfulness and falsehood of your childhood to the deceitfulness and wickedness of your manhood and womanhood,— do you ever remember a time when, if those who are nearest to you, could have seen the working of your sinful heart, as you saw it yourself, that they would love you? Do you not rejoice that man does not see you? Do you not rejoice that your heart is concealed from your friends? are not you thankful to God that no eye can see you, no being on earth can know you but yourselves? —I am sure I am,—I am thankful, that none but God can see the corruption of my vile, sinful heart,—and so must it be with you, if you know yourselves; for "*as in water, face answereth to face, so the heart of man to man.*"—Prov. xxvii. 19. God's testimony of the heart is, that it is "*deceitful above all things, and desperately wicked.*" Jer. xvii. 9,—and God's testimony, borne in His eternal word, will not, as was shown before, be reversed before His glorious tribunal, when He shall bring the thoughts of every sinner's heart into judgment, and weigh them in the balances of the sanctuary. Then, if you know that your fellow-man could not love you, if he saw you as you are, nay, if you must even "*abhor yourself and repent in dust and ashes,*" Job xlii. 6,—what must you seem in the sight of a pure and holy God, "to whom all hearts are open, all desires known, and from whom no secrets are hid?" "Who can stand the thought of that expression, "*Thou hast set our iniquities before thee, our secret sins in the light of thy countenance?*" Psalm, xc. 8, who must not cry, "*Enter not into judgment with thy servant, O Lord?*" If we are saved, it is by God's free, sovereign, rich, eternal grace and mercy. We would never turn one step from the broad way of eternal death, if God did not arrest us by His Almighty power, and bring us to Himself. Yes, it is by God, "*God, who is rich in mercy, for his great love wherewith he loved us, even when we were dead in sins, hath quickened us together with Christ.*" Observe the Apostle in his parenthesis, ("BY GRACE ARE YE SAVED.") Mark this parenthesis, as much as to say, do not forget this, do not forget the true interpretation of this text, it proves that—BY GRACE ARE YE SAVED—Mark, I pray you, this parenthesis.

II. Now we come to consider THE MEANS OF SALVATION. "HE HATH QUICKENED US TOGETHER WITH CHRIST."

This implies, you know, the death of Christ. It is not necessary that the Apostle, in his reasoning, especially as he is referring, as I have shown you, to the mercy that God bestowed on them, and to the greatness of His power exercised when He raised Christ from the dead,—it is not necessary, I say, that he should recapitulate continually, the atonement, the redemption, by the Lord Jesus. Of course, the resurrection of Christ implies His death, but you remember, how he had set that forth in the preceding chapter, 6th verse, "*to the praise of the glory of his grace, wherein he hath made us accepted in the beloved, in whom we have redemption through his blood, the forgiveness of sins according to the riches of his grace.*" Therefore, the means of a sinner's salvation are the death and resurrection of the Lord Jesus Christ.

Now, we must again dwell on the contrast and at the same time the union between Christ and the sinner, as mutually interchanging their condition each with the other. The sinner transferring through God's grace, or rather God transferring through His grace, and the sinner embracing with gratitude by faith the blessed transfer, of all his guilt and misery and curse to Jesus,—"*The Lord hath caused to meet on him the iniquity of us all;*"—and Jesus transferring, God the Father imputing, and the sinner by faith with joyful gratitude receiving all the riches of Christ's righteousness, redemption and salvation, put down to His account as a guilty sinner. If you understand this, then you know, that the only means of your salvation, are the obedience unto death and the resurrection of Jesus.

Alas! if you are looking to any other means of salvation,—I beseech, I implore you, for God's sake, pause, and consider how vain, and false your hope is! "*If righteousness come by the law, Christ is dead in vain.*"—Gal. ii. 21. If man's works could save him, Christ's death is of no value. If then, you are looking to other means of salvation, let me beseech you to turn from them all, to the hope that God sets before you in Christ,—"*Repent and believe the Gospel.*"

Are you looking to your Church for salvation? What is to save the poor Church?—One set of lost sinners looking to another set of lost sinners for salvation! One poor debtor who cannot pay one farthing of his debt, looking to other poor bankrupts like himself to discharge it!—one starving wretch, turning to others, starving like himself, for a morsel of bread! Such is man looking for salvation to his church.

Are you looking to the Sacraments for your salvation? To what are you looking? Is it to the outward sign in the ordinance? Or is it to the truth which it represents? Oh beware! Can water wash away your guilt? Can bread and wine atone for it? Are these your Saviours? The glorious Lord hath left them to us as precious emblems, as blessed memorials of Christ the substance of salvation,—but if the sinner looks from Christ to them, he turns his eyes from the substance to the shadow, from truth to falsehood, from the only hope that God has given to man, to emblems and memorials of that hope! You might as well take a picture, and embrace that picture, and bestow all your affections on it, and call it the being or thing it represents, and put it in the place of that being in your affections, and in your house, as depend your salvation on sacraments or anything that man can do for you, instead of on the Lord of life and glory. Oh think of this. Salvation by sacraments in the Church of England is as great a falsehood as salvation by Sacraments in the Church of Rome. A shadow is a shadow, whether it is projected by the sun in Italy, or by the sun in England, and sacraments can no more save the soul in Britain than they can in Rome. Christ, the glorious Redeemer, the Lord of life and glory, He is the only Saviour of the lost. You must stand on that Rock, if you ever hope to stand firm amidst the coming floods and storms.—If you ever hope to rest with peace upon your dying bed, or to lift up your eyes when the clouds shall be rent asunder, and when the Lord Himself shall be revealed,—if you hope then to join the chorus of the redeemed, and say, "*Lo, this is our God, we have waited for him, and he will save us, this is the Lord, we have waited for him, we will be glad and rejoice in his salvation.*" Isai. xxv. 9. If you hope for these things, you must not be looking to miserable shadows and miserable fallen sinners to save your souls, instead of Christ.

I am sorry to say, it is too necessary to preach on these topics in our pulpits. I am grieved to think that falsehood and heresy should creep into the Church of England to corrupt our congregations from the simplicity that is in Christ. May the Lord keep us "*looking unto Jesus*,"—continually looking to Christ alone for salvation, for this is His word, "*Look unto me, and be ye saved, all ye ends of the earth, for I am God, and there is none else.*" *Isa.* xlv. 22.

When the Apostle saith then, "HE HATH QUICKENED US TOGETHER WITH CHRIST." He sets forth the means of salvation, God quickens the sinner together with Christ, implying, of course, the death of Christ, for Jesus to be quickened must have been dead. Now forgiveness of sins is set forth through the Scriptures, as being proclaimed and secured through the resurrection, as well as the death of Immanuel, so we are told in Romans, iv. 25, He "*was delivered for our offences, and raised again for our justification.*" It was a proclamation that God had accepted the work of Jesus, the atonement of Jesus for the salvation of rebellious man. So, the Apostle speaking to the Corinthians, of some of those in that Church, who had set forth heresies; (for there are always heresies springing up in the Church, there always have been, and always shall be, until the Lord himself shall come to reign over His kingdom, and Satan shall be bound,) referring to those who denied the resurrection of Christ, 1 Cor. xv.—17. "*If Christ be not raised your faith is vain, ye are yet in your sins.*" The Apostle uses an expression, similar to this 5th verse, in Colossians, ii.—13. "*You being dead in your sins and the uncircumcision of your flesh, hath he quickened together with him, having forgiven you all your trespasses,*" raised up with Christ, and your sins buried in his grave and forgotten, never to be mentioned again. Therefore, the means of salvation which the Apostle speaks of here, are the death and resurrection of the Lord Jesus Christ; and he asserts the interest His people have in Him, in virtue of their union with Him, being raised together with Him.

III.—Now, we come to consider THE EFFECTS OF SALVATION, the effect of their being saved in Christ, "AND HATH RAISED US UP TOGETHER, AND MADE US SIT TOGETHER IN HEAVENLY PLACES IN CHRIST JESUS." Let us ask, what meaneth this? Where were the Ephesians at that time? They were at Ephesus, walking about, engaged in their ordinary occupations, or perhaps engaged at home, or in the congregation, as you are sitting in Church, occupied with the word of God, and I hope lifting up your hearts to ask for a blessing on it. Then, what does the Apostle mean by saying, he "HATH RAISED US UP TOGETHER,

AND MADE US SIT TOGETHER IN HEAVENLY PLACES IN CHRIST JESUS?" What is the meaning of that? How can men on earth be said to *have been raised with Christ*, and to have been *made to sit together in heavenly places with him*? Believers are spoken of, and deemed to be now as they shall be. Their blessed inheritance in reversion, is spoken of as in possession, and their faith in God's promises of what they shall be, enables them through His grace to rejoice in what they are. What are they called? "Children of God." "*Ye are all the children of God, by faith in Christ Jesus.*" What is their inheritance as children? The Apostle tells us, in Romans, viii. 17, as indeed we are told in various other passages of Scripture, "*If children, then heirs, heirs of God, and joint-heirs with Christ.*"

Your children, you would say, are your heirs, they are to possess your property. Men make their eldest son the heir of their properties. The law which subverts that of primogeniture, which divides estates, and necessitates that property be divided among all the members of a family, soon reduces the family to beggary, for our poor earthly properties are easily exhausted. But the children of the King of kings, are all heirs of eternal glory. The rays of the sun are undiminished in their bright effulgence, the lustre of that luminary is not dimmed, although the beams of his glorious orb have been diffused throughout the world from the first moment of the morning when God set him in the firmament of the heavens to rule the day; he still pours forth from his redundant fountain floods of unexhausted, and exhaustless light, and every creature that basks beneath his beams enjoys the fulness of their power too much to leave him room to grudge the world beside. But what is all the glory of the orb of day compared with that of Him whose fiat struck that orb but as a spark from solid darkness? and what is the inheritance of him who is an heir of God and a joint heir with Christ? "*The glory that thou gavest me I have given them, that they may be one even as we are one.*" John xvii. 22. Christ's inheritance—Christ's glory is their inheritance and their glory, and there is not one whose glory is diminished by the fulness of glory that all enjoy.

This is the blessed hope—this the glorious inheritance of the saints in light. Oh, you who perhaps are fixing all your thoughts and your anxieties on your little earthly inheritance,—wrapt up in all your comforts, pleasures and enjoyments, without one thought, or fear, or hope as an immortal being,—"*what will you do in the end thereof?*" What will you do when your all is gone? You may be obliged to "*pull down your barns, and build greater.*" but what can this avail when God shall say, "*Thou fool, this night thy soul shall be required of thee.*" Luke xii. 20,—Oh, consider this, and ere it be too late, receive the glorious inheritance that is freely given to sinners in Christ Jesus the Lord. Now, on the other side, there may be some, yea, I doubt not there are some here, who are oppressed with want, poverty-stricken, and often not knowing one day how their wants may be supplied the next. Well, my poor friends, if you are looking to Jesus,—if Christ is your hope and refuge,—think what an inheritance you have! think, what a glorious inheritance is secured to you in Him. Remember, O poor believer, you are an heir of God, a joint-heir with Christ. Whether would you rather be the rich man or Lazarus? Your days of poverty will soon be past—you will soon be beyond the reach of want, or pain, or sin, and your Lord is now watching over you, and numbereth the very hairs of your head. Wherefore lift up your heart—better be poor, and have unsearchable riches in reversion, than be reigning on a throne without Christ. "*Lift up the hands which hang down, and the feeble knees.*" Heb. xii. 12,—and remember, that "*God hath chosen the poor of this world, rich in faith, and heirs of the kingdom.*" James ii. 5. This is the inheritance of which Daniel speaks, when he says, "*a kingdom and dominion and the greatness of the kingdom under the whole heaven shall be given to the people of the saints of the Most High, whose kingdom is an everlasting kingdom, and all dominions shall serve and obey him.*" Dan. vii. 27.—"*Happy is the people that is in such a case, yea, happy is that people whose God is the Lord.*" Psal. cxliv. 15.

Believers then are spoken of, I say, as they shall be, they shall be raised up together, they shall be glorified together with the Lord Jesus Christ, and the Apostle says, they are so. They are so in God's counsels, they are so in God's purposes, they are so in God's promises, they ought to be so in the joyful confidence of faith and hope, and when they believe in the Lord Jesus Christ, it is their happy privilege to know they are so in reality.

Allow me to enlarge a little more on a former illustration. I desire an architect to give me an estimate for building a church, he draws his plan, he furnishes me with the ground, and the elevation, and he gives me a specification of all the various expenses, and if he be a professional man who knows his business, the whole of that church is just as clear in that man's eye, while he is drawing the plan and estimate of it, as when he beholds it erected and completed. Now let me ask, does not Jehovah hold His Church, complete and finished in His eye? Is there a single stone in the building that is not marked in the specification of His counsels, from eternity. The architect may not perhaps know the quarry, where he is to find the stones to erect the building he proposes, or if he expects to find them in a certain quarry, he may be disappointed in his expectations,—but do you think there can be any disappointment in the materials of the Church of the living God? The architect may change his plan, perhaps from caprice, perhaps from necessity, from some unforeseen difficulty, some unlooked-for contingency, which serves but to show the imperfection of the individual himself, or the unavoidable difficulties and disappointments that attend all human plans and calculations. But, do you think, can God encounter these? Do you think, can God's plans be changed? Can unforeseen contingencies arise to make Him vary from the course laid down in the plans of His Omniscient wisdom? Can He be disappointed or deceived in any quarter from which the living stones in the mighty fabric of His spiritual temple are to be collected? Nay, when He gives His command to His angels to gather the elect from the four quarters, from every kingdom and nation and tongue and people,—and to bring them together to Himself—and when He beholds the finished structure of His glorious Church, and sees "*the top stone brought forth with shoutings, crying, Grace, grace unto it*," Zech. iv. 7—there shall not be a single individual—not a single saint in glory in the building that was not marked in the counsels of the eternal God, and his very position allotted in the Church, in which Jehovah sees him. Eternal resurrection life and glory are given—received—embodied into being in the word "HATH." The architect will point out in his plan to his employers—"There is the aisle—there the nave—there the chancel—there the tower," &c.—he calls these things of his ideas and intentions as if they were real existences, but their only being is in his own conception, they may perhaps never have any other. But Omniscience and Omnipotence give present existence to the future. In the fiat of His eternal word, He "*calleth the things that are not as though they were.*" It is the province of faith to embody the existences of her Maker's word, and therefore, "*Faith is the substance of things hoped for, the evidence of things not seen.*" Heb. xi. 1. Therefore they are "RAISED UP TOGETHER AND MADE TO SIT TOGETHER IN HEAVENLY PLACES IN CHRIST JESUS."—These are the privileges of the believer—they are written in the word of his God.

And now, brethren, what shall we say to these things? these glorious present blessings of the Church of Christ? Surely we may say with the Apostle to the Romans, xii. 1, "*I beseech you, therefore, brethren, by the mercies of God, that you present your bodies a living sacrifice, holy, and acceptable unto God, which is your reasonable service.*" Surely we may say with St. Peter, 2 Pet. iii. 14, "*Wherefore, beloved, seeing that ye look for such things, be diligent that ye may be found of him in peace, without spot and blameless.*"

The Church of Rome is very right in her marks of the church,—*Catholicity, unity, apostolicity, sanctity.* Very true they are all marks of the church, they are marks of the church of Christ,—not indeed of the church of Rome, no, nor of the church of England. You will see men contending about the term Catholic, as if its real sense and meaning is not that in which it is to be applied to the whole church of Christ through all the world. That is the Catholic Church;—and so it has that mark of *Catholicity*,—all believers in Jesus that have been, are, or shall be, through the whole length and breadth of the globe, yea, "*the whole family in heaven and earth*" are all in Christ, and are all one in Christ.

And so they have the mark of *Unity*. Recollect that blessed testimony that was given to His Church by the Lord Jesus Himself, in that wondrous prayer He offers up, commencing, as it were, His glorious mediatorial office on earth,—St. John's Gospel, xvii.—9, "*I pray for them*," (that is for His disciples,) "*I pray not for the world, but for them which thou hast given me; for they are thine*." Now, O believer, look at the glorious testimony in the 20th verse, "*Neither pray I for these alone*," (His disciples were then around Him,) "*but for them also which shall believe on me through their word, that they all may be one, as thou, Father, art in me and I in thee, that they also may be one in us*." So that glorious unity of hidden life exists in all the members of His Church, and shall be manifested, when all who have believed on His name, shall be gathered together at His coming in His glory.

So you may see too the *Apostolicity* of the Church. Our Lord saith, "*for them also which shall believe on me through their word*," those who shall believe the testimony of the Apostles, therefore, those whose principles and doctrines will stand the test of God's eternal Word, and therefore, who are one with Christ Jesus, their Lord, "*built on the foundation of the Apostles and Prophets, Jesus Christ, Himself, being the chief corner stone*." Eph. ii. 20.

So is the *Sanctity* of the Church—they are sanctified in Christ Jesus, and so, though holiness is no part of their hope; for Christ is all their hope, it is an inseparable part of their character, an inseparable test of their fidelity; and therefore, though no man can be saved by his works, the Scripture tells us that all men can be judged by their works, because it is thus, and only thus, that the sincerity of the disciples of Christ can really be known. If we be servants of our blessed Master, we cannot be serving another master, "*no man can serve two masters; for, either he will hate the one and love the other, or else he will hold to the one, and despise the other. Ye cannot serve God and Mammon*." Mat. vi. 24.

Let us then deeply consider these things. It is difficult in lecturing through these consecutive portions of the Scripture, not to leave each portion more or less incomplete, because in its full meaning it stands so connected with its context; but still it is, I believe, the most profitable mode of instructing from the sacred Scriptures. It calls all who hear, to study the portion of God's blessed Word, which is under consideration, to bring what we say, always to that standard of truth.

Recollect you are not to be judged by the sermons or the ministry of your pastors, you are to be judged by the Word of God, itself, which it is their province to teach you. "*The word*," says Christ, "*that I have spoken, the same shall judge you at the last day*." John xii. 48.—"*To the law and to the testimony, if they speak not according to this word, it is because there is no light in them*." Isa. viii.—20. And if we speak according to that Word of truth,—woe be to those who neglect our word, not because it is ours, but because it is according to the Word of the living God.

The Lord write His truth in our hearts, and sanctify it to our souls, for His great Name's sake.—Amen.

THIRTEENTH LECTURE.

EPHESIANS II.—7.

"That in the ages to come, he might show the exceeding riches of his grace, in his kindness towards us through Christ Jesus."

WE are now to consider more fully the effects of man's salvation, as set forth in this passage. In part we have seen them to consist in this, the raising man from the death of sin, its curse and condemnation, and the exalting him to be an inheritor of the kingdom of Christ,—*God, who is rich in mercy, for his great love wherewith he loved us, even when we were dead in sins, hath quickened us together with Christ, (by grace are ye saved,) and hath raised us up together, and made us sit together in heavenly places in Christ Jesus.*"

Another result we see is to follow—namely, the manifestation of the glorious attributes of God, and the exceeding riches of his grace, "THAT IN THE AGES TO COME, HE MIGHT SHOW THE EXCEEDING RICHES OF HIS GRACE, IN HIS KINDNESS TOWARDS US THROUGH CHRIST JESUS."

I shall not apologize for adverting again to the first of these subjects briefly to-day; for, if we be indeed the children of God, it ought to be the theme of our continual consideration,—as it must be, it alone can be the joy and consolation of our hearts.

I. Recollect, then, that the state of a believer, is a state of present pardon and acceptance with his God. Remember that. It is not a contingent future forgiveness, as most persons, yea, as all unenlightened sinners believe it to be. It is not, I say, a future forgiveness, contingent upon their own present morality and virtue, —this is not the salvation of Christ—but present pardon, present forgiveness, proclaimed to them through the blood of their Redeemer, in the everlasting Gospel, and ratified on the authority of the eternal God Himself; therefore, their state, being a state of present forgiveness, is a state of present exaltation to the kingdom of Christ,—I say, of present exaltation. Though the believer is on this earth, living in this world, a poor, helpless sinner, yet, in the covenant counsels of his God, as a believer in the Lord Jesus Christ, he is raised up with his Heavenly Head, and as a member of Christ, he is exalted to the right hand of God, so that the glorified members of the human body of Christ are not more exalted with Christ at the right hand of God than the members of His mystical body, that is, all the members of the Church of Christ Jesus are raised up in covenant, and made to sit together in heavenly places in Christ Jesus their Lord. Consider one or two passages on this subject.

In Acts, xxvi. 18, you see the commission which the Lord gave to the Apostle Paul, speaking of His sending him to the Gentiles, He says, "*unto whom now I send thee, to open their eyes, and to turn them from darkness to light, and from the power of Satan to God, that they may receive forgiveness of sins, and inheritance among them which are sanctified by faith that is in me.*" You perceive here what they were to receive. Now compare this with the testimony of the Holy Ghost as to the state of those who received the Gospel. In chapter i. 3, of this Epistle, we see the fact, "*Blessed be the God and Father of our Lord Jesus Christ, who hath blessed us with all spiritual blessings in heavenly places in Christ,*"—*hath* done so.—Compare this again with Colossians i. 12, 13, "*Giving thanks unto the Father, which hath made us meet to be partakers of the inheritance of the saints in light; who hath delivered us from the power of darkness, and hath translated us into the kingdom of his dear Son.*"—Now observe, "*hath* made us meet,"—"*hath* delivered us from the power of darkness,"—"*hath* translated us into the kingdom of His dear Son." This is the actual state of all who truly believe the Gospel—the actual position in which they should consider themselves to be. Look again to 1 Pet. i. 3, 4, 5, he says, speaking of the state of believers, "*Blessed be the God and Father of our Lord Jesus Christ, which, according to his abundant mercy, hath begotten us again unto a lively hope, by the resurrection of Jesus Christ from the dead, to an inheritance incorruptible, and undefiled, and that fadeth not away,*" (there is their inheritance,) "*reserved in heaven for you, who are kept by the power of God through faith unto salvation, ready to be revealed in the last time.*"

Now, this inheritance is reserved for them, and they are kept for it. Then it is to be revealed. It is as secure now as when it shall be revealed. So in St. John's 1st Epistle, iii. 1, you see the same truth set forth, "*Behold what manner of love the Father hath bestowed upon us, that we should be called the sons of God; therefore the world knoweth us not, because it knew him not.*"

Ah, brethren, these truths are above the comprehension of the unregenerate world, "*the world knoweth us not because it knew him not.*"—Consider these facts, verse 2, "*Beloved, now are we the sons of God.*" If Jesus is indeed our refuge, then, beloved, we are, and must be the sons of God; for "*whosoever believeth that Jesus is the Christ, is born of God.*" 1 John v. 1. "*Ye are all the children of God by faith in Jesus Christ.*"—Gal. iii. 26. "*But it doth not yet appear what we shall be.*"—that is not yet known—"*but we know, that when he shall appear, we shall be like him; for we shall see him as he is.*" When He shall be revealed, then His redeemed church shall burst from the earth in light and glory, and in the likeness of their blessed Master, having *their vile bodies* "*fashioned like unto his glorious body.*" Phil. iii. 21, they "*shall meet their Lord in the air, and so shall they be ever with the Lord.*" 1 Thess. iv. 17. So, in the last verses of this same chapter, which we are now considering, the Apostle, having told them to remember what their former condition had been, compares it with their present state, and says, verses 19 and 20, "*Now therefore ye are no more strangers and foreigners, but fellow-citizens with the saints, and of the household of God, and are built upon the foundation of the apostles and prophets, Jesus Christ himself being the chief corner stone.*" You see, therefore, this is the effect of a sinner being brought to Jesus, this is the immediate result of a sinner embracing the glorious Gospel of Christ. But this is an exhaustless subject; for it is a subject that is to be expanded into infinity and prolonged to eternity. Oh, that it may be so with each of us!

II. But we come now to consider another effect of salvation, not merely individually, but collectively, as embracing the salvation of this whole church of Christ, which is the passage before us to-day. Observe, how directly and consequentially it depends on that which precedes it,—"*he hath raised us up together, and made us sit together in heavenly places in Christ Jesus.*—THAT IN THE AGES TO COME, HE MIGHT SHOW THE EXCEEDING RICHES OF HIS GRACE, IN HIS KINDNESS TOWARDS US THROUGH CHRIST JESUS."

The highest privilege, the first duty, the noblest exercise of the faculties of a moral being as such, is the setting forth of moral excellence, the manifestation of moral virtue. Hence, the glory of angels is their holiness—that which becometh the house of God forever, is holiness. This is clear, most especially in all situations of authority, from the father and master of a family to the ruler and governor of nations, in which not only their own individual existence is concerned, but also the relative position which they hold to all that are placed under them. But to do this man cannot set forth, or set up himself. If he does, it is ignorance, it is pride, it is selfishness and falsehood. All the faculties, all the powers of a moral agent, to be exercised as they ought, must be exercised in manifesting, in holding forth the power and glory of the Creator. The perfection of man as a moral agent, would be the observance of the holy law of God. In this, the perfection of Jesus, "*of God manifested in the flesh,*" consisted. The perfection of Jesus was in doing the will of His Father,—"*my meat,*" said He, "*is to do the will of him that sent me, and to finish his work.*" So it must be in all created intelligences, men or angels,—the will of their Creator is the highest summit of perfection. To set themselves up or to set forth themselves is to forget their God.

I must then take occasion here to remark on the objection, the infidel objection that I have heard made against the Scriptures, against such passages of the Scripture as this, in which God sets forth His own glory as the great end of His dealings with man. They say—

"Surely, if man was to set forth himself as the end and scope of his actions would we not call him sinful and selfish and proud in setting himself up. It is in consideration of others that men should show forth moral excellence. Therefore is it not attributing to God that which we admit to be moral evil in man, to make his own glory the end and scope of his government?"

This is like all the other objections against God's word. It only shows the blindness, the corruption, the ignorance of the unconverted, proud, natural heart of man;—stupid, contemptible, worthless, the moment it is put into the balance of the sanctuary. Why is self-exaltation criminal in man? What is the reason why he ought not to set himself up as the end or scope of his actions? Because the standard of perfection is Jehovah, therefore, he rejects that standard, if he does not aim at it,—if he aims at anything lower. But the infinite perfection of God's moral government as it really consists in the exercise, so it can only be exhibited in the display of His own glorious attributes.—I say, the perfection of His government can only consist in this, in the exercise and in the manifestation of His own individual glory. Why? Because He can have no higher standard of perfection than Himself, unless there is something above God. He can have nothing less than Himself, He cannot descend from the Creator to the creature; for that would be to descend from the standard of perfection to imperfection, from the standard of the glory of the Creator to the insignificance of the thing created. Therefore that men or angels should make themselves the end or scope of their actions is sin. But that God should make Himself the end and scope of His actions is the necessary result of His perfection, as the holy God. It could not be otherwise,—not to do so, would be, that He must cease to be God,—it were to abdicate His throne—to take up imperfection instead of perfection, as the standard of His moral excellence and moral glory.

Hence, all the Scripture testimonies on the subject of the manifestation of God's glory, in all His dispensations and all His dealings with man. Hence, the salvation of His people should be the glorious manifestation of the glory of His grace; and hence, the very existence of sin, the wickedness of man, the rage and malice of the devil, shall redound at last to the glorious manifestation of the attributes of Jehovah,—His justice, His power and His mercy, —the power of His justice in judgment, and the power of His mercy in salvation. So you must see—you must acknowledge it, unless you are blind, in all the history of the Scripture.

The overwhelming of a rebellious world by the flood, was as great a manifestation of the glorious attribute of God's righteous judgment and justice, as the saving of Noah and his family in the ark, was of His grace and mercy.

The gaping of the earth, and the swallowing up of Korah, Dathan, and Abiram, was the righteous manifestation of Jehovah's character, as much as the sanctification of Aaron to the priesthood—the miraculous budding of his rod—and the setting up the sacrifices for sin,—the types of that blood of "*the Lamb of God that taketh away the sin of the world.*"

The fire of Sodom manifested the glory of God's righteous judgment, as much as the deliverance of Lot exhibited His mercy. And the sentence of the last day, when "*the secrets of all hearts shall be disclosed*," in the day of the righteous revelation of the holy judgments of the mighty God,—the sentence against those upon his left hand, "*depart ye cursed into everlasting fire, prepared for the devil and his angels*," Matt xxv. 41, shall redound to the righteous justice of the eternal God, as much as the glorious manifestation of His love to those on His right, "*where mercy and truth meet together, where righteousness and peace have kissed each other*," "*Come, ye blessed of my father, inherit the kingdom prepared for you from the foundation of the world*," Mat. xxv. 34. Yea, "*the weeping and gnashing of teeth*" of the damned shall glorify the righteous judgment of Jehovah, as much as the song of the redeemed.

Oh think of this. Remember what it shall be, when instead of man being everything and God nothing, "*the loftiness of man shall be bowed down, and the haughtiness of men shall be made low, and God alone shall be exalted in that day*." Isa. ii. 17. "*Oh, consider this, ye that forget God, lest I tear you in pieces, and there be none to deliver you*." Ps. l. 22.

But our attention in the passage which I have read is directed to the glory of God's grace in the ages to come, in the redemption, the salvation, the exaltation, of His Church,—"THAT IN THE AGES TO COME, HE MIGHT SHOW THE EXCEEDING RICHES OF HIS GRACE, IN HIS KINDNESS TOWARDS US THROUGH CHRIST JESUS." Do you ask the meaning of this,—do you ask, how is this manifested?—how is the "*exceeding riches of God's grace*" shown "*in his kindness towards us through Christ Jesus?*" I will endeavor to explain it and to teach you how it is to be shown even in this very congregation. I will divide you this day—not by persons, for that is not man's province, but by principles, of which I must leave the application to each person's own conscience. I will divide you, as you are divided in fact and truth, if there be, as there are, alas, too many here, who are not servants of God,—and that is, I will divide you into unconverted sinners, and the people of God. You are divided, you must be, into these two classes. There is not a sinner here, or a sinner in all the earth this day, who does not belong to one or the other. You must be an unconverted sinner, or you must be a sinner that is brought to the Lord Jesus Christ, and made a servant of God.

I will show you how the riches of God's grace is manifested,—how, in the ages to come, the exceeding riches of His grace shall be manifested towards you in Christ Jesus,—and I hope and trust in His blessed name, that it shall be manifested this day to the ungodly, unregenerate heart and conscience of every unconverted sinner that is here. For example,—I care not who or what you are—I suppose you to be some wretched, guilty creature, whom all your neighbors know to be a character that ought to be avoided,—there are such people who come into church frequently.

There may be here some this day of whom those who know you say—

"Ah, that is a rogue, that is a thief, there is no dependence to be placed on that man."

Or again—"Look at that poor wretch, that miserable drunkard, he cannot keep himself sober a moment, he has plunged himself and his family into ruin."

"There is a Sabbath-breaker,—what could have brought him to church to day?—I never saw him in church before, what could have led him here?—he spends his Sabbaths in idleness and wickedness." Again

"There is a liar, you cannot depend on one word that comes out of his lips,—he speaks truth and lies, alike with the same facility."

"There is a wretch that is a blasphemer, cursing and swearing from morning to night."

"There, there is one whose hands are stained with blood—that man ought to have been hanged for murder."

Again,—"Ah! there is a woman who is a reproach to modesty, and to her sex—one whom we must shun as a pestilence, whose very touch is contagion."

Perhaps there are some such here of various grades and shades of guilt to-day,—and some perhaps who have never been detected, but whose conscience echoes the charge from the pulpit in the ear of God. Such, I say, may be here to-day, stained even with blood, —yea, if your hands are not, the hearts of many of you are, because it is written, "*whosoever hateth his brother is a murderer.*" 1st John, iii. 15. And there are murderers in this and in every congregation, those of wicked passions, who hate, or who have often hated their brother.

How then are the riches of the grace of God to be manifested here? It is our commission to proclaim, in His blessed name, salvation to every creature—to proclaim mercy to the very chief of sinners, and the exceeding riches of His grace are manifested in the magnitude of the guilt he pardons, and the mercy He extends to those who are ready to perish.

But there is another, and perhaps a more common character,—a white-washed Pharisee! A man who presents a fair exterior, of whom his neighbors say, and as far as man sees, justly say, "that is an upright, moral, worthy, decent, respectable man." But God is not in your heart, and God is not in your house,—His Holy Word is not opened in your family, you do not kneel down with them, and seek His pardoning grace and mercy on your souls,—you do not, in your own closet, kneel down and call upon God to wash away your guilt in the blood of the Lamb—you value not the fountain opened for sin and uncleanness—you think you have but little sin to pardon—your pride is, that you are not as other men. "*God, I thank thee that I am not as other men are, extortioners, unjust, adulterers,*"—this is your consolation, and this is the hope of your salvation, when you look at such characters as I have been describing, to comfort yourself with the thought—"I am not such a character."—Alas, if this be so, you are but a whited sepulchre. God looks through the whitewashing—the varnish of the exterior, and He sees within, the heart of His own description, the corrupt, unwashed, guilty, rebellious heart,—the heart, "*deceitful above all things, and desperately wicked.*" Jer. xvii. 9.—"*The carnal mind is enmity against God.*" Rom. viii. 7.

But now, I care not what you are—in the name of the Lord Jesus Christ, I proclaim to you this day, free and full forgiveness. Oh thou poor, black, and guilty sinner, who would be afraid that your fellow-sinners would look at a single movement of your heart,—Remember God sees you, remember He sees every depth of sin and every winding of deceit,—but God sends you pardon in His everlasting word,—this day he commands you to "*repent, and to believe the Gospel.*" Mark i. 15. He proclaims mercy and forgiveness in your ears,—"*Go ye,*" He says to His ministers, "*go ye into all the world, and preach the Gospel to every creature,*" Mark, xvi. 15—the good news of salvation. Whatever be your character, or whatever the cause why you came into this Church—whether to build up a Babel of your own righteousness—to go through an accustomed form—to salve your conscience by the discharge of a duty—to trifle away an hour of an idle Sabbath, yea, even to hear and scoff—Yet, look unto Christ, and be ye saved, "*He came into the world to save sinners,*" 1st Tim. i. 15. Think of the words of that sacred Hymn which you repeat so often in our Liturgy, "When thou hadst overcome the sharpness of death, thou didst open the kingdom of heaven to all believers." Oh, it is true—it is true—hear it—believe it, and

"Let fools who came to scoff, remain to pray."

I went, last week, to see an old friend of mine, who had been a member of this congregation. He is dying, and he told me, "Oh, sir, I remember when you preached on a text, to illustrate these words, 'When thou hadst overcome the sharpness of death, thou didst open the kingdom of heaven to all believers,'—my heart rejoiced to see such pardon, grace and mercy in Christ Jesus my Lord."

Well—your hearts may rejoice this day, for you are, like him, sinners, and Christ is the same Almighty Saviour.

And is not this "THE EXCEEDING RICHES OF HIS GRACE?" and if the Lord quickens you who are "*dead in trespasses and sins,*"—leads your souls to know and rejoice in his pardoning mercy to-day—if you are enabled, instead of coming here next Sunday, a poor, blind, profligate rebellious enemy of God—or a proud self-righteous Pharisee,—if you are enabled to come, as a believer in Jesus—a reconciled child of God—longing to hear the word of Christ—kneeling down in faith and hope, in truth and love, to call upon your God—not going through the service in mere mockery and form—but worshiping "in spirit and in truth" that God who "seeketh such to worship Him"—if He leads you, who have hitherto been serving the world, the flesh, and the devil, to serve and glorify your God—will not that manifest "THE EXCEEDING RICHES OF HIS GRACE, IN HIS KINDNESS TOWARDS YOU THROUGH CHRIST JESUS." Will it not be "*to the praise of the glory of His grace*" in time and eternity. Oh, think of this, and may the Lord send this message of mercy and salvation to your hearts, to-day, my friends and fellow-sinners! for this is the good news of the Gospel—it is the same alike to all, that which is for you, is for me, we are all by nature vile, rebellious sinners,—if God should enter into judgment with us, we must all perish. Oh, then, "*to-day if ye will hear his voice, harden not your hearts.*" "*To-day, while it is called to-day,*" Heb. iii. 7, 8, 15, "*look unto me,*" saith He, "*and be ye saved.*" Is. xlv. 22.

Believer, you know something of this, but, alas! we know but very little of it, as we ought to know. But are you at a loss to understand—are you at a loss to know, how God manifests the riches of His grace, in His kindness towards you? Were you not such as we have described, once living without God in the world? Do you not remember what you were? Do you not remember your guilt—your enmity against God? Do you not remember when you hated, or at least totally neglected His word? When you never prayed in spirit and truth?—when you turned a deaf ear to the Gospel?—when you disregarded it, and cast it from you? Who remembered you in your low estate?—who found you an outcast in the wilderness? Who "*passed by you, and said unto you, live?*" Ezek. xvi. 6. Who, "*for his great love wherewith he loved you, even when you were dead in sins, hath quickened you together with Christ*"? Ch. ii. 5,—Who "*sent his word and healed you, and delivered you from your destructions?*" Ps. cvii. 20. Who brought His word to your heart, and led you to see Jesus as your refuge, and gave you hope and peace in His salvation? And then—when you look back, and think of what you have been since—your innumerable provocations how you have tempted Him to withdraw His grace from you, and yet, up to this hour, how His patience has borne with you!—How often you have turned back in your heart "to the flesh pots of Egypt!"—how often you have cherished in your soul, instead of detesting, the very thought of sin—and yet, the long-suffering of your God has not cast you off! Oh! how great has been his mercy to you! How many your backslidings, your innumerable sins!—Perhaps the world has seen them,—perhaps they are only known to God and your own conscience!—but, Oh! how often have you fallen, and He has lifted you up!—watched over you—not left you to yourself—not allowed you to depart from Him—followed you with His grace, His mercy, His providences—hedged up your way with thorns—visited you with stripes, to chastise—to reprove—to correct—to humble you, to bring you back—sending a messenger to you, like Nathan—bringing His word to your soul in a thousand different ways,—and here you are to-day, a monument of grace!—and in the ages to come, when it is all known,—Oh! how shall every dealing of his wisdom, providence, and love display "THE EXCEEDING RICHES OF HIS GRACE, IN HIS KINDNESS TOWARDS YOU THROUGH CHRIST JESUS." When "*we know even as we are known.*" 1st Cor. xiii. 12. When we see the precipices on which we have been standing—tho pit-falls from which he has rescued us—the ruin into which we would have rushed, if God had left us to ourselves—if He had not taken us, and dragged us back—and held us in His mighty hand—and not allowed Satan to pluck us out of it!—Oh, dear brethren in Christ, if there can be a contest in eternity, it must be, which of us should sing in the loudest strain, "*Unto him that loved us, and washed us from our sins in his own blood, and hath made us kings and priests unto God and his Father; to him be glory and dominion forever and ever. Amen.*" Rev. i. 5, 6. Well then, may we understand in some degree, yea, I know you feel something—when I speak to you of the blessed hopes and prospects of His servants, and of that love which has opened them to your ears—something of the meaning of these words, "THAT IN THE AGES TO COME, HE MIGHT SHOW THE EXCEEDING RICHES OF HIS GRACE, IN HIS KINDNESS TOWARDS US THROUGH CHRIST JESUS." To Him be praise and glory forever and ever. Amen.

FOURTEENTH LECTURE.

EPHESIANS II.—8, 9.

"For by grace are ye saved through faith; and that not of yourselves; it is the gift of God: Not of works, lest any man should boast."

WE have seen, that one of the effects of the salvation of the Lord's Church, is the manifestation of the glorious attributes of Jehovah Himself, in the exceeding riches of His grace,—as we had in verse 7, "*that in the ages to come, he might show the exceeding riches of his grace, in his kindness towards us through Christ Jesus.*" The Apostle seems to introduce the 8th and 9th verses, as an emphatic repetition, a fuller explanation of the momentous truth which he had inserted parenthetically in the 5th verse, "*by grace are ye saved.*" He had said "*But God who is rich in mercy for his great love wherewith he loved us, even when we were dead in sins, hath quickened us together with Christ,* (*by grace are ye saved,*") and here again he evidently introduces it, for the purpose of reminding them again of the important lesson, which is necessary to be so continually impressed on the heart of the sinner, viz., that the whole of man's salvation from first tc last is to redound, not to his own glory, but to the glory of his God, as you observe by the word "*for*."—" *That in the ages to come, he might show the exceeding riches of his grace, in his kindness toward us through Christ Jesus,*—FOR,—BY GRACE ARE YE SAVED THROUGH FAITH,"—he shows the exceeding riches of his grace, FOR—by grace alone are ye saved.

It is indeed necessary to have this truth perpetually reiterated to man; for it is a truth of which, though the heart, in its constant sense of its own want and sin, has continually need, yet the believer is as continually prone to turn from it. Therefore, you may perceive, how frequently it has been introduced, even in this short portion of the epistle we have read,—as for instance, in verse 2 chapter i. The Apostle uses the term as he always does in his benedictory salutation, " GRACE *be to you, and peace from God our Father, and from the Lord Jesus Christ,*" and he repeats the word in verse 6, " *to the praise of the glory of his* GRACE," wherein " *he hath made us accepted in the beloved,*" and in the 7th verse, " *in whom we have redemption through his blood, the forgiveness of sins, according to the riches of his* GRACE," and then in verse 5th of this chapter, as I have already remarked, "*by* GRACE *are ye saved,*" and in verse 7, " *that in the ages to come he might show the exceeding riches of his* GRACE," and in the verse now before us, " BY GRACE ARE YE SAVED THROUGH FAITH."

Now, when we meet a truth repeated again and again in God's word, we are not to pass over it lightly, and say, " This is the same truth we met in the other verse, we have spoken of this before."—No—God repeats truths in his holy word that we may continually reconsider them, that we may again, and again, and again, and again pray for His Spirit to apply them to our hearts. When we preach—at least for my own part, I can say, that when I come to preach or lecture on these great truths to any of my fellow-sinners, I feel I have need when I have set them forth to others, to preach and lecture upon them again, as it were to myself, that the same truths may be impressed upon my own heart, that I have endeavored to impress on others, which, however we may know them as abstract truths, we are continually ready to forget, if God whose grace teaches them to us, and keeps us, would allow it. So the Apostle exhorts in the 2nd chap. of Hebrews, verse 1, " *Therefore we ought to give the more earnest heed to the things which we have heard, lest at any time we should let them slip.*"

If one of the members of our body is fractured, or dislocated, or distorted, it can be set and bandaged up and bound to some support, to keep it in its natural and right position. But Oh! what human force—what power—what skill—what instruments can we find to bind up and heal those dislocated, disjointed, and distorted thoughts and hearts of ours! If we are attracted for a moment to the holy word of God, and if our attention seems fixed for a time to the standard of truth and sober wisdom, alas! the next moment we fly off again, like a wandering bird. "*The wicked,*" saith the Prophet, "*are like the troubled sea, when it cannot rest, whose waters cast up mire and dirt.*" Isa. lvii. 20,—and we often feel our hearts fluctuating, like the waves of the troubled sea, which, though, as you heard this day, at the moment when the voice of Jesus spake, they were hushed and stilled into a calm, yet were again lashed and convulsed by the very next storm that swept over them, or ruffled and disturbed by the next breeze that passed across their surface. So it is with the heart of sinful man. So do we require the continual impress, the continual acting of the word of God, the grace, the power of the Spirit to move over the face of the waters,—so must we have "*line upon line, precept upon precept, here a little, and there a little.*" Isa. xxviii. 10,—that we be not "*carried about with every wind of doctrine,*" Eph. iv. 14—and turned from the truth of God to fables. Therefore, may the great God bless us and teach us by His Spirit, and by His holy word, while we consider it this day and at all times.

The Lord tells us in these words, expressly by the Apostle,

HOW WE ARE SAVED,

"BY GRACE ARE YE SAVED, THROUGH FAITH, AND THAT NOT OF YOURSELVES, IT IS THE GIFT OF GOD,"—

AND HOW WE ARE NOT SAVED,

"NOT OF WORKS, LEST ANY MAN SHOULD BOAST."

We are saved by grace through faith; and we are not saved by works.

Grace is taken in various senses in the word of God,—sometimes in a very limited, and sometimes in an enlarged sense. It appears to me in this passage to be taken in its most comprehensive sense, embracing within its meaning all that is implied in its application to the salvation of man in the Scripture. Grace is sometimes put to signify the everlasting love of God to His people. As for instance, 2d Timothy, i. 9, "*who hath saved us, and called us with an holy calling, not according to our works, but according to his own purpose and grace which was given us in Christ Jesus before the world began,*"—and you have nearly the same sense of it in this Epistle, i. 5, 6, "*having predestinated us to the adoption of children by Jesus Christ to himself, according to the good pleasure of his will, to the praise of the glory of his grace, wherein he hath made us accepted in the beloved.*"

Sometimes, it signifies the effectual calling of the sinner, by the operation of the Spirit of God, quickening his soul, as we have it in this chapter, verse 5, "*even when we were dead in sins, hath quickened us together with Christ,* (*by grace are ye saved*")*.*

Sometimes, grace signifies abounding mercy, as in Rom. v. 20, 21, "*where sin abounded, grace did much more abound, that as sin hath reigned unto death, even so might grace reign through righteousness unto eternal life, by Jesus Christ our Lord.*" So you have the same idea expressed, though the same word is not used, in Isa. xl. 1, "*Comfort ye, comfort ye, my people, saith your God. Speak ye comfortably to Jerusalem, and cry unto her, that her warfare is accomplished, that her iniquity is pardoned; for she hath received of the Lord's hand double for all her sins.*" Superabounding grace for abounding sin.

Sometimes, it is taken for the free and full pardon of sin, as in Romans iii. 24, "*being justified freely by his grace, through the redemption that is in Christ Jesus,*"—and that was the view taken of it in our last Lecture, in setting forth the riches of God's grace, as proclaiming pardon to ungodly sinners, and the continual exercise of love and mercy to His redeemed people.

Sometimes, it means the being in a state of pardon and acceptance with God, as for instance, in Romans v. 2,—"*by whom also we have access by faith into this grace wherein we stand, and rejoice in hope of the glory of God,*" and you have the same idea in Romans vi. 14, "*you are not under the law, but under grace,*" —under a covenant of grace,—in a state of gracious acceptance through the goodness of God.

Sometimes, it signifies the final salvation of the Lord's people, as in 1st Pet. i. 13, "*be sober, and hope to the end, for the grace that is to be brought unto you at the revelation of Jesus Christ.*"

Now here I conceive it comprehends all these things, all the blessings of the grace which brings salvation to the sinner's soul. "BY GRACE ARE YE SAVED THROUGH FAITH, AND THAT NOT OF YOURSELVES, IT IS THE GIFT OF GOD," from first to last—from beginning to end—from the grace that called you to the grace that shall open the folding doors of eternal glory to your view.

"BY GRACE ARE YE SAVED THROUGH FAITH." It is important to attend to this, it is necessary to put faith into its right place, it is indispensable to have the judgment, the understanding clear upon this subject, for I know of no subject on which the minds of believers are more frequently in error, perplexed and harassed than on this.

They are not saved by works, they say, but they are saved by faith. But, when they find their faith weak, when they find doubts and darkness arise in their minds, then their hope of salvation is gone,—they are all agitated, "Oh we are saved by faith, but I do not believe—I feel I have no faith." Now, it is of the greatest importance rightly to understand this, "BY GRACE ARE YE SAVED THROUGH FAITH." Faith no more saves you than works, considered in itself. It is no more the act of your mind in believing, or it is no more your strongest confidence that saves you, than it is your works. Faith is the channel through which salvation is given to you. Your salvation is Christ,—the glorious grace of God in giving Christ; Christ's righteousness, the gift of grace,—Christ's blood, the gift of grace,—Christ's glorious sacrifice, His finished salvation, the gift of grace,—all, is the grace of God, all, the manifestation of the riches, "*the exceeding riches of his grace in his kindness toward us through Christ Jesus.*" Faith is merely, as it were, the vessel by which this salvation is given to you. If man rejects it and casts it off, of course he must perish,—if a man receives it and embraces it, all the blessings of it are his,—but, remember, the blessings are all in Christ, and not in his faith. Faith receives and embraces the blessing, but is not the blessing itself,—because, salvation is in Christ, and not in faith. It is the medicine that heals the body, and not the cup in which that medicine is conveyed. If a medicine is administered to you in a vessel of gold, silver, china, delph, or glass,—yea, though the vessel be not only fragile, but cracked, or partly broken,—it matters not, it is the medicine and not the vessel, that conveys healing to your body. And it is the balm of Christ's blood, it is the salvation of the Lord Jesus Christ, by which your soul is saved, though the faith may be very weak by which you receive Him—"BY GRACE ARE YE SAVED THROUGH FAITH." An illustration, perhaps, will convey more clearly to your minds, that the important difference lies not between a weak and a strong faith, but between a true and a false one. Let me suppose two shipwrecked mariners, swimming from the waves to a bank of sand, one very confident,—the other, trembling with fear. They reach the bank of sand, but it is a quicksand, and both are engulphed. Why? All the spirit, the courage, and confidence of the one could not save him, because the ground on which he trod sunk under his feet,—the other perishes, not by his fears or apprehensions, but because the ground on which he stood sunk beneath him too. So it is with sinners. *It is not the strength or weakness* of their faith, but it is the *truth* of their faith, that is, the truth of the object in which they believe. It is not the strength or confidence with which one believes, or the weakness with which another believes,—but it is this,—that the thing which we believe is God's eternal truth. So if two men believe a lie as the hope of their soul,—one going on with the utmost possible confidence, and the other, trembling and fearing,—they shall both perish in the lie they have believed; for they have not "*fled for refuge to lay hold on the hope set before them,*" Heb. vi. 18, but they have fled to a refuge of lies.

Let me speak affectionately, and entreat their attention, if I address any of my Roman Catholic friends and neighbors to-day. No doubt there are very different degrees of confidence with which you may believe, that the sacrifice of your Mass is a propitiatory offering that satisfies God for your sins, or that your priest can forgive you. So there are different degrees of confidence, with which many ignorant Protestants may believe, that the Sacrament will be an atonement for their sins, and make their peace on their deathbed, or that their minister can do something for their souls. But it is no matter, whether men believe in such things with confidence or whether they believe in them with trembling doubt and apprehension, they shall perish in their iniquity, if they rest upon such refuges of lies, for there is no offering in either the Mass or the Sacrament of the Lord's Supper nor in anything in earth or heaven for the sinner to save his soul, but the blood of our crucified Redeemer.

Now let me again illustrate true faith. Two shipwrecked mariners buffet their way from the wreck to a rock,—one is confident and joyous—the other trembling and fearing, lest the waves should overwhelm him and sweep him again into the bosom of the deep; —but the rock is inaccessible to the waves, and both are equally secure. Why? It is not the courage or confidence of the one that saves him, but because he is on a rock. All the doubts and fears of the other cannot overwhelm him. Why? Because notwithstanding all his doubts and fears, he is on a rock.—So when sinners have indeed "fled for refuge to lay hold upon the hope set before them," when they have indeed fled to Jesus,—the Rock, the Fortress of their salvation, whether they believe with joyous, lightsome heart, with full assurance of faith, or whether they are, as many are, doubting, trembling, fearing in the weakness and unbelief of their own hearts,—still they are both equally secure;—for both are resting upon the "Rock of ages,"—Jesus is the Hope, Jesus is the Rock, Jesus is the Salvation of them both. Wherefore the babe in Christ is as safe as the father in Christ—the weakest believer is as safe as the strongest,—because it is not their faith, but Christ that saves them—it is not by faith you are saved through grace, but "BY GRACE ARE YOU SAVED, THROUGH FAITH?" Grace is that which gives salvation, and therefore, that may "*be strong in the Lord, and in the power of his might*," Eph. vi. 10, "*strong in the grace that is in Christ Jesus.*" 2nd Tim. ii. 1.

This may seem to some of you not very important,—but if you are distressed and agitated with doubts and fears, as certainly some, perhaps many of you who believe the Gospel are,—you will see, what a blessing it is for a sinner to be taught to look out of himself, and how blessed it is for him to see, that all his salvation is in Christ Jesus his Lord. Oh, how hard it is, when persons have taken up a false system, and have not been rightly instructed in God's truth, to drive these vain fancies out of their minds! How often have I seen the servants of God doubting and trembling, and writing bitter things against themselves, even on the bed of death, because, instead of looking to Jesus as their all, they were looking into themselves for confidence, and expecting comfort and courage from the strength of their faith, instead of from Christ, the strength of their salvation. Remember this.

You who are strong in the faith of Christ Jesus,—you who are resting with joyous confidence on your Lord,—beware—we are in an enemy's land, and always in danger. "*Let him that thinketh he standeth, take heed lest he fall.*" 1 Cor. x. 12. We are often encouraged when faith is strong, to look away from Christ to ourselves, to transfer our confidence from Jesus to our faith. Beware, lest the confidence of faith should degenerate into confidence in faith. Remember David—"*In my prosperity I said, I shall never be moved, Lord, by thy favor thou hast made my mountain to stand strong.*" What are the next words? "*Thou didst hide thy face, and I was troubled.*" Psalm xxx. 6, 7. Oh, brethren, "*watch and pray.*" If you are strong in the faith that is in Christ Jesus, pray that the Lord may keep you strong, keep you humble, and keep you lowly. Remember, the Apostle says, "*when I am weak then I am strong.*" Strong faith is often a very hard tried faith. Recollect strong faith ought to be victorious faith. "*This is the victory that overcometh the world, even our faith.*" 1 John v. 14. If your faith is strong, you may be called upon to put it into exercise against a storm of corruption and sin within, or such power of temptation without, that it may make you tremble, and ask yourselves, "Is it possible I can be a believer?" I repeat then—"*Watch and pray.*" Mat. xxvi. 41.

And those of you who are weak in the faith that is in Christ Jesus,—trembling and doubting,—if indeed you are looking unto Him, take courage. Look out of your faith. It is not your faith,—it is Jesus that saves you. It is not the strength of your own confidence, it is the strength of Him in whom you confide. Think of this.—Lift up your hearts. Remember that Jesus is the same to the weakest as to the strongest. The Rock is the same to the man that trembles on it, as to the man who stands with the stoutest heart upon it. Jesus is the same to both. O weak believer! lift up your hands that hang down,—you may be "*walking in darkness, and have no light,*"—but he that does so,—"*let him trust in the Lord, and stay himself upon his God,*" Isa. l. 10—upon "*his God*" when he is weak as well as when he is strong,—"*his God,*" in darkness as well as in light,—"*his God,*" in doubts as well as in confidence,—"*his God*" in difficulty as well as in the easy course of prosperity. Therefore, "*Lift up the hands that hang down, and the feeble knees.*" Heb. xii. 12. Let the weak take courage,—let the strong "*watch and pray.*" Remember the character of your Shepherd—remember what is said, "*he gathereth the lambs in his arms, and carrieth them in his bosom, and gently leadeth those that are with young.*" Isa. xl. 11. *The* strong walk firmly and boldly on,—he gathereth the weak ones in His arms,—He gently leadeth those that are weary and heavy laden with burdens of anxious doubts and fears—"*I have yet many things to say unto you, but ye cannot bear them now,*" He saith, John xvi. 12. You then that are weak and weary, heavy-laden, burthened with a sense of your sins,—Oh! look out of yourselves to Jesus, cast your burden on Christ,—He is able to sustain it,—He is mighty to bear it. Remember, "*underneath are the everlasting arms.*" Deut. xxxiii. 27. The bearer of your burthen is Omnipotent. What weight of sin or sorrow is too great for Christ to carry? and what burthen ought to be too heavy for us to cast on Him? We cannot bear it, but Jesus can.

"BY GRACE ARE YE SAVED, THROUGH FAITH, AND THAT NOT OF YOURSELVES."—Now, the word "*that*" does not mean either grace or faith. The original does not directly admit of its reference to either, but it means both together, namely, salvation by grace through faith, "BY GRACE ARE YE SAVED, THROUGH FAITH, AND THAT" (namely your salvation by grace through faith) "IS NOT OF YOURSELVES, IT IS THE GIFT OF GOD: NOT OF WORKS, LEST ANY MAN SHOULD BOAST." It is not by your works you are brought into a state of salvation, and it is not by your works you are kept in it, for you can do nothing to save your soul, you are a lost sinner,—you are saved, not by anything you can do, but by the work of Jesus, proclaimed to you in His blessed word, and brought home to your hearts by His mighty Spirit.

Some men will go very far indeed in ascribing salvation to a being they call Christ, and to a thing they call Grace, if you will only allow them to have some little share in their own salvation. Only allow, that there is some little credit due to themselves, and they will give to Christ and Grace as much as you please. I repeat it again, they will ascribe salvation to a being they call Christ, and to a thing they call Grace. But they do not really mean Christ or Grace. It is neither the Christ nor the Grace of the Bible that men really call by such names, when they hold such principles in their hearts. This is of the greatest possible importance to consider, because such awful falsehoods are set forth with such ingenuity and sophistry, and come recommended by such names and such authority, that if men are not built upon the "Rock of ages," if their faith is not established on the Word of the living God, they will be led away by the "cunning craftiness" of men who "lie in wait to deceive."

I shall read for you a brief specimen of this system of religion to which I advert:

"Religious doctrines and articles of faith can only be received, according to certain dispositions of the heart."—That is very true.

"These dispositions can only be formed by the repetition of certain actions."

This is very false, and mark the false principles engrafted on it.

"And therefore, a certain course of action can only dispose us to receive certain doctrines."

And here the writer says,

"It is curious to observe, how entirely Aristotle's system in this respect coincides with Holy Scripture."*

Whether this be the doctrine of Aristotle, it is of no importance to us to investigate; but if it be, the writer of this sentiment is, at least as far as the Pagan author whom he quotes, from either truth or the doctrine of the Bible.—You will perceive how directly the principles here maintained contradict the express testimony of our Lord. This doctrine is—make the fruit good, and you make the tree good. Our Lord's doctrine is, "*Make the tree good and his fruit good.*" Mat. xii. 33. And our Lord expressly testifies, "*Every good tree bringeth forth good fruit, but a corrupt tree bringeth forth evil fruit. A good tree cannot bring forth evil fruit; neither can a corrupt tree bring forth good fruit.*" Mat. vii. 17, 18. Outward actions are not in themselves

* Tracts for the Times, as cited by Mr. Goode, in his excellent Tract "The Case as it is," p. 32, 33.

really good—because they may seem to be so—their goodness depends on the motives and principles of the heart on which they are performed—just as the excellence of the fruit depends not on its outward appearance, but on the taste and flavor when you try it. You may have seen apples that appeared beautiful and tempting to the eye on the tree, but when you tasted them, you found them sour and not fit to be eaten; so actions on false principles, that are not, as it were, flavored with the motive of love to our blessed Master, are only falsely tinted with the seeming glow of virtue. The application, therefore, of this doctrine is as false as the doctrine itself. The writer says,

"For instance charitable works alone will make a man charitable and the more any one does charitable works, the more charitable will he become."

"He only will be humble in heart who does humble actions."

Mark how directly this transposes the order both of truth and Scripture, as if it were not charity and humility of heart that could alone make men either really charitable or humble; as if men might not "*bestow all their goods to feed the poor, and give their body to be burned,*" 1 Cor. xiii. 3, without one spark of charity in their heart; or, "*make broad their phylacteries, and enlarge the borders of their garments,*" Mat. xxiii. 5, and stand praying in seeming humility at the corners of the streets, with the pride of Satan in the heart—garnish and whitewash the sepulchre without, while nought but death and corruption were festering within.

He adds—"He who most of all practises these duties, will be most of all brought by a necessary and moral consequence to embrace the cross of Christ." And by forming men to these actions, there is to be "a preparation of the heart previous to the imparting of the highest knowledge" namely, "the doctrine of the Cross."

How miserably ignorant of divine truth is man when not taught by the Word and the Spirit of the living God. How clearly do such doctrines illustrate that the "*unlearned and unstable*" who "*wrest the Scriptures to their own destruction,*" 2 Pet. iii. 16, do not mean those who are not learned in Classics or in Science, in modern literature or Pagan Philosophy, but those who are untaught in the sacred oracles of truth. For these doctrines, I am ashamed to say are put forth from learned men in one of our English Universities, and this system is but another edition of the falsehoods of Rome.

But this illustrates the use of scriptural terms in an unscriptural or antiscriptural sense. For this is a system that sets forth a thing that is not grace, and a being that is not Christ! Christ and the cross are not for the good, but for the guilty. "*They that are whole need not a Physician, but they that are sick.*" Mat. ix. 12. This is like prescribing to a man in an hospital—"Get up and make yourself better, and walk about a little, and take exercise, and then you will be fit to be healed by a Physician."

This is exactly the same thing. Set men to work, to do some good deeds, in order to make them acquire good habits, and then they will come to the doctrine of the cross by a "moral consequence"! Is this the word of the living God? Is this the salvation of Christ for the lost? Preaching Christ to men who have acquired good habits—preaching the doctrine of the cross to save humble charitable men! Alas! such a system as this can only come from the father of lies. Blessed be God it is written in His word of truth, "*This is a faithful saying, and worthy of all acceptation, that Christ Jesus came into the world to save sinners,*" 1 Tim. i. 15—uncharitable sinners, proud sinners, guilty, rebellious, vile sinners, sinners such as are in this and in every congregation. The glorious Gospel of Jesus is, that Christ came into the world to save sinners such as you and me. Oh, that is the blessing of the Gospel! "BY GRACE ARE YE SAVED, THROUGH FAITH, AND THAT NOT OF YOURSELVES, IT IS THE GIFT OF GOD, NOT OF WORKS, LEST ANY MAN SHOULD BOAST."

If such a system as this were true, what would be the consequence? Why, that man could boast, and must boast. The man who prepares himself by this sort of system, by his charitable works, and humble works, and similar works, to come to Christ, what must that man's song be? what must his principle be? Is it not this? "*God, I thank thee, I am not as other men are, extortioners, unjust, adulterers,*" Luke, xviii. 11. "I have done a variety of charitable actions, and so made myself charitable—I have performed a number of humble actions and so made myself humble—and therefore, I have prepared myself to profit by the doctrine of the cross—I have prepared myself for the reception of this 'highest knowledge'—this neighbor of mine has not done so,—therefore, "*stand by thyself, come not near to me, for I am holier than thou.*" Such must be their language if they speak as they think. But what saith the Lord? "*These are a smoke in my nose, a fire that burneth all the day.*" Isaiah lxv. 5. It is impossible to call principles such as these the principles of the Church of England! Nay—they subvert the very foundation of truth—they pervert the doctrines, not only of the Bible, but of our holy religion!—they deny the truths, which those martyrs whom the Lord raised up, our blessed reformers, to deliver us from Apostacy and superstition, embodied as the principles of God's holy truth into the articles of our religion, and into the whole framework of our Church, to raise a bulwark in this land, against such false and ignorant corruptions of the blessed Gospel, as this. Hear our Article on this subject,—

ARTICLE X.—"The condition of man after the fall of Adam is such, that he cannot turn and prepare himself by his own natural strength and good works to faith, and calling upon God."

He cannot do so, that is, by doing charitable or humble actions or any such thing as this, he cannot even turn himself to faith and prayer, much less give himself a claim upon God.

The Article proceeds ;—

> "Wherefore we have no power to do good works, pleasant and acceptable to God, without the grace of God, by Christ preventing us, that we may have a good will, and working with us, when we have that good will."

Grace must go before any actions that the sinner can do, before they can be called good; therefore good actions cannot lead him to faith, but, as we shall see, if we are spared to consider the next verse, faith in Christ leads him to good actions, to serve his God.

Again, in Article 13—

> "Works done before the grace of Christ, and the inspiration of his Spirit are not pleasant to God, forasmuch as they spring not of faith in Jesus Christ. Neither do they make men meet to receive grace, or (as the school authors say) deserve grace of congruity."

All works that are done before the grace of Christ, are not pleasant to God, because their principle is false and hollow, and when that principle is on the system of making men meritorious, and making them fit to come to Christ, fit recipients of His mercy, making them deserve grace of condignity, or congruity, (as the Popish authors say,) when this is the principle of such works—it is a denial of the Gospel, it is a total subversion of God's holy truth. The Article continues,—

> "Yea, rather for that they are not done, as God hath willed and commanded them to be done,—we doubt not but they have the nature of sin."

And indeed they need not doubt it; for there is not a shadow of doubt upon the subject. They have, and must have the nature of sin; they do not fulfil the law, and the motive they spring from is false, it cannot be love. The works of a believer, although they do not fulfil the law, and all have in them much to be forgiven—yet they are graciously accepted by God, because the man who does them is accepted—the person is accepted, so are his works—and the motive is accepted, because it is love. The sinner whom Christ has washed in His precious blood desires to serve his Lord, because he loves Him—so a cup of cold water given in the name of Christ shall by no means lose its reward. Love—the attractive power that gravitates to the centre of all good—is that which gives weight to acts of obedience. It can cause "*two mites which make a farthing*" to weigh more than "*all the gifts of the treasury,*" and "*a cup of cold water*" more than "*thousands of rivers of oil.*"

But the unconverted sinner is dead in sin, and he is dead in law; his person is condemned, so are his works; and all he does, or can do, will but accumulate sin on his head before God, when God shall enter into judgment with him. He must be saved by grace, or he must perish.

Herein then comes the glory of the blessed Gospel,—"BY GRACE ARE YE SAVED THROUGH FAITH, AND THAT, NOT OF YOURSELVES, IT IS THE GIFT OF GOD, NOT OF WORKS, LEST ANY MAN SHOULD BOAST." It proclaims rich salvation to the very chief of sinners, to man in the depths of his guilt, and to man in the depths of his proud imaginary virtues, the pride, the self-righteousness of the natural rebellious heart—for the one is as deep an abyss as the other, and both alike are alienated from God.

If, then, I say again, a man were to be saved by his works, or if he were to prepare himself for grace by the merit of his own actions, his humility, charity, or anything else, I say, that man must boast over his fellow man, who had not so prepared himself as he has done. "*I do not frustrate the grace of God*," says the Apostle, Galat. ii.—21, "*for if righteousness come by the law, then Christ is dead in vain.*" If righteousness come by anything a sinner can do for himself, that is, by his obedience to the law, then "*Christ is dead in vain*," so in Romans, xi. 6, "*if by grace then is it no more of works, otherwise grace is no more grace. But if it be of works, then it is no more grace: otherwise work is no more work.*" Surely, a man could not possiby be delivered from death, both by the verdict of a jury, pronouncing him innocent—and by the sovereign sending him pardon for his guilt. If the jury pronounce him innocent, he does not want a pardon, he is saved from condemnation, because he is not guilty. If the sovereign send him pardon, then he must have been pronounced guilty by the jury, and his only hope depended on the remission of his sentence. So it is, if a man is saved by his own righteousness, he cannot be saved by Christ. Christ has nothing to say to him, he wants not Christ,—he cannot look to Christ,—Christ never came to save those who can save themselves,—there is no salvation proclaimed to righteous men. A righteous man cannot need salvation,—again, I repeat the Scripture, "*they that are whole, need not a physician, but they that are sick*," "*I came*," saith Christ, "*not to call the righteous, but sinners to repentance.*" The salvation of the Lord Jesus Christ, is a salvation for sinners, for us who know and feel that we are sinners. Glorious indeed is the sound of the gospel to us, "BY GRACE ARE YE SAVED THROUGH FAITH, AND THAT NOT OF YOURSELVES, IT IS THE GIFT OF GOD, NOT OF WORKS, LEST ANY MAN SHOULD BOAST."

Such a system as this—salvation by works, by merit, by preparing the sinner to make himself worthy to receive pardon from God,—such a system completely frustrates the grace of God—subverts, denies the Gospel, and makes Christ dead in vain. It turns away the hope of the sinner's soul from Christ on earth—it would reverse the song of the redeemed in glory; for that song could not be "*Unto him who loved us, and washed us from our sins in his own blood*," but, "Unto me, who have prepared myself, and made myself fit for salvation and glory, and made myself worthy to receive the mercy of God,—unto me be praise and glory"!

Oh, blasphemous abandonment of God's eternal truth! blasphemous subversion of the salvation of Jesus, and of all the hope that God proclaims to man in His eternal word!

Blessed be God, "BY GRACE ARE YE SAVED"! Blessed be God, the same grace is opened for us to-day that was opened for us when first we believed. Blessed be God, we have a Saviour who is "*the same yesterday, to-day, and forever.*" Heb. xiii. 8. Blessed be God, we have "*a fountain opened for sin and for uncleanness,*" Zech. xiii. 1, and though mountains of sin have rolled into it,—it is still as deep, as fathomless as ever,—for it is written, "*Thou wilt cast all their sins into the depths of the sea,*" Micah vii. 19. Oh, grace is the song that we must sing.

> "Grace all the work shall crown,
> Through everlasting days;
> It lays in heaven the topmost stone,
> And well deserves the praise."

Yes, when the top stone is laid in the arch of the Spiritual Temple, "*grace, grace unto it,*" Zech. iv. 7, shall echo through the vault of heaven,—"grace, grace, redeeming grace, salvation to the Lamb for all eternity!"

> "O that with yonder sacred throng,
> We at His feet may fall,
> There join the everlasting song,
> And crown Him Lord of all."

Amen.

FIFTEENTH LECTURE.

EPHESIANS II.—10.

"For we are his workmanship, created in Christ Jesus, unto good works, which God hath before ordained that we should walk in them."

NOTHING can be more opposed to true religion or to common sense, than to suppose that any dispensation could come from God to man, in which he did not provide for the authority and observance of his holy law. The relation between Creator and creature, Governor and subject, God and man, precludes the possibility of such a monstrous anomaly; for, as long as that relation subsists, it must be regulated according to some rule, it cannot be undefined. There must be a rule, according to which the governor is to govern, and the subject to obey,—and that rule can only be the holy law of God.

Can you imagine a sovereign, ruling over his subjects without any law? Or, can you imagine a sovereign so absurd as to make any proclamation to his subjects, which would give them license to tread his laws under foot? So soon might you suppose the Almighty Ruler of the universe making any revelation of His will to man, in which there could be any dispensation for His holy law or any relaxation of its divine obligation.

The objectors to the Gospel scheme of salvation, by which it is provided, that "*by the deeds of the law*," (i. e. by man's obedience to the law,) "*no flesh can be justified*," cry out against this Gospel, because they say, it relaxes obedience to the law, on the part of man; it relaxes the obligation of the law, on that of God. In this they only show their own ignorance, both of the law and of the Gospel: for it is because the law cannot be relaxed, it is because the perfection of its authority must be maintained, it is because "*It is easier for heaven and earth to pass, than one tittle of the law to fail*,"—this is the very reason why by that law, no flesh can be justified before God. It is admitted, that if man keeps the law, he shall be saved. This is a principle laid down in Scripture over and over again, as in St. Matthew, xix. 16, 17, where the young man came to our Lord and asked him "*Good master, what good thing shall I do that I may have eternal life?*" and our Lord answers him, "*if thou wilt enter into life keep the commandments.*" If man will attain eternal life by the good that he is to do, that good must be to "*keep the commandments*," And again in Romans, x. 5, you see the same principle stated, "*Moses describeth the righteousness which is of the law, that the man that doeth these things shall live by them;*" therefore, it is a principle laid down in the Scripture, that if a man keeps the law, he shall be saved.—But if we suppose that a man were only to break the law in one single instance, and that with that single exception he could be justified by his previous and subsequent obedience to the law, then the law must be relaxed for him in that instance;—his violation of the law in that instance must be passed over, and his obedience, before or after, must be taken as a satisfaction for his disobedience in that one point. But it is because, this is utterly impossible, it is because the law of God cannot be relaxed in a single particular, that therefore, it is written in St. James, ii. 10, "*whosoever shall keep the whole law, and yet offend in one point, he is guilty of all.*" So to prove the impossibility of justification by obedience to the law, it is written in Gal. iii. 10. *Cursed is every one that continueth not in all things which are written in the book of the law to do them.*" And so, when the Apostle proves in Rom. iii. 20, that "*by the deeds of the law there shall no flesh, be justified in his sight; for by the law is the knowledge of sin*,"—and when he concludes from his argument in verse 28, "*Therefore we conclude that a man is justified by faith, without the deeds of the law*,"—so far from relaxing the obligations of the law of God, the Apostle demonstrates that it is by this alone the law can be maintained,—verse 31, "*Do we then make void the law through faith? God forbid, yea, we establish the law.*" So in this chapter, in the passage we had under our consideration, in our last Lecture, "*by grace are ye saved, through faith, and that, not of yourselves, it is the gift of God, not of works, lest any man should boast*,"—while the law is there excluded from the justification of the sinner, provision for obedience to the law is immediately set forth, as we have it in our text,

"FOR WE ARE HIS WORKMANSHIP, CREATED IN CHRIST JESUS, UNTO GOOD WORKS, WHICH GOD HATH BEFORE ORDAINED THAT WE SHOULD WALK IN THEM." In the very place where he tells you, that the law can have no place whatever in the salvation of the believer, he tells you in the very next verse, which we have now under consideration, that it must have a place in his conduct and character. So that, though it is clear from the Scripture, that no man keeps the law of God *absolutely*, so that he can never call himself a fulfiller of the law,—on the contrary, it is written, "*in many things we offend all.*" James iii. 2—on the contrary, it is written, that at any time or under any circumstances, "*if we say we have no sin, we deceive ourselves, and the truth is not in us.*" 1 John i. 8,—yet it is as clearly set forth in Scripture, that the believer must be a keeper of the law *relatively;* that is, in a manner totally different from his own former life, and totally different from the customs and practices of an unregenerate and ungodly world; "FOR, WE ARE HIS WORKMANSHIP, CREATED IN CHRIST JESUS UNTO GOOD WORKS, WHICH GOD HATH BEFORE ORDAINED THAT WE SHOULD WALK IN THEM." So you see this is set forth of the believer in 1 Pet. iv. 2, 3, "*that he no longer should live the rest of his time in the flesh, to the lusts of men, but to the will of God, for the time past of our life may suffice us to have wrought the will of the Gentiles, when we walked in lasciviousness, lusts, excess of wine, revellings, banquetings, and abominable idolatries.*" Such had been their walk, but now it is changed—and all their former companions see it to be so—ver. 4 "*wherein they think it strange, that you run not with them to the same excess of riot, speaking evil of you.*" You did run with them, but now they think it strange that you do not do so,—and that is the very case this moment with the sinner who is brought through grace to know Christ. He was a merry pleasant fellow, as his companions thought him,—but now, what a great change has come over him!—he will not go with them as he used to do, he no longer joins with them in their former pursuits, he has become a new man. They tell him most truly, but alas! for them, in mockery, "*He has become a saint.*" He has become a changed character. It must be so, it could not be otherwise. "*If any man be in Christ, he is a new creature. Old things are passed away; behold, all things are become new.*" 2 Cor. v. 17. So you see the same thing in 1 Cor. vi. 9, 10, 11, "*Know ye not, that the unrighteous shall not inherit the kingdom of God. Be not deceived, neither fornicators nor idolaters, nor adulterers, nor effeminate, nor abusers of themselves with mankind, nor thieves, nor covetous, nor drunkards, nor revilers, nor extortioners, shall inherit the kingdom of God. And such were some of you*"—(that is, what they were, their former character)—"*but ye are washed, but ye are sanctified, but ye are justified in the name of the Lord Jesus, and by the Spirit of our God.*" "Such were some of you," but now you are no longer such—you are totally changed. So you have it in this very chapter, verse 2, "*wherein in time* *past ye walked, according to the course of this world, according to the prince of the power of the air, the spirit that now worketh in the children of disobedience;*"—and then Paul includes himself,—"*among whom also we all had our conversation in times past in the lusts of our flesh, fulfilling the desires of the flesh and of the mind, and were by nature the children of wrath, even as others*"—"*But*"—a mighty change hath passed on us—"*God who is rich in mercy, for his great love wherewith he loved us, even when we were dead in sins, hath quickened us together with Christ, (by grace are ye saved,) and hath raised us up together, and made us sit together in heavenly places in Christ Jesus, that in the ages to come, he might show the exceeding riches of his grace, in his kindness toward us through Christ Jesus; for by grace are ye saved through faith, and that not of yourselves, it is the gift of God; not of works, lest any man should boast.*"* But are we now living as we once were, among an ungodly world? are we walking with them as they walked? No, God's mercy hath been revealed to us, God hath stretched out His hand over us, He hath quickened us,—and now, "WE ARE HIS WORKMANSHIP, CREATED IN CHRIST JESUS UNTO GOOD WORKS, WHICH GOD HATH BEFORE ORDAINED THAT WE SHOULD WALK IN THEM."

Now we have in this text—

I. *The power that acts on the sinner to bring the sinner into obedience to his God*—"WE ARE HIS WORKMANSHIP."

II. *The mode in which that power acts upon him, so as to produce this effect,* "CREATED IN CHRIST JESUS UNTO GOOD WORKS."

III. *The certain security for the operation of this power and for the effect it will produce,* "WHICH GOD HATH BEFORE ORDAINED THAT WE (his people) SHOULD WALK IN THEM." It is His appointment—it is His will—it shall be done.

We consider then—

I. THE POWER THAT ACTS ON THE SINNER TO BRING HIM INTO OBEDIENCE TO HIS GOD. What is the power? The power of God alone,—no other power. Oh that men knew this! then instead of looking to men and means, they would look to God! instead of resting on preachers, and running about, as many do, from one preacher to another, to try and derive profit from them,

* Some readers may think it very unnecessary to quote at length these passages of the chapter which have been lately so frequently cited, and so much dwelt on, and that a mere reference to the verses would be quite sufficient. The Editor does not think so—he has often felt in reading religious books that mere references to the passages in the Word of God on great principles of doctrinal or practical truth, lose their power and effect when not fully inserted—for few will open their Bibles to refer to them, they take them for granted, and pursue the thread of the subject—but the Editor is persuaded, that the greatest blessing to be hoped for in any work, is to be found most especially in this, how far the Author in his work, may be able through grace to set forth, in truth and faithfulness, the mind of God by His own blessed word. Here the whole course of the Apostle's reasoning, which had been considered in its doctrinal meaning, is now brought forward in its practical bearing on the subject of this Lecture, so that the truth is applied which was before explained.

—and turning from one religious book to another, and often from one error to another,—Oh! that they would remember that the only real profit a sinner can find for his soul, is not to be derived from his fellow-man, but from God!—that "*men are born, not of blood, nor of the will of the flesh, nor of the will of man, but of God.*" John i. 13.

There is no truth more clearly set forth in Scripture, than that it is impossible for man to reform himself.—"*Can the Ethiopian change his skin, or the leopard his spots? then may ye also do good that are accustomed to do evil.*" Jer. xiii. 23. And now, consider, how opposite this is to your own natural sentiments, because there is not a single person in this congregation who is not brought to the Lord Jesus Christ, that admits this principle. You do not believe it,—you think you can amend your life, you think you can reform your character. You might as well imagine that an Ethiopian could wash himself white, or a leopard change his skin! God who knoweth all things tells you, that "*then*"—when they do so—"*then may you do good who are accustomed to do evil.*" This is repeatedly shown in those portions of this Epistle which we have been considering. We should consider them over again, to prove the principle from them. Man is represented as dead, and God as the quickener. The same power must be put forth to quicken the dead soul, that Jesus Christ put forth to quicken the dead body, when he said, "*Lazarus come forth.*" John xi. 43. If man cannot quicken his own soul, how can he reform his own life? If man cannot set the cause in operation, how shall he be able to produce the effect? If you cannot make the tree good, how will you make the fruit good? and, if you cannot generate in yourselves good principles, how can you possibly produce in yourselves, the conduct that flows from good principles? It is impossible. "WE ARE HIS WORKMANSHIP." God's power alone can produce holiness of life. So we have this repeatedly set forth in God's holy word, as for instance in Jeremiah xxxi. 33, where the Lord speaks of men becoming new creatures,—what does he say, "*I will put my law in their inward parts, and write it in their hearts, and will be their God, and they shall be my people.*" "*I will do it,*" saith the Lord. There is the royal fiat of the King of kings, "*I will put my law in their hearts, I will be their God, they shall be my people.*" And again, xxxii. 39, 40, "*I will give them one heart and one way, that they may fear me forever, for the good of them and of their children after them. And I will make an everlasting covenant with them, that I will not turn away from them to do them good, but I will put my fear in their hearts, that they shall not depart from me.*" "*I do it,*"—they do not do it for themselves,—it is God's work, "WE ARE HIS WORKMANSHIP." So you have in 2d Cor. v. 5, "*he that hath wrought us for this selfsame thing is God, who also hath given unto us the earnest of the Spirit.*" And so in Philippians i. 6, "*being confident of this very thing, that he who hath begun a good work in you, will perform it unto the day of Jesus Christ.*" He does not say, I am confident, that as you have begun to reform your lives, you will continue to do so. No, but "*being confident of this very thing, that he who hath begun a good work in you, will perform it unto the day of Jesus Christ.*" Oh, what a blessing,—what a blessing it is, that it is God's work.

All of you who are ignorant of this, in the pride of your heart are angry at it, you think that it is an unreasonable thing to suppose, that you are not to have some strength in your own power—some share in quickening your own soul,—in your own deliverance—you, I say, are displeased. But you who know the Gospel of Christ, and you who know the corruption of your own hearts,—you thank God, that it is God's work—you bless God, that it is His power you have to look to, and not your own—your hearts rejoice when you pray to Him and say: "*forsake not thou the work of thine own hands!*" Ps. cxxxviii. 8. Yes, those who know their own helplessness, know, that if they had not the Almighty hand of God to take them and keep them, and bring them to Zion, they must perish forever.

Now we consider—II. THE MODE IN WHICH THE POWER OF GOD ACTS UPON THE SINNER. It is God's power that brings the sinner to obedience. "WE ARE HIS WORKMANSHIP"—this is His power. Then "CREATED IN CHRIST JESUS UNTO GOOD WORKS,"—this is the mode in which His power acts on the sinner, he is "CREATED IN CHRIST JESUS UNTO GOOD WORKS," and thus brought in Christ to serve his God.

Now this is again opposed to the natural sentiment of the unregenerate Christian; I use the term unregenerate Christian; I am sorry to say, that a vast mass of those who are called Christians, are so,—so false is the principle, that men are spiritually regenerated by the ordinance of baptism, (who live and die, alas! what countless thousands of them) ignorant, impenitent, unbelieving, and consequently unregenerate and unredeemed to eternity!

Now, I say, this is totally opposed to their opinion, for what do they think? They directly reverse the truth. They think that they are created in good works unto Christ Jesus,—not that they are "*created in Christ Jesus unto good works.*" Pray consider this.

They think that they are created in good works unto Christ Jesus.

Ask them how are they to be saved? They will say, "we must endeavor to make ourselves fit to come to Christ."

Do you depend on Christ?—Have you a solid hope that your soul is saved in Christ? "No. I trust I shall have, but I have not now."

Why? "I am not yet worthy of Christ."

I beg of you to consider whether or not this is the religion of many of you?

"I am not fit. I am not worthy. I must be a different creature before I can have that hope. I must make myself fitter to come to Christ. I must prepare myself to come to Christ."

What will you do? "Well, I will endeavor to read more—to pray more,—I will attend the ordinances of grace better, and I trust that, after I have persevered in this for some time, then I may have some hope."

Now all these things are very right to do. It is right to read, it is right to pray,—it is very right to attend the ordinances of grace,—all these are very important—but when you do this as a means of making yourselves fit to come to Christ,—do you not see what your religion is? It is this:—"*we are created in good works unto Christ Jesus,*" *or we hope to be.* Now you perceive this is the very reverse of the truth; for the Scripture is, We are "CREATED IN CHRIST JESUS UNTO GOOD WORKS." When we are enlightened by divine grace to believe the Gospel, and thus united by faith to Christ—grafted into the Living Vine—then "WE ARE HIS WORKMANSHIP CREATED IN CHRIST JESUS UNTO GOOD WORKS." So the Apostle tells us in 2nd Cor. v. 17, "*if any man be in Christ he is a new creature,*"—a new creation; he must be in Christ, to become a new creature. Would you expect fruit from a branch, before it was grafted into a tree, or after?—this is a simple question. Consider it simply. What would you think of a gardener who should take a branch which was to be grafted into a tree, and expect to find fruit on the branch before it was grafted into the tree? Would you think him a wise man or a fool? Certainly a fool. Such are you, when you think you can bring forth fruit before you are grafted into Christ. What saith the Lord Jesus Himself? St. John xv. 3. "*now are ye clean through the word which I have spoken unto you.*" Mark that,—they do not make themselves clean, they are clean through His Word, through His Gospel. Verse 4. "*Abide in me, and I in you. As the branch cannot bear fruit of itself, except it abide in the vine; no more can ye, except ye abide in me.*" You must be grafted into Him, and abide in Him, ere you can bring forth fruit unto God. So, though your works can never produce justification, justification must produce works. Bearing fruit will never graft you into the vine, but being grafted into the vine, then afterwards you are to bear fruit; so we have in the text, "WE ARE HIS WORKMANSHIP, CREATED IN CHRIST JESUS UNTO GOOD WORKS." The sinner that is brought to Christ, washed in the blood of Christ, clothed in the righteousness of Christ must necessarily produce fruit unto God. Thus you see in Romans vi. 17, 18, how clearly this is set forth, "*God be thanked, that ye were the servants of sin, but ye have obeyed from the heart that form of doctrine that was delivered unto you; being then made free from sin,* (through the Gospel of Christ) *ye became the servants of righteousness.*" Then in verse 21, "*What fruit had you then in those things whereof ye are now ashamed; for the end of those things is death; but now being made free from sin,* (that is, being delivered from its curse, being delivered from its condemnation,) *and become servants to*

God, ye have your fruit unto holiness, and the end everlasting life." So in the Epistle to Titus ii. 11, 12, 13, 14, "*The grace of God that bringeth salvation hath appeared to all men, teaching us, that denying ungodliness and worldly lusts, we should live soberly, righteously, and godly in this present world, looking for that blessed hope, and the glorious appearing of the great God, and our Saviour Jesus Christ, who gave himself for us, that he might redeem us from all iniquity, and purify unto himself a peculiar people zealous of good works.*" The Gospel brings salvation first, and then teaches men to live soberly, righteously, and godly. They are redeemed from all iniquity, and so they are purified unto Christ, and thereby made zealous of good works. So in 1st Peter i. 15, 16, "*as he which hath called you is holy, so be ye holy in all manner of conversation: because it is written, be ye holy; for I am holy;*"—therefore, I say, as it is utterly impossible that God could, by any dispensation, relax the obligation of His law, so it is only by the Gospel of Jesus that provision for the observance of that law is made by God for sinners,—they must be "CREATED IN CHRIST JESUS UNTO GOOD WORKS."

The law of God, proclaimed to the sinner, in its spirituality and its justice, shows his guilt, his condemnation, his state of death and ruin. So it was with the Apostle Paul "*when the commandment came, sin revived and I died.*" Rom. vii. 9, 10. Then, the Gospel, proclaiming Christ as our glorious surety, fulfilling the law for sinners—bearing its curse—proclaiming thereby, deliverance from the wrath to come—staying the sentence of eternal judgment,—satisfying the demands of eternal justice through the blood of the Lamb—speaking peace and pardon to the sinner's conscience, leads his heart by the Spirit to know the love of his Redeemer, and draws his heart to respond to that love. What is that response? That response is love. And what is that love? "*Love is the fulfilling of the law.*" Love is a spontaneous movement of the heart, it can neither be enforced nor restrained by obligation. The practical glory of the Gospel is that it leads the sinner into the Law, because it draws him into love. The impulses of gratitude and affection become identified with the obligations of obedience. "*I delight in the law of God after the inward man.*" Rom. vii. 22. An obligation embraced by the heart, and the affections, turns duty into happiness, and, therefore, our glorious Deliverer and Benefactor saith, "*my yoke is easy, and my burden is light.*" Mat. xi. 30. Holiness is the burden of the unconverted sinner,—sin is the burden and the cross of the redeemed saint.

III. WHAT NOW IS THE SECURITY FOR THIS? HOW IS IT THAT IT MUST BE SO? God hath ordained—God hath appointed it. God hath ordained that His people should walk in good works. We are "CREATED IN CHRIST JESUS UNTO GOOD WORKS, WHICH GOD HATH BEFORE ORDAINED THAT WE SHOULD WALK IN THEM." You have this set forth in this Epistle, i. 3, 4, "*Blessed be the God and Father of our Lord Jesus Christ, who hath blessed us with all spiritual blessings in heavenly places in Christ, according as he hath chosen us in him before the foundation of the world, that we should be holy and without blame before him in love."* So you have in 1st Peter i. 2, "*Elect, according to the foreknowledge of God the Father, through sanctification of the Spirit, unto obedience, and sprinkling of the blood of Jesus Christ*"—"*elect unto obedience*"—"*created in Christ Jesus unto good works, which God hath before ordained that we should walk in them.*" Therefore, you perceive, why throughout the Scriptures, the works of man are made the test of his salvation. He is not to be justified by them, but he is to be judged by them;—and this is a difficulty that often occurs to the mind,—how is man to be judged by his works if he is not to be justified by them? because they are taken as the test of his faith, they are taken as the proof of his sincerity. A cup of cold water could not purchase salvation for the sinner,—but "*a cup of cold water*" given in the name of Jesus, "*shall in no wise lose its reward,*" Mat. x. 42, because it is the test that the believer loves his Master.

An act from the principle of love to Christ never was done, and never can be done, by the unconverted sinner. Of all the motives to moral action, which can influence the heart of man (and there are innumerable motives,) the love of Jesus can have no place among them; for man by nature does not know what to love Him for,—he fears and hates Him as his Judge. The brightness of Christ's example, so far from alluring, repels the heart of man. So it was in His own day. You see how the Scribes and Pharisees hated Him, because He was holy. So He is just as hateful this moment to the natural heart of man.—But when the sinner is enlightened to see that Jesus is the Refuge for his soul,—that Jesus is the Friend of sinners,—that he can come to Christ as a Saviour,—that he can pour out his heart at His feet,—that He can depend upon His blood to wash away all his sin,—that he can come as a vile sinner, as we had in the language of the Psalm to-day, "*for thy name's sake, O Lord, pardon mine iniquity, for it is great*"—Psal. xxv. 11, instead of thinking, as the sinner in his natural state thinks, that he can, at least in some degree, make himself clean, and come with the prayer, "*pardon mine iniquity, for it is little,*"—when he knows, he can say, "*pardon mine iniquity, for it is great*"—when he knows, he can thus come to Christ, with his sins, and cast them into the fathomless ocean of eternal love, "*the fountain that is opened*" in the blood of Jesus for the guilt of sinners,—when he knows this—then he loves his Lord and Master; and then, the least work of love becomes the test of his faith, and is certain of acceptance and of reward,—not for its own value, for it is nothing; but because it is a proof that this man is a disciple of Jesus—that he had fled to Jesus as the salvation of his soul—"*fled for refuge to lay hold on the hope set before him,*" Heb. vi. 18.

The act that brought sin and death into the world was, not in itself, an act of good or evil. There was no moral good or evil in the act of eating the fruit of a certain tree more than of any other tree;—but when that act was made a test of the law, that is, of love to Him who commanded it, then the very lightness of the test itself aggravated its guilt ten thousand fold, and it became sin, pregnant with death and ruin to the world. So, the act that is a test of love to God,—that act, however little, is graciously received and rewarded.

Allow me to entreat you to consider again the articles of our church on this subject, that you may compare and see how sound and scriptural they are. Our text says, "WE ARE HIS WORKMANSHIP, CREATED IN CHRIST JESUS UNTO GOOD WORKS."

ARTICLE X.

"The condition of man after the fall of Adam is such, that he cannot turn and prepare himself, by his own natural strength and good works to faith and calling upon God."

Now, is not this an epitome of the instruction I have been endeavoring to give you?

"Wherefore, we have no power to do good works, pleasant and acceptable to God, without the grace of God, by Christ, preventing us," (that is, going before us,) "that we may have a good will, and working with us, when we have that good will."

So again in Article xiii., the same principle is laid down.

"Works done before the grace of Christ and the inspiration of his Spirit, are not pleasant to God, forasmuch as they spring not of faith in Jesus Christ."

They want the motive, they want the test, they want the true principle of moral action.

"Neither do they make men meet to receive grace, or, (as the School authors say,) deserve grace of congruity; yea, rather that they are not done as God hath willed and commanded them to be done, we doubt not but they have the nature of sin."

Now, "WE ARE HIS WORKMANSHIP CREATED IN CHRIST JESUS UNTO GOOD WORKS." Consider Article xii.

"Albeit, that good works which are the fruit of faith, and follow after justification, cannot put away our sins, and endure the severity of God's judgment."

We cannot be justified by them, nor challenge God to enter into judgment with us for them.

"Yet, are they pleasing and acceptable to God in Christ, and do spring out necessarily of a true and lively faith; insomuch, that by them a lively faith may be as evidently known, as a tree discerned by the fruit."

They necessarily flow from it. It must be, that a man if he is a believer in Jesus, must show that he is so. It is impossible that the heart can love any human being, if it have an opportunity of showing that love, and that it will not show it. We cannot conceal our affection, if we love any one. Much less, if the heart is filled with love to Jesus, when we love our blessed Redeemer, we cannot but endeavor to prove it by our life. Therefore, all who are grafted into the Living Vine, are "CREATED IN CHRIST

JESUS UNTO GOOD WORKS," "insomuch, as by them a lively faith may be as evidently known as a tree discerned by the fruit."

You see, how sound the articles of our church are on this subject,—and therefore, it is no wonder, that those who endeavor to subvert the Gospel of Christ in our communion, should endeavor to explain away the articles with sophistry and falsehood. They are a solid bulwark for the faith of the church, because they stand the test of comparison with the word of God, and because, when you search the Scriptures, and bring them "*to the law and to the testimony*," Isa. viii. 10—there you find, that they are sound in the faith.

I would now address unbelievers in this congregation. My dear friends, what is all your morality, if you are not in Christ Jesus? Whatever be your character before men, you are, alas! guilty, condemned sinners before God,—and it is in vain you struggle to deliver yourselves from your sin. You cannot do it,—all these efforts that you make, and that you think you are making, for which, as you expect God will give you credit, and which you shall have put down to your account, are all vain, they can profit you nothing, they evince nothing but this, that you are ignorant of yourselves and ignorant of God.

What are you to do? Hear the glorious proclamation of divine grace and mercy to you in Christ Jesus,—The Gospel addresses us all, each and every sinner only in one character—as sinners. It makes no allowance for our morality. Whatever we may have, comparatively before men, we have none before God,—"*there is none righteous, no, not one.*" Psalm xiv. 3—Rom. iii. 10. God's judgment is proclaimed against us—God's judgment is written in this book against us. Read your Bible. There you read the sentence of God against your souls, when you think of your sins, and your deserts in His sight. Now we do not mean to drive you to despair, by such testimony as this, but on the contrary to bring you out of despair,—a state of real despair, though yet not felt;—to bring you out of that, to the hope of the Gospel. For Oh, my friends, when you read that Bible, you see also the good news, that the sentence has been executed on Him who came into the world to bear it for sinners. How mad a man would be, who was indictable for a capital crime, if there were conclusive proofs against him—if it were wholly impossible he could escape when brought to trial—whose sovereign should issue a command that he might go free, and not be indicted or prosecuted to conviction,—how mad he would be to say, "I will insist on a trial,—I demand a prosecution." That is the mode in which you act. Depending on your own claims—your own morality—your virtue—your own miserable efforts to save your soul,—you are going on to judgment, challenging God to condemn you, and refusing the glorious deliverance that is proclaimed to you in the Gospel of Christ. David says, "*Enter not into judgment with thy servant, O Lord, for in thy sight shall no man living be justified.*" Ps. cxliii. 2. Now we proclaim to you mercy, that God has entered into judgment with

Christ for you. Some will say, "you speak of this very often, you preach this doctrine continually,"—most certainly I do so; God forbid, I should ever leave the pulpit without preaching it—for as there is no other hope of salvation, so there is no other sound principle of Christian conduct. Do you not come here as sinners?—Do I not address some who are under the wrath of God? some who have not fled to Christ for salvation? some who come here vainly endeavoring to save their own souls, rejecting the hope of the Gospel? and must I not set that Gospel before them again and again? How many, alas! shall never hear its blessed sound once more. Besides, I want to keep it ever upon my own heart; every day of my life, I want to have the Gospel preached to my own soul. May the Lord bring it home to our hearts by the Holy Spirit.

Are you looking to Christ for salvation? Remember if you are not in Christ, you cannot bring forth good works. You who are indeed looking unto Christ as your hope and refuge, remember this, —"WE ARE HIS WORKMANSHIP, CREATED IN CHRIST JESUS UNTO GOOD WORKS, WHICH GOD HATH BEFORE ORDAINED WE SHOULD WALK IN THEM." Remember, that the same testimony of God's word that gave you hope in the faith of the Gospel, gives you also directions for the walk of those who embrace that faith. The same word, the same Gospel which tells you, that, "*there is no condemnation to them that are in Christ Jesus*," tells you too that they "*walk not after the flesh, but after the Spirit.*" Rom. viii. 1,—tells you that they who are in Christ are "CREATED IN CHRIST JESUS UNTO GOOD WORKS, WHICH GOD HATH BEFORE ORDAINED THAT WE SHOULD WALK IN THEM."

Remember my friends, my beloved brethren, that if you are walking carelessly with God, you cannot be walking safely or peacefully with God. If you are not watching against your own sins, you are not enjoying confidence in your Lord. Do you remember what the Apostle says? "*I therefore so run, not as uncertainly; so fight I, not as one that beateth the air.*" 1st Cor. ix. 26. There is great uncertainty in the faith and hope of the believer, where there is unsteadiness in the walk of the believer. Our own experience tells us so, I know it from my experience, and you know it from yours,—and therefore, though there is no reward for the works of the law, considered in themselves,—there is an amazing reward in the works of the believer, "*in keeping of them, there is great reward.*" Psalm, xix. 11. Even the ungodly world will tell you, that "virtue is its own reward,"—and if that is a maxim, even of those who know not Christ, how much more do those who know Christ, feel that in walking carefully with their Lord and Master, they are walking happily and confidently? This is what the Apostle means, when he says, "*If our heart condemn us, God is greater than our hearts, and knoweth all things, if our heart condemn us not, then have we confidence toward God.*" 1 John iii. 20, 21. It is not if our heart condemn us not of sin, for our heart must always condemn us of sin,—but if, instead of coming to our Lord Jesus Christ, with our sins, and pouring them out at his feet, and crying for strength against them, we cherish any of them in our heart,—we must feel the bitter consequence, the Lord will made us feel it. He loves his people too much, not to make them feel it. Thus He visits them with the rod,—this is the reason why, "*whom the Lord loveth, he chasteneth, and scourgeth every son whom he receiveth.*" Heb. xii.—6. Therefore, dear friends, if we are under the chastening of the Lord, let us take the chastening thankfully, gratefully; remembering how much we need it—remembering, how much we have drawn it on ourselves—remembering, how tender our Father is to chasten us, to humble us, to prove us, that we may know what is in our heart, and to bring us again out of the furnace, strengthened and refreshed, to His feet, that we may "*run in the way of his commandments, when he shall enlarge our hearts.*" Ps. cxix. 32.

Oh think of this, and may the Lord, in His great mercy supply the innumerable defects and deficiencies of these instructions, and bring home His own truth with demonstration of His own Spirit and with power to our hearts and consciences for Jesus' sake Amen.

SIXTEENTH LECTURE.

EPHESIANS II.—11, 12, 13.

"Wherefore remember, that ye being in time past Gentiles in the flesh, who are called Uncircumcision by that which is called the Circumcision in the flesh made by hands; That at that time ye were without Christ, being aliens from the commonwealth of Israel, and strangers from the covenants of promise, having no hope, and without God in the world. But now in Christ Jesus ye who sometimes were far off are made nigh by the blood of Christ."

It is a common exhibition of the evil of the human heart, that when a man has been raised from some low condition by the favor of his sovereign, and placed in one of rank and influence, he is apt, as we say, to forget himself,—to forget the mean estate in which he formerly was—to forget, that he has been raised to that which he now enjoys, only by the favor of his sovereign—to forget what he owes to his benefactor, what he owes to his superiors, what he owes to his equals, what he owes to all over whom he is placed, in every relative position of duty.

If this be a common evil with respect to our fellow-men,—how much more in reference to God. What innumerable mercies have we all received! what temporal mercies!—How could we ever enumerate them? What spiritual mercies!—what a mercy that we are here this day with the sound of the Gospel in our ears,—yet, which of them have we remembered as we ought? which of them have we not forgotten?

If we were asked, what is it that man ought most to remember, and what is it that man most forgets? The answer must be—His God. Well may He complain, then, as He does in Jeremiah, ii. 32, "*Can a maid forget her ornaments, or a bride her attire? Yet, my people have forgotten me, days without number.*" So, we perceive, when God warns the Jews against departing from Him, he warns them against forgetting Him,—we see this in Deuteronomy iv.—9. "*Only, take heed to thyself, and keep thy soul diligently, lest thou forget the things which thine eyes have seen, and lest they depart from thy heart all the days of thy life.*" We have the same in chap. viii. 11, speaking of their readiness to forget the blessings they have received from God, "*Beware that thou forget not the Lord thy God in not keeping his commandments, and his judgments, and his statutes, which I command thee this day; lest when thou hast eaten and art full, and hast built goodly houses, and dwelt therein, and when thy herds and thy flocks multiply, and thy silver and gold is multiplied, and all that thou hast is multiplied,—then thine heart be lifted up, and thou forget the Lord thy God, which brought thee forth out of the land of Egypt, from the house of bondage.*" And, as He warns them thus not to forget Him, so in the promises of His covenant love to the Jews, to gather them to their own land, and to pour upon them the blessings He has promised; He provides for their fidelity by providing, that they shall remember all their own sin, and all His mercies to them. You see this in Ezekiel xvi. 60. "*Nevertheless, I will remember my covenant with thee.*" (namely with the people of the Jews,) "*in the days of thy youth, and I will establish unto thee an everlasting covenant.*" then in verse 62 and 63, "*And I will establish my covenant with thee, and thou shalt know, that I am the Lord, that thou mayest remember and be confounded, and never open thy mouth any more, because of thy shame, when I am pacified toward thee for all that thou hast done, saith the Lord God.*" You see the same in Ezek. chap. xx. 42, 43, "*And ye shall know that I am the Lord, when I shall bring you into the land of Israel, into the country for the which I lifted up my hand to give it to your fathers. And there shall ye remember your ways, and all your doings wherein ye have been defiled; and ye shall loathe yourselves in your own sight, for all your evil that ye have committed.*" The same is in chap. xxxvi. when the Lord promises to give them a new heart, 26th and following verses, "*A new heart also will I give you, and a new spirit will I put within you; and I will take away the stony heart out of your flesh, and I will give you an heart of flesh. And I will put my Spirit within you, and cause you to walk in my statutes, and ye shall keep my judgments, and do them. And ye shall dwell in the land that I gave to your fathers, and ye shall be my people, and I will be your*

God. I will also save you from all your uncleannesses; and I will call for the corn, and will increase it, and lay no famine upon you. And I will multiply the fruit of the tree, and the increase of the field, that ye shall receive no more reproach of famine among the heathen." Now, mark,—"*then shall ye remember your own evil ways, and your doings that were not good, and shall loathe yourselves in your own sight, for your iniquities and for your abominations.*

If such is to be the humility of the saints in that blessed time of promise when the "*earth shall be full of the knowledge of the Lord as the waters cover the sea.*" Isa. xi. 9,—surely, it ought to be the humility of the saints now. One of the offices of the promised blessed Spirit is, that he shall be a Remembrancer.

What wonder, then, that the Apostle, having enumerated the misery and guilt of the saints at Ephesus, and having set before them, as we have seen, the glory to which they had been raised, by the Lord Jesus Christ,—what wonder that he should come to the conclusion with which my text commences, "WHEREFORE, REMEMBER," remember what you have been, and remember what you are. He had showed them, from verses 1 to 3 (which I need not now recapitulate to you, as we have gone through them so lately,) he had showed them there, their state of sin by nature,—he had showed them from verses 4 to 10, their present state by grace, "*raised up together, and made to sit together in heavenly places in Christ,*"—and now he calls them to remember from what they had been rescued, and to what they had been brought.

You will observe, that in this place, he addresses especially the Gentile converts at Ephesus,—and it is necessary for the understanding of the passage, that you should attend to this, and that you should refer to the history of the fact. You perceive, on referring to the history, which you find in Acts xix., that the Church at Ephesus consisted of Jews and Gentiles. When St. Paul came to Ephesus, as you see in verse 1, he found certain disciples, and then he asked them, as we find in verse 3, "*Unto what were ye baptized? They said, unto John's baptism,*"—therefore they must necessarily, have been Jews. John had never come to Ephesus, nor had the idolatrous worshippers of Diana gone to Jerusalem; but the Jews had gone up to Jerusalem, and there some of them who believed, had been baptized unto John's baptism. So, you perceive, they had a synagogue at Ephesus, as is evident from Acts, xix. 7, 8, "*all the men*" (that is the disciples) "*were about twelve. And he went into the synagogue, and spake boldly for the space of three months, disputing and persuading the things concerning the kingdom of God.*" The Jews, in the synagogue at Ephesus, rejected Paul, they rejected his testimony, and then we are told, verse 9, "*when divers were hardened, and believed not, but spake evil of that way before the multitude, he departed from them, and separated the disciples*"—that is, those who did believe the Gospel,—he separated them from the unbelievers and scoffers, and he "*disputed daily in the school of one Tyrannus.*" He left the synagogue, and went to the school of Tyrannus; and there, we are told, this daily disputation, "*continued by the space of two years, so that all they which dwelt in Asia heard the word of the Lord Jesus, both Jews and Greeks.*" verse 10.

We see, then, that the church consisted of a mixed assembly,—of believing Jews and believing Greeks,—and likewise the immense progress which the Gospel made among the idolatrous Greeks at Ephesus at this time. If you read the whole chapter, you will see it more fully, I can only cite a few verses, 18, 19, 20, "*And many that believed, came and confessed, and showed their deeds.—Many also of them which used curious arts brought their books together, and burned them before all men, and they counted the price of them, and found it fifty thousand pieces of silver. So mightily grew the word of God and prevailed.*" And then, you perceive, one of the idolatrous workmen at Ephesus, who made silver shrines for Diana, named Demetrius—called together his fellow workmen, and said to them, verse 26, "*ye see and hear, that not alone at Ephesus, but almost throughout all Asia, this Paul hath persuaded and turned away much people, saying, they be no gods which are made with hands. So that not only this our craft is in danger to be set at nought, but also, that the temple of the great goddess Diana should be despised, and her magnificence should be destroyed, whom all Asia and the world worshippeth.*" St. Paul had no notion of that unchristian charity of the present day which is to be found among Protestants. He had no notion of saying, or believing in his heart and conscience, that people were idolaters, and then professing, that indeed he did not wish to proselytize them. There was no such unbelief, no such ignorance of his own apostolic mission—no such contempt of his duty—no such abandonment of his Master and his Master's cause, and of the souls of men, there was nothing like that in St. Paul. He *did* wish to proselytize those who, he knew, were idolaters,—and he testified before God and before them, that "*they were no gods that were made with hands*"—no matter of what they were made—whether made of stone or iron, or brass, or wood, or flour, he testified, "*they are no gods that are made with hands.*" Paul asserted this, and God's blessing rested upon his testimony, and God's power accompanied His word, and God's salvation was brought to the souls of men,—many believed. So it would have been in this country, if there had been fidelity, apostolical fidelity, as there ought to be among those who profess to call themselves the servants of Christ. So you see the testimony against Paul,—they cried out against Paul that he said, "*they be no gods which are made with hands,*"—therefore said Demetrius, "*not only this our craft is in danger to be set at nought, but also, that the temple of the great goddess Diana should be despised, and her magnificence should be destroyed, whom all Asia and the world worshippeth.*" You see, how the

Lord, by the fidelity of His apostle, battered down the temples of idolatry. This was by Christian fidelity, turning men, through God's grace, in the spirit of faithfulness and love, "*from darkness to light, from the power of Satan unto God*"—as he had been sent by his Lord to do. Acts xxvi. 17, 18.

It is clear, then, from the history, that the church at Ephesus was composed of Jews and Gentiles. We perceive how numerous were the converts from the worship of Diana,—and the Apostle, in the passage which I have read to you, is addressing, as you perceive, these Gentile converts, reminding them of their state of aggravated guilt and misery, and of the great blessing which God had vouchsafed to them, in bringing them "*from darkness to light, and from the power of Satan unto God*," he says, "REMEMBER, THAT YE BEING IN TIME PAST GENTILES IN THE FLESH, WHO WERE CALLED UNCIRCUMCISION BY THAT WHICH IS CALLED THE CIRCUMCISION IN THE FLESH,"—he reminds them, that they had been looked down upon as Gentiles, by all who knew anything of the true God, as the Jews,—that they had been in a despicable state, they "*were called uncircumcision*." The rite of circumcision was that especially, which separated the Jew, from the time of his birth, from all the other people of the world; it was one of the great distinctions that God had placed between them, and all the other nations; therefore, the "uncircumcision" was the name given by the Jews to all those persons who were separated from God, outcasts from God;—so you remember the story of David and Goliath,—you recollect David's contemptuous sneer at the giant,—he did not care for his being a giant, or for his staff, or for his spear, but he said—"*who is this uncircumcised Philistine that he should defy the armies of the living God?*" 1st Sam. xvii. 26. He was an "uncircumcised Philistine," such is the term of contempt with which David brands him. And so in Acts, xi. 3, you see the charge that all the Apostles brought against Peter, "*thou wentest in to men uncircumcised, and didst eat with them*." They were angry with him for doing so. It was a thing totally unknown to the Jews, and unknown to the world, that the Gentiles—that any nation except the Jews should be brought into the covenant of Christ; therefore we perceive, when the Lord intended to send Peter to Cornelius, he sent a vision from heaven to Peter to show him that the distinction between clean and unclean, was now done away. "*What God hath cleansed that call not thou common*," Acts x.—15,—and if you look to Ephesians iii.—2, you perceive this subject clearly set forth, "*if ye have heard of the dispensation of the grace of God which is given me to you-ward*," 5th, "*which in other ages was not made known unto the sons of men, as it is now revealed unto his holy apostles and prophets by the Spirit,—that the Gentiles should be fellow heirs, and of the same body, and partakers of his promise in Christ by the Gospel*." It was not known to the sons of men, but it was now revealed, that the Gentiles should be fellow-heirs; therefore the Apostle reminds them of their state of former separation from God, and of the contempt in which they had been held by His people, before the mercy of the Lord had visited them, "*Ye know*" saith the Apostle Peter, "*how that it is an unlawful thing for a man that is a Jew to keep company, or come unto one of another nation.*" Acts, x. 28. The Apostle Paul had set forth, as we have seen in the first part of the chapter, the state of the Jews and Gentiles universally as sinners. He had set forth their state positively, "*dead in trespasses and sins,*" utterly insensible to their guilty, miserable condition—unable either to feel it, or deliver themselves from it—walking "*according to the course of this world,*"—under the power of the devil—walking in the lusts of the flesh—"*fulfilling the desires of the flesh and of the mind,*" and "*by nature the children of wrath, even as others.*" This was the *positive* state of them all. But now, in this passage he sets forth the state of the Gentiles, *negatively,*—he shows what they were not. "*Remember,*" he says, in addition to your state of positive sin,—remember, that "*at that time, you were called uncircumcision,*"—you were not circumcised—shut out, by that means, from the only people upon the face of the earth who were the recognized, acknowledged people of God.—"*You were without Christ,*"—you had no Saviour, in type, or ordinance, or promise,—you were "*aliens from the commonwealth of Israel,*"—you had no lot or part in the commonwealth of God's Church—you were "*strangers from the covenants of promise,*" you knew nothing about the glorious salvation provided in the Covenant of Grace. You had "*no hope*"—eternity was a dark and fearful precipice—a gulf that yawned before you. And you were "*without God in the world.*" You knew not Him who formed you—your idol Diana was a senseless image, made with hands. That was their condition.

Not so the Jews. We see in Galatians, iii. 8, that God had "*preached the Gospel unto Abraham.*" We see, in Romans, iii. 1, 2, when the Jew is supposed to ask, "*what advantage then hath the Jew?*" (because the Apostle had proved that "*both Jew and Gentile were all under sin,*") "*or what profit is there of circumcision?*" He answers, "*Much every way: chiefly, because that unto them were committed the oracles of God.*" They had much blessing, much profit, of which all other nations were destitute—but the greatest blessing of them all was this, that "*unto them were committed the oracles of God.*"

You perceive, that the Scriptures are counted the greatest blessing that a people can enjoy,—therefore, the privation of the Scriptures is the greatest curse with which a nation can be visited,—the worst of all famines is "*a famine of hearing of the word of the Lord.*" Amos, viii. 11. Compare these advantages of the Jews again with those mentioned, Romans ix. 4, 5, "*Who are Israelites, to whom pertaineth the adoption, and the glory, and the covenants, and the giving of the law, and the service of God, and the promises; whose are the fathers, and of whom, as concerning the flesh, Christ came, who is over all, God blessed forever.*" So you see in 1 Corinthians x. 2, "*they were all baptized unto Moses in the cloud and in the sea, and did all eat the same spiritual meat, and did all drink the same spiritual drink, for they drank of that spiritual Rock that followed them, and that Rock was Christ.*" 1 Cor. x. 3, 4. So in St. John's Gospel our Lord saith, v. 45, 46, "*Do not think, that I will accuse you to the Father, there is one that accuseth you, even Moses in whom ye trust; for had ye believed Moses, ye would have believed me, for he wrote of me.*"

Therefore, the Jews had Christ revealed to them in the Sacred Volume,—they were not "*without Christ,*" as the Gentiles were. The Gentiles were deprived of the oracles of God, therefore "WITHOUT CHRIST, ALIENS FROM THE COMMONWEALTH OF ISRAEL, AND STRANGERS FROM THE COVENANTS OF PROMISE," which promised Christ, whom Abraham knew—in whom he believed and rejoiced.—"*Your father Abraham,*" saith Christ, "*rejoiced to see my day, and he saw it, and was glad.*" John viii. 56. They were strangers from the promise of the coming of Messiah to save—strangers from the promise of the coming of the glorious King, who was to "*arise and to reign over the Gentiles, in whom the Gentiles should trust.*" They were strangers from the covenant of the glorious priesthood to be fulfilled in Christ Jesus the Lord, the "*priest forever, after the order of Melchisedech.*" Ps. cx. 4. They had no prophets, no promises, no sacrifices to the true God, no types, no shadows, no law, no blessing or privilege derived from the Gospel covenant which the Israelites possessed. Therefore, they had "*no hope.*"

In what an awful state a sinner is, without hope! Did you ever see a man die without hope? and feeling he was without hope? I have—it is an awful sight. This was the state of all the Gentiles, they had "no hope." They had not, indeed, a clear revelation of the awful eternity that was before them,—but they had within, the conscious apprehension of an immortal existence, a sense of sin that barbed the arrow of death, and made that which is the sting of death rankle in their consciences; and they had no balm of mercy to pour into the wound,—being "*without Christ, without hope, and without God in the world.*" It is of great importance that we should know and consider this,—we had in the second of the Psalms of this day, xcvi. 5, "*as for all the gods of the heathen, they are but idols, but it is the Lord that made the heavens,*" and again, xcvii. 7, "*confounded be all they that worship carved images, and that delight in vain gods, worship him all ye gods,*" and the Apostle says, "*the things which the Gentiles sacrifice, they sacrifice to devils, and not to God.* 1 Cor. x. 20.

It is of vast moment that all who bear the name of Christians should remember these things, for what were the privileges of the Jews compared with the blessings that we enjoy! We ought to form our judgment and our opinion respecting the state of the heathen world, not from the ignorance of man, but from the records of God's eternal truth. This would give us, both a right sense of the privileges and blessings we enjoy ourselves, and make us feel as we ought, for the destitution of those who have "*no hope,*" and who are "*without God in the world.*"

But while the Apostle calls on them to remember what their state had been, he teaches them also to remember the blessing of their present condition, "BUT NOW IN CHRIST JESUS YE WHO SOMETIMES WERE FAR OFF ARE MADE NIGH BY THE BLOOD OF CHRIST." Amazing mercy! made nigh—by what means?—"*made nigh by the blood of Christ,*"—brought to behold the "*glory of the only begotten of the Father, full of grace and truth,*" John, i. 14—brought into a state of pardon, peace, and salvation through Him. The change that had passed upon them was like the light bursting on the dark world, when "*God said, let there be light, and there was light.*" For "*God who commanded the light to shine out of darkness had shined into their hearts, to give the light of the knowledge of the glory of God, in the face of Jesus Christ.*" 2 Cor. iv. 6. There they behold all the prophecies of Jesus fulfilled, "*to him give all the prophets witness, that through his name, whosoever believeth in him should receive remission of sins.*" Acts x. 43. All the glorious promises of God are accomplished in Jesus, for, "*all the promises of God in him are yea, and in him, amen.*" 2 Cor. i. 20; in Him, are all the blessed covenants ratified, as you see in the song of Zechariah, St. Luke, i. 67—75, where he so beautifully sets that forth, as he speaks, being "filled with the Holy Ghost,"—"*Blessed be the Lord God of Israel, for he hath visited and redeemed his people, and hath raised up an horn of salvation for us, in the house of his servant David; as he spake by the mouth of his holy prophets, which have been since the world began; that we should be saved from our enemies, and from the hand of them that hate us; to perform the mercy promised to our fathers, and to remember his holy covenant; the oath that he sware to our father Abraham, that he would grant unto us, that we, being delivered out of the hand of our enemies, might serve him without fear, in holiness and righteousness before him, all the days of our life.*" Here they were no longer "*strangers from the covenants of promise,*" they behold them all fulfilled in Christ. Here, they were not brought merely into the shadows of the Jewish law, but into the substance of the glorious Gospel, not offering daily sacrifices, but resting on the one finished sacrifice of Christ. Hebrews, x. 11, 12, "*Every priest standeth daily ministering, and offering oftentimes the same sacrifices which can never take away sins; but this man, after he had offered one sacrifice for sins forever, sat down at the right hand of God.*" And so, they had the antetype instead of the type. Though they had not the covenant of the priesthood of the Jews, they had the everlasting covenant of Christ's glorious priesthood, "*Christ being come an high priest of good things to come, by a greater and more perfect tabernacle, not made with hands, that is to say, not of this building, neither by the blood of goats and calves, but by his own blood, he entered in once into the holy place, having obtained eternal redemption for us.*" Heb. ix 11, 12. That precious blood of Jesus, the "fountain opened for sin and for uncleanness" hath been revealed to them, that they who bathe in that blessed fountain, though like Naaman, full of leprosy, should come up healed and clean as a little child.

Oh, the blessing of being "BROUGHT NIGH BY THE BLOOD OF CHRIST!" Then, instead of having no hope, they had "*hope as an anchor of the soul, both sure and steadfast.*" Heb. vi. 19. Instead of being "without God in the world," they were made "*children of God, by faith in Christ Jesus,*" Gal. iii. 26; brought nigh to Him as a reconciled Father in Jesus. Brethren, if the state of the Jews who neglected the privileges they enjoyed, although these privileges were only typical, was awful—if the state of the Gentiles who were without these privileges that the Jews possessed, was such as described in this passage by the Apostle.—What must be the state of those who have all those privileges, which "*many prophets and kings desired to see, and have not seen them?*" if we speak of the Jews. And who have all the privileges and blessings enjoyed by these Gentiles when they were "*brought nigh by the blood of Christ,*" and yet who "*neglect such great salvation?*"

It may be,—it must be, that I address some, perhaps many in that state to-day. Remember, "*all were not Israel who were of Israel.*" Remember, all are not Christ's who are Christians in name and profession. Remember, that "*a name to live when we are dead,*"—privileges when neglected—the blood of Jesus as a fountain, when it is despised—the righteousness of Christ, as a robe to clothe our nakedness, when it is cast by as an unclean thing—remember that these, instead of blessings, are all turned into curses, judgments, accumulated causes of ruin on the heads of those who thus trample on these mercies.

If I address some, as I trust I do, who are awaking to a sense of the state in which they have been living in the midst of blessings and privileges,—who are asking "*the way to Zion with their faces thitherward,*"—who say in their hearts, "Oh that my lot were cast among the people of Christ." Remember, my dear friends, the means by which these persons were brought from their awful state of ignorance, of guilt, and misery, both Jews and Gentiles—remember it is all contained in that one word, "*made nigh by the blood of Christ,*"—alone.—There was no process to be gone through by them,—no long and labored return from their dark idolatry and guilt, to come to God, but to believe the glorious proclamation of God's everlasting mercy, of His eternal love, of His rich grace, of His free and full salvation sounding in their ears—this was enough,—even all that they could want.

The blood of Jesus Christ has been poured out, a ransom for the guilty. The ransom is paid down, the prison doors are opened,—come forth ye prisoners of hope into life, and light, and liberty,—the life that Christ has purchased with His blood.—The light of "*the Sun of righteousness,*" of Him who is "*the light of the world.*"—The liberty of the everlasting Gospel,—"*If the Son therefore shall make you free, ye shall be free indeed.* John viii. 36. Oh, think what brought them nigh,—why should it not bring you nigh to-day? Remember, the fountain of Immanuel's blood is like Himself, "*the same yesterday, to-day, and forever.*"

And you, brethren, who see, and taste, and hope, and rejoice in the glad tidings of salvation, who can repeat in spirit and truth, "*O come, let us sing unto the Lord, let us heartily rejoice in the strength of our salvation.*" Ps. xcv. 1. Remember what you were; in one sense, far worse than these Ephesians; you were not brought up like them to worship Diana, or to believe that that image had fallen down from Jupiter,—you were not placed in the midst of darkness and idolatry, without the Word of God, "ALIENS FROM THE COMMONWEALTH OF ISRAEL,—STRANGERS FROM THE COVENANT OF PROMISE, HAVING NO HOPE, AND WITHOUT GOD IN THE WORLD." No, you were baptized in the name of Jesus—when you were born into the world, you were brought to that holy ordinance, which Jesus has appointed as the instrument of confessing His faith—being adopted into His family—entering into His church. You were brought to that ordinance as the sign and seal of salvation, a fountain of water, emblematic of a fountain of blood,—bathed in that, or sprinkled with it, it matters not which, it is emblematical of the cleansing power of the blood of the Lamb. You were brought by that means into all the blessings and privileges of the Christian church,—and how have you used them? Alas! how long you despised these mercies! how long you slighted them. Even when your Ministers perhaps have been endeavoring to explain to you,—listen to me, children—listen to me, my beloved young friends—listen to me, you who are learning your Catechism,—when your Ministers have been endeavoring to explain to you, and to set before you the privileges and blessings, the solemn obligations and responsibilities of those who are brought into, and brought up in the Christian church.—Oh! how have you neglected and turned a deaf ear,—slighted them, disregarded the instructions you received, and provoked the Lord to cut you off in your sins. Remember this.

But God hath touched your hearts—God hath reached your consciences—God hath visited you with His mercy—God hath led you to the feet of Jesus—and now you see, that "*you who some times were afar off*" in spirit, though near in profession, are now "*made nigh by the blood of Christ.*" Wherefore, remember what you were, and remember what you are,—"*ye are not your own; for ye are bought with a price: therefore glorify God in your body, and in your spirit, which are God's.*" 1st Cor. vi. 19, 20. You are no longer debtors to the world, or to the flesh, to live after the flesh—you owe to Jesus all you have, and all you are; for Jesus hath "*redeemed you from the curse of the law.*' He hath bought you with his precious blood—And "Now IN CHRIST JESUS YE WHO SOMETIMES WERE FAR OFF ARE MADE NIGH BY THE BLOOD OF CHRIST."

Oh! then hear the words of the Apostle, "*I therefore, the prisoner of the Lord, beseech you that ye walk worthy of the vocation wherewith ye are called, with all lowliness and meekness, with long-suffering, forbearing one another in love; endeavoring to keep the unity of the Spirit in the bond of peace. There is one body, and one Spirit, even as ye are called in one hope of your calling; one Lord, one faith, one baptism, one God and Father of all, who is above all, and through all, and in you all.*" Ephes. iv. 1—6.

"*Now unto Him that is able to keep you from falling, and to present you faultless before the presence of his glory with exceeding joy, to the only wise God our Saviour, be glory and majesty, dominion and power, both now and ever. Amen.*" Jude, 24, 25.

SEVENTEENTH LECTURE.

EPHESIANS II.—14, 15, 16, 17.

"For he is our peace, who hath made both one, and hath broken down the middle wall of partition between us; Having abolished in his flesh the enmity, even the law of commandments contained in ordinances; for to make in himself of twain one new man, so making peace; And that he might reconcile both unto God in one body by the cross, having slain the enmity thereby: And came and preached peace to you which were afar off, and to them that were nigh."

WE have seen in our last Lecture, the distinction between Jews and Gentiles,—that although all were alike sinners before God, as we see from the first to the third verses of this chapter, yet that there was, in the case of the Gentiles, a peculiar degree of alienation from God, they were in a much more deplorable condition than the Jews. This has been shown in our last Lecture. "*At that time ye were without Christ, being aliens from the commonwealth of Israel, and strangers from the covenants of promise, having no hope, and without God in the world.*" But he adds, "*But now in Christ Jesus, ye who sometimes were far off, are made nigh by the blood of Christ.*" Then the Apostle proceeds to explain *how* they were made nigh.—He shows the mode in which it was effected, that Jews and Gentiles should be brought nigh, both to each other and to God, "FOR HE IS OUR PEACE, WHO HATH MADE BOTH ONE,"—&c.

Now, observe,—First, "PEACE" between Jew and Gentile, making them, who were so totally separated from each other, "BOTH ONE." Then, "PEACE" between both and God,—having been both separated from Him, and being both brought nigh to Him. Now, I say, first, that this passage shows us, that peace was made between Jew and Gentile. You know what a barrier God had erected between the Jews and all the other nations of the earth,—what an impenetrable barrier. We should go through the whole of the Jewish polity, civil and ecclesiastical, if we were to enumerate all the means by which this separation had been effected.

There was circumcision—their sacrifices—their passover—their priesthood—their daily food—the whole system of their worship and ordinances,—by all these means they were separated from all the other nations of the earth. God had placed these as an impassable barrier between them. You see this mentioned in a variety of passages in the Scripture, but I shall only point your attention to one or two,—for instance, Esther iii. 8, you see here what the Gentiles thought of the Jews,—"*And Haman said unto king Ahasuerus, there is a certain people scattered abroad and dispersed among the people in all the provinces of thy kingdom; and their laws are diverse from all people; neither keep they the king's laws.*" This was the ground on which Haman induced Ahasuerus to issue his decree for the destruction of the Jews,—the complete separation there was between them and all the rest of the nations. And again, you see that marked in a passage, familiar no doubt, to you all, Acts x. 28, where Peter says to Cornelius, "*ye know how that it is an unlawful thing for a man that is a Jew to keep company or come unto one of another nation. But God hath showed me that I should not call any man common or unclean,*"—as the Jews had always considered the Gentiles.

Now, I need not quote other passages, to prove to you a fact with which, of course, you are all acquainted, but the argument of the Apostle in the passage I have read is this, that all these ordinances, all these means by which the Jews were separated from all the other nations of the earth, had all been done away by Christ. Consider the verses in reference to this point, the reconciliation of Jew and Gentile, "FOR HE IS OUR PEACE, WHO HATH MADE BOTH ONE, AND HATH BROKEN DOWN THE MIDDLE WALL OF PARTITION BETWEEN US; HAVING ABOLISHED IN HIS FLESH THE ENMITY,"—and you see what that enmity was,—what it was that constituted that enmity,—"EVEN THE LAW OF COMMANDMENTS, CONTAINED IN ORDINANCES; FOR TO MAKE IN HIMSELF OF TWAIN ONE NEW MAN, SO MAKING PEACE; AND THAT HE MIGHT RECONCILE BOTH UNTO GOD IN ONE BODY BY THE CROSS, HAVING SLAIN THE ENMITY THEREBY; AND CAME AND PREACHED PEACE TO YOU WHICH WERE AFAR OFF, AND TO THEM THAT WERE NIGH."

Now we shall see that all these things were done away in Christ. Circumcision is done away, as you see in Colossians iii. 10, 11, "*And have put on the new man, which is renewed in knowledge after the image of him that created him: where there is neither Greek nor Jew, circumcision nor uncircumcision, Barbarian, Scythian, bond nor free: but Christ is all, and in all.*" The rite of circumcision is superseded by baptism, "*for in Christ*

Jesus neither circumcision availeth anything, nor uncircumcision, but a new creature." Gal. vi. 15,—He saith in another passage, "*for as many of you as have been baptized into Christ have put on Christ. There is neither Jew nor Greek, there is neither bond nor free, there is neither male nor female: for ye all are one in Christ Jesus.*" Gal. iii. 27, 28.

Again, the Sacrifices were done away. You see this in innumerable passages, I shall merely quote one, Hebrews x. 4, where the Apostle says, "*It is not possible that the blood of bulls and of goats should take away sins,*" speaking of the sacrifices as "*a shadow of good things to come,*" "even of the sacrifice of Christ," "*wherefore when he cometh into the world, he saith, sacrifice and offering thou wouldest not, but a body hast thou prepared me:*" &c.—he quotes here Psalm xl. 6, 7, 8, and then mark the Apostle's reasoning upon it, "*above*"—that is, "*in the first place, when he said, sacrifice and offering, and burnt-offerings and offering for sin, thou wouldest not, neither hadst pleasure therein; (which are offered by the law;) then said he, Lo, I come to do thy will, O God, he taketh away the first,*"—that is, all the legal sacrifices, He sweeps them all away at once, "*that he may establish the second,*"—that is, His own sacrifice,—"*by the which will*" (by His doing His Father's will, or by the decree of which will, since He hath fulfilled it,) *we are sanctified, through the offering of the body of Jesus Christ once for all.*" Therefore, in writing to the Hebrews, he tells them, that, while the continual repetition of their sacrifices proved that they could not take away sin, they are all done away by the one atoning sacrifice of the Lord Jesus Christ, because by Him is the remission of sins. So he argues conclusively in this chapter, and proves, that the sacrifices were repeated because they could not take away sin; but that the sacrifice of Christ was offered once for all, because in it, there is full and everlasting remission of sin.

Then, their Passover was taken away. You recollect the remarkable words of our blessed Lord, in St. Luke xxii. 15, 16, "*He said unto them, with desire I have desired to eat this passover with you before I suffer; for I say unto you, I will not any more eat thereof, until it be fulfilled in the kingdom of God.*" What did our blessed Lord mean by these words, "*until it be fulfilled in the kingdom of God.*" If you turn to 1st Corinthians, v. 7, you will find the explanation of it,—"*Christ our passover is sacrificed for us.*" When He bowed that blessed head upon the cross, and said, "*It is finished,*" then that passover was fulfilled in the kingdom of God, the Lamb of God, typified by the paschal lamb, being then slain upon the accursed tree—the blood, typified by that sprinkled on the lintels and door posts of the Israelites, was then poured out from the side, hands and feet of the dying Saviour, and that precious blood proclaimed in the record of His eternal word both to Jew and Gentile, guilty sinners like us, that it might be sprinkled upon our consciences and our souls, and that we might be passed over in the day of God's vengeance. Oh, that it may be so! Oh, remember that passover is "*fulfilled in the kingdom of God,*"—remember, "*Christ our passover is sacrificed for us, therefore let us keep the feast, not with the old leaven, neither with the leaven of malice and wickedness, but with the unleavened bread of sincerity and truth.*" 1st Cor. v. 7, 8.

Again, the Priesthood was another barrier between the Jews and all the other nations of the earth. But that priesthood is all done away in our glorious Redeemer. You see this argued at length in Hebrews, vii. The Apostle argues in verses 11, 12, of that chapter, "*if perfection were by the Levitical priesthood,—(for under it the people received the law,) what further need was there that another priest should rise after the order of Melchisedec, and not be called after the order of Aaron? for the priesthood being changed, there is made of necessity a change also of the law.*" He then speaks of our blessed Lord; of Him, he says, verse 16, "*who is made, not after the law of a carnal commandment, but after the power of an endless life,*" and then, verses 23, 24, 25, "*and they truly were many priests, because they were not suffered to continue by reason of death: but this man, because he continueth ever, hath an unchangeable priesthood. Wherefore, he is able also to save them to the uttermost that come unto God by him, seeing he ever liveth to make intercession for them,*" and he closes the chapter in these words, "*for the law maketh men high priests which have infirmity; but the word of the oath, which was since the law, maketh the Son, who is consecrated for evermore.*" Therefore, the Lord Jesus Christ has superseded the whole of the Levitical priesthood; but He has not come to establish another priesthood as a priesthood to offer sacrifice for sin. Recollect, that all the Lord's people are called "*an holy priesthood,*" and so, we call the ministers of our church, whose business it is to offer up prayers, whose business it is to administer the ordinances of the Lord, we call these priests, as being appointed in the Christian covenant, "*to offer up spiritual sacrifices, acceptable to God, by Jesus Christ.*" 1 Pet. ii. 5. But when this principle is set forth, that the priesthood of the church is appointed to offer sacrifices for sins—when, for example, that blessed ordinance, the commemoration of our blessed Lord's sacrifice, is corrupted from its glorious intention—and instead of being made, as it is, the blessed memorial of the finished sacrifice of Immanuel—when it is corrupted and perverted into a sacrifice, propitiatory unto God for sin,—the priesthood of the Lord Jesus Christ is denied—the work, the sacrifice of Christ is denied—the axe is laid to the very root of the Gospel, and instead of preaching "*Jesus Christ, and him crucified,*" men, whether in the church of Rome or in the church of England, who preach such falsehood as that, preach not Jesus Christ, but themselves as the priests and ministers to take away sin from men. Mark this. Christ hath finished transgression, Christ is the priest, the only priest to offer up sacrifices to God for sin. Beware, how you turn your poor guilty consciences from the Lord Jesus Christ to priests or ministers.

Now, my dear Roman Catholic friends, if I address, as I trust I do, some of you to-day, this is one of the desperate corruptions of your church, that your priests are called sacrificing priests,—they profess to offer sacrifice for your sins, they call the mass "a propitiatory sacrifice." Beloved friends, the good news of the Gospel is, that our precious Redeemer hath offered one sacrifice for sins.—Oh, look unto Him. There can be no repetition of it. Repetition must prove its utter insufficiency. That is the argument of the Apostle on the Jewish sacrifices, that the repetition of the sacrifices proves their inefficiency, their imperfection, but the oneness of the sacrifice of the Lord Jesus Christ proves that our blessed Redeemer's sacrifice was sufficient once for all, as he says in Hebrews x. 11, 14, "*Every priest standeth daily ministering and offering oftentimes the same sacrifices, which can never take away sins:—but this man, after he had offered one sacrifice for sins forever, sat down at the right hand of God; from henceforth expecting till his enemies be made his footstool. For by one offering he hath perfected forever them that are sanctified.*" Why? because it was finished, the work was done, salvation was completed, the good tidings of the Gospel which He commissioned His Apostles to preach to sinners, now proclaim finished salvation through His precious blood shed once for all. Through Him this barrier of the priesthood between Jew and Gentile is swept away, and both Jew and Gentile pointed to the great High Priest, who "*ever liveth to make intercession for us.*"

Their daily food was also another barrier. You see that in Acts x., where the Apostle Peter, in the vision that he had of a sheet let down from heaven, in which were numbers of beasts of all kinds, four-footed beasts and creeping things, all mingled together, which, if you recollect, were separated by their law for the use of the Jews,—you remember the distinction marked between clean and unclean beasts, so that the Jews were obliged in their daily food to take care that they eat nothing unclean; and even to this day, most Jews will not touch a morsel of meat that has been slain by any one but their own Rabbies; they must have their meat slain by them, that they may be sure, that according to their law, not a drop of blood is left in it. At the same time that this vision appeared to Peter, "*there came a voice to him, rise, Peter, kill and eat,—but Peter said, not so, Lord; for I have never eaten anything that is common or unclean. And the voice spake unto him again the second time, what God hath cleansed, that call not thou common.*" Acts x. 13, 14, 15. God hath broken down now, the barrier between Jew and Gentile, which consisted so much in the use of certain food, in things clean and unclean. God hath abrogated that now, God hath cleansed it, therefore thou art no longer to call that common. You see this set forth in Romans xiv. This principle could not be brought immediately into operation among the Jewish converts. The Jewish converts had been all their lives accustomed to the strictest care and vigilance in what they eat; and they could not be brought at once to see, that there was no difference between clean and unclean meats: and therefore, their consciences were in a great number of instances, extremely scrupulous, and could not touch the things that they had been accustomed to consider unclean. This is that principle on which the Apostle writes in Romans xiv., to which it is important to advert. It begins, "*Him that is weak in the faith, receive ye, but not to doubtful disputations; for one believeth that he may eat all things, another who is weak, eateth herbs.*" Some of the Jews did not think that they might eat all things, others of them did. Then the Apostle is here exhorting them to patience and forbearance and tenderness with one another on such points as these,—because, if a man's conscience is not sufficiently enlightened on a subject, provided he believes the truth, you are to receive him as a Christian brother, but not "*to doubtful disputations.*" This shows us, that there are many points on which the consciences of many may be weak, that is, not clearly enlightened, and that we should be tender and kind, and charitable, and careful of wounding them on minor indifferent points, if they are, by God's grace, brought to hold the head, and lean on Christ Jesus the Lord, as you observe the Apostle says, "*Him that is weak in the faith,*"—"*in the faith,*"—though "*weak*" in it. He says, verse 14, "*I know and am persuaded by the Lord Jesus, that there is nothing unclean of itself, but to him that esteemeth anything to be unclean, to him it is unclean.*" I read this verse to show you the complete abrogation of the ceremonial law on this subject. "*I know and am persuaded by the Lord Jesus, that there is nothing unclean of itself.*" Now, that text completely shows, that the whole system of clean and unclean meats is abrogated by the Christian dispensation. But I have known some instances, of devoted servants of God, who have had a tenderness of conscience about eating blood, they would not therefore eat game, or any animal that was shot. I have known highly intelligent Christians whose consciences are tender on the subject. I merely mention it to illustrate what the Apostle means—namely, persons whose consciences are weak in things in which the mind is not enlightened. But you see the ordinances as to all unclean meats were completely done away by the Lord Jesus, "*nothing is unclean of itself,*" says the Apostle, "*but to him that esteemeth anything to be unclean, to him it is unclean.*" If a man thinks he is doing wrong in anything, let him not do it,—"*happy is he that condemneth not himself in that thing which he alloweth.*" verse 22.

The whole system of the worship of the Jews was another barrier.—It is unnecessary for me to dwell on this for a moment, because you know it must have separated them from the whole world. You will find that dwelt on at large, in Hebrews, ix. 9, 10, 11, 12, where the Apostle speaks both of their worship and its abrogation, by the fulfilment of its types, "*Which was a figure,*" (that is, their worship, their tabernacle worship,) "*for the time then present, in which were offered both gifts and sacrifices, that could not make him that did the service perfect, as pertaining to the conscience; which stood only in meats and drinks, and divers washings, and carnal ordinances, imposed on them till the time of reformation. But Christ being come an high priest of good things to come, by a greater and more perfect tabernacle, not made with hands, that is to say, not of this building; neither by the blood of goats and calves, but by his own blood, he entered in once into the holy place, having obtained eternal redemption for us."* All that worship of theirs, was but an emblem of the great and glorious work of Jesus—their sacrifices finished in the sacrifice of Christ—their priesthood abrogated in the priesthood of Christ. No longer was the High Priest to enter into the holy place with blood of others—when the blessed Jesus bowed His head on the cross, the vail was rent in twain from the top to the bottom, to show that the way into the Holiest of all was now made manifest to the sinner—when He Himself, the Great High Priest, passed into the heavens, there "*to appear*," once for all, and that forever, "*in the presence of God for us.*" Therefore, you perceive that all the ordinances that had separated the Jew from the Gentile, had been completely done away. Now, let us read over the passage again, and I trust you will all understand it clearly, "HE IS OUR PEACE, WHO HATH MADE BOTH (Jew and Gentile) ONE, AND HATH BROKEN DOWN THE MIDDLE WALL OF PARTITION BETWEEN US; HAVING ABOLISHED IN HIS FLESH THE ENMITY, EVEN THE LAW OF COMMANDMENTS CONTAINED IN ORDINANCES; FOR TO MAKE IN HIMSELF OF TWAIN ONE NEW MAN, SO MAKING PEACE; AND THAT HE MIGHT RECONCILE BOTH UNTO GOD IN ONE BODY BY THE CROSS, HAVING SLAIN THE ENMITY THEREBY; AND CAME AND PREACHED PEACE TO YOU WHICH WERE AFAR OFF, AND TO THEM THAT WERE NIGH." So these are His own blessed words, speaking of the Gentiles, "*Other sheep I have, which are not of this fold: them also I must bring, and they shall hear my voice; and there shall be one fold, and one shepherd.*" John x. 16, "*Where there is neither Greek nor Jew, circumcision nor uncircumcision, Barbarian, Scythian, bond nor free: but Christ is all, and in all.*" Col. iii. 11.

But this passage of Scripture, not only shows, that He had made peace between Jew and Gentile, but further, "THAT HE MIGHT RECONCILE BOTH UNTO GOD IN ONE BODY, BY THE CROSS, HAVING SLAIN THE ENMITY THEREBY."

Now let me call your attention to the difference that there is between these two words, or rather this same word in these two verses. The word "enmity" in the 15th verse, and the word "enmity" in the 16th verse. The enmity in the 15th verse is the enmity between Jew and Gentile, "HAVING ABOLISHED IN HIS FLESH THE ENMITY," and He tells you what that enmity was, "EVEN THE LAW OF COMMANDMENTS, CONTAINED IN ORDINANCES." But the "enmity" in the 16th verse, is the enmity that both Jew and Gentile have to God. This is the enmity that you read of in Romans viii. 7, "*the carnal mind is enmity against God.*" But mark, too, the different expressions that are used—"HAVING ABOLISHED IN HIS FLESH THE ENMITY, (between Jew and Gentile) EVEN THE LAW OF COMMANDMENTS, CONTAINED IN ORDINANCES"—but the enmity between God and man is spoken of differently,—"HAVING SLAIN THE ENMITY THEREBY." The first enmity is "ABOLISHED"—the enmity between Jew and Gentile is taken away, the commandments and ordinances are abrogated. The second enmity between them and God, is "SLAIN," because the carnal mind, the carnal nature, the carnal heart, the old man, all the rebellion of the believer against his God, is slain forever—dead upon the cross of Christ. I pray you attend to this. He says "HAVING SLAIN THE ENMITY THEREBY." Look to Romans vi. 6, 7, "*Knowing this, that our old man is crucified with him, that the body of sin might be destroyed, that henceforth we should not serve sin. For he that is dead is freed from sin.*"

I have dwelt very often on this passage of Scripture and the glorious truth contained in it. But now, let me dwell on it again, for we ought all to dwell on it every day,—"*our old man is crucified with him, that the body of sin might be destroyed, that henceforth we should not serve sin, for he that is dead is freed from sin.*" There is no sin chargeable upon a dead body, a dead body can have no sin. He that believeth in Christ Jesus the Lord is accounted by God as dead with Christ upon the cross; he is accounted as one with Christ, and dead with Christ. As the justice of God had been fully satisfied, all the demands of God's righteous law had been finished when Jesus died—finished forever, not only for the Jew, but for every sinner that believeth on Him,—so all who believe are dead with Christ, as you have in this chapter, Romans vi. 11, "*Likewise reckon ye also yourselves to be dead indeed unto sin, but alive unto God through Jesus Christ our Lord,*" and in Colossians iii. 3, "*Ye are dead, and your life is hid with Christ in God.*" What is the practical application of this? Look to the next chapter, Romans vii., and you will see it practically applied by the Apostle Paul;—he, speaking of his own sense of sin, his own corruption, his own burden, says, "*I see a law in my members warring against the law of my mind, and bringing me into captivity to the law of sin which is in my members.*" He felt what you, believer, feel. I say, you believer,—every one of you who believe the Gospel of Jesus, feels as Saint Paul felt—if you believe, you feel within, your own corrupt heart, rebellious against your conscience, against your own standard of right, which is the holy law of God, and when you would desire to do good, you find evil present with you, you feel that "*law in your members, warring against the law of your mind, and bringing you into captivity to the law of sin that is in your members,*"—it is the law of your body of sin and death,—you feel that law evermore contending against the law of your mind, and bringing you into captivity every day. This very day, since you came into this congregation, there is not a single one among you, that has been able to worship God as you desire to do. There is not a single one among you who feels you have worshipped God as you ought to do. Any of you who are dead in trespasses and sins,—you think you are very good—you have come to church,—you have said your prayers,—as you call it, and you think you are very good for doing so. But you, believer, feel very differently, you feel your poor heart distracted, vain and foolish thoughts have come into your mind since you came into this house, and defiling all your prayers, you feel how little you worship God as you long to do,—you mourn that you are continually more inclined merely to "say your prayers" than to pray—thus you feel that corrupt heart of yours warring against the law of your mind, you feel you cannot do as you ought,—so did the Apostle Paul, and then he cries out, "*Oh, wretched man that I am, who shall deliver me from the body of this death?*" then he adds, "*I thank God, through Jesus Christ our Lord,*"—as much as to say, "I am delivered from it, it is dead with Christ, though it is living in me—working in me—though it is bringing my heart down—making me sink under a sense of my own guilt and vileness,—yet, I thank God it is dead with Christ—it is crucified with Him—its transgression is finished—its sin is made an end of—it never can come against me—my God has blotted it out—the blood of the Lamb has washed it away, and therefore, '*I thank God through Jesus Christ.*' My blessed Redeemer has slain the enmity of this guilty heart to God, and so has reconciled me, a guilty sinner to my God and Father." Oh! then, rejoice, believer, lift up your heart, look to your Lord and Saviour, triumph over death, sin, and hell, and thank your God through Jesus Christ our Lord. Then—when groaning and brought low as he was—then—when like him constrained to cry out, "*Oh, wretched man that I am, who shall deliver me from the body of this death?*" let faith triumph over sin and death, and say, "*I thank God through Christ Jesus.*" That is faith, that is trust, that is confidence in God's blessed word. "*Lord increase our faith.*"

So then, "HAVING SLAIN THE ENMITY THEREBY," and reconciled Jew and Gentile unto God, "IN ONE BODY BY THE CROSS, HE CAME AND PREACHED PEACE TO YOU WHICH WERE AFAR OFF, AND TO THEM THAT WERE NIGH,"—peace to the Gentile, and peace to the Jew, "PEACE TO THEM THAT WERE AFAR OFF, AND TO THEM THAT WERE NIGH." And is not this peace? Is it not peace to see your sins blotted out through the blood of Jesus? When Jesus has made peace by the blood of His cross, what can make war? If God is satisfied, if eternal justice is satisfied, what have you to fear then? "*It is God that justifieth, who is he that condemneth?*" Who can condemn when God acquits? when the Judge of heaven and earth pronounces the sinner innocent? Oh, what an amazing expression! what a paradox! But what a truth!! when God pronounces the sinner innocent?—Innocent sinner! Did you ever hear of such a thing? Yes, blessed be God! though a sinner, yet counted innocent,—though guilty, yet counted clear, through the blood of the Lamb! Oh, is not this peace? "HE CAME AND PREACHED PEACE TO YOU WHICH WERE AFAR OFF AND TO THEM THAT WERE NIGH." How did Christ preach peace? How does He preach peace? He preached peace by His prophets, Isaiah xxvii. 5, "*Let him take hold of my strength, that he may make peace with me;*" (that is, Christ,) "*and he shall make peace with me.*" Then again He saith, lii. 7, "*How beautiful upon the mountains are the feet of him that bringeth good tidings, that publisheth peace; that bringeth good tidings of good, that publisheth salvation; that saith unto Zion, thy God reigneth!*" And again, lvii. 19, "*I create the fruit of the lips; peace, peace to him that is far off, and to him that is near, saith the Lord; and I will heal him.*" This appears to be the very passage that the Spirit suggested to Saint Paul, when he quoted this verse, "PEACE TO YOU THAT ARE AFAR OFF, AND TO THEM THAT ARE NIGH."

Again, He preached peace by His angels. What was the song of the angels when the blessed Redeemer was born?—when they came to announce the birth of the Saviour? "*Glory to God in the highest, and on earth, peace, good will towards men.*"

Again, He came and preached peace by His own word, as he says in St. John's Gospel, xiv. 27, "*Peace I leave with you, my peace I give unto you, not as the world giveth, give I unto you. Let not your heart be troubled, neither let it be afraid.*" Again, He closes His conversation with His disciples in these words, "*These things have I spoken unto you that in me ye might have peace.*" John xvi. 33. And what was that peace? You see that peace explained in chapter xx. 19. After our blessed Lord arose from the dead, when He came on the first day of the week to the room where the disciples were assembled for fear of the Jews, what were His first words, when He came and stood in the midst of them? The first accents that fell from His blessed lips were these, "*Peace be unto you!*" The very men that "*forsook him and fled.*" Peter that denied Him with an oath—to him He saith, "*Peace be unto you.*" And again, in eight days after, to Thomas, who said he would not believe unless he put his finger into the print of the nails, and thrust his hand into His side,—what is the first word that Jesus speaks to them all? "*Peace be unto you, and when he had so said, He showed them his hands and his side.*" As much as to say, "*Peace be unto you,*" and, behold here is the purchase of that peace—here is the price of peace, here is the security of peace,—"*Behold my hands and my side.*" Well indeed may those words be added, "*Then were the disciples glad, when they saw the Lord.*" v. 21. "HE CAME AND PREACHED PEACE TO YOU WHICH WERE AFAR OFF, AND TO THEM THAT WERE NIGH." To His disciples, who were Jews—to Saul, a Jew too, a persecutor and blasphemer—to you, poor idolatrous worshippers of Diana at Ephesus,—and blessed be His name, it is the same peace to us who are far off, poor Gentiles in these islands.

So He preaches peace by His Apostles. What is His commission to them? "*Go ye into all the world, and preach the Gospel to every creature.*" Mark xvi. 15. What is that Gospel? Peace with God, through Jesus Christ our Lord, pardon through His blood, and peace through His salvation. So you see the Apostles preaching. I should go through the whole of the Apostolical epistles, were I to quote on this subject. How do they commence all their epistles? "*Grace, mercy, and peace from God the Father, and from our Lord Jesus Christ.*" How did St. Peter preach his first sermon? To whom was the first proclamation of peace made? To whom did the Apostles make the first proclamation of peace? To the men whose hands were embrued in the blood of Christ. See Acts ii., when Peter had testified against them for their crimes, and when they cried out, what shall we do? "*Repent, and be baptized every one of you, in the name of Jesus Christ, for the remission of sins, and ye shall receive the gift of the Holy Ghost, for the promise is unto you, and unto your children, and to all that are afar off, even as many as the Lord our God shall call.*" v. 38, 39. Come to the Saviour whom you have slain, come to Him, whose blood has stained your guilty hands, come to Him, receive pardon and peace. He preaches "PEACE TO YOU WHICH WERE AFAR OFF, AND TO THEM THAT WERE NIGH."

He preaches peace by His ordinances. What is that feast? What is that which is spread on that table? Who instituted that ordinance? For what purpose was it instituted? Was it not by Him "*who in the same night that he was betrayed took bread, and when he had given thanks, he brake it and gave it to his disciples, saying: take, eat, this is my body which is given for you: do this in remembrance of me. Likewise after supper, he took the cup, and when he had given thanks, he gave it to them, saying, drink ye all of this, for this is my blood of the new testament, which is shed for you and for many for the remission of sins. Do this, as oft as ye shall drink it, in remembrance of me.*" The pledge of peace—the memorial of peace, purchased by the blood of Jesus, just as fresh this day as when it came from His own blessed hands. There is the ordinance remaining, immutable to this day, from the night He instituted it among His disciples to this moment. There it is, just as it was, broken bread and poured out wine, the memorial of peace, and this "TO YOU WHO WERE AFAR OFF," says the Apostle, "AND TO THEM THAT WERE NIGH."

Oh, blessed be God! peace is purchased for them that are afar off, and I dare say, I address some sinners who are very far off from God, to-day. I have no doubt, I address many who are very far off from Him indeed—sunk in sin and wickedness—coming into a church—perhaps, they do not know why—perhaps some—who seldom attend a place of public worship—sabbath-breakers—liars—drunkards—thieves—murderers—adulterers—all, or any other class of sinners. If such be your character, you are far from God—you have no peace with God—no comfort—terror at the thought of death—trying to forget that you are immortal beings—hating anything that forces you to remember it—perhaps greatly displeased, now, at my thus addressing you—perhaps anxious to go, but ashamed to go out of the church—ashamed to get up and go out—hating me, for testifying against your guilt and misery; and thinking I am speaking to your case—perhaps you think so—an accusing conscience has a fearful power in applying the Word of God. You are far from God. What shall I say to you? What is my commission to you? "PEACE, PEACE TO YOU WHO ARE AFAR OFF."

However guilty your poor soul is, the message of the Gospel is peace. The message of God's law indeed is terrible—the message of God's justice is terrible—it is vengeance, judgment, curse, death and hell. Oh! "*consider this, ye that forget God, lest he pluck you away, and there be none to deliver you.*" But that is not the message of the Gospel. I must speak of these things to you, but for what purpose? to enhance to you the glory of the everlasting Gospel, the riches of Immanuel's grace, who sends a message of peace and mercy to your souls, "PEACE, PEACE TO YOU WHO ARE AFAR OFF."

I address, I doubt not, some, who compared with you, think they are very nigh, some who may be very diligent in all their observances of religion, some Pharisees who are strict in all the ordinances of their Church, and who would not for the world, omit one of them,—but who still are resting their souls on these observances and ordinances, resting their souls on what they are doing for themselves. They may be said in one sense to be nigh to God; for they attend on the worship of God, "*they draw nigh with their lips*," but "*their heart is far from Him*," they are just as far from peace as you, such persons are all alike far from peace,—they are as far from peace as the publicans of old. The Pharisees and Scribes were just as far from peace and from God, as the publicans and harlots; and so it is with them. Indeed, often as of old, the publicans and harlots go into the kingdom of God before such, and often it is, that to a poor, wretched, guilty, vile sinner, whose character is blasted among men—the sound of the Gospel will reach his ear—the peace of Christ Jesus will touch his heart—his soul will be melted at the foot of the cross, and he will come, like her who had her mighty debt forgiven—lie down at his Saviour's feet and wash them with his tears.

Oh, that it may be so among you to-day! And remember, dear fellow-sinner, whoever you are, there is but one peace. "PEACE TO YOU WHO ARE AFAR OFF AND TO THEM THAT ARE NIGH," peace to the Gentile—peace to the Jew,—peace to all who bear the name of Christian, whose heart may be as far from God, as Jew or Pagan—our message is, peace to all through the blood of Christ.

Oh! that God, by the blessed power of His Spirit, may bring this home to your hearts and consciences, my friends, that you may know what it is to have peace with God through Christ. May the Lord apply it,—may the Lord bring it home with demonstration of the Spirit and of power to your souls, that you may know the sweetness of having the blessed message of God's mercy.

and the blessed ordinance of Christ's salvation spread before you, and that your souls may be enabled to feed on Him who is our Peace, our Rest, our Rock, our Salvation,—to "feed on Him in your hearts, by faith, with thanksgiving." Amen.

EIGHTEENTH LECTURE.

EPHESIANS II.—18.

"For through him we both have access by one Spirit unto the Father."

ON the last day, we considered the state of the Gentiles by nature, as expressed in 11th and 12th verses—severed from the people of God, the Jews—severed from the ordinances and the revelation of God, and consequently from God Himself. "*Having no hope, and without God in the world.*" We considered the means by which they were brought nigh to the people of God—brought from a state of guilt and condemnation, into a state of union with God's people, and into a state of peace with God Himself, even by Christ Jesus. "*Now in Christ Jesus,*" adds the Apostle, in the 13th verse, "*ye who sometimes were afar off are made nigh by the blood of Christ,*"—made nigh to the Church of the Jews,—Jew and Gentile united together, and both made nigh to God—all one in Christ Jesus; "*for he is our peace.*" He—that is Christ Jesus, "*who hath made both one,*"—Jew and Gentile who believe in Him, —"*and hath broken down the middle wall of partition between*" us, —which separated the Jew from the Gentile,—"*having abolished in his flesh the enmity, even the law of commandments contained in ordinances, for to make in himself, of twain, one new man, so making peace, and that he might reconcile both unto God in one body by the cross.*" Recollect, then, the way in which alone we can be reconciled to God,—by the blood of Christ, by the cross, "*having slain the enmity thereby:*" having slain the enmity between man and God by the cross, having "*borne our sins in his own body on the tree,*" 1 Pet. ii. 24,—having taken our flesh, "*that through death, he might destroy him that had the power of death, that is the devil; and deliver them, who through fear of death, were all their lifetime subject to bondage.*" Heb. ii. 14, 15, and so "*having made peace by the blood of his cross, he came and preached peace to you which were afar off, and to them that were nigh:*"—to the Gentiles who were afar off, and to the Jews who were nigh, who had the oracles of God, and the ordinances of God, and the means of grace, but who still, though nigh in outward form and privileges, were just as far separated in spirit and truth as you were.

Outward forms, ordinances, and privileges, may be said, in one sense, to bring a sinner nigh to God, as they do. They bring him within the means of grace, they enable him to come and hear the Gospel preached, to come and attend instruction from the word of the living God, as in Lectures, to come and attend the ordinances of God, as in public Worship and Sacraments, these things all bring a sinner, in a certain sense, outwardly nigh to God. You are all, of course, in this sense, far nigher to God than many of your poor countrymen and countrywomen, who have no Bible, no Gospel preached to them, no message of peace or salvation to their souls, but vain superstitions substituted for the Gospel of Christ;—you are much nearer to God in that sense than others. But remember that these things do not bring the sinner *spiritually* nigh to God; you may enjoy all these outward ordinances, and be just as far from God as the heathen, or the idolater who never heard His name. The Scribes and Pharisees were just as far from Christ as the worshipper of Diana of Ephesus, though they enjoyed all His ordinances, and in that sense were nigh to God; they disbelieved the record of the eternal Gospel, and were, in that sense, as far from God as the remotest heathens. Therefore, remember this distinction, and it is very important, for Alas! my dear friends, we are so apt to rest in outward means, and outward ordinances, to mistake *the forms of religion for religion itself*, the *privileges* of spiritual religion for *spiritual religion itself*—that we have great need to be driven every moment back into our own hearts, and to stop in the midst of ordinances and privileges, and ask ourselves,—"What is this to me? Is my soul brought nigh to God by the blood of Christ? Have I peace with God through Him that died on the cross? Am I ready and watching when my Master calls me? or when my Master comes?" These are important questions;—take heed, you do not rest in outward privileges. Outward privileges are only aggravations of guilt, if they do not bring us nearer to God in spirit and truth, therefore mark and recollect this distinction in reading this passage of Scripture—He "*came and preached peace to you which were afar off, and to them that were nigh.*"

The Apostle proceeds, "FOR THROUGH HIM WE BOTH HAVE ACCESS BY ONE SPIRIT UNTO THE FATHER." This is the text at which we commence this day. Observe in this passage, the only way in which a sinner can come to his God: "THROUGH HIM, WE BOTH HAVE ACCESS;" Jew and Gentile alike—none other access for either. Observe how this agrees with the expression of our blessed Lord Himself, in the 14th chap. of St. John's Gospel, 6th verse, "*I am the way and the truth and the life, no man cometh to the Father but by me,*" and again he says in the 10th chapter, 9th verse "*I am the door, by me, if any man enter in, he shall be saved, and shall go in and out and find pasture.*" Therefore, observe, through Him *alone* we have access. Now consider, what need of access a sinner has to his God. "*We must all appear before the judgment-seat of Christ, that every one may receive the things done in his body.*" 2 Cor. v. 10. Time is hurrying us on. We are, as it were, grasped in the mighty hand of time, and dragged or driven along, however reluctant we may be, to the precipice of death. Like the poor culprits of old, who were sentenced at Rome, to be hurled down from the summit of the Tarpeian rock, we are, as it were, hurried along under the sentence of death to the verge of the precipice of eternity;—on—on—down—down we must go. We cannot turn about and parley with the officers that are hurrying us along; we cannot turn about, and say to the minutes, hours, and days—"Oh! stop,—wait,—linger a little slower,—give me a little more time,—do not fly so fast,—a little space—a little respite." *Impossible!* on, on, on, on we must go; who or what shall arrest the rapidity of our progress? What barrier can be erected to stay the flight of time? Is it not necessary then, for the poor sinner to have access to his God? If you could suppose a culprit, such as I have been speaking of, doomed to be cast from the summit of the Tarpeian rock—if, when he was in the act of being dragged to the execution of his sentence, it were possible that he could even then have access to the means of pardon—if it were possible that even then, his voice might reach the ears of the judge who could reverse his sentence—Oh! with what joy would he pour forth that cry, would he send forth that supplication to the judge's ear, if haply indeed, his fate might be arrested, and he might be restored to liberty and life! Though we cannot pause on our progress to eternity, yet may we have access every moment to the ear of our Judge; and remember, that it is not a sinner crying to God for respite, and for pardon.—No—but this is the awful point of the case, that it is God crying to the sinner to receive respite and pardon; "*turn ye, turn ye, why will ye die?*" Remember this;—it is not, only, come you to God, cry you to the judge, for the judge will have mercy upon you. But the language of the Gospel is a message from your God to you, crying to you.—Oh! sinner, peace, peace, pardon, pardon, "*come unto me and I will give you rest,*" "*look unto me and be ye saved.*" Oh! think of this; "*he came and preached peace to you who were afar off,*" here is the access; you may have access continually to your God. God invites you,—commands you,—to cry to Him, to come to Him, He proclaims peace to you, however far—pardon, however guilty.

Now, "*through Him, we have access*"—then if we feel the need we have of this access, let us consider the nature of it. Let us open the 4th chapter of Hebrews, and we shall see, that such is the nature of the access which the sinner has to his God, that he is not only privileged to come, invited to come, but *to come with confidence and boldness.* Look at the last verse, "*let us therefore come* BOLDLY *unto the throne of grace, that we may obtain mercy, and find grace to help in time of need.*"

"*Let us therefore*"—wherefore?—what is the reason?—what is the means? You observe, it is exactly the same that is set before us in this text, for in this text it is said, "THROUGH HIM, WE HAVE ACCESS, BY ONE SPIRIT UNTO THE FATHER." Now, if we look at the reason, 4th chapter of Hebrews, why it is said, "*let us therefore come boldly to the throne of grace*,"—if we look at the word "*therefore*" and ask ourselves the question, *wherefore?* We shall find it answered in the 14th and 15th verses, "*Seeing then that we have a great high priest that is passed into the heavens, Jesus the Son of God, let us hold fast our profession. For we have not an high priest who cannot be touched with the feeling of our infirmities; but was in all points tempted like as we are, yet without sin. Let us* THEREFORE *come boldly unto the throne grace.*" Mark—"*Seeing then that we have a great high priest that is passed into the heavens.*" Who is this High Priest? what is the office of this Priest? what is the necessity of a Priest? what has a Priest to say to us? "*Every high priest is ordained to offer gifts and sacrifices.*" Heb. viii. 3. We see the office of a priest is to offer gifts and sacrifices. Then, we find in the 7th chapter of the Hebrews, 26th verse, "*Such an high priest became us*," was suited to us "*who is holy, harmless, undefiled, separate from sinners, and made higher than the heavens; who needeth not daily, as those high priests, to offer up sacrifices, first for his own sins, and then for the people: for this he did once, when he offered up himself; for the law maketh men high priests which have infirmity; but the word of the oath which was since the law, maketh the Son, who is consecrated for evermore.*"

Now we are told, in this passage of Ephesians which we have been reading, that sinners are "*made nigh by the blood of Christ*"—we are told that He slew the enmity between God and man, on the cross, by giving His own life on that cross for sinners—we are told that He offered up Himself as an atonement for man's transgressions,—He was a Priest, He was a victim,—such is the language of St. John, "*Behold the Lamb of God, that taketh away the sin of the world!*" Behold the Lamb of God slain on the cross for sin:—now, behold the Lamb risen from the dead, and ascended into heaven, not only a Lamb and a victim, but *a Priest*, "*he is passed into the heavens, Jesus, the Son of God*," "*having obtained eternal redemption for us.*" We read in the 9th chapter Hebrews, from the 24th verse, "*Christ is not entered into the holy places made with hands, which are the figures of the true; but into heaven itself, now to appear in the presence of God for us. Nor yet that he should offer himself often, as the high priest entereth into the holy place every year with blood of others; for then must he often have suffered since the foundation of the world: but now once in the end of the world hath he appeared to put away sin by the sacrifice of himself.*" And in the next chapter, from the 11th verse, "*Every priest standeth daily ministering, and offering oftentimes the same sacrifices, which can never take away sins; but this man, after he had offered one sacrifice for sins forever, sat down at the right hand of God; from henceforth expecting till his enemies be made his footstool; for by one offering he hath perfected forever them that are sanctified. Whereof the Holy Ghost also is a witness to us: for after that he had said before, this is the covenant that I will make with them after those days, saith the Lord: I will put my laws into their hearts, and in their minds will I write them: and their sins and iniquities will I remember no more. Now where remission of these is, there is no more offering for sin."* Where is remission of sins? whence is it? How is it to be found? In the blood of Christ. "*The blood of Jesus Christ cleanseth from all sin.*" Then, "*where remission of these is, there is no more offering for sin,*"—there is nothing more to be done.—"*Having, therefore, boldness to enter into the holiest by the blood of Jesus, by a new and living way, which he hath consecrated for us, through the veil, that is to say, his flesh; and having an high priest over the house of God; let us draw near with a true heart, in full assurance of faith, having our hearts sprinkled from an evil conscience, and our bodies washed with pure water. Let us hold fast the profession of our faith without wavering; (for he is faithful that promised:) and let us consider one another to provoke unto love and to good works: not forsaking the assembling of ourselves together, as the manner of some is; but exhorting one another: and so much the more, as ye see the day approaching.*" Heb. x. 19—25.

Now, to compare these passages of Scripture. We have here, in Ephesians, the blood of Christ bringing the sinner nigh—we have that blood poured out on the cross as a way of access—we have, in the 4th chapter of Hebrews, and in other passages to which I have called your attention, Jesus, the high priest, who is passed into the heavens, the Son of God, a merciful and faithful High Priest—we have his two offices as a Saviour:—his office as a victim, an atonement; and His office as a priest to carry that atonement into the presence of the Father—we have both these brought together, in the 10th chapter of Hebrews,—and in these three passages, we have announced this blessed truth, that a sinner, a guilty sinner,—you,—I,—any—every sinner, has access to God, freely, boldly, continually, through the blood of the victim, and the glorious intercession of the great High Priest, who hath taken that blood into the heavens, and appears with that blood as an all sufficient offering, to cleanse the chief of sinners, "THROUGH HIM WE BOTH HAVE ACCESS BY ONE SPIRIT TO THE FATHER." Thus, as in the 4th chapter of Hebrews, "*let us, therefore, come boldly to the throne of grace, that we may obtain mercy and find grace to help in time of need;*" and as in the 10th Hebrews, "*having, therefore, brethren, boldness to enter into the holiest by the blood of Jesus, by a new and living way which he hath consecrated for us, through the veil, that is to say, his flesh; and having an high priest over the house of God, let us draw near with a true heart, in full assurance of faith.*" Oh! sinner, see what an access there is for you here! There is no qualification necessary for you, except that which you possess; there is not one of us who has not this qualification,—the only qualification that is necessary for us to come with the greatest confidence to the throne of grace,—and what is that? It is that *we are sinners, that we are guilty sinners;* that is our qualification. What is our plea? There is the victim offered for the guilty,—there is the Great High Priest who is passed into the heavens, and who has carried that victim, His own pierced hands, and feet, and sides, to the throne of grace; that victim, that bleeding victim is the sinner's plea; the One who offers it, is the sinner's Priest, his Friend, his Refuge, his Redeemer, his God. What more can we want? Oh! my friends, that we were all but enabled to enjoy this blessed Refuge as we ought to do! When we think of the constant, the ever-during need the sinner has of access to the throne of grace! and of the glorious way of access,—Christ "*the way, and the truth, and the life,*" how can we sufficiently appreciate THE NATURE of this access. It is a free access, an open access, an access in which the sinner may have boldness with confidence, as we see in the very next chapter, Ephes. iii. 12, "*in whom we have boldness and access with confidence by the faith of Him.*" How blessed, then, is the thought that it is an *ever open access*, the way is always open, so saith David, "*Be Thou my strong habitation whereunto I may continually resort:*" Ps. lxxi. 3, "*continually resort:*" there is not a moment of our life, not a circumstance of our existence, there is not a state of want, misery, destitution, wretchedness, bereavement, guilt, ruin, there is no earthly position in which we can be placed, in which the cry of the Gospel is not just the same to us, "*come unto me, all ye that labor and are heavy-laden, and I will give you rest,*" Mat. xi. 28, "*look unto me and be ye saved.*" Is. xlv. 22.

Oh then consider, dear friends and fellow-sinners, consider what a privilege is here open to us! Here may we all have access, every Jew and every Gentile. But there is an important word here, there is an important person, an important agent, that must not be left. I fear not to assert, that the truths which I have just laid before you, and the passages of God's eternal Word which I have quoted to substantiate these truths, are as irrefragable as the foundations of the earth itself—for they are the truths of the living God. But such is your state, such is my state, that—important and true as they are, and supported as they are on the foundations of God's eternal Word—I might as well address them to the seats you sit on, as address them to you, or to myself, unless the Spirit of the Living God, who indited these truths, should bring them home to your hearts, and to mine. Therefore observe, "THROUGH HIM, WE HAVE ACCESS BY ONE SPIRIT TO THE FATHER." You see, how the Three Persons of the ever-blessed Trinity are brought together, in this verse, in their different offices, as they are in so many passages of God's Word. You see the Three Persons so distinctly mentioned here, that they cannot be confounded or mistaken.

"THROUGH HIM," through whom?—Christ, the mediator of the new covenant, God the Son.

"WE HAVE ACCESS" unto whom?—"UNTO THE FATHER," from whom the sinner is separated by nature—from whom he is at a distance—cast off by his own rebellion.

THROUGH HIM, WE HAVE ACCESS TO THE FATHER.

But who brings us? Do we come of ourselves? Are we willing, are we ready? *Never:—"you will not come to me, that you might have life."* John v. 40, is language that is just as suited to our hearts as to the hearts of those to whom it was addressed—the Scribes and Pharisees,—"*You will not come to me that you might have life.*" How are you brought?—"*Thy people shall be willing in the day of thy power.*" Ps. cx. 3. Our Lord saith, "*It is written in the prophets, and they shall be all taught of God; every man, therefore, that hath heard and hath learned of the Father, cometh unto me.*" John vi. 45. And thus "THROUGH HIM WE HAVE ACCESS, BY ONE SPIRIT UNTO THE FATHER."

The Spirit of God must quicken the soul, the Spirit of God must open the understanding, the Spirit of God must bring the truth home to the sinner's heart and conscience, or the sinner remains dead in trespasses and sins, and perishes in his iniquity, for "*no man can say, that Jesus is the Lord, but by the Holy Ghost,*" 1 Cor. xii. 3.

What therefore are we to do? We find these truths written in the word of the Living God,—our own guilt, our own misery, our own condemnation. We see written in that Volume, our own entire inability to do or think anything good. We see written in that word, the glorious testimony of salvation proclaimed fully, freely, through the blood of Christ, to the chief of sinners—we see that this is brought home to the sinner's heart by the word of God; accompanied by the Spirit of God; and we see that the Spirit of God is freely given to every poor sinner who asks for it. "*If a son shall ask bread of any of you that is a father, will he give him a stone? or if he ask a fish, will he for a fish give him a serpent? or if he shall ask an egg will he offer him a scorpion? If ye, then, being evil, know how to give good gifts unto your children, how much more shall your heavenly Father give the holy Spirit to them that ask him.*" Luke xi. 11, 12, 13. Now, there is Christ's promise,—take that promise, plead that promise on your knees before the Throne of God. Did you ever try it? Did you ever take your Bible and go into your closet, and take one of the promises of God, for example that promise in the 11th chap. Luke,—did you ever take that promise, kneel down on your knees, and cry to God thus:—

"Oh, God, I am a poor, lost, helpless, vile sinner: I have no inclination to come to Thee, I have no power to come to Thee; Lord, Thy word tells me, thy precious promise assures me, that Thou wilt give Thy Holy Spirit to them that ask Thee; Lord, I come, I would plead Thine own promise before Thee, it is Thy word, Lord; it is written, Lord, as a promise to poor guilty sinners

I come to Thee for bread, Thou wilt not give me a stone! My Father, my earthly father never cast me off; he never, when I went to him for bread, sent me empty away, or gave me a stone; O Lord, wilt Thou do so? Oh, no, Lord, I know that Thou wilt not, yea, how much more wilt Thou give Thy Holy Spirit to them that ask Thee. Oh, give it to me, incline my heart to read Thy blessed word, bring Thy promises home to my understanding, to my conscience, to my heart, teach me to know Christ as my refuge, teach me to bathe in the fountain of His precious blood, to wrap my soul in His spotless righteousness, give me access with confidence by the faith of Him to Thee. Lord hear me—Lord fulfil Thy promises for Jesus' sake to my soul."

Now did you ever do this? If a friend, a patron wrote to you, giving you a promise of anything that you wanted, and that you could not possibly obtain through any channel or from any person but Him, what would you do? Suppose he delayed to give it to you; suppose you did not get it in time as you required; suppose your need of the fulfilment of his promise pressed on you, what would you do? You would take his promise, go to him, or write to him, remind him of his own letter, tell him what he had promised you, tell him your want, ask him to fulfil his word. And is not that the use to make of the promises of the living God? Would you not expect your friend, if he were true—if he were a person of integrity and power,—would you not expect he would keep his word—that he would fulfil his promise? And shall we not trust in the truth—the faithfulness and power of our God? Did you ever know or hear of any one who trusted in the promises of God, and was disappointed? You never did, and you never shall. "*Heaven and earth shall pass away, but my words shall not pass away.*" Mat. xxiv. 35.

Then think of these things, consider, what a blessing is comprehended in this one verse; it is quite sufficient to consider at one time;—"THROUGH HIM, WE BOTH HAVE ACCESS BY ONE SPIRIT TO THE FATHER."

May the Lord the Spirit enable you and me to profit by this great and precious truth of the word of God this day, through our Lord Jesus Christ. Amen.

NINETEENTH LECTURE.

EPHESIANS II.—19.

"Now therefore ye are no more strangers and foreigners, but fellow-citizens with the saints, and of the household of God."

I HAVE endeavored in the course of my Lectures on this chapter, to impress on your minds the great truth which is so continually brought before us in the word of God,—namely, the actual state of every individual on the face of the earth, either that he is before God in the actual condition of guilt and condemnation, so that, if cut off in that state, he must perish. Or that he is, before God, in the actual state of acceptance and salvation; so that whenever he is called away in that state, he departs and is with Christ; so that he may say with the Apostle, "*whether we live, we live unto the Lord, or whether we die we die unto the Lord, whether we live therefore, or die, we are the Lord's.*" Rom. xiv. 8. And I wish you to bear this continually in mind, because I believe there is no one truth of which persons are more entirely ignorant than this. They believe they are in an *uncertain* state, they believe that they are in a *doubtful* condition, they will not say, that they are children of God; that, they think, would be too much to assume; they will not admit that they are children of Satan,—that, they consider would be too awful to contemplate: but remember, my friends, *you must be in one state or the other.* If you believe, that all sinners when they die, must go to either of two places, either enter into that "*rest which remaineth for the people of God,*" or that they must have their portion among those to whom the Lord shall say, "*depart ye cursed into everlasting fire, prepared for the devil and his angels:*" if you believe that that is the condition of every individual at the hour of their death, remember, they must be fitted for one or the other of these conditions, at every moment of their existence. You and I must be so now, and I entreat you to consider this chapter over and over again, with reference to this one great truth. Observe the condition in which the Apostle again and again asserts that men are by nature; and observe the state in which the Apostle testifies, that believers are by grace. It is to this latter view of the subject, our attention is called to-day.

On the last day, you recollect, we considered the access which the sinner has, through Christ, unto the Father, by the Spirit; and in the 19th and following verses, you see the state of every believer who enjoys this blessed access. "*Now therefore ye are no more strangers and foreigners, but fellow-citizens with the saints, and of the household of God; and are built upon the foundation of the Apostles and Prophets, Jesus Christ himself being the chief corner-stone, in whom, all the building, fitly framed together, groweth into an holy temple in the Lord, in whom ye also are builded together for an habitation of God through the Spirit."* Now, I pray you, refer to the 12th verse, and contrast it with the 19th. You see, in the former, the state in which he describes them as having been. "*At that time ye were without Christ, being aliens from the commonwealth of Israel, and strangers from the covenants of promise, having no hope, and without God in the world:*" that was their state;—observe now their present condition, 19 v. "NOW THEREFORE YE ARE NO MORE STRANGERS AND FOREIGNERS, BUT FELLOW-CITIZENS WITH THE SAINTS, AND OF THE HOUSEHOLD OF GOD:" you were "*aliens from the commonwealth of Israel, and strangers from the covenants of promise,*" but now "YE ARE NO MORE STRANGERS AND FOREIGNERS," you had "*no hope, and were without God in the world,*"—but now you are "FELLOW-CITIZENS WITH THE SAINTS, AND OF THE HOUSEHOLD OF GOD." Can there be a more plain or striking contrast between the two conditions than there is in these two verses, the 12th and 19th.

Now, there is one great blessing contained in these verses—and that is, that these two verses refer to the same individuals. Observe, you *were* so and so, you *are now* so and so. You and I certainly were, and perhaps, too, many among us yet are, as he describes in the 12th verse "*without Christ,*" and as to all real spiritual blessings, "*aliens from the commonwealth of Israel, strangers from the covenants of promise, having no hope, and without God in the world.*" These same individuals, who were in that condition, are now brought out of it; you are not what you were, the Apostle says, you are "NO MORE STRANGERS AND FOREIGNERS, BUT FELLOW-CITIZENS WITH THE SAINTS." Now, dear friends, is not this a most important question for us to consider? There may be many among us who have never seriously considered it; for certainly if there are any (as it is to be feared there are,) who are not brought to the knowledge of the Lord Jesus Christ, you never have considered this question—how am I brought from the one condition to the other, from being "*an alien and a stranger, without hope and without God in the world,*" how am I brought from this, to be made a "FELLOW-CITIZEN WITH THE SAINTS, AND OF THE HOUSEHOLD OF GOD?" Is it not most important that you should be brought from one state to the other? Consider what is your condition if you are not brought. And then consider, what is your blessed condition, if you are. Remember then, remember the way, 13th verse, "*Now in Christ Jesus ye who sometimes were far off, are made nigh by the blood of Christ.*" Let me dwell on this, for those whose consciences testify that they are not brought nigh, and let me illustrate the truth

We have just sung that beautiful hymn of Cowper's containing these lines:

"There is a fountain filled with blood,
Drawn from Immanuel's veins;
And sinners plunged beneath that flood,
Lose all their guilty stains.

The dying thief rejoiced to see
That fountain in his day;
And there may I, as vile as he,
Wash all my sins away."

Let us then consider the case of the Thief on the Cross. When he hung there as a malefactor, having joined his fellow-culprit as we know he did (Mat. xxvii. 44) in mocking Christ—in reviling that blessed Saviour who was hanging on the Cross beside him; what was his condition? Was he not, as those mentioned in the 12th verse, an "*alien from the commonwealth of Israel, and a stranger from the covenants of promise, having no hope, and without God in the world?*" But we see in his case the work of the Holy Ghost—there was no preaching to that thief, he had no Bible in his hand or in his heart when he was nailed to the cross—it was the Holy Ghost's work, whose special office it is, to take of the things of Christ, and show them to the sinner. He alone can enlighten by means—or, as in this case, without means. But when that blessed Spirit touched the poor thief's heart, and taught him to know, that he who was hanging crucified beside him, was the Lord of life and glory, that He was indeed the King of kings, in whom it was to be fulfilled, "*Lift up your heads, O ye gates, and be ye lift up, ye everlasting doors, and the King of glory shall come in.*" Ps. xxiv. 7.—I say, when that blessed Spirit touched this poor thief's heart, and taught him to know Christ, to turn to Him, whom but a moment before he had been reviling—to look to Him as his Refuge, and to cry to Him, "*Lord, remember me when thou comest into thy kingdom*"—what was then his condition? he was then "*no more a stranger and a foreigner, but a fellow-citizen with the saints, and of the household of God,*" his Lord's answer of mercy sealed his inheritance and adoption to his dying ear,—"*This day shalt thou be with me in Paradise.*" He was then ready to be transplanted to glory.

Now the same fountain that washed that thief is open to you and to me,—there is no other means to cleanse the least stain of sin, "*there is no other name under heaven given among men whereby we must be saved,*" Acts iv. 12. And if there be any of you who have not come to bathe in this fountain, Oh, come and bathe there to-day! See how soon the poor sinner can be washed in it! See, how soon the dying thief was washed in it! Turn ye then, and behold the blessed condition of those who are "*made nigh by the blood of Christ,*"—they are "NO MORE STRANGERS AND FOREIGNERS, BUT FELLOW-CITIZENS WITH THE SAINTS AND OF THE HOUSEHOLD OF GOD."

Consider the image used here by the Apostle—how it illustrates the difference between the state of man as unreconciled, and as reconciled to God.

A stranger and a foreigner in a city has no home there—he has no property—no privileges, no rights, in the city—no habits, interests, pursuits, in common with its inhabitants. Therefore his heart, his desires, his affections, his feelings, are alien from that city where he is a stranger, and are given to his own city and his home.

He is in all these points contrasted with the inhabitant of the city. There is his home—there his property—all the privileges and rights of the city belong to him; even though he is absent from it—still they are his—his interests and his cause are one with its inhabitants—therefore his heart, his desires, his affections, his feelings, are all identified with his city and his home.

How truly does this apply to the difference between the unconverted and converted sinner. Speak to a man who is not "*made nigh by the blood of Christ*," of the blessings, the rights, the privileges, the possessions, and the home of the saints—tell him of the great Charter of their Salvation, and all its glories in the blessed word of God—and you see he evinces that he is "*a stranger and a foreigner*," he shows he has neither home, property, privileges, interest, feeling, care, or concern in the matter. To dwell on such subjects—to engage in the pursuits, or to be occupied in the company of those who are "FELLOW-CITIZENS WITH THE SAINTS, AND OF THE HOUSEHOLD OF GOD," would be to him intolerable. His possessions, his home, his interests and his heart are in the world.

But not only are they strangers and foreigners, but enemies—men are more than aliens from a city, when the very name of its inhabitants is a term of reproach, as that of Samaritan was with the Jews. So they said to our Lord, "*Say we not well that thou art a Samaritan, and hast a devil.*" John viii. 48.

And alas! my friends, as I have before remarked, in what an awful state is the nominal Christian church.—In what an awful state is the Protestant Church, when there are so many thousands, nay, tens—hundreds of thousands belonging to it, who in their blindness and ignorance, take the very name of God's servants—the very name of those, of whom some serve Him here on earth, and some surround the Throne of His glory—to be fellow-citizens with whom is the highest privilege of man—and make it a nickname to mock at,—"SAINTS!!" The very term with multitudes is a name of scorn. Is not this an awful state of blindness and ignorance, when *even the title that God bestows on his people, is borrowed from His holy Word, as a name of reproach?* Are not these "*aliens?*" Are not these "*strangers and foreigners?*" But remember that the Church of Christ—those who are "*made nigh by the blood of Christ*," are truly enrolled among the saints; they are "FELLOW-CITIZENS WITH THE SAINTS," they are sanctified in Christ Jesus. Recollect the means whereby they are brought to God and sanctified. Recollect our Lord's own words to the Apostle Paul, when He sends Him to preach the Gospel to the Gentiles, He says, "*To whom now I send thee, to open their eyes, to turn them from darkness to light, and from the power of Satan unto God, that they may receive forgiveness of sins, and an inheritance among them which are sanctified, by faith that is in me.*" Acts xxvi. 17, 18. And recollect, in the 13th of Hebrews, the same truth is set before us, 11th and 12th verses, "*The bodies of those beasts, whose blood is brought into the sanctuary by the high priest for sin, are burned without the camp, wherefore Jesus also, that he might sanctify the people with his own blood, suffered without the gate.*" Thus they are sanctified by the blood of Christ, by faith in Christ, through the teaching of the Holy Ghost by the Word, that is, they are made saints, they are "*made nigh by the blood of Christ,*" they are made holy, they are taken from the mass of a guilty world, and they are "*washed, they are sanctified, they are justified, in the name of the Lord Jesus, and by the Spirit of our God,*" 1st Cor. vi. 11; therefore he says, "YE ARE FELLOW-CITIZENS WITH THE SAINTS." We have this expression used by the Apostle in the 3rd chapter of Philippians, though our translation does not exactly convey it, yet the original word is the same, —it is according to our translation, "*our conversation is in heaven,*" but the original word is, "*our citizenship* (πολιτευμα) *is in heaven,*" we are citizens of heaven;—our citizenship is there. St. Paul was a Roman citizen, he had the privileges, and enjoyed the privileges belonging to one. He demanded, as you recollect from Claudius Lysias the rights of Roman citizenship. But he was a citizen of a far higher city than that of Rome, he was a citizen of the Kingdom of God, he was a "FELLOW-CITIZEN WITH THE SAINTS."

We have this subject expanded more in the 12th chapter of the Hebrews, where the Apostle contrasts the state of those under the law, with that of those under the Gospel—of the Jews when in unbelief, with that of Jews as believers—of those under condemnation, with that of those who are sanctified in Christ, 18, 19, 20, 21, verses, "*For ye are not come unto the Mount that might be touched, and that burned with fire, nor unto blackness, and darkness, and tempest, and the sound of a trumpet, and the voice of words; which voice they that heard entreated that the word should not be spoken to them any more; for they could not endure that which was commanded, and if so much as a beast touch the mountain, it shall be stoned, or thrust through with a dart: and so terrible was the sight, that Moses said, I exceedingly fear and quake:*"

That is—ye are not come to the Mount that was to be seen and touched, namely, Mount Sinai—where the Law was given amidst thunderings and lightnings, and clouds and tempest—where blackness and darkness, and flame, and the terror of the trumpet, and the sentence of death pronounced against any, even a beast that should touch the mountain, all proclaimed aloud that "*the law worketh wrath.*" Rom. iv. 15, and that by its deeds "*no flesh could be justified.*" Rom. iii. 20, that it was—as it was, and is—a ministration not of life, but of death to the soul.

Ye are not come, saith the Apostle, to that Mount;—"*But,*" he adds in the 22, 23, 24, verses, "*Ye are come unto Mount Zion, and unto the city of the living God, the heavenly Jerusalem, and to an innumerable company of angels, to the general assembly and church of the first-born, which are written in heaven, and to God the Judge of all, and to the spirits of just men made perfect, and to Jesus, the Mediator of the new covenant, and to the blood of sprinkling, which speaketh better things than that of Abel.*"

The contrast in this passage of the Hebrews between the condition of the unbeliever and the believer, is the very same that we find in this chapter of the Epistle to the Ephesians, only expressed in different terms. Let me entreat those who hear, who have not fled to Christ for refuge, to consider how solemn that contrast is.

Some there are of you, perhaps, whose hearts are wholly occupied about this passing, perishing world,—taking anxious thought for "*what ye shall eat, and what ye shall drink, and wherewithal ye shall be clothed.*" Mat. vi. 31—thinking how you shall maintain yourselves—improve your trade—increase the profits of your shop or farm—advance yourselves in your profession—or perhaps only considering how you may amuse yourselves, if—in the lan guage of the poet, you are

> "Cursed with means
> To dissipate your days in quest of joy—"

but never—never thinking of your God, "*as for the ungodly, he careth not for God, neither is God in all his thoughts:*" Ps. x. 4, —never contemplating that awful eternity to which you are rushing on, as fast as time can hurry you; and never considering the fearful condition of the sinner, passing, in such a state, into the presence of his Judge.

Some perhaps there are again different from these—religious, not in God's way, but in their own. Many are religious in their own way, "*we have turned every one to his own way:*" Isa. liii. 6.—man has his own way of religion, as well as his own way of iniquity, and some of you may be very religious thus—laboring to wash your Ethiopian skin—to qualify yourselves to come into the presence of your Creator—abstaining from certain sins, and hoping that God will give due merit to your self-denial,—practising certain virtues, and expecting that God will give you credit and reward for them. So you may be either, perhaps *careless*, without *any religion*, or secure, as you vainly imagine, in a *false* religion—"*going about,*" like the Jews, "*to establish your own righteousness, and not submitting yourselves to the righteousness of God.*" Rom. x. 3. To whichsoever of these classes you belong, (and to some grade of these every unenlightened sinner may be reduced,) consider to what you are come. "*You are come to the mount that might be touched, that burns with fire, unto blackness and dark-*

ness, and tempest, and the sound of the trumpet, and the voice of words"—that sinners' ears could not endure.

That is, you are come to the mount of the Holy and Eternal Lawgiver—the flames of justice and the clouds of the outer darkness surround His throne—the tempest that shall sweep away every refuge of lies rolls before Him—the sound of the trumpet that shall summon the guilty to judgment, heralds the sentence of your doom—and the thunder of that voice that the ear of the unpardoned sinner can never bear to hear, peals from His lips.

You are come to the law, which, as a careless sinner, you are daring to despise—or, which, as a self-righteous Pharisee, you are vainly and ignorantly expecting to fulfil. You come to "*the ministration of death, written and engraven in stones,*" 2 Cor. iii. 7; you are come to "*the ministration of condemnation*" v. 9.—you are come to the law that condemns you—to the Judge that pronounces sentence upon you—you are drawing near to the mountain—and as certain as you come to it, you shall be, not "*stoned or thrust through with a dart,*"—but bound hand and foot, and cast into outer darkness, as a rebel against God! Such must be your state, if either living carelessly in your sins, or "*going about to establish your own righteousness,*" you know not Christ, and seek Him not. He is dead in vain for you. You are a "*stranger and a foreigner.*"

But if you have indeed "*fled for refuge to lay hold on the hope set before you,*" Heb. vi. 18,—if you know your sin and misery, and know Christ as the Hope and Refuge of your souls, Oh, lift up your head, and see the blessed testimony of your God concerning all who are indeed, "*made nigh by the blood of Christ,*"—you have access by Christ unto the Father, "*you are come unto mount Zion, unto the city of the living God,*" to "*the city which hath foundations, whose builder and maker is God,*" Heb. xi. 10, you are "FELLOW-CITIZENS WITH THE SAINTS." And, then, see what that city is,—"*the heavenly Jerusalem,*" there is your home—there the place which Christ hath gone to prepare for His people—there is your "*house not made with hands, eternal in the heavens,*"—2 Cor. v. 1, there your "*inheritance incorruptible, undefiled, and that fadeth not away.*" 1st Pet. i. 4. But you are not only come to His city, but His Household, ye are "FELLOW-CITIZENS WITH THE SAINTS, AND OF THE HOUSEHOLD OF GOD,"—and who are your fellow-citizens? who are members of this household? You are come to "*the innumerable company of angels, the general assembly and church of the first-born, which are written in heaven.*" Their names are enrolled there in the book of life, and you are their "FELLOW-CITIZENS," so your names must be written there too.

Who reigns in this city? "*and to God the Judge of all,*"—the Judge that has pronounced the sentence, not of condemnation, but of acquittal upon you, for "*it is God that justifieth, who is he that condemneth?*" Rom. viii. 33, 34, you are "*washed in the blood of the Lamb.*" You are come to Him, then, not as a Judge, but as a Father—not only to His city, but to His household—and you have come "*to the spirits of just men made perfect*," those who have gone before you, through the wilderness—some, perhaps near and dear to your hearts, who have trodden the pilgrimage through trials, sufferings, sorrows and sins—through vexations, cares, temptations, perplexities—tears often starting from their eyes—and many sighs bursting from their hearts—but who are now "*rested from their labors*," and departed "*to be with Christ, which is far better.*" Phil. i. 23,—you are come to these—and to Him who saved both them and you, "*to Jesus, the Mediator of the new covenant, and to the blood of sprinkling, which speaketh better things than that of Abel.*" "*You, who sometimes were far off, are made nigh by the blood of Christ*," "YOU ARE NO MORE STRANGERS AND FOREIGNERS, BUT FELLOW-CITIZENS WITH THE SAINTS, AND OF THE HOUSEHOLD OF GOD, AND ARE BUILT UPON THE FOUNDATION OF THE APOSTLES AND PROPHETS, JESUS CHRIST HIMSELF BEING THE CHIEF CORNER-STONE." Oh, what a blessed privilege it is for a sinner to be enabled to look to such a rest, such a city, and such a home.

Observe, he says, "*ye are not come unto the mount that might be touched*;" Sinai, with all its terrors and judgments, was visible and tangible, as the fruits of sin are sensibly felt and suffered here below—and so "*in this tabernacle we groan being burthened.*" But the blessings which are purchased for sinners by our glorious Lord are all as yet unseen. That for which we hope is hid from our eyes, for "*what a man seeth why doth he yet hope for? But if we hope for that we see not, then do we with patience wait for it.*" Rom. viii. 25,—so saith the Apostle, "*your life is hid with Christ in God.*" Col. iii. 3, the life that you enjoy is a hidden life;—you see it not, it is not a life of sense or of sight, it is a life of faith, "*we walk by faith, and not by sight.*" 2nd Cor. v. 7. Faith indeed may give substantializing views of this, but still it is "*the substance of things hoped for, the evidence of things not seen.*"

Oh, believers, consider what a blessed privilege it is to realize by faith the things we hope for! Oh, that we all could see, and feel, and rejoice by faith as we ought to do!

How would it lift up our hearts in the midst of our trials, cares, and conflicts within, and without, in our pilgrimage,—if, as we are toiling along in our weary journey, we could lift up our eyes and look at the turrets of the city whither we are going, and behold by faith the pinnacles of the New Jerusalem! Oh, blessed cheering prospect! Like the poor weary traveller, when he comes within sight of his home, and sees the smoke curling among the trees, and anticipates his reception, his welcome, and his rest. Oh, how blessed for a poor sinner, if he knows his privileges, to "*look for, and haste unto the coming of the day of God.*" 2 Pet. iii. 2. That is what St. Paul means in the passage of Philippians to which I have adverted, when he says "*our citizenship is in heaven.*" Observe the use he makes of it—"*from whence also, we look for the Saviour, the Lord Jesus Christ, who shall change our vile body, that it may be fashioned like unto his glorious body, according to the working whereby he is able to subdue all things unto himself.*" Phil. iii. 20, 21. And this, too, is what the Apostle John says in his first Epistle, 3rd chap. 1st and 2nd verses; —"*Behold, what manner of love the Father hath bestowed upon us, that we should be called the sons of God! therefore, the world knoweth us not, because it knew him not; beloved, now are we the sons of God; and it doth not yet appear what we shall be, but we know, that when he shall appear, we shall be like him; for we shall see him as he is.*"

You see with what confidence the Apostle speaks "*Beloved,* NOW ARE WE THE SONS OF GOD, *and it doth not yet appear what we shall be, but* WE KNOW *that when He shall appear, we* SHALL BE LIKE HIM, *for we shall see Him as He is.*" We are *His children,* we are "OF HIS HOUSEHOLD," we are "FELLOW-CITIZENS WITH HIS SAINTS," and, therefore we are "*looking for the coming of our Lord Jesus Christ, who shall change our vile body, that it may be fashioned like unto his glorious body, according to the working whereby he is able even to subdue all things to himself.*" This is the very same idea that the Apostle uses in the next chapter, "*for this cause I bow my knees to the Father of our Lord Jesus Christ, of whom the whole family in heaven and earth is named.*" Observe, "*the whole family in heaven and earth;*" one family:—part of the family are at home, part of the family are abroad, part are still travelling in the wilderness, and part have travelled through it, and have reached the end of their journey, and are at rest on the bosom of their Lord,

"The toilsome way thou 'st travelled o'er, and borne the heavy load,
But Christ hath taught thy languid feet, to reach his blest abode:
Thou 'rt sleeping now like Lazarus, upon his Father's breast,
Where the wicked cease from troubling, and the weary are at rest."

Part of the family are safe in Canaan, part are on their journey coming up to the River Jordan—

"One army of the living God,
At his command we bow,
Part of the host have crossed the flood,
And part are crossing now."

Some are beyond the flood, some coming up to the banks, but it is one family, "*the whole family in heaven and earth.*" And think you, that that family in heaven, are safer than the family on earth? No; for those who are on their way, are "*kept by the power of God through faith unto salvation.*" All who are looking to Jesus "*are no more strangers and foreigners, but fellow-citizens with the saints and of the household of God.*" Well then, is not this a blessed truth?

And now, believer, perhaps, you may be often weary in your earthly household. There may be many things in your tabernacle here that distress and afflict you. Your habitation may be poor, and very sad, and melancholy, in many respects. But, pause and look at the fact—Is that your household? Is that indeed your home? Is the place that you are living in here—is this your real rest? Nay, have you not another and a better household? Is not this rather your little tent, pitched here for a few nights, or the inn you are lodging at for a few days? Are you indeed a "FELLOW-CITIZEN WITH THE SAINTS"? Are you "OF THE HOUSEHOLD OF GOD?" What! "OF THE HOUSEHOLD OF GOD!!" think of this expression; "OF THE HOUSEHOLD." It is one word; it occurs but three times in the New Testament,—

I.—Galatians, vi. 5, where we are exhorted, "*while we have time let us do good unto all men especially unto them that are of* THE HOUSEHOLD *of faith.*"

II.—It occurs here where those who are of "THE HOUSEHOLD OF FAITH," are declared to be of "THE HOUSEHOLD OF GOD."

The last place it occurs is in 1st Tim. v. 8, in which it is said that "*if any man provide not for his own and specially for those* OF HIS OWN HOUSE *he hath denied the faith and is worse than an infidel.*" Shall the Lord commend to our special love and care, "THE HOUSEHOLD OF FAITH?" Shall he assure us that they are HIS HOUSEHOLD, HIS FAMILY? Shall He tell us, that he that "*provideth not for* HIS OWN HOUSE *hath denied the faith and is worse than an infidel?*" and shall not He provide for His OWN HOUSEHOLD? Yes! my brethren, "JEHOVAH-JIREH," is written on every page of the history of His Church. When He provided the Lamb for the burnt offering, He provided all things in Jesus; for "*He that spared not his own Son but delivered him up for us all, how shall he not with him also freely give us all things?*" Rom. viii. 32. Fear not, believer, "*all things are yours, whether Paul, or Apollos, or Cephas, or the world, or life, or death, or things present, or things to come, all are yours, and ye are Christ's, and Christ is God's.*" 1st Cor. iii. 21, 22, 23.

Fear not, believer, whatever be your wants, spiritual or temporal, fear not. It is written, "*my God shall supply all your need, according to his riches in glory by Christ Jesus,*" Phil. iv. 19. Surely this is the inheritance you derive under your Father's will—this is the possession which your Lord assures you is your own, as of His household. Therefore, lift up your heart, and look unto Jesus. "*Gird up the loins of your mind, be sober, and hope to the end for the grace that is to be brought unto you at the revelation of Christ Jesus.*" 1 Pet. i. 13.

And Oh! unbelievers, my poor unbelieving friends, if there be any here, who as yet know not, and belong not to this "HOUSEHOLD"—you too are uneasy perhaps, about your earthly habitation; and thinking how you may embellish, enlarge, adorn, improve it—perhaps meditating how you may exchange it for a better, thinking how happy you would be, if you were in such or such circumstances—or how much better off, if you were in such or such a place. Well—suppose your wishes gratified—your expectations realized—and that you had all your hearts could desire This question comes—"*what will you do in the end thereof?*" If this is your all, what a miserable all it is. Is it a cottage? Or is it a palace? How poor is a palace when the unhappy owner has no hope beyond it!—how poor is a throne!—how poor is a perishing world! Alas! "*what shall it profit a man, to gain the whole world and lose his own soul?*" Mat. xvi. 26. But, Oh! there is a better household, there is a better inheritance. Think what it is to be "OF THE HOUSEHOLD OF GOD!" Oh! look unto Christ, and be ye saved.—You have, no doubt, a wounded conscience, and a troubled heart. You have tried, perhaps, many physicians to heal your distempered soul, and you are nothing better, but rather worse,—and so must it be to the end unless you come to Jesus. Come, then, and touch the border of Immanuel's garment; the woman mentioned in the Gospel said, "*If I may but touch his garment, I shall be whole.*" Mat. ix. 21. Come now—He is as near to you as He was then to her,—come touch the border of His garment. It was not only that poor woman, but "*as many as touched him were made perfectly whole.*" Mat. xiv. 36. "*The blood of Jesus Christ cleanseth from all sin.*" Remember, what Christ saith to His disciples in the 14th ch. St. John, "*Let not your heart be troubled; ye believe in God, believe also in me; in my Father's house are many mansions, if it were not so, I would have told you. I go to prepare a place for you, and if I go and prepare a place for you, I will come again, and receive you unto myself, that where I am, there ye may be also.*" If He is gone to prepare a place for you—then, lift up your eyes to those mansions! that household of God where Christ is gone to prepare a habitation for His people; look to that, there is a rest, a rest indeed—and indeed there is no rest in anything beside. There is no rest for the sole of our foot on the troubled waters of this weary world, no more than there was for the dove on the waters of the deluge. And it is well for those who look for a better rest, that they cannot find a rest on earth—how ready would we be to make nests for ourselves, to nestle here below—but our God, our Father will not allow us. If we are looking to Christ, He has prepared some better things for us. If your father and mother expected you at home, and if they thought, you were lying lazily down to sleep in some hovel on the road-side, instead of hastening on to them, how would they be disappointed and distressed. They would send, if a messenger could reach you, and say to you, "Oh, come home, why rest in such a place as that? We are waiting for you, expecting you at home." Thus, our heavenly Father will not let us take up our abode in hovels on the road side, He will compel us, He will constrain us to come home, He will send His messenger to reprove, to quicken us, to chide our dull delay. He will make us "*gird up the loins of our mind,*" and teach us to "*be sober and hope to the end.*" How can we sufficiently appreciate the blessing till we reach our Father's house, of being "FELLOW-CITIZENS WITH THE SAINTS, AND OF THE HOUSEHOLD OF GOD!"

I said, St. Paul was a Roman citizen, and therefore had a right to the privileges of his citizenship. And do you remember how he used them? Do you recollect when the chief captain bound him, and would have scourged him, he asks, "*Is it lawful for you to scourge a man that is a Roman, and uncondemned?*" Acts xxii. 25. And do you remember how, when the chief captain heard he was a Roman, he was afraid, and let him go, the terror of the Roman name was upon him, and he dare not scourge or bind a Roman citizen. And do you think there are no privileges belonging to the citizenship of the city of the living God? If the chief captain feared the Roman Emperor, if he should dare to invade the privileges of a Roman citizen, or to infringe the rights of Rome, do you think, the King of Glory is not watching over his citizens, and vindicating their privileges and their rights in all their trials? Oh! remember—Satan, and the flesh, and the world, shall no longer have power to hold you captive—"*sin shall not have dominion over you, for you are not under the law, but under grace.*" Remember, all your foes *can* do nothing that the King your Father does not permit. They *shall* do nothing but what is for your good, for "*all things are working together for good to them that love God, to them who are the called according to his purpose.*" Rom. viii. 28.

Think, then, of these things! Oh blessed thought! we shall never reach the end of our privileges—they are for eternity. Oh, may we be enabled, through the grace and mercy of our God, to know—enjoy—live on them as we ought, to live to the glory of our God and Father—to "*glorify God in our body and in our spirit, which are God's.*" I beseech you consider these things, compare these two verses, the 12th and 19th—study the intermediate verses, and they will show, how man is brought from the state of an unbeliever, in the 12th verse, to the state of a believer, in the 19th. Mark—how in that short compass you have laid before you "*the fulness of the blessing of the Gospel of Christ,*" and let us pray that the Lord may enable us to know, to understand, to believe, and rejoice in the unsearchable riches of our adorable Redeemer. Amen.

TWENTIETH LECTURE

EPHESIANS II.—20, 21, 22.

"And are built upon the foundation of the apostles and prophets, Jesus Christ himself being the chief corner-stone: in whom all the building, fitly framed together, groweth unto an holy temple in the Lord, in whom ye also are builded together for an habitation of God through the Spirit."

ON the last day, we considered some of the privileges of believers, as they are set forth in the 19th verse. We contrasted the state in which they had been, as "*aliens from the commonwealth of Israel, and strangers from the covenants of promise, having no hope and without God in the world*," with that in which they now are; being "*made nigh by the blood of Christ*," having "*through him access by one Spirit unto the Father*," "*no more strangers and foreigners, but fellow-citizens with the saints, and of the household of God*." The Apostle proceeds to show them the stability of all their privileges, in the 20th verse, which we consider to-day, "AND ARE BUILT UPON THE FOUNDATION OF THE APOSTLES AND PROPHETS, JESUS CHRIST HIMSELF, BEING THE CHIEF CORNER-STONE."

You are "BUILT UPON THE FOUNDATION,"—this is an expression, or rather an image, which is repeatedly used throughout the whole of the Scriptures;—the Church of Christ is compared to a building, and the Lord Jesus Christ Himself, to the foundation. We meet it in the Prophet Isaiah, xxviii. 16th verse, the Lord there declares "*Behold I lay in Zion for a foundation, a stone, a tried stone, a precious corner-stone, a sure foundation, he that believeth shall not make haste*." We find the Apostles repeatedly using this image; we see it, in the sermon of Peter, in the 4th chapter of the Acts, where he says, alluding to our Saviour who was foretold in the prophecy that I have just read to you—to His rejection by the Jews, and His exaltation as foretold Ps. cxviii., 22, he saith 11th and 12th verses, "*This is the stone which was set at nought of you builders, which is become the head of the corner, neither is there salvation in any other, for there is no other name under heaven given among men, whereby we must be saved*." And so the Apostle in the 3d chapter 1st Cor. 11th verse, "*Other foundation can no man lay, than that is laid, which is Jesus Christ*." The Lord Jesus Christ, is set forth as the foundation on which the sinner must rest all his hope, He is the foundation on which rests all our salvation, the foundation, on which, as on a rock, the whole Church of Christ is built.

Now, before we consider this any farther, let me pause, and ask all who are here, or rather let me entreat you my dear friends to ask yourselves,

"Is Jesus my foundation?—Is all the hope of my salvation built on Christ?"

It is a question, which perhaps every nominal Christian would be ready to answer in the affirmative, "Oh, yes," he would say, "I have no hope of being saved but by Christ, I could not be saved without Christ."

But we shall find on examination, that while many persons make this confession, nevertheless, He is not the foundation of their hope. Their confession is a sentiment which they have been accustomed to admit in words, not in principle. They prize it, and they have learned to confess it with their lips; but in saying, that they cannot be saved without Christ;—They mean this,

"I know that my own righteousness—my own works—my own merits—my own efforts, are not a sufficient foundation for me to rest my hope on, if I had not Christ to make them so; if Christ's merits were not to be added to the best that I can do, I know I could not be saved, but I trust through Him that my humble efforts will be accepted."

Such is, I fear, the hope of multitudes who call themselves Christians. If this is your opinion, be assured that Christ is not the foundation of your hope at all. If we say, "this house is founded on a rock," we do not mean, it is partly founded on a rock, and partly on the sand, but we mean to say, it is altogether founded on a rock. Now, your hope, if it be as I have described, is founded partly on a rock, and partly on the sand; and if a house is partly founded on a rock, and partly on the sand, it might as well be all founded on the sand; for the foundation of the half will be soon washed away, and then it must fall to ruin. If you think that Jesus makes your works and efforts acceptable to God for your salvation—and that therefore, He is necessary, so that, in this sense, you cannot be saved without Christ—if you mean this —then Christ is not your foundation at all; He is merely the helper of your salvation,—He is not your Saviour. The foundation that is laid on Christ, or rather the hope that is built on Christ, is *entirely* built on Christ. The whole of Christ's righteousness, without any mixture of your own whatever, that is the righteousness of the sinner whose hope is built on Jesus. The whole of Christ's redemption—the finished pardon that He has bought with His blood—which gives the soul complete and full acceptance with God, without any reference to his own works—except this—that they are sinful, and therefore unable to save him—that is the resting place for the soul of every sinner who trusts in Jesus. He can say "Jesus hath paid my debt, He '*is the end of the law, for righteousness*' Rom. x. 4.—for me. He hath satisfied the divine justice for me. He hath passed into the heavens, as my Great High Priest, having obtained eternal redemption for my soul. Christ is my peace. He is my Lord, my Master, my eternal

Salvation. If I look to myself, I am all doubt, all fear, all apprehension. If I look unto Christ, I have no doubt, no fear, no apprehension, because Christ has done all, '*finished transgression, made an end of sin, made reconciliation for iniquity, brought in everlasting righteousness.*' Dan. ix. 24. Therefore, '*Why art thou cast down, Oh my soul, and why art thou disquieted within me, hope thou in God.*' Ps. xlii. 5, lean on this rock, rest on this foundation." Such is the language of a soul that is built on Christ.

Here an expression is used, which is a peculiar one, "ARE BUILT UPON THE FOUNDATION OF THE APOSTLES AND PROPHETS." What is the meaning of being "*built on the foundation of the Apostles and Prophets?*" There are two passages in Scripture which seem similar, one in the 16th chapter of St. Matthew, where our Lord says to Peter, "*I say unto thee that thou art Peter, and upon this rock will I build my church, and the gates of hell shall not prevail against it.*" This is the passage from which the members of the Church of Rome take their doctrine, that Peter is the foundation of the Church, that the Church is built upon Peter. If the Church is built on the Apostles at all, we see it is built, not alone on Peter, but on all of them; for here it is said, "BUILT UPON THE FOUNDATION OF THE APOSTLES AND PROPHETS," and we have a similar expression in the 21st chapter of Revelations, 14th verse, "*the wall of the city had twelve foundations, and in them the names of the twelve Apostles of the Lamb.*" But what is the meaning of being "*built upon the foundation of the Apostles and Prophets?*" Is it that the Apostles or Prophets, Peter or all of them, are a foundation on which sinners are to rest their hope or their salvation? No more on them than any other sinners. We might just as well say, that we are built on one another, or on any sinner on the face of the earth, as built on one or all of the Apostles, if you consider the Apostles or Prophets in reference to themselves, or their persons. It does not signify built on them as a foundation, but built on that which was their foundation. The foundation of a wall or city does not mean the wall or the city itself, but the foundation on which the wall or city is built—so it is here. "*The foundation of the Apostles and Prophets,*" is not they themselves, but the foundation on which the Apostles and Prophets were built—and the testimony which the Apostles and Prophets bore, was a testimony of Christ, and a testimony to Christ, as the foundation of our salvation; so they say, as we have said before, "*other foundation can no man lay, but that is laid, which is Jesus Christ.*" This is equally true, whether we consider with some, that the word "*Prophets*" refers to the inspired Prophets of the Old Testament—or to the evangelical preachers of the New. I am rather inclined to adopt the former opinion, and if that be right, then of them it is true, "*To him give all the Prophets witness, that, through his name, whosoever believeth in him shall receive remission of sins.*" Acts x. 43. If the latter opinion be correct, then to testify of Jesus as the foundation, is the office of all faithful preachers since Jesus died. I need not enter into the question of the Church of Rome, in reference to Peter, further than to quote the Apostle himself. He cites this very passage from the Prophet Isaiah, to which we have referred a little before; and he gives the interpretation of that passage, he says, 1 Peter ii. 4, 5, speaking of the Lord Jesus Christ, "*To whom coming, as unto a living stone, disallowed indeed of men, but chosen of God and precious, ye also as lively stones are built up a spiritual house, an holy priesthood, to offer up spiritual sacrifices, acceptable to God by Jesus Christ.*" If Peter were to have been called, in himself, the foundation of the Church, we see he here deserts his post—he abandons his place as the foundation of the Church, and leaves the Church built on him to fall, because he renounces such a title, and calls the Church to its true foundation, even to Christ;—and then he quotes the passage, verse 6, "*Wherefore also, it is contained in the Scripture, behold, I lay in Zion a chief corner stone, elect, precious; and he that believeth on him shall not be confounded;*" verse 7, "*unto you therefore who believe he is precious.*" Here he describes believers; then alluding to those who reject the testimony of God, he says, "*but unto them which be disobedient, the stone which the builders disallowed, the same is made the head of the corner, and a stone of stumbling and a rock of offence, even to them that stumble at the word, being disobedient.*" He shows us what their disobedience is—stumbling at the Word, and denying the Gospel of the Lord Jesus Christ. Therefore, "*the foundation of the Apostles and Prophets*" is the very same thing which our Lord means, in that passage where he addresses Peter, when, in reply to the question, "*Whom say ye that I am? Simon Peter answered and said, thou art the Christ, the Son of the living God; and Jesus answered and said unto him, blessed art thou Simon Barjona, for flesh and blood hath not revealed it unto thee, but my Father which is in heaven. And I say unto thee that thou art Peter, and upon this rock will I build my church, and the gates of hell shall not prevail against it.*" "*On this rock.*" This is the foundation laid by the Apostles and Prophets in their testimony,—the Prophets prophesying of Christ as a foundation—the Apostles testifying of Christ as a foundation—Peter here acknowledging and confessing Christ as a foundation, as we see him calling sinners, and calling the Church in his Epistle to rest on that foundation. So "*upon this rock will I build my Church, and the gates of hell shall not prevail against it.*" So the Apostle here speaks of it in a consolatory manner, to the Church of Christ, "YOU ARE BUILT UPON THE FOUNDATION OF THE APOSTLES AND PROPHETS,"—that which is laid in their testimony and in their word, and in which they trusted themselves—on which they themselves are built, and on which they call the world to rest. As they were first built on Christ, and, as it were, the stones immediately laid on Him, and then the Church called by them laid next to them—so, in this sense, it might be said, you are built upon that foundation, "JESUS CHRIST BEING THE CORNER STONE" on which the building rests—on whom, and by whom, Jew and Gentile are united, and thus, "IN WHOM ALL THE BUILDING FITLY FRAMED TOGETHER, GROWETH INTO AN HOLY TEMPLE IN THE LORD."

Here then, the church of Christ, its foundation, and superstructure are described.

Its foundation—the Lord Jesus Christ.

Its superstructure—all the members who rest on Him—all the other parts of the building. He it is "IN WHOM, ALL THE BUILDING IS FITLY FRAMED TOGETHER." And in Him the building itself, "GROWETH INTO AN HOLY TEMPLE IN THE LORD." And then, that the Church at Ephesus might know their own place in the building, he adds, "IN WHOM YE ALSO ARE BUILDED TOGETHER FOR AN HABITATION OF GOD THROUGH THE SPIRIT."

We may here remark how the grace of God, of which the Apostle had been speaking throughout this chapter,—is prominently set forth in this image. As well might we say, that the stones, of which the walls of this building in which we are assembled, are composed, could quarry themselves out of the mountain—convey themselves to this spot—fit themselves together into that wall—and raise this structure which we behold around us—as say, that the church of Christ is collected and gathered together by the natural good will—good inclinations—good understanding—reason—faith—excellence—or merits of the persons who compose it! Not more certainly does the hand of the workman quarry the stones—bring them together—lay them in order on the foundation—and erect them into the superstructure which they compose; than the Lord of life and glory calls sinners by His Spirit and His power, out of their state of natural darkness, ignorance and death—brings them to the Lord Jesus Christ—layeth them on Him as a foundation—buildeth them up on Him, and fitly frameth them together as a holy temple in the Lord.

We may observe then, in the first place, *the grace of God*, in gathering His Church. "*By grace are ye saved, through faith.*" Then we observe, *the stability of that Church;* they are "BUILT ON THE FOUNDATION OF THE APOSTLES AND PROPHETS"—their foundation is Immanuel. Their "*builder and maker is God;*"—they have been brought by sovereign grace, every individual among them, to know the "*truth as it is in Jesus*"—There is no member of the church of Christ that is not taught these lessons; their guilt—their ruin—their utter helplessness—their utter inability to deliver their own souls,—none who are not instructed in Christ as their hope—their only hope and refuge—yea, all their salvation. They are all taught of God, though their degrees of knowledge and experience in all the doctrines of truth may be very different. One man may have a much greater fear of his guilt and condemnation—another man may have much deeper views—more humbling, self-prostrating views of his own corruption and abomination—another may have much clearer and brighter views of the finished work of his glorious Redeemer—a much more lively assurance of faith and hope,—these principles may be, and are exceedingly varied, not only in different believers, but in the same believers at different times; but they all learn the same lesson, they are all brought to renounce themselves—to fly to Christ as their hope and refuge; they are all brought to know —to look to—to lean on, and rejoice in Christ. So the Apostle Peter, in the passage I have quoted, speaking of the church being built on this living stone, says, "*Unto you therefore who believe, he is precious.*" This is the characteristic of every true child of God. Yes, "*to you who believe, he is precious,*" whatever may be your state, whatever may be your circumstances or feelings, now or at any other time, Christ is precious to your soul. Those who know not Christ, as the foundation of their hope—He "*hath no form or comeliness,*" Isaiah liii. 2, to them. But to those who know Christ, he is indeed precious, "*the chiefest among ten thousand,*" yea, "*altogether lovely.*" Cant. v. 10, 16.

Some may say perhaps, "Alas! I wish it were so with me, but I find my heart so cold and dead, that this is the very thing that distresses me, I do not feel that I love Christ as I ought to love Him, and therefore I am cast down, that thought casts me down, to those who believe Christ is precious, but I do not feel Him so, as he ought to be to me."

Well, I say unto you, if this be your feeling, lift up your heart; for if He was not precious to you, and if you did not love Him, your own coldness and deadness could not be a source of grief to you: you would not feel that coldness and deadness if you did not love Christ: and those who love Him most, feel how little precious He is to them, compared to what He ought to be. For Oh! how precious ought Christ to be to us! How contemptible everything else on this earth ought to be, when it comes into competition for a moment with Christ! "*Whom have I in heaven but thee, and there is none on earth that I desire besides thee,*" saith the Psalmist. Ps. lxxiii. 25. There is no sin, no earthly joy or pleasure, no carnal gratification—nothing that the whole world could bestow that we could not count it all loss for Christ, if He was precious to us as He ought to be. Let us seek that we may know Him more and more, for if He is not precious to us as He ought, it is because He is not known to us as He ought. Let us all consider what we are, what Christ has suffered, what He has done for us,—let us remember how He has borne with us—let us reflect what provocations, what innumerable provocations He has received from us, since He taught us that He was our Hope and Refuge,—let us consider our ingratitude—what vile returns we have made to Him for all His love and tenderness—and yet how He has kept us—and has borne with us,—and has not withdrawn His grace and mercy from us! He has brought us here to-day—He has opened His glorious Word before us—again He calls us to Himself—again He testifies of the riches of His love—the exceeding riches of His grace, His invitation is—"*Come unto me and I will give you rest.*" Mat. xi. 28. Oh yes! Christ ought to be precious to us, indeed—and cold, compared with what we owe to Him, are the warmest affections of our hearts.

We behold then, the grace of the Lord in building His church, as set forth in this chapter—and this stability of the church, as resting on that foundation. The church is founded on a rock, and the stability of this foundation is one of the things which makes Christ precious to the soul. Do not be doubting, O believer! do not be distrusting your Lord—do not allow your own sin, your own ingratitude, your own unbelief to make you doubt your Lord's love. Surely it was not for anything good in you that He loved you first, and brought you to Himself; and He will not cast you off now, for all your unworthiness, and all your vileness, when you bring it all to Him,—"*Trust in him at all times ye people, pour out your hearts before him, God is a refuge for us.*" Ps. lxii. 8.

We are told continually that this is great encouragement to licentiousness, an encouragement to go on in sin; nay, but, it is the encouragement the Lord gives to His people, to love and serve him, and if the grace and love of Christ is abused, as we grant, that the doctrines of grace, have been abused, and may be abused again to licentiousness, yet, if they are so, is that a reason that we are to stint the children of God of the "Bread of life," because the devil chooses to mix poison with it for his own children? The children of God will not turn the grace of God to licentiousness, they shall not do so. We have seen, verse 10, that they "*are his workmanship created in Christ Jesus, unto good works, which God hath before ordained that they should walk in them.*" They shall be taught to know and feel the power of this truth, "*Shall we continue in sin that grace may abound, God forbid. How shall we that are dead to sin live any longer therein?*" Rom. vi. 1, 2; they shall be taught to know and feel, that as "*where sin abounded, grace did much more abound:*" It is not that they are to "*continue in sin that grace may abound,*" but "*that as sin hath reigned unto death, even so might grace reign through righteousness unto eternal life by Jesus Christ our Lord.*" Rom. v. 20, 21. Nay, this is only the means of lifting up the sinner's heart from the love and power of sin. It was the grace and love of Christ that first brought your soul to know, and to rejoice in Christ, and it is the same power alone that shall keep, and carry you on to trust and serve Him, so saith the Apostle, "*the love of Christ constraineth us, because we thus judge, that if one died for all, then were all dead, and that he died for all, that they which live should not henceforth live unto themselves, but unto him that died for them, and rose again.*" 2 Cor. v. 14, 15. Therefore, consider, that God is the foundation on which your soul rests, and the stability of the Church is derived, not more from the security of her foundation, that she rests on Christ, than from the power of her Lord, who keeps, and guards, and preserves her for evermore, "*I the Lord do keep it; I will water it every moment: lest any hurt it, I will keep it night and day.*" Isa. xxvii. 3—He saith by the Prophet. So they are kept, "*kept by the power of God through faith unto salvation,*" saith the Apostle Peter, i. 5.

Then we are to consider, not only the grace of the Lord, and the stability and security of His Church, but also, *the unity of the Church in Christ.* This is, perhaps, a view of the question which it requires as great an exercise of faith to see distinctly, as any truth connected with it; for alas, what divisions do there appear in the Church of Christ! yea, even among those who clearly profess to believe the Gospel—among those, who from their life and conversation, we suppose make a true profession that they know Christ—that they love Him, and that He is precious to their souls! Yet alas! what divisions appear among them! how we see them "*contending about words to no profit but to the subverting of the hearers!*" 2nd Tim. ii. 14. What contentions exist about forms of government—of discipline—forms of worship—forms of words—ordinances of various kinds—modes of administering ordinances—opinions, on points of speculation—some looking in the church on earth for the purity of the church in glory; separating—dividing among themselves—causing divisions and schisms in search of a pure church—trying "*to bring a clean thing out of an unclean,*" Job xiv. 4, foolishly and ignorantly anticipating the work of the angels in separating the tares from the wheat, and forgetting that both must grow together till the harvest!!! Alas, what a heart-rending view the state of disunion among believers, presents to one that really knows and feels, what the spirit of union ought to be among all the children of Christ! Yet, in spite of all this, whatever it may appear to the eye of sense, still, "THE WHOLE BUILDING FITLY FRAMED TOGETHER, GROWETH INTO AN HOLY TEMPLE IN THE LORD." Out of all the various outward churches, and outward denominations of those that profess the name of Jesus, the Lord is gathering in His own flock into His fold—the stones of His own temple, they are all "FITLY FRAMED TOGETHER" in His eye, and all "GROWING INTO AN HOLY TEMPLE IN THE LORD."

This is the proposition that is written here, it must be true, it is as true as His word,—and yet, there is nothing, perhaps, connected with the Church of Christ, that requires a greater exercise of faith than the belief of that truth. But so it was even in the days of the Apostles. See what a dissension arose even between Paul and Barnabas, a contention so sharp "*that they departed one from the other,*" Acts xv. 38.—and that too, about Mark. Yet, the Lord overruled this, one goes one way, and the other goes another. And while their contention is calculated to humble them both, and make them feel what they are; the Lord can overrule the evil to make them go and declare His Word in different countries, and bring the message of salvation to the souls of sinners in different places. The Lord can thus overrule even evil for good in gathering the stones of His spiritual temple. Paul was obliged to withstand Peter to the face, for Peter was temporizing with the Jewish believers. Yet that stands recorded in the word of eternal truth, and a blessed record it is; for that, among other testimonies stands as a witness against the awful delusion of that fatal apostacy, which would make that Apostle the foundation on which men were to build the hope of their salvation!

You see then, the Lord can overrule even the evil in His Church for good; and to this very moment, although we have to mourn over the contentions and divisions in the church, yet the Lord overrules, and will overrule them, as the very means of making His people more watchful, more vigilant, more circumspect, and drive them more from resting on their forms, and trusting in themselves, to the pure spiritual principle of faith in Christ, and love to the brethren.

Pure and undefiled religion cannot consist in outward ordinances, it cannot consist in outward privileges, however important they may be, but it must consist in genuine faith and love—in a real trust in the Lord Jesus Christ, and the vital principle of a real Christian spirit that will lead the heart not only to love its Lord, but all who love Him, for His sake, and to say and feel the last words of this Epistle;—"*Grace be with all them that love our Lord Jesus Christ in sincerity.*" *Amen.* "IN WHOM ALL THE BUILDING, FITLY FRAMED TOGETHER, GROWETH UNTO AN HOLY TEMPLE IN THE LORD."

Then, again, consider what a beautiful view this presents to us of the different circumstances of the members of the church of Christ,—the different circumstances in which they are called. One is called in a higher, another in an humbler walk of life, one is called as a parent, another as a child—one, as a master, another, as a servant—one may be called as a king, another, as a subject—one may be called as a noble, another as a commoner;—persons are called in all the different departments of life:—and remember, that in all their circumstances and situations they are called, for what? that in those circumstances, and in that situation, they may glorify God. The king on his throne. If he is a servant of his God, his faith in his Lord and Master is the brightest jewel in his crown. The great and good George the Third, in his own prayer-book, in the prayer for the King, where the words occur, "*our most gracious Sovereign Lord King George,*" —wrote in the margin,—"*a poor guilty sinner,*" What a blessing it is to see a king, laying down his crown at the feet of Jesus. He knew and loved his Lord and Master—and he has now cast a crown far brighter than his earthly diadem, at the feet of his Redeemer.

But, now, I address, no doubt, persons moving in varied circumstances of life. If I address any in poor and humble stations, I would say to them, remember, that as surely as you are brought to the Lord Jesus Christ, he has placed you, as a living stone in His temple, in the very position in which you are—He has called you, and fixed you in the very spot which you occupy—all the circum stances of the Lord's people, how different soever they may be, and all things connected with them, are all arranged by the infinite wisdom of God—because we know that "*all things work together for good, to them that love God, to them who are the called according to his purpose.*" Rom. viii. 28. Therefore, I say, whatever your circumstances in life may be—whatever your situation—how poor and humble soever,—however overlooked or disregarded by men—how numerous soever your trials—how weighty soever the cross you have to carry—how humble, how low, how poor, how mean, how despised soever you may be—you are placed exactly in the very position in the temple of the living God, in which He has been pleased to call you, to glorify your Lord and Master, "THE WHOLE TEMPLE IS FITLY FRAMED TOGETHER." The Lord requires for His own All-wise and mighty purpose, every single stone in His temple—not one is to be left out, all are to be gathered—placed—fixed in their own position, no matter what it is. The smallest stone that the mason takes, to fill up and fit in the wall, is just as necessary in his eye to the building, as the large stone, the thorough stone, or the quoin, he lays beside it. And remember, it must be true of every single stone in His spiritual temple, that the Lord is the one who has laid it there—who has fitted it there—who keeps it there—and there, in your position, whatever it be, you are called upon to serve and glorify your Lord and Master. Therefore our true happiness is, as it is well and simply expressed in our Catechism, "to do our duty in that state of life unto which it shall please God to call us."

Oh! how contented that should make us, how thankful in all our situations, in all our circumstances! We should each remember, "I am just as the Lord has placed me." And therefore, believer, in any purpose—in any desire—in any thought of change of position, you should seek the Lord's guidance, you should seek the Lord's gracious and special providential direction. Look to Him, cast all your care upon him, "*in all thy ways acknowledge him, and he will direct thy paths.*" Prov. iii. 6. What a beautiful view this gives us of the temple of Christ, the temple of the living God, "THE WHOLE BUILDING FITLY FRAMED TOGETHER, GROWETH INTO AN HOLY TEMPLE IN THE LORD." We have the church of Christ spoken of in another chapter under the image of the body and the members, iv. 15, 16, you "*may grow up into him in all things, which is the head, even Christ, from whom the whole body, fitly joined together, and compacted by that which every joint supplieth, according to the effectual working in the measure of every part, maketh increase of the body, to the edifying of itself in love.*" What a beautiful view that is! Every muscle, nerve, and fibre is necessary for the body—so every believer, whatever he be in place or condition in the church, is necessary, and they are all, every one of them, growing together in one body, exactly adapted and formed by Him. Well may we say of the body of the church, it is "*fearfully and wonderfully made.*" Ps. cxxxix. 14. Each is to hold their own place—to serve their Lord's purpose, and to glorify that God, who has "*called them out of darkness into his marvellous light.*" 1st Pet. ii. 9.

And then, dear friends, consider this, "THE WHOLE BUILDING FITLY FRAMED TOGETHER, GROWETH INTO AN HOLY TEMPLE IN THE LORD." Consider, it is not only a temple, but a "HOLY TEMPLE;" and we see the reason why it is a holy temple, "IN WHOM YE ALSO ARE BUILDED TOGETHER FOR AN HABITATION OF GOD THROUGH THE SPIRIT." He saith, "*I will dwell in them, and walk in them,*" 2 Cor. vi. 16, "*I will put my laws into their hearts, and in their minds will I write them, and will be their God, and they shall be my people.*" Jer. xxxi. 33, with Heb. x. 16. This is the way in which the charges of licentiousness that are brought against the freedom and glory of the doctrines of grace are to be answered. We are not to cramp, to contract the glorious liberty of the everlasting Gospel, we are not to confine, to curtail, or explain away the blessed privileges of the Lord's people, to meet the ignorance and carnal objections of an ungodly world. We are to walk through the land of promise, in the length and in the breadth of it, unshackled by what men may say or think. But we are to prove—to manifest—to demonstrate to all, that we give no just ground for such a charge. Not only is it to be denied in our doctrine, but practically disproved in our lives. Our whole life and conversation is to be the answer to the charge that is made against us. "*For so is the will of God, that with well doing, you may put to silence the ignorance of foolish men; as free, but not using your liberty for a cloak of maliciousness, but as the servants of God.*" 1 Pet. ii. 15, 16. "*Holiness becometh thy house, O Lord, forever.*" Ps. xciii. 5. Oh yes! and if Christ hath called us, and "*loved us, and washed us from our sins, in his own blood.*" Rev. i. 5.—"*what shall we render to the Lord for all his benefits toward us.*" Ps. cxvi. 12. How shall we serve Him? How shall we glorify Him? Surely, that ought to be the inquiry—the aim of our existence.

Consider then, what a blessed portion of Scripture this chapter is. It might be very justly compared to the history of a magnificent building—a Palace for the residence of a king. As if you were to describe an architect, who employed his workmen to go to some vast quarry; who there quarried the stones—took them out—drew them—brought them together—wrought—squared—chiselled—fitted, and erected them into such or such a mighty structure, which you behold for the habitation of a monarch. This chapter is, as if even thus, the history of the Church of Christ. Here the materials are represented as in a mass of sin in the beginning, "*dead in trespasses and sins*"—quickened by the grace of God—called out of that state by "*his great love wherewith he loved us, even while we were dead in sin*"—*quickened together with Christ*—all their sins blotted out—reconciled to God—given free access through Christ, to God by the Spirit—"*no more strangers and foreigners, but fellow-citizens with the saints, and of the household of God*"—brought together—fitted—prepared—"BUILDED TOGETHER AS A HOLY TEMPLE IN THE LORD, FOR AN

HABITATION OF GOD THROUGH THE SPIRIT," and the Lord dwelling in the midst of them, and choosing them as His habitation forever! Oh! think, what blessed privileges are brought before us in this chapter.—Read it over, pray over it. May the Lord grant, that it may be sanctified to us, that we may derive from it spiritual blessing—instruction and edification, that we may be built up indeed, "A HOLY TEMPLE IN THE LORD," "BUILDED TOGETHER, FOR AN HABITATION OF GOD THROUGH THE SPIRIT." Amen.

TWENTY-FIRST LECTURE.

EPHESIANS III.—1, 2, 3, 4, 5, 6.

For this cause, I Paul, the prisoner of Jesus Christ for you Gentiles, (if you have heard of the dispensation of the grace of God which is given me to you-ward; how that by revelation he made known unto me the mystery; (as I wrote afore in few words; whereby, when ye read, ye may understand my knowledge in the mystery of Christ,) which in other ages was not made known unto the sons of men, as it is now revealed unto his holy apostles and prophets by the Spirit; that the Gentiles should be fellow-heirs, and of the same body, and partakers of his promise in Christ by the Gospel.

THIS Chapter contains a long and rather difficult parenthesis, on which it is necessary to offer some prefatory observations. The parenthesis begins with the second verse.

"FOR THIS CAUSE, I PAUL, THE PRISONER OF JESUS CHRIST, FOR YOU GENTILES;" then commences the parenthesis "(IF YE HAVE HEARD OF THE DISPENSATION OF THE GRACE OF GOD," &c. Now this parenthesis terminates at one of two verses. It may end at the close of the 13th verse; or, as our authorized version makes it end, at the middle of the 1st verse of the next chapter. We shall read it in both ways, and then consider which seems to be preferable. If we read it as terminating at the 13th verse, and omit the intervening verses, then we suppose the Apostle to mark the sense, and limit the parenthesis by repeating the words "*For this cause*," with which the 14th verse commences—then the sense will run thus:—"FOR THIS CAUSE, I, PAUL, THE PRISONER OF JESUS CHRIST FOR YOU GENTILES," "*bow my knees unto the Father of our Lord Jesus Christ, of whom the whole family in heaven and earth is named, that he would grant you*," &c., v. 14, 15.

Or if we read it as it is marked in the Bible, continuing the parenthetic reading to the middle of the first verse in the next chapter—then we suppose the Apostle to mark the sense, and to limit the parenthesis by the words "*the prisoner of the Lord*," then it will read thus:—"FOR THIS CAUSE, I, PAUL, THE PRISONER OF JESUS CHRIST, FOR YOU GENTILES," "*beseech you that you walk worthy of the vocation wherewith ye are called, with all lowliness and meekness, with long-suffering, forbearing one another in love,*" &c. iv. 1, 2.

Now, each of these is very important for us to consider. In the first place; remark, what the cause is to which the Apostle alludes; in the first words of the chapter, "*For this cause.*" What cause? He had stated in the close of the last chapter, as we have seen, the great and blessed privileges of believers in the Gospel of Jesus—"*Ye are no more strangers and foreigners, but fellow-citizens with the saints, and of the household of God, and are built upon the foundation of the Apostles and Prophets, Jesus Christ himself being the chief corner-stone, in whom all the building fitly framed together, groweth unto an holy temple in the Lord; in whom also ye are builded together for an habitation of God through the Spirit.*" And "*for this cause,*"—viz.—because ye are so—because ye are "*of the household of God*"—because ye are "*built on the foundation of the Apostles and Prophets*"—because ye are "*builded together for an habitation of God through the Spirit:*" "FOR THIS CAUSE, I, PAUL THE PRISONER OF JESUS CHRIST, FOR YOU GENTILES," "*bow my knees unto the Father of our Lord Jesus Christ, of whom the whole family in heaven and earth is named, that he would grant us according to the riches of his glory to be strengthened with might by his Spirit in the inner man, that Christ may dwell in your hearts by faith,*" &c. Or, if you continue the parenthesis to the next chapter, "FOR THIS CAUSE, I, PAUL, THE PRISONER OF JESUS CHRIST, FOR YOU GENTILES," "*beseech you, that you walk worthy of the vocation wherewith you are called, with all lowliness and meekness, with long suffering, forbearing one another in love, endeavoring to keep the unity of the spirit in the bond of peace,*" &c.

It is important to consider in either case, that professors of the Gospel of Christ are too apt to think when they are brought to the knowledge of the truth as it is in Jesus—when they are brought to know the great fundamental doctrine of justification by the righteousness and blood of a crucified Redeemer—called out of darkness into the marvellous light of God's truth—thereby brought into the state of which the Apostle speaks in the latter part of the preceding chapter, "*no more strangers and foreigners, but fellow-citizens with the saints, and of the household of God*"—when they are brought, I say, into this condition, then they think, as it were, that all is done. "Now they are Christians, now they are servants of Christ." True—so they are—and in one sense, all is done—in one sense all is completed—the work on which depends their salvation is finished by Him who died on the cross—the glorious work of redemption is accomplished. But then begins the conflict of those who are partakers of this great salvation—then, from that moment begins the conflict of which you read throughout the Scriptures, as existing in the breast of every believer: as for instance, in Galatians v. 17, "*the flesh lusteth against the Spirit, and the Spirit against the flesh, and these are contrary the one to the other, so that ye cannot do the things that ye would.*" From that time, the new principle, the regenerating power of the Spirit, is shed abroad in their hearts, and then they begin to feel the conflict that they must have with the world, the flesh, and the devil. Then begins the time, when they have need of these blessings and this watchfulness which, in whatever view we take the parenthesis in this chapter, the Apostle brings, either in one or the other, so prominently before them. They have need continually of prayer to God for strength and grace, "*that they may be strengthened with all might by his Spirit in the inner man, that Christ may dwell in their hearts by faith, that they may be rooted and grounded in love, and able to comprehend with all saints, what is the length and breadth, and depth, and height, and to know the love of Christ which passeth knowledge, that they may be filled with all the fulness of God.*" 16–19. They have need of continual prayer for these inestimable blessings, and this is the subject of the Apostle's prayer, for them, because they are of "*the household of God,*" if you read the parenthesis as ending at the 13th verse.

And again, they have no less need of watchfulness, that they "*may walk worthy of the vocation wherewith they are called,*" if you read the parenthesis as ending in the 1st verse of the next chapter. They have need then of prayer for all that they require, to enable them to carry on their warfare; and they have need of grace, that, from that time forth, they may "*glorify God in their body and in their spirit, which are God's,*" for they "*are not their own, but are bought with a price.*" 1st Cor. vi. 20. They are "*children of light,*" and should "*walk in the light.*" 1st Thes. v. 5, 1st John i. 7.

Bear this, then, in mind; and, if it pleases God when we come to these passages, we shall resume this subject, as to the proper place of closing the parenthesis. In the meantime, we shall consider the parenthesis itself, and the subject which the Apostle introduces in it.

"FOR THIS CAUSE, I, PAUL, THE PRISONER OF JESUS CHRIST, FOR YOU GENTILES." This epistle was written to this Gentile Church the Ephesians, from Rome, where St. Paul was a prisoner; and he calls himself "A PRISONER OF JESUS CHRIST FOR THE GENTILES," because it was the faithful testimony which he bore to the salvation of Christ for the Gentiles, by which he had excited so much the wrath and enmity of the Jewish people. Therefore the Jews persecuted him—therefore he appealed to Cæsar—therefore he was brought as a prisoner to Rome, as we see in the four last chapters of the Acts. He says, "*If ye have heard of the dispensation of the grace of God, which is given me to you-ward, how that by revelation he made known unto me the mystery, as I wrote afore in few words; whereby when you read, you may understand my knowledge in the mystery of Christ, which in other ages was not made known unto the sons of men, as it is now revealed unto his holy Apostles and Prophets by the Spirit, that the Gentiles should be fellow heirs, and of the same body, and partakers of his promise in Christ by the Gospel, whereof I was made a minister according to the gift of the grace of God, given unto me by the effectual working of his power."* The Apostle had communicated to the Ephesian Church his own conversion, he says, "IF YOU HAVE HEARD OF THE DISPENSATION OF THE GRACE OF GOD, WHICH IS GIVEN ME TO YOU-WARD." The word translated "IF," is rather affirmative than hypothetical, it means "since indeed;" and the Apostle uses it, not because they had not heard of it, but because it was necessary they should remember, and dwell on it; that they might consider the Apostolical authority and power, by which he proclaimed to them the Gospel of Christ, and know the certainty of their own calling in Christ, being called by him to the knowledge of His precious Gospel.

The Apostle calls his divine mission; "THE DISPENSATION OF THE GRACE OF GOD, WHICH IS GIVEN ME TO YOU-WARD." This subject "THE GRACE OF GOD,"—you perceive, he brings before them by frequent repetition throughout the whole of his epistle. He commences his epistle with it,—"GRACE *be to you, and peace from God the Father, and from the Lord Jesus Christ."* Then speaking of their election and adoption in Christ in the 6th verse, he says, it is "*to the praise and glory of his* GRACE, *wherein he hath made us accepted in the beloved."* Then speaking again of the riches of the pardon of their guilt, in the next verse, "*in whom we have redemption through his blood, the forgiveness of sins, according to the riches of his* GRACE." Then again, as we see in the chapter we have just finished, he says, speaking of their being quickened, their being delivered out of their state of nature, of guilt, darkness and condemnation, "*even when we were dead in sins, hath quickened us together with Christ, by* GRACE *ye are saved,"* then again in the 7th verse he repeats the same thing, "*that in the ages to come, he might show the exceeding riches of his* GRACE, *in his kindness towards us by Christ Jesus,"* 8th verse, "*By* GRACE *are ye saved, through faith, and that not of yourselves, it is the gift of God; not of works, lest any man should boast."* And so, throughout the whole of this epistle, he reminds them over and over again of this GRACE, and so he says in this verse, "IF YE HAVE HEARD OF THE DISPENSATION OF THE GRACE OF GOD WHICH IS GIVEN ME TO YOU-WARD." We do not consider it good taste in writing to be guilty of tautology, that is, repeating the same expression over and over. Why then do we see that this is the case in the Scriptures, which furnish a model, a perfect model of taste and beauty in composition—the most perfect model in the world? Why are these terms repeated so continually in the Sacred Volume?—Because it is indispensably necessary that they should be repeated—they should be impressed again and again on the ears and heart of every sinner. God's grace is continually brought before us in every part of His word because we need it every moment. Every day, every hour we sin against our God, and provoke his righteous judgments against us: if He were to enter into judgment with us. And if there be any here that have been quickened and called out of their natural state of ignorance, of guilt and condemnation, to the knowledge of the Lord Jesus Christ, as I trust there may be many,—it is, as we have seen, because "*God, who is rich in mercy, for his great love wherewith he loved us, even when we were dead in sins, hath quickened us together with Christ, (by grace are ye saved.*") And if there be any, who, having been brought to the knowledge of the Lord Jesus Christ, for any time past, for months or years, are here this day, still knowing Christ as their refuge—enabled in any respect to serve our God—kept from bringing reproach, dishonor, disgrace, on His blessed cause through our guilt and wickedness, if these things are so, each may say with the Apostle, "*By the grace of God, I am what I am,*" 1st Cor. xv. 10. By Grace we are called, and by Grace we are kept,—"*kept by the power of God through faith unto salvation.*" 1st Pet. i. 5.

Let me address myself to you especially, Believer. I know you feel—for God's word tells me so; and I know I feel—my own heart corroborates the word that testifies it, the continual working of sin, of corruption and evil within; so that you are obliged to complain with the Apostle Paul, "*to will is present with me, but how to perform that which is good, I find not.*" and again, "*when I would do good, evil is present with me.*" Rom. vii. 18—21. You are obliged to confess with him, "*We that are in this tabernacle do groan, being burthened,*" 2 Cor. v. 4, you are obliged to exclaim with him, "*O wretched man that I am, who shall deliver me from the body of this death?*" Rom. vii. 24. I say, when you feel, when you experience this in yourselves, you know that every moment you have need to cast yourselves down at the footstool of the Throne of Grace that you may obtain mercy—strength—salvation, and all the blessings that flow from salvation—not for anything you have done—not on account of your holiness—your prayers—your hearing of the Word of God—your attendance on ordinances—nor on account of anything you have in yourselves—but that you may receive the blessing of salvation, and all those blessings that accompany it; and that flow from the free, sovereign grace, love, and mercy of your God through Christ and Christ alone. Your cry is, O Lord, "*receive me graciously, and love me freely.*" This is a prayer which is suited to every sinner, this is language which the Lord Himself by His prophet puts into the mouth of His people, as you will find it written in the 14th ch. of Hosea in the 2d v., and let me call you to consider this. The Lord does not merely from the throne of Grace invite sinners to come to Him, but He puts words into their lips, He tells them the very words they are to speak when they do come to Him. "*Take with you words, and turn to the Lord. Say unto him,*"—now mark what they are to say, "*take away all iniquity, and receive us graciously, so will we render unto thee the calves of our lips.*" He does not say, take with you words, and tell the Lord what you have done for Him, how you have served Him—alas! what could we have to recount!—He does not say, take with you resolutions and vows—come to the Lord, and tell the Lord what you will do for Him, and how you will serve Him—alas! what could we venture to promise! But He commands—invites—encourages you to come to Him, as guilty, helpless sinners, and say to Him these words which He authorizes you to adopt, "*take away all iniquity, and receive us graciously.*" Now dear friends is not this what we want to-day? Is not this the very language that, if we know ourselves, we feel is suited to our case? Lord, I am nothing but a poor, vile, guilty sinner, "*take away all iniquity, and receive me graciously.*" What can a sinner desire more than that such a plea should be heard—and how can he doubt that it will be received, when his Heavenly Father Himself puts the very words into his lips. Oh! hear His word, and avail yourself of His infinite mercies; for therefore it is that this grace is brought before us in the Scripture so repeatedly, because we so continually need it, and therefore observe, what the Apostle says, "*If ye have heard of the dispensation of the grace of God.*"

The dispensation of the Gospel is a dispensation of grace; and so when the Apostle alludes to this, he speaks of the dispensation of the grace of God given to the Gentiles. He speaks of that peculiar dispensation which was expressly committed to him, when he was on his journey to Damascus. He was himself, the most eminent example of divine grace. Grace found him "*breathing out threatenings and slaughter,*" Acts ix. 11, blasphemy on his lips, and murder in his heart,—going on his way to carry believers in Christ bound unto Jerusalem. Such was Saul of Tarsus, when the sovereign grace of God arrested him in his progress. And before we advert to the dispensation, committed to the Apostle Paul, let us turn to the 1st chapter of the first epistle to Timothy, where he speaks of this grace as a special manifestation to himself in his own person. The dispensation of grace was committed unto him for the Gentiles; and in order that he might speak from experience, and that he might be a glorious example of the grace which he preached, and of which the dispensation was committed to him, he was arrested by that divine grace in the midst, as we see, of blasphemy and persecution, and so he tells us in this chapter, 1st Timothy, i. 12–15, he says, "*I thank Christ Jesus our Lord, who hath enabled me, for that he counted me faithful, putting me into the ministry, who before was a blasphemer, and a persecutor, and injurious, (but I obtained mercy,) because I did it ignorantly in unbelief. And the grace of our Lord Jesus Christ was exceeding abundant, with faith and love which is in Christ Jesus. This is a faithful saying and worthy of all acceptation, that Christ Jesus came into the world to save sinners, of whom I am chief.*" Now, mark the 16th verse—he tells us in it, by the Holy Spirit, the reason why he obtained mercy—namely, that when the dispensation of grace was committed unto him for the Gentiles, he might stand out himself as a most prominent example of grace to the world, "*Howbeit for this cause I obtained mercy, that in me first, Jesus Christ might show forth all long-suffering, for a pattern to them which should hereafter believe on him to life everlasting.*" That is, that every sinner to whom he, Paul, preached the Gospel, might say, "If Saul of Tarsus was pardoned in the midst of blasphemy and persecution, and if in such a state, grace and mercy were extended to him, why should I fear to trust in grace—when I hear the Gospel of Christ proclaimed to such a wretch as I am?" Mark, then, the reason of his own calling, as he gives it in this Epistle to Timothy; then turn back to the history of his conversion, in the 26th chapter of the Acts; I say the 26th chapter, because, although the first mention of his conversion is in the 9th chapter, yet it is in the 26th chapter, when he is speaking before Agrippa, that he mentions at large the peculiar dispensation that was given to him, of grace to the Gentiles. He describes his journey to Damascus—his previous life—his commission from the chief priests, in the 12th verse—the light that shone around him, and the voice he heard from heaven, testifying that it was Jesus whom he was persecuting;—and then look at the 16th verse, "*But rise and stand upon thy feet; for I have appeared unto thee for this purpose, to make thee a minister and a witness both of these things which thou hast seen, and of those things in the which I will appear unto thee, delivering thee from the people and from the Gentiles, unto whom now I send thee*"—(here is "the dispensation of grace,") "*to open their eyes, and to turn them from darkness to light, and from the power of Satan unto God, that they may receive forgiveness of sins and inheritance among them that are sanctified by faith that is in me.*" 17, 18, 19.

This is the testimony given to the Apostle Paul, or rather the dispensation, committed to him, of grace to the Gentiles.

Let us recollect we are all Gentiles. And there may be some poor unbelieving sinner, a Christian only in name here, to whom this dispensation of grace, if you attend to it, will be indeed, a message of joy and mercy to your soul. For if you are not converted to God, you are in the very state in which Gentiles are here described by the Lord Jesus Christ, when he sends the Apostle Paul to them. Observe their state, blind—in darkness—unpardoned—unsanctified—under the power of Satan—without any inheritance of eternal life. That is exactly the state of every unconverted sinner.

Observe, the Lord saith, I send thee "*to open their eyes,*" therefore, they must be blind.

"*To turn them from darkness to light,*" of course they must be in darkness.

"*From the power of Satan unto God,*" of course they must be under the power of Satan.

"*That they may receive forgiveness of sins;*" of course then their sins are unpardoned.

"*And inheritance among them that are sanctified through faith that is in me;*" of course they were unsanctified, and without any such inheritance.

Observe, this is an exact parallel to the beginning of the 2nd chapter of this epistle, "*In the words which the Holy Ghost teacheth, comparing spiritual things with spiritual,*" they are here described, "*dead in trespasses and sins,*" walking "*according to the course of this world, according to the prince of the power of the air, the spirit that now worketh in the children of disobedience;*" and so, "*aliens from the commonwealth of Israel, strangers from the covenant of promise, having no hope and without God in the world.*" You perceive how these descriptions of the Apostle exactly agree together.

If you are not brought to Christ, if you are not brought to know the Lord Jesus, as the refuge and salvation of your soul, this must be your state. Consider then, what this Gospel is, which is sent to such persons. Does it send them a message of condemnation? does it give them up to despair and abandon them? does it say, "Go—you are in a state of rebellion—in the service of Satan—blind—dark—enemies to God,—go on to perdition, perish as you deserve"? No, no, my dear friends, no,—it is a dispensation of grace, of free and full forgiveness, pardon, peace, mercy, life, salvation, sanctification, inheritance among them that are sanctified. Oh! consider what a blessed message the Gospel of Christ is! and if there be any of you who are oppressed, under a sense of sin, then let me say with the Apostle, "*to you is the word of this salvation sent.*"

We often hear people saying, "If I was religious, I would do, and feel so and so, but I feel my own heart is so evil—so hard—I feel so dead and so sinful, that I do not think there can be any hope, or peace, or comfort for me, till I am in a different state from this." Believe me this is ignorance of the Gospel of Christ, this is the blindness spoken of here. What is the Gospel? A full, free pardon to sinners just as they are.—The Gospel does not say, "When you are religious, when you are good, when you are improved, then hope." But it says—"When you are lost—guilty—vile—then hope, look unto Christ, come to Christ, in the midst of your sins—as you are." The only way on earth to fly from sin is to fly to Jesus.—The only refuge from guilt is Jesus. Come to Him who came to save the lost, the guilty, the vile—"*they that are whole need not a physician, but they that are sick.*" These are His own words, three times recorded by the Holy Ghost. It is the blind, that want their sight—it is those in darkness, who want light—it is those bound by Satan, that need deliverance—it is those who are unpardoned, that require forgiveness—those who are unholy, require to be sanctified—and those who have no inheritance and no hope, that need an inheritance among the saints in glory. It is not for anything you have to do, not by anything you are able to do, but by the glorious work He has wrought Himself that all these blessings are given. This is a

"DISPENSATION OF THE GRACE OF GOD TO YOU-WARD Christ has borne the guilt of all that weary heart of sin that you feel, that heavy heart of guilt, that deadness, rebellion, unbelief, blindness, He "*himself bare our sins in his own body on the tree, that we, being dead to sins, should live unto righteousness.*" 1 Pet. ii. 24—He has carried away all the judgment of God that is recorded against this iniquity, and the message of his Gospel is a message of full and free salvation, "*Ho, every one that thirsteth come ye to the waters, and he that hath no money; come ye, buy and eat; yea, come, buy wine and milk without money and without price.*" Isa. lv. 1. "*Come unto me all ye that labor and are heavy laden, and I will give you rest.*" Mat. xi. 28, "*look unto me, and be ye saved, all the ends of the earth.*" Isa. xlv. 22. Consider, my dear friends, how often this mercy and grace is repeated; and surely it is that we may learn to dwell on it as repeatedly—to recur to it—to repose on it—to draw forth from it continual refreshment and strength for the conflicts, the trials, the necessities of our earthly pilgrimage. Alas! how many persons there are to whom this subject instead of refreshment, is a burthen: who would prefer something that might entertain their imagination, or amuse their fancy, rather than that truth which goes directly to enlighten the understanding, and to renew the heart by the Gospel. But we must adhere steadily to the page of Truth—"*necessity is laid on us, yea, woe are we, if we preach not the Gospel,*" 1st Cor. ix. 16,—we must maintain and set forth "*the grace of God which bringeth salvation,*" for it is that alone which "*teacheth us, that denying ungodliness and worldly lusts, we should live soberly, righteously and godly in this present world.*" Tit. ii. 11, 12.

It is a very bad sign of a man's spiritual state, when a sinner complains of the repetition of the Gospel—it is a very bad symptom of his condition; it is not likely, in that state, that such persons shall be among the number that will never tire of that song throughout eternity;—we are not told that the redeemed tire, or that they shall ever be weary of their song, "*Worthy is the Lamb that was slain to receive power, and riches, and wisdom, and strength, and honor, and glory, and blessing.*" Rev. v. 12. We are not told that they ever tire of the song, "*Blessing, and honor, and glory, and power, be unto Him that sitteth upon the throne, and unto the Lamb, forever and ever.*" v. 13. The cadences may be varied indeed—varied symphonies and harmonies may resound from ten thousand times ten thousand harps and voices—but the words of the song are the same throughout eternity. Oh, consider this! We want "*the fulness of the blessing of the Gospel,*" Rom. xv. 29, every moment; and, blessed be our God, it is, like its glorious Author, "*the same yesterday, to-day, and forever.*"

The Apostle proceeds, "HOW THAT BY REVELATION HE MADE KNOWN UNTO ME THE MYSTERY." We have seen that it was an immediate revelation from heaven to Paul, he saw the Lord Jesus Christ, 1 Cor. xv. 8. He saw "*a light from heaven above the brightness of the sun,*" and he heard the voice of the Lord Jesus giving him a direct revelation and commission. This same Jesus who died and rose again, was He that commissioned Paul to go and preach salvation, through His precious blood, to the Gentiles; and, through that very commission, we have this glorious Volume of His Divine Revelation given to us—we have "*life and immortality brought to light through the Gospel.*" 2nd Tim. i. 10.

The Apostle saith therefore, that "BY REVELATION HE MADE KNOWN UNTO ME THE MYSTERY, AS I WROTE AFORE IN FEW WORDS," alluding to his statement in the beginning of his epistle, ch. i. 9, 10, where he says, "*Having made known unto us the mystery of his will, according to his good pleasure which he hath purposed in himself, that in the dispensation of the fulness of time, he might gather together in one all things in Christ, both which are in heaven, and which are on earth, even in him.*" Here alluding to this mystery, in that first part of his epistle, he then proceeds to explain it. "WHEREBY WHEN YE READ, YE MAY UNDERSTAND MY KNOWLEDGE IN THE MYSTERY OF CHRIST, WHICH IN OTHER AGES WAS NOT MADE KNOWN UNTO THE SONS OF MEN, AS IT IS NOW REVEALED UNTO HIS HOLY APOSTLES AND PROPHETS BY THE SPIRIT, THAT THE GENTILES SHOULD BE FELLOW-HEIRS, AND OF THE SAME BODY, AND PARTAKERS OF HIS PROMISE IN CHRIST BY THE GOSPEL." Now this mystery which the Apostle here unfolds, appears to comprehend two things.

The first is; that it was not known in the whole world, among the sons of men, that God would extend the glory of this salvation to the Gentiles. It was not known to the Gentiles themselves, carried away, as they were, with their dumb idols. Nor was it known to the Jews, or to their prophets; for they believed that the whole blessings of the dispensation of the promised Messiah should be given to themselves alone. This is a subject into which we cannot enter at length, but if you will examine the prophecies—read them simply as you would a book in which you expected that its meaning would be plainly expressed—read with prayer, for a simple, child-like heart of faith—read thus the prophet Isaiah, study that prophet, consider his prophecy in its plain and obvious sense; and you will find that the great glory which is promised to the earth, shall flow to the world through the Jewish people, even through the reign of the Lord Jesus Christ over that nation. I shall not enter into this view of the subject, nor consider whether the reign of our blessed Lord be a personal, or a spiritual reign; but this is clear as light, to those who peruse the prophecies, that, whatever be the nature of the reign of our glorious Redeemer—at His second advent that reign shall be commenced—His kingdom shall then be established over Jerusalem, and that from thence, His government shall flow throughout all the nations of the earth.

Let me refer you to Isaiah ii. 2, 3. Consider the plain literal meaning of that passage. "*And it shall come to pass in the last days, that the mountain of the Lord's house shall be established in the top of the mountains, and shall be exalted above the hills, and all nations shall flow unto it; and many people shall go and say, come ye, and let us go up to the mountain of the Lord, to the house of the God of Jacob, and he will teach us of our ways, and we will walk in his paths; for out of Zion shall go forth the law, and the word of the Lord from Jerusalem.*" Look at the first verse,—"*The vision, that Isaiah the son of Amos, saw concerning Judah and Jerusalem.*" Observe the vision is, "*concerning Judah and Jerusalem.*" Then, consider again how plain these words are. "*And many people shall go and say, come ye, and let us go up unto the mountain of the Lord, to the house of the God of Jacob, and he will teach us of his ways, and we will walk in his paths, for out of Zion shall go forth the law, and the word of the Lord from Jerusalem.*" 4th v. "*And he shall judge among the nations, and shall rebuke many people, and they shall beat their swords into plough-shares, and their spears into pruning-hooks, nation shall not lift up sword against nation, neither shall they learn war any more.*"

Just ponder these verses—the plain truth set forth in them, and you will see this same truth repeated throughout all the prophecies. You will see there, that the reign of the Lord upon the throne of His Father David, whatever you may consider the nature of that reign to be, shall be certainly the time in which the glory and blessing that is predicted of this earth shall be fulfilled. It is to this, the Apostle Paul alludes, as we observed, in his prophecy in Romans xi. 15, where he speaks of the calling in of the Jews. "*If the casting away of them be the reconciling of the world,*" meaning, that if when they rejected Christ as they did, and when in consequence they were themselves cast away, and that then He sent His dispensation of grace to the Gentiles, "*If the casting away of them be the reconciling of the world, what shall the receiving of them be but life from the dead?*"

Now the Jews were totally unable to distinguish the first from the second advent of the Lord Jesus Christ. The advent of Jesus Christ in his humiliation when he was to come to be "*made a curse for us.*" Gal. iii. 13, "*to die, the just for the unjust, that he might bring us to God,*" 1st Pet. iii. 11, they entirely overlooked; and therefore, they despised and rejected the Lord Jesus Christ. This mystery then—that the Gentiles should be gathered in, called into His church, that they should be called into that glorious dispensation of love and mercy, in which "*there is neither Greek nor Jew, circumcision nor uncircumcision, Barbarian, Scythian, bond or free,*" Col. iii. 11, this mystery was not known to the Jews or to their prophets, "AS IT IS NOW REVEALED UNTO HIS HOLY APOSTLES AND PROPHETS BY THE SPIRIT."

But the Second point comprehended in this mystery, seems to be not only as we have seen in the first, that the salvation of Christ should embrace the Gentiles, as well as the Jews, and that they should be "*one fold and one shepherd*"—John x. 16, but also the development to the nations of the earth of the redemption which is proclaimed to them—the glory of the salvation itself that is sent to the Gentiles, that they "SHOULD BE FELLOW-HEIRS AND OF THE SAME BODY, AND PARTAKERS OF HIS PROMISE IN CHRIST BY THE GOSPEL." That they should understand that great mystery of godliness that "*God was manifest in the flesh*,"—that mysterious work of redeeming love by which the vilest can be pardoned, and yet God can be just in justifying the chief of sinners,—that mysterious dispensation of grace, by which, those who were following their dumb idols can be brought to the God and Father of their salvation,—the polluted sinner can be brought unto Him "*who is of purer eyes than to behold iniquity*," and presented to Him "*without spot, or wrinkle, or any such thing*,"—covered in the righteousness and washed in the blood of Christ.

The words of the Apostle indicate still more the nature of this mystery, "*That the Gentiles should be* FELLOW-HEIRS," the same word that is used in the passage, Rom. viii. 17. "*heirs of God, and* JOINT-HEIRS *with Christ*."

"*And of the* SAME BODY,"—the same thought that is in the passage, Rom. xii. 5, "*We being many are* ONE BODY *in Christ*."

And partakers of HIS PROMISE *in Christ*." The same glorious privilege on which the Apostle reasons so fully in Galatians iii., concluding with the words, "*There is neither Jew nor Greek, there is neither bond nor free, there is neither male nor female, for ye are all one in Christ Jesus. And if ye be Christ's then are ye Abraham's seed, and heirs* ACCORDING TO THE PROMISE."

Each word indicating the glorious mystery of the union of the Church with Christ. "FELLOW-HEIRS" *in Christ*—"OF THE SAME BODY" *in Christ*—"PARTAKERS OF HIS PROMISE IN CHRIST BY THE GOSPEL." These showed the Apostle's "*knowledge in the mystery of Christ*." "*Whereof*," he adds, "*I was made a minister, according to the gift of the grace of God, given unto me by the effectual working of his power, unto me who am less than the least of all saints, is this grace given, that I should preach among the Gentiles the unsearchable riches of Christ*." This mystery of grace and love, proclaiming salvation to the chief of sinners, through all the earth—this mystery of gathering in the Gentiles to the fold of the Good Shepherd—of the union of His Church in Him—of preaching the Gospel to every creature—proclaiming among all nations, "*the unsearchable riches of Christ*,"—going to the philosophers and votaries of Minerva, at Athens—to the worshippers of Diana, at Ephesus—of Jupiter, at Rome—and proclaiming the glorious salvation of God through the blood of the Redeemer, and the resurrection of the dead to all, this was committed to him, and its blessings were all condensed in that one expression, "*that I should preach among the Gentiles, the unsearchable riches of Christ*."

We must reserve this for another occasion. But the rejection of the Jews—the calling of the Gentiles—their dispensation—and the future prospects of Jews, Gentiles, and the earth—open a most interesting field for the examination of the prophecies. It is a subject which has been lamentably neglected in the Church; and though much has been said, and much must be expected to be said, of vain speculation, even by sober persons who may make mistakes, and by others who will seek perhaps to be "*wise above what is written*;" still it is no reason, because many mistake, and others abuse what the Divine Word reveals, that therefore, it should not form the subject of deep, and close, and prayerful attention and investigation, by all who desire to be instructed in the truth of the living God. There are many reasons, into which I shall not enter at present, which should lead us to consider and examine the subject. Men speak of the danger of mistakes. But there is no grosser mistake, and no greater danger, than to be ignorant of what God has graciously written for our learning. Let us read, and watch, and pray, humbly,—faithfully,—and then we shall read safely.

Let us beware indeed of vain speculations, of questions to no profit. Let us pray that we may be kept like Mary at her Master's feet, that nothing may divert our attention from the great simplicity of the Gospel of Christ, as applied to our own soul. That is the great point.—The foundation of all sound knowledge, the basis of all solid hope, and all real, or stable peace, and the only true principle of all holiness of life.

Be assured that the genuine power of "all holy conversation and godliness," is simply the Gospel—applied to the sinner's soul by the Holy Ghost, in the constant exercise of faith and hope and prayer, looking unto and leaning on Christ—covering our nakedness by faith, with His righteousness—washing away our sins by faith in the fountain of His precious blood—leaning by faith on the arm of His strength—and looking to His eye to guide and keep us in the way wherein we ought to go. Let us pray, dear friends, that we may be brought to "*the simplicity that is in Christ*," and let us beware that we be not corrupted from that simplicity. May our God teach and direct us all according to the riches of His grace! for we may preach—or we might hear truth, not from a poor, weak fellow-sinner, but from an inspired Apostle, and yet both that Apostle himself and those who hear, must be indebted solely to the sovereign grace and power of God for fixing that truth in their heart, and keeping it practically influential upon their life in every moment of their existence.

May the Lord teach us all by the power of His Spirit, and bring us to eternal life, for Christ's sake. Amen.

TWENTY-SECOND LECTURE.

EPHESIANS III.—7, 8.

"Whereof I was made a minister, according to the gift of the grace of God, given unto me by the effectual working of his power. Unto me, who am less than the least of all saints, is this grace given, that I should preach among the Gentiles the unsearchable riches of Christ."

THE mystery of which the Apostle speaks, which "*in other ages was not made known unto the sons of men, as it is now revealed unto his holy apostles and prophets by the Spirit,*" we considered in a two-fold sense.

One, as it refers to the glorious work of Christ,—redemption by the righteousness and blood of a crucified Saviour.

And the other, that the Gentiles should be called in, and made partakers of this, and fellow-heirs of that glorious kingdom which is promised in Christ to the Jews. The Apostle proceeds to mention his own ministrations in this dispensation of love to the Gentiles—he says, "WHEREOF I WAS MADE A MINISTER," (namely, of the Gospel,)—"WHEREOF I WAS MADE A MINISTER, ACCORDING TO THE GIFT OF THE GRACE OF GOD GIVEN UNTO ME BY THE EFFECTUAL WORKING OF HIS POWER. UNTO ME, WHO AM LESS THAN THE LEAST OF ALL SAINTS, IS THIS GRACE GIVEN, THAT I SHOULD PREACH AMONG THE GENTILES THE UNSEARCHABLE RICHES OF CHRIST."—That is the dispensation of the grace of God of which he speaks in the 2d verse, "*If ye have heard of the dispensation of the grace of God which is given me to you-ward.*" We referred to the place where the Lord committed this ministration to him (Acts xxvi.) and he says here, speaking of himself and this ministration, "UNTO ME, WHO AM LESS THAN THE LEAST OF ALL SAINTS, IS THIS GRACE GIVEN, THAT I SHOULD PREACH AMONG THE GENTILES THE UNSEARCHABLE RICHES OF CHRIST. The Apostle speaks of his own character as "LESS THAN THE LEAST OF ALL SAINTS," and he tells us the reason of this in 1st Cor. xv. 9, "*I am the least of all the Apostles, and am not meet to be called an Apostle, because I persecuted the church of God.*" This is a very important reason. The character of St. Paul, in his natural state, we have on the testimony of the Holy Ghost, speaking by the mouth of the Apostle himself, Phil. iii. 4—6. It was a character of the very highest order. The highest order of morals, the highest order of religion, in a certain sense, was Paul's—he says himself, "*If any other man thinketh he hath whereof he might trust in the flesh, I more:*" v. 4,—there was sincerity, morality, devotedness, conscientiousness, zeal, indomitable courage, to be found in the character of the Apostle Paul. But you see, that so far is this sincerity, conscientiousness, and devotedness to what he believed to be the truth—so far is this from being accepted before God, when it is not the truth—that is, when not founded on the truth as it is in Jesus—so far is it from being approved or accepted before God—that the Apostle brings forward this very zeal and devotedness in a wrong cause, not as a proof of his excellence, but of his guilt and vileness. He says, that "*he is not worthy to be called an apostle, because he persecuted the church of God.*" This is a very important point to consider, because as we have had frequent reason to remark, this is the common principle of the natural mind, that if persons are really upright, sincere and zealous in their religion, it is not of much moment whether or not they hold certain doctrines or opinions; as if the truth of God consisted of mere vague statements, which it is of no consequence whether men believe or not, provided they are sincere in what they profess. Sincerity and conscientiousness are only the means of sinners running farther from God, and rebelling with a higher hand against Him, if they are not sincere and conscientious in God's truth, because the more a man is devoted to a false religion, the more opposed he is to the truth as it is in Jesus. The most bitter opponents of the Gospel whom I have ever met, were men considered by the world as very religious, as the Scribes and Pharisees were, the chief enemies of Christ.

One of the Articles of our Church is very clear on this subject, and although the Articles of the Church are not the authority of Scripture, they will be found to derive their authority from the Bible. One is very plain on this point, Art. xviii. It states—

"They are to be held accursed that presume to say, that every man shall be saved by the law or sect which he professeth, so that he be diligent to frame his life according to that law, and the light of nature; for holy Scripture doth set out unto us only the name of Jesus Christ, whereby men must be saved."

I would observe, our Church does not pronounce, of her own power, as if she had a right to curse any one, but she says, they are to be held so. What an awful but common state of delusion for men to think, that provided they are zealous and sincere in the sect they profess, they will be saved: whereas, if they believe not the Gospel, the wrath of God abideth upon them, they are under the sentence of death. So the Apostle, speaking of himself, says, he is "LESS THAN THE LEAST OF ALL SAINTS," and he gives the reason, "*Because I persecuted the church of God, but by the grace of God, I am what I am.*"—That grace of which we have been speaking in the last chapter—that sovereign grace, arrested Saul in the midst of his blasphemy and persecution—seized him on his way to Damascus—revealed to him the glory of Jesus—his own guilt and misery—the riches of pardoning love,—and sent him forth to testify of that faith which he once destroyed, of that Christ whom he was persecuting. And you do not forget the passage to which we referred on the last day, in 1st Tim. i., wherein the Apostle shows the reason why he received mercy; he says, "*I thank Christ Jesus our Lord who hath enabled me, for that he counted me faithful, putting me into the ministry, who was before, a blasphemer, and a persecutor and injurious, (but I obtained mercy,) because I did it ignorantly in unbelief.*" Let me again call your attention to this verse for there is an important error connected with it, into which I did not sufficiently enter on that occasion.

Some person may say, "If one is ignorant, he will obtain mercy, because the Apostle says, ignorance is no sin, he obtained mercy, because he sinned ignorantly in unbelief, and God will pardon us when we sin ignorantly."

The Apostle Paul says no such thing; and if you look at the passage, you will clearly see this. He does not mean, "*I obtained mercy because I did it ignorantly in unbelief,*" but these words refer to the other clause, "*I was a blasphemer, and a persecutor, and injurious, because I did it ignorantly in unbelief.*" The sense is shown by placing the words, "*but I obtained mercy,*" in parenthesis. The 16th verse proves unequivocally the meaning of the passage, "*howbeit, for this cause I obtained mercy,*" not "*because I did it ignorantly in unbelief.*" But "*for this cause I obtained mercy, that in me first, Jesus Christ might show forth all long-suffering, for a pattern to them which should hereafter believe on him to life everlasting.*"

The Apostle Paul holds himself forth as we have said, as an eminent example of the grace of God, that no sinner should despair, when such grace was given to such a wretch as Saul of Tarsus, the persecutor and blasphemer. And see, what a blessing it is to us! how often have we blasphemed the Lord in our hearts! how often resisted his providences and his ordinances! how often has our heart risen in unsubdued opposition in a thousand ways against Him! perhaps it is so even now, perhaps there are many things, against which some hearts amongst us rise in proud rebellion against our God; perhaps even at this very moment we are complaining and murmuring against him. Well! Paul was "*a persecutor, and a blasphemer, and injurious,*" and he is held out to you as an example, that you may know that the grace of God can pardon any sinner—and that you may bring your sinful heart, laden with iniquity as it is, to the foot of the cross of Christ—and that you may know that in Christ there is full salvation, free salvation for the very chief of sinners. Blessed be God for the pardon of the persecuting Saul! blessed be God for the pardon of the thief on the cross! blessed be God for the pardon and the raising up of fallen Peter! Blessed be God for the pardon and bringing back of guilty David! Blessed be God for the riches of His grace to the bloodthirsty Manasseh! Blessed be God for the glorious Gospel, which is a dispensation of grace to the chief of sinners.

The dispensation of grace given to St. Paul for the Gentiles, is that which we have to contemplate in this passage. He says, "UNTO ME WHO AM LESS THAN THE LEAST OF ALL SAINTS IS THIS GRACE GIVEN, THAT I SHOULD PREACH AMONG THE GENTILES THE UNSEARCHABLE RICHES OF CHRIST."

There was a very eloquent and able minister of our Church, who went to labor among his flock, ignorant of the Gospel of Christ, but at the same time very zealous and devoted in his own way of religion. He was sedulously endeavoring to deliver them from their sins, and to promote morality and virtue among them by every means in his power; and you may suppose with the same success that must always attend such vain efforts as these, to make the law do "*what the law could not do, in that it is weak through the flesh*," Rom. viii. 3. Whitewashing the sepulchre can never purify the corruption within. "*Daubing the wall with untempered mortar*," Ezek. xiii., can never build it on a solid foundation. Outward reformation can never renew the heart and save the soul, or bring the sinner nearer to his God. But this clergyman was reading this chapter one day, and when he came to this verse, "UNTO ME WHO AM LESS THAN THE LEAST OF ALL SAINTS, IS THIS GRACE GIVEN, THAT I SHOULD PREACH AMONG THE GENTILES THE UNSEARCHABLE RICHES OF CHRIST;" he began to consider what the doctrine was which St. Paul was preaching, "PREACH AMONG THE GENTILES THE UNSEARCHABLE RICHES OF CHRIST!" "What is that?" said he. "Is this what I preach? I am preaching virtue, amiability, goodness, devotedness to God, attendance on ordinances, I am preaching against all sort of sins; St. Paul was preaching 'THE UNSEARCHABLE RICHES OF CHRIST!' what is that? what can he mean?"

See, how the Holy Ghost is pleased to use various means in bringing sinners into the light of truth! The blessed Spirit fastened that word on that man's mind, "THE UNSEARCHABLE RICHES OF CHRIST" and led him to see that that was not the doctrine which he taught: he did not even understand the meaning of the expression. This led him to inquire into what that meaning was, and the same blessed Spirit satisfied the inquiry, and led him to discover the treasure hid in the field, even "THE UNSEARCHABLE RICHES OF CHRIST," and then he went forth and preached these "UNSEARCHABLE RICHES," and the blessing of God attended his labors, he experienced in his congregation the truth of the Apostolic testimony, that the Gospel is "*the power of God unto salvation to every one that believeth*." Rom. i. 16. And now, perhaps, there are some in this congregation as ignorant as this Clergyman* was. Let me ask, do you know the meaning of "THE UNSEARCHABLE RICHES OF CHRIST?" Let me, I entreat, ask you this question, did you ever find this treasure in the sacred Scriptures? Do you know the meaning of it? When you take the word of God into your hand, can you open that book, and can

* This story is told, and the name of the Clergyman is given, to the best of my recollection, by Newton, in one of his letters.—ED.

you find in it, any portion of "THE UNSEARCHABLE RICHES OF CHRIST?" Can you lay your hand on any passage and say, "here is a portion of 'THE UNSEARCHABLE RICHES OF CHRIST,' a treasure, a rich treasure for my poor soul, here are the real riches which I want to give me true and solid happiness?" Can you do this? Remember, the Lord Jesus Christ saith—"*the kingdom of heaven is like a treasure hid in a field.*" Mat. xiii. 44. If you know the meaning of these words, let me not say the meaning, for who can fully know the meaning?—who hath searched out these "UNSEARCHABLE RICHES?" But if you know, in any degree, the meaning of these words, you have found the treasure hid in the field; you know there is in this blessed book a treasure greater than all the world or ten thousand worlds! you know that the only treasure for your soul to give you rest, peace, and happiness in time and in eternity, is to be found in this blessed word: and if you do not know this, then you are poor indeed. How destitute the sinner is, that has not "THE UNSEARCHABLE RICHES OF CHRIST." If he had all the world beside, the question still is to be answered, the sum is still to be calculated, "*what shall it profit a man, if he shall gain the whole world, and lose his own soul, or what shall a man give in exchange for his soul?*" Mat. xvi. 26. The monarch of a world were a miserable pauper if destitute of "THE UNSEARCHABLE RICHES OF CHRIST."

What are they? Go to a man in an arid desert, lying on the ground, gasping with thirst, at the gate of death, beneath a burning sun, take to him gold—and jewels—offer them to him—promise him a kingdom; and what do you bestow on him? There is that for which, if he had it, he would barter them all.—A cup of water, one draught from the stream—for this he pants—this would be wealth and a kingdom for him.

Go again to another in the jaws of famine, dying from hunger, pour out silver and gold—the wealth of a world at his feet, and what do you confer upon him? he would give a world, or a thousand worlds, for a single morsel of bread.

Again, take a man gasping on the field of battle, mortally wounded, writhing in agony, offer him riches, offer him a crown, will he thank you? No. If you could heal his wounds,—if you could raise him up from the cold bed of death,—if you could restore him to the life and health he enjoyed an hour before, that would be wealth and riches for the dying man.

Take a poor criminal, led out to execution, offer him all that earth could give—what could he do with it? what is the earth to him? But procure a pardon for him,—gain for him a reprieve, there is a world, and more than a world for him.

Well then, if you knew your own actual state, you would see that your spiritual condition before God, is just as hopeless, just as miserable, just as desperate, as the temporal condition of any one of these sufferers I have described; you are spiritually the poor wretch in the burning desert, without a drop of water, and if you die in your unconverted state, you must be without a drop of water to cool your tongue for eternity. You are worse than the poor creature who is famishing with hunger,—worse, far worse than him writhing in agony on the field of battle,—worse than the criminal about to be led to execution; these, however agonizing their state, are merely suffering for time; considered in reference to man's mere animal existence, their pangs soon must terminate; but the misery in which your immortal soul is sunk, unless you are delivered, must endure for eternity.

Now Christ is the Water to the soul that is dying of thirst. John iv. 10. vii. 37.

Christ is the Bread of life to the sinner, perishing for hunger. John vi. 32, 33, 35.

Christ is the Great Physician that can heal the dying man. Mark ii. 10, 11.

Christ is the King that extends his pardon to the criminal led forth to execution. Luke xxiii. 43.

These serve as a partial illustration, of "THE UNSEARCHABLE RICHES OF CHRIST." You understand the application, if you know Christ as the Deliverer, the Healer, the Saviour of your immortal souls.

The knowledge of that grace of God which pardons sin, and delivers those who are under its curse and power, from death and hell—of that blessed Saviour who has "*borne our guilt in his own body on the tree*,"—and who sends a proclamation of His mercy to a lost and perishing world, illustrates the meaning of the Apostle, when he says "THAT I SHOULD PREACH AMONG THE GENTILES THE UNSEARCHABLE RICHES OF CHRIST."

Now, who were the Gentiles? They composed a world sunk in every species of crime; there is no description of iniquity into which man could be degraded, no degree of utter alienation of his will or his affections from God, no prostration of intellect in the worship of dumb idols, the work of his hands, into which you will not find the Gentile nations fallen and debased. Now, what did Christ send Paul to do? What was the message of the Gospel with which He charged him? The Apostle declares he was sent to them, "THAT I SHOULD PREACH AMONG THE GENTILES," —the original word is stronger,—that I should *proclaim*,—go as an ambassador from God, and *proclaim* "AMONG THE GENTILES THE UNSEARCHABLE RICHES OF CHRIST,"—tell them of a Redeemer that came to save the vilest sinner,—tell them of the justice, the judgment, the mercy, and love of God,—tell them of the justice that pronounces sentence on sinners,—but which Christ had satisfied—tell them of the judgment that is to be executed on them, but which Christ had borne—tell them of the mercy that they had forever forfeited, but which Christ had purchased for them—tell them of the wisdom that devised, the faithfulness that carried out, and the love that began, continued, and carries on the glorious plan of salvation for a guilty world—tell them that this is the True, and Holy Lord, the Judge of quick and dead—call them thus to turn from their idols and their vanities, to serve the living God.

Now, if we look to the history of the Acts of the Apostles, we see through their various labors, how the Apostle executed his divine commission. Let us take one instance; let us turn to Acts xiii. St. Paul came into the synagogue in Antioch of Pisidia, and stood up to preach the Gospel to those assembled. We find him beginning at the 16th verse; he gives a brief history of the Jewish people,—the promise of the Messiah,—and the fulfilment of that promise, in the birth, life, character, and death of Christ. After giving a brief sketch of these, he testifies, not only of His death, but His resurrection from the dead; that He was raised up, and that He saw no corruption, 37th verse. And then we find, afterwards he testifies what the end and object of His coming was, "*Be it known unto you, therefore, men and brethren, that through this man is preached unto you the forgiveness of sins, and by him, all that believe are justified from all things from which ye could not be justified by the law of Moses.*" v. 38, 39.

Then he warns them to beware, lest they despise this testimony, "*Beware lest that come upon you which is spoken of in the prophets, behold ye despisers, and wonder, and perish; for I work a work in your days, a work which ye shall in no wise believe, though a man declare it unto you.*" v. 40, 41.

Then look at the 42nd verse, "*When the Jews were gone out of the synagogue, the Gentiles besought that these words might be preached to them the next Sabbath.*" He proclaimed to them "THE UNSEARCHABLE RICHES OF CHRIST"—namely, the pardon of their sins, through a crucified and risen Saviour, "*through this man is proclaimed unto you the forgiveness of sins;*" then the "*Gentiles besought that the same words might be proclaimed to them the next Sabbath;*" and so it is always the case, the moment the sinner is brought to know the Lord Jesus Christ, the proclamation of His great salvation is the joy of his soul,—he desires to hear the same things over again and again.

I knew a lady once, who had heard the Gospel of Christ for many years, but she had neglected that great salvation, and continued in darkness and ignorance till she was very old. She was taken very ill at one time, her daughter was sitting by her bed side, and speaking to her of the riches of Christ. She was reading the Word of life to her, telling her of the pardon of sin. It pleased the Lord to bring His word with power home to her heart, and she did the very same thing that the Gentiles did at Antioch, she raised herself up in the bed, and said, "*Oh, my dear child, tell me that again,—tell me these words again.*" She had heard the same words a thousand times, but she had never believed them, never attended to them before,—now she heard them and understood the blessing they conveyed, and cried, "*Oh, tell me that again.*" Whenever a sinner is brought to Christ, he says, "tell me that again, tell me more of Christ, the refuge of my soul, more, more of the unsearchable riches of Christ." When a man finds a gold mine, what does he do? he digs deeper and deeper still, till he discovers more and more of the treasure. When the sinner finds Christ, that is, when through grace he understands and believes the Gospel, he longs for more of the inestimable treasure—more of the unsearchable riches—he "*counts all things loss for the excellency of the knowledge of Christ*," he longs for more of the happy privilege of trusting on Christ,—more of the power of leaning and resting on Christ,—casting all his soul, all his sins, all his sorrows, all his cares, all his wants, all his hopes, doubts, fears, anxieties, upon Him,—he longs for an increase of faith, and learns more and more to wrap his naked soul in the spotless righteousness of his Redeemer, to bathe continually more and more by faith in the fountain opened for sin and for uncleanness,—he finds the riches of Christ unsearchable, because he finds his own sin inexhaustible, he finds the deceit of his own heart, he finds the depth of his own guilt and wants unfathomable; daily he finds more and more sin, and corruption, and varied wants and evils in himself, and sees more and more his bankrupt poverty, and his need to draw on "*the unsearchable riches of Christ.*" Hence, sincere Christians who are not well and scripturally instructed, are grievously cast down because they do not feel their heart growing better, but rather growing worse; for they feel more unbelief—more deadness—more sin, than they have ever felt before. It is not that your heart really grows worse, for worse it cannot be, but you begin to discover its evil more and more, to understand—to feel it more and more, your mind is more enlightened to comprehend the spiritual nature of the law of God, how it reaches to every desire, wish, thought and imagination of the heart—you learn more of what you ought to be, and you learn by painful experience more truly what you are. It is then you are brought to know somewhat of the meaning, and to see the blessing of "*the unsearchable riches of Christ*," whatever be the painful experience of your own want and sin, you find the Lord Jesus Christ commensurate to all your necessities.

His righteousness is unsearchable, "*his righteousness is like the great mountains.*" Ps. xxxvi. 6.

His wisdom is unsearchable, "*in him are hid all the treasures of wisdom and knowledge.*" Col. ii. 3.

His grace is unsearchable, "*Where sin abounded, grace did much more abound.*" Rom. v. 20.

His love is unsearchable, "*many waters cannot quench it.*"—"*Strong as death.*" Cant. viii. 6, 7,—It "*passeth knowledge.*" verse 19.

His faithfulness is unsearchable, "*Thy counsels of old are faithfulness and truth.*" Isa. xxv. 1. We would turn from Him, we would go back, we would run the broad way to ruin as fast as ever we ran, but that His faithfulness will not let us go. What would become of us, if it were not written, "*My sheep shall never perish, neither shall any pluck them out of my hand.*" John x. 28. Oh, "*the unsearchable riches of Christ!*"

Then His power is unsearchable, "*By thee have I been holden up from the womb.*" Ps. lxxi. 6. "*In him dwelleth all the fulness of the Godhead bodily.*" Col. ii. 9. "*God is our refuge and strength.*" Ps. xlvi. 1. "*My strength is made perfect in weakness,*" "*most gladly therefore,*" saith the Apostle, "*will I rather glory in my infirmities, that the power of Christ may rest upon me.*" 2nd Cor. xii. 9. It is a wonderful experience for a sinner to attain to, to be able to look at his infirmities as a subject of glorying, because they magnify and endear his Saviour more and more to his soul, and lead him to discover more and more of "*the unsearchable riches of Christ.*"

Then the tenderness and compassion of our blessed Saviour are unsearchable, his long-suffering is unsearchable; which of you who knows the Gospel cannot tell, (I am sure I can,) what a "*God of patience,*" Rom. xv. 5, He has proved to us? how many years He hath "*suffered our manners in the wilderness.*" Acts xiii. 12.

But time would fail were we to enter into any detail of these gracious attributes of our adorable Redeemer. If those who love the treasures of this earth take pleasure in counting their silver and their gold, we may be permitted to take some time to dwell on that which we prize more than all the wealth of the world; and we shall dwell yet once again on the "*unsearchable riches of Christ,*" "*for we have not been redeemed with corruptible things, as silver and gold, from our vain conversation received by tradition from our fathers, but with the precious blood of Christ, as of a lamb without blemish, and without spot.*" 1st Peter i. 18, 19.

May our souls so feel their need continually of Christ, that we may love to dig deeper into the mine where his unsearchable treasures are to be found; here is the mine, the Bible; all who once have found the "*treasure hid in this field,*" the deeper they go, the richer veins of ore, do they discover; the more we search the Scriptures, the more we find of their treasure, and remember the reason of it is this, "*Because,*" saith our blessed Lord, "*they are they which testify of me;*" John v. 39, "*the testimony of Jesus is the spirit of prophecy,*" Rev. xix. 10, "*we preach Christ crucified,*" saith the Apostle, 1st Cor. i. 23. "*I am Alpha and Omega, the beginning and the ending, saith the Lord, which is, and which was, and which is to come, the Almighty,*" Rev. i. 8. Let us pray that our souls may be enriched, more and more with "THE UNSEARCHABLE RICHES OF CHRIST," that our hearts, filled with the joyful hope of their undefiled, unfading, incorruptible, inheritance, may be less careful and anxious for the passing vanities of a transitory world, which like a mirror that reflects a shadow, gives back to the eager eye but the unsubstantial image of a shade, that our hearts may be filled more and more with these "UNSEARCHABLE RICHES OF CHRIST," "*The blessing of the Lord that maketh rich, and he addeth no sorrow with it.*" Prov. x. 22.

Yes, O Thou bounteous Giver of all good,
Thou art of all thy gifts, Thyself the Crown!
Give what Thou canst, without Thee we are poor,
And with Thee rich, take what Thou wilt away.

TWENTY-THIRD LECTURE.

EPHESIANS III.—8, 9, 10.

"Unto me, who am less than the least of all saints, is this grace given, that I should preach among the Gentiles the unsearchable riches of Christ; and to make all men see what is the fellowship of the mystery, which from the beginning of the world hath been hid in God, who created all things by Jesus Christ: to the intent that now, unto the principalities and powers in heavenly places might be known by the church the manifold wisdom of God."

IF a ship freighted from a foreign clime for our shore, with the invoice of a cargo of inestimable value, were consigned to a merchant, for his own emolument; when the intelligence of her arrival in port had reached his ears, how anxiously would he hasten to investigate the contents of his expected prize. How earnestly would his mind be exercised in the various thoughts, arrangements, and occupations which this rich consignment entailed on him.

Now, beloved brethren, when the Apostle Paul was commissioned to "PREACH AMONG THE GENTILES THE UNSEARCHABLE RICHES OF CHRIST." He was charged with a freight of blessings, richer than all the merchandize that all the vessels of the world have ever carried on the bosom of the deep; and this too a freight consigned to every sinner who hears the gracious message of the Gospel. "*Men and brethren, children of the stock of Abraham, and whosoever among you feareth God, to you is the word of this salvation sent,*" Acts xiii. 26. These are his own words in the very passage which I quoted in my last Lecture, as addressed by him to those in the synagogue at Antioch, in Pisidia, "*To you is the word of this salvation sent,*" and let me add that those who have received this blessed freight consigned to them, would not barter it for all the treasures of the earth or of the sea.

How inexpressibly important is the question then, whether we have received it, or know its inestimable value? whether we have received the invoice of the Holy Ghost, that the Gospel carries the freight to us of the "UNSEARCHABLE RICHES OF CHRIST." May our God lead us to examine the rich consignment, and enable us to draw forth treasures from these unsearchable riches, that "*our souls may be satisfied as with marrow and fatness,*" and that our "*mouth may praise him with joyful lips!*" Ps. lxiii. 5.

The heart of man is continually panting after something it imagines to be good; continually longing for something to satisfy its vast desires; and as long as it pursues the things of time and sense, which in its natural state, it always will pursue; turning from one unsatisfying vanity to another, so long, the very nature of the immortal soul, precludes the possibility of its happiness, and keeps it in continual misery. Because, nothing but "UNSEARCHABLE RICHES," can really satisfy the wants of an immortal being; and therefore, the invitation sent to sinners, are invitations to come to God Himself. "*Ho, every one that thirsteth come ye to the waters,*" Isaiah iv. 1, "*Come unto me all ye that labor and are heavy-laden, and I will give you rest,*" Mat. xi. 28; "*If any man thirst,*" saith Christ, "*let him come unto me and drink,*" John vii. 37; "*My oxen and my fatlings are killed, and all things are ready, come unto the marriage.*" You that thirst for happiness, that seek for enjoyment,—for rest,—for peace,—come unto me saith Christ. He knows what is in man. He knows that "UNSEARCHABLE RICHES" alone can satisfy the desires of the immortal soul. So He saith, "*Riches and honor are with me, yea, durable riches and righteousness. My fruit is better than gold, yea, than fine gold, and my revenue than choice silver. I lead in the way of righteousness in the midst of the paths of judgment, that I may cause those that love me to inherit substance, and I will fill their treasures.*" Prov. viii. 18, 19, 20, 21. When Christ saith, "*I will fill their treasures,*" then must the treasures of the soul be filled indeed! The immortal soul is not formed by God to be satisfied with anything, but enjoyment commensurate with its own existence, therefore, it is not to be found in time or in the world,—eternity and Christ, alone can fill its infinite capacity, therefore the riches of Christ are called "UNSEARCHABLE RICHES," because they satisfy the desires, they quench the thirst of an immortal being,—the soul is never cloyed, never left to pine, as in finite enjoyments for the brief duration of its bliss: it never reaches the end of its unsearchable and inexhaustible possessions until it has found its treasure and its rest in the bosom of the Infinite God.

The suitability and all-sufficiency of Christ, for the wants of the sinner, constitute one reason why the blessings of Christ are called "UNSEARCHABLE RICHES." I said, we should count over some of the items in our treasure.

Take then, in the first place, the WISDOM OF CHRIST, nothing less than an Omniscient Saviour could possibly be suited to the wants of sinners like us. Hence, the absurdity as well as the awful idolatry of praying to saints or angels; for if they have not the attributes of an Omniscient God, they cannot be suited to the wants of man. Christ is the Omniscient God, "*in him are hid all the treasures of wisdom and knowledge,*" "*in him dwelleth all the fulness of the Godhead bodily,*" Col. iii. 3, 9. "*He knows what is in man,*" how could we kneel down and pour out our hearts to Him, if He did not know our sins, our wants, if He could not enter into all our necessities and fears? If we were to tell our feelings, wants, sins, to any friend on earth, they could not understand—they could not enter into them—impossible! But Christ can, and does, "*He knoweth our frame, he remembereth that we are dust,*" Ps. ciii. 14; "*in that he himself hath suffered, being tempted, he is able to succor them that are tempted.*" Heb. ii. 18. O! what an inestimable blessing!

The Apostle says, "*all things are naked and open to the eyes of Him, with whom we have to do.*" Heb. iv. 13. What a frightful thought for the ungodly sinner, that would try to hide from God.—for the sinner who is looking for salvation in himself!—trying to deliver himself—to make himself clean in God's sight! What a fearful thought for such an one to have a God, that sees all the turnings of his deceitful and desperately wicked heart!—what a frightful thought for a poor sinner, who is trying to make himself fit for the inspection of Him, who is of purer eyes than to behold iniquity!

But what a blessing for the soul who knows, that instead of delivering himself, all his deliverance is in Christ! His very wants,—sins,—necessities,—weaknesses, these are the very reasons why he comes to Christ; these are the very reasons why Christ is precious, because he wants a Saviour such as this. And therefore, what a blessing to think, that the wisdom of Christ is unsearchable, and that he knoweth all things! If we are sick, and a physician is called in, we are most anxious to let him know our case; and we very often hear persons say, of a physician long attending them and their families, "Oh, such a man knows my constitution—he knows my case—he is accustomed to my disease—I value him above all others!" If we value such a physician for the body, what a blessing it is to have such a Physician for the soul. To have ONE who is familiar with our case, who understands our disease, who knows all our wants,—to have Him watching over us—watching by our sick beds, "*Thou wilt make all his bed in his sickness,*" Ps. xxi. 3; watching by us in health, "*Behold he that keepeth Israel shall neither slumber nor sleep,*" Ps. cxxi. 4; watching over us with the Omnipresent eye of infinite wisdom,—of everlasting love, and of Almighty power!

Then again, the LOVE OF CHRIST, how unsearchable!—the very nature of God's love to sinners is unsearchable. We do not love anything on earth in which we do not see something to make it loveable or lovely in our eyes. But the love of God, the free, full, and everlasting love of God for sinners cannot be derived from anything attractive in the sinner; on the contrary there is everything repulsive to make God hate us, to make Him turn from us. Yet His language to His people is, "*I have loved thee with an everlasting love, therefore with loving kindness have I drawn thee.*" Jer. xxxi. 3. The love of Christ is then an everlasting love to His people. I believe I quoted on some former occasion the remark of an old woman, "I am sure, if the Lord did not love me before I was born, he never saw anything in me to make Him love me since," if He did not love sinners with an everlasting love, He never would love them at all; but He does, as we have seen. "*God, who is rich in mercy, for his great love wherewith he loved us, even when we were dead in sins, hath quickened us together with Christ.*" ii. 4; and again, "*according as he hath chosen us in him before the foundation of the world, that we should be holy and without blame before him in love.*" i. 4. Then if His love is unsearchable in its commencement, surely it is equally so in its continuance. There is no affection on earth so strong as that it may not be weakened or totally dissolved by repulse, ingratitude, baseness, unkindness. The various evils of our own natural tempers will often obliterate any affection that can be conceived in the human heart. But Oh! what can quench the love of God to His people! Surely, coldness—unbelief—distrust—ingratitude—baseness,—repulse,—and provocation, if these could banish from His bosom the love of Jesus; I am sure there is not one in this assembly—nay, not a sinner in the world who could look up to God with any ground of hope for a continuance of His love. But "*Christ is the same, yesterday, to-day, and forever.*" Heb. xiii. 8. "*I am the Lord, I change not, therefore ye sons of Jacob are not consumed.*" Mal. iii. 6. Surely this is as true of the Gentiles as of the Jews. So we see, "*having loved his own which were in the world, he loved them unto the end.*" Thomas would not believe in Him, he would not even believe his own eyes, "*Unless I put my finger into the print of the nails, and thrust my hand into his side, I will not believe,*" but Jesus when he cometh saith to him, "*reach hither thy finger and behold my hands, and reach hither thy hand and thrust it into my side, and be not faithless, but believing.*" John xx. 25–27. He would take the hand of His unbelieving disciple, and let it probe His own wounded side, sooner than give him up, or withdraw His love from Thomas.

Peter denied Him with an oath, and yet He sends a messenger, to "*Go, tell his disciples and Peter,*" He particularizes him, "*that he goeth before them into Galilee, there shall ye see him.*" Mark xvi. 7.

Saul was "*breathing out threatenings and slaughter against the disciples of the Lord.*" Acts ix. 1. He was going to "*Damascus with authority from the chief priests to bring them bound to Jerusalem.*" but the love of Christ stops him on the way, and calls him to Himself; so that, whether in its commencement or its continuance, the love of Christ is unsearchable and unchangeable.

Persons continually say, that to speak of the unchangeable love of Christ is an excitement to sin. If ingratitude will not provoke—then let us be ungrateful. If rebellion will not force Him to withdraw His love—let us rebel. If sin and provocation will not incite him to forsake us—let us sin and provoke. Is that the language of your hearts? Then you know nothing of Christ.—Nay, this is the very thing that melts the heart, and draws us to Jesus, if we are taught of Him. His holy word commands us, "*If thine enemy hunger, feed him; if he thirst, give him drink; for in so doing, thou shalt heap coals of fire on his head.*" Rom. xii. 20. He desires us to melt down our enemies by heaping coals of fire,—that is, kindness and affection on their heads. Thus it is that Christ acts too. He draws us, when our hearts would stray from Him—when we turn to idols, to vanities, as we are so continually doing—the Lord Jesus Christ meets us, He draws us back to Himself. Perhaps as sometimes, by overwhelming testimonies of His love—the tenderness of reproof mingled with love, as we may suppose beamed from His eye full upon the face of Peter, when "*the Lord turned and looked upon Peter,*" and "*Peter went out and wept bitterly.*" Luke xxii. 61, 62. Or sometimes, by leaving our idols to chasten and reprove us, till we find "vanity of vanities" written on them all, and we turn with all our hearts again to Jesus, as our best—our only good.

The love of Jesus, the believer finds to be unsearchable, *by experience.* Oh, how inexhaustible it is! We know too well how often we have sinned against Him, in a thousand—thousand, ways; and yet He is just the same unchangeable Saviour to us! He is sending to us the messages of his unwearied love, as He does this day, in His everlasting Gospel; and telling us to look into his glorious Word for the "UNSEARCHABLE RICHES" of that love. And so, this is the very subject of which the Apostle speaks in the latter end of this chapter. The climax of his prayer for this church is this, "*that ye may be able to comprehend with all saints, what is the breadth, and length, and depth, and height, and to know the love of Christ, which passeth knowledge, that ye might be filled with all the fulness of God.*" verses 18, 19, 20. But His love is the love of a wise and tender Saviour. It is very mistaken love of a parent, that gives way to the selfishness, and wilfulness, and folly of his child.—A petted child is an unhappy child, and an over-indulgent parent is a foolish parent. Christ manifests His love continually, in the visitations He sends to His people; therefore he says, "*As many as I love, I rebuke and chasten.*" Rev. iii. 19. So, those "*whom the Lord loveth, he chasteneth; and scourgeth every son whom he receiveth.*" Heb. xii. 6. The child who has been corrected—wisely corrected by a wise parent—wisely brought into subjection—prudently kept in order—carefully restrained and kept from evil,—there is no child in the world that loves and respects his parent so much; and in no way can parents so effectually evince their love to their child. So, Christ shows His love to His children, and that very thing draws them nearer and nearer to Him; the very chastenings of His love are precious to His people;—His rod as well as His staff comfort them. So the Apostle testifies, "*No chastening, for the present, seemeth to be joyous, but grievous; nevertheless, afterward it yieldeth the peaceable fruit of righteousness to them that are exercised thereby.*" Heb. xii. 11. The knowledge of His love is derived continually from the visitations and trials with which He graciously afflicts His servants. And I dare say, the experience of all will testify, if we are taught to know the Lord, that when we look back to His dispensations, we shall mark His chastenings, trials, visitations,—some perhaps of those that have pressed most heavily on our hearts, when under His afflicting hand,—we shall look back at them, as some of the sweetest proofs of His love, issuing in the richest blessings to our souls. These are some of the lessons by which he trains us to learn that LOVE holds a prominent place among the "UNSEARCHABLE RICHES OF CHRIST."

Then take another.—THE POWER OF CHRIST;—the wisdom, love, and power of God must combine to form a Saviour suited to our necessities. Now we may be very wise to know what would be good for those we love, and we may have hearts full of affection for them, so that we would gladly do anything for them in our power, but we may be totally unable to do what we know their necessities require. Not so Christ.—There is nothing that He knows to be good that He *cannot* do, and there is nothing He knows to be good that he *will* not do;—His love *will* do all, and His power *can* do all that His wisdom sees fit for His children.—What a blessed thought that is!—that we have an omnipotent arm to lean on,—an almighty hand to hold us! "*Who is this that cometh up from the wilderness, leaning upon her beloved?*" Cant. viii. 5, resting upon Him, knowing how faithfully tender He is,—how mighty is His arm! Oh, what a privilege it is to have the arm of Omnipotence to lean on! and so He saith, you know, speaking of His love and power exercised towards his sheep, "*I give unto them eternal life, and they shall never perish, neither shall any pluck them out of my hand: my Father who gave them me is greater than all, and no man is able to pluck them out of my Father's hand. I and my Father are one.*" John x. 28, 29, 30. None shall pluck them out of my hand,—the tongue of everlasting *love* declares, what the hand of *Omnipotence* accomplishes. What a blessing this is!

Remember, then, you can never be in any difficulty, Oh believer! never in any straits—in any trials—any sorrow—in which you have not such a Saviour as this, with the "UNSEARCHABLE RICHES," of His wisdom—His love, and His power to relieve you. What more can you want? Let us add HIS FAITHFULNESS. The faithfulness of Jesus! the "UNSEARCHABLE RICHES" of Christ's faithfulness! This it is, that gives to all the promises of God, that certainty which enables the soul to repose on them, in Christ;—which testifies, that "*all the promises of God in him are yea, and in him Amen, to the glory of God by us,*" 2 Cor. i. 20, all yea, and all amen. It is not yea and nay—it is not that He promises what he declares to be good from his wisdom,—that he promises what He desires to do from His love,—and it is not that He promises to do what He can do by His power,—but He promises what He knows,—what he desires,—what He is able,—and what He will do from His faithfulness and truth. Yes! All his promises are yea and amen. It shall be said at the last to every redeemed soul around the throne, as Joshua said to Israel, "*Ye know in all your hearts, and in all your souls, that not one thing hath failed of all the good things which the Lord your God spake concerning you; all are come to pass unto you, and not one thing hath failed thereof.*" Joshua xxiii. 14.

Well, then, what a privilege it is for the believer to walk through the fields of promise, when he remembers the faithfulness of his covenant God! Oh think of that. Man may deceive you, and will deceive you, and you may and will deceive yourselves; Christ never can deceive. Oh, what a blessing, to have the faithfulness of Christ to trust in; the "*brother born for adversity*," Prov. xvii. 17, the "*friend that sticketh closer than a brother;*" "*when my father and mother forsake me, the Lord will take me up.*" Ps. xxvii. 10. These are some of the "UNSEARCHABLE RICHES OF CHRIST."

Then, if we speak of the riches of His grace in pardoning sin, O! how unsearchable! The riches of HIS BLOOD,—that fathomless ocean, Oh! how unsearchable! What sinner has ever sounded the depths of that atoning sea? The riches of HIS RIGHTEOUSNESS, that spotless robe, that hides "*the shame of our nakedness.*" Rev. iii. 18, which is "*unto and upon all them that believe.*" Rom. iii. 22,—with which the Father is well pleased, Oh! how unsearchable! Who can ever estimate the privilege of having such a Saviour as this to come to! Well might the Apostle magnify his glorious office—"THAT I MIGHT PREACH AMONG THE GENTILES THE UNSEARCHABLE RICHES OF CHRIST."

I have before remarked that the word "*preach among the Gentiles,*" means "*proclaim among the Gentiles.*" Recollect, then, it is the proclamation of the King of kings. If you saw a proclamation issued from the Sovereign, to any city, or to any district or province in rebellion, and that it was a proclamation of pardon;—as surely as that proclamation was issued—as surely as it was posted up—all those who desired protection under it would come in with confidence to claim protection—why?—because it was a proclamation from the Sovereign, of pardon; because in that royal proclamation, the royal word was pledged to pardon. So, if there is a proclamation of pardon for any crime committed in a country, the criminal who chooses to come in, comes in under that proclamation; he is sure he cannot be arrested, tried, and executed. The word of the Sovereign is pledged that he shall be protected, and he comes in on the faith of it. Now remember, the riches of God's grace are proclaimed to sinners. This is the Gospel of Christ—every poor sinner is invited, encouraged, commanded to come in. The Apostle saith, "THAT I MIGHT PROCLAIM AMONG THE GENTILES THE UNSEARCHABLE RICHES OF CHRIST."

Now, perhaps, there are some of you who never thought of this; for, though you may continually hear the Gospel—Alas! how many there are who never think of it. Did you ever consider, that the Gospel was a proclamation of God's mercy to your soul? That His glorious Word,—the glorious Gospel preached or proclaimed—is a proclamation of the King of kings of illimitable pardon to the chief of sinners. This is to "PROCLAIM AMONG THE

GENTILES THE UNSEARCHABLE RICHES OF CHRIST." Well then, you are Gentiles, and it is proclaimed among you to-day. God's message of pardon is proclaimed to you this day. You are rebels, have you come in under the proclamation? Are you out yet in arms, or have you come in at the proclamation—at the word of the King of kings—to receive pardon? If you have not, Oh! come in to-day. Come in this moment—"*all things are ready*"—"*To-day if ye will hear his voice harden not your hearts.*" Psal. xcv. 7, 8. You do not know when he may cut you off! If you continue but another night in arms, He may send His judgments, and sweep you into eternity!

But, if you have come in under the proclamation of mercy, then, see to what a King you have come! Remember "THE UNSEARCHABLE RICHES OF CHRIST,"—these are the blessings proclaimed to you in the Gospel. You recollect, as we have seen, when the Apostle Paul went to preach or proclaim this Gospel in the synagogue in Antioch, "*the Gentiles besought that these words should be preached to them the next sabbath.*" Now, if Paul had preached any other words, they would have been sadly disappointed, for they requested that "*these words should be preached to them,*" namely, the gracious pardon of sin, "*be it known unto you, men and brethren, that through this man is preached unto you the forgiveness of sins.*" So they "*besought that these words should be preached to them*" again,—"Let us hear that glorious proclamation again." What a blessing it is, that the "UNSEARCHABLE RICHES OF CHRIST" is the glorious proclamation of God's love to sinners like you and me! The Apostle goes on to show the result, in the divine dispensation of preaching the "UNSEARCHABLE RICHES OF CHRIST." "AND TO MAKE ALL MEN SEE, WHAT IS THE FELLOWSHIP OF THE MYSTERY, WHICH FROM THE BEGINNING OF THE WORLD HATH BEEN HID IN GOD, WHO CREATED ALL THINGS BY JESUS CHRIST." Now, you see he refers again to the subject of the beginning of the chapter, "*if ye have heard of the dispensation of the grace of God, which is given me to you-ward, how that by revelation he made known unto me the mystery,*" and here it is "TO MAKE ALL MEN SEE, WHAT IS THE FELLOWSHIP OF THE MYSTERY WHICH FROM THE BEGINNING OF THE WORLD HATH BEEN HID IN GOD, WHO CREATED ALL THINGS BY CHRIST JESUS." This mystery, as I remarked to you, appears to be two-fold,—1st, the mystery of the union of Jew and Gentile in the church of Christ. And 2dly, the great mystery of the union of both with the Lord Jesus Christ in one body as their Covenant Head. We spoke at length of the mystery of the union of Jew and Gentile, and we touched then rather briefly on the mystery of the union of Christ and His people.

This subject is greatly illuminated in that wonderful chapter, 17th chapter of the Gospel of St. John, in which our blessed Lord gives His Church, to see Himself standing, as if in His priestly office before the Throne, commencing even while on earth the office of Mediator; showing them how He acts as their Intercessor, and revealing to them as it were, the nature of His mediation, that as He saith verse 13, "*They might have my joy fulfilled in themselves.*"

He acts as Mediator in the character of a man who prays, and He acts as Mediator, in the character of God who wills. He acts in the character of man who prays, as you see in the 1st verse of the chapter, "*These words spake Jesus, and lifted up his eyes to heaven, and said, Father, the hour is come; glorify thy Son, that thy Son also may glorify thee:*" and so He says in the 5th verse, "*And now, O Father, glorify thou me with thine own self, with the glory which I had with thee before the world was.*" Here and in several other parts we hear the voice of the man who prays.

But He acts as Mediator in the character of God who wills, 24th verse, "*Father, I will that they also, whom thou hast given me, be with me where I am; that they may behold my glory, which thou hast given me: for thou lovedst me before the foundation of the world.*"

Christ does not pray for what may not be good, as we often pray, "*We know not what we should pray for as we ought.*" Rom. viii. 26. We might pray, and the very granting of our prayer might be our destruction. Even the heathen saw, that the granting of men's prayers might be and often was their ruin, so the heathen poet says,* "the compliant Gods have overturned whole families by granting their own petitions." And so, if God were to grant all our petitions, or the things we might desire or pray for, they might be our destruction. But Christ cannot pray thus, He prays for nothing that ought not to be granted, and that must not be good. We see Him then, I say, here in His character as Mediator. And mark the wondrous mystery of union with Himself, of which he speaks in that chapter, speaking of His people in the 9th, 10th, and 11th verses, He saith, "*I pray for them: I pray not for the world, but for them which thou hast given me; for they are thine. And all mine are thine, and thine are mine; and I am glorified in them. And now I am no more in the world, but these are in the world, and I come to thee. Holy Father keep through thine own name those whom thou hast given me, that they may be one as we are.*" Then in 20th and 21st verses, we see a prayer for the whole Church to the end of time; "*Neither pray I for these alone, but for them also who shall believe on me through the word; that they all may be one; as thou Father, art in me, and I in thee, that they also may be one in us: that the world may believe that thou hast sent me,*" 22nd and 23rd verses, "*and the glory which thou gavest me I have given them; that they may be one, even as we are one: I in them, and thou in me, that they may be made perfect in one;*

* "Evertêre domos totas, optantibus ipsis,
Dii faciles." JUV. SAT. X.

and that the world may know that thou hast sent me, and hast loved them, as thou hast loved me."

These verses afford not only a theme of amazement and grateful adoration to the Church in time, but they shall afford a subject of wonder, thanksgiving and glory to the Church and to all the Hosts of heaven; yea, and of astonishment to the hosts of hell for eternity! And it is now one end of the proclamation among the Gentiles of "*the unsearchable riches of Christ*," "TO MAKE ALL MEN SEE WHAT IS THE FELLOWSHIP OF THE MYSTERY, WHICH FROM THE BEGINNING OF THE WORLD HATH BEEN HID IN GOD, WHO CREATED ALL THINGS BY JESUS CHRIST, TO THE INTENT, THAT NOW UNTO THE PRINCIPALITIES AND POWERS IN HEAVENLY PLACES MIGHT BE KNOWN BY THE CHURCH THE MANIFOLD WISDOM OF GOD."

And this mysterious fellowship of Christ and His church, this amazing work of the Son of God, in which God the Son stands in the place of his fallen creatures, becomes their Surety—becomes responsible for them—takes all their debts, as their fellow-man in His humanity upon Himself—pays all their debts—discharges all their obligations both of obedience and of penalty—delivers them from death and hell, to which eternal Justice must else consign them—carries them on with the wisdom, power, and love of which we have been speaking, as one with Himself—members of His own mystical body, to eternal life—taking all along their guilt and misery, and giving them all along His righteousness and His glory—this union in its manifestation "TO THE PRINCIPALITIES AND POWERS IN HEAVENLY PLACES BY THE CHURCH," shall be the subject of adoration, joy, wonder and glory throughout all eternity. Therefore the song of the redeemed shall ever be a song of thanksgiving and praise to Him—"*Amen: Blessing, and glory, and wisdom, and thanksgiving, and honor, and power, and might, be unto our God forever and ever. Amen.*" Rev. vii. 12.

This is the subject of which we have spoken so much in the 6th chap. of Romans, and in the 1st and 2nd chap. of this epistle,—the union of Christ with His people—so that in His death, they are to reckon themselves dead with Him, and in His resurrection, alive with Him,—their sins all cancelled—their penalty all paid, in His death—their glory and their everlasting life secured in His resurrection and identified with His life; they are counted one—"*raised up together, and made to sit together in heavenly places in Christ Jesus, that in the ages to come, he might show the exceeding riches of his grace, in his kindness toward us by Christ Jesus.*" chap. ii. 6, 7. For "*When Christ, who is our life shall appear, then shall we also appear with him in glory.*" Col. iii. 4.

And Oh! my friends, if we are indeed "*looking for that blessed hope, and the glorious appearing of the great God and our Saviour Jesus Christ.*" Tit. ii. 13—even here, with all our blindness, ignorance, and self-love; with all our deadness and insensibility to the awful nature of sin, with all our obstinacy and unbelief as to the riches of the grace of God's glory, His love, His attributes, and all the wonders of the person, work, and character of Christ, even here, when we see by faith a little of these things, and are able to realize them at all, so as to live on them substantially by faith,—what wonder do they awaken in our souls! what thankfulness! what feelings of joy! We see some persons, when they realize these things, enabled to live above the world; to "look," in the language of a beloved and sainted friend, "not as if up from earth to heaven, but as from heaven down on earth."

Seldom we see it, when the old man, the vile body of sin and death is strong and active;—but often in death we see the happiness of the Lord's servants—their triumph, their glory, in treading under foot the last enemy,—so amazing sometimes to those who behold, that they seem, as if they were in another world, almost in possession of the joy and glory which faith realizes to their view. "*I see the heavens opened*," said Stephen, "*and the Son of man standing on the right hand of God.*" Acts vii. 56. And if it is so here, what shall it be when all is past? when we shall no longer "*see through a glass darkly, but face to face?*" 1 Cor. xiii. 12.—when we shall be enabled to look back at ourselves, and to see all our sins, all our vileness, ingratitude and unbelief—and all the way that the Lord hath led us, through the wilderness; how untiring has been His patience—how immeasurable His grace—how inexhaustible the resources of His wisdom—how unwearied the watchfulness of His love—how unremitting the exercise of His power—how unchangeable the constancy of his faithfulness,—or, in the one summary expression of the Apostle, how UNSEARCHABLE THE RICHES OF CHRIST, as they have been expended, lavished on such sinners, in calling and keeping us, and bringing us to Zion!

Oh! that we may be enabled to enter a little more into—to know more of these wondrous truths—to know them experimentally, practically—that we may learn more to be dead to the world—dead to the things of time and sense—more to look on them as they are, vain, passing shadows!—more to substantialize by faith, the great, approaching realities of eternity!

What a thought that we *may* be in a moment in the midst of it!—that we *must* be so very soon—that all this world shall be to us like clouds that have flown along the face of the sky,—gone,—passed,—and where are they? So shall all the things of time be to us then; we shall carry nothing with us but the remembrance of ourselves, our sins, and the unsearchable riches of our Lord's grace, goodness, and glory, all He has been to us, and done for us!

Let us pray, that we may lay these things to heart, that they may be brought home to us in demonstration of the Spirit and of power, then we shall be more enabled "*by the mercies of God to present our bodies a living sacrifice holy and acceptable unto God, which is our reasonable service, not to be conformed to this world, but to be transformed by the renewing of our mind, that we may prove what is that good and acceptable and perfect will of God.*" Rom. xii. 1, 2.

TWENTY-FOURTH LECTURE.

EPHESIANS III.—9, 10, 11.

"And to make all men see what is the fellowship of the mystery, which from the beginning of the world hath been hid in God, who created all things by Jesus Christ: to the intent that now unto the principalities and powers in heavenly places might be known by the church the manifold wisdom of God, according to the eternal purpose which he purposed in Christ Jesus our Lord."

WE considered on the last day some of the blessed truths enfolded in those words, "*the unsearchable riches of Christ*," and something of "THE FELLOWSHIP OF THE MYSTERY WHICH FROM THE BEGINNING OF THE WORLD, HAD BEEN HID IN GOD, WHO CREATED ALL THINGS BY JESUS CHRIST,"—of that mysterious fellowship which exists between Christ and His Church, in that they are one body with him, accounted one before God in all the covenant blessings of salvation which Jesus has purchased, and which He has covenanted to all His people. The Apostle says, that the preaching of the Gospel is "TO MAKE ALL MEN SEE WHAT IS THE FELLOWSHIP OF THE MYSTERY," for this purpose, "TO THE INTENT, THAT NOW UNTO THE PRINCIPALITIES AND POWERS IN HEAVENLY PLACES, MIGHT BE KNOWN BY THE CHURCH THE MANIFOLD WISDOM OF GOD, ACCORDING TO THE ETERNAL PURPOSE WHICH HE PURPOSED IN CHRIST JESUS OUR LORD."

All created things, animate or inanimate, intelligent beings or things without sense, that do not show forth the glory of their Creator, must fail of the highest end of their creation. All things bespeak the glory of God, that are really in their true position. "*The heavens declare the glory of God, and the firmament showeth his handy-work; day unto day uttereth speech, and night unto night showeth knowledge.*" Ps. xix. 1, 2. All God's intelligent creatures ought to glorify their God as all inanimate creation does. Thus in any view that is given to us of the beings that surround the throne of God, in any revelation given of them to us in the Bible, we find that the occupation of all the heavenly intelligences, is the praise, and glory of their Creator. So we see in Isaiah vi. 1, when the Prophet has a vision of the Lord sitting on His Throne, when the curtain of heaven is lifted up, and the eye of the Seer is permitted to pierce through it, he says, "*I saw the Lord sitting upon a throne, high and lifted up, and his train filled the temple, above it stood the seraphim; each one had six wings, with twain he covered his face, and with twain he covered his feet, and with twain he did fly.*" "*With twain he covered his face;*"—an old writer remarks, as if he were ashamed to lift up his eyes,—unworthy to stand in the presence of God;—"*with twain he covered his feet,*" as if he were ashamed of his obedience. "*And one cried unto another and said, holy, holy, holy, is the Lord of hosts, the whole earth is full of his glory.*" And again, in another vision which the Apostle John is permitted to see, as we have in Rev. iv., when he was in the spirit and beheld "*a throne set in heaven, and one sat on the throne. And he that sat was to look upon like a jasper and a sardine stone; and there was a rainbow round about the throne in sight like unto an emerald. And round about the throne were four and twenty seats, and upon the seats four and twenty elders sitting clothed in white raiment, and they had on their heads crowns of gold; and out of the throne proceeded lightnings and thunderings and voices and there were seven lamps of fire burning before the throne, which are the Seven Spirits of God. And before the throne there was a sea of glass like unto crystal: and in the midst of the throne and round about the throne were four beasts,* (it would be better translated, four living creatures,) *full of eyes before and behind. And the first creature was like a lion, and the second creature like a calf, and the third creature had a face as a man, and the fourth creature was like a flying eagle. And the four creatures had each of them six wings about him, and they were full of eyes within, and they ceased not day nor night, saying, holy, holy, holy Lord God Almighty, which was, and is, and is to come. And when these living creatures give glory, and honor and thanks to him that sat on the throne who liveth forever and ever, the four and twenty elders fall down before him that sat on the throne, and worship him that liveth forever and ever, and cast their crowns before the throne, saying, Thou art worthy, O Lord, to receive glory, and honor, and power; for thou hast created all things, and for thy pleasure they are and were created.*" I say, then, in every view that is given to us in God's word that shows us intelligent creatures in His holy presence, we see all their intelligence and all their affections, and powers, consecrated to the praise and glory of their God; and surely it ought to be the position, and is the duty of all intelligences that are created, in heaven and earth and under the earth.

But man, fallen man, that blot on the face of nature, degraded, apostate man refuses to glorify his God: he will not glorify his great Creator, he bows before the prince of this world, Satan. Yet, even out of this state of ruin, even out of this abyss of degradation, God can raise up, and God has raised up, and will raise up to all eternity, a church, a people that shall glorify Him; and thus, from the very apostacy of man, from the very fall of man, from the very guilt and rebellion of intelligent, rational, voluntary, accountable agents, even through their means, God shall show forth His own manifold wisdom, manifest His own power, and build His glory on the very ruins of a guilty world,—"TO THE

INTENT THAT NOW UNTO THE PRINCIPALITIES AND POWERS IN HEAVENLY PLACES MIGHT BE KNOWN BY THE CHURCH THE MANIFOLD WISDOM OF GOD."

And here, though it be a subject which we cannot presume to enter into with any degree of dogmatism, yet I would humbly say, that we can see, even in this, a reason, why man has been allowed to fall. A great part of the moral character of Jehovah must have been unknown, unrevealed to His intelligent creatures, unless there was allowed in some part of His dominions, some part of the vast territory over which He presides, unless, I say, there was allowed a positive rebellion against His holy will, we could not see the nature of His moral government, the glory of His moral attributes unless His law was violated. How could justice be manifested in punishing sin, if there was no sin to punish?—The mercy of God could not be known, unless there was rebellion.—How could mercy be manifested in pardoning rebels, unless there were rebels to pardon? Take these two attributes, justice and mercy, which constitute the perfection of moral government, consider these two attributes, and how could they be manifested unless in the sin of rational, intelligent, accountable moral agents, as men are? If we add to that, if we enter into the subject of the wisdom of God, "*the manifold wisdom of God*" spoken of here, how "*justice and mercy can meet together*," how "*righteousness and peace can kiss each other*," how perfect holiness that must banish sin forever from His presence, can yet admit the vilest sinner into that presence, and only glorify holiness still! How justice, that sentenced the sinner to perdition forever—that banished him forever from his Maker's sight—this justice can take the sinner and bring him out of the very depths of guilt and condemnation, and exalt him to the throne of glory, while justice is only magnified still! How mercy may be extended to the very chief, the vilest of sinners, and yet that that mercy shall not infringe on that justice, while all but reflect glory on the Creator Himself, and all can centre in "*Christ the brightness of his glory, the express image of his person*," one with Himself forever! The subject is too vast for human intellect to attempt to expatiate on it. But short as our sight is, we can perceive in it, the manifold wisdom and wonderful glory of our God:—and what shall it be, when we shall "*know even as we are known!*" 1 Cor. xiii. 12, when every redeemed individual of those who are of the fallen race of man, shall be in himself an exemplification of that justice and mercy, and all the glorious attributes of God, wisdom, power, faithfulness, love, and all these attributes shall be glorified in their behalf who are rescued and brought from the jaws of hell to heaven. Oh how shall God be exalted and glorified in that day! We see it not now, but yet, the principalities and powers even now behold it, even now to "THE PRINCIPALITIES, AND POWERS IN HEAVENLY PLACES, IS KNOWN BY THE CHURCH THE MANIFOLD WISDOM OF GOD."

Here we perceive this expression, "IN HEAVENLY PLACES"

occurring again, as in Chap. ii. 6,—and some persons may consider that it means exclusively the angels. We cannot reasonably doubt that it includes them; no doubt it comprehends the hosts that surround the throne of God, the cherubim and seraphim, those hosts of which we were speaking this moment in Isaiah vi. We know "*there is joy in the presence of the angels of God over one sinner that repenteth.*" Luke xv. 10. We know that "*these things the angels desire to look into.*" 1 Pet. i. 12. But it may mean also Satan and all his hosts, these may be included in "THE PRINCIPALITIES AND POWERS IN HEAVENLY PLACES." They are spoken of in Scripture as being "IN HEAVENLY PLACES," but if you consider the meaning of that word, you will find, it does not mean what we call in heaven,—in the place of happiness and glory with God. It is indeed in some places applied thus, but it is also applied to places, as it were, over our heads, which we call, when we look up to the sky, the heavens,—that is the firmament above us. It is thus the term is applied to the "*celestial bodies,*" 1 Cor. xv. 40. And Satan seems to have his seat, as it were, above us, over our heads, so he is called, as we have seen, in the 2nd chapter "*the prince of the power of the air, the spirit that now worketh in the children of disobedience.*" And again, if you look into this Epistle, vi. 12, you see this expressly stated, "*we wrestle not against flesh and blood, but against principalities, against powers, against the rulers of the darkness of this world, against spiritual wickedness in high places,*" or "*in heavenly places,*" it is the same word which is used in both passages. There you perceive, in the vi. chapter, the word is expressly limited to Satan; and when our Lord saith, Luke x. 18, "*I beheld Satan as lightning fall from heaven,*" you do not suppose He means to say that Satan was enjoying the presence of the Lord, except as he is under his eye and in his presence in the territory of apostate spirits; but it means, fallen from his power in heavenly places, he is "*the prince of the power of the air,*" where he does exercise his power as it were with a rapid ubiquitous domination of his agency. There is no room from which you can exclude the air, and there is no room from which you can shut out the power and agency of Satan; you cannot go into any closet, where Satan will not follow you. Hence the absurdity of the idea of monasteries and nunneries shutting out as they pretend, the world, as if they could thus shut out the world, the flesh and the devil from the heart. It cannot be so, there is no place into which Satan has not access, —you know this, believer, you know this from your own sad experience; you go into your closet, and you shut to the door, and you pray to your Father in secret, but you know full well that you cannot shut out the enemy of your soul, and you cannot shut him out of your own heart, he has power there, you know and deeply feel what is the meaning of that expression, "*the prince of the power of the air.*" I myself have no doubt that the fallen angels are included in this passage, "TO THE INTENT THAT NOW UNTO THE PRINCIPALITIES AND POWERS IN HEAVENLY PLACES MIGHT

BE KNOWN BY THE CHURCH, THE MANIFOLD WISDOM OF GOD." I think it means collectively, to include all intelligent creatures, angelic and satanic, that all the thrones and dominions of heaven shall know the wondrous wisdom of their Creator the wondrous glory of the Redeemer; and all the powers of hell shall know and tremble at the majesty of the glory of Christ, who makes even the very sins of sinners, and the very snares and temptations of Satan redound to his own everlasting glory.

You see how often He has met and conquered Satan, and made many of Satan's snares redound to his own glory in this world.

Thus, see how Satan ensnared David, how awfully he entrapped him; he thought when he had allured David into crime, that David was his own. But mark, the Lord sent His prophet with His word to the heart of David, and He rescued him out of the grasp of Satan, and David remains to this day an example to a poor, fallen, backsliding sinner who might be perhaps otherwise hopelessly trembling in the fangs of Satan, David remains to him an example that "*where sin abounded, grace did much more abound*," Rom. v. 20, and that God will rescue a poor fallen sinner, and bring him back to Himself, and enable Him to say, as David did, "*Purge me with hyssop, and I shall be clean: wash me, and I shall be whiter than snow. Make me to hear joy and gladness that the bones which thou hast broken may rejoice.*" Psa. li. 7, 8. That very 51st Psalm, which David composed after his fall, has been, and ever shall be, a prayer of deep humiliation, of grace, of gratitude, and of blessing, to poor backsliding, broken-hearted, fallen, but repentant sinners.

See, again, the thief on the cross, how Satan was triumphing there, not only when he brought that poor wretch into thefts, made him steal, and then left him as he is continually leaving those who trust him,—in the lurch,—left him to fall into the hands of justice, when he was sentenced to death for his crimes; —no doubt Satan was triumphing, rejoicing, thinking that he had gained another soul into his grasp, and when, still further, he got him to blaspheme the name of the only Hope and Refuge of sinners, Christ Jesus; how Satan was rejoicing when he was joining his fellow-thief, and when he heard the two thieves blaspheming Christ, as well as the multitude before him, how Satan must have triumphed then! But mark, how divine grace touched the heart of that poor thief, even when in the moment he hung on the cross in the agonies of death, grace enlightened his eyes, and enabled him to see that Christ was the King of glory,—that, though hanging on that cross as a malefactor, He was "King of kings, and Lord of lords," and the certainty of Christ's kingdom was brought to the eye of that thief by faith, by the Spirit of God, and he said, "*Lord remember me when thou comest into thy kingdom.*" See how, in the very midst of the wickedness, the blasphemy of that poor man, he was brought to see the Lord. See how all Satan's rage was over-ruled in that instance, and how it has been made a glorious exhibition, by God's grace, of love and mercy to many a sinner to this day. Thus, from this example, we may go to the den of the vilest wretch—grovelling in the lowest and darkest abyss of human wickedness, we may tell him in the depths of his iniquity to turn like the dying robber to a dying Saviour—we may tell him there is salvation in Christ, even while trembling as it were on the very jaws of hell—we can proclaim to him that "*all sins shall be forgiven unto the sons of men, and blasphemies wherewith soever they shall blaspheme.*" Mark iii. 38. We can encourage and exhort him to "*repent and believe the Gospel.*"

Again, how Satan must have triumphed when he had led Judas to betray his Master! how he must have rejoiced when, entering into his own son, John xiii. 27, "*the son of perdition,*" John xvii. 12—he instigated him to betray his Lord—when he had prompted him to lead a band of officers into the garden to take Christ! how he must have triumphed when he had led that unhappy traitor to betray Him too with a kiss! just as at this moment his servants use the words *charity* and *peace* for the very purpose of betraying the truth, the salvation, and the cause of Christ. When we speak a word in defence of the glorious Gospel, against Popery, Arianism, Socinianism, or any anti-Christian system that prevails in any part of the world,—"It is want of charity—it is illiberal to find fault with the religion or principles of any other body of Christians." Such is the common cant—"Every man has a right to think and worship God as he pleases, and we have no right to say a word on the subject." Here is Judas's kiss of charity, and as Satan triumphed when he had inspired Judas to kiss his Master! so he triumphs this day when under the cloak of charity, liberality, and peace, he covers the most awful blasphemies and apostacy, and the most wicked attacks on Christ and His kingdom.

But mark how Satan's wrath was overruled. He instigated Judas to betray the Lord Jesus—the high priest to condemn—the mob to denounce—and Pilate to put him to death,—he filled the hearts of the multitude when they cried, "*Away with him, away with him, crucify him, crucify him,*"—the rage of the fiend, all his malice, and all his power, were concentrated, as it were, on the head of the suffering Redeemer. But mark how God overruled them all! These were the very means of Satan's overthrow, and of our salvation. All that the fiend could do, served but to promote by his very malice the glory—and to make known by the Church the manifold wisdom of God. For "*Forasmuch as the children are partakers of flesh and blood, he also himself likewise took part of the same, that through death he might destroy him that had the power of death, that is the devil, and deliver them who through fear of death were all their lifetime subject to bondage.*" Heb. ii. 4,—He caught Satan in his own snare; "*Surely the wrath*" of devils as well as "*of man shall praise thee: the remainder of wrath shalt thou restrain.*" Psa. lxxvi. 10.

And thus is "MADE KNOWN BY THE CHURCH THE MANIFOLD WISDOM OF GOD"—by the Head and the members. By the manifestation of Christ's love and power in the salvation of every sinner—by the individual exercises of His grace—the individual application of His precious blood—His spotless righteousness—by His faithfulness—by the infusion of His strength into every member of the whole body—by all the deliverances that are wrought for them—all the snares that are broken—all the temptations from which they are rescued—all the precipices from which they are held back—all the abysses of sin and sorrow out of which they are raised—all the whole chain of providences by which they are surrounded. I say, by every one of these things, Satan is made to see, and to feel "THE MANIFOLD WISDOM OF GOD;" and he is made to feel that all his power, all his efforts are nothing when he strives in vain to pluck the sheep of Christ out of His hand. The howling of the wolf but makes the sheep run together into the fold.

How was he triumphing, when he was filling Saul's mouth with blasphemy and rebellion against God! when under his inspiration, as it were, Saul was "*breathing out threatnings and slaughter against the disciples of the Lord,*" Acts ix. 1—along the way from Jerusalem to Damascus, going to drag the saints to prison. The procession of Saul and his companions was an ovation for Satan. But what was the issue? That very man was stopped on his journey, arrested in the middle of his career, not only to be the most eminent chosen instrument to overthrow the powers of darkness—but the very blasphemies and persecutions in which Satan chiefly rejoiced, became a beacon of the light and glory of the Gospel—of the power—of the wisdom—of the grace of God to the vilest sinners that should ever exist in the world. "*I obtained mercy,*" saith Paul, "*that in me first Jesus Christ might show forth all long-suffering, for a pattern to them which should hereafter believe on him to life everlasting.*" 1st Tim. i. 16. So that out of the depths of sin we may turn to the example of Saul, and say—"Grace pardoned the blaspheming Saul, Christ rescued Saul, '*breathing out threatnings and slaughter,*'" "*Christ is the same yesterday, to-day, and forever,*" and I may look to Christ as well as Saul did." This is all that Satan gained by inspiring Saul with this blasphemy and wickedness. The Lord Jesus took that very man to be his most honored servant—to "*preach the faith he once destroyed;*" and this is the man who is now telling the Church at Ephesus, that to him "*is this grace given, that he should preach among the Gentiles the unsearchable riches of Christ,* AND TO MAKE ALL MEN SEE WHAT IS THE FELLOWSHIP OF THE MYSTERY, WHICH FROM THE BEGINNING OF THE WORLD HAD BEEN HID IN GOD, WHO CREATED ALL THINGS BY JESUS CHRIST, TO THE INTENT THAT NOW UNTO THE PRINCIPALITIES AND POWERS IN HEAVENLY PLACES, MIGHT BE KNOWN BY THE CHURCH THE MANIFOLD WISDOM OF GOD."

The Apostle saith in another place "*We are made a spectacle unto the world, and to angels, and to men.*" 1st Cor. iv. 9. If then the Church is a spectacle to angels, celestial and satanic, most assuredly to these angels, these principalities and powers, is "MADE KNOWN BY THE CHURCH THE MANIFOLD WISDOM OF GOD."

All—all who shall be brought to glory hereafter, shall be seen as monuments, individually and collectively, monuments of "THE MANIFOLD WISDOM OF GOD."

Look back at your life, believer, look back at your own experience of your whole course. Could you not recount many sins, many evils into which you had fallen, many pitfalls—many snares—many temptations—many afflictions spiritual and temporal—out of which you have been kept and brought by the grace and by "THE MANIFOLD WISDOM OF GOD?" What stories I could tell of my own sinful heart! what grace—what mercy—what patience—what long-suffering, have I not experienced at the hand of a compassionate and merciful Lord! And I suppose you could say the same for yourselves, who is there who is really looking to Christ who cannot say it? Think of your rebellions since you were a believer in Christ, think of your sins against light and knowledge—of the waywardness of your will—the vileness of your heart—the wandering of your affections from your Lord—the blindness of your understanding—think of all the evils you feel and know in yourselves, and yet see, there you are, hearing the sound of the glorious Gospel of Christ, and if you are taught of God, saying to yourself, "Oh! merciful Jesus, Oh! my precious Lord, if it were not for Thee, if Thou wert not the very Saviour that Thou art, I should be, as I deserve, in hell! But here I am, blessed be Thy Name, hearing Thy gracious voice in Thy glorious Gospel. The volume of Thy grace is open before me, Thy faithfulness, Thy truth, Thy righteousness, Thy precious blood, Thy love, Thy compassion, Thy long-suffering, are all developed before me in Thy blessed Word, and here I am, '*kept by the power of God through faith unto salvation.*' 1st Pet. i. 5. Often, often as it seemed to me ready to perish—to be plucked out of thine hand, still thou sayest, '*none shall pluck them out of my hand.*' John x. 28—still Thou keepest me, Thou teachest me to lift up my prayer, to look unto Thee my Lord as the Hope, the Refuge, the Salvation of my soul!"

What is this but exhibiting in you, as one member of the Church, "THE MANIFOLD WISDOM OF GOD?" Does not Satan learn it, when he retreats like a baffled foe from all his attempts to destroy you? When he sees you are kept from his power safe in the protecting grasp of an Almighty hand? When after all the thorns in the flesh that he sends as messengers to buffet you, he hears your Saviour say, "*My grace is sufficient for thee?*" 2nd Cor. xii. 9. When he sees you are enabled to catch all his fiery darts upon the shield of faith, from which they rebound and fall before you quenched in the blood of the Lamb—Does he not see you on his throne of darkness, where he sits as "*Prince of the power of the air,*" a prominent example of "THE MANIFOLD WISDOM OF GOD?"

Do not the angels of light behold you, as they are led from wonder to wonder in the manifestation of Redeeming love—as they are "*sent forth to minister*" to you as an heir of salvation—you know not how indeed, but is it not written that they are so? Heb. i. 14—Is it not written, too, "*The angel of the Lord encampeth round about them that fear him, and delivereth them?*" Psalm xxxiv. 7.—And if the Lord were to open your eyes as he opened those of the Prophet's servant, how often might you see, like him, "*the mountains full of horses and chariots of fire,*" 2nd Kings vi. 17—round about you and the church of Christ. What visions of unimagined existences are given to a blind man if it pleases God to grant him sight! and what might not eyes to see spiritual beings disclose to our astonished view? But there are the angels of God looking on you—"*a cloud of witnesses*" surrounding you—devils watching you—trying to draw you away—but greater is He who is for you than they who are against you. And then at the last, when shall be revealed all the righteous judgments of God, all the amazing developments of His glorious dealings with His church, Oh! what shouts shall rend the skies, when all the church shall be exhibited as manifesting the manifold wisdom and love of the Lord! the very cries of the damned shall resound to the glory of the eternal justice of the living God! There is not a devil or a fiend in hell, or an angel or saint in heaven, whose cry or whose song shall not resound to the glory of God—to the God of justice, who condemned, or to the God of love and mercy, who has kept the elect angels, and redeemed fallen sinners; while "TO THE PRINCIPALITIES AND POWERS," to angels, men and devils, "SHALL BE KNOWN BY THE CHURCH THE MANIFOLD WISDOM OF GOD."—Thus shall it be openly known to all "*when he shall come to be glorified in his saints, and to be admired in all them that believe.*" 2nd Thess. i. 10.

"ACCORDING TO THE ETERNAL PURPOSE WHICH HE PURPOSED IN CHRIST JESUS OUR LORD." There is nothing fortuitous, no chance, no accident, in God's dealings. "*Known unto God are all his works from the beginning of the world,*" Acts xv. 18,—yea, from the beginning to the end. None of God's remedies for sin are accidental, such as a physician prescribes on the contingent emergencies that spring up before him. God's remedies are not like these—Omniscience cannot feel succession of knowledge. Succession implies imperfection, and cannot exist in the Eternal mind—from eternity to eternity He is the First and the Last, so all things relating to His Church are "ACCORDING TO THE ETERNAL PURPOSE WHICH HE PURPOSED IN CHRIST JESUS."

It is not necessary to enter again on the subject, which has been before so largely discussed, of the consistency of the voluntary agency of man, as a responsible being, with the overruling power of God, which makes that agency subservient to His own eternal purposes. It could not be more perfectly illustrated, than in the inspired testimony of the very stupendous fact, which is here presented to us, the crucifixion of our Lord and its glorious results

If we speak of the purposes of God. Then Jesus was "*the Lamb slain from the foundation of the world.*" Rev. xiii. 8. If we speak of this in connection with the perpetrators of His death; then this is the testimony of the Holy Ghost, "*Him being delivered by the determinate counsel and foreknowledge of God, ye have taken and by wicked hands have crucified and slain.*" Acts ii. 23.

It is impossible that the eternal purpose of God could be more distinctly expressed, and the wickedness of the voluntary agents who executed it, more clearly and emphatically denounced. It was thus that all its cruelty and all its crime, were overruled by God for good; but as yet the development is only partially unfolded; for the full intent is not as yet accomplished, by the proclamation of the unsearchable riches of Christ to the nations of a guilty world. "TO MAKE ALL MEN SEE WHAT IS THE FELLOWSHIP OF THE MYSTERY, WHICH FROM THE BEGINNING OF THE WORLD HATH BEEN HID IN GOD, WHO CREATED ALL THINGS BY JESUS CHRIST: TO THE INTENT THAT NOW UNTO THE PRINCIPALITIES AND POWERS IN HEAVENLY PLACES MIGHT BE KNOWN BY THE CHURCH THE MANIFOLD WISDOM OF GOD, ACCORDING TO THE ETERNAL PURPOSE WHICH HE PURPOSED IN CHRIST JESUS OUR LORD."

The Lord Jesus was the agent in the creation of the world, as we see here and in numberless passages of Scripture, as John i. 3, Col. i. 16, 17, Heb. i. 2. And He is the glorious "*Word*," in whom is revealed, and exhibited, the end and object of its creation. As "*the heavens declare the glory of God, and the firmament showeth his handy-work.*" So the Sun of Righteousness, in the firmament of His church, shall declare the fulness of the glory of all His moral attributes to all the principalities and powers, as all the system is attracted, supported, illuminated, and animated by His life, His light, His power, and His love.

But when we know our own character, and the character of our foes—when we have a real Scriptural view of our own corruption—of the power of sin—and the malice of Satan—we never can rest on any promise as immutable, or any hope as secure, till we know that all things relating to His church are founded on the eternal purpose of God. And it is a blessing to think that we have a God whose purposes are unchangeable; that, in a changeable world, such changeable creatures as we are, have an unchangeable God to rest on as our salvation. What a blessing it is to have a hope, that in those "*immutable things in which it is impossible for God to lie, we might have a strong consolation, who have fled for refuge to lay hold upon the hope set before us: which hope we have as an anchor of the soul, both sure and steadfast.*" Heb. vi. 18, 19. What has a sinner to rest on in this world, till he learns to rest on Christ? What can this world give? See how God sends us continually lessons to teach us the vanity of all below. We have been praying, and I do hope have prayed from our hearts, for those whom the Lord has been pleased to visit with heavy affliction. Alas for beauty, rank, wealth! what are they all? We see the young, with all their ardent inexperienced hearts fixed with eager hope of anticipated enjoyment on the world. The phantom form of happiness seems to rest like the gorgeous image of the rainbow on the earth, but still, like it, retreats from the pursuit of their eager footsteps. We have seen one possessed of rank, of youth, and health, and beauty, of everything that could be desired—that earth could give—to make her happy. We have seen in a moment, how God can teach a solemn lesson to an extensive neighborhood—can place the form of youth, and rank, and beauty, on a yawning tomb—to speak this solemn text to all around, as she sinks into its cold embrace—"*All flesh is grass, and all the glory of man as the flower of grass; the grass withereth, and the flower thereof falleth away.*" But Oh! what a blessing for sufferer and survivors, when her dying accents too can speak the rest, "*but the word of the Lord endureth forever.*" 1st Pet. i. 24, 25.

What a blessing that she was able to know, through grace, the Lord on whom to lean! and that she was able, through grace, to lean upon her Lord.*

Now, ye parents who are looking with anxiety for what you call the settlement of your children in this world,—and who perhaps live, and leave them to live, without thinking of the settlement of their eternal peace—without laying to heart a thought for their "*inheritance with the saints in light.*" Alas! if you saw your children cut off before your eyes—cut off without a hope in Christ, and remembered, that you had ever been more anxious about "*what they should eat, and what they should drink, and wherewithal they should be clothed,*" and educated, and accomplished, for this world,—than in thinking how their souls might be nourished with the "*Bread of life,*" or with the "*Living water,*" —how they might be washed in the blood, and clothed in the righteousness of Christ. Oh! think what pangs of conscience, if your conscience was not dead in sin, would wring your hearts in such a case as this!

And you young friends who hear,—Consider what is the world to you if you know not Christ? You may think you would have been happy if your lot was cast as hers was:—yet had she possessed a thousand worlds, what were they all compared with the knowledge of Christ? If she had not known Christ, what would they be all to her now?—when her youthful brilliant eye is closed on all below; her young and warm heart is become "*a clod of the valley!*"

Oh! consider these things,—pray that God my incline your hearts to His truth, and your footsteps to His ways. These warnings are not sent, to be spoken of, as an event of the passing day, and then forgotten; but as solemn lessons, each speaking with a voice that bears life or death in the sound, "*Ye know not what*

* Lady E. S. had just entered into her rest, in the early bloom of life, 1837.

shall be on the morrow. For what is your life? It is even a vapor, that appeareth for a little time, and then vanisheth away." James iv. 14. "*Therefore be ye also ready: for in such an hour as ye think not the Son of man cometh.*" Mat xxiv. 44.

TWENTY-FIFTH LECTURE.

EPHESIANS III.—12.

"In whom we have boldness and access with confidence, by the faith of him."

HAVING seen in an imperfect sketch—Alas! how imperfect is the best that man could draw!—"*That now unto the principalities and powers in heavenly places is made known by the church the manifold wisdom of God, according to the eternal purpose which he purposed in Christ Jesus our Lord,*"—we may observe how the Apostle applies to himself and to all believers the blessings that belong to the Church—that they were individually partakers of these, individually possess, and have a right to enjoy the access to God, which is inspired by the confidence of reconciliation through Christ Jesus. "IN WHOM WE HAVE BOLDNESS AND ACCESS WITH CONFIDENCE BY THE FAITH OF HIM."

We see, the Apostle here speaks of blessings common to all believers, present blessings,—"IN WHOM WE HAVE BOLDNESS." All who believe the Gospel have these présent blessings, too happy if they but knew and enjoyed them as they ought.* And what are these blessings? Access to God—boldness in access—confidence in access—by the faith of Christ Jesus.

This is a most important point for us to consider—the individual application of these blessings to our own souls. It is nothing to us to hear, that there are blessings belonging to the Church of Christ, if we do not partake of them ourselves. It is nothing to us to hear, that sinners may have access to God by Christ Jesus, if we do not come to God. It is nothing to us to hear that they may come with boldness—with confidence,—if we do not come with boldness and confidence. One great glory of the Gospel is, that it is a blessing individually to the souls of all sinners, who through grace are taught to look unto Christ Therefore now, let us consider this blessing.

We have had this subject before, in the 18th verse of the preceding chapter, and on that occasion we referred to this verse. There it is written, "*through him we both have access by one*

* "O! fortunati nimium sua si bona nŏrint."

Spirit unto the Father," and here again, "IN WHOM WE HAVE BOLDNESS AND ACCESS WITH CONFIDENCE BY THE FAITH OF HIM."

I have remarked to you frequently before, and we cannot too often consider it, that when God is pleased to bring before us truths repeatedly in His holy Word, He brings them before us, that we may study them with reiterated attention. Recollect, it is children who have "ACCESS WITH CONFIDENCE" to their Father, and it is only as children of God that we can have this access. Then if so—we must come in the spirit of children. Remember it is written, "*Whosoever shall not receive the kingdom of God as a little child shall in no wise enter therein.*" Luke xviii. 17. It is those whom God instructs—and children must have children's lessons. How beautifully is this set forth by the Prophet thus—"*Whom shall he teach knowledge, or whom shall he make to understand doctrine? Them that are weaned from the milk, and drawn from the breasts. For precept must be upon precept, precept upon precept, line upon line, line upon line, here a little and there a little.*" Isa. xxviii. 9, 10. How this too, accords with the words of our blessed Lord, "*Thou hast hid these things from the wise and prudent, and hast revealed them unto babes.*" Luke x. 21. How often as children have we repeated our lessons over, and over, and over, to learn them by heart! All the lessons of our Heavenly Father require to be learned by heart by His children, and therefore must be repeatedly impressed on the memory. A master on the subject says, that Attention—Repetition—Pleasure—and Pain, are the chief means of producing impressions on the memory. All these are more or less employed by our Heavenly Teacher, and we should learn to profit by them all. He opens our heart like that of Lydia to attend—He employs, as we see here, continual repetitions of His instructions—He cheers our hearts, as he seeth fit, by the refreshing consolations of the Gospel—and inflicts on us, "*if need be*," in love, the chastenings of His rod.

Thus, when the Lord repeats instruction to us again and again, we are not to say—"We have met this verse or this subject before, and we may pass on to another." No, God brings it before us again and again, to show that we are particularly called on to attend to it; for when he is graciously pleased to instruct us so frequently, it is because it is His holy will that we should give our earnest repeated attention to it, and therefore He reiterates instruction in His blessed Word.

Let us then again consider this subject. Believers have access—yea, "BOLDNESS AND ACCESS WITH CONFIDENCE BY THE FAITH OF CHRIST." THEY HAVE BOLDNESS. We may observe how totally opposite is this, to the view which the natural mind takes of God, and the feeling it entertains in reference to Him. If there be one object of terror more than another to a fallen sinner, that object is God. Adam had enjoyed the privilege of communion with Him, when he came forth fresh moulded from his Creator's mighty hand, when "*God saw everything that he had made, and behold it was very good.*" Gen. i. 31. But when Adam's conscience told him he was a sinner, that communion was gone—and as far as human power could redeem it, it was gone forever. He fled with a blinded understanding and an alienated heart, among the trees of the garden, and when the voice of God summoned him from his vain retreat—he exhibited the fall of his intellect, as well as the conscious sin of his soul, he said, "*I heard thy voice in the garden, and I was afraid because I was naked, and I hid myself.*" Gen. iii. 10. Now though we do not hear God's voice, we are afraid of God for the very same cause. Sin is on the conscience, and sin on the conscience, brings into the heart the terror of an All-seeing and an Almighty Judge. Therefore when a sinner has any boldness whatever in approaching to God—when he can approach his Maker with any degree of confidence in his heart—it can only arise from this, that he has a confident expectation and security, that sin, which separated him from his God—sin—which lay with terror upon his conscience, is removed from him—that his conscience is now clear, and thus being clear of sin, he can confidently approach his Judge, his Creator, his God.

This is the reason why those persons who are ignorant of the Gospel, and who are seeking for justification by their own righteousness—by Sacraments—Priests—penances—fastings—alms—any moral or superstitious observances, never can approach to God with confidence; or if they think they can, it is a delusion—they cannot maintain it by the authority of His divine Word; and therefore they generally consider that the very mention of confidence, or assurance in the believer's mind, is the grossest possible presumption, because it is a thing so entirely opposite to all their own feelings and experience. For when persons imagine, that, by their own righteousness, or any of the means I have mentioned, they are to fit themselves to approach to the presence of God—their conscience bears witness against them that they have not this righteousness, on which they think they must depend; so they never can have confidence in approaching to God, because they never can feel that sin is removed from their conscience, they never can believe they are clear from sin in his sight. On the contrary, it is the privilege of a believer to know that he is clear from sin before God—perfectly clear from sin. "What!" you may say, "Is not that gross presumption? Is it not great audacity in any sinner to say, he is clear from sin?" The question demonstrates, that the person who asks it is ignorant of the means whereby a sinner is to be delivered from sin. Consider this.

It is manifest, he thinks, that the way in which a sinner is to be cleared from sin, is, that he is not to have any sin, in other words, to be no longer a sinner. There is no such thing as a sinner being cleared from sin before God, in that sense, "*If we say that we have no sin, we deceive ourselves, and the truth is not in us.*" 1st John i. 8. Then, the question is, how can we have sin, and yet be clear from sin? how can we be sinners, and yet be free from our sins? How can this be? Because, sin is taken away, not by its non-existence in the sinner—but by its non-imputation to the sinner. It is not that he is clear from sin by not having sin—but it is, that he is clear from sin, by not having sin laid to his charge—"*Even as David also describeth the blessedness of the man unto whom God imputeth righteousness without works, saying, blessed are they whose iniquities are forgiven, and whose sins are covered. Blessed is the man to whom the Lord will not impute sin.*" Rom. iv. 6, 7, 8.

The privilege of the believer is to know, that his sin is thus taken away—not imputed to him. Why? because it was imputed to Christ,—laid on Christ,—taken off the sinner and laid on his Redeemer. "*The Lord hath laid on him the iniquity of us all.*" Is. liii. 6. Now, if the sinner is brought through grace, to see and know this glorious truth, "*to believe the record that God hath given of his Son,*" 1 John v. 10, then he is free from sin, then he says, my conscience now is delivered from its guilt, because, I see from God's eternal Word, that my blessed Redeemer, "*bare our sins in his own body on the tree,*" 1 Pet. ii. 24; that "*he hath once suffered for sins, the just for the unjust, that he might bring us to God.*" 1 Pet. iii. 18. This is the truth on which we have been dwelling so repeatedly, in the preceding chapter, "*Now in Christ Jesus, ye who sometime were afar off, are made nigh by the blood of Christ;*" Ephes. ii. 13. Thus we come near to God—for "*the blood of Jesus Christ, his Son, cleanseth us from all sin.*" 1 John i. 7. Then, if we are cleansed from all sin, of course, we can have no sin remaining; when sin is taken away, sin cannot remain; so that, though sin exists in the believer,—though he feels it in himself,—though he knows it, and mourns over it bitterly in his heart—yet it is his privilege to know, that it is all cancelled, and that it cannot hinder him from coming to his God, "HAVING BOLDNESS AND ACCESS WITH CONFIDENCE BY THE FAITH OF CHRIST."

Oh! dear friends, it is a most wonderful privilege to be able to understand the grand simplicity of the Gospel of Christ,—so to understand it, as to apply it practically,—daily,—hourly,—momentarily to our own sinful consciences. When sin is taken away we have nothing to fear. The man who has nothing to fear is bold. Having no fear is synonymous with boldness, so St. John saith, "*herein is our love made perfect, that we may have boldness in the day of judgment, because as he is, so are we in this world.*" As Christ is, so are his people,—as He is righteous, so are they righteous—as He is dead to sin, they are dead to sin,—as He is alive unto God, they are alive unto God—as He has access to God, so have they access in Him; because they are accounted one with Him: accordingly, (as we have been often dwelling on this subject) you recollect the Apostle says, "*reckon yourselves to be dead indeed unto sin, but alive unto God through Jesus Christ our Lord:*" Rom. vi. 11—reckon yourselves to be so. Therefore, it is He, "IN WHOM WE HAVE BOLDNESS AND ACCESS WITH CONFIDENCE BY THE FAITH OF HIM." So assuredly it is our privilege thus to come to God by the faith of Jesus; it is our privilege to know that we shall not be cast away, that there is no doubt of our acceptance, no doubt but that we shall inherit eternal life. This is the privilege of all those who believe the Gospel of Christ. "*This honor have all his saints. Hallelujah.*" Psal. cxlix. 9. I say, it is their privilege. I do not say they all enjoy it; they ought to enjoy it: but alas! all believers do not enjoy their privileges, they go on doubting and fearing, and trembling, instead of going on their way with trust, and confidence, and joy, and boldness, looking unto their Lord and Master, their blessed Redeemer "*heartily rejoicing in the strength of their salvation.*" Psa. xcv. 1. There is indeed a sense of holy fear and trembling, which is inseparable from true faith; but it is the reverential fear of joy and love, and not the slavish terror of enmity and unbelief. The fear of grieving a loving, gracious Father, is very different from that of being sentenced to be hanged by a just Judge. St. John speaks of the latter when he saith, "*There is no fear in love, but perfect love casteth out fear, because fear hath torment.*" 1st John, iv. 18. St. Peter speaks of the former when he saith, "*If ye call on the Father, who without respect of persons judgeth according tc every man's work, pass the time of your sojourning here in fear: Forasmuch as ye know that ye were not redeemed with corruptible things, as silver and gold, from your vain conversation received by tradition from your fathers; But with the precious blood of Christ, as of a lamb without blemish and without spot:*" 1st Pet. i. 17, 18. The loving confidence of faith is the cause of the latter fear. The unloving terror of unbelief is that of the other fear which "*hath torment.*"

This is the reason why there is so little of a true, genuine exhibition of the power of the Gospel in the church, because there is really such unbelief—such unbelief in believers. Instead of going on with strength and confidence, boldness, and faith, and love, united to Christ and united in Christ, and thus "striving together for the faith of the Gospel," you see them doubting and trembling, and fearing—some running to one of their beggarly elements, others to other beggarly elements, not firmly united together, exalting their respective forms, and separated from each other; and why? because they are not trusting in faithful simplicity in their Lord and Master, with ardent love to Him "*who hath called them out of darkness into his marvellous light,*" 1st Pet. ii. 7,—for the glorious work He wrought for them and all His people.

Ignorance and unbelief blind the eyes of men who are called Christians, so that they do not comprehend the ground of a sinner's confidence—they know not what is that ground—what is the cause why he has this boldness. It is vain to talk of boldness to those who do not know the foundation of it. If you see persons in fear, and desire them not to be afraid, you never can take away their apprehensions thus, all your exhortations will not calm their fears; but if you can prove to them, and convince them, and make them confident, that there is no ground for apprehension; then their fears naturally subside. So it is, that it is in vain to tell men to have confidence in coming to God, unless their understandings are enlightened to see and know the solid ground of confidence that God gives them in His blessed word. Therefore let us consider more fully what is the ground of this confidence. Why have believers "BOLDNESS AND ACCESS WITH CONFIDENCE BY THE FAITH OF CHRIST?" We answer on account of

The work of Christ.

The office of Christ.

The character and person of Christ.

Consider these three things.

I.—THE WORK OF CHRIST GIVES BOLDNESS AND ACCESS WITH CONFIDENCE THROUGH THE FAITH OF HIM.

The finished work of Christ Jesus is a full remission of sins, by the one offering of himself once offered on the cross. You have this set forth repeatedly in the Word of God; you may see it reasoned and argued out in Hebrews x, where the Apostle compares the legal sacrifices with the sacrifice of Christ, and shows the inefficiency of all those sacrifices from the fact of their continual repetition; and the completeness and fulness of the sacrifice of the Lord Jesus Christ, from its being offered once, and but once, and that, once for all, 10th verse, "*By the which will we are sanctified, through the offering of the body of Jesus Christ once for all.*" I have cited this chapter before; and almost lectured on every verse, but let me again call your attention to the 11th v. "*Every priest*" (meaning the priests of the Levitical law,) "*every priest standeth daily ministering, and offering oftentimes the same sacrifices, which can never take away sins. But this man, after he had offered one sacrifice for sin forever, sat down on the right hand of God, from henceforth expecting till his enemies be made his footstool; for by one offering he hath perfected forever them that are sanctified.*" The priests stand daily ministering, they offer a sacrifice to-day, they are obliged to stand up the next day and offer the same sacrifice, and the next day to offer the same, and the next day to offer the same, and so on,—and by standing up to-day to offer sacrifice, they confess that the sacrifices of yesterday were not sufficient; therefore the daily repetition of sacrifices daily proves the insufficiency of these sacrifices. "*But this man, after he had offered one sacrifice for sin forever, sat down at the right hand of God.*" There was no rising up to come from his throne to offer another sacrifice for sin, there was no repetition of his glorious offering on the cross. *It is finished*—once for all. It was "*one sacrifice for sins forever.*" So "*He sat down at the right hand of God,*" 14th v. "*for by one offering he hath perfected forever them that are sanctified.*" Now observe, "*by one offering he hath perfected forever.*" Surely if a thing is forever perfected, nothing more can be done to perfect it. Perfection cannot be added to. And if a thing is perfected once, it cannot need to be perfected again. If Christ has perfected all His saints, that is, those who are sanctified, which is another term for believers, if He has perfected all His saints forever, nothing more can be done to take away their sins. Christ Himself cannot do anything more to take away sins than he has already done. Think of this, consider it in your own heart, and see whether you believe or understand this truth. I say, the Lord Jesus Christ cannot do anything more to take away your sins than He has already done. Now do you believe this? Ask your own conscience if you are satisfied that it is truth? If you are not, then ask yourself this question, "What is to be done to take away my sins?" What do you suppose is to be done? Some will say, "Oh, I must pray, I must attend the Sacraments, I must change my life." That will not take away your sins. If you were to spend from this time to the end of your existence on your knees, it would not take away one sin. If you were to go to the Sacrament every hour in the day, it would not help to take away one sin. Nothing that you can do, or that the whole world can do for you, or that God Himself can do for you, can take away one sin, but what is already done. This is true indeed,—that God, and God alone, can, by His eternal Spirit, enlighten your eyes to see, and know, and understand His great salvation; but that is not doing anything to take away your sins,—it is opening your eyes, that you may see the glorious work that has been done already to take them away,—namely, the glorious work of the Lord Jesus Christ, which He has finished on Mount Calvary for sins, that "*by one offering he hath perfected forever them that are sanctified.*" Therefore when God puts a work perfect out of His hands, He does not resume that work to do anything more. If an artist or a mechanician gives you a work, and says "that is finished," he tells you thereby that he can do nothing more for it. When the Lord Jesus Christ tells you "*He hath perfected, by one offering, them that are sanctified,*"—that is, all His saints, He cannot do anything more to perfect them. Now consider this—think of it—reason on it—digest it—and if you do not believe it, then you know not "*the fulness of the blessing of the Gospel of Christ.*"

The Apostle saith, "*Whereof the Holy Ghost also is a witness to us, for after that he had said before, this is the covenant that I will make with them; after those days, saith the Lord, I will put my laws into their hearts, and in their minds will I write them, and their sins and iniquities will I remember no more. Now where remission of these is, there is no more offering for sin.*" Heb. x. 18. Observe, "*where remission of these is,*"—He has told you where remission of sins is to be found—namely, that it is to be found in the finished atonement of Christ—that it is to be found in the perfect sacrifice of the Lord Jesus on the Cross; and then, having told you, that it is to be found in this perfect sacrifice—and having told you, that the Holy Ghost witnesses this—and that this is God's covenant, that He will remember their sins and iniquities no more—then, he comes to the conclusion, "*where remission of these is, there is no more offering for sin.*" There fore it is, that nothing you can do can take away your sins—nay, that (I repeat it) God Himself cannot do anything more to take away your sins;—for if the Lord were to make any other offering to take away sin, that offering would be an acknowledgment that the whole work before was not sufficient; and that all that has been revealed is delusion on the subject. Thus the truth of the Gospel annihilates the Sacrifice of the Mass—that awful superstition of the Church of Rome;—not to say that a piece of paste is made an object of worship, or called God—the very idea of making an offering to God for sin, is a total denial of the finished work of Christ—a total rejection of the Gospel of Christ. The very thought that Christ Himself could make another offering for sin, would subvert the whole foundation of the Gospel, and totally obliterate the finished work of salvation. Hence all the modified mummeries of Rome that are sought to be introduced again into our Church, arise from an utter ignorance of the Gospel of Christ; indeed, the chief movers and conductors of the heresy, confess that their great enmity is to the doctrine of justification by faith in Christ; and their vain superstitions could not be entertained for a moment by any, but those who are lamentably ignorant of the Gospel. But they are perfectly congenial to the natural pride, corruption, and ignorance of the human mind, and hence those who hold them, pass over by an easy and natural transition to the Church of Rome.

Now then, mark the conclusion which the Apostle draws, "*Having therefore, brethren, boldness to enter into the holiest, by the blood of Jesus.*" You perceive the work of Christ is the ground of the sinner's boldness, and observe, he saith, "*therefore,*" viz., for these reasons—on account of the work of Christ—the finished work of Immanuel—on account of this, that nothing more can be done to take away sin;—"*Having therefore, brethren, boldness to enter into the holiest, by the blood of Jesus, by a new and living way which he hath consecrated for us, through the vail, that is to say, his flesh; and having a high priest over the house of God, let us draw near with a true heart, in full assurance of faith. Having our hearts sprinkled from an evil conscience, and our bodies washed with pure water.*" Heb. x. 19, 22.

And now, let me entreat you to consider what a ground of boldness is set forth here, for you, and me, and all sinners to draw near to the throne of Grace. You say and feel, each of you I suppose, "Alas! I am a vile sinner before God." I feel the same, I am a vile sinner before Him; if God were to enter into judgment with you or me, we must perish. So the language of our souls must be the language of David, "*Enter not into judgment with thy servant, O Lord, for in thy sight shall no man living be justified.*" Psa. cxliii. 2. This then is our case, all of us are on a level, all alike, "*there is no difference, all have sinned and come short of the glory of God.*" Rom. iii. 22, 23. Consider, then, what is placed before us here—the finished work of Christ—that

Jesus, by one offering, hath perfected forever every sinner that rests upon Him—every sinner that is a believer on Him—He hath perfected them forever—they are all in this sense perfect—they are not judged by different degrees of character as among men, but they are all viewed as one complete whole, perfect, delivered from all their guilt, because their blessed Surety has died for them. Suppose one man owes ten pounds, another twenty, another fifty, five hundred, a thousand, ten thousand—were some man of adequate wealth to take all their debts upon himself, and pay them all, all would be clear, every debt would be cancelled, every debtor be delivered from his burthen.

We owe a countless debt, all of us; we may form some conception of some few of the items against us. But who could pretend to count the number? Oh, "*who can tell how oft he offendeth?*" Ps. xix. 12. How little can we conceive of the amount of the black catalogue of our transgressions before God!—but "*the blood of Christ cleanseth us from all sin.*" There is remission of sins in Him, and "*where remission of these is, there is no more offering for sin.*" "*Having therefore, brethren, boldness to enter into the holiest.*" So we come into the holiest, we come and stand in the presence of God. True we must say indeed, O Lord, behold I am vile, "*I abhor myself, and repent in dust and ashes.*" Job xlii. 6; but vile as I am, "*Thy blood cleanseth from all sin.*" Thy blood, the blood of the cross, Thy blood, the blood of my Redeemer, is the fountain where I bathe, I come as one of the flock "*which he hath purchased with his own blood.*" Acts xx. 28.

Is not this then enough to give a sinner boldness? what fear, what doubt—what cause for fear or doubt have we, if indeed we are enabled to trust on Immanuel's Redemption—on the work that Jesus has finished on the cross?

Now, my dear friends, if you do not understand this—if you are not brought to know the Gospel, you must have some other ground of hope, some vain refuge, whatever it be—your moral character—your virtue—your religious observances—good resolutions—sacraments—charities—Church—or something of this nature—you are looking to some false hope, if you are not brought to the Lord Jesus Christ,—therefore you are not happy, you have no access to God,—no peace in the prospect of meeting Him,—your heart is far from Him,—you are living without Him in the world,—seeking your happiness where it cannot be found,—following after a phantom—a floating image—an airy vision—a cloud—a delusion—an "unreal mockery," turning away from the only solid ground of peace the sinner can have—peace with God through Christ,—"BOLDNESS AND ACCESS WITH CONFIDENCE THROUGH HIM," as going to a reconciled God and Father, your sin cancelled—blotted out forever—and the blessed hope of everlasting life opening before your eye, through the dark vista of the grave, a light from the glorious portals of eternity. Such prospect does the work of Christ open to the eye of the believer.

But I said, we have not only the work, but

II.—THE OFFICE OF CHRIST, TO GIVE US "BOLDNESS AND ACCESS WITH CONFIDENCE." Recollect that the Lord Jesus Christ has not only finished that glorious work on the cross, but He has risen and ascended to the right hand of His Father; and there He appears as our great High Priest, having carried into the presence of God, for us, the blood of the everlasting covenant. When the high priest offered the great annual atonement, he carried the blood of the victim into the holy of holies, where the presence of God was manifested, over the mercy-seat, between the cherubims. That was, you know, the emblem of the Lord Jesus Christ; who, having poured out His precious blood as the great atonement, of which all others were types and shadows, has gone into the presence of God, there to appear for us. And so the Apostle continues, Hebrews x., let me entreat you to consider this chapter, for it gives the most clear and simple view of the Lord Jesus Christ, 19th verse, "*Having therefore, brethren, boldness to enter into the holiest by the blood of Jesus, by a new and living way which he hath consecrated for us, through the vail; that is to say, his flesh, and having an high priest over the house of God;*"—he not only points the view to the work of Christ—His work—as having made atonement, but he points you to the office of Christ, as being a high priest, and as having carried that blood into the presence of the Father, there to appear as the advocate of His people. So the Apostle John saith, "*these things I write unto you, that you sin not;*" but he adds, "*and if any man sin, we have an advocate with the Father, Jesus Christ the righteous; and he is the propitiation for our sins.*" 1st John, ii. 1, 2. He is our advocate and our propitiation, our high priest and our sacrifice—He has made an offering, and He has gone into the presence of God, and carried that blood into the holy of holies, there to appear in the presence of God for us. So the Apostle says, in Hebrews ix., in the 6th and 7th verses, where he is mentioning the subject of which I am speaking;—"*Now when these things were so ordained, the priest went always into the first tabernacle, accomplishing the service of God, but into the second, went the high priest alone, once every year, not without blood, which he offered for himself, and for the errors of the people.*" 11th v. "*But Christ, being come an high priest of good things to come, by a greater and more perfect tabernacle, not made with hands, that is to say, not of this building; neither by the blood of goats and calves, but by his own blood, he entered in once into the holy place, having obtained eternal redemption for us.*" He has gone, once for all, as the high priest into the holy place; that is, into the presence of God, "*having obtained eternal redemption for us.*" And in Hebrews iv., he gives the same ground for the confidence of the sinner, 14th verse, as we saw in reference to chap. ii. 18, "*Seeing then, that we have a great high priest that is passed into the heavens, Jesus, the Son of God, let us hold fast our profession; for we have not an high priest who cannot be touched with the feeling of our infirmities, but was in all points tempted like as we are, yet without sin; let us therefore come boldly unto the throne of grace, that we may obtain mercy, and find grace to help in time of need."* You see, then, the priestly office of Christ affords a ground of confident access to the believer.

III.—But THE PERSON AND CHARACTER OF CHRIST ARE SET FORTH AS A GROUND OF BOLDNESS. And the Apostle also brings this before us in Heb. x. 21. "*Having an high priest over the house of God, let us draw near with a true heart, in full assurance of faith.*" Observe, "*full assurance of faith,*" full confidence—not doubting your Lord, not hesitating to confide in His word, or His work, but "*in full assurance of faith, having our hearts sprinkled from an evil conscience, and our bodies washed with pure water.*" It is not that you have not an evil conscience, or a consciousness of evil—it is not that your conscience does not tell you, you are a sinner; for it must be a subject of continual exercise of conscience, to avoid sin; "*herein do I exercise myself,*" saith the Apostle, "*to have always a conscience void of offence both toward God and toward man.*" Acts xxiv. 16. It is a continual conflict of the believer to endeavor to keep his conscience void of offence in the various circumstances in which he may be placed in life. But every day he lives he will feel that his conscience accuses him of sin. How is he then to cleanse that conscience? It must be sprinkled with the blood of Christ. "*Having our hearts sprinkled from an evil conscience.*" When he is accused of guilt his conscience says, "True, I am guilty, but '*the blood of Jesus Christ cleanseth me from all sin.*' 1st John i. 7. '*I am black, but comely,*'—black—'*as the tents of Kedar,*'—comely—'*as the curtains of Solomon.*'" Cant. i. 5.

Therefore, when your conscience charges you with sin, should you try to silence its accusing voice by prayers?—by resolutions? —by promises, like a child, that you will do wrong no more? No —you must go directly to the blood of Christ, you must go to the blood of sprinkling, must have your conscience cleansed from sin by Christ before you can do anything in the service of Christ. How is that to be done? Come to Christ in prayer by faith, say to Him,

"Lord I am a fallen sinner, behold I am vile, my conscience is defiled with sin, I come to Thy precious blood, there is no refuge, no help for me but in thee; I come to Thy precious blood—Thy word assures me that it cleanses from all sin; I come to that blessed Fountain—there let me bathe. Oh, let my soul cast all its heavy load on Thee, who wast wounded for our transgressions. Let me rest on Thy faithfulness, Thy glorious work, Thine exceeding great and precious promises. There let me rest forever!"

When you are enabled to commit your soul to Christ, to trust in Him thus;—then you can rest on the blood of your Redeemer as all-sufficient to wash away your sins; thus is your heart "*sprinkled from an evil conscience,*" when "*the blood of sprink-*

ling that speaketh better things than that of Abel," Heb. xii. 24—saith "*peace be still.*"

Come then to Christ for pardon, and in pardon you find strength to enable you to contend against your sins, not to save yourself, for salvation is in Christ alone, but to serve and glorify your Lord who hath loved you, and given himself for you. It is thus you "HAVE BOLDNESS AND ACCESS WITH CONFIDENCE BY THE FAITH OF HIM." For "*being justified by faith, we have peace with God through our Lord Jesus Christ. By whom also we have access by faith into the grace wherein we stand, and rejoice in hope of the glory of God.*" Rom. v. 1, 2.

The character and person therefore of Christ are full warrant for our having BOLDNESS. "*Let us draw near with a true heart, in full assurance of faith, having our hearts sprinkled from an evil conscience, and our bodies washed with pure water, let us hold fast the profession of our faith without wavering, for he is faithful that promised.*" Heb. x. 23. Here we have the faithfulness of Christ. And in Heb. iv., he brings before us the sympathies of Christ, 15th v.; "*we have not an high priest which cannot be touched with the feeling of our infirmities, but was in all points tempted like as we are, yet without sin.*" He brings us to the faithfulness of Christ as God—"*He is faithful that promised.*" He brings us to the sympathies of Christ as man—as one who is so "*touched with the feeling of our infirmities.*" And on both grounds gives us encouragement to come boldly to Christ—"*let us therefore come boldly to the throne of grace, that we may obtain mercy and find grace to help in time of need.*" Heb. iv. 16. And again, "*Having boldness to enter into the holiest by the blood of Jesus.*" Heb. x. 19. And here in this passage, "IN WHOM WE HAVE BOLDNESS AND ACCESS WITH CONFIDENCE BY THE FAITH OF HIM."

Thus then in happy faith in the *Work*, the *Office*, and *Person* of our beloved Lord—His work of Righteousness and Atonement—His Office as Priest and Mediator—His Person as God and man—let us consider what a glorious privilege it is for a sinner to have such a way of access to God! what a wondrous blessing it is, to have such a path opened not only of approach, but of approach with boldness, so that instead of leaving our salvation as a matter of doubt and uncertainty, thinking as multitudes who bear the name of Christian think, that it is presumption to suppose we can be in a safe state until after the day of judgment—till God has decided on our respective merits whether we have deserved to inherit eternal life!—It is our privilege to have through grace a blessed hope, a joyful assurance of salvation, not indeed through our own merits, but through the merits and death of our adorable Redeemer, and to approach through Him with boldness and confidence to God, not as a dreaded Judge, but as a reconciled Father.

Hence—the faith and love of Christ, give boldness in the prospect of judgment, as saith the Apostle, "*Herein is our love made perfect, that we may have boldness in the day of judgment.*" 1st John iv. 17. Hence—the proper attitude of a Christian, is not that of awaiting with apprehension, a judgment which he would be thankful to avoid; but looking with hope to the appearance of the Judge, as his Deliverer, and his Salvation. This, so far from being the terror, is the joyful expectation of the Church. Thus were the Christians instructed by the Apostles as saith St. Paul, "*Ye turned to God, from idols to serve the living and true God, and to wait for his Son from heaven, whom he raised from the dead, even Jesus, which delivered us from the wrath to come.*" 1st Thes. i. 9, 10. So he saith that "*To them that look for him he shall appear the second time without sin unto salvation.*" Heb. ix. 28. So, it is with grace, and with the gift of salvation, that all sound principle of genuine moral action is inseparably united, as with the joyful hope of the coming of the Lord Jesus. We see them all associated together in their scriptural place in the Epistle to Titus, "*For the grace of God that bringeth salvation hath appeared to all men, teaching us, that, denying ungodliness and worldly lusts, we should live soberly, righteously, and godly, in this present world; looking for that blessed hope, and the glorious appearing of the great God and our Saviour Jesus Christ; Who gave himself for us, that he might redeem us from all iniquity, and purify unto himself a peculiar people, zealous of good works.*" Tit. ii. 11, 12, 13, 14.

Here we see what the grace of God brings—namely, "*salvation*" —not means to help us to save ourselves, but SALVATION.

We see what the grace which brings this salvation teaches; namely, to "*deny ungodliness and worldly lusts, and to live soberly, righteously, and godly, in this present world.*"

We see what the grace which brings this salvation teaches us to look for, namely, the glorious manifestation and everlasting enjoyment of the salvation which it brings, "*looking for that blessed hope, and the glorious appearing of our great God and Saviour, Jesus Christ.*" For then shall be revealed, bestowed, enjoyed, the glorious inheritance which Jesus has purchased for his risen saints. So saith the Apostle Peter when he testifies of this salvation, and this glorious inheritance, which is reserved for them in heaven. "*Be sober and hope to the end for the grace that is to be brought unto you, at the revelation of Jesus Christ.*" 1st Pet. i. 13. For, as St. Paul saith, "*when Christ who is our life shall appear, then shall ye also appear with him in glory,*" Col. iii. 4; and it is in this "*blessed hope*"—this "*glorious appearing*"—this everlasting life at the coming of Christ in glory, that he teaches the saints to comfort one another for those that are gone to rest, and for their own everlasting consolation. 1st Thess. iv. 13–18. Therefore, how well may those who look unto Jesus, when they know the solid ground of Hope for eternity, have access with confidence through the faith of Him to the Throne of Grace in time.

"*Blessed are the people that know the joyful sound.*" Psal. lxxxix. 5,—blessed those who receive the great salvation which this grace bestows—walk in the path of holiness and peace which it teaches—and shall partake of the glory that it shall bring at the coming of the Lord Jesus, to whom be praise and glory forever, Amen.

TWENTY-SIXTH LECTURE.

EPHESIANS III.—13, 14, 15, 16.

"Wherefore I desire that ye faint not at my tribulations for you, which is your glory. For this cause I bow my knees unto the Father of our Lord Jesus Christ, of whom the whole family in heaven and earth is named, that he would grant you, according to the riches of his glory, to be strengthened with might by his Spirit in the inner man."

WHEN we were beginning this chapter, I mentioned, that in the first verse there was the commencement of a very long parenthesis, which might be considered as terminating either at the 13th verse of this chapter, or in the middle of the first verse of the next;—that you might either suppose that the words, "*for this cause*" were those referred to by the Apostle at the close of the parenthesis, as in the 14th verse, so that the reading in this case would be,

"*For this cause, I, Paul, the prisoner of Jesus Christ for you Gentiles, bow my knees unto the Father of our Lord Jesus Christ.*"

Or—you might suppose that the word "*prisoner*" was that referred to at the conclusion of the parenthesis; and that it was taken up at the 1st verse of the 4th chapter.

"*For this cause, I, Paul, the prisoner of Jesus Christ for you Gentiles; beseech you that ye walk worthy of the vocation wherewith you are called.*" chapter iv. 1.

Now, I rather think that the proper termination is at the 13th verse; and my reason is this. St. Paul commences this chapter thus, "*For this cause, I, Paul, the prisoner of Jesus Christ for you Gentiles.*" Then, as if he feared that the mention of his being a prisoner would cast a great damp on the spirits of his brethren at Ephesus; he commences in this parenthesis, not only to account for his being a prisoner, but to show that his imprisonment —so far from being a matter of grief to his Gentile brethren—ought to be a subject of great joy to them. Why was Paul a prisoner? Because (as you will find, on referring to the history in the Acts of the Apostles) he preached the Gospel of the Lord Jesus Christ to the Gentiles.

You recollect, when he said in his speech to the Jews, that the

Lord had said unto him, "*Depart; for I will send thee far hence unto the Gentiles. They gave him audience unto this word, and then lifted up their voices, and said, Away with such a fellow from the earth: for it is not fit that he should live.*" Acts xxii. 21, 22. In consequence of his persecution by the Jews, who were aided by Felix and Festus; Felix kept him in prison "*to do the Jews a pleasure,*" Acts xxiv. 27, and Festus wished to bring him to be judged at Jerusalem, for the same reason, Acts xxv. 9. But he not choosing to be carried to Jerusalem to be judged, appealed unto Cæsar, and when he appealed to Cæsar, Festus said, "*To Cæsar thou shalt go,*" Acts xxv. 12,—therefore he went and was a prisoner at Rome; and thence he writes to them, "*I, Paul, a prisoner of Jesus Christ for you Gentiles,*" &c. But then he takes occasion to unfold to them the mystery which was now revealed by God, that the Gentiles were to be fellow-heirs, and that to him was given the glorious office "*to preach among the Gentiles the unsearchable riches of Christ,*" and having thus set forth, as we have seen, the glory of that mystery—the union of Jews and Gentiles in Christ;—and the glory of the salvation of Christ, how that "*to the principalities and powers in heavenly places was made known by the Church the manifold wisdom of God, according to his eternal purpose which he purposed in Christ,*" and having shown the glorious access which Jew and Gentile have with "*boldness and confidence by the faith of Christ;* he concludes v. 13, "WHEREFORE, I DESIRE, THAT YE FAINT NOT AT MY TRIBULATIONS FOR YOU, WHICH IS YOUR GLORY." I think, therefore, that the parenthesis from the second verse to the end of the 12th, contains the premises from which he draws the conclusion, to cheer and console them on account of his imprisonment, "WHEREFORE," that is, for these reasons, "I DESIRE THAT YE FAINT NOT AT MY TRIBULATIONS FOR YOU, WHICH IS YOUR GLORY."

When he saith, "*I, Paul, a prisoner of Jesus Christ,*" "Ah," thought he, "these poor Ephesians will be cast down—they will say, 'What! Paul a prisoner! this great Apostle Paul a prisoner! Hath the mighty God abandoned his servant to a prison?'" "Yes," saith he, "I am a prisoner, but consider for what I am a prisoner." Then he tells them the glorious cause in which he suffered, and concludes "WHEREFORE I DESIRE, THAT YE" be not discouraged—"I DESIRE THAT YE FAINT NOT"—but remember that my being a prisoner, instead of being your grief, is your glory.—It is for preaching the Gospel to you and the heathen nations, that I am a prisoner—I am a prisoner for being commissioned to declare the glorious salvation of Christ to the Gentiles; and therefore, so far from being cast down at this, you ought to rejoice, as it is your joy—your salvation—your glory.

Consider how needful is this encouragement—we are continually prone to be cast down whenever we see outward afflictions or tribulations befall the church of Christ. We look at outward things, and are ready to be overwhelmed. If we hear of our brethren being persecuted or afflicted, or suffering for the sake of Christ, we are almost fainting at heart by it. If we heard of some of our ministers being sent to prison, or brought perhaps to the scaffold or the stake for their faithful testimony, as might be the case, we should be nearly driven to despair at this. But let us remember, that the covenant of God for all His people is, that "*all things are working for their good;*" and let us remember, that the history of the whole church proves, that "the blood of the martyrs has been the seed of the church." What was the first signal for the diffusion of the Gospel?—The persecution that arose on the death of Stephen. You see in the history of that, in the Acts of the Apostles;—the disciples went everywhere, preaching the gospel of Christ—they went through all the country testifying. "*They that were scattered abroad went everywhere, preaching the word.*" Acts viii. 4. And so it has been in our own church;—so it was when Latimer and Ridley were brought to the stake:—when Latimer said to Ridley, "Be of good cheer, brother, we shall light a candle this day that never shall be extinguished in England." And so, the very means taken by Satan to oppose and put down the glorious Gospel of Christ—those very means, God uses for the diffusion, promulgation and maintenance of His truth. He can support and strengthen His people in suffering—enable them to endure affliction—persecution—death for His glorious Gospel; if it was only to show, that the very persecution of the Church of Christ exhibits the glory of the everlasting Gospel. So the Apostle, in this parenthesis, on which we have been dwelling for some time, having explained the commission he had received, "*to preach among the Gentiles the unsearchable riches of Christ,*" adds, "WHEREFORE, I DESIRE, THAT YE FAINT NOT AT MY TRIBULATIONS FOR YOU, WHICH IS YOUR GLORY."

Let us recollect, that the testimony of our Lord to His Apostles was, that they should be called to suffer for His sake; and let us remember that the testimony of the Apostles themselves to the churches was, that they should suffer for the cause of truth, "*All that will live godly in Christ Jesus must suffer persecution.*" 2nd Tim. iii. 12. And perhaps, the ease that the church of this nation enjoyed for so long a period, has been owing to this, that there has been so little faithful testimony, either in doctrine or practice, to the glorious Gospel of Christ. So little faithful testimony in doctrine against the ignorance—the falsehood—the infidelity—the idolatry—and superstition of the nation; and so little faithful testimony in practice, in coming out from an ungodly world, and being separate in life and conversation from those who have a mere "*form of godliness, but who deny the power thereof.*" 2nd Tim. iii. 5. We are told of this Apostle and Barnabas, at Derbe, that "*when they had preached the Gospel to that city, and had taught many, they returned again to Lystra, and to Iconium, and to Antioch, confirming the souls of the disciples, and exhorting them to continue in the faith; and that we must, through much tribulation, enter into the kingdom of God.*" Acts xiv. 21, 22.

The Apostle saith in the epistle to the Philippians, i. 12, "*I would ye should understand, brethren, that the things which happened unto me have fallen out rather unto the furtherance of the Gospel.*" He comforts them also for his imprisonment at Rome, and you know, there were several in Cæsar's household called by this very means to the knowledge of Christ; so he saith of these events "*So that my bonds in Christ are made manifest in the palace, and in all other places; and many of the brethren in the Lord, waxing confident by my bonds, are much more bold to speak the word without fear.*" So, you see, that the Apostle had cause to desire his Ephesian brethren "NOT TO FAINT AT HIS TRIBULATION FOR THEM, WHICH WAS THEIR GLORY." It was the glory of the Gentiles that Paul should be called to suffering and to tribulation for the testimony which his heavenly Master had commissioned him to bear to the nations of the earth. The Lord said, "*He is a chosen vessel unto me, to bear my name before the Gentiles, and kings, and the children of Israel. For I will show him what great things he must suffer for my name's sake.*" Acts ix. 5, 16. So that he might well say to his Ephesian brethren, "I DESIRE THAT YE FAINT NOT AT MY TRIBULATIONS FOR YOU, WHICH IS YOUR GLORY." This seems then to me, to be the close of the parenthesis; and I am quite satisfied that the Apostle introduces this for the express purpose of comforting them, when they knew that he was a prisoner for their sake.

I therefore think, he here resumes his subject repeating the first words of the chapter, "FOR THIS CAUSE I BOW MY KNEES UNTO THE FATHER OF OUR LORD JESUS CHRIST."

"FOR THIS CAUSE."—This brings us back to inquire, what was the cause to which he alludes? and we find the cause in the conclusion of the 2nd chapter, and thus adduced in the 1st verse of the 3rd—viz., that they had been called out of their natural darkness into the marvellous light of the glorious Gospel—that they were, as the Apostle had thus stated, "*Now therefore ye are no more strangers and foreigners, but fellow-citizens with the saints and of the household of God, and are built upon the foundation of the Apostles and Prophets, Jesus Christ himself being the chief corner-stone, in whom all the building, fitly framed together, groweth into an holy temple in the Lord, in whom ye also are builded together for an habitation of God through the Spirit.*" Eph. ii. 19–22. Wherefore, since you are so called, so founded on Jesus Christ, builded together into an holy temple, for an habitation of God through the Spirit, "FOR THIS CAUSE, I BOW MY KNEES UNTO THE FATHER OF OUR LORD JESUS CHRIST." Connect the four last verses of the second chapter with the 14th verse of this chapter, and you have, I think, the true continuity of the sense.

We learn from this, that, when persons are first brought to the knowledge of the Gospel of Christ, then indeed, they become subjects of anxious prayer, both for themselves and for all who watch over them and love them as their Ministers. No man prays for himself, till he is brought to know Christ as the only way of access to God—till he comes unto the Father through Christ, "*no man cometh unto the Father but by me*," saith the Lord, John xiv. 6, and although Paul "*after the straitest sect of his religion lived a Pharisee*," Acts xxvi. 5, yet it was not until Christ had smitten him down on his way to Damascus, and revealed Himself to him as Jesus whom he persecuted—it was not till then, that Paul ever uttered a prayer that God acknowledged as a supplication at the footstool of the throne of grace. But then God sent Ananias to him, "*For*," saith the Lord, "*behold he prayeth*." Acts ix. 11. So when sinners are brought to the knowledge of Christ, they see their need of prayer, they see their utter helplessness, their utter destitution of all spiritual light and spiritual strength, they begin to feel the plague of their own hearts, that they are indeed "*deceitful above all things, and desperately wicked*." Jer. xvii. 9—that their "*carnal mind is enmity against God*;" Rom. viii. 7; they see therefore their need of waiting on God continually in prayer and supplication. "*A prayerless sinner*," an old writer says, "*is a Christless sinner*," and we may convert the proposition, and say, "A Christless sinner is a prayerless sinner." He knows not God, if he comes not to Him in prayer and supplication—and he comes not in prayer and supplication till he comes through Christ.

Persons too frequently think, and it seems to be a great error of the present day, that, if we are brought to the knowledge of the Gospel of Jesus,—to know that Christ is the Saviour of sinners—the Refuge of our souls—in opposition to the general systems of error and falsehood that are current among the professors of religion under the name of Christianity—that if we are brought to this, all is well.

Now, so far, in a certain sense, *all is well*. It is a great blessing when sinners are taught to know Christ. But let us remember, that this is the time when they most especially have need of continual prayer and supplication at the throne of grace. It is then, for the first time in their lives that they are brought into a capacity of serving God—It is then their conflict begins against the world, the flesh, and the devil—It is then they have need of prayer, in order that the truths they know, may be fastened more and more deeply in their hearts, that they may be given more of the Spirit of God, and be enabled more to trust Him, to love Him, to know this great truth, "*Ye are not your own, for ye are bought with a price; therefore glorify God in your bodies and in your spirits, which are God's*." 1st Cor. vi. 19, 20.

In this prayer, which the Apostle by the Spirit of God offers here for the Ephesian Church, we see what the Holy Ghost inspires, as the subject of prayer in behalf of all who believe the Gospel of Jesus, and let me entreat your earnest attention to it. "FOR THIS CAUSE I BOW MY KNEES UNTO THE FATHER OF OUR LORD

JESUS CHRIST, OF WHOM THE WHOLE FAMILY IN HEAVEN AND EARTH IS NAMED, THAT HE WOULD GRANT YOU, ACCORDING TO THE RICHES OF HIS GLORY, TO BE STRENGTHENED WITH MIGHT BY HIS SPIRIT IN THE INNER MAN; THAT CHRIST MAY DWELL IN YOUR HEARTS BY FAITH; THAT YE, BEING ROOTED AND GROUNDED IN LOVE, MAY BE ABLE TO COMPREHEND WITH ALL SAINTS, WHAT IS THE BREADTH, AND LENGTH, AND DEPTH, AND HEIGHT; AND TO KNOW THE LOVE OF CHRIST WHICH PASSETH KNOWLEDGE, THAT YE MIGHT BE FILLED WITH ALL THE FULNESS OF GOD." Now, I think you will see the explanation I have given of the parenthesis in this chapter very beautifully illustrated, if you connect not only the 14th verse, but the 15th verse also, in its order with the latter part of the preceding chapter. Observe that beautiful expression, "I BOW MY KNEES UNTO THE FATHER OF OUR LORD JESUS CHRIST, OF WHOM THE WHOLE FAMILY IN HEAVEN AND EARTH IS NAMED:" you perceive he had said in the preceding chapter, "*ye are no more strangers and foreigners, but fellow-citizens with the saints, and of the household of God.*" You are now brought to God's family, you are now not only "*fellow-citizens with the saints,*" but of the very "*household of God,*" wherefore "I BOW MY KNEES UNTO THE FATHER OF OUR LORD JESUS CHRIST, OF WHOM THE WHOLE FAMILY IN HEAVEN AND EARTH IS NAMED,"—that family of whom you are become members—that blessed family of whom ye are one, and with whom ye dwell—what a glorious name, my dear friends is this to be given to the Church of Christ—"THE WHOLE FAMILY IN HEAVEN AND EARTH!—the family on earth—part of the family, and as much a part—as all, or any part of the family in heaven; "*For ye are all the children of God by faith in Christ Jesus.*" Gal. iii. 26—adopted into the family of God, "*And because ye are sons, God hath sent forth the Spirit of his Son into your hearts, crying, Abba, Father.*" Gal. iv. 6.

"THE WHOLE FAMILY IN HEAVEN AND EARTH!"—What a blessed thought! If we turn our eyes from this poor world, and look with the eye of faith to the company that surround the throne. If we turn to the vision that the Apostle John saw in the Apocalypse, when he "*beheld, and lo, a great multitude, which no man could number, of all nations, and kindreds, and people, and tongues, stood before the throne, and before the Lamb, clothed with white robes, and palms in their hands; and cried with a loud voice, saying, Salvation to our God which sitteth upon the throne, and unto the Lamb.*" When we behold those "*who came out of great tribulation, and have washed their robes, and made them white in the blood of the Lamb,*" who "*are before the throne of God, and serve him day and night in his temple: and he that sitteth on the throne shall dwell among them. They shall hunger no more, neither thirst any more; neither shall the sun light on them, nor any heat. For the Lamb which is in the midst of the throne shall feed them. and shall lead them unto living fountains of waters: and God shall wipe away all tears from their eyes."* Rev. vii. 9–17—if we turn our eye—the eye of faith to that blessed assembly, we should say, "How happy—oh! how blessed, how glorious are they! How blessed should we be, if we were brought to join that celestial company!—all our troubles, sins, sorrows, conflicts, temptations, trials past,—yea, the body of sin and death left below, or transfigured into a glorious body like the body of Christ! Oh! how blessed if we are brought to join that glorious throng!" But if we exercise that faith which it is our privilege to exercise at this very moment; we may turn our eyes upon this world, this wilderness of sin and sorrow, we may look at ourselves, if indeed we "*love the Lord Jesus Christ in sincerity,*" vi. 24—and at all the Lord's people, in the midst of all their conflicts, trials, and afflictions—and it is our privilege to know, yea our privilege to be assured, that they are just exactly as safe—that every believer in Christ, whatever his calling—whatever his station—however, poor, unknown, or despised he may be—is just exactly as safe—as much in the presence of his Lord—under the protection, the guardianship of His arm, as much an object of his care and love, as any of the hosts that surround the throne of God, and cast their crowns at his feet; for "THE WHOLE FAMILY IN HEAVEN AND EARTH" is one family. "*There is one body, and one spirit, even as ye are called in one hope of your calling. One Lord, one faith, one baptism, one God and Father of all, who is above all, and through all, and in you all,*" saith the Apostle to this very Church, chap. iv. 4–6. Therefore the same blessings belong to them all, and are just as secure to those who are following through the wilderness, as to those who have reached their heavenly rest. The language of the believer, in the full enjoyment of his blessed hope, may be that of the hymn:

> "Yes, I to the end shall endure,
> As sure as the earnest is given;
> More happy, but not more secure,
> The glorified spirits in heaven."

Nor can this blessed hope even for a moment be ever separated from, but rather must be ever identified, with "*repentance toward God, and faith toward our Lord Jesus Christ.*" Acts xx. 21—and with the love and service of our Heavenly Master.

What a blessed truth, then, is conveyed in these words, "THE WHOLE FAMILY IN HEAVEN AND EARTH!" Oh! let us consider—are we brought indeed, through faith in Christ, to belong to this glorious family? Is God our Father? If so, what a sure inheritance! what great security and blessing to belong to the family of the Omniscient, Omnipresent, Omnipotent Jehovah! How are we called on to trust our Father! to believe all his "*exceeding great and precious promises!*" How are we called on to fear our Father with a holy fear, not the fear of a slave or a culprit, but the holy fear of a reconciled and adopted child! How are we called on to love our Father, Him who hath "*so loved us, as to give his beloved Son to die for us!*" How—this "*brother born for adversity*," our Covenant Head, "*who loved us, and gave himself for us!*" How are we called on to serve our Father! Think, what a Father he hath been to us! Oh, what a Father hath God been to every one of His children! There is not one who can look to Him with the eye of faith, as their Father in Christ Jesus, who must not say, "Oh what a Father God hath been to me! what a sinful, rebellious child I have been! But, Ah! my patient, tender, loving, gracious God and Father! what a God and Father he hath been to me,!" How then can we ever sufficiently appreciate those words, "THE WHOLE FAMILY IN HEAVEN AND EARTH!"

There is also a beautiful mode of expression adopted here by the Apostle, when he reminds them by this name, of the character of the God to whom he prays. He does not say, "I BOW MY KNEES UNTO GOD," but "UNTO THE FATHER OF OUR LORD JESUS CHRIST"—as much as to remind them of the confidence of his access,—v. 12—the certainty of his acceptance—ii. 13—the power of His intercession—Heb. ix. 24, and the assurance of the response to that prayer—John xiv. 13–14.

Then consider—what is this prayer for the family on earth? "THAT HE WOULD GRANT YOU, ACCORDING TO THE RICHES OF HIS GLORY, TO BE STRENGTHENED WITH MIGHT BY HIS SPIRIT IN THE INNER MAN; THAT CHRIST MAY DWELL IN YOUR HEARTS BY FAITH; THAT YE, BEING ROOTED AND GROUNDED IN LOVE, MAY BE ABLE TO COMPREHEND WITH ALL SAINTS, WHAT IS THE LENGTH, AND BREADTH, AND DEPTH, AND HEIGHT, AND TO KNOW THE LOVE OF CHRIST WHICH PASSETH KNOWLEDGE, THAT YE MIGHT BE FILLED WITH ALL THE FULNESS OF GOD."

"THAT HE WOULD GRANT YOU, ACCORDING TO THE RICHES OF HIS GLORY"—what a wondrous prayer that is! that is the true way of praying to God. Look at the measure of this prayer of the Apostle—"THAT HE WOULD GRANT YOU, ACCORDING TO THE RICHES OF HIS GLORY!" The Apostle's commission was "*to preach among them the unsearchable riches of Christ*," and the measure of his prayer for them is, that God would grant them—not according to their poor petitions—nor according to their weak faith—nor according to their narrow views of God's dealing out his mercy and compassion to sinners;—but "THAT HE WOULD GRANT YOU, ACCORDING TO THE RICHES OF HIS GLORY." It is an admitted principle, that the child should be provided for according to the rank of the parent. A peer will desire that all the wants of his child should be supplied according to the rank that he is to fill in society. A king will take care that his sons should be brought up in all things according to the rank of princes, suitable to the station they are to hold in the world; that is, not with reference to their individual merit—person, or character—but in reference to the station of their Father as king, and in reference to their own position, as his sons and as princes.

So it is the will of the King of kings, that His children shall be provided for "ACCORDING TO THE RICHES OF HIS GLORY." Recollect, this is not a prayer which the Apostle Paul utters from his own imagination; remember, this is a prayer inspired of the Holy Ghost—recorded for our instruction in the blessed word of the living God: this is a prayer, an inspired prayer of that blessed Spirit, of whom the Apostle saith in his Epistle to the Romans, "*Likewise the Spirit also helpeth our infirmities: for we know not what we should pray for as we ought: but the Spirit itself maketh intercession for us with groanings which cannot be uttered. And he that searcheth the hearts knoweth what is the mind of the Spirit, because he maketh intercession for the saints according to the will of God.*" Rom. viii. 26, 27. Remember, that every prayer of the children of God is a prayer aided by that blessed Spirit. Consider then that this is a recorded prayer of the direct plenary inspiration of that Spirit. It is He who teaches the Apostle to pray, that the King of kings should grant unto His people, "ACCORDING TO THE RICHES OF HIS GLORY."

But then, the measure which the King of kings is pleased to grant to His children is not a measure of earthly pomp, or power, or riches, or rank, or any of those things that men call great, and which we might say was a suitable provision for the children of an earthly king; "*But God has chosen the poor of this world rich in faith, and heirs of the kingdom which he hath promised to them that love him,*" James ii. 5, and the provision that He makes for them "ACCORDING TO THE RICHES OF HIS GLORY," is a spiritual provision.

Lazarus was provided for "ACCORDING TO THE RICHES OF HIS GLORY," when he was "*laid at the rich man's gate, full of sores, and desiring to be fed with the crumbs which fell from the rich man's table: moreover, the dogs came, and licked his sores.*" Luke xvi. 20, 21. We know, he was a child of God, "*he was carried by the angels into Abraham's bosom.*" v. 22.

The poor widow was provided for, "ACCORDING TO THE RICHES OF HER FATHER'S GLORY, when all she had was but "*two mites, which make a farthing,*" "*even all her living,*" Mark xii. 42; but she was given, "ACCORDING TO THE RICHES OF HIS GLORY," a heart to cast it into her Lord's treasury. All the treasures of the rich men were nothing of a provision, "ACCORDING TO THE RICHES OF HIS GLORY," compared to the two mites of that poor widow. Therefore, remember, that the great provision "ACCORDING TO THE RICHES OF HIS GLORY," is a spiritual provision for his children. Oh! look to this, and remember that since the Holy Spirit inspired this prayer to the Apostle Paul, whatever we are given to pray for, according to the will of God, we are entitled to pray for it, according to the same measure,—that is, that "HE WOULD GRANT TO US, ACCORDING TO THE RICHES OF HIS GLORY." What a blessed thought is this for poor sinners like us! But alas! how little we feel this as we ought! When we go to prayer, we measure our petitions according to our own contracted thoughts. We are looking to ourselves, groaning over our sins, and our vile hearts, and the troubles—the cares—the spiritual and temporal trials that encompass us—the many evils within and without, under which "*in this tabernacle we groan being burthened*;" 2 Cor. v. 4—our minds and hearts are turned to these things, and we forget—alas! how we forget!—what a privilege is open to us, of coming to the King of kings, believing and praying that for all our wants, He shall make provision, "ACCORDING TO THE RICHES OF HIS GLORY."

Such is the measure of this prayer—now what is the subject?—"THAT HE WOULD GRANT YOU, ACCORDING TO THE RICHES OF HIS GLORY, TO BE STRENGTHENED WITH MIGHT BY HIS SPIRIT IN THE INNER MAN." As you are called to be parts of a spiritual temple, as you are built on Christ Jesus, as you are made members of the household of God, and builded together in Christ for an habitation of God through the Spirit. So He prays that you may be "STRENGTHENED WITH MIGHT BY HIS SPIRIT IN THE INNER MAN." If we are indeed built in Christ, "*for an habitation of God by the Spirit*," it is only by the indwelling power of that Spirit, that we can be enabled to know—to trust—to love—or serve our God. There is nothing good in us by nature, in us "*dwelleth no good thing*," Rom. vii. 18; "there is no health in us." There cannot be a more beautiful, a more just and forcible expression, than that in our most scriptural Confession,—"there is no health in us;" therefore "*Every good gift, and every perfect gift is from above, and cometh down from the Father of lights*;" James i. 17, and it is by the in-pouring of the Spirit—the in-dwelling of the Spirit in our hearts alone, that our understanding can be enlightened—our wills subdued—our affections sanctified, and drawn from the creature to our God; and just in proportion to the Spirit's in-dwelling, and the Spirit's abiding power over us;—just in such proportion shall we understand—choose—love—and walk in the ways of God.

Now consider that if this was a prayer, an inspired prayer for the Ephesian church, it is an inspired prayer for us—if they wanted it, we want it—if it was a blessing for them, it is a blessing for us. Consider the words of our Lord, in that gracious encouragement to prayer, given to His disciples; for the Holy Spirit, Luke xi. 5th to 13th verses, "*Which of you shall have a friend, and shall go unto him at midnight, and say unto him, Friend, lend me three loaves; For a friend of mine in his journey is come to me, and I have nothing to set before him? And he from within shall answer and say, Trouble me not, the door is now shut, and my children are with me in bed; I cannot rise and give thee. I say unto you, Though he will not rise and give him, because he is his friend, yet because of his importunity he will rise and give him as many as he needeth. And I say unto you, Ask, and it shall be given you; seek, and ye shall find, knock, and it shall be opened unto you. For every one that asketh receiveth; and he that seeketh findeth; and to him that knocketh, it shall be opened.*"

If a son shall ask bread of any of you that is a father, will he give him a stone? or if he ask a fish, will he for a fish give him a serpent? Or if he shall ask an egg, will he offer him a scorpion? If ye then, being evil, know how to give good gifts unto your children: how much more shall your heavenly Father give the Holy Spirit to them that ask him?"

What promise can be more explicit—what encouragement more certain? Let us remember that this is a blessing, for which we are warranted, *unconditionally* to pray. It is not permitted us, I think, to pray unconditionally for temporal blessings; for the very concession of our prayers, as we have before observed—the very granting us the desires of our hearts might be our ruin, if the Lord gave us what we might call good. We know not what temporal blessings might be fit for us. Every mercy of time—all the comforts of our existence—health—the greatest of earthly blessings—even life itself ought to be asked conditionally from God.—"If it be Thy blessed will"—"If Thou seest it good." But as for the gift of the Spirit of God, we are to ask it *unconditionally*—it must be good, it must be a blessing which we want, it must be a gift of which we have need, and we see it is fully, graciously, positively, emphatically, promised in this passage. The Lord Jesus Christ Himself commands His people to ask it urgently, importunately—and so the Holy Spirit inspires the prayer of which we have been speaking, into the heart of the Apostle Paul, and records it for our learning, that we should ask it unconditionally, immeasurably—yea, "ACCORDING TO THE RICHES OF GOD'S GLORY, THAT HE WOULD GRANT US, TO BE STRENGTHENED WITH MIGHT BY HIS SPIRIT IN THE INNER MAN."

Then, think, dear friends, how encouraging this is to us poor sinners—these promises—these records—this inspiration—this example—these exhortations—these commands. We shall hereafter consider the work of the blessed Spirit. What is His influence—what, His mode of operation on a sinner's heart. And may the Lord grant, "ACCORDING TO THE RICHES OF HIS GLORY, THAT YOU MAY BE STRENGTHENED WITH MIGHT BY HIS SPIRIT IN THE INNER MAN!" Amen.

TWENTY-SEVENTH LECTURE.

EPHESIANS III.—17, 18, 19, 20, 21.

"That Christ may dwell in your hearts by faith; that ye, being rooted and grounded in love, may be able to comprehend with all saints what is the breadth, and length, and depth, and height; and to know the love of Christ, which passeth knowledge, that ye might be filled with all the fulness of God. Now unto him that is able to do exceeding abundantly above all that we ask or think, according to the power that worketh in us, unto him be glory in the church by Christ Jesus, throughout all ages, world without end. Amen."

WE come now to consider this prayer, which, as we have observed, is inspired by the Holy Ghost, and given to the Apostle to pour out at the footstool of the throne of grace for his Ephesian brethren.

Recollect the glorious measure, according to which he is inspired to ask of God, that is, the measure of "*the riches of his glory.*" And, recollect, the blessing which the Lord is thus called upon to grant to His people,—that they may be "*strengthened with might by his Spirit in the inner man,* THAT CHRIST MAY DWELL IN THEIR HEARTS BY FAITH." The Apostle here shows, what is that strength which the Spirit imparts in the inner man of the sinner—namely, the abiding testimony, which it is the office of the Spirit to bear in his soul to the Lord Jesus Christ.

Our blessed Lord, when he promised the Spirit to His disciples, told them what one great office of that Spirit should be,—"*He shall glorify me; for he shall receive of mine, and shall show it unto you;*" John xvi. 14. And you recollect our Lord saith to Nicodemus, "*Except a man be born again,*"—"*except a man be born of water and of the Spirit, he cannot enter into the kingdom of God.*" John iii. 3, 5. Now, if you compare 1st John v. 1, with this testimony of our Lord, you will find what the meaning of being born again of the Spirit is:—for there we read, "*Whosoever believeth that Jesus is the Christ is born of God.*" This is the spiritual birth—the believer is brought thus into God's family, and this spiritual birth or regeneration is the work of the Spirit; and the means by which this is effected are, that the sinner is taught his own guilt, helplessness, and misery, and is enlightened to see Jesus as the refuge and salvation of his soul. So we see, Gal. iii. 26, "*Ye are all the children of God, by faith in Christ Jesus.*" See also John i. 12, 13.

It is of the utmost importance to understand this, that you may have a scriptural view of the influences and effects of the Holy

Spirit. I believe there is nothing that brings believers more frequently into darkness and distress, and keeps them so, than looking for some vague, undefined operation of the Spirit, which they expect is to be wrought in their hearts, and by which they hope those hearts are to be made so much better, that they will be delivered or purified, if not altogether, yet in a great measure, from sin. And when this expected work of the Spirit takes place, then, they think, they may begin to hope well of themselves, and to hope that they are the children of God; but they cannot indulge this hope, while they feel a power and indwelling of sin within, from which they think it is the peculiar office of the Spirit to purify them.

Now, as far as I have been able to judge of believers, whom I have seen bound in darkness of spirit, I think there is nothing that keeps them more suffering in that darkness, than this unscriptural view of the work of the Spirit. They are looking for some change they know not how—for some undefined improvement, they cannot exactly tell what it is—but it is some sanctifying change which they expect to feel; and until they feel this, they cannot suppose they are entitled to consider themselves children of God.

Now the testimony of Scripture is "*Whosoever believeth that Jesus is the Christ is born of God,*" 1st John v. 1, for, as the Apostle testifies in 1st Cor. xii. 3, "*No man can say that Jesus is the Lord, but by the Holy Ghost.*"

When the soul, then, is enabled to know Jesus as its peace, (Chap. ii. 13, 14), when the soul has fled to Jesus as its refuge, and is leaning on Him as its hope;—that soul is born of God. True it is indeed, that the sanctifying influences of the Spirit are ever to be looked for by the believer—ever to be prayed for, to enable him "*to bring forth fruit unto God,*"—to serve and glorify his heavenly Master; yet as certainly as it is by being brought to Jesus by the Spirit, that he is born of God—so it is by being kept in the faith and love of Jesus, that all the sanctifying influences of the Spirit are produced. Therefore when the Apostle here prays, "*That he would grant you, according to the riches of his glory, to be strengthened with might by his Spirit in the inner man,* THAT CHRIST MAY DWELL IN YOUR HEART BY FAITH," he does not pray for two distinct gifts or blessings for the Ephesians,

First that they "*may be strengthened with might by the Spirit in the inner man.*"

And secondly, "*that Christ may dwell in their hearts by faith,*" &c.

No, it is one and the same petition, but the latter part is explanatory of the former. He shows how strength is given to the heart by the Spirit—namely, by the indwelling of Christ in the heart by faith. Subjoin that word—"*namely*" to the 16th verse, and this shows the Apostle's meaning, as I trust we shall see.

Let us turn to the Gospel of St. John ch. xv., to that consolatory address of our blessed Lord to His disciples—observe what he says in the 4th verse of this chapter, "*Abide in me, and I in you, as the branch cannot bear fruit of itself, except it abide in the vine, no more can ye, except ye abide in me.*" The branch by abiding in the vine is supported by it alone—derives its life, its verdure, its fruit, its beauty, its all, alone from the stem; and if dissevered from the stem, that all is gone. The believer derives his life, his spiritual existence, his fruit, his all, from abiding in Christ; severed from Christ, he is withered—dead—only fit for fuel for the fire. So saith our Lord, "*If a man abide not in me, he is cast forth as a branch, and men gather them, and cast them into the fire, and they are burned.*" v. 6. The Apostle saith, Col. iii. 3, "*Your life is hid with Christ in God. When Christ, who is our life, shall appear, then shall ye also appear with him in glory.*" Therefore the whole life of a believer is derived from his abiding in Christ. Since then our Lord saith "*Abide in me, and I in you,*" the question is—how does the believer abide in Christ? and how does Christ abide in the believer? You have that explained in this prayer, "THAT CHRIST MAY DWELL IN YOUR HEARTS BY FAITH, THAT YE, BEING ROOTED AND GROUNDED IN LOVE, MAY BE ABLE TO COMPREHEND WITH ALL SAINTS, WHAT IS THE BREADTH, AND LENGTH, AND DEPTH, AND HEIGHT, AND TO KNOW THE LOVE OF CHRIST, WHICH PASSETH KNOWLEDGE, THAT YE MIGHT BE FILLED WITH ALL THE FULNESS OF GOD."

Let us now consider the idea of "CHRIST DWELLING IN THE HEART." Before he can *dwell* in the heart, he must *be* in the heart. Now, Christ being in the heart, means simply this, that the understanding has been enlightened by the Spirit of God, to see the righteousness and blood of Jesus as all its righteousness and its justification—that the will has been brought by the same Spirit to receive and embrace Christ as all its confidence—that the affections have therefore been drawn to love Christ, and to cling to Christ as all the hope and salvation of the soul. Therefore, Christ dwelling in the heart means, that the idea of the Lord Jesus Christ is kept present in the heart, as its Peace,—its Hope,—its Refuge,—its Joy,—its Life,—its All. And whereas, whenever the mind is enlightened to know the spiritual nature of the law, there is in the heart a continual consciousness of sin, self-conviction and self-condemnation before God—a continual consciousness, that if God were to deal with us after our sins, we must perish and be cast away. So there is, by the Spirit of God in the heart, testifying of Christ and His great salvation, a continual refuge in Christ from all these evils. Thus, as the Apostle saith in the Hebrews, the heart is "*sprinkled from an evil conscience.*" When the charges of the law are brought against the heart, and our conscience accuses us of sin; the Spirit testifies of Jesus, as in the 10th chapter of Romans, that "*Christ is the end of the law for righteousness to every one that believeth.*" He testifies that "*the blood of Jesus Christ cleanseth us from all sin,*" 1st John, i. 7; therefore the heart flies from its own self-accusations—its fears—

apprehensions—convictions—terrors of God—of death—of judgment—of hell—it flies from all to Jesus—He is the first thought that is ever present for its relief.

As a man subject to attacks of a dangerous disease, who has perfect confidence in a certain physician, of whose skill he has often experienced the benefit—He has been often attacked—often apprehensive of death; this physician has come—prescribed for him a certain remedy—he has been relieved, and restored to health. He is attacked again with the same disease—he immediately recurs to this physician for this remedy—his heart turns to him—his hope is fixed on him—he sends for this man—he confides in him—he believes that he will again restore him by the same means. So the heart, conscious of sin, having been enabled, through grace, to look to Christ,—having experienced the healing efficacy of Immanuel's precious blood—trusts His love—His faithfulness—His truth and power;—turns to Him—looks to Him—leans on Him—rests on this Great Physician,—reposes on Jesus for pardon and peace. Therefore Christ dwells in this heart; because the heart, in its want, its continual necessity and grief, turns to Christ, and confides in Him with all its affections and desires, as its hope, its refuge—its salvation. This is the work of the Spirit of God. It is for this the Apostle prays in these words, "THAT CHRIST MAY DWELL IN YOUR HEARTS BY FAITH." And we shall find that, when our consciences are distressed on account of the evil of indwelling sin, it is because Jesus is not dwelling in our hearts by faith. If we are not delivered from the apprehensions which result from sin, and brought to trust, to love, and rejoice in our glorious Master in liberty; we shall find, by experience, that it is, because, either the heart is not trusting in Christ, in the exercise of faith; or is turning after some earthly pursuits,—earthly idols—earthly vanities; so that they are occupying the place that Jesus ought to hold in the heart and affections; in this state, darkness, doubt, and sorrow, must necessarily oppress the believer. "*If our heart condemn us, God is greater than our heart and knoweth all things.*" 1st John iii. 20. But if it is looking away from these to Christ, and is still cast down—then it is not looking to Him in the fulness of His glorious character, in which He is set forth in the Word of God. It has some doubts or apprehensions, either of his want of power to heal it, or of the full and complete efficacy of His blood,—or it is apprehensive that these particular sins that are afflicting and distressing it, are so great in number or degree, that it is not sufficiently warranted to trust in Christ,—that is, it is doubting the glorious completeness and fulness of Christ. Because, whenever the Lord Jesus Christ dwells in the heart by faith, whenever the Lord Jesus Christ is really leaned upon, trusted—confided in, as a full and all-sufficient Saviour for our souls, then, the heart is strengthened, we are enabled to go on our way rejoicing. Therefore, the Apostle prays, that this work of the Spirit, namely—strength, through Jesus, dwelling in the heart by faith, may be wrought in his Ephesian brethren.

Our Lord saith, Rev. iii. 20. "*Behold I stand at the door and knock; if any man hear my voice, and open the door, I will come in to him, and will sup with him, and he with me.*" Like a friend coming in to us, and sitting down with us at our table, and cheering us with his presence,—with his conversation,—his love,—his affection,—his faithfulness;—so the Lord Jesus Christ comes into the heart of him who opens his heart. He knocks at the sinner's heart,—He knocks now at your heart,—at my heart,—He is knocking at our hearts this moment by His word,—by the testimony of his blessed truth. He saith, "Open the door,—take me in,—I will come in and sup with you,—I will come into your heart and cheer and refresh you by my presence, as your Saviour,—your Lord." So the disciples whom he joined on the way to Emmaus, said, "*Did not our hearts burn within us, when he talked with us by the way, and opened unto us the Scriptures.*" Luke xxiv. 32. Thus the Lord Jesus enters into the heart by faith, and the heart through the teaching of the Spirit, opening the door of its will and affections to receive the blessed Guest, in His Scriptural character, as an all-sufficient and adorable Saviour, rejoiceth in the strength of His salvation.

So the Apostle prays, "THAT CHRIST MAY DWELL IN YOUR HEARTS BY FAITH;" "*I will dwell in them and walk in them,*" this is his covenant, "*I will dwell in them and walk in them.*" How dwell in them? By faith—by the Spirit continually testifying of Jesus to their heart, and making their heart look to Him, and lean on Him,—to "*rejoice in Christ Jesus, and have no confidence in the flesh.*" Phil. iii. 3.

And now, the great subject of this inspired prayer is vitally necessary to every one of us, viz.:—"THAT CHRIST MAY DWELL IN OUR HEARTS, BY FAITH." We know what it is to have beloved objects dwelling in our heart—their image will be present to us—we will be always thinking of them. If we were in distress or difficulty, and we knew one who could, and would relieve us, our hearts would turn to him—if he were absent, we would say, "If thou wert with me, or I with thee, I should be delivered from this distress." The poor culprit, in prison, and under sentence of death, if he thinks there is a friend who would have interest and inclination to obtain his pardon;—all his thoughts are dwelling on that person—his expectations—his anxieties—his affections, are turned to him—he thinks of nothing else—his heart turns to none other upon earth but him. So the soul, when enabled to know Jesus as its Hope and Refuge, turns to Him—looks to Him—leans on Him. So you remember what Mary and Martha said. First, one meets the Lord Jesus—then the other meets Him; and the first word that bursts from the lips of each is, "*Lord, if thou hadst been here, my brother had not died.*" John, xi. 21, 38. So they were looking to Jesus—they were loving Him—leaning on Him—and they knew, if Christ had been there, their brother had not died. Now, it is the privilege of the believer to know, that Christ is always here; we need never say, "If thou hadst been here," for He is always present to His people that are looking to Him; therefore the Apostle prays, "THAT CHRIST MAY DWELL IN YOUR HEARTS BY FAITH,"—that He may be always present in their hearts; as David says, "*God is our refuge and strength, a very present help in trouble; therefore will we not fear.*" Ps. xlvi. 1, 2. What a wonderful blessing to have Christ dwelling in the heart! Oh, that we might be able to enjoy this blessing continually! This is to be "*strengthened with might, by the Spirit in the inner man.*" For the way by which the Spirit imparts His strength is by testifying of Jesus—of His love—His faithfulness—His power—His blood—and righteousness—to the soul, as its continual refuge and comfort; and thus having Jesus dwelling in the heart.

We see an eminent example of this in the Apostles. When the Lord Jesus Christ was taken from them, they did not either appreciate or understand the blessing or the meaning of the work of His salvation. As far as the Lord's bodily presence could attach them, they were attached to Him. They had been with Him,—walking with him,—conversing with Him,—hearing and seeing His miracles, partaking of His favor, and rejoicing in His presence, so that as far as His personal association, communion, friendship, and love, considered merely in reference to His character as a man, could attach them to Him they were attached, yet, when He was taken from them and crucified, "*they all forsook him and fled;*" they did not, at that time know the work of Christ; they knew he was Messiah, the Son of God, but what He was to do for them, or how their guilt was to be removed, or how their souls were to be comforted—how they could rest on Him, or trust in Him, or lean on Him, or rejoice in Him they did not know: and you recollect what the two disciples said to Him on the way to Emmaus—having mentioned the circumstances that had happened at Jerusalem in His crucifixion, "*we trusted it had been he who should have redeemed Israel:*" Luke xxiv. 21, as much as to say, we know it is not He, because He was taken and crucified. In ignorance of this—weak and without strength, "*all the disciples forsook him and fled.*" Matt. xxvi. 56. Peter, after all his declarations and professions, was, as you know, overcome with terror,—you know how the words of a servant girl made him deny his Master, and declare with an oath, "*he did not know the man.*"

Now look at this same Apostle, when the Holy Ghost was sent down from heaven according to the Lord's promise to the disciples: when that Holy Spirit testified of Jesus to them, when their eyes were opened to see the glorious work wrought on Calvary by their crucified Redeemer, and when that Blessed Spirit enabled them to know the glory of "*Jesus Christ and him crucified,*" and to understand the full meaning of this glorious commission, "*that repentance and remission of sins should be preached in his name among all nations, beginning at Jerusalem.*" Luke xxiv. 47, and when Christ was brought into their hearts by faith, as a refuge for their own souls; then mark how they were "*strengthened with might by the Spirit in the inner man,"*—see what they did. —"*Behold Peter standing up with the eleven, and lifting up his voice.*" Acts ii. 14—that same Peter who had trembled and denied with an oath the accusation of a servant girl that he had been with Jesus—behold him standing up boldly on the day of Pentecost in the midst of all the Jews, and charging them with their guilt; that they had crucified and slain this Jesus, the Lord of life! Behold Peter and John, standing out boldly in spite of all the Chief Priests and Pharisees, and preaching in the name of Christ—going from prison to the temple to testify of His salvation.

What made them do so? They were "*strengthened with might, by his Spirit, in the inner man;*" and that strength was proved by this, "THAT CHRIST DWELT IN THEIR HEARTS, BY FAITH." They were enabled to turn to Him themselves, as their Saviour, and the Refuge of their souls—they knew their guilt was pardoned—that the blood of Christ blotted out all their sins—and they testified of that great salvation to all the people. They were "*strengthened with might,*" by the Spirit showing to their hearts the fulness of the salvation of Christ; and the inspiration of that same Spirit taught them therefore to testify of Jesus, from the abundance of their hearts, to others; and so they went into the world, preaching the everlasting Gospel of Christ, in the face of power, persecution, and death. It was their own joyful assurance that their guilt was pardoned by the atoning blood of the Lamb of God, taught to their heart by the inspiration of the Spirit, whose office it is to reveal the character and work of Christ to the sinner, as it is written here—It is by faith—and faith alone—that the Apostles themselves, or that any sinners could be strengthened with might, under any circumstances in the world. It is by this alone we can be strengthened to bear up under all our trials, whatever they may be. It is this alone that bears the Christian up against inward, as well as outward conflicts. How it bore up the Church against outward persecutions—led the martyrs to the stake, and cheered them in the furnace! It is this alone that can bear us up under trials and conflicts not less perilous;—rather, I might say, more perilous—more difficult—that gives us strength against "the world, the flesh, and the devil,"—the temptations that surround us—earthly thoughts, feelings, affections—sins that are within us—that are continually drawing us away from Christ—continually setting up idols and vanities in the heart, instead of Christ. Nothing but the faith of Christ—the indwelling of Christ by the Spirit of God—nothing but this, can enable us to carry on our warfare against these.

Therefore, when the Apostle prays, "THAT CHRIST MAY DWELL IN YOUR HEART BY FAITH;" think what he prays for! think what it is to have Jesus dwelling in our hearts! our hearts continually turning to him! so that wherever we roam in all the wilderness, we may say, in the language of the Poet,

"Where'er I roam, whatever realms I see,
My heart untravelled, fondly turns to thee—
Still to my brother turns!—"

A Brother "*born for adversity*," a "*Friend that sticketh closer than a brother*," a Saviour—a God—whose covenant promise is, "*I will never leave thee, nor forsake thee.*" Oh, what a privilege it is to have such a Saviour dwelling in the heart!

We shall all know, by sad experience, that everything in this poor world is passing away. But Christ, is an enduring Treasure. The more our hearts turn to any one, or anything in this world except Christ, the greater trial we shall feel in that very thing; for all things are vanity, all are shadows;—there is nothing substantial for the heart to lean on but Christ; when therefore, the Apostle prays for his brethren, "THAT CHRIST MAY DWELL IN YOUR HEART BY FAITH, THAT YE BEING ROOTED AND GROUNDED IN LOVE, MAY BE ABLE TO COMPREHEND WITH ALL SAINTS, WHAT IS THE BREADTH AND LENGTH, AND DEPTH AND HEIGHT, AND TO KNOW THE LOVE OF CHRIST, WHICH PASSETH KNOWLEDGE, THAT YE MIGHT BE FILLED WITH ALL THE FULNESS OF GOD." He prays for all blessings for them in time and eternity; for "*in Christ are hid all the treasures of wisdom and knowledge*," "*in him dwelleth all the fulness of the Godhead, bodily, and ye are complete in him.*" Col. ii. 3, 9, 10.

"THAT YE, BEING ROOTED AND GROUNDED IN LOVE." He uses here the image of a tree, which shoots forth its roots, and all their fibres into the soil in which it is planted, and takes fast hold by these roots and fibres, and is maintained in its position by the hold that these have in the ground. So, he prays, "THAT YE BEING ROOTED AND GROUNDED IN LOVE," that is—that your hearts may spread forth, as it were, all the fibres of their affections, and take root, as a tree in the ground, in the love of Christ. Although it is true, that faith worketh by love, and that love is the great principle which faith produces in the sinner's heart,—and that from that love, all acceptable obedience alone can spring; it is not this love, I think, which is spoken of here. I do not conceive St. Paul to mean,—being rooted and grounded in your own love—for independent of the incorrectness of the figure that a tree could be rooted and grounded in itself—the love that exists in our warmest affections would be a poor ground of strength to the believer. No—it means "THAT YE BEING ROOTED AND GROUNDED" in the love of God towards you: it appears to me to be a parallel with Rom. v. 5, where the Apostle says, "*hope maketh not ashamed, because the love of God is shed abroad in our hearts by the Holy Ghost which is given unto us.*"* It is the office of the

* The first time I ever knew the meaning of Rom. v. 5, it was conveyed to me under circumstances which I can never forget. I was called many years ago when but a short time in the Ministry, to visit a poor creature dying of a fever.

It was a hovel on a mountain side in the county of Wicklow. The door leading from the miserable chamber to the kitchen (the only other room in the habitation,) was built up to prevent infection, and the only entrance was through a window about a

Holy Ghost, as I mentioned, to reveal Christ; and the Holy Ghost reveals the *love* of Christ;—so he saith, "*because the love of God is shed abroad in our hearts by the Holy Ghost which is given unto us.*" Then, observe, how that love is exhibited. "*For, when we were yet without strength, in due time, Christ died for the ungodly; for scarcely for a righteous man will one die, yet, peradventure, for a good man some would even dare to die, but God commendeth his love towards us, in that while we were yet sinners, Christ died for us.*" Rom. v. 6, 7, 8. This is that love, of which, I think, the Apostle speaks in this passage, "YE BEING ROOTED AND GROUNDED IN LOVE,"—having full confidence by the Spirit in the love of the Lord, having your hearts established in the riches of His grace and love, spreading out, as it were, all the roots and fibres of your affections into the vast field of the love of God—the love of the Father in giving the Son—and of the Son in coming on such a mission of love and mercy—trusting and confiding in Him in every office of His love, as a Prophet, as a Priest, as a King. See how He has taught us—see how He has borne with our manners—our ignorance—our stupidity! See how He

foot and a half square, out of which the frame had been taken for that purpose. In the corner of that wretched apartment on some straw lay a young man of 21 dying, but in the fullest possession of his faculties. A few moments' conversation convinced me that I was there, not to teach, but to learn, in witnessing the triumph of a believer over sin, death, and hell.

The young man was rejoicing in Christ, and as a passage of Scripture which seemed appropriate to his state of mind, I opened the 5th of Romans, and began to read it, applying each successive sentence to the young man, as according with his experience, to which he gave a most cordial response. When I reached the 5th verse I said, "Now you feel how true this is—you have that blessed hope which maketh not ashamed, for you feel such love to God shed abroad in your heart, that it must be by the Spirit of God which is given to you."

"Ah, Sir," said he, "that is not the meaning of that text at all."

"What!" said I, "not the meaning!" and I looked at the verse again, never having thought that any other could be attached to it—"what meaning, then, do you give to it?"

"Ah, Sir," he replied, "it would be a poor hope I should have, if it was derived from any love I feel to God. When I think of what He has done for me, and how I ought to love Him, I feel so cold and dead compared to what my love ought to be, that I would be in despair, instead of having a hope that maketh not ashamed, if my love to Him was to be the ground of my hope. No, Sir, it is God's love to us poor sinners, that the Holy Ghost sheds abroad in our hearts, and it is that gives us the hope that maketh not ashamed. Read on, Sir, and you will see it is."

I read on, and the next three verses convinced me at once, that he was right—and that I had taken an erroneous view of the text—which of course I immediately acknowledged, and never can I forget either the Comment or the Commentator, both may well serve to illustrate this passage.

That poor youth had, not many months before, been brought to the knowledge of the Gospel through the means of my lecturing in the cottages in that, a distant district of the parish. Too poor, too old, and too much engaged in labor to go to school, he had learned from a young companion to read, in the evenings when his work was over, that he might read that book which had revealed a Saviour to his soul. He had read—and had been taught by Him who can teach not as man teacheth. I had not known him—I had not to my knowledge seen him before, though God had taught him under my ministry. I saw him but once again—the next day—entering into "the valley of the shadow of death," and fearing no evil. That night or next morning he entered into his rest. His name was never printed in this world before, but as certainly as it is recorded here, so surely in "*the Lamb's book of life*" is written the name of CHARLES ARMSTRONG.—ED.

has died for us; how He has carried in His precious blood into the Holy of Holies, "*there to appear in the presence of God for us.*" Behold how "*he ever liveth to make intercession for us.*" See, how, as a King, He has watched over us—led us—kept us—preserved us from evil—guarded us from dangers—guided us through difficulties and perplexities. We can raise our Ebenezer here and say, "*hitherto hath the Lord helped us,*" and is this not a vast field of wondrous love in which our hearts may be "ROOTED AND GROUNDED" forever.

"THAT YE, BEING ROOTED AND GROUNDED IN LOVE, MAY BE ABLE TO COMPREHEND WITH ALL SAINTS, WHAT IS THE BREADTH, AND LENGTH, AND DEPTH, AND HEIGHT, AND TO KNOW THE LOVE OF CHRIST." This passage proves, that it is of the love of Christ the Apostle is speaking. It is by tasting that the Lord is gracious—by having the heart taught to know and trust in His love, that an experimental knowledge and comprehension of its nature alone can be acquired. It is thus alone His saints can learn to comprehend "THE BREADTH, AND LENGTH, AND DEPTH, AND HEIGHT."

They learn how vast its breadth—that it is spread over the Volume of eternal life through every promise, from that of the Seed to bruise the serpent's head, to the invitation to drink of the waters of life in the last chapter of the Apocalypse.

They know how immeasurable is that love, which is from everlasting to everlasting. "*The mercy of the Lord is from everlasting to everlasting upon them that fear him.*" Psal. ciii. 17. "*Yea, I have loved thee,*" saith He, "*with an everlasting love, therefore with loving kindness have I drawn thee.*" Jer. xxxi. 3. So our Lord "*Having loved his own which were in the world, he loved them unto the end.*" John xiii. 1. "*For he hath said, I will never leave thee nor forsake thee.*" Heb. xiii. 5.

They understand how unfathomable are the depths of that love, which can stoop to the lowest abysses of human guilt and misery, and raise up the sinner from the very gates of perdition to everlasting life. "*He raiseth up the poor out of the dust, and lifteth up the beggar from the dunghill, to set them among princes, and to make them inherit the throne of glory, for the pillars of the earth are the Lord's, and he hath set the world upon them.*"—1 Sam. ii. 8. "*Though ye have lien among the pots, yet shall ye be as the wings of a dove covered with silver, and her feathers with yellow gold.*" Ps. lxviii. 13.

They learn the height of it—that it reaches to the very throne of God, and bringeth those who were afar off, nigh to "*the High and Lofty one, that inhabiteth eternity, whose name is Holy.*" Isa. lvii. 15. It taketh those who "*have come out of great tribulation, and have washed their robes, and made them white in the blood of the Lamb,*" and carrieth them up, even "*before the throne of God, to serve him day and night in his temple.*" Rev. vii. 14, 15. "*I go,*" saith he to his disciples, "*I go to prepare a place for you, and if I go and prepare a place for you, I will come again and receive you unto myself, that where I am there ye may be also.*" John xiv. 2, 3. "*To him that overcometh will I grant to sit with me in my throne, even as I also overcame and am set down with my Father in his throne.*" Rev. iii. 21.

The Saints can comprehend the nature,—the faithfulness,—the truth,—the certainty,—and security of these promises, these deeds and gifts of love. But who can scan their glory? Who can ever measure this "BREADTH AND LENGTH, AND DEPTH AND HEIGHT?" Therefore, the Apostle adds, "AND TO KNOW THE LOVE OF CHRIST WHICH PASSETH KNOWLEDGE"—as much as to say, after all you have heard, learned, and known of the love of Christ, it transcends the utmost limits of human knowledge, or of human thought; you can so measure—as to discover that it is immeasurable, so comprehend it—as to find that it is incomprehensible.

And what is the end or the scope of this inspired petition? "THAT YE MAY BE FILLED WITH ALL THE FULNESS OF GOD."

When Christ dwelleth in the heart by faith, He is in His people, as the Apostle saith, "*Christ in you the hope of glory.*" Col. i. 27. He "*is made of God unto you, wisdom and righteousness, and sanctification and redemption.*" 1 Cor. i. 30. Now "*it pleased the Father that in him should all fulness dwell.*" Col. i. 20. "*In whom are hid all the treasures of wisdom and knowledge.*" Col. iii. 3. "*In him dwelleth all the fulness of the Godhead bodily, and ye are complete in him, which is the head of all principality and power.*" Col. ii. 9, 10.

When therefore, Christ dwelleth in the heart by faith, the whole fulness of the Godhead dwelleth in it. All that Jesus has, and all that Jesus is, dwelleth in the heart and filleth it, for "*Christ is all, and in all.*" Col. ii. 11. Nothing then, that can be needful for the perfection of the believer, in blessing here and in glory hereafter, is wanting in this prayer. It comprehends all that he could want for time and eternity. Here is strength,—faith,—love,—knowledge,—power,—completeness,—fulness in Christ, and Christ in him; therefore, saith the Apostle, "*All things are yours, whether Paul, or Apollos, or Cephas, or the world, or life, or death, all things are yours, and ye are Christ's, and Christ is God's.*" 1 Cor. iii. 21, 22, 23.

When this Prayer then is a prayer to be "*strengthened with might, by the Spirit in the inner man,*" it implies all the gifts of the Spirit; it is evidently then connected, as I have shown, with the last verse of the preceding chapter, in which they are said to be "*builded together for an habitation of God by the Spirit,*" and seems more clearly to illustrate, that it is to be considered as belonging to that context.

It is impossible that the believer can be "*strengthened with might by the Spirit in the inner man*"—that he can be builded in the Church "*for an habitation of God by the Spirit*"—that he can be as the Apostle saith in another place, "*What! know ye not that your body is the temple of the Holy Ghost, which is in you, which ye have of God?*" 1 Cor. vi. 19—and again, "*Ye are the temple of the living God, as God hath saith, I will dwell in them, and walk in them, and I will be their God, and they shall be my people,*" 2 Cor. vi. 16. It is impossible, I say, that the believer can be thus, without bringing forth the fruits of the Spirit. And if we consider this prayer in its results, we shall see how the fruits of the Spirit are to be cultivated and produced, which seems a subject that is very generally much mystified, because, not simply and scripturally received or understood.

It is not denied by any professing Christian, that "*faith worketh by love;*" that is, when faith in Christ as the Refuge of the soul, is produced in the heart, it makes love to Christ, the motive of the conduct.

In the catalogue of the fruits of the Spirit, Gal. v. 22, the first on the list is *Love.* Now as our blessed Lord teaches us, as we have seen, that it is the office of the Holy Ghost to glorify Him—and as here the strengthening power of the Spirit is exercised, in causing Christ to dwell in the heart by faith, and causing the heart to take root in the love of Christ, it is manifest—that this faith in Christ and in His love to sinners, in which the Spirit teaches the heart to repose its confidence and its affections, must necessarily produce the fruits of the Spirit, "*love, joy, peace,*" &c. It is when the knowledge of His love is "*shed abroad in the heart by the Holy Ghost which is given unto us,*" Rom. v. 5, that we have that "*hope which maketh not ashamed;*" so this is that love of which the Apostle speaks when he saith, "*The love of Christ constraineth us;*" 2 Cor. v. 14; it influences,—actuates,—inspires us,—produces love in our hearts to Him who hath so loved us, as the Apostle John saith, "*We love him because he first loved us,*" 1 John iv. 19, and thus are the fruits of faith produced by love. "*He that abideth in me and I in him, the same bringeth forth much fruit;*" John xiv. 5; and thus the Apostle prays for his Philippian brethren as here for the Ephesians, "*this I pray,*" saith he "*that your love may abound yet more and more in knowledge and in all judgment, that ye may approve things that are excellent, that ye may be sincere and without offence until the day of Christ; being filled with the fruits of righteousness, which are by Jesus Christ, unto the glory and praise of God.*" Phil. i. 9, 10, 11.

It is thus the harmonizing power and glory of the Persons of the ever-blessed Trinity are manifested and illustrated in the salvation of the soul! The Father, in the gift of His Beloved Son! The Son, in the pouring out of His own precious blood! The Spirit, in the illuminating testimony and instruction of the heart by the Word, as to the perfection and spirituality of the holy law—as to the glorious gift of the Father, and the glorious offices and work of Christ!—all resulting in the happiness—the blessedness—the holiness—the glory of His people.

The very scheme of salvation, "*by faith without the deeds of the law,*" being thus made, by infinite wisdom, the means to "*establish the law*"—inscribing it on the heart, as it were in the blood of Him who hath redeemed us from its curse; thus causing the Gospel to produce in the heart, love—which is the law, and making that law—which is love—the motive of obedience in those who believe the Gospel.

If then, we feel, as we so often do, sinful and cold—groaning in these bodies of sin and death—suffering under the power of our three-fold enemy the world, the flesh, and the devil—how are we to be lifted up? how strengthened and refreshed? How enabled to meet and conquer our foe?

Not by abstract desires of spiritual aid, to be given to us in some vague and undefined way, we know not how, and know not what —but by coming in the spirit of this prayer, directly for strength in God's appointed way;—strength from the Spirit, through the faith and love of Christ;—strength to take Christ in all His love and fulness of His salvation, against every foe within and without, to take Him as our Refuge, our Fortress, our Defence, our Power against them all; and answer all with the precious blood of the Lamb. It is thus we "*put on the whole armor of God.*" chap. vi. 11, thus we take "*the shield of faith, wherewith we shall be able to quench all the fiery darts of the wicked:*" vi. 16; and are "*more than conquerors through him that loved us.*" Rom. viii. 37.

The Apostle concludes his prayer with a doxology, an ascription of glory to God. "Now UNTO HIM THAT IS ABLE TO DO EXCEEDING ABUNDANTLY ABOVE ALL THAT WE ASK OR THINK, ACCORDING TO THE POWER THAT WORKETH IN US."

After having prayed for them, that God would grant this petition "*according to the riches of his glory,*" how beautiful is this doxology! It is as much as to say, no matter what the magnitude or extent of our prayer may be, whatever it may comprehend, our God is "ABLE TO DO EXCEEDING ABUNDANTLY, ABOVE ALL THAT WE ASK OR THINK." What a glorious view that is of the character of God! To behold Him sitting on the throne of grace, and hearing prayer! Pray as much as you please—for what you please—for all things you can want in earth or heaven —pray for them "*according to the riches of his grace,*" still "HE IS ABLE TO DO EXCEEDING ABUNDANTLY, ABOVE ALL THAT WE ASK OR THINK." Well might the Apostle say, "*O ye Corinthians, our mouth is open unto you, our heart is enlarged, ye are not straitened in us, but ye are straitened in your own bowels,*" 2nd Cor. vi. 11, 12. It is in our own narrow, niggard, unbelieving hearts we are straitened my friends; for if we asked according to our privilege of asking, thought could not reach the blessings it is our privilege to ask. After all we can pray for, we come to a God, "WHO IS ABLE TO DO EXCEEDING ABUNDANTLY ABOVE ALL THAT WE CAN ASK OR THINK." So the Apostle then con cludes "UNTO HIM BE GLORY IN THE CHURCH BY CHRIST JESUS, THROUGHOUT ALL AGES, WORLD WITHOUT END."

The business of a Christian Church is to glorify its Master—the business of every individual Christian is to glorify his Master.

It is a melancholy proof of the spiritual state of a church, when she begins to set up her own power and authority, instead of her Lord's, and to magnify herself instead of her Heavenly King. If God reveals the riches of His glory to us, in our redemption by Christ Jesus! If he hath bought us with such a price! What is it for, but that we should remember we are not our own, and that we should glorify Him with our bodies and spirits? Oh! that we might be enabled to live to His glory—that our God would enable us to live more and more above the world—to mortify more and more our corrupt affections—to crucify and deny ourselves—and live to Him who has lived for us, and died for us! Yea "*rather who is risen again, who also maketh intercession for us*"—Rom. viii. 34. Who "*is alive for evermore, Amen,*" and "*hath the keys of hell and of death.*" Rev. i. 18. Who "*will never leave nor forsake*" the poor sinner whom He has taught by His Spirit to look to Him as his refuge and strength.

"NOW UNTO HIM WHO IS ABLE TO DO EXCEEDING ABUNDANTLY, ABOVE ALL THAT WE ASK OR THINK; ACCORDING TO THE POWER THAT WORKETH IN US, UNTO HIM BE GLORY, IN THE CHURCH, BY CHRIST JESUS, THROUGHOUT ALL AGES, WORLD WITHOUT END." Amen.

TWENTY-EIGHTH LECTURE.

EPHESIANS IV.—1, 2.

"I therefore, (the prisoner of the Lord,) beseech you, that ye walk worthy of the vocation wherewith ye are called, with all lowliness and meekness, with long-suffering, forbearing one another in love."

WE perceive in this, as in others of the Apostolical Epistles, the order in which the Holy Spirit brings the Word of Truth before the mind of the Church. There is an order in teaching, as there is order in receiving: and the order which the Holy Spirit observes in teaching, is the same which He preserves, in leading the hearts of men to receive His truth.

The order which we perceive in this, and other Apostolical Epistles in teaching, is this,—

The Apostles lay down, first, the doctrines of the Gospel of Jesus; and then, they enforce on those, whom they address as persons who have received the faith of that Gospel, the holy precepts of the Law. And this order, which we perceive in the teaching of the Holy Ghost, is the order which that Blessed Spirit preserves in enabling sinners to receive the truth: that is—all who are taught of God, receive first, the faith of the Gospel—they are "*given repentance to the acknowledging of the truth*"—2 Tim. ii. 25, they learn to believe in the Lord Jesus as all their salvation —to look to Him—to trust in Him—to love Him, and thus through faith they are led by love into the sincere desire of walking according to the will and law of God.

Let me entreat you to remember this. In this is involved the whole Scriptural principle of true Christian moral action. This is directly the reverse of the principle of all unconverted men. All unconverted men go, according to their natural ignorance, in direct opposition to God the Holy Ghost, in the mode of teaching and receiving Christianity. Their doctrine—the doctrine of every man educated or uneducated, until he is taught by the Word and Spirit of God, is this—"I must endeavor to observe God's law, and by the observance of God's law, I hope I shall be able to attain his favor, and thus I trust I shall endeavor to gain salvation," (and perhaps, he adds,) "*through Jesus Christ our Lord.*"

Now the doctrine of the Gospel is this, you must first receive salvation through Jesus as a sinner—not because you *keep* the law, but because you *break* the law: you are a breaker of the law, that is the only ground on which salvation is proclaimed to you. It is sent to you, not as a righteous man but as a sinner. If you are ever saved—you must receive salvation, because you are a breaker of the law, acknowledging and feeling that you are so, and receiving it on these conditions as a lost sinner. Then, when you receive the salvation of Christ, you are called to serve your Lord and Master, not that you may be saved by your own works; but because He *has* saved you by His works—His righteousness, and His death. Now, if there be any of you who do not subscribe to this; rest satisfied, you are ignorant of the very foundation of man's hope and of the Christian faith—you do not know the very first principles of the Gospel of Christ—you know nothing as yet, of God's appointed means for the salvation of your soul. Therefore, consider—reflect on it well—investigate the subject fully. Search the Scriptures. Examine them faithfully, with prayer—and if you now deceive yourself with the imagination that you are to be saved by your own efforts instead of by Christ, if you are taught of God you will learn, that you must be saved entirely by Christ, and not by your own efforts. For remember that "*if by grace then it is no more of works, otherwise grace is no more grace; but if it be of works then it is no more of grace, otherwise work is no more work.*" Rom. xi. 6. Remember as we had in chapter ii. 10, that "*we are his workmanship created in Christ Jesus unto good works,*" not created in good works unto Christ Jesus. This truth cannot be too continually kept before the mind. It ought to be present with us as the principle and foundation of every hope of life. It ought to direct us as the motive in the discharge of every moral duty. It should never be absent from us, for there is incorporated with it, the vital existence of the Christian religion in our hearts.

We have had now, in these three preceding chapters, the whole doctrine of the Gospel clearly and faithfully laid down by the Apostle. From this 4th chapter we commence that portion, in which the Apostle enforces the practical influences of the Gospel, pressing on the Church to cultivate from its blessed principles, the fruit of good works, of holiness, of every relative duty to God and our fellow-creatures.

Where there is no fruit, we must argue there is no faith, "*Faith if it have not works is dead, being alone.*" James ii. 17. It has no existence—it is a mere lifeless form like a dead body. Where there is no influence of the Gospel, we necessarily conclude there is no faith of the Gospel. Where men are living in the service of Satan, they cannot be the servants of God, "*No man can serve two masters,*" saith the Lord, Mat. vi. 24. "*Know ye not, that to whom ye yield yourselves servants to obey, his servants ye are to whom ye obey;*" Rom. vi. 16. We must put works away, as far as pole from pole, when we speak of a sinner's justification before God. That is not their position—they have no place there—with that they have nothing to do. But we must bring them and put them into their own proper place—the place they hold in the Bible—in the believer's conduct and character before God, as the true Scriptural test and evidence of the sincerity of his profession. Here indeed, obedience, holiness, have their place, not a place of merit, or justification, or redemption, or salvation; not, in supplanting or dividing the glory with Christ. His is all the merit—He is our Justifier—He is our Redeemer—He is our Saviour. His is the exclusive office to give pardon to the sinner—peace to the conscience—and salvation to the soul.

We know, alas! how common it is for men to make a Saviour of their own imaginary virtues. We sometimes read accounts of men deriving hope and consolation from these, even in the hour of death; we read of their dying happy in the consciousness of a well-spent life, and looking to a heavenly reward. Those who composed such eulogies, would far more truly state, that they died, blinded by ignorance—by unbelief—by sin, and Satan. The man whose conscience is taught of God, so far from being happy in the sense of his virtues—or, his excellence—is humbled and bowed down to the dust in the consciousness of his guilt and sin. He feels that he is unworthy to lift up his eyes to heaven—the language of his heart and of his lips is that of the Publican, "*God be merciful to me a sinner.*" Luke xviii. 13.

Let us then proceed—and we shall find in the very beginning of this chapter, as through all the rest of the Epistles, how the principle that I have stated is brought before the Church at Ephesus. How the Gospel is kept ever before them as the as sured foundation of all their hope, and how this is pressed on them throughout, as the principle and motive of their conduct.

The Apostle commences, "I THEREFORE THE PRISONER OF THE LORD, BESEECH YOU, THAT YE WALK WORTHY OF THE VOCATION WHEREWITH YE ARE CALLED."

Now remember, what that vocation was, wherewith they were called. Remember what the state was from which they had been called. And recollect the state to which they had been called.

The state from which they had been called, is fully set forth in the 2nd chapter. They are there represented as having been "*dead in trespasses and sins,*" walking in them "*according to the course of this world,*" under the dominion of "*the prince of the power of the air,*" v. 2—"*in the lusts of their flesh fulfilling the desires of the flesh and of the mind,*" "*children of wrath,*" v. 3—"*without Christ,*" "*aliens from the commonwealth of Israel, strangers from the covenants of promise, having no hope and without God in the world.*" v. 12.

Such was the state from which they had been called; and what state of moral misery and degradation more deplorable, could be conceived.

But what was the state to which now they had been called? "*God who is rich in mercy for his great love wherewith he loved them, even when they were dead in sins, had quickened them together with Christ.*" chap. ii. 4, 5. They were now "*accepted in the beloved, in whom they have redemption through his blood, even the forgiveness of sins,*" chap. i. 6, 7—"*In whom they have obtained an inheritance, being predestinated according to the purpose of him who worketh all things after the council of his own will,*" i. 11—Now, they are "*raised up together and made to sit together in heavenly places in Christ Jesus,*" ii. 6—"*Now in Christ Jesus, they who sometime were afar off, are made nigh by the blood of Christ,*" ii. 13—"*Now therefore they are no more strangers and foreigners but fellow-citizens with the saints, and of the household of God, and are built on the foundation of the Apostles and Prophets, Jesus Christ himself being the chief corner-stone, in whom all the building, fitly framed together, groweth into an holy temple in the Lord, in whom they also are builded together for an habitation of God through the Spirit.*" ii. 19–22.

This was now their present condition. It was impossible they could have been called from a lower state of spiritual destitution, or called to a higher state of blessedness or glory in this world, than that, to which they had been called by the Spirit through the faith of the Gospel.

This then is "THE VOCATION WHEREWITH THEY ARE CALLED." And mark, the Apostle does not urge the observance of any precepts on the Church, as the cause of their being called into the enjoyment of these blessed privileges. But on the contrary, he urges their vocation to these great and glorious privileges, as the ground on which he presses on them, the observance of the precepts which he proceeds to inculcate.

"I THEREFORE, THE PRISONER OF THE LORD, BESEECH YOU, THAT YE WALK WORTHY OF THE VOCATION (or calling) WHEREWITH YE ARE CALLED." As much as to say,—"Bear this ever in your mind—Remember what ye are called from, and what ye are called to. Ye are called to be members of the household of God—children of the Most High—heirs of eternal glory." And if the Church were really in all things as it ought to be, a true spiritual Christian church—that is, if it were in the power of man, by rules and regulations, and means and ordinances, to enlighten and convert the heart of man, and that all who are brought into the outward profession of the Church of God, were indeed really believers of the Gospel—and spiritually, and truly members of Christ's mystical body—His disciples by faith in Jesus, and children of God—they would be, as those whom the Apostle addressed in the Church at Ephesus, "*Saints and faithful in Christ Jesus,*" chap. i. 1, part of that Holy Catholic Church in which we profess our belief, that is, of the holy, spiritual Church of Christ—of that spiritual body of God's elect people—who shall be gathered together in Christ out of every kindred, nation, tongue, and people, which is indeed, not now, and never was visible to the human eye, which is known only to God, and shall only be revealed, "*in that day when he shall make up his jewels.*" Mal. iii. 17.

But there is not one of you who does not profess the faith of Christ. You cannot be members of our Church, which, in all the doctrines of the great salvation of the Gospel which it teaches, is "*built upon the foundation of the Apostles and Prophets, Jesus Christ himself being the chief corner-stone.*" chap. i. 20. You cannot be members of that Church, without at least making your public profession of the faith of the Gospel. You profess that faith every time you come to our public services, as clearly as the Church at Ephesus could; you profess it when you go into the church and repeat or join in our Liturgy. Examine it well, compare what you say in it with God's Word, and you will see what a profession you make there of being disciples of Christ, and to what you profess to be called.

You there profess yourself a lost and miserable sinner. Read your Confession and your Litany.

You there profess the glorious Gospel of Christ—His pardoning love and mercy.—Read your absolution.

You testify your conviction that "*when he had overcome the sharpness of death, he did open the kingdom of heaven to all believers.*"—Read your Te Deum.

You profess, sinners as you are, to rejoice in this salvation,—"*O come let us sing unto the Lord, let us heartily rejoice in the strength of our salvation.*"

You say of yourselves—"*we are his people and the sheep of his pasture.*"

Look at the various Psalms and portions of Scripture that you find in the Liturgy expressive of the hope, the joy, the peace, the salvation of the redeemed saints—look at these—remember this is your profession—this is your religion—you take it in your lips into the house of God and call him to witness that these are your principles, in confession—and these your hope, in praise and prayer when you come to worship before Him. But alas! how many come "*with a lie in their right hand*" to church, when they repeat our solemn Scriptural services! How many come there with a profession in their lips, which, if you hear their real principles as they express them out of church, you find they totally deny! They reject, when enforced from the pulpit, the very truths to which they not only assent when used in the reading desk, but which they profess to adopt as their own in the worship of God, and for the truth of which they appeal to God. Alas! the Liturgy of the Church of England shall rise in terrible judgment, against those who belong to her communion, but who reject the Gospel of Christ.

Remember then, that when you were baptized into the faith of Christ, and brought into the outward Church of Christ, you were called into the profession of the faith of His Gospel.

Remember, you have now arrived at maturity of understanding, and full responsibility to God, at the time when you make this profession.

Now, the Apostle's argument and exhortation to all who are real Christians, on the principle of their conduct is, that it ought to be this, "*I am called to be a fellow-citizen of the saints and of the household of God*," and therefore, let me walk worthy of my vocation. Suppose any of you were taken into the household of an earthly sovereign, the first thing you would think of must be, that you should frame your conduct according to the situation which you were called to fill. And if you profess to be members of the household of the King of kings, the first thing to consider is how you are to walk according to the high station to which you are raised. You are all called to be members of God's household by the Gospel of Christ; if you do not really become so—if you reject the Gospel—consider, that for all this God will bring you into judgment—reflect, that you cannot for one moment alter, escape, or evade the condition of your own responsibility.

Those who indeed believe the Gospel of Jesus, are really members of God's household, members of God's family—and therefore, as such, they are exhorted from the "VOCATION WHEREWITH THEY ARE CALLED," to serve their God.

Oh! then forget not—ye, who do really know and believe the Gospel—ye, who know that these things are true—then, knowing the Gospel of Jesus—forget not the principle—the blessed principle according to which you are called to serve your God.

The Apostle does not say, "Walk so as to bring yourselves into a state of reconciliation and peace with God—walk so as to entitle yourselves to God's favor—walk so as to make yourselves fit to become fellow-citizens with the Saints—to qualify yourselves to become members of the household of God—to entitle yourselves to an inheritance among the Saints in light." The Apostle does not speak thus. If this were the language of the Scripture, alas! who could stand? What conscience, that is in the least enlightened to know its own guilt and misery, that must not give up the hope of salvation in despair, if such were the conditions of its attainment? And there are few consciences so devoid of sensibility as to enjoy a ray of bright and cheerful hope and consolation, when the mind is so blind and ignorant as to expect salvation on these conditions.

But this is not the language of truth and of the Bible. You are not called to serve God on the base and slavish principle of mere self-interested efforts in virtue, no—but on a principle of liberty, of loyalty, of gratitude, and love. When man expects salvation by his own exertions, this service which he calls the service of God, is a service of intolerable bondage and slavery. When man is brought to serve his God on the principle of the Gospel of Truth, then his service is indeed "perfect freedom." So this is the language of the Apostle—"*Now in Christ Jesus ye who sometimes were afar off, are made nigh by the blood of Christ, for He is our peace,*" chap. ii. 13, 14. He hath cancelled your mighty debt. "*He himself bare our sins in his own body on the tree, that we being dead unto sin should live unto righteousness, by whose stripes ye were healed. For ye were as sheep going astray, but are now returned unto the Shepherd and Bishop of your souls.*" 1st Pet. ii. 24, 25. "*Now therefore ye are no more strangers and foreigners but fellow-citizens with the saints and of the household of God, and are built upon the foundation of the Apostles and Prophets, Jesus Christ himself being the chief corner-stone,*" chap. ii. 19, 20.

Seeing then, that ye are redeemed by such a ransom—purchased at such a price—called to inherit such a blessing—exalted to such glory.—"I THEREFORE, THE PRISONER OF THE LORD, BESEECH YOU, THAT YE WALK WORTHY OF THE VOCATION WHEREWITH YE ARE CALLED," worthy of that high position in which God has placed you—worthy of that high calling to which God has called you—even to be members of his own household—the household of the King of kings.

And think, dear friends, what a mighty privilege this is—what a blessing in every sphere of human existence from the highest to the lowest.

What a blessing to the rich! What it is for the sinner, who is rich in everything in this world—who has all his heart can desire to gratify him, and make him feel it is good to be here—O what a blessing to be called to know that he has still a "*better and an enduring substance,*" even "*an inheritance incorruptible and undefiled, and that fadeth not away, reserved in heaven for him, who is kept by the power of God, through faith unto salvation,*" 1st Pet. i. 4, 5, and that, as he knows that his tenure of earthly goods is very slender, even a thread to be snapped in a little moment—that he has indeed a treasure beyond the reach of rust, and moth, and time, and death—that God has not left him to his own sleepy and foolish heart, but "*called him out of darkness into his marvellous light,*" 1 Pet. ii. 9, and given him "*a house not made with hands, eternal in the heavens.*" 2 Cor. v. 1.

And think, what a blessing it is for the poor—for those struggling with difficulties and poverty, and who have many trials to afflict them in this weary world. Think what it is for such to lay their hand on the Bible and say, "Well, I am tried here, but it is but for a short time, and my God has given me a rich reversion, my Father has given me too *an 'inheritance incorruptible and undefiled, and that fadeth not away.'* He has called me to glorify him in this humble rank, in this lowly state of poverty and want, this is the place in which my glorious Master has been pleased to call me to honor Him, and He Himself made poverty and want honorable. He had not where to lay His blessed head, and has called me to follow Him here below, in the path He trod before me. I have unsearchable riches and glory in prospect—if I have an humble portion in possession; but this is for a moment, they are for eternity. He has given me the assurance and pledge of that glorious inheritance which is before me, to which every day and hour brings me nearer!"

Oh I have seen many poor creatures suffering—dying in poverty and pain, yet I have seen them smiling, rejoicing, triumphing, in the midst of it all, in the glorious Gospel of Christ. There is not a more glorious sight on earth, than to see a poor afflicted saint, even while bent beneath the pressure of distress, enabled to rejoice in that blessed Saviour, who has called him out of darkness into his marvellous light, washed away his guilt and given him the glorious hope of this inheritance. In such a case we see how suffering enhances the prospect of relief—we see how Grace divinely adjusts the apparent inequalities of Providence in His church; and balances every difference in the lot of time, by a blessed compensation in eternity.

Think then, what it is to be called into the Lord's household! what a privilege it is to be a member of the Lord's family! You need not envy a king his birth, his crown, or his kingdom, if you are called to be a child of the King of kings. How glorious is that happiness which God holds forth before us in his eternal word! How can it be that man is so blind, so ignorant, and lost, as to trample on or "*neglect such great salvation.*"

But we see, the obedience of the Gospel, is not a burden that the Apostle lays upon us—it is not a hard burden of subjection—a hard obedience—a hateful obedience—a slavish and an unwilling obedience.

Such is the obedience which the unconverted sinner in his best efforts tries to render—he strives against his grain—his heart—his feelings—to render an obedience to God's commands. But this obedience to which the children of God are called, is, as I have said, that of freedom, liberty, loyalty, and grateful love. See, what David saith, "*I will walk at liberty; for I seek thy precepts,*" Psal. cxix. 45. "*I will run in the way of thy commandments when thou shalt enlarge my heart,* (*or when thou shalt set my heart at liberty,*") Psal. cxix. 32. When the heart is set free from the bondage of the law—liberated from doing works as a condition of salvation, and enabled to lean its hope on Christ, then—

but not until then, it is at liberty to love and serve its God—then—when we can serve him, not on the slavish principle of obtaining a reward, but on the principle of love for the great redemption He hath wrought for us, then we serve Him freely—serve Him heartily—and serve Him happily. But never until then, can any service from man be either rendered to, or accepted by, his Creator.

What then is the first duty which the Apostle impresses on believers? "I THEREFORE THE PRISONER OF THE LORD, BESEECH YOU, THAT YE WALK WORTHY OF THE VOCATION WHEREWITH YE ARE CALLED, WITH ALL LOWLINESS AND MEEKNESS." One of the master sins of man's heart is pride. "*The lust of the flesh, the lust of the eye, and the pride of life,*" 1st John ii. 16, may be said to comprehend most of the practical iniquities of man. Pride was the sin by which our first parents fell; it is at least one reigning passion, if not the reigning sin, in the heart of every one of us.

To set up self—to have something—to be something—and to do something—is our heart's prime ambition. We cannot be content to prostrate self—to have nothing—to be nothing—and to do nothing. Pride was the very first sin which the devil called into action in our first parents. The temptation which he brought before Eve was a lure to her pride, "*your eyes shall be opened; ye shall be as gods knowing good and evil.*" Gen. iii. 5.

We believe pride to have been the sin that cast Satan from heaven; and we know it was the sin which cast out man from paradise. So also the very first sin, to the root of which the Gospel lays the axe, is pride. And therefore, when the sinner is brought to believe the Gospel; the very principle on which he believes in Christ is the fact of his lost condition—this is the prostration of pride. Pride is the cause, the chief cause of opposition to the Gospel of Christ: "*They being ignorant of God's righteousness and going about to establish their own righteousness, have not submitted themselves unto the righteousness of God.*" Rom. x. 3; they have not bowed their necks down to submit themselves—they are too proud to do so.

So David saith, "*The wicked, through the pride of his countenance will not seek after God.*" Ps. x. 4. The feeling in the natural mind that takes offence at the cross of Christ, is pride. You tell man, "You are a lost sinner"—you tell him "you can do nothing whatever to justify your soul before God—you are a breaker of God's law, and stand a condemned and convicted criminal." Then the pride of man's heart takes fire, he bursts out at once.

"What sort of doctrine is this? then it is no matter what I do—I am on a level with the vilest criminal—all virtue and vice is reduced to the same standard.—What is this? I—who am so and so—virtuous, moral, excellent, honest, upright, good-tempered, amiable—you reduce me to a grade with a man, the reverse of all this."

Thus, we see pride is ever setting itself above others. "*But,*' saith the Apostle, "*they, measuring themselves by themselves, and comparing themselves among themselves, are not wise.*" 2nd Cor. x. 12. If God's standard of judgment were, comparing men, one with another, that language might suit very well. But when God's law is the standard of his righteous judgment of man, then the blind sinner who is ignorant of that law, is offended when you tell him, that he is a violator of it in every particular, and that he cannot save himself—his pride is angry, because he has been all his life congratulating himself, like the Pharisee, "*God, I thank thee that I am not as other men are, extortioners, unjust, adulterers,*" &c. When you bring then to his pride, the principles of truth that lay him in the dust, he cannot endure it. But the Gospel prostrates him there. It is for sinners. And he never can receive the Gospel until he receives it in the dust. The Gospel addresses him in no other character but as a corrupt and guilty sinner; gives him no credit for his amiability—morality—or anything of the sort—but addresses him as a lost and guilty sinner, on whom, as under the law, the wrath of God abideth. In that position the Gospel finds him—in that alone, it recognizes him and addresses him—and there it proclaims to him, full—free—finished pardon and salvation, as a condemned sinner; and brings to him, for his deliverance, the righteousness, and the blood of Christ.

See those proud rebels, who had been crying out against Christ, "*Away with him, away with him, crucify him, crucify him,*" when the Lord brought home conviction to their consciences, by the preaching of the Apostle Peter, on the day of Pentecost—how did they act? "*When they heard this, they were pricked in their hearts, and said, men and brethren, what shall we do?*" So every sinner on earth that is ever brought to the knowledge of the Gospel of Christ, is brought in the same way. Some may have deeper conviction of sin than others. In some, those convictions may be more slowly produced; in others, they may be more sudden and violent;—but every individual that is saved, is saved in the same way—as a helpless, ruined sinner—brought down to the dust, and looking to Jesus for free and full salvation.

Now, although they are brought thus to Christ, pride is not eradicated from the heart. Remember this. The pride of the natural heart remains as long as there is a throb of life in it. Pride, like all other sins, remains lusting against the Spirit, in the natural heart; the natural heart remains unchanged—struggling forever against the Spirit. In that struggle consists the constant conflict of the Christian—and in the mortification and subjection of that nature, by the Spirit, consists the Christian's triumph of faith and his practical religion.

One of the most common and dangerous mistakes into which many believers fall, is, that the natural heart of man undergoes some improvement in itself and its dispositions. This is alike opposed to the Word of God, and the experience of every redeemed soul. It never does so. The natural heart of man remains the same in itself to the end. The man, on the whole is changed—"*If any man be in Christ, he is a new creature.*" 2nd Cor. v. 17.

He is a new man—but he is so thus, because he receives a new principle—a new heart—another heart, a heart which is called, "*a heart of flesh*,"—which is the gift of the Holy Spirit, opposing—resisting—subjugating his natural heart. Hence, I repeat, the conflict that continually exists in the believer, and under which he is constantly harassed—"*the flesh lusteth against the Spirit, and the Spirit against the flesh: and these are contrary the one to the other; so that ye cannot do the things that ye would.*" Gal. v. 17. So saith the Apostle of himself, "*I see another law in my members, warring against the law of my mind, and bringing me into captivity to the law of sin, which is in my members.*" Rom. vii. 23.

Our Article on original sin, the 9th, is very plain on this point, and describes our state by nature, both before and after conversion, it says,

> "This infection of nature doth remain, yea in them that are regenerate, whereby the lust of the flesh, called in Greek *phronema sarkos*, which some do expound the wisdom—some sensuality—some the affection—some the desire of the flesh is not subject to the law of God. And although there is no condemnation for them that believe and are baptized, yet the Apostle doth confess that concupiscence and lust hath of itself the nature of sin."

Indeed the Apostle disposes of the question in a single text, for using these very Greek words which we translate "the carnal mind," he saith "*The carnal mind is enmity against God, for it is not subject to the law of God, neither indeed can be.*" Rom. viii. 7.

Hence, therefore, this Apostolic exhortation, and all other exhortations in the Gospel of Christ, are directly or indirectly against ourselves; we must "*deny ungodliness and worldly lusts,*" Titus, ii. 12—"*crucify the flesh with its affections and lusts,*" Gal. v. 24—"*mortify our members which are on earth,*" Col. iii. 5—"*not yield our members as instruments of unrighteousness unto sin.*" Rom. vi. 13. The whole Christian walk is a walk of conflict;—that is, a conflict between our own corrupt, natural inclinations, and the mind of the Spirit. It is very important we should know and recollect this. For there are many believers going on their way, mourning, in anguish and darkness of soul, because they do not feel the change they are looking for—that is, the absence of sin in themselves. They think they are to be improved to a certain state, in which there is to be, in a great degree, if not altogether, an absence of sin.* But they are like men waiting for the river to flow by. The corrupt fountain of evil—the natural heart, remains a corrupt fountain still; but the mind of the Sprit is given as a gift by the Lord Jesus to oppose—to contend against—and to

* A late writer, whose theology is as false as it is fashionable, speaking of Mat. v. 8, says, "Truth itself is here manifesting its own eternal essence; to 'see God' being the one only happiness; and purity of heart—the one only qualification." Meaning—not a "*heart sprinkled from an evil conscience*" by the blood of Jesus—which is true—but a heart purified from the indwelling of sin, which is utterly without even a shadow of truth.

subdue the flesh, "*Casting down imaginations, and every high thing that exalteth itself against the knowledge of God, and bringing into captivity every thought to the obedience of Christ.*" 2 Cor. x. 5. The Apostle therefore exhorts them "TO WALK WORTHY OF THE VOCATION WHEREWITH THEY ARE CALLED, WITH ALL LOWLINESS AND MEEKNESS." If a Christian were necessarily made lowly—if pride were removed by conversion—there would be no necessity for calling on believers to watch against it;—men could not in this case, mortify evils—for there would be nothing to mortify. The very command to watch against their affections and lusts, implies and proves their existence.

"WITH ALL LOWLINESS AND MEEKNESS." These words are different in their signification: Lowliness signifies *lowliness of mind;* it is elsewhere translated, "*in lowliness of mind let each esteem other better than themselves.*" Phil. ii. 3. And in this respect it differs from meekness—the one referring to the conduct and demeanor; the other, to the principle of the mind. A lowly mind will produce a meek deportment, and a gentleness of manner. A man who thinks humbly of himself, will not act proudly and haughtily to others; and this exhortation first goes to the root of the evil in the mind, and then to the conduct.

You have been called to the feet of the meek and lowly Jesus, and brought to the foot of the cross, there then abide, and as becometh those bought at such a price, "WALK WITH ALL LOWLINESS AND MEEKNESS." "*Let this mind be in you which was also in Christ Jesus.*" Phil. ii. 5. And, my dear friends, if we are really taught by the Spirit of God, this, among other graces, is that in which the Christian especially grows, lowliness and humility. Some old divine, when asked what is the first Christian grace in which the Christian grows? answered—Humility. And when asked what was the second? he replied—Humility. And what was the third?—Humility. I appeal to the experience, of any of you who know the Gospel, and who feel the burthen of an evil heart, and I will venture to assert that your experience testifies, that, the more you know of yourselves, the more evil you have found, and continually find in your heart, therefore, if you are taught of God, this is your experience, and this is the reason why you should grow in humility. Let us remember to mark the difference between true humility and that sort of mock humility which is very often the fruit of pride. We affect to value ourselves at a far lower rate than we really do, and to seem much lower in our own estimation than we really wish to stand in that of others. But true humility is a just and sober sense of our own guilt and misery, which teaches us, not before man, but before God, in our own closets and in our own hearts, to prostrate ourselves at His feet and cry, "*God be merciful to me a sinner,*" Luke xviii. 13. When we are taught of God, as we grow in the knowledge of His truth, we see cause of deep humiliation, not only in our general conduct in which we so frequently fall into sin—but we learn to see cause of humiliation, most especially in all our holy things, yea—in our best thoughts; we find our best deeds and thoughts defiled and polluted by sin.

Perhaps our friends may say, whether we be ministers or not, how earnestly we pray—how devoted we are—how warmly we write—how faithfully we preach—or how exemplarily we discharge our duties in all our stations.—But we feel before God, that it is in the discharge of our most holy duties we have most cause of humiliation in His sight; no matter what man may think, or say—we feel, if taught of God, that God sees us all vile, polluted, guilty creatures. This must follow from the knowledge of God, "*I have heard of thee by the hearing of the ear, but now mine eye seeth thee, wherefore I abhor myself and repent in dust and ashes*," Job xlii. 5, 6. Therefore, growth in the knowledge of our own hearts teaches us to grow and walk in humility. It is thus we learn to grow in grace and in the knowledge of our blessed Lord and Saviour Jesus Christ, we grow in the knowledge of His character as applicable to our wants, as suited to our deep necessities and sins.

If we have prized the righteousness of Christ when first we heard of it, when first we were given to believe it—it is more precious to us every day, because we discover daily more and more the truth of the Prophet's words, "*All our righteousnesses are as filthy rags.*" Is. lxiv. 6.

If we prized the fountain of Christ's blood at the first, we learn to prize it every day, more and more, for we learn that it is not merely all our sins, but all our righteousness—all we have and are that we have constant need to cast into that blessed fountain. Christ grows more precious to us as we grow continually lower in our own eyes. And if we are not growing in the humiliating knowledge of ourselves continually more and more, believe me, it is because we are not growing in the knowledge of our own hearts—our own real character. True humility is the fruit of the real knowledge of ourselves: it is not, as I have seen it stated, the undervaluing of ourselves, but the real knowledge—the real, solid judgment of our hearts—a sober, solid principle, arising from a sound and sober knowledge of truth. The more we know of the purity and holiness of the law of God, the more we find, not only our own actual violations of that law, but our short comings in everything, that in everything we may say with the Psalmist, "*Who can understand his errors, cleanse thou me from secret faults*," from faults I know not, and then, "*keep back thy servant also from presumptuous sins; let them not have dominion over me: then shall I be upright, and I shall be innocent from the great transgression.*" Psal. xix. 12, 13.

Lowliness and meekness evince their practical effects, especially in all our conduct to our fellow-creatures, so he adds, "WITH ALL LOWLINESS AND MEEKNESS, WITH LONG-SUFFERING, FORBEARING ONE ANOTHER IN LOVE." Lowliness always teaches us patience and forbearance. Knowledge of ourselves, teaches us how to bear with the evils we see in others; and therefore, while we sometimes see in the young Christian a proud, arrogant, or censorious disposition—the experienced Christian bears with the faults of his fellow-sinners, having learned in some degree how God graciously bears with him. Increased knowledge of our hearts teaches us to comprehend and calculate some portion of that mighty debt of ten thousand talents which we owe to God, and thus instructs us to have patience with our fellow-servant that owes us fifty pence; we learn to exercise "LONG-SUFFERING," with others, in proportion as we learn how long-suffering our Master is with us.

"FORBEARING ONE ANOTHER IN LOVE." This is the best commentary on the text, "*charity covereth a multitude of sins*," which is, I might say, blasphemously applied to prove the principle, that alms-giving and benevolence, and acts of kindness to others, cover our sins in the sight of God; thus putting man's works into the place of Christ, and laying the axe to the very root of the Gospel. Charity, that is Christian kindness and love, "*covereth the multitude of sins*" that appear in us to each other. The text is quoted by the Apostle Peter from Proverbs, where we see it in its own place in contrast with its opposite, "*hatred stirreth up strife, but love covereth all sins.*" Prov. x. 12. And that is the very thing, bearing and forbearing with each other, throwing a mantle of love over another's transgressions. In our natural state, we are all ready to remark on our neighbor's defects and imperfections—to expose them—to whisper them—to laugh at them, because pride and Satan foster in our hearts the impression, that we thus exhibit ourselves as superior to others, in those defects which we are so ready to point out in them; hence that spirit of slander—of scandal—of whispering—of backbiting and satire, that is so common in general conversation among persons who are ignorant of God. And alas! there is a lamentable defect in Christian conduct among those who profess the Gospel of Christ. There are many who are too ready to speak of the faults of their neighbors and to blazon their errors. "*But love covereth all sins*," so he saith "FORBEARING ONE ANOTHER IN LOVE;" implying that we have need of forbearance, and ought to exercise it.

In our own family—among our friends—our acquaintances—our neighbors—in every relation in life, who has not to bear with some peculiar tempers—eccentricities—weaknesses—and failings in others? and who has not a great necessity that others should bear with their own?

What countless peculiarities and infirmities do those who are near us see in us, as we see in them, and what would become of us—surely every house would be almost a hell—if mutual forbearance, kindness, and patience, did not "*cover the multitude of sins.*" And that forbearance which we would exercise toward a friend whom we loved, the Gospel teaches us to practice towards all, "FORBEARING ONE ANOTHER IN LOVE."

What a blessed standard of happiness as well as holiness the Gospel erects for men. How happy would the genuine exercise of these short precepts make a family, or a circle of friends or acquaintances, "WITH ALL LOWLINESS AND MEEKNESS, WITH LONG-SUFFERING, FORBEARING ONE ANOTHER IN LOVE."

May the Lord Jesus bring these principles into our hearts and these precepts into our lives, for His Name's sake, Amen.

Now we shall part till after Christmas.—So beloved friends I must wish you a happy Christmas; Oh that we may all know the rich source of happiness to be derived from the return of the anniversary of our glorious Saviour's birth! Alas, what a blight it is on the Christian church at this day, that the very time which was set apart by those of the early faith for celebrating the glorious advent of our blessed Lord and Master, is so lamentably perverted and abused! Look at that season now, among nominal Christians.

"*I wish you a merry Christmas;*"—that means, I wish you a season of carousing and feasting, of eating and drinking and revelling, and a full indulgence in all the follies and vanities of the world. I was struck with the newspaper the other day in looking at the vast number of advertisements of Christmas games of all descriptions, for children:—foolish and absurd amusements, adapted to what they call a merry Christmas, without a shadow of even religious instruction in them! Oh, how the many returns of what is called a happy Christmas, shall rise in judgment against those who profess His name, but who know not the blessing of His coming into the world. It is indeed a happy, and ought to be a happy season; we should have a continual recollection, an everlasting remembrance of the time when the Son of God came down from heaven and "*took upon him the form of a servant,*" Phil. ii. 7,—that time ought, indeed, to be a time of joy and thankfulness, spiritual joy, spiritual thankfulness, when "*Christ came into the world to save sinners,*" 1 Tim. i. 15. What a wonder in time, what a wonder in eternity, that the Lord of glory came to be born in a stable, and to lie in a manger, to live "*a man of sorrows*" without where to lay His head, and die on a cross for guilty rebels like us! Oh, the true celebration of Christmas is, to think, with gratitude and joy, what our Master has done for us—what His love demands from us.—Oh, may we know this! And I wish you, my dear friends, a happy Christmas, and this is the happiness I wish you—"*That Christ may dwell in your hearts by faith, that ye being rooted and grounded in love, may be able to comprehend with all saints, what is the breadth, and length, and depth and height; and to know the love of Christ which passeth knowledge, that ye may be filled with all the fulness of God.*" chap. iii. 17, 18, 19.—Amen.

TWENTY-NINTH LECTURE.

EPHESIANS IV.—3, 4, 5, 6.

"Endeavoring to keep the unity of the Spirit in the bond of peace. There is one body, and one Spirit, even as ye are called in one hope of your calling; One Lord, one faith, one baptism, one God and Father of all, who is above all, and through all, and in you all."

THE Apostle continues his practical exhortations to his believing brethren to walk worthy of their vocation, and the next characteristic mark of that walk which he mentions, is, "ENDEAVORING TO KEEP THE UNITY OF THE SPIRIT IN THE BOND OF PEACE."

There are two grand principles in the Gospel of Jesus, *Faith* and *Love*. The belief of the truth, and the influence of that truth produced by the belief of it, which is love. It is utterly impossible that the sinner can really believe the Gospel of Jesus, without that faith producing love to Jesus. We cannot believe the work that Christ has wrought for us, and rest upon that work, and upon him who has wrought it, as our Hope—our Peace—our Joy—our Salvation—we cannot do so, without loving the Lord Jesus; and therefore, you see, that love is always given as the true characteristic of genuine faith, as in that text, "*in Christ Jesus, neither circumcision availeth anything nor uncircumcision, but faith which worketh by love.*" Gal v. 6.

Now these—as "*Every good gift and every perfect gift is from above,*" James i. 17, these are the gifts of the Spirit of God, "*no man can say that Jesus is the Lord but by the Holy Ghost;*" 1st Cor. xii. 3. And so you see, these are numbered among the fruits of the Spirit, in Gal. v. 22, 23, "*The fruit of the Spirit is love, joy, peace, long-suffering, gentleness, goodness, faith, meekness, temperance:*" now, "*the flesh lusteth against the Spirit;*" and the natural workings of the corrupt heart are always contravening the mind of the Spirit of God: you see this stated in the chapter from which I have quoted, Gal. v. "*The flesh lusteth against the Spirit, and the Spirit against the flesh, and these are contrary, the one to the other: so that ye cannot do the things that ye would.*" The natural unbelief of the heart of man is always conflicting against the faith of the Gospel—as the natural corruptions, the evil lusts and passions of the heart of man, are always conflicting against the love of the Gospel; therefore, all believers are continually exhorted throughout the Scriptures to faith, and to the fruits of faith; which are therefore always requiring an effort on the part of man against his own evils, so the Apostle says. "ENDEAVORING TO KEEP THE UNITY OF THE SPIRIT IN THE BOND OF PEACE"—as much as to say, your natural mind is opposed to the great principle of Christian love, just as the pride of the natural heart is opposed to lowliness and meekness; the impetuousness and evil tempers of the natural mind are opposed to "*long-suffering, and forbearing one another in love;*" so the same corrupt principle is opposed to "KEEPING THE UNITY OF THE SPIRIT IN THE BOND OF PEACE." Therefore, you see the Apostle says, "ENDEAVORING TO KEEP THE UNITY OF THE SPIRIT IN THE BOND OF PEACE"—that is to say, you must strive to do so. "*I labor for peace,*" saith David; and hard work it is sometimes, both for ourselves and others.

If those who profess the Gospel, attended diligently to these great leading principles, the pure faith of the Gospel of Jesus, and the love that flows from that faith, we should not see the Church of Christ so distracted as it is at this moment. Look at the Protestant Churches, you hear continually the objection that Popery advances against the Word of God, it says,

"Look at the result of reading the Scriptures; Protestants have the free use of the Bible, and see what it produces in them; see their divisions, their contentions, see the different sects and parties into which they are divided."

This, alas! is awfully true in fact, but utterly false in principle. For—it arises, not from reading the Scriptures, but from neglecting the Scriptures. Union may arise from ignorance and unbelief of the Gospel of Christ, "*teaching for doctrines, the commandments of men.*" Such is the state of the Church of Rome itself, whose unity is that of darkness, ignorance, and death; and such the unity that those would effect among ourselves, who would transfer the authority of Rome to the Church of England. In general, divisions arise from an imperfect, and inadequate view of the value and importance of the faith and love of Christ, and from giving an undue unscriptural preponderance, to things, of which some are comparatively of lesser moment, and some of none at all. In some cases the spirit of dissension seems in itself to rule in the hearts of men. It is astonishing how some men seem born with a spirit of discontent, insubordination, and contradiction,—few there are, who do not feel something of these in themselves, and he who tries to bring men to unity, where discipline does not forbid resistance, is well aware how those evils reign in various proportions in the hearts of others.

The only contention that ought to have a place in the Church ought to be that of which we see so little—"*striving together,*" as St. Paul saith, "*for the faith of the Gospel*"—Phil. ii. 27, or in the language of St. Jude, "*contending earnestly for the faith once delivered to the saints,*" Jude 3, and as here "ENDEAVORING TO KEEP THE UNITY OF THE SPIRIT IN THE BOND OF PEACE."

But it really would seem, as if some persons thought, that their Christian duty consisted in the opposite of this; in endeavoring to break the unity of the Spirit in contention and war. For instead of persons asserting and maintaining the great principles of the Gospel, that ought to keep and hold them together; there are many who seem to search the Scriptures for points of contention and division—who think they may dissent, and that they may separate themselves, and excite to dissension the consciences of others, on the most minute and most contemptible trifles, the beggarly elements of forms and ceremonies, and different things of that kind, to the utter neglect of the great fundamental principle of maintaining the faith of Christ, and "ENDEAVORING TO KEEP THE UNITY OF THE SPIRIT IN THE BOND OF PEACE."* Creating divisions appears, I confess, to me to be an awful act of evil, separating and dividing from the unity of those that hold the truth of the Gospel; whether it is effected by those who would force unessential matters on the consciences of others; or by those who give to such matters an unscriptural weight and authority over their own.

I trust I can say, and feel with all my heart, "*Grace be with all them that love our Lord Jesus Christ in sincerity*," chap. vi. 24—yet, I cannot, for this very reason, but mourn as sincerely the divisions among those, who, I believe, hold the essentials of Gospel truth. Oh! my friends, if those that profess the Gospel of Jesus were as anxious to unite together in maintaining the faith of the Gospel of Christ, and in walking, as here enjoined, "*worthy of the vocation wherewith they are called, with all lowliness and meekness, with long-suffering, forbearing one another in love*,"—"ENDEAVORING TO KEEP THE UNITY OF THE SPIRIT IN THE BOND OF PEACE," this country would present a very different picture, from that which it presents at this moment;—an awful exhibition of dissensions, divisions, and contentions—not merely among those who are ignorant of the Gospel of Christ, but even among those who know it! You see, the command of the Holy Ghost is, "ENDEAVORING TO KEEP THE UNITY OF THE SPIRIT IN THE BOND OF PEACE." Men may differ—and, no doubt, will continually do so, on various subjects connected with religion. It is utterly impossible, that the minds of men can all be brought to think alike—I do not believe the Lord ever intended it;—but, though men cannot all agree in all unimportant, non-essential points—those who agree together on the great foundations of the Gospel of Christ ought to walk together—to love one another, in "THE UNITY OF THE SPIRIT AND THE BOND OF PEACE." If

* I recollect a lamentable illustration of the evil here spoken of, in a body who separated from the Church and all other sects, and who would not even kneel down to pray with a person who did not belong to their own body, on the ground that those who did not observe all the Apostolic precepts, were "walking disorderly." One of them at last introduced the Apostolic precept, "*Greet one another with a holy kiss*," and then they separated into parties themselves, having divided on this question of the salutation. When will men learn that schisms and divisions, except where the vital principles of the Gospel are involved, are a positive violation of the most express commands of the Scripture, and a greater evil than any, that those who cause them can seek to avoid?

there were no differences in opinions and tempers, how could men bring into practice, "*forbearing one another in love*"?—what need of "ENDEAVORING TO KEEP THE UNITY OF THE SPIRIT IN THE BOND OF PEACE"?—it is the difficulty, that makes it necessary to endeavor to do so. Surely, if we hold the great foundations of the truth as we ought to hold them, we shall agree in trusting and in loving our Lord, and loving one another, for our Lord's sake; and we shall agree in maintaining the great principles of the Gospel of our God and Saviour, against all the ignorance, error, and falsehood, that are endeavoring to undermine them.

Oh! shall it ever be, when we shall be permitted to say, "*Behold, how good and how pleasant it is for brethren to dwell together in unity.*" Surely, "*It is like the precious ointment upon the head, that ran down upon the beard, even Aaron's beard; that went down to the skirts of his garments.*" Surely it is "*As the dew of Hermon, and as the dew that descended upon the mountains of Zion: for there the Lord commanded a blessing, even life for evermore.*" Psalm cxxxiii. 1, 2, 3.

Surely, a spirit of union and love—an unction flowing from Him, the Glorious Head, whose name is Love, descending down to the skirts of His garment, even from the highest to the lowest in the Church—might well be compared to the perfumed oil, wherewith Aaron was anointed, flowing down on his garments;—or, the dew that distilled from heaven on the mountains of Zion bringing verdure to the cedars of Lebanon, and perfume and refreshment to the flowers that grew beneath them.

Surely, we have a sad experience of how evil and how bitter a thing it is for brethren to dwell together in contention.

I have seen much of dissension and divisions in my life; and I can truly say, I never knew a blessing rest, in any single instance, on them! I can only view them as the work of the enemy of souls. I have seen many who have separated from the Church, but I never knew in my life, an instance, in which practical evil did not result from it, both to the individuals themselves, and others. I have seen it too often narrow the heart of Christian love, and embitter the spirit—stirring up dissensions, "*which minister questions, rather than godly edifying, which is in faith.*" 1st Tim. i. 4.

I trust there is not any person who has a more Catholic spirit than I have, in this case. I can give, cordially, the right hand of fellowship to those who I believe love the Lord Jesus in sincerity, to whatever outward denomination of Christianity they belong; yet, I must say, that I think there is in these realms, at this moment, an awful evil among many who make a high profession of the Gospel, but who dissent from the Church which God has been pleased to establish amongst us. Men may hold different opinions about various points of government, and forms, and discipline, and cavil at expressions—but all the great vitalities of eternal truth—all the great foundations of the Gospel of Jesus, are incorporated with the principles of the Established Church, as plainly as they are written in the Bible. The Articles, the Homilies, the Liturgy, of our Church, contain the doctrines of the Gospel of Jesus, as plainly as they are written in the Word of God. And, although there are of course, as there must be in all human institutions, various ordinances that are, confessedly, of human appointment,—and which are, and must be, left at large, and adapted to various circumstances, and times, and nations, for the utility and edification of the Church;—yet all the great fundamental truths, on which a sinner can alone rest his soul before God, are to be found at the very foundations of the Established Church. And, when God did please to establish that Church in this nation,—all those who call themselves Christians, if, as they say, their conscience leads them to dissent themselves,—I think it ought to lead them, not to sow dissension, but to "ENDEAVOR TO KEEP THE UNITY OF THE SPIRIT IN THE BOND OF PEACE."

I have said, I never saw a blessing rest on divisions. I love many that are dissenters, as Christian men; yet, the principle, I think, has been, and is at this moment, lamentably tested and exhibited in this empire*—for I see many who make a loud profession of the Gospel, united at this time with Apostacy, with Popery, with Infidelity, to pull down the Established Religion! This is clear;—no person who reads the public journals can doubt the fact. Then, I say, that this presents an awful exhibition of the evils of divisions, and of the substitution of other things, for the grand principles of faith and love, which are the vital essence of true religion. I trust that God will lead such persons to see the evil of taking part with Satan, against the cause of Christ! I have known men, to whom I have gladly given the right hand of fellowship, as members of Bible Societies, mantaining cordially, as I supposed, the Bible—vindicating and asserting its authority;—I have seen such persons stand forward and take part with Popery and Infidelity, for the establishment of that awful system of anti-Christian education in this country, that empowers priest-craft to shut out the Word of the Living God from the instruction of our poor countrymen. Nor do I see one to this day stand forward faithfully against it.

Again, I have met with persons belonging to our Church, with whom I have taken sweet counsel, and enjoyed Christian fellowship, yea—who have labored with me in the cause of Christ—who have quitted the Church, and afterwards, in a spirit of division, and dissent, and schism, have turned from me, or argued bitterly against me—as being a member of Babylon, which they call the Established Church! This is neither like "*lowliness*,"—nor "*meekness*,"—nor "*long suffering*,"—nor "*forbearing one another in love*,"—still less, "ENDEAVORING TO KEEP THE UNITY OF THE SPIRIT IN THE BOND OF PEACE."

When men either arrogate an unscriptural authority for themselves—their office—and their Church—setting them up instead

* This Lecture was delivered in 1837, and the truth of this statement was too mournfully proved, in many ways, at that period.

of Christ—and unchristianize all who do not belong to them, as some do in our own Church.

Or, when men—forgetting the great principles of the Gospel of Jesus—the great principles of faith and love—dispute, and dissent, and divide, about forms and ceremonies, and ordinances, which are no part of the vital truth and power of the religion of Jesus.

Or, when men choose to anticipate the commands of Christ, and the office of the angels, in separating the tares from the wheat, and seek to form a Church for themselves—consisting purely of the saints—such as is only to be looked for when Christ shall come; and when they strive to sow dissensions, and cause divisions among believers—really doing the work of the enemy. It appears to me, that such persons, of all classes, seem to know little—and to prize still less, the glorious Gospel of Jesus, in its faith, and love, and power; and that they have much need both to learn these, as well as the meaning of this exhortation, "ENDEAVORING TO KEEP THE UNITY OF THE SPIRIT IN THE BOND OF PEACE."

These things ought to be laid to heart; for certainly, "*God is not the author of confusion, but of peace, as in all the churches of the saints.*" 1st Cor. xiv. 33. "*If ye have bitter envying and strife in your hearts, glory not, and lie not against the truth. This wisdom descendeth not from above, but is earthly, sensual, devilish. For where envying and strife is, there is confusion, and every evil work.*" James, iii. 14, 15, 16.

The Apostle proceeds to give an unanswerable reason for this exhortation to unity of Spirit,—"THERE IS ONE BODY AND ONE SPIRIT, EVEN AS YE ARE CALLED IN ONE HOPE OF YOUR CALLING."

There will be no divisions at the right hand of the Lamb! There, these two great principles of Faith and Love shall appear to have been the grand doctrines which God inculcated, with all their power and their fruits, on His Church, and which God's Church ought to have ever kept in view. You will always find, when divisions exist, that it is for want of maintaining these two principles; some "*beggarly elements*" are brought in, and put into a place which they ought not to occupy. Nothing should sever the members of Christ from each other—nothing should sever the children of God—the brothers and sisters of "*the whole family in heaven and earth.*" There are no divisions in heaven, and it is earth alone that causes any here below. For—

"THERE IS ONE BODY AND ONE SPIRIT, EVEN AS YE ARE CALLED IN ONE HOPE OF YOUR CALLING; ONE LORD, ONE FAITH, ONE BAPTISM, ONE GOD AND FATHER OF ALL, WHO IS ABOVE ALL, AND IN YOU ALL."

THERE IS ONE BODY.

What a beautiful image that is, in which all the members of the Church of Christ are compared to one body, of which their risen Lord is the Head! Christ the Head, and all the individual members of His Church, members:—"ONE BODY AND ONE SPIRIT." What a blessed privilege for a dying sinner, to look upon himself as a member of the body of Christ!—to recollect that Christ is his Head—that, whatever place he holds in the body, he is still a member of the body—however high or low he may be—however adorned with gifts and graces, or however feeling himself destitute of these—however he may be placed, on high in the eyes of man—or however low, so that the eye of man sees and regards him not;—still all—all that are looking to Jesus—that are resting on Jesus, are "ONE BODY." And there is "ONE SPIRIT," too. The same spirit that moves my hand or my finger, is the same spirit that animates my heart, and my head, and every member of my body. The same Spirit that rules on high, even the Spirit of the Lord Jesus Christ, is the Spirit that dwells in every member of His mystical body, wherever that member may be. The sole of my foot is as much a part of my body, as the crown of my head—and the life that animates one part, animates the other. So, the poorest, lowliest, humblest believer in the Church is as much a member of the body, wonderful to speak, even as the glorious Head Himself! So the Lord Jesus, in His prayer for His Church, in John, xvii., saith, "*Neither, pray I for these alone*," namely, the Disciples who were surrounding Him at the time, "*but for them also which shall believe on me through their word.*" Now, mark what He prays—"*that they all may be one; as thou, Father, art in me, and I in thee, that they also may be one in us: that the world may believe that thou hast sent me. And the glory which thou gavest me I have given them; that they may be one, even as we are one:*" John, xvii. 20, 21, 22. See how also the Apostle sets forth this truth to the Romans, "*For as we have many members in one body, and all members have not the same office; so we, being many, are one body in Christ, and every one members one of another.*" Rom. xii. 4, 5. The same truth is set forth to the Corinthians, "*As the body is one, and hath many members, and all the members of that one body, being many, are one body: so also is Christ.*" 1st Cor. xii. 12.

What a wonderful truth, my dear friends—that sinners, like us, should be privileged to think ourselves members of the body of Jesus! And ought one member of the body to injure another? Does not the Apostle say, "*Whether one member suffer, all the members suffer with it; or one member be honored, all the members rejoice with it.*" 1st Cor. xii. 26. Again, he saith, "*The eye cannot say unto the hand, I have no need of thee; nor again the head to the feet, I have no need of you.*" verse 21. Shall I, with my hand injure my head, or my feet, or any part of my body? Shall I not rather defend and preserve them? Surely, if one member of my body is in pain, will not all the members sympathize in suffering with it? Oh! if we but knew the value of the Gospel of Jesus, as we ought to know, so should it be with all the members of His mystical body. They would love one another—be united with one another, in heart; as they are, in fact, one in Christ. They would endeavor to defend, and protect, and sympa thize with, and help each other. As one member of the body will help, instinctively as it were, all the other members—so all the members of the Church of Christ (if they recollected, as they ought, that they are all one in Jesus) would feel for—love—help, and cherish one another. Oh! that we knew, and appreciated as we ought, the privilege of being united together in Christ; and then we would feel it our privilege, as well as our duty, to "ENDEAVOR TO KEEP THE UNITY OF THE SPIRIT IN THE BOND OF PEACE."

The Apostle proceeds, "THERE IS ONE BODY AND ONE SPIRIT, EVEN AS YE ARE CALLED IN ONE HOPE OF YOUR CALLING." The body must be one—the Spirit one—as the hope to which ye have been called by that Spirit is one. You have all the same hope—all, the same refuge. The blood of Christ is the common fountain for your sins; the righteousness of Jesus is the common robe for your nakedness; the power of Jesus is the common safeguard and dependence for your weakness; the faithfulness of Jesus your common security in your waywardness and wavering; and the glorious thought of meeting at the right hand of your Lord, is the same bright prospect for you all. Therefore, the "HOPE OF YOUR CALLING" is the same. You should all then remember this, and should have but one heart and one mind. The same Spirit that calls the whole body of Christ, should, in this one blessed hope, rule in the heart of that body, and animate every member from the crown of the head to the sole of the foot. So it would be, were it not for Satan and sin. We may say of all divisions in the Church, like the sowing of the tares in the field, "*an enemy has done this*," Mat. xiii. 28.

Then the Apostle proceeds from the members to the Head. He adds, "ONE LORD, ONE FAITH, ONE BAPTISM." There is but one Lord—one Head over all—one Saviour of all—one common Redeemer; ye are servants of the same Master—soldiers of the same Captain—children of the same Father—and heirs of the same glory.

So there is "ONE FAITH,"—one genuine agreement in believing the glorious Gospel, and all the great truths revealed in the Word of our God—one common salvation—one only object of common trust—one sole ground of dependence.

"ONE BAPTISM," all baptized into Jesus; as the Apostle saith, "*as many as have been baptized into Christ have put on Christ*," Gal. iii. 27, "*buried with him in baptism, wherein also ye are risen with him through the faith of the operation of God, who hath raised him from the dead.*" Col. ii. 12. Every consideration, all the truths of the Gospel—all consolations in time—all hopes for eternity—all the blessings derived from God to man here—all that can be expected and looked for hereafter—all conspire to this one end, to draw the members of the Church of Christ into one body, to "*strive together for the faith of the Gospel*," Phil. i. 27; to "*contend earnestly for the faith once delivered to the Saints*," Jude 3; to "*love one another with a pure heart fer-*

vently," 1 Pet. i. 22; "ENDEAVORING TO KEEP THE UNITY OF THE SPIRIT IN THE BOND OF PEACE."

For as there is "ONE LORD, ONE FAITH, ONE BAPTISM." So, there is, "ONE GOD AND FATHER OF ALL, WHO IS ABOVE ALL. AND THROUGH ALL, AND IN YOU ALL."

The Apostle brings forward the privileges and blessings which believers enjoy, as the ground for his exhortations. All the Apostolical exhortations are based on the same foundation—all made to rest on the position in which believers are placed, with respect to their God. They are not exhorted to these things, to make them believers, or give them privileges;—but because they are believers, and because they have privileges. There is "ONE GOD AND FATHER OF ALL." Are you not members of the same family—children of the same Father? If you saw your children quarrelling, and contending with each other, you would say, "Is it not a shame for you to disagree in this manner?—you are brothers and sisters—you are members of the same family—you have one father—one mother—you ought to live together in unity and in the bond of peace." And if any child was to allege to you any reason whatever for quarrelling with their brother or sister, you would say—"That is no reason for your quarrelling—nothing can be a reason for violating the great duty of love to each other." The same principle holds good in God's family:—if we be indeed children of the Lord, we are brethren and sisters; and, surely, we ought to say, as Joseph to his brethren, "*see that ye fall not out by the way.*" Gen. xlv. 24. We should recollect, that we are children of the same family—brethren and sisters—if we are indeed in Christ, if we are indeed looking unto Jesus. But it is in vain for persons to imagine that outward forms can ever prove a substitute for inward principle.—Forms and ordinances, however useful in their place, are miserable ties and bonds to unite a Church together. It is the great principle of faith and love that alone can really hold them in one—and it is that which the Apostle impresses on them.

"THERE IS ONE GOD AND FATHER OF ALL." Our blessed Lord, when He teaches you to pray, instructs you all to kneel down, and call God your Father; and surely, when you thus unite in this appellation, you ought to love as brethren.

But he sets before them the attributes and power of God, and the relation in which He stands to them, "WHO IS ABOVE ALL, AND THROUGH ALL, AND IN YOU ALL."

He "IS ABOVE ALL." Your Father's eye is upon you. Oh! my friends, how all divisions shall vanish, when the trump of God shall echo through the world! There shall then be no disputes among believers. Where then shall all the trifles be, which led men to differ from each other, and about which there were so many loud and fierce contentions—when they shall see the one Grand Object—the Lord coming in His glory? And if we remember, that though we see not God, the eye of God is over us—that we are as fully revealed in His sight, as we shall be when "*He com-*

eth in the clouds"—when "*every eye shall see Him.*"—If we thought of this, and gave to His omnipresence and to His coming in His kingdom, and glory, the weight these thoughts ought to have in our hearts,—there would be no such thing as divisions among those who love the Lord Jesus Christ. Now then, remember this—Your Father's eye is upon you. Children, when they are out of the sight of their parents, will quarrel and contend. But, if the eye of the parent is near, and that they catch that eye watching them, their quarrels are over—they are ashamed—they are silenced at once. So it would be, if Christians but felt, as they ought, that the eye of God is over them.

You recollect how ashamed the Disciples were, when our blessed Lord asked them, "*What was it that ye disputed among yourselves by the way? But they held their peace; for by the way they had disputed among themselves who should be the greatest.*" Mark ix. 33, 34. Then observe, the lesson He taught them—"*He sat down and called the twelve, and saith unto them, If any man desire to be first, the same shall be last of all, and servant of all. And He took a child and set him in the midst of them, and when he had taken him in his arms, he said unto them, whosoever shall receive one of such children in my name, receiveth me, and whosoever shall receive me receiveth not me, but him that sent me,*" Mark ix. 35, 36, 37. What "*lowliness and meekness,*" so humble as that of a little child? What exaltation so great, as to be taken into the arms of Jesus?

But, as if to furnish a practical comment on the necessary connexion, as in this passage, between lowliness and meekness, and the preservation of unity and love, we are told, in the very next words, "*John answered him, saying, Master, we saw one casting out devils in thy name, and we forbade him because he followeth not us,*" as much as to say, If we are not to set ourselves up individually, one above another, at least we may set ourselves up as a body above all others who do not join us. But what saith our Lord, "*Forbid him not, for there is no man which shall do a miracle in my name, that can lightly speak evil of me.*"

Surely, if ever a visible body on earth had a claim, to silence, and put down all who did not join with them, even Rome would admit that it was our Lord and His Apostles. Yet mark His answer to John, as well as the reproof to His Disciples, and see the lesson He inculcated; and let those learn meekness and Christian forbearance, who make an idol of uniformity; and let those learn humility, unity, and Christian love, who make so light of schisms and divisions.

If there is one lesson which our Lord more inculcates than another, it is humility and unity of spirit amongst His Disciples, He enforces it—He illustrates it—He prays for it on their behalf. "*By this shall all men know that ye are my disciples, if ye have love one to another.*" John xiii. 35. So the Apostle John, "*Be loved, let us love one another, for love is of God, and every one that loveth is born of God, and knoweth God,*" 1st John iv. 7.

Yea, he saith, "*We know that we have passed from death unto life, because we love the brethren, he that loveth not his brother abideth in death.*" 1st John iii. 14.

You see what the state of the early churches was, when they were united and walking in love. "*Then had the churches rest throughout all Judea, and Galilee, and Samaria, and were edified, and walking in the fear of the Lord, and in the comfort of the Holy Ghost, were multiplied.*" Acts ix. 31. Ah, my friends, there is the reason, when the churches "*had rest, and were edified,*" they walked in unity of faith and love, and they "*were multiplied,*" multitudes were gathered into them, because of their union in the Lord.

Look now at the state of Christendom! Look at the Gentile churches, see what an example they have set to the Jews and Pagans! What wonder, humanly speaking, that the Jews should reject, and should contend against Christianity, when all they have to do is to lift up their finger and point, saying, look at the Christians! Surely, too, the Pagan nations may say the same. Cruelties and crimes have tracked the path of those who bore the name of Christians for centuries among them.

Come a little nearer home—look at the poor Roman Catholics of Ireland! What wonder, that these poor creatures should remain bound together in the chains of darkness, ignorance, and superstition, and that they should oppose and object to reformation and Protestantism, when all they have to do, is to lift their finger and say, look at the Protestants, look at the men who profess to reform us! look at their faith, their walk! ungodliness, unbelief, wickedness, schisms, sects, contentions, contempt of God and all religion, mark the conduct of numbers. Alas! where is unity and faith and love to our Master? where is the walking together like those that love the Lord Jesus Christ, and who could aid, by their example, as well as by the fidelity of truth, to bring our poor fellow-sinners out of darkness to the truth of God? Oh, there would be little boasting, if we thought of ourselves as we ought to think, we should be humbled to the dust. And God is humbling us, yea, and will humble us more, I fear, if we do not humble ourselves, and bow down in deep repentance at the footstool of His throne.

The belief then of the relation which God bears to His people as the "FATHER OF US ALL."—The remembrance of His presence as a reconciled Father who is "ABOVE ALL" may well be urged by the Apostle as a powerful incentive to lowliness, meekness, love and unity. It is this sense of His presence impressed on the hearts of His children by the Spirit, that seems the true fulfilment of the promise; "*I will instruct thee and teach thee in the way wherein thou shalt go—I will guide thee with mine eye.*" Psalm xxxii. 8.

And this inward spiritual instruction is contradistinguished by the Spirit from that outward visitation of the lash which is necessary to scourge into a sense of duty, or to restrain from evil, for the Lord adds—"*Be ye not as the horse, or, as the mule: which have no understanding, whose mouth must be held in with bit and bridle, lest they come near unto thee.*" verse 9.

But the Apostle saith not only that He is "ABOVE ALL," but "THROUGH ALL AND IN YOU ALL."

Recollect he is writing, "*To the Saints that are at Ephesus, and to the faithful in Christ Jesus.*" chap. i. 1. It is only to such it can truly be said, He is "THROUGH ALL AND IN YOU ALL." For if a sinner is unconverted, it is not the Spirit of God, but the spirit of the Prince of the power of the air that is in him. He is walking "*according to the course of this world, according to the prince of the power of the air, the spirit that now worketh in the children of disobedience.*" Eph. ii. 2. That is the spirit that worketh in all unconverted men; so it cannot be said that the Spirit of God is through them, and in them.

Let us recollect, that when the Lord dwells in men, He walks in them—that is His promise. "*I will dwell in them, and walk in them.*" 2nd Cor. vi. 16. And let us not forget how peculiarly this is connected with the Spirit and walk inculcated here. "*Thus saith the high and lofty One that inhabiteth eternity, whose name is Holy; I dwell in the high and holy place, with him also that is of a contrite and humble spirit, to revive the spirit of the humble, and to revive the heart of the contrite ones.*" Isa. lvii. 15.

And now, my dear friends, these practical exhortations, as well as all the doctrines and promises, must have all their place in the Church, and in the heart of real Christians. Recollect, they are given by the same Spirit that gives us the testimony of the Gospel of Jesus. The God who proclaims to us the glorious pardon and salvation of our souls—who teaches us how we can approach Him, as a reconciled Father—teaches us also how we are to walk and serve Him. And, although we are never to put our works, or our walk, into the place of Christ—let us remember, also, we are not to put the Gospel of Jesus into the place of practical duties—or to suppose, that the neglect of the one, can be sanctioned by the profession of the other; so as to say, because we have grace, and faith, and hope, and joy—therefore, these things are not to be attended to by us. That were indeed an awful state for a sinner! On the contrary, it is because we are called with this vocation, that therefore we are to walk worthy of it, as the Apostle saith; or, as St. Peter expresses it, "*According as his divine power hath given unto us all things that pertain unto life and godliness, through the knowledge of him that hath called us to glory and virtue.*" 2nd Peter, i. 3. Recollect that, as our blessed Lord saith, "*As the branch cannot bear fruit of itself, except it abide in the vine; no more can ye, except ye abide in me.*" So He addeth, "*He that abideth in me, and I in him, the same bringeth forth much fruit; for without me ye can do nothing.*" John xv. 4, 5. And let us not forget that He saith, too, "*Ye shall know them by their fruits.*" Matt. vii. 16.

We have come, now, dear friends, to the close of another year! This is our last lecture for this year—where shall we be, at the close of the next? Who can tell, what a day—much less a year—may bring forth? In all human probability, some of those who are here to-day shall have passed from this scene, before another year shall close;—as some who were here at the beginning of this, have "gone to that bourne whence no traveller returns."

What a solemn thought it is to consider—Shall the privileges which we enjoy rise in judgment against us? Have we all been brought, through grace, to know Jesus as our refuge? Or, has another year flown off—another year's opportunities passed by—while yet the souls of any here have not "*peace with God through our Lord Jesus Christ*," Rom. v. 1, while any have not "*fled for refuge to lay hold upon the hope set before us.*" Heb. vi. 18. Alas! shall any have to say, "*the harvest is past, the summer is ended, and we are not saved!*" Jer. viii. 20. If we are not brought to look unto Jesus—every day God's long-suffering spares us, must rise in judgment against us. "*How shall we escape, if we neglect so great salvation.*" Heb. ii. 3.

But if, on the other hand, we are brought to look unto Jesus—years may fly on. Let them come—let them go,—the last year of our life shall be the best of all, for "*the day of death is better than the day of one's birth*"—Eccl. vii. 1, that is, if a man is a child of God. What a blessing is it then, if we are brought to Jesus! Oh! then, whatever time we are spared, let the prayer of our hearts be, that we may be enabled to love Him, whether He gives us years, or months, or weeks, or days, whatever our time may be, that it may be spent in the service of our God. Let us "*no longer live the rest of our time in the flesh to the lusts of men, but to the will of God.*" 1st Pet. iv. 2. Time and all its concerns are passing away; "*Seeing, then that all these things shall be dissolved, what manner of persons ought we to be in all holy conversation and godliness. Looking for and hasting unto the coming of the day of God.*" 2nd Peter iii. 11, 12.

May the Lord sanctify His word to us, and give us to meet in the fulness of joy on that blessed birth-day of everlasting love and glory, when Christ shall come "*to be glorified in His Saints, and to be admired in all them that believe in that day.*" 2 Thess. i. 10. "*Now unto him who is able to keep you from falling, and to present you faultless before the presence of his glory with exceeding joy. To the only wise God our Saviour, be glory and majesty, dominion, and power, both now and forever. Amen.*" Jude 24, 25.

THIRTIETH LECTURE.

EPHESIANS IV.—7, 12.

"But unto every one of us is given grace according to the measure of the gift of Christ. Wherefore he saith, when he ascended up on high, he led captivity captive, and gave gifts unto men. (Now that he ascended, what is it but that he also descended first into the lower parts of the earth? He that descended is the same also that ascended up far above all heavens, that he might fill all things.) And he gave some, apostles; and some, prophets; and some evangelists; and some, pastors and teachers: for the perfecting of the saints, for the work of the ministry, for the edifying of the body of Christ."

WE considered in our last Lecture the exhortations to unity in the commencement of this chapter:—exhortations founded on the great fact, that those who are believers, are one body in Christ, all united in Jesus as their living head, and all in Christ Jesus united to each other; and that, therefore, keeping continually in remembrance the great fact of their union by faith to their Lord, and in Him to each other, they should regulate their conduct to each other accordingly;—abhor divisions and dissensions—"*Endeavoring to keep the unity of the Spirit,*" as united in one body "*in the bond of peace.*"

But the inequality of circumstances, the diversities of gifts, the differences of the operations of grace in the church of Christ, are very likely from that very cause, to produce discord and disunion. One is apt to be jealous of another—One is anxious to occupy the place of another—Some desire to be teachers—Some aspire to places that God has not been pleased to give them in the church; hence, envyings, jealousies, strifes and contentions creep in—and Satan availing himself of the corruption of the human heart, sows the seeds of discord and division in the church which have produced, and do produce such lamentable fruits of bitterness. The Apostle had said, 4, 5, 6 verse, "*There is one body and one Spirit, even as ye are called in one hope of your calling, one Lord, one faith, one baptism, one God and Father of all, who is above all, and through all, and in you all.*" "BUT," he adds, (as much as to say, recollect,) "UNTO EVERY ONE OF US IS GIVEN GRACE, ACCORDING TO THE MEASURE OF THE GIFT OF CHRIST;" all are not alike, all have not the same gifts or the same graces. He reminds them here, that all they possess of grace, is a gift—and that every gift, is of grace. And he reminds them, that in these gifts there are differences, according as it pleaseth the Gracious Giver. "WHEREFORE HE SAITH, WHEN HE ASCENDED UP

ON HIGH, HE LED CAPTIVITY CAPTIVE, AND GAVE GIFTS UNTO MEN." Having stated, that there were different gifts, and that these gifts come from Christ, he quotes a passage from the Prophet in the Book of Psalms, in which he saith, that Jesus was exalted on high and had received gifts for men—intimating hereby the fact, that all the gifts that are given and received by men, are purchased by the blood of our crucified, risen, and ascended Lord—and are all the gifts of His grace, as "*The head over all things to his church.*" You find the quotation in the 68th Psalm, "*Thou hast ascended on high, thou hast led captivity captive, thou hast received gifts for men; yea for the rebellious also, that the Lord God might dwell among them. Blessed be the Lord who daily loadeth us with benefits, even the God of our salvation.*" Ps. lxviii. 18, 19. This passage then, the Apostle quotes here to show, that Jesus, when He ascended on high, after His resurrection, having "LED CAPTIVITY CAPTIVE," gave these different gifts unto the church.

We must pause a little on this verse, "WHEN HE ASCENDED UP ON HIGH, HE LED CAPTIVITY CAPTIVE, AND GAVE GIFTS UNTO MEN." Here the Apostle alludes to the glorious conquest of our blessed Master over the powers of darkness, who are here called "CAPTIVITY." They held, and hold the ungodly world captive. Satan, with his mighty power, holds mankind by nature captive. All were in a state of captivity, and all by nature are in a state of captivity and bondage. The unconverted feel not this; they talk of their freedom, they pride themselves on their liberty, not knowing that they are indeed bond-slaves to Satan—that "*whosoever committeth sin is the servant of sin.*" John viii. 34. The converted feel this, every believer feels the power of the captivity of Satan, and therefore the Apostle Paul, speaking of himself, as we have so fully entered into, and dwelt upon in the 7th of Romans, says, "*I see another law in my members warring against the law of my mind, and bringing me into captivity to the law of sin which is in my members,*" Rom. vii. 23. I find the power of sin and Satan so distressing that I call it a law, "*I delight in the law of God after the inward man,*" but I find another law, another power, dragging me "*into captivity to the law of sin which is in my members, so that when I would do good, evil is present with me,*" Rom. vii. 21, 22, 23; "*to will is present with me; but how to perform that which is good, I find not.*" v. 18.

To explain this from my own experience, I would say—When I would give up my thoughts to God, I feel sin and Satan hurrying my imagination into evil. When I would remember all the Lord's past mercies to me, I find sin and Satan diverting my memory into past scenes of wickedness and folly. When I would kneel down in prayer, and pour out my heart to God, I find sin and Satan filling my heart with a thousand vanities and distractions. When I would open my Bible, and study the word of my God—I feel sin and Satan diverting my attention from it, by a thousand artifices. When I would have my will brought into subjection to my Master, and when I would kneel down and say to Him, "*Thy will be done*"—I find sin and Satan exciting my will into rebellion against my God, and urging my thoughts to murmur against my Master's ordinances. When I would have my affections given to my God and desire to love Him with all my heart—I find sin and Satan drawing my affections to some earthly idol. Therefore, I can truly say, "*I find then a law that when I would do good evil is present with me,*" I feel "*a law in my members, warring against the law of my mind, and bringing me into captivity to the law of sin which is in my members.*" Rom. vii. 21—23.

But "WHEN JESUS ASCENDED UP ON HIGH, HE LED CAPTIVITY CAPTIVE," or as the Apostle says in Colossians, speaking of the work of the Lord Jesus, "*Having spoiled principalities and powers, he made a show of them openly, triumphing over them in it.*" Col. ii. 15. So the Apostle John says, "*For this purpose the Son of God was manifested, that he might destroy the works of the devil.*" 1st John iii. 8. And so, the Apostle Paul says, writing to the Hebrews, "*Forasmuch then as the children are partakers of flesh and blood, he also himself likewise took part of the same, that through death, he might destroy him that hath the power of death, that is the devil, and deliver them, who through fear of death were all their life-time subject to bondage;*" Heb. ii. 14, 15; therefore, when the Lord Jesus Christ "ASCENDED UP ON HIGH, HE LED CAPTIVITY CAPTIVE."

This is an image taken from the processions of the ancient triumphs, in which the conqueror used to bind the kings or distinguished warriors whom he had conquered and taken captive, and lead them as the trophies of his victory, bound at the wheels of his chariot, in the array of his triumphal procession. This appears to be the very same image which David uses in that psalm from which the Apostle makes the quotation, for in reading it with the preceding verse, it is thus, "*The chariots of God are twenty thousand, even thousands of angels, the Lord is among them, as in Sinai, in the holy place. Thou hast ascended on high, thou hast led captivity captive; thou hast received gifts for men, yea for the rebellious also, that the Lord God might dwell among them,*" Ps. lxviii. 17—19. As much as to say—He that "*layeth the beams of his chambers in the waters, and maketh the clouds his chariot, and walketh upon the wings of the wind,*" Ps. civ. 3—He when He ascended up on high, destroyed the works of the devil—led captive at his chariot wheels, amidst the attendant hosts of heaven, the fiend who had held His people in bondage—and only waits the approach of the appointed time, to trample him under His feet, and under the feet of His Church, and to cast him into the abyss, forever and ever.

Remember, therefore, believer, that though you feel this law in your members, and though you feel the power of your enemy, remember, that he is virtually conquered, and that you are delivered from his captivity forever. You feel yet in your body the bondage of sin and death, but your soul is forever emancipated from his chains, you are delivered from his thraldom, and as surely as your risen Head is ascended to glory, so surely you are "*raised up together, and made to sit together in heavenly places in Christ*," chap. ii. 6. And therefore, you see, how when Satan is spoken of in the book of Revelation, as "*the accuser of the brethren, which accused them before our God day and night*," you see, how the church is declared to have gained the victory, "*they overcame him by the blood of the Lamb, and by the word of their testimony*," Rev. xii. 10, 11.

We shall see more at large, if we are spared to reach the 6th chapter of this Epistle, how—when the Apostle is commanding them to "*Put on the whole armor of God, that they may be able to stand against the wiles of the devil*," he says, "*above all, taking the shield of faith, wherewith ye shall be able to quench all the fiery darts of the wicked*," chap. vi. 12, 16. That is to say, "Remember, O ye Saints at Ephesus, your Blessed Master—your glorious Redeemer—your crucified Lord—your risen Head—your ascended High Priest—remember that He has conquered your foe—He has "LED CAPTIVITY CAPTIVE;" and though you feel the attacks and malice of your enemy, remember "*The God of peace shall bruise Satan under your feet shortly*," Rom. xvi. 20; and that He has delivered you out of his hands, for ever and ever.

Let me entreat you to consider, especially in the passage which I have quoted from Romans vii., the practical and experimental use of this doctrine. Consider how it was used by the Apostle Paul. In that passage in which he is groaning under the power of this captivity, he is not cast down; he says, "*I see another law in my members, warring against the law of my mind, and bringing me into captivity to the law of sin which is in my members*," then he utters his complaint of sorrow, "*O wretched man that I am, who shall deliver me from the body of this death;*" Rom. vii. 23, 24; observe then, I say, the experimental use he makes of this doctrine, he "*takes the shield of faith*," "*to quench the fiery darts of the wicked*." For when groaning he asks, "*Who shall deliver me from the body of this death?*" he answers by faith, "*I thank God through Jesus Christ our Lord*." Rom. vii. 25. And consoles himself with the joyful assurance, "*There is therefore, now, no condemnation to them which are in Christ Jesus*." Rom. viii. 1.

Mark here the glorious triumph of faith, looking up in the very midst of the conflict to Christ—gaining the victory over the law in the members, and delivering him from the captivity and bondage he felt even at the moment, when he was groaning beneath its yoke Surely, "*This is the victory that overcometh the world, even our faith. Who is he that overcometh the world, but he that believeth that Jesus is the Son of God*." 1st John v. 4.

The Apostle then having stated that there is a difference of grace, "ACCORDING TO THE MEASURE OF THE GIFT OF CHRIST,' reminds them thus that all their graces and all their gifts come from the Lord Jesus. We have nothing of our own; no sinner can ever have anything good in himself, "*Every good gift and every perfect gift is from above, and cometh down from the Father of lights.*" James i. 17. Having quoted this text from the Psalms, then in the parenthesis of 9th and 10th verses, he calls to their recollection the person and work of Jesus. The Apostles continually delight to dwell on Jesus; in all their practical exhortations, bringing the soul back to Him. They keep Christ continually in view; they show in their doctrine what the Apostle Paul testified and exemplified in his own experience, "*The life that I now live in the flesh, I live by the faith of the Son of God, who loved me, and gave himself for me;*" Gal. ii. 28.

Therefore he saith, as it were to keep the Lord before them, "NOW THAT HE ASCENDED, WHAT IS IT BUT THAT HE ALSO DESCENDED FIRST INTO THE LOWER PARTS OF THE EARTH, HE THAT DESCENDED IS THE SAME ALSO THAT ASCENDED, FAR ABOVE ALL HEAVENS, THAT HE MIGHT FILL ALL THINGS."

As much as to say,—remember that this same person who ascended is the King of glory. Remember who Christ is. Do not forget, "HE THAT DESCENDED IS THE SAME ALSO THAT ASCENDED," that he is not a mere man, born on this earth, and ascending from this earth. True, he is indeed man, perfect "*man of the substance of his mother, born in the world;*" but remember, He is the God of Glory that hath descended into that flesh on earth. Remember that this is the great "*mystery of godliness, that God was manifest in the flesh,*" 1st Tim. iii. 16; remember, "HE THAT DESCENDED IS THE SAME ALSO THAT ASCENDED, FAR ABOVE ALL HEAVENS THAT HE MIGHT FILL ALL THINGS."

So our Lord also himself saith in St. John's Gospel iii. 13, "*No man hath ascended up to heaven, but he that came down from heaven, even the Son of man who is in heaven;*" and so again, in chapter vi. 33, our blessed Lord uses the same expression of Himself, "*The bread of God is he that cometh down from heaven, and giveth life unto the world;*" and so He says in the 62nd verse, "*What, and if ye shall see the Son of man ascend up where he was before?*" and so, in His blessed prayer, in xvii. 5, "*And now, O Father, glorify thou me with thine own self, with the glory that I had with thee, before the world was.*" Arians and Socinians could not be allowed to be Christians by St. Paul He reminds them, that He who gave them these gifts was the eternal God; and as Moses saith in the blessing of Israel, "*The eternal God is thy refuge, and underneath are the everlasting arms,*" Deut. xxxiii. 27; so, when they think of Jesus, they should remember, that He who gave them these gifts is the eternal God, the Lord of Glory; who has "ASCENDED FAR ABOVE ALL HEAVENS THAT HE MIGHT FILL ALL THINGS"—all Time—all Space—Eternity. When and where was He not? When and where is He not? When and where shall He not be? Alas! how miserable is Infidelity!!!

The Apostle then speaks of these gifts, which the Lord had given to the Church, "HE GAVE SOME APOSTLES AND SOME PROPHETS, AND SOME EVANGELISTS, AND SOME PASTORS AND TEACHERS, FOR THE PERFECTING OF THE SAINTS, FOR THE WORK OF THE MINISTRY, FOR THE EDIFYING OF THE BODY OF CHRIST, TILL WE ALL COME IN THE UNITY OF FAITH, AND OF THE KNOWLEDGE OF THE SON OF GOD, UNTO A PERFECT MAN, UNTO THE MEASURE OF THE STATURE OF THE FULNESS OF CHRIST." Now we may observe, that there are some gifts which are common to all the Church of Christ. Every individual member of the Church of Christ has and must have the gift of the Holy Ghost, or he could not be a child of God.—The Holy Spirit must be given to every individual believer to teach him his state as a sinner.—The Holy Spirit must be given to every individual believer—to take of the things of Christ and show them to his soul—that is His office; for "*no man can say that Jesus is the Lord, but by the Holy Ghost.*" 1st Cor. xii. 3. "*The natural man receiveth not the things of the Spirit of God: for they are foolishness unto him, neither can he know them, because they are spiritually discerned.*" 1st Cor. ii. 14. No power of the natural understanding of man, however exalted, however enlightened—cultivated—endowed with all the gifts of literature and science, can arrive at the simple knowledge of the Gospel of Christ Jesus. Man must have the gift of the Spirit of God, to "*know the things that are freely given to him of God,*" 1st Cor. ii. 12. Therefore, I say, all believers must have the gift of the Spirit of God. They mnst be born of the Spirit—as they have the gift of eternal life; for "*Whosoever believeth that Jesus is the Christ is born of God;*" 1st John v. 1, "*the gift of God is eternal life, through Jesus Christ our Lord,*" Rom. vi. 23; "*And he that hath the Son hath life.*" 1st John v. 12; therefore, these gifts are common to all the children of God. They are sanctified in Christ Jesus by the Holy Spirit.

But as we have in 1st Cor. xii. "*There are diversities of gifts, but the same Spirit. And there are differences of administrations, but the same Lord. And there are diversities of operations, but it is the same God that worketh all in all. But the manifestation of the Spirit is given to every man to profit withal; for to one is given by the Spirit the word of wisdom:*" one believer has a peculiar degree of wisdom given to him whereby he is more gifted to advise and guide his brethren. "*To another the word of knowledge by the same Spirit.*" 1st Cor. xii. 8. Some have a much greater degree of spiritual knowledge than others: "*to another faith, by the same Spirit;*" the faith of different believers is given in very different proportions; some have strong faith by which they can encounter any difficulty, any danger, or any conflict—others again are among the weaklings of the flock, whose faith is very weak, and who require continually to be strengthened, helped, cheered on by their stronger brethren. The Great Shepherd watches over them, however, with care, "*He gathereth the lambs in his arms and carrieth them in his bosom, and gently leadeth those that are with young."* Is. xl. 11.

Then the Apostle speaks of the outward gifts that were given in Apostolic days; "*To another the gifts of healing by the same Spirit; to another the working of miracles; to another prophecy; to another discerning of spirits; to another divers kinds of tongues; to another the interpretation of tongues. But all these worketh that one, and the self-same Spirit, dividing to every man severally as he will, for as the body is one, and hath many members, and all the members of that one body, being many, are one body, so also, is Christ.*" 1st Cor. xii. 7—12. Now observe the very same figure in that chapter of Corinthians, which he uses in this, of Ephesians, under our consideration; he proceeds, v. 13, "*For by one Spirit we are all baptized into one body, whether we be Jews or Gentiles, whether we be bond or free, and have been all made to drink into one Spirit. For the body is not one member but many. If the foot shall say, because I am not the hand, I am not of the body; is it therefore not of the body? And if the ear shall say, because I am not the eye, I am not of the body; is it therefore not of the body? If the whole body were an eye, where were the hearing? if the whole were hearing, where were the smelling? But now God hath set the members, every one of them as it hath pleased him; and if they were all members, where were the body? But now are they many members, yet but one body. And the eye cannot say unto the hand, I have no need of thee; nor again the head to the feet, I have no need of you, nay much more, these members of the body which seem to be more feeble are necessary; and those members of the body which we think to be less honorable, upon them we bestow more abundant honor, and our uncomely parts have more abundant comeliness. For our comely parts have no need; but God hath tempered the body together, having given more abundant honor to that part which lacked; that there should be no schism in the body; but that the members should have the same care one for another. And whether one member suffer, all the members suffer with it, or one member be honored, all the members rejoice with it. Now, ye are the body of Christ and mem bers in particular.*" 1st Cor. xii. 13—27.

I read this passage at length, because it is more clear, full and perspicuous than anything I could say to illustrate the great truths it contains.

Read it over—study and consider it; and remember, that in this passage the Holy Spirit is showing under the beautiful simili tude of a human frame, the different gifts that the Lord has been pleased to bestow on different individuals, members of His Church, and the different places in which He has been pleased to fix them, and the perfect unity and harmony that ought to subsist among them. And therefore, your duty and my duty is, not to try and get out of our place in the body, not to try to seek for some higher distinction, or some higher honor, or higher office or place in the

Church, or in the world, than we have, but to remember, that God has been pleased to place us in our present position, and that all we have to do is this, to know our own place, in whatever sphere God has appointed us, and to endeavor to discharge our duty, humbly, faithfully, and devotedly in that station in which we are placed by our heavenly Father. Our duty is to know simply what is our place? where has God fixed us? and to say, "Wherever His Providence has fixed me, that is my position, and there let me serve and honor my Heavenly Master." And if the different individuals of the Church did this, instead of "*all seeking their own, not the things which are Jesus Christ's*," Phil. ii. 21; seeking to divide and split from one another. One desiring one object, and one another—some finding fault with one real or imaginary evil, and some with another—one contending for this observance, and another against it—they would all in their own places, humbly walk together, and try to serve and glorify their God, in the position in which He has been pleased to place them.

Recollect, that the humblest individual in the Church of Christ has as great an opportunity of glorifying his Heavenly Master in that place, as the highest. The humblest servant—the humblest operative can glorify the Lord, as much as the Sovereign on the throne. It is not by mighty acts, in exalted situations, that God alone may be glorified—but by humble duty, in every station, whatever that station be, done for the service, the honor, and the glory of God.

No doubt, if we had been standing in the temple when Christ was there, and had seen a great number of individuals, "*casting their gifts into the treasury*;" and if we had been asked—"Who do you think, of all these persons that you see casting their gifts into the treasury, is most serving and glorifying God?" Perhaps we should have looked among the rich and the great men who were casting in their gifts, and whom we saw approach with the largest offerings to God, bearing a sober and sanctified demeanor, and presenting their gifts with the most seeming devotion. I suppose, we should have said, "This or that man appears to be most especially glorifying God—look at his manner—see, he is offering a vast gift."

But whom did our Lord point out as serving Him most? Who is that person, whose character he has recorded in His eternal Word, as the individual who glorified Him most among them all? A poor creature, whom perhaps we should never have looked at, or even thought of for a moment,—"*a certain poor widow, and she threw in two mites, which make a farthing*." Mark, xii. 42. Now, remember this; and remember whatever your condition in life may be,—if God has been pleased to give to you the precious gift of salvation in Christ, if He has given you to know Him as your hope and refuge,—remember, I say, whatever your situation in life may be, if the Lord has given you that unspeakable gift, your calling is not to get out of your place, but to serve the Lord and glorify Him in your place. He has placed you, perhaps, an humble member of the body, perhaps a weak member of the body; but you are as much a member of the body, as the highest—you are one with Christ.

Oh, poor believer, if there be any such here; poor—destitute—tried—afflicted believer! remember the Lord has put you into a place, in which, perhaps, the very difficulties—the very trials that afflict you, may be in His eye, the very means by which you can honor and serve Him most. If the Lord had given that poor woman a large fortune, He would not have given her so much to honor Him with, as when He was pleased to give her but two mites as her all, but gave her too a heart to cast that all into the treasury. Consider this. And what a blessing it is to think, that the poorest and humblest of His flock is not overlooked by that God who is "no respecter of persons." He hath "*chosen the poor of this world rich in faith, and heirs of the kingdom.*" James ii. 5. If indeed Christ is the Refuge of your soul, His heart—His hand is over you—He will "*never leave you nor forsake you.*" Oh, think of that;—and whatever be the different gifts which God has been pleased to bestow on us or to withhold from us—it is of the utmost moment to us, to remember that it is the Lord who giveth, and the Lord who taketh away, or withholdeth—that whatever be our circumstances or position, it is not more our duty than our happiness to remember, that we are just where the Lord has seen fit to place us—that there we are called to serve and glorify our Heavenly Master. In the simple, but expressive and comprehensive words of our Catechism, "To do our duty in that state of life unto which it shall please God to call us."

You observe, this subject is more enlarged on, in 1st Cor. xii., than it is here. But I have called your attention to that chapter, in order that, in considering this portion of Ephesians, you may refer to it, and dwell upon the enlarged statement of the subject that is given in that passage; and look to all the references, in the various parts of the Word of God, in which these great truths are brought before us. That is the profitable way to study Scripture, "*not in words which man's wisdom teacheth, but which the Holy Ghost teacheth, comparing spiritual things with spiritual.*" 1st Cor. ii. 13.

Here the Apostle speaks, not merely of spiritual gifts as bestowed on the individuals themselves, but as bestowed on them for the edification of the Church; and he speaks of the individuals on whom they were bestowed as being themselves gifts to the Church This is the conclusion of the passage which I have quoted from Corinthians, for the Apostle proceeds there, "*And God hath set some in the church, first, apostles; secondarily, prophets; thirdly, teachers; after that miracles, then gifts of healings, helps, governments, diversities of tongues. Are all apostles? are all prophets? are all teachers? are all workers of miracles?*" 1st Cor. xii. 28, 29. So here the Apostle, omitting the gifts to the individuals, by which they were respectively qualified for their offices, speaks of them, as being themselves the gifts of Chr st to His Church.

"He gave some apostles;" that is, men specially called—and directly inspired—and sent by God Himself. Those who were thus sent were called Apostles;—all other teachers in the Church were appointed and sent forth by these Apostles. The Apostle's office, deriving its immediate authority and mission from God, was, of course, the highest office of teacher in the Church. With them He promised to continue—"*Lo, I am with you always; even unto the end of the world.*" Mat. xxviii. 20. And those Apostles, and their instructions, we have to this day.

He gave "some prophets;" this is used in the New Testament rather as referring to teaching or preaching than to foretelling; the gift of prophecy is rather a gift of preaching and edifying the flock, than of predicting; therefore, I rather think it means here, those who were gifted to teach and to preach in the Church. So saith the Apostle, "*Ye may all prophesy one by one that all may learn and that all may be comforted.*" 1st Cor. xiv. 31.

"And some evangelists;" those whose office it was to go forth and preach the Gospel. It seems from this name being applied to Philip, Acts, xxi. 8, and from what we read of Philip, Acts, viii.; and from the command to Timothy, to "*do the work of an evangelist,*" 2nd Tim. iv. 5; in which places alone this word occurs; that this office was that of a missionary, itinerating to preach the Gospel, as the Apostles did themselves; an office necessary at all times in the Church, and too lamentably neglected in our own.

"And some pastors and teachers;" the exact difference between those gifts, we may, perhaps, not be able, adequately or fully to determine. But "pastors" seem to be those, whose especial gift it was to visit and to feed the flock. "*Feed my lambs. Feed my sheep,*" saith the Lord Jesus. John xx. 15, 16, 17. Some are peculiarly gifted to converse—to take the Scriptures and read them—to open out their meaning, and to strengthen and nourish the flock.

"Teachers" are those again, perhaps, whose office it was to instruct children in the church, and to expound the Word of God to them and others, who required especial instruction. Whether these were exactly distinct offices in the Church, or persons specially gifted to discharge these varied functions, they were all given as gifts to the Church; for the purposes, which the Apostle proceeds afterwards to explain.

There are many persons at this day, who think that there are men who have different gifts of this kind, and who should be accordingly appointed to those several offices; and that we ought to discern them; that they ought to be sent out in the Church, as evangelists, prophets, pastors and teachers. But that appears to be a very erroneous opinion. It is very true, that God has been pleased to bestow different gifts on His servants. He has made some men powerful in one way, and some in another—some powerful in preaching—some more competent to act as pastors in feeding the flock, going among them—visiting—instructing them—

strengthening and building them up in Christ. But we are not competent to form a true estimate or judgment of these persons or their respective gifts, as the Apostles did. All the different means of spiritual instruction, all the varied writings of these inspired Apostles, are now collected together for us, as the written Word of God, and are given to us as the Word of inspiration, by the Apostles themselves; so that these gifts which were at that time the direct and immediate qualifications given by the Spirit of God—given by inspiration or by intuition—without the written collected Word—are now to be attained by men in the study of that Word, and to be used by them from thence in edifying and instructing others. And we might as well expect, I think, that miraculous gifts of tongues were to supersede the use of learning—or an immediate inspiration of the Holy Ghost to prevent the necessity of taking thought what we should say—as, suppose that these distinctive gifts were now discernible in every character, in such a mode, as to determine the place appointed for them by God in the Church.

Every minister ought to be a prophet—that is, a preacher—an evangelist—a pastor—a teacher. Every minister ought to be a well-instructed scribe—"*to bring out of his treasure things new and old*"—Mat. xii. 52, to draw forth out of the Word of God, the treasure of instruction which he may be called upon to administer, in the different parts of his vocation, to the flock of Christ—to expound—to instruct—to teach—to admonish—to "*reprove—rebuke—exhort*"—to comfort—to encourage—to preach the Word, as it may be needful in the calling of his sacred office to do.

However great or varied the gifts of men may be—it is not great intellectual gifts—not great powers of eloquence, that really constitute a faithful and efficient minister! It is drawing out of the treasury of the Word of God—bringing forth the holy truth that is written there, as a means of instructing—feeding—refreshing—nourishing—strengthening, and directing the soul.

I have, for my own part, gone away from listening to some, considered most eloquent men in the Church—and from hearing very eloquent sermons—and I have thought, that the person was a very powerful and highly gifted man; and that his discourse was a fine oratorical display;—still my heart has derived no refreshment from it. And I have gone away from hearing a man, with not the least pretensions to what the world might call eloquence;—while my soul has been refreshed, and fed with the Word of Life—my heart instructed, and comforted by the precious truths of the glorious Gospel. As far as my own experience goes—and I have been now for many years, a hearer, more than a teacher—I could say, I have derived from the exposition of the Word of God, by men who were not highly gifted with eloquence, at least as much, if not more profit, than from those who were. When eloquence is devoted to simplify and to impress pure Scriptural truth—I know how important and valuable it is. But there is a very great danger, both to preachers and hearers, lest the gratification of the taste, or the intellect might supersede the edification of the soul—lest men should be led away by the "*wisdom of words*," more than edified by the simplicity of the Gospel. This is what the Apostle says to the Corinthians, "*I, brethren, when I came to you, came not with excellency of speech, or of wisdom, declaring unto you the testimony of God: For I determined not to know anything among you, save Jesus Christ, and him crucified.*" 1st Cor. ii. 1, 2. And again, "*Christ sent me not to baptize, but to preach th gospel; not with wisdom of words, lest the cross of Christ should be made of none effect.*" 1st Cor. i. 17. Our feelings may be excited sometimes, by glowing appeals, that may address our fancy or our imagination—but depend upon it, the only solid food for the soul, is that which comes by the Holy Spirit of God, bringing the truth as it is in Jesus, home, through the understanding, to our hearts and consciences.

Therefore, whatever may be the importance of the gifts, considered in themselves, they derive all their real utility, and all their blessing, from this—that they are sanctified by the Holy Spirit of God, to the service of the Lord of Glory. And if the gift of eloquence may not be very great in a minister, let us remember, that the gift of eternal life is very great;—and that the simplest testimony and proclamation of that great salvation, is the richest eloquence that can reach the ears of a dying sinner. Let us remember, the power of Christ is very great; and let us remember, that it is by the simplicity of truth the heart is instructed, and the soul saved—not by the wisdom of words. As saith the Apostle, "*After that, in the wisdom of God, the world by wisdom knew not God, it pleased God by the foolishness of preaching to save them that believe.*" 1st Cor. i. 21.

It is very important for us to consider this. There really seems a great evil in the Church of Christ on this very subject. You go into what is called religious company—you hear what is called religious conversation. Persons think, that if they speak of religious men and of religious things—of this preacher and that society—this sermon and that religious meeting—they are conversing on religion. There is a vast deal of talk about these things, but very little indeed about Christ—very little about the precious Word of eternal life—little of "*considering one another to provoke unto love and to good works: . . . . exhorting one another: and so much the more, as we see the day approaching.*" Heb. x. 24.

Talking of religious things and of preachers, is not religion. Sometimes it merely ends in "*One saith I am of Paul, and I of Apollos, and I of Cephas, and I of Christ.*" 1st Cor. i. 12. It often degenerates into a mere contemptible sort of gossip, religious gossip instead of worldly gossip. Ah, my friends, Christ in the heart, ought to bring forth Christ in the closet—Christ in the drawing-room—Christ in private, and Christ in public. Is not this the meaning of the Apostle when he saith, "*Let the word of Christ dwell in you richly, in all wisdom, teaching and admon-*

ishing one another; in psalms and hymns and spiritual songs, singing with grace in your heart to the Lord; and whatsoever ye do in word or deed, do all in the name of the Lord Jesus, giving thanks to God and the Father by him." Col. iii. 16, 17.

We have not now time to enter upon the consideration of these various offices, of which the Apostle speaks as gifts to the Church, in reference to the edification of the body of Christ. If the Lord spares us, we shall on the next day consider from the 12th verse, and see what the end and use of these different instructors was to be. May the Lord sanctify His Word to us, and bring it with "*demonstration of the Spirit and power*" to our souls.

It is a great comfort, my dear friends, in opening the Bible and reading, or hearing it read or expounded to think that all the blessing comes from God: that although we should endeavor to speak the Word in simplicity and faithfulness according to the truth, still that it is not a person's language, or their manner, or any power they could possess to communicate instruction, that can really convey any truth to a sinner's soul. It is a great comfort to think, that it is all the power of God:—That the power of the Holy Spirit alone can bless His Word to our understandings, consciences, or hearts. However weak or feeble we may be—how imperfect soever our instruction—(and, alas, how imperfect and inadequate to the mighty subject are our best instructions! how very poor and meagre are our best expositions of God's Word!) still let them be ever so inadequate, and ever so weak;—the hope—the comfort of the minister for his own soul and the souls of others, is the thought, that all the blessing comes from God—that his is the power, that His is the glory. And therefore, he may hope, if he addresses a people, who are looking up in prayer and supplication for God's blessing—that however humble his instructions, God's blessing will attend them—the people will be edified and instructed—souls will be fed with the Bread of life—they will be enabled to know more of themselves—more of Christ—their affections will be drawn out to their Lord and Master, and so, they will be established in the faith of Jesus—their life will be influenced by the power of faith and love, and this because it is not man's work but God's. Oh, let us pray, that the work in our hearts may be God's work, and then He will "*perfect that which concerneth us: and not forsake the work of his own hands.*" Ps. cxxxviii. 8.

He will keep us in trials, difficulties, dangers—in life and in death; so that, "*Whether we live, we live unto the Lord, and whether we die, we die unto the Lord, whether we live, therefore, or die, we are the Lord's.*" Rom. xiv. 8.

THIRTY-FIRST LECTURE.

EPHESIANS IV.—12, 13, 14, 15, 16.

"For the perfecting of the saints, for the work of the ministry, for the edifying of the body of Christ: Till we all come in the unity of the faith, and of the knowledge of the Son of God, unto a perfect man, unto the measure of the stature of the fulness of Christ: That we henceforth be no more children, tossed to and fro, and carried about with every wind of doctrine, by the sleight of men, and cunning craftiness, whereby they lie in wait to deceive; But speaking the truth in love, may grow up into him in all things, which is the head, even Christ: From whom the whole body fitly joined together and compacted by that which every joint supplieth, according to the effectual working in the measure of every part, maketh increase of the body unto the edifying of itself in love."

WE come now to consider the object, which the Spirit tells us by the Apostle here, the Lord had in giving to His Church these "*Apostles, Prophets, Evangelists, Pastors, Teachers.*" And we see, in the 12th verse, what that object was, "FOR THE PERFECTING OF THE SAINTS, FOR THE WORK OF THE MINISTRY, FOR THE EDIFYING OF THE BODY OF CHRIST: TILL WE ALL COME IN THE UNITY OF THE FAITH, AND OF THE KNOWLEDGE OF THE SON OF GOD, UNTO A PERFECT MAN, UNTO THE MEASURE OF THE STATURE OF THE FULNESS OF CHRIST: THAT WE HENCEFORTH BE NO MORE CHILDREN, TOSSED TO AND FRO, AND CARRIED ABOUT WITH EVERY WIND OF DOCTRINE, BY THE SLEIGHT OF MEN, AND CUNNING CRAFTINESS, WHEREBY THEY LIE IN WAIT TO DECEIVE; BUT SPEAKING THE TRUTH IN LOVE, MAY GROW UP INTO HIM IN ALL THINGS, WHICH IS THE HEAD, EVEN CHRIST: FROM WHOM THE WHOLE BODY FITLY JOINED TOGETHER AND COMPACTED BY THAT WHICH EVERY JOINT SUPPLIETH, ACCORDING TO THE EFFECTUAL WORKING IN THE MEASURE OF EVERY PART, MAKETH INCREASE OF THE BODY, UNTO THE EDIFYING OF ITSELF IN LOVE." Here we have the inspired description of the Church of Christ, and how it ought to be instructed and built up by those ministers whom God gives to it as gifts. This passage might be applied or interpreted in a two-fold sense:—

FIRST.—It might be considered in an enlarged prophetic sense. Namely that the Lord has given these different ministers as gifts to the church—who should continue to gather in—to complete—or perfect the number of His elect, and build up the stones of His Spiritual Temple, until all are brought in, and until at the last all shall come to the full perfection of growth in Christ—until the Spiritual Temple shall be finished, and the Head-stone is laid, "*with shoutings, crying, Grace, grace, unto it.*" Zech. iv. 7.

If it is limited to this sense, it is manifest that the words, "PERFECTING,"—"EDIFYING,"—"A PERFECT MAN,"—"MEASURE OF THE STATURE OF THE FULNESS OF CHRIST," must refer to the completion of the number of the elect. I believe that this is, at least, fully implied and intended in the passage.

But SECONDLY.—It might be considered as being applied to these ministers, as gifts, for the individuals in every particular branch of the universal Church, and for their work in the edification—in the salvation, of the members individually, and of the Church collectively. In this sense, these words must be considered in reference to individuals, and individual Churches.

But indeed the former sense of the passage must also imply this. For it is by the perfecting and building up of the saints individually, in every Church, and every successive generation, by each successive generation of ministers whom the Lord shall raise up and send as His faithful witnesses and laborers, that the whole body of the elect shall at last be brought to "THE MEASURE OF THE STATURE OF THE FULNESS OF CHRIST." When the Glorious Head and the glorified members shall all be manifested in the fulness of the glory that shall be revealed at His appearing.

Let us then consider in this latter sense of the passage, that these ministers are given "FOR THE PERFECTING OF THE SAINTS." Are not the saints then perfect?—Yes, in one sense, they are. "*Ye are complete in him,*" Col. ii. 10, saith the Scripture. Again, it is written, "*By one offering he hath perfected forever them that are sanctified.*" Heb. x. 14. The saint—that is, the sinner who is brought by the Spirit to the Lord Jesus Christ, and sanctified in Christ—sanctified "*through his blood,*" Heb. xiii. 12—sanctified "*through the truth,*" John, xvii. 17—is accounted perfectly sinless before God:—for, though a sinner himself, his sins are entirely removed, being taken away from him, and laid on Christ; they are no longer imputed unto the believer. "*The Lord hath laid on him the iniquity of us all;*" Is. liii. 6. Therefore, "*Blessed is the man to whom the Lord will not impute sin.*" Rom. iv. 8. He is perfectly righteous before God—for having no righteousness of his own, the righteousness of his glorious Lord and Master is put down to his account—as if he had entirely performed it, "*For Christ is the end of the law for righteousness to every one that believeth.*" Rom. x. 4. "*He who knew no sin was made sin for us, that we might be made the righteousness of God in him.*" 2nd Cor. v. 21. So, "*There is therefore now no condemnation to them which are in Christ Jesus.*" Rom. viii. 1. And so in that sense, the saint is perfect—perfectly sanctified in Christ—set apart in Him—consecrated—dedicated to God, in Him and by Him—and one with Jesus, forever. "*For,*" saith the Apostle, "*of him are ye in Christ Jesus, who of God is made unto us wisdom, and righteousness, and sanctification, and redemption.*" 1st Cor. i. 30. Therefore we say in this sense, the saint is indeed wholly and completely perfect.

But, in another sense, the saint is very imperfect. He inhabits a body of sin and death—he is in the midst of a world that lieth in wickedness—he is subject to temptation—to the power of an adversary, that "*like a roaring lion, walketh about, seeking whom he may devour.*" 1st Pet. v. 8. He is not perfect in his understanding—nor in his will—nor perfect in his affections—nor in his walk;—in all these things he is very imperfect. He is also very imperfect in his views of the Sacred Word. How little does he know of himself—his own ignorance—sinfulness—weakness—want—and how little of "*the unsearchable riches of Christ,*" out of which he is to be instructed—strengthened—pardoned—nourished—and directed by the Spirit;—how little of the mind and purposes of God, as revealed in His Sacred Truth. How much has he need to read—to hear—to learn from the exhaustless stores of God's Eternal Word. How often is he involved, both within and without, in perplexities—in doubts—in fears—in difficulties. And therefore, when we consider these things, and they are but a small part of those that are to be considered—we see how imperfect are the saints—we see how the Church requires a continual ministration of the Word of God. Hence, the Lord hath given these gifts to the Church, "FOR THE PERFECTING OF THE SAINTS, FOR THE WORK OF THE MINISTRY, FOR THE EDIFYING OF THE BODY OF CHRIST.

The Apostle John speaks of three stages in the life of a believer, a child, a young man, and a father in Christ. When we are first brought to the knowledge of the Gospel of Christ, when "*the Sun of righteousness arises with healing in his wings*" on our souls. Mal. iv. 2—when we see the first light of divine truth gilding with its beams all objects around us—brightening every prospect in time and opening a glorious vista into an illuminated eternity,—we think, very frequently that we are so established—so strong—that the Word of Truth—the power of the Gospel is so great, so glorious, that the effect in our hearts is such, that we shall never again fall into the evils with which we know our previous course has been continually defiled. "*In my prosperity I said, I shall never be moved, Lord by thy favor thou hast made my mountain to stand strong.*" Ps. xxx. 6, 7.

But Oh, my friends, how very soon the believer begins to feel the imperfection of his knowledge—the weakness of his faith—the corruption of his will—and the power of the sin that dwelleth in his deceitful and desperately wicked heart.

Then commences the conflict within—the struggle between the flesh and the spirit—the new man and the old man—"*the law in the members,*" and "*the law in the mind:*" and he requires, therefore, a continual increase of knowledge to be derived from the Word of God, of his own character—of his own heart, and of the character—offices and power of his Lord and Saviour.

Therefore, you remember in this Epistle, iii. 16, the prayer of the Apostle for this Church "*that he would grant you according to the riches of his glory, to be strengthened with might, by his*

Spirit in the inner man." You see they want the strength of the Spirit in their souls. "*That Christ may dwell in your hearts by faith,*"—they want the indwelling of Christ through the Spirit in their hearts by faith,—the habitual turning of the heart to Christ—the habitual leaning of the heart on Christ,—the habitual confidence of the soul in the person and work of their Lord and Saviour;—in his spotless righteousness and His precious blood. "*That ye being rooted and grounded in love*"—just as the plant, as it grows from a seedling into a sapling, and from a sapling into a tree, requires to spread forth its roots continually below, to take deeper hold in the soil in which it is planted, that it may spread forth its branches above, both to yield fruit and to sustain the pressure of the storm; so the believer, who is like "*a tree planted by the rivers of waters that bringeth forth his fruit in his season,*" Ps. i. 3, as he requires to have his branches spreading forth continually and bearing fruit and blasts of trial in faith, so does he need as constantly to have his roots, the fibres of his heart's desires, affections, confidence and hope, spread deeper and deeper into the love of his Lord and Saviour.

Therefore the vast subject, "THE PERFECTING OF THE SAINTS, THE WORK OF THE MINISTRY, THE EDIFYING OF THE BODY OF CHRIST," might be enlarged upon as the continual application of the whole of God's truth to the continual wants of all the members of His church and the constant exhibition to them of His power, faithfulness, and love.

There is not one who hears me, who is a believer in the Gospel, and who, therefore, knows anything of his own heart, that does not feel continually his need of strengthening, of refreshing, of edification in Christ.

Why do we meet together? why do we read the Bible? why pray? why expound or converse about the Scriptures? Is it not because we feel our continual want of being built up and strengthened in our Lord and Saviour Jesus Christ? Omit, for a little season, the reading of your Bible—neglect, for a time, prayer—forsake the means of grace—abandon the ordinances of God, and see how you will droop and languish in your spirit. See how your heart will grow faint in faith and hope—how your desires and affections will be debased into wilful disobedience to God, and clinging to all things of earth! It is only by the study of the Word of God—it is only by diligent attendance on His appointed ordinances—on the means of grace—by prayer, public and private; it is only by these means, (and these are the means of profiting by the ministry) it is only by these means, I say, that we can derive strength or power in our spiritual life, or growth in grace to carry on our conflict with the world, the flesh, and the devil. Therefore, look into your own hearts, for your sins—your wants—your weaknesses—temptations—trials—corruptions—whatever they be; look into your hearts, I say, for these, and then you will understand, by your necessities, what is the need of the perfecting of the saints. You will see your innumerable wants;—and the continual sense of your wants will lead you to feel how much you require for the perfecting and the edifying of your own soul.

But it is always most important to keep in view,—that while the believer must ever feel his own wants, and what he requires continually for his soul's strength and edification,—he is never to allow his sense of those wants, or of all that he requires, to hinder his view of his perfection, as he is complete in Christ Jesus. If his heart does not condemn him of insincerity or double-dealing with God—if he is indeed sincerely looking unto Jesus—he is not to allow his view of his own wants—sins—and imperfections, to hinder him from believing with confidence, that he is accepted, and perfectly delivered from all condemnation, in Christ his Lord and Saviour. When the Apostle as we have seen was groaning under the pressure of his body of sin and death, he triumphed at the same moment in deliverance in Jesus, "*O wretched man that I am! who shall deliver me from the body of this death? I thank God, through Jesus Christ our Lord.*" Rom. vii. 24, 25.

And this is a point, very important for us carefully to distinguish and examine. For unless believers are well instructed in the Truth of God, it is a frequent error among them, as we have before observed, to think, that although they are privileged to believe that the work of Christ is indeed a refuge for their souls,—yet they cannot have perfect confidence in their acceptance through the work of Christ, until they find in themselves a certain growth towards perfection, which they do not find;—and therefore, they look off Christ, and the perfect work of Christ, as the ground of their acceptance,—and they look into themselves—they feel their own innumerable sins and imperfections, which keep them thus continually back from trusting and rejoicing in Christ. They look for a certain purifying work of the Spirit, yet to be wrought in their hearts,—and, until this is wrought, they cannot really find perfect confidence before God in Christ,—not knowing that the purification of the heart is by faith, "*purifying their hearts by faith,*" Acts xv. 9, and by the blood of Jesus, "*having our hearts sprinkled from an evil conscience,*" Heb. x. 22. That is a great delusion—a great error. Let us never forget, for a moment, that it is the privilege of the believer to rest with confidence on his complete acceptance, through the finished work of Jesus; and while he is fully conscious of all his own imperfections, and all his own wants and sins, he has to seek for strength against these, and pray in the midst of these—not to complete—or to strengthen—or to increase his acceptance before God,—but to enable him to serve and glorify his God, who "*hath made him accepted in the Beloved,*" Chap. i. 6, by the continual subjugation of his own corrupt affections—by a continual conquest over his own carnal mind—and a continual exhibition of Christian holiness—and a devoted life—and Christian fruitfulness in the service, and for the glory, of his Lord and Master. So observe what our Lord says, "*Let your light so shine before men, that they may see your good works,*" not that you may derive pardon—or peace—or acceptance from your good works,—but that men may "*glorify your Father which is in heaven.*" Mat. v. 16. Our good works—our holy and devoted life, are for the glorifying of our Lord and Master, and not for the acceptance of our own souls—they are manifested as the effects of our acceptance, but are no part of the cause of it; for our own peace. Christ is the Alpha and Omega—Christ is all.

Consider these vast truths, they are of deep moment. When the Apostle then says that these ministers endowed with various powers are "FOR THE PERFECTING OF THE SAINTS," he does not mean to imply that the saints are to doubt of their complete and perfect acceptance in Christ, for you recollect he says, Ephesians, i. 3, 4, "*Blessed be the God and Father of our Lord Jesus Christ, who hath blessed us with all spiritual blessings in heavenly places in Christ, according as he hath chosen us in him before the foundation of the world, that we should be holy and without blame before him in love.*" Remember he blessed God for this being their actual condition, and therefore, there is nothing to be done in order to give them that perfect acceptance which they already have.

But these are gifts to the church.

"FOR THE WORK OF THE MINISTRY," who can attempt to tell what the varied work of the ministry is—what the varied work of the ministry must be? None,—Unless he can tell the varied wants of man and the varied fulness of the blessings which are contained in this blessed Book, as given to man by God, and which it is the province and duty of the minister to draw forth from that Word, for the conversion, the edification, and the salvation of his poor guilty fellow-sinners:—"THE WORK OF THE MINISTRY" is as extensive as man's wants, and God's grace and glory, as it is revealed in Scripture. It is only necessary to state the meaning of the Apostle; we could not enter into the vast field which it opens.

"FOR THE EDIFYING OF THE BODY OF CHRIST." "*Edifying*" —building up the body of Christ—increasing it—strengthening it —establishing it—compacting it—uniting the members of the body of Christ together—building up each individual soul—and building all up together in Christ. What is the work of a builder in a building? Some employed in the work, hew out stones from the quarry—some draw them to the foundation—some hammer and square them—the builder lays every single stone firmly and evenly on the foundation; and from the moment he lays the first stone on the foundation, he applies his plumb-line as the wall goes up, to see that he lays every stone evenly on the same foundation; and the top stone of the wall rests as much on the foundation stone, as the stone that immediately presses over it. All rest on the foundation, from the bottom to the top. So it is the business of all the ministers of Christ to take care that all are placed on the foundation, and every man is to "*take heed how he buildeth thereupon.*" 1st Cor. iii. 10. All must rest alike on the Lord Jesus Christ. The minister has the same Gospel for the salvation of all —the same Rock for all to rest on—the same Hope to set before them all,—but he must regulate his admonitions and exhortations to them, according to their different circumstances of life, as the Apostle himself exemplifies in this Epistle. He must direct his varied exhortations to parents—children—husbands—wives—masters—servants—those in high stations, and those in the humbler walks of life—those in power, and those in subjection. He has different admonitions to give them all, according to their different circumstances. It is his business to instruct them, according to the position in which God has been pleased to place them in the Church, in the several duties of their respective spheres in life. While all are laid on the foundation of Christ alone as their hope, they are all to be built up in Him, to glorify their Lord and Saviour, wheresoever He hath been pleased to place them in His Temple. For these gifts are given, "FOR THE WORK OF THE MINISTRY, FOR THE EDIFYING OF THE BODY OF CHRIST."

We considered, on the last day, and indeed we cannot too frequently advert to it, that there never was a greater or a more common delusion than this:—that believers should think, that if they were in some circumstances, different from those in which they are placed, they would serve the Lord better, and glorify Him more. I believe that is a frequent temptation and snare of their heart—I am sure it is of mine. We are continually prone to say, or at least to think:—"If it was not for such and such a difficulty—or for such and such a want of means, or power, or opportunity—if I were placed in a different position from what I feel I am placed in—then I would be able to serve the Lord better." Now, this is a gross delusion—a snare of our enemy. For God is to be glorified by His people, in every position of difficulty—of danger—of distress. He is to be glorified by us, in overcoming the very obstacles of which we complain. In the difficulty is the victory and the glory of divine grace. We are seeking for facilities of the flesh, and not of the Spirit. Let us remember all things are alike easy to Him in whom is all our strength, "*I can do all things, through Christ, which strengtheneth me.*" Phil. iv. 13. Therefore our duty and our happiness is, not to change the place that our Heavenly Father has allotted to us, but to glorify Him there with our bodies and spirits, which are His. If we be low, not to seek to be high, "*Seekest thou great things for thyself, seek them not.*" Let us rather seek, in our different circumstances, whatever they are, to make them and ourselves subservient to our Master's glory. There is not a single individual, from the highest to the lowest on earth, that cannot serve and glorify the Lord, in the situation in which he is placed. So "THE EDIFYING OF THE BODY OF CHRIST" is, in this sense, the building up of the Church of Jesus—not only, as it may be interpreted, in gathering in the stones of the temple, but in establishing them all individually in the faith of our Lord and Saviour—in directing and strengthening them all, and establishing them all in the service of their Divine Master, in the various places in which the Lord has been pleased to fix them in His Church, for His glory.

"TILL WE ALL COME, IN THE UNITY OF THE FAITH, AND OF THE KNOWLEDGE OF THE SON OF GOD UNTO A PERFECT MAN, UNTO THE MEASURE OF THE STATURE OF THE FULNESS OF CHRIST."

This part of the passage seems to me to indicate that the more enlarged prophetic interpretation of it, of which we spoke, is, if not its direct and primary meaning, at least expressly included in the Apostolic view and intention; for we can scarcely conceive that so full and perfect an image would be meant by the inspired writer, to express that, which presents to the mind so very inadequate an idea of it, as that state, to which either the Church at Ephesus or any other church has ever attained. Besides, it seems too contracted a view by far, to suppose that the words "WE ALL," are applied to the mere Church at Ephesus,—they seem plainly to comprehend not only that Church but all the Churches of Christ,—and not only those of Apostolic times, but the whole mystical body with their glorious Head. It seems to comprehend the same idea as that, in our Blessed Lord's own prayer, "*Neither pray I for these alone, but for them also who shall believe on me through their word; that they all may be one, as thou, Father, art in me, and I in thee, that they also may be one in us: that the world may believe that thou hast sent me.*" John xvii. 20, 21.

But, no doubt, as all the gifts of the ministry were given by the Lord to His Church to be continued till that glorious consummation, when all are to be gathered together in Christ—so the same blessed standard of unity in the faith and doctrine of the Gospel, and in the edification of holiness and love, in which the glorified Church shall appear, is that, into which it should be the object, as it is the duty, of the ministry to labor to bring every part of the Church in its present dispensation. And this brings us to the practical application of the passage. For that state, to which it is the object of the whole appointed ministry of the dispensation to bring the whole Church at the last, must be the proper aim of every minister, with reference to every Church and every individual in their present state—till they "ALL COME IN THE UNITY OF THE FAITH AND OF THE KNOWLEDGE OF THE SON OF GOD UNTO A PERFECT MAN, UNTO THE MEASURE OF THE STATURE OF THE FULNESS OF CHRIST;" till they all are perfectly edified, strengthened, and built up in the unity of the Lord Jesus Christ, like the members of one body. Without any doubt this ought to be the object of the work of the ministry; for let us recollect, that although it is true, that no church ever has arrived, on this earth, at the fulness of this blessed state, still the measure of man's attainment, whether individually or collectively—the measure of the attainment of the individual believer, or the measure of the attainment of any collective body of believers in a church, is not to be the standard, according to which either men or churches are to be, collectively or individually edified. Though we never at tain to perfection, still perfection is the standard at which we all should aim. We attain not to the fulfilment of God's holy law, still the law of God is the true and only standard of perfection, that standard is the measure of our duty, and at that standard we are consequently bound to aim. Therefore, that standard should be the only measure of the believer's judgment of himself. And this is the reason why a man when his eyes are opened to see the holy and spiritual nature of the law, sees his own lost condition as a sinner, and so the Apostle saith, "*When the commandment came sin revived and I died.*" Rom. vii. 9. And this is the reason, why, the more believers grow in grace—the more clearly and deeply the law of God is written in their heart, this is the reason why, (as we have before explained at length) the more they grow in humility, because as they acquire increased knowledge of the spiritual nature and perfection of the law of God—as they acquire increased knowledge of the spiritual dominion which it claims over their wills, desires, affections, thoughts, and imaginations—as they acquire a knowledge of this heavenly standard,—so they acquire an increased knowledge of their own violations—their short-comings—their constant transgressions; they see and learn continually how totally they fail of approaching the standard of perfection. Thus the perfect standard of the law of God, ought to be the aim of every believer for himself, and every collective body of believers as a church; and it ought to be the aim of every minister—of every person, whose office and whose object it is to edify the body of Christ, to hold up this holy law as the standard and rule of their duty.

It is the perfection of the standard of duty that magnifies the nature of sin, and it is the extent and magnitude of the nature of sin that exalts and glorifies the unsearchable riches of Christ in the souls of his people, showing that "*where sin abounded grace did much more abound.*" Rom v. 20.

Now as the law is the standard of the believer's duty; and as it is by his transgressions of the law he learns to prize the salvation of the Gospel—so the standard of perfect faith, and unity, and love, and glory in the Gospel, ought to be the standard of the believer's aim, and of that of all the Church; and consequently, to this, it is the duty of the ministry to labor to bring the Church. The love and harmony of the Church above, surrounding the throne of God and the Lamb, with the praises of redeeming love, ought to be the standard and model for the Church below.

It does not at all follow, that a Church must necessarily attain to this state, any more than that it must attain to a perfect obedience to the law, because that is the standard of its duty. But it is true, nevertheless, that this is the standard of attainment for the Church, and ought to be the object of every minister, in endeavoring to edify the Church, "TILL WE ALL COME, IN THE UNITY OF THE FAITH, AND OF THE KNOWLEDGE OF THE SON OF GOD, UNTO A PERFECT MAN, UNTO THE MEASURE OF THE STATURE OF THE FULNESS OF CHRIST." We know, indeed, how impossible the full attainment of this glorious stature is in the Church now—we know that, even under the teaching of the Apostles themselves, the different understandings of men—the different orders of their minds—their several sins and failings, hindered them from all having the same clear, distinct view of the truth—and from having in uniform exercise or power, the faith or trust in the truths they did know. But still, this ought to be the end and object of every individual minister and of every believer in the Church.

Dear friends, persons imagine, when they know the doctrine of justification by faith, that they know Christ; but we never know Christ as we ought to know Him, we never know the Lord Jesus Christ, just as we never know ourselves—The Lord saith, "*The heart is deceitful above all things, and desperately wicked, who can know it?*" Jer. xvii. 9. So we may say, "Christ is glorious above all things, infinitely precious, infinitely suitable to all the wants of poor sinners, who can know Him?" So, you see, the Apostle saith in this Epistle that to him was given, to "*preach among the Gentiles the unsearchable riches of Christ.*" chap. iii. 8, and when he speaks of knowing the love of Christ he saith," *and to know the love of Christ which passeth knowledge.*" chap. iii. 19.

Yes indeed, it passeth knowledge,—we never can know it; let any of us look back at our course and see what He has been to us! let us see what Christ has done for us! let us just consider what every individual member of his Church has experienced from Him,—of His grace—His pardoning love—His redeeming power—His long-suffering—His sympathy—His compassion—His tenderness—His vigilance—His faithfulness—His truth! Think how He has borne with us.—Think what He has borne from us! We may well repeat the language of the hymn,

> "Could we bear from one another,
> What He daily bears from us?
> Yet this glorious Friend and Brother,
> Loves us, though we treat him thus!
> His is boundless love indeed,
> Jesus is a friend in need."

When we think of what Christ has been to us, we may say, we never could have anticipated what He has done in time past, any more than we can tell all He shall do in time to come, we never can comprehend the grace and the glory of Christ. Therefore, here too, the necessity for the believer to grow continually in the knowledge of Christ, as the Apostle says, "*grow in grace, and in the knowledge of our Lord and Saviour Jesus Christ.*" 2nd Pet. iii. 18. Hence, both the need of these gifts of ministers and of the constant exercise of their ministration "TILL WE ALL COME IN THE UNITY OF THE FAITH AND OF THE KNOWLEDGE OF THE SON OF GOD UNTO A PERFECT MAN, UNTO THE MEASURE OF THE STATURE OF THE FULNESS OF CHRIST."

If men really believed the Gospel of Christ in the pureness and brightness of its truth, and gave to it the weight and value it deserves, we should have no divisions in the Church.

Observe, the Apostle saith, "THE FAITH," "THE KNOWLEDGE OF THE SON OF GOD." There is but one faith—one truth—one Gospel—dissension is produced from the multiplicity of ignorances and errors by which that faith—that truth—that Gospel are corrupted, perverted, denied.—When the salvation of Christ was first proclaimed with the power of the Holy Ghost on the Day of Pentecost,—when the pride and presumption of sinners, had neither time or opportunity to mix up their works, whether moral or ceremonial with the righteousness and blood of the Lord Jesus Christ, as the ground of a sinner's justification before God.—When remission of sins through the name of Jesus, was freely and fully proclaimed to the very men who "*with wicked hands had crucified and slain*" Him, and when they "*who gladly received his word were baptized*" then they "*continued daily with one accord in the Temple, and breaking bread from house to house, did eat their meat with gladness and singleness of heart.*" Acts ii. 23, 38, 46. Then "*The multitude of them that believed were of one heart and of one soul.*" Acts v. 32. "THE UNITY OF THE FAITH AND OF THE KNOWLEDGE OF THE SON OF GOD" then produced that unity of love, that oneness of heart and soul, which filled their own bosoms with joy, and manifested to others the truth and power of the doctrine they believed. But soon, alas! the evils of sin produced discord and disunion in the body. Soon "*when the number of the disciples was multiplied, there arose a murmuring of the Grecians against the Hebrews, because their widows were neglected in the daily ministration.*" Acts vi. 1. Soon persecution superinduced other trials and scattered the disciples. Soon again, when the Gentiles were brought into the Church, the Pharisaic teachers arose preaching circumcision and keeping the law of Moses, corrupting and perverting the Gospel, till the assembled Apostles and Elders were obliged to issue a letter to the Church against them. Contentions about beggarly elements, eating certain meats, observances of days, as in the Church of Rome, Rom. xiv. Contentions and divisions, one saying "*I am of Paul, and another I am of Apollos,*" as in the Church of Corinth. Corruptions of the Gospel through ceremonial observances and the merit of works, as in the Churches of Galatia, which struck at the very root of the Christian faith; these and similar evils indicated the necessity of men to labor in the work of the ministry in every Church, till they were brought to "THE UNITY OF THE FAITH, AND OF THE KNOWLEDGE OF THE SON OF GOD."

Hence the earnest exhortations of the Apostle, as in this chapter, to unity in faith and love. Hence his prayer as for the Romans, "*That ye may with one mind and one mouth glorify God, even the Father of our Lord Jesus Christ.*" Rom. xv. 6. Hence the duty of all the ministers of Christ in the exercise of their holy calling, which cannot be more scripturally and faithfully enforced, than in the exhortation in our own solemn service, in the Ordering of Priests, which is a practical application of this very passage, and of which the following is an extract:

EXHORTATION IN THE ORDERING OF PRIESTS.

"Wherefore consider with yourselves the end of your ministry towards the children of God, towards the spouse and body of Christ, and see that you never cease your labor, your care and diligence, until that you have done all that lieth in you according to your bounden duty, to bring all such, as are or shall be committed to your charge, unto that agreement in the faith and knowledge of God, and to that ripeness and perfection of age in Christ, that there be no place left among you, either for error in religion or for viciousness of life."

We perceive, by the subsequent illustration, what the evil is, against which the Apostle desires particularly to guard them, namely—the instability of ignorance. It is by the edification of the ministry, that the Church is to be brought to ripeness and perfection of maturity in Christ—from the weakness of childhood, to the strength and stability of age. So he saith, "THAT WE HENCEFORTH BE NO MORE CHILDREN, TOSSED TO AND FRO, AND CARRIED ABOUT WITH EVERY WIND OF DOCTRINE, BY THE SLEIGHT OF MEN AND CUNNING CRAFTINESS, WHEREBY THEY LIE IN WAIT TO DECEIVE."

This is a peculiarly apposite illustration. If a child hears a number of stories, from different persons, that are contrary to, or inconsistent with each other, about which it has no experience or knowledge,—it is led off, and carried away by the various impressions produced by the most opposite opinions. It does not know what to believe, or whom to follow. So it is with all those in the Church, who are not established in the truth—they are like weak and ignorant children.

They hear one man's sermon, and they say, "*I am of Paul.*"—Then they hear another man's, and they say, "*I am of Apollos.*" They take up a book, and read the opinions that one man writes on a subject of Theology—they think that is truth. They take up another book, and read the opinions of a man on the other side of the question—they think that is truth. The false opinion being more congenial to the natural mind than the true, they are generally swayed by what is wrong—they have no knowledge—no experience of truth—they think it is candid, as they say, to hear all sides of the question. I know one individual, of whom I happen to think at this moment, who has read the most opposite doctrines of truth and error;—and, not knowing what to believe, or what to think, he has ended in scarcely believing anything at all on the subject—"TOSSED TO AND FRO, AND CARRIED ABOUT WITH EVERY WIND OF DOCTRINE,"—like a weather-cock, the sport of every breeze.

There never was a time, when persons are in more danger of this than now.—There are such a multiplicity of books published—such inundations of falsehood from the press—such false principles poured forth, on every subject connected with divine truth. I might mention many,—but I do not wish even to bring them to your notice—but their effects are lamentably exemplified, as one goes among individuals, in what is called the religious world, and converses with them. We hear the most extraordinary and absurd opinions, as contrary to the Scriptures, as if those who uttered them had never read the Bible.

They are "LIKE CHILDREN, TOSSED TO AND FRO AND CAR-

RIED ABOUT WITH EVERY WIND OF DOCTRINE." Thus some of the very fundamental truths of the Gospel—the very fundamental principles of the Christian religion, are sapped at this very moment, in the minds of thousands, who are led away by the fanciful torturing of Scripture—by rationalism, and philosophy, falsely so called, on the one side,—and by mysticism—superstition—fanaticism, and idolatry, on the other;—so that, even from institutions which ought to be the fortresses of true religion in the land,—falsehoods are poured forth, which strike at the very root of the hope of man's salvation—and turn the minds of men, not "*from darkness to light*," but from any little light they may have seemed to have, to utter darkness.*

And what does this arise from?—from ignorance of "*the faith*"—from want of "*the knowledge of the Son of God;*" and this springs, either from the fundamental principles of divine truth not being soundly taught by the ministry—or received by the flock. Where the great foundations of the truth are laid in the soul, and where the soul is firmly built up and established on Christ,—then, it cannot be carried about by the various winds of doctrine—whereby some persons are like children, tossed to and fro. And the Holy Spirit knew well the state of the human mind, and the state of the Church, when He inspired the Apostle to write this verse,—since it is only, by being built and established in "THE UNITY OF THE FAITH, AND OF THE KNOWLEDGE OF THE SON OF GOD," we shall "HENCEFORTH BE NO MORE CHILDREN, TOSSED TO AND FRO, AND CARRIED ABOUT WITH EVERY WIND OF DOCTRINE, BY THE SLEIGHT OF MEN, AND CUNNING CRAFTINESS, WHEREBY THEY LIE IN WAIT TO DECEIVE."

It was, in the days of the Apostles, as in our own, that souls were "*beguiled by the sleight of men, and cunning craftiness, whereby they lay in wait to deceive.*" Then, as now, and at all ages of the Church, such men were the agents and ministers of the Prince of Darkness. The Apostle had warned the elders of this very Church, when he had summoned them to Miletus, not only that there should "*grievous wolves enter in among them, not sparing the flock,*" Acts, xx. 29,—but that those wolves should arise even from themselves. "*Also of your own selves shall men arise, speaking perverse things, to draw away disciples after them.*" v. 30. And nothing can more clearly establish that men were never intended to surrender their judgment and conscience to their teachers, than the many safeguards against false teachers and blind guides, with which the Word of God abounds. For as

* The progress of Tractarianism, or rather of Popery in disguise which had gone so far when these Lectures were delivered, in 1837–8, has too lamentably developed itself into the only system to which, from its first commencement, it inevitably tended. False principles are not at all less false, when put forth in the name of the Church of England, than in that of the Church of Rome—they are only the more dangerous, as being less suspected; and the more treacherous, as being taught by those who have solemnly abjured them. But wherever that apostacy begins to develop itself—the mark which God has written on it, is equally legible on its brow, "*Speaking lies in hypocrisy; having the conscience seared with a hot iron.*" 1st Tim. iv. 2.

faithful shepherds were the gifts of God, for a blessing to His Church,—to strengthen and build them up in Christ,—so were false teachers the curse and pest of the flock—"*grievous wolves*" corrupting the Gospel of Jesus, as the Apostle saith to the Corinthians, "*I fear, lest by any means, as the serpent beguiled Eve through his subtilty, so your minds should be corrupted from the simplicity that is in Christ.*" 2nd Cor. xi. 3. And their "*sleight and cunning craftiness*" were to be especially guarded against. The word translated "*sleight*" occurs only in this place, and it is a metaphor taken from gamblers playing with dice, implying trick and cheating. So the word cunning craftiness is the same which is translated "WILES *of the devil,*" chap. vi. 11, and it only occurs in these two places in the New Testament.

He proceeds "BUT" (instead of being thus deceived—distracted—and beguiled) "SPEAKING THE TRUTH IN LOVE, MAY GROW UP UNTO HIM IN ALL THINGS, WHICH IS THE HEAD, EVEN CHRIST." These are the two vital principles—the two pillars of Christianity. Faith and Love. Faith—providing for the whole trust and confidence of the soul in its God. And Love—providing for the whole walk of man, with God and his fellow-creatures.—Faith, taking root in Christ,—and Love, produced by faith, and manifesting its fruits, in the life and conversation—devotedness to God—and love to man. So he saith, "SPEAKING THE TRUTH IN LOVE, MAY GROW UP UNTO HIM IN ALL THINGS, WHICH IS THE HEAD, EVEN CHRIST."

You see where there is true faith wrought in the heart, there is love, and there is open, honest profession of it. No hesitation about it,—no mincing of it, no accommodation of it, no surrender of principle, no compromise with base iniquitous expediency,—no trying how far it is expedient to accommodate God's truth to man's wickedness;—"BUT SPEAKING THE TRUTH IN LOVE," boldly and faithfully doing so. But then, in the true spirit of love, not as is the case with nominal charity—with pretended charity—with Satan's charity—by which he is so fond of alluring men to come to him. Not disturbing them at all, nor offending them, nor saying a word to wound their prejudices. Such charity regards not how far God's truth be abused, perverted or put down, so that we neither say or do anything to offend man. This is Satan's charity, to get man's soul into his power, not "SPEAKING THE TRUTH IN LOVE," but "*speaking lies in hypocrisy,*" 1st Tim. iv. 2, accommodating their doctrines to the taste and inclination of their hearers who say unto them "*speak unto us smooth things, prophesy deceits.*" Is. xxx. 10. Such is not the love spoken of here. Such was not the love our Blessed Lord had, nor such the love the Apostles had. All false religion, all false principles they faithfully exposed, but speaking the truth, in the spirit of genuine love for the souls of men, to deliver those from evil who are in evil, and to establish those in the truth who are in the truth, that they might grow unto Christ in all things. What important training for the Church of Christ, for every individual member of that Church! It is impossible not to give offence to those who hate the truth! if men will speak the truth, however much in a spirit of love. What man can be gentler than Christ? Who can be meeker than Christ? Can any be wiser than Christ? Is it possible to be more simple—more charitable—more tender—more inoffensive than Christ.—Yet, who gave such offence? "*Say we not well that thou art a Samaritan and hast a devil?*" "*Now we know that thou hast a devil.*" John viii. 48, 52. This was the language to Christ of those to whom he spoke the truth in love—and the disciple is not above his Lord, so was it with the Apostles, with this very Apostle who "was all things to all men," "SPEAKING THE TRUTH IN LOVE." Yea, and "*all that will live godly in Christ Jesus must suffer persecution.*" Tim. iii. 12. It may be only the persecution of opinion, or of words, though the Church has often felt it heavier than either, but if men are really faithful to their Lord and Master in all their conversation and dealings with one another, they can scarcely escape giving offence to men; until the offence of the cross ceases, still you see the standard, "BUT SPEAKING THE TRUTH IN LOVE MAY GROW UP UNTO HIM IN ALL THINGS WHICH IS THE HEAD, EVEN CHRIST; FROM WHOM THE WHOLE BODY, FITLY JOINED TOGETHER AND COMPACTED BY THAT WHICH EVERY JOINT SUPPLIETH, ACCORDING TO THE WORKING IN THE MEASURE OF EVERY PART, MAKETH INCREASE OF THE BODY UNTO THE EDIFYING OF ITSELF IN LOVE."

As the human frame "*fearfully and wonderfully made,*" Psalm cxxxix. 14, is formed and adapted in every part of its wondrous mechanism with the most perfect fitness—harmony—unity—sympathy and co-operation of all its parts, for their mutual support, increase, and growth in strength and energy, till it reaches the full maturity of its appointed stature—and as every part of it is formed and adapted by the almighty power of Him "*by whom all things were made*"—so by the same power, and by the same hand alone, are all the parts of his mystical body formed—adapted—fitted—harmonized—adjusted for that unity—sympathy—co-operation—and increase that ought to characterize the visible Church of Christ, and which though all unseen by us, does really belong to his mystical body. But it is from Christ the glorious Head alone that all the blessings flow to the body. It is from Him "THE WHOLE BODY IS FITLY JOINED TOGETHER, AND COMPACTED BY THAT WHICH EVERY JOINT SUPPLIETH."

Through the head is all the nutriment and life derived to the human body. The head thinks for it—sees for it—hears for it—speaks for it—rules it—guides it—every fibre, muscle, and joint is moved at the will of the head. How beautifully, yet how inadequately, does the image illustrate the glorious character of Him, who is, "*The head over all things to his church, which is his body, the fulness of him that filleth all in all?*" chap. i. 22, 23. Life through the head, wisdom—guidance—government—direction—safety—movement to every place—motion of every limb—

sympathetic guidance and government of every member—all that can be needful for the body is treasured up in its glorious Head. "*In him dwelleth all the fulness of the Godhead bodily, and ye are complete in him, which is the head of all principality and power,*" saith the Apostle Col. ii. 9, 10. In Him the whole body ought to be joined together in love. Love should supply the band, and lubricate the motion of every joint, while every part should contribute to the increase and edification of the whole.

I must enter a little more into particulars on this verse again, please God. But, what a blessed picture of a Church on earth does this figure present to us! All united in the pure faith of the everlasting Gospel. All one in Christ by a living faith, and one with each other in sympathy and love, as members of one body in Him—All drawing together with one heart and one soul. Each in his proper place discharging exactly the functions of the sphere, in which the Lord has been pleased to appoint him, as every joint and muscle of the body moves in its appointed station, performing its exact and proper office. All from the highest to the lowest growing up into Christ, and firm and steadfast in the faith, moving onward in the path of holiness and peace, as a strong man pursueth his way.

Such shall be the pattern presented to the world "*when Christ who is our Life shall appear,*" and when, "*Then shall we also appear with him in glory.*" Col. iii. 4. But though the visible Church attain not to this in its present state, in this dispensation, —let us not forget that this and nothing less is the standard of her growth—"THE MEASURE OF THE STATURE OF THE FULNESS OF CHRIST." May our God in His great mercy teach us to aim at this! May we learn in the varied disappointments which we meet in this, in ourselves and others, to look for and haste unto His coming and His kingdom! May He enable us to "*Present our bodies a living sacrifice unto God holy and acceptable which is our reasonable service!*" Rom. xii. 1; to "*glorify God in our body and in our Spirit which are God's!*" 1st Cor. vi. 20, both individually and collectively here! and may He bring us by the riches of his grace, and the might of His power, to meet at His right hand in the glory of His kingdom. Amen and Amen.

THIRTY-SECOND LECTURE.

EPHESIANS IV.—17, 18, 19, 20.

"This I say therefore, and testify in the Lord, that ye henceforth walk not as other Gentiles walk, in the vanity of their mind; Having the understanding darkened, being alienated from the life of God through the ignorance that is in them, because of the blindness of their heart: Who, being past feeling, have given themselves over unto lasciviousness, to work all uncleanness with greediness. But ye have not so learned Christ."

MAN'S natural condition is that of being severed and alienated from God; and therefore, before he can serve God, he must be brought back, and reconciled to Him. A servant who is dismissed from your household cannot serve you—a child, who has fled from his home, cannot render you the duty and obedience of a child. The man who is not a servant of God, and a child of God, can neither render to God the duty of a child, or the service of a servant;—therefore, we must be first brought back and reconciled to God, before it is possible to render Him any obedience.

You recollect how we dwelt, in the 2nd chapter of this Epistle, on the state of man by nature, as being "dead in trespasses and sins"—therefore, you will observe, in these chapters, 4th, 5th, 6th, of this Epistle, in which the Apostle presses practical duties on the servants of God. He assumes throughout the principle that they are reconciled and brought back to God—and it is therefore, as we have seen, he urges on them, to "*Walk worthy of the vocation wherewith they are called, with all lowliness and meekness, with long-suffering, forbearing one another in love.*" Thus you perceive it is, in consequence of the relation in which believers stand to Jesus, as being united unto Him, as members of that body of which He is the living Head, that the Apostle proceeds in the exhortation in this chapter.

Is Christ spoken of as a vine—His Church are the branches. Is Christ spoken of as the head—his Church are the members! as the body severed from the head, or as the branches broken off from the vine, so is the sinner without Christ:—and just exactly as the branch in the vine draws all its sap and life, and flower and fruit from the stem, and as the body derives all its vital power, or functions, and its very existence from its union with the head, so the believer derives all spiritual fruit, power, and existence from his union with the Lord Jesus Christ. Quickened by the Holy Spirit, grafted into Christ, "*brought nigh by the blood of Christ*" and reconciled to God; thus they are called to walk and glorify the Father in Him. Therefore our Lord saith, "*As the branch cannot bear fruit of itself, except it abide in the vine, no more can ye, except ye abide in me.*" John xv. 4. Now in this image of the vine every living branch and every single fibre, in every ramification of every branch from the joint where it is united to the stem, to the remotest bud that bursts from its extremity derives all its vitality, its verdure, and fruit from the stem. And in the image of the body, and the members, &c., the very same relation exists in reference to the Head. The Apostle says, "FROM WHOM THE WHOLE BODY, FITLY JOINED TOGETHER AND COMPACTED BY THAT WHICH EVERY JOINT SUPPLIETH, ACCORDING TO THE EFFECTUAL WORKING IN THE MEASURE OF EVERY PART MAKETH INCREASE OF THE BODY UNTO THE EDIFYING OF ITSELF IN LOVE." As the whole body is composed of a great variety of members—a great variety of bones—joints—muscles—nerves—fibres, &c.;—so the whole body of the Church of Christ is composed of a great variety of members. We cannot see the mechanism of its movements, or the mode in which the nutriment is conveyed—how the powers of its vitality are derived, and its motions communicated from the Head. But God sees it! And the Church may take up the words of the Psalmist, and apply it to all her members, as David to his body—"*Thine eyes did see my substance, yet being unperfect; and in thy book all my members were written, which in continuance were fashioned, when as yet there was none of them.*" Psalm cxxxix. 16. And the body of the Church is as perfect and complete, in God's eye, as the body of Adam, when He formed it from the dust of the earth—and beheld him—and all was very good. There is nothing wanting—no member wanting in the Church of Christ—no joint—no member deficient. It is as true of His mystical body, as of His human form, "*A bone of him shall not be broken.*" John, xix. 36. Everything is complete, though we cannot see it;—but we shall see it—when the body shall, in the Lord's time, be raised a glorified body; and it shall be beheld by angels, men, and devils,—as all complete—all perfect in one—united in its Glorious Head, Christ Jesus.

I have often mentioned to you before, but we ought to think of it every day, and so we must have "*precept upon precept, precept upon precept; line upon line, line upon line; here a little, and there a little.*" Is. xxviii. 10—that it is one important lesson for every Christian to learn, the place which he has in the body. What place have I in the body? Let me ask, what place has my hand—my finger—my eye—or any member of my frame, in my body?—The answer is, the place that God has appointed it. And, as every joint and muscle in the body, has that place in the body, that God has appointed it—so, every Christian in the Church of Christ has a place in the Church, that God has appointed him to fill. Where they are—there they are called—there they are to rest—and there they are to serve the Lord.

I do not think this can be too often, or too particularly insisted on—for in fact, the murmuring and discontent of individuals with their respective lots would cease, if they were really Christians, and felt that they were placed in the position they fill by God. It is ignorance of God that makes the world miserable. It is forgetfulness of God that makes His people murmur. It is the discontent, the murmuring of individuals that arises, accumulates, and swells into the storms that disturb social happiness, and peace, and order, and agitate, convulse, and overturn nations. It may be applied to every murmurer—"*Of the Rock that begat thee thou art unmindful, and hast forgotten the God that formed thee.*" Deut. xxxii. 18. Therefore in every state and stage of existence to know and feel that we are in our appointed place, and there to serve and glorify our God is our only happiness and peace. Now this is a most important consideration for every single one of you;—the child who is called to the knowledge of the Lord Jesus Christ, is called as a child to serve and glorify the Lord who has called him in the relation in which he stands as a child;—and the youth who is called to know and serve his God has his own peculiar department in which he is placed by his Lord to love and serve Him, he has peculiar circumstances and duties attendant on his position, peculiar trials and snares attendant on his youth; he has all these difficulties against which to watch and pray that he may be enabled to glorify his God in that sphere and stage of his existence.

The man who is called in a more advanced period of life, he has his peculiar position, his appointed place in the body;—the cares of his family, the difficulties of his circumstances—the snares and temptations peculiar to these that surround him; against these he is also called to watch and pray, and in the midst of them he is called on to glorify his God. The young female too, has her snares, her difficulties, her besetting sins, her trials, she is called on in these to serve her Lord. The married female, grown up with the cares of her family resting on her, has her position too in which to serve her Heavenly Father; and in all spheres in which we can be called to move, and in each sex, from youth to age, from the lisping tongue of infancy to the hoary head which is "*a crown of glory if it be found in the way of righteousness*"—Prov. xvi. 31. All have their peculiar places in the body, where they are to serve and glorify their God. Thus too in the different ranks of life, the poor creature who is suffering in poverty, in want, and distress, is called on in those circumstances in which God has been pleased to place him, to serve and glorify his Heavenly Father. The man again, who is in a higher sphere, blessed with competence and comfort, is called on in his position to serve and glorify his God:—if one is called on to suffer from trials, the other is called on to enjoy the privilege of knowing, that "*it is more blessed to give than to receive.*" Acts xx. 35. Those in still a higher sphere are called on, according to the increased variety and value of the talents with which God has entrusted them, to glorify the Giver.

Solomon—the Lord was pleased to place in a situation of pomp and magnificence, and he was called to magnify his God in that sphere.

Joseph, of Arimathea, a rich man, who could purchase and hew out his own tomb in a rock—he was called on to glorify his Master, and honored by being allowed to provide a sepulchre for his Redeemer.

Lazarus, lying on his humble bier to be carried about from door to door, to watch for the crumbs that fell from the rich man's table, while the dogs came to lick his sores, was called on to glorify his God there, and carried from that bier by angels to Abraham's bosom.

The women that followed our blessed Lord, and ministered unto him of their substance,—the Queen of Sheba, that "*came from the uttermost parts of the earth to hear the wisdom of Solomon.*" Matt. xii. 42. Ruth, the Moabitess, and Rahab, the harlot, who was brought to Christ, were called to glorify that God whom they adored in the various spheres of their existence. The poor widow, who had but two mites to cast into the treasury, was called to glorify her God with these. They were all she had, but God gave them to her for His own glory, and you see how she used them for that end. Every member and every muscle is arranged and fixed in the body in its place, and all the joints are fitly compacted together, and fitly work together. We may not see, we cannot understand the wisdom of this wondrous mechanism in the body, we are just as ignorant of the various fittings of all the members and joints of the church, as a person unacquainted with anatomy is ignorant of the nerves, and joints, and muscles of the animal frame. But notwithstanding, we may be assured—we ought to know that there is a harmony, a perfection, a glorious wonderful magnificence in the structure of them all: we are "*fearfully and wonderfully made,*" and as His works are marvellous in the world of nature, so are they no less marvellous in the world of grace. All the joints and members of His mystical body are "*fitly framed together, and compacted by that which every joint supplieth.*" As every muscle and joint of the body, contributes to the perfect growth and completion of the frame, so, every member of the church of Christ contributes to the model of perfection which the Lord Jehovah has wrought, and is continually working in the church for his own eternal glory.

Why should I dwell on this again in this place? Because I do not know anything that is more necessary to dwell on. And although it is more properly strictly belonging to the last passage, yet it is as we shall see the motive and argument of the Apostle by which he presses on believers the duty enforced in these verses which form the subject of our consideration.

It is one of the strongest temptations of Satan.—It is one of the most ensnaring corruptions of our hearts, to be discontented with our respective circumstances, to desire to leave the place in which God has fixed our lot, to get out of our sphere and the present trials we endure instead of reflecting thus:—

"In whatever place I am this day,—this day is all I can call my own, to-day is the only portion of time on which I have a right to reckon, and this day, it is my privilege to serve my Father here, where He has placed me, and to know that I am placed here by the ordinance of my Father's will."

This ought to be the Christian's language and the Christian's principle—to learn "*in whatsoever state we are therewith to be content.*" Phil. iv. 14—and there to serve and glorify our Lord. He will surely place us in our proper sphere, and it is ours to glorify Him there. "*In all thy ways acknowledge him, and he will direct thy paths.*" Prov. iii. 6. This is the real receipt for true happiness to the believer: as the Apostle shows at length Phil. iv. 4, "*Rejoice in the Lord alway, and again I say, rejoice. Let your moderation,*"—that is, your gentleness, forbearance—"*be known unto all men,*"—manifested in your whole life and conversation—"*The Lord is at hand. Be careful for nothing; but in everything by prayer and supplication, with thanksgiving let your requests be made known unto God. And the peace of God, which passeth all understanding, shall keep your hearts and minds through Christ Jesus.*" Phil. iv. 4—7.

Therefore, observe, where we really enjoy this happy, patient, gentle, submissive, thankful, prayerful acquiescence in the Lord's dispensations, and are looking by faith to Him, you see the blessed fruits of it, happiness and peace that passeth understanding. What unity must there be in the body if all the members were thus—surely "*the whole body, fitly framed together, and compacted by that which every joint supplieth, according to the effectual working in the measure of every part,*" must thus "*make increase of the body unto the edifying of itself in love.*" Imagine a household, in which the master, mistress, children, and servants, were all servants of God—imagine a household, in which the master and mistress were setting, as they ought, an example to their families of reverence and love to their Lord and Master, in the sphere in which He was pleased to place them;—the children brought up "*in the nurture and admonition of the Lord,*" and touched by the grace of God, trained in His fear, and manifesting by His grace the power and influence of His truth in their obedience, their diligence, their humility, their love in the service of God:—imagine the servants of that household, in spirit and truth the Lord's servants, serving their earthly master and mistress "*with good will, doing service, as to the Lord, and not to men.*" ch. vi. 7,—imagine the master and mistress treating them as "*remembering that their master also is in heaven,*"—in fact, walking in the ways in which the Lord is pleased to point out for His children in His word.—Imagine this, and conceive how every member of that family would help and edify one another, and comfort one another in love. And wherever there is a body together, consisting of high and low, young and old, rich and poor, if the course of conduct and the principles that are here laid down were carried out, conceive if you can what a blessing it were for every part of the Church of Christ, and therefore for the whole. Oh, how different the Church of Christ would be in itself, and would appear to the world!

It is the more necessary, as it appears to me, to dwell at greater length on this subject, because it is the foundation of the solemn and emphatic exhortation contained in the 17th and succeeding verses. The union of the members of the Church of Christ, with Christ and with each other, form the premises of the conclusion, which the Apostle presses on the saints at Ephesus, as to the manner in which they should walk, to serve and glorify their God. "THIS I SAY, THEREFORE;" mark the word "THEREFORE,"—that is—because you are united to this glorious Head—because you are members of so glorious a body—so blessed a brotherhood—because you are children of your Heavenly Father—"*brought nigh by the blood of Christ,*" and members of the body of Christ—because you are so—"THIS I SAY, THEREFORE, AND TESTIFY IN THE LORD, THAT YE HENCEFORTH WALK NOT AS OTHER GENTILES WALK, IN THE VANITY OF THEIR MIND." If the Gospel of Christ were to make no difference in this world between man in his former state and his redeemed state, what blessing would the Gospel confer on this earth? What moral capability could an unholy being possess of happiness in the presence of a holy God, if he had not been taught to feel that holiness and happiness are inseparable to a redeemed spirit? But we say on the authority of all the Word of God, that wherever the Gospel does reach the sinner's heart, it must make a difference and a mighty difference too—"*If any man be in Christ, he is a new creature, old things are passed away; behold, all things are become new.*" 2nd Cor. v. 17. So he says "I TESTIFY THAT YE HENCEFORTH WALK NOT AS OTHER GENTILES WALK, IN THE VANITY OF THEIR MIND." They who are ignorant of God, mark how they walk.—Ye, who know God, how ought ye to walk? How do they walk? In the vanity of their mind, in the ignorance, guilt, folly, wickedness, corruption, of their natural heart. All vanity:—"*Spending their money,*" as the Prophet saith, "*for that which is not bread, and their labor for that which satisfieth not.*" Isa. lv. 2. But he describes their state more particularly, "HAVING THE UNDERSTANDING DARKENED." You see, here is the first place where sin, and the power of sin is manifested in the fallen heart of man, "HAVING THE UNDERSTANDING DARKENED."—That was the first proof of his fall that Adam gave;—he ran to hide himself from the Lord among the trees of the garden. What must have been the prostration of his intellect, what the blindness of his understanding, when he could have become such a fool as to think, that he could hide himself from God!—to forget the Omniscience,—Omnipresence,—Omnipotence of his Creator! We see in all his fallen children how this blindness of the understanding pervades the race of men from infancy to the grave. The child thinks if he can hide himself from his parents or his teachers, that it is no matter what he does. If he can escape their observation he is content—that is, his natural mind—his understanding being darkened, the child does not reflect or know that God sees him. Let him but think that the eye of his parent or teacher, or of any person who will give them information of his misconduct, is fixed on him, he immediately stops whatever he is doing that he is afraid should come to their knowledge, or that his conscience tells him is wrong, but the thought that God sees him, never enters his mind, his understanding is darkened. So it is with man in his natural state, wherever he is;—that principle which is illustrated by the child, is the same in the man. His moral condition in this respect is described by the Psalmist, "*God is not in all his thoughts. His ways are always grievous. Thy judgments are far above out of his sight. He hath said in his heart, God hath forgotten. He hideth his face, he will never see it.*" Ps. x. 4, 5, 11.

Look at him again in the objects of his worship,—the idols he sets up. What can exhibit the desperate fall and blindness of the human mind more than the idols of the Gentiles? The idol formed by them of gold, silver, brass, stone, wood, or whatever it may be, they mould that image, whether large or small, they place it in their mighty temples, as Jupiter at Rome—Juggernaut in Hindostan—Diana at Ephesus—Minerva at Athens—the Virgin at Loretto—or they keep in their chambers or houses, be they large or small, it is no matter—they form these idols and bow before them with reverence, and worship them, as if these things, or some real or imaginary beings identified with them, or represented by them, as if these had made the heavens, or could intercede for them or deliver them—they bow before them as God. They would not say to the idol, although it is present to their eyes, "regulate my house, rule my children, govern my servants." They would feel the absurdity of asking the idol, or supposing it competent to perform a single act which a child, or a servant, or even a beast could perform—they are not so foolish as to say that, to an inanimate thing—yet they bow before it—worship it, and say that this thing made the world. What could exceed the blindness, the ignorance, and folly of Aaron and the Israelites, when he made their calves for them—"*These be thy Gods, O Israel, which brought thee up out of the land of Egypt.*" Exod. xxxii. 4. Such is the sort of being they worship, though they know it could not really perform one act of a human being, or even of a brute. What then must be the desperate blindness and darkness of the human heart!

This is what the Apostle says, "HAVING THE UNDERSTANDING DARKENED." Every man on the earth has his understanding in a spiritual sense perfectly dark; the nominal Christian has no more spiritual light—no clearer spiritual view of the real character of God than the Pagan idolater. He is accustomed to call a Being whom he imagines in his own mind, and of whom he has read in the Bible, or heard of—God—but he has no more notion of the real Scriptural character of that God than the heathen. He knows indeed that the gods of the heathen are but the work of men's hands, wood and stone, and that the God who made the world is an invisible Almighty being—but this gives him no knowledge of God's moral character as just, holy, merciful, faithful and true. Even the attributes of God which he acknowledges and believes as abstract truths are of no spiritual use to him, and he has no real understanding of them. He calls God Omniscient and Omnipresent, but has no regard for Him—no sense of his Omniscience and Omnipresence. If, like the child of whom we spoke, he escapes the eye of man, he cares not for the eye of God. He has no more sense of the wickedness of his own heart and thoughts, desires and imaginations, which are all open before God, than if there were no God. He is so blind as to God's moral character and government, that he thinks God is pleased with some punishment inflicted on his body for his sins, and that some deeds which he calls good, will atone for others which he knows to be evil, and that the justice of God is satisfied with this, and with the outward form of service, when his heart is far from Him. If you were to ask him, would you be satisfied or pleased, if a servant or one in an humbler situation in life were to approach you with great reverence, and to ask with great apparent submission and sincerity, and in most respectful and decorous language some petition, while you knew that that man disregarded and slighted you, and did not care for either you or what he asked for, or whether you granted his petition or not, how would you receive such a petitioner? He would answer, I would turn him away as a hypocrite and an impostor. Yet that is the way in which he himself approaches God;—that is the way in which an unconverted man who is called a Christian, goes to Church to worship, or to the Sacrament, or to read his Bible, or to say his prayers, as he calls it. He kneels down, mutters a portion of prayers, and never thinks or cares whether God hears him or not. If you speak to such a man, and ask him, Does God hear and answer your prayers? Does He grant what you pray for? Do you watch for, or expect an answer to your petitions? He will say, you are an enthusiast or a fanatic for even supposing such a thing. So blind and ignorant is the natural understanding of man. "*There is none that understandeth, there is none that seeketh after God, they are all gone out of the way, they are together become unprofitable, there is none that doeth good, no, not one.*" Rom. iii. 11, 12.

So here "HAVING THE UNDERSTANDING DARKENED;"—and what is the consequence? "BEING ALIENATED FROM THE LIFE OF GOD, THROUGH THE IGNORANCE THAT IS IN THEM, BECAUSE OF THE BLINDNESS OF THEIR HEART;" blindness of the understanding necessarily produces alienation from the life of God;—there is no such thing as the worship or service of God, no fear, no love, nor any knowledge of God, while the understanding remains darkened. This exactly corresponds with the description given of the Gentile world, in Acts xxvi. 18, where the Apostle Paul recites the words used by the Lord Jesus Christ to himself, when He arrested him on his way to Damascus, and declares the commission which he had received from the Lord, when He sent him as His Apostle to the Gentiles. It was this—"*To open their eyes, to turn them from darkness to light, from the power of Satan unto God.*" They are "ALIENATED FROM THE LIFE OF GOD, THROUGH THE IGNORANCE THAT IS IN THEM, BECAUSE OF THE BLINDNESS OF THEIR HEARTS," and therefore, the first thing is, "*to open their eyes, and to turn them from darkness to light.*" This is the same blessing which every sinner wants—to have his eyes opened. You require not only to have the Word of God set before you—but to have the Spirit of God opening your eyes and enlightening your mind to receive the sense of God's eternal truth—you require to have your understanding enlightened, that you may know and believe the plain meaning of the words you read or hear. The angel with the drawn sword was before Balaam, but his eyes were blinded, and he could not see or fear him, Num. xxii. 31.—The chariots of fire were round about the Prophet and his servant, but the servant's eyes must be opened by the Lord before he could see them, 2d Kings vi. 17. So it is with the sinner in his natural state—the sword of justice and the golden sceptre of mercy—death and life—condemnation and salvation are in every page of the Bible, but he neither sees nor regards—neither fears nor hopes, he is "ALIENATED FROM THE LIFE OF GOD." His heart is ignorant and blind.

I do not know any greater change exhibited in the sinner by conversion than in his understanding. His will and his affections are not more effectually renewed in their purpose and objects than his understanding; he is improved and advanced by the illumination of God's Holy Word—he learns to see at once the difference between truth and falsehood—he has got a standard of right and wrong—good and evil—a sound judgment of what renders a man happy and unhappy—of what renders a character excellent or wicked. He learns to form a right estimate of man, of books, of all principles which he had not before. He receives and exhibits the proofs of an intelligent understanding which no other instruction could possibly bestow. No education in sciences, classics, languages, literature, nothing on earth can enlarge or enlighten the mind of a sinner so much as the light of the Gospel. The real character of the most enlightened man on earth, if he is not enlightened by the Word and Spirit of God, is that given by the Apostle here, "HAVING HIS UNDERSTANDING DARKENED, BEING ALIENATED FROM THE LIFE OF GOD THROUGH THE IGNORANCE THAT IS IN HIM, BECAUSE OF THE BLINDNESS OF HIS HEART;" and the poorest, the most illiterate creature in the world, who never read anything, but the Bible, or who, perhaps, cannot read at all,—that poor sinner if brought to Christ, and reconciled unto God, through the blood of the covenant, has more real understanding than all the unconverted, learned men on earth; for his understanding is enlightened, he is "*turned from darkness to light, and from the power of Satan unto God,*" he has "*received forgiveness of sins, and inheritance among them that are sanctified, through faith, which is in Christ Jesus.*" Therefore, when the Apostle exhorts that "THEY HENCEFORTH WALK NOT AS OTHER GENTILES WALK, IN THE VANITY OF THEIR MINDS,"—he then gives the real and universal source of the wicked walk of men,—they have "THEIR UNDERSTANDING DARKENED, BEING ALIENATED FROM THE LIFE OF GOD THROUGH THE IGNORANCE THAT IS IN THEM, BECAUSE OF THE BLINDNESS OF THEIR HEARTS." You perceive the very same truth set forth in 2d Cor., chap. iv., 3, 4, in which the Apostle speaks of the state of those who do not know the Gospel, "*If our Gospel be hid, it is hid to them that are lost; in whom the god of this world hath blinded the minds of them which believe not, lest the light of the glorious Gospel of Christ, who is the image of God should shine unto them;*"—this is their natural state.—Now observe the converted state in the 6th verse, "*For God, who commanded the light to shine out of darkness, hath shined in our hearts, to give the light of the knowledge of the glory of God in the face of Jesus Christ.*" You perceive the difference here stated between the converted and unconverted man; the one lost—unbelieving—blinded by the devil—his understanding all dark; the other enlightened by the same power which "*commanded the light to shine out of darkness,*"—his understanding illumined by the Divine Spirit—the light that shines is, a "*light of knowledge,*"—the subject of that knowledge,—is "*the knowledge of the glory of God:*" and the knowledge is revealed, "*in the face of Jesus Christ,*"—in the glorious face of a crucified Redeemer, bowed in death on the cross for our sins, blotting out our transgressions, "*receiving us graciously, and loving us freely,*" forgiving all our iniquities, bringing us nigh to God by His precious blood, as a reconciled Father—then the sinner sees indeed the blessed light of eternal day, when "*the Sun of righteousness ariseth on his soul with healing on his wings.*" Mal. iv. 2.

But now mark the necessary result of the blindness and alienation from God here spoken of—"WHO, BEING PAST FEELING, HAVE GIVEN THEMSELVES OVER UNTO LASCIVIOUSNESS, TO WORK ALL UNCLEANNESS WITH GREEDINESS." Such is the result of this dark and blinded understanding. "BEING PAST FEELING,"—no sense of fear, or shame, or remorse—conscience stifled and hardened, so that it is only fear of consequences without, and no compunction from within, that holds them back from any sin. He mentions these peculiar sins;—but every sin is exactly the result of the same thing. The Apostle enumerates the various iniquities that deform the world, under the head of the fruits of the flesh, Gal. v. 19—21, and in Rom. i. 29—31. These are sins that are manifest—they "*work all uncleanness with greediness,*" or as the word is also "covetousness"—swallowing down iniquity as water—so Job saith—he "*drinketh in iniquity like water.*" Job xv. 16. All that man wishes for in his natural state is this, power to fulfil the desires of his flesh and his mind, whatever they are;—the greediness, the covetousness, the great ambition, of the natural mind is this,—"Oh, that I was able to do what I like to do!" This is the master-desire of the natural heart—and from the child that hates the restraint of his parent, of the servant that attends, or of the teacher that instructs him—to the man who hates the restraints of the laws of his country that will not allow him to act according to the wicked disposition of his mind—or who trembles at the law of opinion lest he should lose or injure his character, and so he should be consigned to contempt, which he fears more than he loves his lusts—I say, from the infant to the full grown man, the natural, the universal, the absorbing desire of the mind is, "Oh, that I was able to do what I like to do"!!!

But how widely different the principle of the true Christian! He knows he would like to commit sin—his natural, corrupt heart would follow after sin—but he has received a purer and higher principle—a holy and heavenly desire. He is now reconciled to his God, and at peace with Him—he remembers that the eyes of God are on him, and he says, "Oh! that my God may ever keep me from doing what my natural heart would like to do! Oh! that He may subdue my iniquity—conquer, and bring into subjection my wicked lusts! Oh! that my God may cast down every imagination that exalteth itself against the knowledge of Christ!" So, David, "*Oh that my ways were directed to keep thy statutes!*" Psalm cxix. 5. So, that, though man's laws never reach or touch the believer—yet God's law is written in his heart. So, this Apostle, "*I delight in the law of God after the inward man; But I see another law in my members, warring against the law of my mind, and bringing me into captivity to the law of sin, which is in my members. O wretched man that I am! who shall deliver me from the body of this death?*" Rom. vii. 22—24.

Hence, the conflict of the believer—hence the walk of the believer—hence his strength to mortify his corrupt affections. Hence the exhortations in the Bible—to mortify his members—to crucify the flesh. Hence the struggle in the believer; there is a deep struggle. The warfare commences from the time he is brought to his God—and against whom?—against himself. You see, the unregenerate "*who being past feeling have given themselves over unto lasciviousness, to work all uncleanness with greediness.*" But, saith the Apostle to the believers, "*Ye have not so learned Christ.*" We shall see hereafter what this means.

I trust the Lord will teach us these lessons—sanctify His blessed instruction—and seal it to our souls. Think of these truths, dear friends!

And now, let us review this—let us consider our place; whatever that place be in which the Lord has been pleased to appoint our lot—Let us glorify him there with our body and spirit which are His—Let us commit ourselves—our souls and bodies to Him in well doing—Let us wait on Him, "*As the eyes of servants look unto the hand of their masters; as the eyes of a maiden unto the hand of her mistress; so let our eyes wait on our God.*" Ps. cxxiii. 2.

Let us consider well whether we are yet in darkness or brought into the light. If indeed "*we are children of the light and of the day let us not sleep as do others, but let us watch and be sober.*" 1st Thess. v. 5, 6. "*Let us lay aside every weight, and the sin that doth so easily beset us, and let us run with patience the race that is set before us, looking unto Jesus.*" Heb. xii. 1, 2.

And if we are "*looking to Jesus,*" let us not walk as those who know Him not; let us manifest the difference in our principles—our state—and our hopes by our conduct. Let us remember, it is only by our works that we can prove we are the servants of God—works do not make the sinner a servant of God, but they prove that he is a servant of God; it is grace, washing him in the blood of Christ—covering him in the righteousness of Christ, the Spirit testifying of Jesus in his heart, this makes him a son by adoption and grace; but we can only prove ourselves children of God, by loving and serving our Lord and Heavenly Father.

THIRTY-THIRD LECTURE.

EPHESIANS IV.—20, 21, 22, 23, 24.

"But ye have not so learned Christ; if so be that ye have heard him, and have been taught by him, as the truth is in Jesus: that ye put off, concerning the former conversation, the old man, which is corrupt according to the deceitful lusts; and be renewed in the spirit of your mind; and that ye put on the new man, which after God is created in righteousness and true holiness."

It has been universally admitted by all persons professing to call themselves Christians, that the wickedness of the human heart and of human conduct ought to be corrected by true religion; and this is indeed the very principle on which men affect, even at this very day, to make light of the doctrines of religion. "Because," they say, "since it is on all hands agreed, that people ought to live a holy and godly life, and that religion ought to produce good works, we should all unite in that practical point," as they call it, "in which we are agreed, namely, that religion ought to produce good works, and not dispute about doctrines in which we are not agreed." This is one of the delusions of the devil, by which all true religion is sought to be subverted under the name of Christian peace and Christian charity.

But, although all men who call themselves Christians agree in this, that good works ought to be the fruit of true religion, yet, they do not agree with God's Word in this principle, that there is but one means of producing these good works. They do not agree, that these good works can be produced alone by good principles, and that these good principles can only be such, as are given to us in the Word of the living God. Therefore we never can admit, that we are to assent to the opinion of ungodly men, that good works are to be the result of true religion, and yet abandon the only principle on which these works can be produced, namely, the doctrines of truth as they are revealed in the Gospel.

Nothing is more absurd than for a man to suppose, that, as long as men hold false principles, they can produce good fruits; therefore we have to contend for two things, we have to contend, first for principles, and then, we have to contend for the fruits of these principles.

Nothing can more clearly illustrate this than the passage from which our Lecture commences this day. The Apostle shows, as we have seen in our preceding Lecture, that those who believed in Jesus were all one body, united together, under one head, Christ Jesus, and because they are so, he presses upon them the consequent obligations. "*This, I say, therefore, and testify in the Lord.*"

You see as we proved that he draws the inference with respect to their conduct—that they should not walk as other Gentiles walk, from the premises he had laid down, namely, their position, their union with Christ, and with each other in Christ. "*This I say, therefore, and testify in the Lord, that ye henceforth walk not as other Gentiles walk.*" Then he shows how they, the Gentiles walked, "*in the vanity of their mind, having the understanding darkened, being alienated from the life of God, through the ignorance that is in them, because of the blindness of their hearts, who, being past feeling, have given themselves over unto lasciviousness, to work all uncleanness with greediness.*" This is his description of the Gentile world. Now observe the contrast which he presses on the minds of his believing brethren at Ephesus, "BUT" saith he, 20 v., "YE HAVE NOT SO LEARNED CHRIST;"—he does not say, ye have not so learned the law, because the law could give them no help whatever against the sins of the Gentiles. The law as the Apostle saith "*was weak through the flesh.*" Rom. viii. 3. The Jews who had learned the law were not strengthened by the law against practising the sins of the Gentiles; on the contrary, it is the Lord's complaint of them, "*they were mingled among the heathen, and learned their works.*" Psa. cvi. 35. So he does not say, "Ye have not so learned the law," he does not say, "ye have not so learned your duty to God," because the knowledge of our duty will never enable us to perform that duty; but he says, "YE HAVE NOT SO LEARNED CHRIST;"—as much as to say, that is the only means by which you can be kept from following the conduct of the unconverted world.

And so it is, we never can have the course of our conduct changed unless our hearts are renewed again by the Spirit, "*created anew in Christ Jesus*;" we never can serve God till we are made his servants, made "*children of God by faith in Christ Jesus.*" Gal. iii. 26. Therefore he says, "YE HAVE NOT SO LEARNED CHRIST," because the knowledge of Christ is the only means by which you can be delivered from the ungodly walk of an ungodly world. We never then can admit the principle, that doctrines, the only principles of virtue, are not to be contended for, and that certain practical duties constitute true religion. We must contend for *principle*, both in others and in ourselves; for if we would cultivate fruit, let us remember, it can only be produced by making the tree what it ought to be; if we would produce any fruit unto God, it only can be by being grafted into Christ: so our blessed Lord himself tells us, "*As the branch cannot bear fruit of itself, except it abide in the vine, no more can ye except ye abide in me.*" Therefore he saith, "YE HAVE NOT SO LEARNED CHRIST, IF SO BE YE HAVE HEARD HIM, AND HAVE BEEN TAUGHT BY HIM AS THE TRUTH IS IN JESUS." That is to say—As surely as ye have "LEARNED CHRIST," As surely as ye have been "TAUGHT BY HIM AS THE TRUTH IS IN JESUS," so surely a vast and mighty change from the principles, the life and conversation of the Gentiles is, and must be, produced in you. He then proceeds to show what instruction is to be derived from the truth as it is in Jesus; namely, v. 22, "THAT YE PUT OFF, CONCERNING THE FORMER CONVERSATION, THE OLD MAN, WHICH IS CORRUPT, ACCORDING TO THE DECEITFUL LUSTS." This is the description of the natural heart of every one of us, which is to be put off,—v. 23, 24, "AND BE RENEWED IN THE SPIRIT OF YOUR MIND, AND THAT YE PUT ON THE NEW MAN, WHICH, AFTER GOD IS CREATED IN RIGHTEOUSNESS AND TRUE HOLINESS."

You see here the lesson that is derived from the knowledge of Jesus,—"THAT YE PUT OFF, CONCERNING THE FORMER CONVERSATION, THE OLD MAN," that is, that ye put off, concerning your former habits in your unconverted state, which were the same as those of all unconverted men;—the fulfilling of your natural evil propensities whatever they be—"THAT YE PUT OFF, CONCERNING YOUR FORMER CONVERSATION, THE OLD MAN."

The "OLD MAN" is called in Scripture by various other names; —sometimes, it is called "*The flesh,*" as for instance in Galatians v. 17, "*The flesh lusteth against the Spirit, and the Spirit against the flesh, and these are contrary, the one to the other, so that ye cannot do the things that ye would.*"

Sometimes it is called "*the carnal mind,*" as in Romans viii. 7, "*The carnal mind is enmity against God, for it is not subject to the law of God, neither indeed can be.*"

Sometimes it is called "*The natural man,*" as in 1st Cor. ii. 14, 15, "*The natural man receiveth not the things of the Spirit of God; for they are foolishness unto him, neither can he know them; because they are spiritually discerned.*" Here it is called

"THE OLD MAN." "THAT YE PUT OFF, CONCERNING THE FORMER CONVERSATION THE OLD MAN," that is, your own natural disposition, the natural corrupt inclinations of your own wicked heart. That is—If ye have learned Christ, If ye have been taught of Jesus, this is the lesson ye have learned, that ye put this off.

Now, there is a sense in which "the old man" is completely and forever put off by the believer: and there is a sense in which the "old man" is to be put off every day. These are two importan points for us to attend to. There is, I say, a sense in which "the old man" is put off completely and forever by the believer. This subject I have entered into very often at length, I shall therefore only now call your attention to it to-day, by reminding you of a passage in Romans vi., on which we dwelt so much at large, and in which the Apostle says, "*We are buried with him by baptism into death; that, like as Christ was raised from the dead by the glory of the Father, even so we also, should walk in newness of life; for if we have been planted together in the likeness of his death, we shall be also in the likeness of his resurrection, knowing this, that our old man,*" (observe now) "*is crucified with him, that the body of sin might be destroyed, that henceforth we should not serve sin. For he that is dead is freed from sin.*" Rom. vi. 4—7. In that sense, "the old man" is crucified with Christ, the body of sin is destroyed, that is, all the sins of the believer, all the guilt and corruption of his sinful nature, all the condemnation and curse due to his iniquity, is put away forever with respect to its power to condemn his soul; all his iniquity, past, present, and to come, is cancelled forever on the cross of Christ: Christ "*bare our sins in his own body on the tree.*" 1st Pet. ii. 24; and in that sense he has "*finished transgression, and made an end of sin;*" —we are reconciled to God—"*The blood of Jesus Christ his Son cleanseth us from all sin.*" 1st John i. 7—in that sense, as the Apostle says, "*the old man is crucified with him, the body of sin is destroyed;*" in that sense, we are to "*reckon ourselves dead indeed unto sin.*" Rom. vi. 11. This is a blessed refuge for the believer, so that, though I feel my sinful, corrupt heart—my vile, wicked, carnal, earthly affections—my rebellious will, although I feel these things working in me, and struggling in me against God's will, and lusting within to turn my heart from God continually, to this vile earth,—though I feel these things in myself,—and therefore feel myself to be a poor, vile, helpless, sinful worm, unfit to lift up my eyes to God, yet it is my privilege by faith, to look out of sin and self to Jesus, and to rest on Jesus whose precious "*blood cleanseth from all sin:*" and I therefore can "*pour out my heart before him,*" because "*God is a refuge for me.*" Psalm lxii. 8, and I therefore can bring all my sins, and pour out at His feet, those sins and that wickedness that I could not acknowledge to any fellow-sinner—those sins that I feel in my own wicked heart, —I can pour them all out at the feet of my blessed Lord and Saviour, because He is a Refuge for me, because He is the Salvation of my soul; therefore I may count my body of sin and death, dead with Jesus;—therefore, I may say with the Apostle, "*God forbid that I should glory, save in the cross of our Lord Jesus Christ, by whom the world is crucified unto me, and I unto the world.*" Gal. vi. 14.

Therefore I say, there is a sense in which the old man is put off forever—made an end of—dead with Christ,—he has no power whatever, with all his working and struggling, to condemn the sinner; because "*there is no condemnation to them that are in Christ Jesus, who walk not after the flesh, but after the Spirit.*" Rom. viii. 1. He may fight and rage, as he does continually within, and Satan may take advantage of his dispositions and propensities as he does, to tempt us, but still, it is the privilege of the believer to say, "*This is the victory that overcometh the world, even our faith,*" 1st John v. 4, and to say, "*The life that I now live in the flesh, I live by the faith of the Son of God, who loved me, and gave himself for me.*" Gal. ii. 20. It is his privilege thus to look unto Jesus, still to believe and trust, and still to hope, in spite of sin and self, that none shall pluck him out of the hand of his Lord and Saviour: for He saith of His sheep, "*I give unto them eternal life; and they shall never perish, neither shall any pluck them out of my hand. My Father which gave them me is greater than all, and none is able to pluck them out of my Father's hand. I and my Father are one.*" John x. 28, 29.

But now there is another sense in which the old man is never entirely put off, and in which he is to be put off every day—I say, though he is completely made an end of, as to his *power to condemn*, he is not made an end of in the corrupt workings of our own sinful hearts; therefore the Apostle shows them what they have learned from Christ if they are "TAUGHT BY HIM AS THE TRUTH IS IN JESUS;" "THAT YE PUT OFF, CONCERNING THE FORMER CONVERSATION, THE OLD MAN WHICH IS CORRUPT ACCORDING TO THE DECEITFUL LUSTS, AND BE RENEWED IN THE SPIRIT OF YOUR MIND." Now, observe—you know he had told his believing brethren, as we have seen, that they were "*blessed with all spiritual blessings in heavenly places in Christ.*" chap. i. 3. He had told them, that they had "*obtained an inheritance in Christ Jesus, being predestinated, according to the purpose of him who worketh all things, after the counsel of his own will.*" chap. i. 11. He had told them, that they "*who were sometimes afar off, were made nigh by the blood of Christ,*" chap. ii. 13, that they were "*no more strangers and foreigners, but fellow-citizens with the saints and of the household of God, built upon the foundation of the apostles and prophets, Jesus Christ himself being the chief corner-stone.*" chap. ii. 19, 20. He had told them, that "*they were builded together for an habitation of God, through the Spirit;*" v. 21; therefore, observe the state in which they were —"*kept by the power of God, through faith unto salvation.*" 1st Pet. i. 5.

Yet, he exhorts them, on this very ground—if they had learned Christ, "IF SO BE THEY HAD BEEN TAUGHT BY HIM, AS THE

TRUTH IS IN JESUS;" to "PUT OFF, CONCERNING THE FORMER CONVERSATION, THE OLD MAN, WHICH IS CORRUPT, ACCORDING TO THE DECEITFUL LUSTS." Therefore, I say, in every one of these men—these saints at Ephesus—this "OLD MAN," as it is called, that is, this natural corrupt heart existed; and they were called on, every day, to put it off. And there is not one of you who believes the Gospel of Christ, who does not feel that it is in yourselves—as it is in every one of you. It is a subject of grief—it is a burthen and trial to you; and you have often learned, by fatal experience, the workings of this corrupt "old man." He says, you see, it "IS CORRUPT, ACCORDING TO THE DECEITFUL LUSTS." Now, that is the statement of inspiration, the old man "IS CORRUPT." We have all our lusts in our hearts, and they are all naturally "*deceitful above all things, and desperately wicked*," and we do not know their iniquity, we are not aware of their deceits; we are tempted and tried in various ways; and the deceitful lusts of our heart are drawn out in ways that we have not anticipated, and by temptations that we never thought of. One man is tempted to one iniquity, another to another, and they find evil inclinations arise, as temptations are presented to them—inclinations in their own sinful hearts, to yield to these temptations whatever they be. There are temptations to various sins, covetousness—self-righteousness—pride—anger—ambition—vanity—vain glory—impurity—intemperance—and excess of various kinds; we are tempted to these and countless other sins, in various ways, and as temptations are presented, we find the inclinations in ourselves to give way to them; and according as Satan sees our peculiar points of natural corruption, and where our hearts are most easily tempted and deceived, there Satan is sure to ply us with temptations, just exactly as a skilful sportsman lays his snare, or his trap to catch his game; or as a fisherman will bait his hook or tie his fly, in whatever way he thinks most likely to allure the fish it is his object to take, so will Satan bait his hook to catch us, or he will lay his trap, or his snare, to deceive us in whatever way he thinks he is most likely to entice us, that we may not see him and be deceived. So saith David of him and his emissaries, "*He lieth in wait secretly as a lion in his den: he lieth in wait to catch the poor: he doth catch the poor, when he draweth him into his net. He croucheth, and humbleth himself, that the poor may fall by his strong ones.*" Psalm x. 9, 10. Therefore our great need of the armor of which we read in the 6th chapter of this Epistle, and the great blessing, as the Apostle saith, that we be not "*ignorant of his devices.*" 2nd Cor. ii. 11,—otherwise we are entrapped before we are aware, and know not until we find ourselves caught in some snare by Satan. The old man is "CORRUPT ACCORDING TO THE DECEITFUL LUSTS." If sin was presented to us by Satan in its own natural, hideous shape, we would start back from the monster. The devil knows this well; just exactly as if the trap were presented without any bait to the bird or the wild beast, they would run away from it; so, if sin was presented to us in its naked deformity, without some lure for our "DECEITFUL LUSTS," we would run away, we would avoid it. When the trap is covered or baited with something that the animal likes, then it is caught:—so it is with us;—the sin is hid, the end of sin—the evil of sin—the deformity—the bitterness—the remorse—the curse of sin, is hid from us, we do not see—we do not suspect, it: something is presented to allure and to entice us, and so, the devil gains an advantage over us. He told our fallen mother, "*You shall not surely die.*" He concealed death—expulsion from paradise—the misery—the curse—the ruin of herself, her husband, and their posterity, from her view—and he only presented to her the fruit, "*good for food, and pleasant to the eyes, and to be desired to make one wise.*" Gen. iii. 6. Which of you who knows the Gospel of Christ, who has not fallen a hundred times, not, perhaps through mercy, into sins and iniquities that would expose you to man's judgment or the penalty of human laws, but who among you has not fallen in your own heart, and been wounded in your own consciences, and heavily afflicted under the sense and burthen of sin? This is "THE OLD MAN, WHICH IS CORRUPT, ACCORDING TO THE DECEITFUL LUSTS," that continually harasses us and draws us aside. Consider this, and think with what bitter triumph the enemy of our souls rejoices if he can allure us into snares and evils. And therefore you see the exhortation of the Apostle, "THAT YE PUT OFF, CONCERNING THE FORMER CONVERSATION, THE OLD MAN, WHICH IS CORRUPT, ACCORDING TO THE DECEITFUL LUSTS, AND BE RENEWED IN THE SPIRIT OF YOUR MIND, AND THAT YE PUT ON THE NEW MAN, WHICH AFTER GOD IS CREATED IN RIGHTEOUSNESS AND TRUE HOLINESS."

If these are great and solemn duties—let us never forget how they are to be performed;—"YE HAVE NOT SO LEARNED CHRIST. IF SO BE YE HAVE HEARD HIM, AND HAVE BEEN TAUGHT BY HIM, AS THE TRUTH IS IN JESUS." There is no use in pressing duties on others or on ourselves, no exhortation will be efficacious to help us in the discharge of them, unless we have the means prepared by God, and use those means which the Lord prescribes, and with which He supplies us:—and you see the mighty instrument—"THE TRUTH AS IT IS IN JESUS." What is the power by which to overcome the malice of the devil? Only the Lord Jesus Christ. So the Apostle John says in the Apocalypse, speaking of the brethren whom Satan accuseth day and night before God, "*They overcame him by the blood of the Lamb, and by the word of his testimony.*" Rev. xii. 11. We shall see—if we are permitted to consider that beautiful chapter, the 6th, in which the whole armor of God is presented to the Christian to take for defence against his foe,—we shall see, that every part of that armor is only another name for Christ. "*Having your loins girt about with truth.*" What is truth? The Lord Jesus Christ,—"*I am the way and the truth, and the life.*" John xiv. 6. "*The breast-plate of righteousness.*" What is that? Christ—"*The Lord our righteousness.*'

Jer. xxiii. 6. "*Your feet shod with the preparation of the Gospel of peace.*" What is that? Christ—"*He is our peace.*" chap. ii. 14. "*Take the helmet of salvation.*" What is our salvation? Christ—"*Behold God is my salvation.*" Isa. xii. 2. "*And the sword of the Spirit, which is the word of God.*" Who is the Word? Christ—John i. 1. He is the Word, and the power of the Scripture is in the revelation of Him. "*Above all, taking the shield of faith, wherewith ye shall be able to quench all the fiery darts of the wicked one:*" Faith in whom, but in Christ as our Redeemer? The only way to conquer our sin, or our enemy, is to take the shield of faith; to say thus, "True, I am guilty, I am such a vile sinner, my spirit trembles under the power of this sin, or this lust or corruption, but I fly to my Lord and Saviour, I rest beneath the cross of my Lord and Master, I come to my Redeemer and lean on Him, I will '*come up from the wilderness leaning on my beloved.*' Satan tempts me into evil, and then charges me with it, he draws me into sin, and then makes sin an accusation against my conscience, to turn me away from Christ; but I will meet Satan with Christ—I will take Christ by faith, and meet the foe—I will resist the devil in the strength of my Lord and Master." And so, when the Apostle here exhorts to put off the old man, and speaks of the guilt of the Gentiles, who were walking in darkness, he says, "YE HAVE NOT SO LEARNED CHRIST:"—as much as to say, This is the power whereby alone you can be able to conquer your sins or yourselves, and to fly from the sins of those who know not His salvation.

And thus, dear friends, you see that the Lord, by the riches of His mercy, overrules the various evils and corruptions of His people, to teach them more of His own love, otherwise we never could comprehend the grace or the love of Christ. It is in dangerous diseases we learn the skill of the physician, and it is in the trials and temptations of the world, the flesh, and the devil, that we learn the character and glory of our Heavenly Physician. The Lord overrules even the workings of sin in us to make Himself more precious to our souls, and to teach us deeper experimental lessons of His power, faithfulness, truth and love, and so to draw forth from us more and more of love to our Lord and Master.

Therefore, what need we have to watch and pray that we may learn more and more of Christ, that Satan may have no advantage over us! If, in our temptations we come to Christ, bring all our inward trials, conflicts and sins by faith to Christ, Satan shall have no power against us. Let us therefore bring "THE OLD MAN, WHICH IS CORRUPT, ACCORDING TO THE DECEITFUL LUSTS," to Christ. Let us cast him down, as it were, at the feet of Jesus, and say to him thus,

"Ah, thou art crucified!—Thou wicked heart—thou vile nature,—thou corrupt, rebellious will—ye grovelling affections, earthly, sensual, devilish—although I feel you all within, a body of sin and death—yet Christ hath made an end of you—you shall never condemn me—you were all hung on the cross with Christ, there you are crucified, dead with Him, who died to bear the curse you have brought on my soul. True, I feel your power within, but that power cannot extend to condemn my soul, I fly to my Lord and Saviour. '*He that believeth on him is not condemned.*' John iii. 18,—as I receive from his salvation pardon for your guilt, so shall I gain strength to stand against your power: '*Nay, in all these things we are more than conquerors through him that loved us.*' Rom. viii. 37."

Thus, though we are tried and afflicted with sins and corruptions, if we bring them to Christ, and cast them on Christ, we feel their power conquered in the strength of Jesus—so saith the Apostle, chap. vi. 10, "*Be strong in the Lord, and in the power of his might,*"—thus we learn more to feel what a privilege it is for a sinner, to be able to know that he has such a precious Saviour as this, one who is "*able to save them to the uttermost that come unto God by him.*" Heb. vii. 25, and of whom he can say with the Apostle, "*I can do all things through Christ which strengtheneth me.*" Phil. iv. 13.

But he not only says, "THAT YE PUT OFF THE OLD MAN, WHICH IS CORRUPT, ACCORDING TO THE DECEITFUL LUSTS," but he adds, "AND BE RENEWED IN THE SPIRIT OF YOUR MIND." Now, they had been renewed, they had been born again, for "*Whosoever believeth that Jesus is the Christ, is born of God.*" 1st John v. 1. And so the Apostle says to these Ephesians, "*We are his workmanship, created in Christ Jesus unto good works.*" chap. ii. 10, and though they were so, yet he says, "BE RENEWED IN THE SPIRIT OF YOUR MIND;" as the Apostle says in another place, "*Though our outward man perish, yet the inward man is renewed day by day.*" 2nd Cor. iv. 16. We need refreshing grace and strength every day. As we require continually, daily nutriment, and nightly repose for our bodies, so do we need daily spiritual food, "The Bread of life;"—daily drink, "The Fountain of living waters;"—daily air, the breath of the Holy Spirit of God—daily repose, rest in Jesus:—we want these all for our souls every day, and we cannot do without them; and none but those who are renewed in spirit, know their need of daily renewal. So David, "*He restoreth my soul.*" Ps. xxiii. 3.

This truth is fully and beautifully set forth in our Collect for the Sunday after Christmas Day:—

> "Almighty God, who hast given us thy only-begotten Son to take our nature upon him, and as at this time to be born of a pure Virgin,—Grant that we being regenerate, and made thy children by adoption and grace, may daily be renewed by thy Holy Spirit, through the same our Lord Jesus Christ, who liveth and reigneth with thee and the self same Spirit, ever one God, world without end. Amen."

Satan tries by all means to hinder us from these blessings; and just as an enemy who thought he had it in his power to starve us, would use his best efforts to do so, thus our foe tries to hinder us from feeding on the "*Bread that cometh down from heaven, and giveth life unto the world.*" John vi. 33. He tries to draw us aside from "*The Fountain of living waters, to hew out to our-*

selves cisterns, broken cisterns that can hold no water." Jer. ii. 13. He tries to hinder us from "*entering into his rest.*" Heb. iv. 1. Therefore the constant need of the exhortation, "BE RENEWED IN THE SPIRIT OF YOUR MINDS," look for, aim at continually, watch and pray for the constant renewal of the Holy Ghost in His power and influences on your heart and spirit.

What a comfort the believer has, when he remembers, that this is not a thing to be attained by his own struggling;—the Lord is engaged in it for him; the Lord—his covenant God, has undertaken it for him, and will carry him through all his trials, conflicts, and difficulties, till he brings him at last to the haven where he would be. But the Apostle explains the effects of this renewal; he shows what he means by it, "AND THAT YE PUT ON THE NEW MAN, WHICH AFTER GOD IS CREATED IN RIGHTEOUSNESS AND TRUE HOLINESS." The knowledge of Jesus teaches two lessons. To put off the old man—and to put on the new man. A true change of mind must necessarily superinduce a change of habits. The sins of the natural disposition—the old Adam—the fruits of the flesh, are to be put off. The holy will of the Lord—the new man—Christ, and the fruits of the Spirit, are to be put on. So the Apostle says, in Romans xiii. 14, "*put ye on the Lord Jesus Christ, and make not provision for the flesh, to fulfil the lusts thereof.*" So here, "PUT ON THE NEW MAN, WHICH AFTER GOD IS CREATED IN RIGHTEOUSNESS AND TRUE HOLINESS."

Now the Apostle says, "PUT ON THE NEW MAN," although they *had* put him on, because the same Apostle teaches us, Gal. iii. 27, "*As many of you as have been baptized into Christ, have put on Christ;*" and yet he says here, "PUT ON THE NEW MAN." For just as the old man, in the sense I have mentioned to you, was forever crucified and made an end of, yet they were called upon to "PUT OFF THE OLD MAN;" so they had been united by faith to the Lord Jesus Christ, and had put on Christ; yet they are called on here to "PUT ON THE NEW MAN." For as there is a sense in which sin is made an end of,—in which the believer is severed forever from the "old man," yet is called daily to watch and fight against him. So there is a sense in which he is made one with Christ forever, yet is daily called to put on the Lord Jesus, or the "new man:" "PUT ON THE NEW MAN, WHICH AFTER GOD IS CREATED IN RIGHTEOUSNESS AND TRUE HOLINESS."—He says, "PUT ON THE NEW MAN,"—that means, put him on as a robe. This is an image frequently used in Scripture, to indicate the completeness with which the gift or attribute belongs to a person. It is used in reference to God Himself. "*The Lord reigneth, he is clothed with majesty. The Lord is clothed with strength, wherewith he hath girded himself.*" Psa. cxiii. 1. So the Prophet saith, "*He hath clothed me with the garments of salvation; he hath covered me with a robe of righteousness as a bridegroom decketh himself with his ornaments, and as a bride adorneth herself with her jewels.*" Isa. lxi. 10. So the Apostle applies it in several places to putting on Christ—Which is used for putting on His righteousness, as by the

Apostle for himself, Phil. iii. 9, by our Lord to the Church at Laodicea, Rev. iii. 18. But it seems here, as well as in Rom. xiii. 14, quoted above, to mean that you are to put Him on, in your practical walk and conversation; we might say as the whole habit of your life. We are called on therefore, to "*abhor that which is evil, and cleave to that which is good.*" Rom. xii. 9; we are called on, therefore, to mortify our corrupt members and affections, to "*deny ungodliness and worldly lusts.*" Tit. ii. 12; not to "*yield our members as instruments of unrighteousness unto sin.*" Rom. vi. 13. This implies a continual solicitation on the part of sin, as there is both from temptation without and corruption within,—we are solicited to do what is wrong by the world, the flesh, and the devil. There is a crowd without us, saying, "Come with us, enjoy yourselves with us," and there is a crowd of sins within ready to lend an ear, and to go. But we must deny—we must resist—we must remember him who saith, "*My son, if sinners entice thee, consent thou not.*" Prov. i. 10. We must "PUT OFF THE OLD MAN, WHICH IS CORRUPT ACCORDING TO THE DECEITFUL LUSTS, AND PUT ON THE NEW MAN, WHICH AFTER GOD IS CREATED IN RIGHTEOUSNESS AND TRUE HOLINESS." We must walk in practical godliness; "*yield not your members,*" saith the Apostle, "*as instruments of unrighteousness unto sin, but yield yourselves unto God, as those who are alive from the dead, and your members as instruments of righteousness unto God.*" Rom. vi. 13. So the believer should say, "Let me yield my tongue to God, let me no more speak in the ways of sin, let me not give my tongue to wickedness. Let me yield my hands, my feet, to God,—let me yield my eyes to God,—let me pray, "*Turn away mine eyes from beholding vanity, and quicken thou me in thy way.*" Psa. cxix. 37;—let me yield all my members to God, for "*I am not my own, I am bought with a price.*" Let me therefore "*glorify God in my body, and in my spirit, which are God's;*" 1 Cor. vi. 20; let me "PUT ON THE NEW MAN, WHICH AFTER GOD IS CREATED IN RIGHTEOUSNESS AND TRUE HOLINESS;" or "holiness of the truth," as in the Greek. This seems to refer to v. 21, "IF YE HAVE BEEN TAUGHT AS THE TRUTH IS IN JESUS—PUT ON THE NEW MAN, WHICH AFTER GOD IS CREATED IN RIGHTEOUSNESS AND HOLINESS OF THE TRUTH." The "TRUTH AS IT IS IN JESUS" brings forth the righteousness and holiness that are derived from it and belong to it—true practical godliness of life,—true separation from the world of sin, and true devotedness to God.

The difference between holiness and righteousness appears to be this. Righteousness is the practical fulfilment of the law of God. Holiness is a state of separation unto God, a state of devotedness to God. As the vessels of the temple were said to be holy, because they were devoted, consecrated to God,—so believers are said to be holy, because they are sanctified in Christ, as I explained to you fully when on the term saint—sanctified in Christ Jesus, and set apart unto God; and therefore, as we are set apart to God if we be his people, let us walk in the ways of God, "IN RIGHTEOUSNESS AND TRUE HOLINESS." Righteousness of life is the effect of holiness unto God.

The Apostle proceeds afterwards to explain the practical details of the righteousness and true holiness in which believers are to walk.

And now, dear friends, what need we have of continual exhortation on this subject! what need to have the blessed Word of God lying continually open before us, showing us, not only our sin, but the glorious remedy for sin! Oh, what a blessing that the Word of God does not come, like a rough, unskilful, unfeeling surgeon, to probe and to tear open the wounds of a guilty conscience, and to leave them then to bleed and fester unto death; but that, while with skilful hand it comes to probe the wound, it comes, too, like the good Samaritan, to pour in balm, and oil, and wine, to heal it! We can have no earthly sin, trouble, sorrow, which, if we come to the Lord Jesus Christ, the precious blood of Christ is not a sufficient balm to cure. Let us think of this; how precious is the balm of Immanuel's blood! Oh, may it be applied to our consciences! Let us pray that it may be applied to our hearts, that we may be enabled to know the blessing of the Gospel of Jesus! that our hearts may "*rejoice in Christ Jesus, and have no confidence in the flesh,*" Phil. iii. 3,—and that thus we may feel ourselves "*strong in the Lord, and in the power of His might,*" chap. vi. 10,—and be made "*more than conquerors through Him who loved us.*" Rom. viii. 37.

May the Lord apply this to your heart and mine and sanctify it to us according to our several necessities! He knows our wants, and He is able to make His word efficacious to bless, to heal, and strengthen us—to enable us to live to Him who hath lived, and died, and risen again for us. To whom be glory and dominion forever and ever. Amen.

THIRTY-FOURTH LECTURE.

EPHESIANS IV.—25, 26, 27, 28.

"Wherefore, putting away lying, speak every man truth with his neighbor: for we are members one of another. Be ye angry, and sin not: let not the sun go down upon your wrath: Neither give place to the devil. Let him that stole steal no more: but rather let him labor, working with his hands the thing which is good, that he may have to give to him that needeth."

IN our last Lecture, you recollect the double exhortation given by the Apostle to his Ephesian brethren, from the 22nd to the

24th verse. The first—"*That ye put off, concerning the former conversation, the old man, which is corrupt according to the deceitful lusts;*" and the second—"*That ye put on the new man, which after God is created in righteousness and true holiness.*"

The Apostle now proceeds in the passage where we commence to-day, 25th verse, to explain his meaning, and he shows what they are to understand both by putting "*off the old man,*" and by putting "*on the new man.*" Therefore, let us look through these verses to the end of the chapter, and see the character of the "*old man,*" which the believer is called upon to put off,—Lying,—Vengeance,—Giving place to the Devil,—Stealing,—Uttering corrupt communication,—Grieving the Holy Spirit of God,—Bitterness,—Wrath,—Anger,—Clamor,—Evil-speaking,—Malice,—these are the characteristics of the "*old man,*" which the Apostle exhorts his brethren to put off.

Then again, let us observe the characteristics of the "*new man,*" of which he speaks, and we find, instead of Lying—Truth. Instead of Vengeance—Cessation from Wrath. Instead of giving place to the Devil—Not giving him any. In opposition to corrupt Communication, "*That which is good to the use of edifying, to minister grace unto the hearers.*" In opposition to Grieving the Holy Spirit of God, not to grieve or wound Him. In opposition to Bitterness, Wrath, Anger, Clamor, Evil-speaking, and Malice,—Kindness, Tender-heartedness, forgiveness of each other for their various wrongs;—"*Even as God for Christ's sake, hath forgiven you.*" v. 32.

Let me first call your attention to the principle which the Apostle ever maintains as the groundwork of these exhortations. You find this in the last verse. "*Even as God, for Christ's sake, hath forgiven you,*" so do ye. Always remember, that exhortations to the performance of moral duties are only addressed in the Apostolical Epistles, and can only be scripturally addressed to believers, as such. The Moral Law is indeed of equal obligation upon all. No unbelief—no rejection of God's Holy Word, can in the least exonerate from that obligation. The belief of the Gospel, while it can scarcely, in one sense, be said to add to an obligation which is, and must be, full and perfect on all mankind, yet in another sense, may be said to increase it, by adding the further obligation of love to Christ for His redemption. "*If ye love me keep my commandments,*" John xiv. 15,—and thus supplying the motive to obey.

But the Law to the unbeliever must ever come, not only with its obligation, but its curse. So it came to the Young Man, who was so blind and ignorant as to tell our Lord he had observed it from his youth, Mark x. 17—22. So to the Lawyer, who stood up to tempt our Lord, Luke x. 25—37. So must the Law ever be to man in his unregenerate state—and therefore it but blinds and deceives men, to exhort them to perform their duty as if they were servants of God, until they are first made servants of God by faith in the Lord Jesus Christ. We must call on men first to "*repent and believe the Gospel*," to flee to Him who "*hath redeemed us from the curse of the law.*" Gal. iii. 13. How absurd to exhort a man under sentence of death for his crimes, to discharge the duties of a good citizen! His first object must be to obtain pardon of his Sovereign—then we must press on him the duties of a citizen, when he is restored to the liberty and privileges of that state. So, it but tends to deceive and blind a man in his unregenerate state, to tell him that he can serve or please God. "*They that are in the flesh cannot please God*," Rom. viii. 8—that is the testimony of Scripture. Therefore the first point for our conscience is, to have it settled within, that we are believing in Jesus, and that faith in His salvation and love to Him is the motive which we acknowledge of obedience to God; not to purchase salvation from Him, but because of the salvation which is freely given to us through Christ Jesus, who has died to purchase it. Let us never forget this, my dear friends, for a moment: we cannot take one step in the Christian life, as I have often endeavored to impress on you, till our minds are enlightened and settled in that truth. No efforts to serve God on false principles are, or can be, but displeasing to Him. We must have the principles that God inculcates before we can pursue the conduct that God commands. Therefore, know your motives,—watch your motives, and carry those that are true, through all your conduct—your motives are the best test of your state in the sight of God.

Let us now consider the characteristics of the "*old man*" which are to be put off, and the principles of the "*new man*" which are to be put on by the believer.

"WHEREFORE, PUTTING AWAY LYING, SPEAK EVERY MAN TRUTH WITH HIS NEIGHBOR." Lying is the first characteristic of the "*old man*" mentioned here, and certainly it is one of the most indigenous and precocious vices, if I may use the expression, of the human heart. As certainly as the earth brings forth thorns and thistles, so certainly does the natural heart of man bring forth its innate corruptions, and lying is among the earliest seeds of sin that burst in the spring of life from the infant mind. "*The wicked are estranged*," saith the Psalmist, "*from the womb; they go astray as soon as they be born, speaking lies.*" Psa. lviii. 3. I dare say, that all here who are parents will agree with me, that this is one of the first vices we discover in the heart and conduct of our children. Lying is the necessary consequence of sin, it is the refuge of an accusing conscience from the fear of accountability to judgment. The child is conscious it does what is wrong, what it has been forbidden to do; it knows it is accountable to its parent, and it hopes to escape the penalty of its fault by concealment, therefore it tells a lie. The first thing Adam did, you know, was not indeed to tell a lie, but to *act* a lie. Instead of going, when he heard the voice of his God in the garden, instead of going to confess his sin, "Lord, I have sinned against Thee," he tried to conceal himself, "*I was afraid because I was naked, and I hid myself.*" Gen. iii. 10. That was a lie,—it was not because he was naked, but because he knew he had violated the commandment of his God, and he was afraid to meet his Judge.

But it is not only in concealing faults and sins that lying is evinced in our heart and conduct, but also in justifying ourselves, in palliating, and excusing the evils of which we are conscious, or even those of which we are convicted. We see this also in Adam, instead of acknowledging his sin when he was convicted of it, "*Hast thou eaten of the tree whereof I commanded thee, that thou shouldest not eat?*" Instead of at once acknowledging his sin, he justifies himself, and throws the blame on his wife, and through her on God. "*This woman whom thou gavest to be with me, she gave me of the tree, and I did eat.*" Gen. iii. 12. As much as to say, "I am not in fault,—I am not the person on whom the blame is to rest,—the woman gave me of it, and the fault rests immediately on her, and ultimately on you; for you gave me such a woman. "*The woman whom thou gavest to be with me, she gave me of the tree, and I did eat.*" It is thus with all his fallen posterity. In the concealment of our sins, in our self-justification, in the palliation of our offences, the principle of lying is pre-eminently exhibited in the natural heart and character of man. It is not only discoverable in our children, as we have seen, but in our servants, in all those who are placed in a state of accountability to persons whom they fear. It would be exactly the same in ourselves if we were placed in similar circumstances. If we were accountable to others, the very same principle would be manifested by us, in our natural character, although there is, no doubt, a diversity in this; as falsehood, however general, is not equally conspicuous in all. But Oh! what a common sin is lying throughout the whole world. Simulation, that is the pretence or affectation of what does not exist, is lying—Dissimulation, that is the concealment of what does exist, is lying. Every sort of artifice that is opposed to truth, whether in word or deed, may be justly termed lying. If this be so, how it shows that the intercourses of social life are carried on too generally in the world by a system of hypocrisy, falsehood, and deceit. The appearance of pleasure, where pleasure is a stranger to the heart—The affectation of enjoyment in the society of others, whose company or presence is not only joyless, but irksome—The ordinary intercourse that is carried on, as it were, in masquerade, in the world, among those who know not God, is discovered by these, the private detraction—the secret whisper—the slanderous report—the satirical inuendo—the unkind expression—the dark allusion—the malevolent hint,—as to persons whom we have met with a face of blandness and civility, perhaps with expressions of regard and friendship—all these things evince, with what a system of lying and deception the social intercourse of the world is carried on. This corresponds with the divine testimony, "*Full of envy, murder, debate, deceit, malignity, whisperers, backbiters, haters of God, despiteful, proud, boasters, inventors of evil things.*" Rom. i. 29, 30. So "*serving divers lusts and pleasures, living in malice and envy, hateful, and hating one another.*" Tit. iii. 3. Now consider this—think of it. Is it not so? There is not one sin of the heart of man which is more interwoven with its natural deceit, than that of lying. When we consider the evil that defiles us in this, we may well say, "*Who can tell how oft he offendeth? Oh, cleanse thou me from my secret faults.*" Psa. xix. 12.

Not to speak of the deliberate and intentional falsehoods which many persons tell without remorse, are there not innumerable "*white lies,*" "*harmless lies.*" Do we not hear these things continually? Do you not hear continually falsehoods glossed over with such names?—as the Church of Rome calls them, "officious lies, which hurt nobody."

But "PUTTING AWAY LYING," is the command of Scripture,—that is the "*old man,*" the corrupt nature. Let us remember this, my brethren, the least lie that you or I have ever told, and Oh! how many have we told!—the least lie that we ever told, would cast us into everlasting death if there were not another sin to be charged against us—and if God were to enter into judgment with us, unless Jesus had hung on the cross to save us from eternal ruin.

When then a person is brought to believe the Gospel of Jesus, his principles, as well as his conduct, are to be totally renewed and changed; not only wilful falsehoods, but also, the deceit—duplicity—hypocrisy—insincerity—hollow profession—the lying mockery of masquerade, in which the world walks, is to be put off from the servants of God. There is no sin which is more particularly specified through the Scripture as casting the soul into perdition, than lying. "*But the fearful and unbelieving, and the abominable, and murderers, and whoremongers, and sorcerers, and idolaters, and all liars, shall have their part in the lake that burneth with fire and brimstone, which is the second death.*" And again, "*And there shall in no wise enter into it, anything that defileth, neither whatsoever worketh abomination, or maketh a lie; but they which are written in the Lamb's book of life.*" Rev. xxi. 8, 27.

Let us then consider this, and see, not only that we cultivate, (if we be servants of God,) the spirit of truth, and avoid any departure from strict veracity, but that we also, in our life and conversation, evince that "*simplicity and godly sincerity,*"—that singleness of eye to truth in our life and conversation, which becometh those, and which we are expressly told must be the character of those, who are really the servants of God. Remember, that no determination to adhere, and no adherence to truth, can purchase for you eternal life. But remember, if you be servants of God, disciples of Him whose name is "FAITHFUL AND TRUE," Rev. xix. 11,—lying is to be put away from you, as a proof, one of the many proofs, that you are indeed the servants of God, as you profess to be.

"WHEREFORE, PUTTING AWAY LYING, SPEAK EVERY MAN TRUTH WITH HIS NEIGHBOR." I remember reading a story, when I was a child, with which, perhaps, some who hear me may be acquainted, but which struck me very forcibly even then as illustrating the deceit and wickedness of the human heart. It is a tale.

The tale was called "THE PALACE OF TRUTH." The writer describes a place into which every person who enters is bound by a certain spell, so that they speak actually the thoughts of their hearts, whatever they be, while, at the same time, they are not at all conscious of the power that influences them, or of the words they utter, but imagine they are saying what they would intend to say in the ordinary language of the duplicity or compliment of the world. Therefore, when friends meet friends, and relatives meet relatives, while they are carrying on the farce which in too many instances they do carry on in social life, expressing, as they imagine, regret or kindness, compliments or pleasure, they are really giving vent to the genuine feelings of their heart. When they are brought into the test of the palace of truth, the mask is there torn off, and all the vain fantastic mockery of kindness, of regard, or of affection, they had once professed, is now exchanged for the genuine expression of envy, malice, hatred, or disgust, and all the other passions which really possessed their breasts. Then they are manifested in their true character to each other, and consequently all these evil passions produce their natural result, in severing almost all the ties of social and domestic life. What a blessing is the truth expressed in the language of the Poet:—

> "Heaven's Sovereign saves all beings but Himself
> That hideous sight,—a naked human heart."

The believer has learned to feel in some degree the burthen and evil of his own heart, and he knows the necessity of hearing the Apostolical exhortation, "PUTTING AWAY LYING, SPEAK EVERY MAN TRUTH WITH HIS NEIGHBOR." And now mark the principle on which this is especially enforced by the Apostle. It is the spirit of Christian love, of union by faith and love with the Lord Jesus Christ and with each other, by which alone men can really learn to speak the truth in sincerity. "FOR," saith the Apostle, "WE ARE MEMBERS ONE OF ANOTHER:" we are united to Jesus, and united to one another in Jesus; therefore the principle of faith in Christ, and love to Christ, union with Him and with each other, is pressed throughout on the believer as the motive of his conduct, and therefore, "PUTTING AWAY LYING, SPEAK EVERY MAN TRUTH WITH HIS NEIGHBOR, FOR WE ARE MEMBERS ONE OF ANOTHER." As one member of our body will not hurt another member of our body, so, saith the Apostle, as we are all members of one body, united under one head, Christ Jesus, let us deal with truth, sincerity and love, one with the other. Consider this, then, "WHEREFORE, PUTTING AWAY LYING, SPEAK EVERY MAN TRUTH WITH HIS NEIGHBOR, FOR WE ARE MEMBERS ONE OF ANOTHER." How blessed are the genuine fruits of true Christianity, where those who bear the name are truly Christians, but when we see that the very fundamental truths of the Gospel—the only hope of man's salvation, are rejected, denied, or neglected by those who are called Christians, it is hopeless to expect the fruit. "*Do men gather grapes of thorns, or figs of thistles?*" Matt. vii. 16.

Another evil he mentions of the old man is anger, "BE YE ANGRY, AND SIN NOT; LET NOT THE SUN GO DOWN ON YOUR WRATH." You see, anger is an evil of the "*old man*," which is to be put off, and restraining anger is the "*new man*," which is to be put on. This is another corruption of the heart which we see so prominent in the character of children. When they are left unrestrained together, how soon they begin to quarrel and to contend with each other, how easily their angry passions are excited: we see it pre-eminently in them, for this reason, they have not the restraint over their tempers and passions that the laws of society, education, or fear of the opinion of others, may impose. But anger, wicked tempers, are not confined to children. What misery they excite in every family! Are there members of any family here who have not in some way experienced it? If you have not experienced it among the members of your own family, and your own immediate relatives and friends, surely, you have experienced it in yourselves—there is no one who has not experienced it in their own hearts. How easily are we excited to anger and revenge! Some are more amiable in their natural temper than others, as some are by nature more sincere and true, but there are few, if any, who are not excitable to anger; some are peculiarly irritable, some are provoked by things that do not produce any emotion in others, but anger is one of the corrupt indigenous principles which has its seeds more or less prolific in their growth and progress in the heart of every sinner. Now the natural propensity of every individual among us is, to indulge our anger,—and you will see persons where there is no restraint placed on them, where they are not afraid, they will give way to their wicked passions and tempers; but where restraint is placed on them, where they are afraid to show it, there it is quite the reverse. Now the Scripture does not admit the principle of outward restraint as the means of conquering sin—does not admit that wicked tempers are to be indulged when the eye of man beholds not—and to be concealed where character—fear of man—fear of the law—fear of reproach, subdue or compel them to be still. All the commands of Scripture bring the sinner before his God, teach him to feel, to think, to act, as in the presence of the Lord of Glory, there to regulate his conduct, and there to regulate his heart, "BE YE ANGRY, AND SIN NOT." Sin not as in the eye of men—but in the sight of God.

Persons differ on the exact interpretation of this verse; some imagine that it should be read interrogatively, thus—"Are ye angry?" as much as to say, "Can you be angry, and sin not? Can you be angry without sin?" Some persons imagine that it is, "BE YE ANGRY, AND SIN NOT," admitting, that there are circumstances in which you may be provoked to be angry, and can be angry without sin. This, I think, is the proper interpretation of it; there is such anger, a righteous anger, a just anger. "*God is angry with the wicked every day.*" Psa. vii. 11. The Lord Jesus represents Himself as being angry—"*The Master of the house being angry.*" Luke xiv. 21. It is the same word as in this passage. Righteous, holy indignation and anger, is a necessary part of real, solid, Christian duty. We ought to be angry at that which is displeasing to God, we ought to be angry at it in others, and more angry at it in ourselves, but "SIN NOT;" whenever anger exceeds that rule, namely, that it is a holy, just, and righteous displeasure against that which is wrong, there anger becomes sin, and even in that case we should watch that it does not lead to sin. It is righteous that a father should be angry at his disobedient child; it is righteous that a master should be angry at his disobedient servant; it is righteous that man should be displeased in the various relations of life at those things that are wrong, "BE YE ANGRY," but then, "SIN NOT." Take care, it does not lead you into practical transgression of the law of God,—take care it does not lead you into the transgression of the law of God in your own heart. If you are angry with sin, take care you are not angry with the sinner. "BE YE ANGRY, AND SIN NOT,"—this is a high standard. dear friends, and one which we feel far beyond our attainment; for alas, let us remember how often by this very sin we have brought on ourselves condemnation, eternal judgment, yea, a thousand, and ten thousand times. How often you and I should have been cast into hell for this sin, if God had dealt with us after our iniquities! How often anger has produced enmity, hatred, in our breasts against the individual who has provoked us, how often have they burned in our bosoms! How often have we committed murder in the Scriptural sense! Our hands may not be stained with blood, we may not have embrued them in the blood of a fellow-creature, as I trust none of us have, but what saith the Word of God? "*Whosoever hateth his brother is a murderer.*" 1st John iii. 15. If this be, as it surely is, the spiritual meaning of the Law, I suppose, there is not a single one in this room that has not, in the Scriptural sense, committed murder. How often have we been provoked and angry at an individual, and felt hatred towards that individual, though it might be but for a time, and although we would not murder, we would be glad he were dead out of our sight. Have we not felt so? I am sure I have; yea, and I am sure you have. How often in this Law have we sinned against God! Alas! what vile, wicked, ungodly, devilish tempers, there are in the natural heart! Oh! my friends, what need we have to receive continually strength and power from God, to restrain the corruptions of our hearts, even in this one sin. But look on a little, and see the rule the Apostle lays down for this in the last verse of this chapter, "*Be ye kind one to another, tender hearted, forgiving one another, even as God, for Christ's sake, hath forgiven you.*" You remember the parable of our Lord, by which He illustrates this principle. You recollect the servant that was brought to his Lord, "*who owed him ten thousand talents; but forasmuch as he had not to pay, his lord commanded him to be sold, and his wife and children, and all that he had, and payment to be made,"*—and you recollect that servant coming to his Lord, and asking him, "*have patience with me, and I will pay thee all,"*—though he undertook to do what he could not do, though he undertook to pay him what he could never discharge, "*The Lord of that servant was moved with compassion, and loosed him, and forgave him the debt.*" Then he went out, you recollect, "*and found one of his fellow-servants, who owed him a hundred pence, and he took him by the throat, saying, pay me that thou owest.*" His fellow-servant used the same expostulation and entreaty to him, "*have patience with me, and I will pay thee all; and he would not, but went and cast him into prison till he should pay the debt.*" And do you remember the remonstrance and judgment of his Lord against him? "*O thou wicked servant, I forgave thee all that debt, because thou desiredst me: shouldest not thou also have had compassion on thy fellow-servant, even as I had pity on thee? And his lord was wroth, and delivered him to the tormentors, till he should pay all that was due unto him. So,*" you see, our Lord adds, "*likewise shall my heavenly Father do also unto you, if ye from your hearts forgive not every one his brother their trespasses.*" Matt. xviii. 24–35.

Observe, this is the principle that the Lord keeps continually in view in the hearts of His people; you recollect in the Lord's prayer, "*forgive us our trespasses, as we forgive them that trespass against us.*"

Now do you suppose that forgiving others their trespasses is the condition on which God pardons ours? Never was a principle more false than that,—and it is the natural, corrupt principle of the human heart. I have heard that principle often professed on the bed of death. Often and often have sinners said to me, when I have asked them, what is the hope you have in going before God in expecting pardon for your sins? I have often received for answer, "I forgive all men, and am at peace with all the world." I have heard that melancholy expression a thousand times, they make a merit of pardoning others, by which they think to purchase forgiveness from God. Nothing can be more false; for if this were so, forgiveness could not be by the blood of the Lord Jesus. But it is charged by the Lord on the consciences of his believing people, as a test of their sincerity in coming to Him for pardon, "*forgive us our trespasses, as we forgive them that trespass against us,*"—that is, can you come to the Lord "*in spirit and truth,*" with the sense of the weight of ten thousand talents which you owe Him, on your soul? Can you come to Him, and ask Him for pardon, for that which your conscience tells you, you owe to Him, when you are cherishing some unforgiving principle in your heart to your fellow-sinner that owes you an hundred pence? There can be no sense of the depth and magnitude of our own debt to God, when we come to Him for pardon, there can be no sense of the magnitude of our debt, no genuine sincerity in seeking forgiveness, if our conscience tells us that we have come to ask God for the pardon of our own sins, with unforgiving tempers towards any of our fellow-sinners,—and therefore observe, the Lord puts this test on the consciences of men in that prayer.

Therefore, "BE YE ANGRY, AND SIN NOT." If you are excited, if your tempers are excited, if your passions are excited, if you are stirred up to indulge a wicked temper, beware how you cherish it—go to the Lord, take it to Him—"LET NOT THE SUN GO DOWN ON YOUR WRATH," go to your Lord for pardoning grace, bring your guilt, your debt of ten thousand talents, to the foot of the cross. See, what a mighty debt you are forgiven! what vast wickedness! what innumerable sins! See all that debt cancelled by the blood of the cross; and beware, lest your heart accuses you, and your conscience charges you with coming to God, with the mockery of seeking such pardon—of trusting in such forgiveness—when you do not forgive the hundred pence your fellow-sinner owes to you. Yes, dear friends, there is nothing that leads us to estimate the provocations we receive from our fellow-sinners aright so much, as this one reflection—

"Alas, why should I be so angry? Let me think of the provocations wherewith I have provoked my God!"

Let us remember this. In every relation of life, whatever injuries we receive from our fellow-sinners, let us remember, what is all that man can do to us, compared with the provocations with which we have provoked God! How this would humble us—subdue our heart—bring us down to the dust, and enable us to remember what we are, what a Saviour we have—what a God! "*who pardoneth iniquity, transgression and sin, and retaineth not his anger forever, because he delighteth in mercy.*" Mic. vii. 18.

"NEITHER GIVE PLACE TO THE DEVIL." Do not allow the devil any place in your mind—give him no quarter—grant him not a moment's admission or entertainment in your breast. As in contending against an enemy who was attacking you, you would not let him gain an inch of advantage against you,—as you would not let him plant his foot on a spot of ground where he could have a position of superiority,—as you would not let him into your house, or to your door, or give him a place where he could have an opportunity to wound or injure you—so, remember, you have an enemy that is continually attacking you, "*going about as a roaring lion, seeking whom he may devour.*" 1st Pet. v. 8,—do not give him a point to stand on: if he gains entrance into your hearts, thoughts, imaginations, he will have the advantage over you; do not let him in for a moment. Perhaps you do not understand how this can be done. When thoughts come into your minds, when desires come into your hearts, that you know in your conscience are contrary to God's word and God's will, what do you do with them? If you take them, and keep them, and cherish them, and entertain them, you give place to the devil; you give the devil the advantage over you, of getting into your heart with his temptations and suggestions, and you give him a lodgment there. Now do not do this—do not give place to him—do not allow him a moment's admission within you; dismiss every thought—every desire—every wish—as soon as it comes into your heart; bring it to the Cross at once, bring it to Christ, bring it to the feet of Jesus, and say to him, "*Lord, deliver me; make haste to help me.*" That is what we have need to do. Therefore do not "GIVE PLACE TO THE DEVIL," for every advantage he gains in this way, you give him a stronger hold, a stronger position, a firmer lodgment in your heart, whence he can more effectually attack you, and draw you into sin against your God.

Now this is one of the most remarkable features of the natural mind. The natural man or woman—that is, man or woman in their unregenerate state—believe, that, provided they do not carry out their sins into practice, it is no matter what they may think, or how far they may indulge their imaginations in sin.—Nay it is our natural propensity to indemnify ourselves for subduing the outward practices of sin, by the inward cherishing and indulgence of it. We delight ourselves in the wicked and corrupt thoughts and imaginations of our own hearts, we revel in them—we enjoy ourselves in them,—and thus console ourselves by the secret indulgence of sins in our imagination, for not carrying them into practical effect. We may be prevented from doing it; the law of the land—respect for character—the laws of society may not allow us to do it; but we cherish these sins in our hearts. It does not occur to the natural man that these things are evil, he thinks he is very good, if he is not practically indulging in wickedness. The believer is taught to see that the power of sin is in his heart, that there he is to meet the enemy—there to guard against the evil—there to watch and "*keep his heart with all diligence, for out of it are the issues of life.*" Prov. iv. 23. It is there then, dear brethren, in our hearts, as well as in our lips and lives, we are specially to watch against the wiles of the devil.

These practical fruits which the Apostle inculcates on his believing brethren, let us remember, are the exhibitions of the Gospel on earth, the manifestations of the Gospel of Jesus,—of the fruit and power of religion in the heart. If religion were to consist in mere notions, mere speculative opinions, that Gospel would produce no benefit in this world. If it were possible that man, by the belief of the Gospel of Jesus, could enter into eternal life, and that that faith were to be a principle totally inoperative on his life here below, what blessing would the Gospel be to man on earth? or what difference would religion make between the servants of God and the servants of the devil? None. But let us remember, though the Gospel of Christ does proclaim that glorious truth, that through the faith of it, man does enter into eternal life, let us remember that the faith of that Gospel is practical. It "*worketh by love.*" The principle that is given into the heart is the faith of Jesus, and the love of Jesus is the result; to turn man "*from darkness to light, from the power of Satan unto God,*" that he may live to that Redeemer, "*who died for him, and rose again.*" Therefore, consider this, and you shall see that these practical exhortations given in the Apostolic writings supply the manifestations,—the only manifestations of the servants of Jesus on this earth, as these principles are brought unto their hearts, and their existence in their hearts manifested in their lives. Let us pray, that we may have clear, full, simple views of the Gospel of Christ for the hope of our souls, that our hearts may be enabled to embrace Christ, to rest on Christ, in simplicity and sincerity as the whole of our salvation, and that we may be able to manifest that we do so, by living to Him, showing that we are the servants of God, by turning from the service of the world, sin and Satan. Let us apply through grace these practical exhortations to ourselves, "*putting off the old man, which is corrupt, according to the deceitful lusts,*" "*putting on the new man, which after God is created in righteousness and true holiness.*"

I may conclude with the words of the Apostle to the Philippians, "*This I pray, that your love may abound yet more and more in knowledge and in all judgment; That ye may approve things that are excellent; that ye may be sincere, and without offence, till the day of Christ; Being filled with the fruits of righteousness, which are by Jesus Christ, unto the glory and praise of God.*" Amen. Phil. i. 9, 10, 11.

THIRTY-FIFTH LECTURE.

EPHESIANS IV.—28, 29, 30, 31, 32.

"Let him that stole steal no more: but rather let him labor, working with his hands the thing which is good, that he may have to give to him that needeth. Let no corrupt communication proceed out of your mouth, but that which is good to the use of edifying, that it may minister grace unto the hearers. And grieve not the Holy Spirit of God, whereby ye are sealed unto the day of redemption. Let all bitterness, and wrath, and anger, and clamor, and evil-speaking, be put away from you, with all malice: And be ye kind one to another, tender-hearted, forgiving one another, even as God for Christ's sake hath forgiven you."

AGAIN we must take up the principle on which these exhortations are given by the Apostle. Let us never lose sight of it in our hearts and consciences, either when we speak practically of the Gospel, or think practically of our own duty. This is the principle to which I called your attention in our last Lecture, which is to be found in the last verse of this chapter, "BE YE KIND ONE TO ANOTHER, TENDER-HEARTED, FORGIVING ONE ANOTHER, EVEN AS GOD FOR CHRIST'S SAKE HATH FORGIVEN YOU."

There the Apostle is addressing those persons, who as believers in Jesus, trusted on the Lord for the pardon of their sins. They were not to do any of these things in order to obtain pardon, which is the corrupt principle of duty in the natural heart of man, but they were to do these things, and to love one another, because they had received pardon, "*Being justified freely by his grace through the redemption that is in Christ Jesus.* Rom. iii. 21. Therefore, remember this is always the point for the sinner to have settled in his conscience, when he is coming to the Lord. He should ask himself,—"Am I coming through the precious blood of Jesus, leaning on my Lord alone for my salvation? having that blessed hope that all my sins are cancelled through that great offering which he has made on the cross? Oh! let my soul come thus to God! let my soul bring nothing but the righteousness and blood of Immanuel! let my soul repose with joy and peace in Him, thus let me "*heartily rejoice in the strength of my salvation*, Ps. xcv. 1. "*Let me enter into his gates with thanksgiving, and into his courts with praise.*" Ps. c. 4.

Think of these things again and again, my friends. Observe, he says, "EVEN AS GOD, FOR CHRIST'S SAKE HATH FORGIVEN YOU." Mark the distinction. It is not, that God, for Christ's sake *may* forgive you,—but he says, "AS GOD FOR CHRIST'S SAKE HATH FORGIVEN YOU."

Well then, recollecting this, you will remember, that the Apostle is here drawing a parallel between the old man and the new man, that is, between man's own natural corrupt heart, and that new heart which is given to him by the Holy Spirit through the faith of the Gospel, "*That ye put off the old man, which is corrupt according to the deceitful lusts,*" and "*put on the new man, which after God is created in righteousness and true holiness.*"

We have seen that the Apostle is drawing a parallel in several particulars between the old man and the new man in their workings. We have seen Lying, and Revengeful Anger, and Admission of Satan into our minds, contrasted with their opposite duties.

In the 28th verse we have Stealing as the work of the old man —we have Honesty—Industry, as the work of the new man. We have taken away by theft the property of others—and we have that contrasted with giving in Christian love to the wants of others. "LET HIM THAT STOLE, STEAL NO MORE, BUT RATHER LET HIM LABOR, WORKING WITH HIS HANDS THE THING THAT IS GOOD, THAT HE MAY HAVE TO GIVE TO HIM THAT NEEDETH."

Stealing is the natural propensity of the old man. All men covet—and many men steal. Let us remember that this sin may be committed in many ways that the law cannot take hold of. Many a man who never in a legal sense stole a shilling, may have stolen much in the sight of God. How many a man is pleased with what he calls a good bargain, disposing of something he has to sell, for more than in the sight of God he knows it to be worth; or getting something from his neighbor by some means or other, for what in his conscience he knows to be less than its value—counting himself very clever if he skilfully and strongly depreciates whatever he wants to buy, and as skilfully and deceitfully puffs beyond its worth whatever he wants to sell. What a mixture of theft and falsehood there is in some of your great bargain-makers. "*It is nought, it is nought, saith the buyer, but when he is gone his way then he boasteth.*" Prov. xx. 14. But remember the word of God is, "*That no man go beyond and defraud his brother in any matter, because that the Lord is the avenger of all such.*" 1 Thess. iv. 6. Then if I have been such an one, let me put off that; but let me manifest the life of the "*new man,*" let me "LABOR, WORKING WITH MY HANDS THE THING THAT IS GOOD." The Gospel of Christ, or true religion is anything but idleness,—true religion inculcates industry, spiritual industry and temporal industry;—spiritual industry, "*The soul of the sluggard desireth, and hath nothing; but the soul of the diligent shall be made fat.*" Prov. xiii. 4—temporal industry, "LET HIM LABOR, WORKING WITH HIS HANDS THE THING THAT IS GOOD." "*When we were with you, this we commanded you, that if any man would not work, neither should he eat.*" 2 Thess. iii. 10. The Christian, in whatsoever station of life he is placed, ought to be the most active and diligent person in that station of life. The persons who are placed at the head of a property ought to be most diligent in the discharge of their duty as Christians. The duties that devolve on them, having a number of persons depending on them, for example, for employment, for provisions, for education,—all these and others are great responsibilities which God has laid on the man to whom he has committed the talent of wealth in this world. The persons who are to provide for their families in any profession should be diligent and attentive to the calling of their profession. The merchant at his counting-house,—the shopkeeper in his shop, active in his business, faithful and upright in his dealings, accurate in his accounts. The Christian soldier ought to be the best, the most obedient and the bravest soldier. The Christian sailor ought to be the man to nail his colors to the mast. The Christian servant should be the most diligent in his labor, "*not with eye-service, as men-pleasers, but as the servants of Christ, doing the will of God from the heart.*" chap. vi. 6,—not serving his earthly master, but his Heavenly Master. Whatever station the Lord has been pleased to place us in, our religion should be manifested in the fidelity—in the zeal and activity with which we discharge our duty in that situation. Therefore, while the Gospel of Christ does not describe our works as having anything to do with the justification of our souls before God, you observe, that the Word of God points out our duties or our works as being the means of both testing and proving the sincerity of our profession, and the only means we have of manifesting it before man, and the mode in which it shall be finally approved and tested before God.

Then again, it is not merely for our own support that we are commanded to work, or for the due discharge of the duty that God has been pleased to annex to our calling, whatever it be, but also that we may be liberal, "WORKING WITH HIS HANDS THE THING THAT IS GOOD, THAT HE MAY HAVE TO GIVE TO HIM THAT NEEDETH." Christianity, you see, is not only industrious and just, but it is generous too; it opens not only the hand to work, but the heart and the hand to give. If we remember what God has done for us, and bestowed on us, and if we remember it as we ought to do, we should be anxious to manifest love to our fellow-sinners in whatever way we can, continually—effectually—liberally—according to our means, to help our poor brethren. Alas! these are duties, that I am afraid are commonly neglected among those who call themselves Christians, and even who are Christians. We think a great deal too much of supporting ourselves in a certain style, in the different circumstances in which the Lord has been pleased to place us, we think many more things necessary for us than really are. How many are not contented with the necessaries or even the comforts, but they must have the luxuries, yea, the extravagancies of life, while their poorer brethren have not even the necessaries. I do not mean that persons should not maintain the station in life in which God has been pleased to place them. There is not a more awful mistake than to suppose that the Gospel of Christ was meant to level ranks or distinctions in society. God has been pleased to establish order, and there is nothing for which we see Satan and the servants of Satan more anxiously laboring, than to annihilate order, to lower rank, to level distinctions, to establish what they call liberty and equality; but what in reality is anarchy and plunder. These are the doctrines of the devil. Authority and order, that is the doctrine of God. But generous liberality is the best security for rank and property in a nation. If the rich by their liberality would teach the poor to reverence and love them, no knaves could ever induce them to revolution or to plunder.

Our positions in life are relative—we are higher in the middle ranks of life than those who are placed below us, as those above us are higher than we are; and in all our situations, whatever they may be, let us remember, there is no way in which the duties of high stations are discharged in such a real Christian manner, as in kindness—humbleness—liberality—condescension to those who are placed below us. "*It is more blessed to give than to receive*," is a maxim of the Lord, and that is the very principle which the Apostle sets forth to the elders of this church, the church of Ephesus, when he called them together at Miletus, Acts xx., where he shows his own blameless walk and conversation among them. He says, "*Therefore watch, and remember, that by the space of three years, I ceased not to warn every one night and day with tears. And now, brethren, I commend you to God, and to the word of his grace, which is able to build you up, and to give you an inheritance among them that are sanctified. I have coveted no man's silver, or gold, or apparel; yea, ye yourselves know that these hands have ministered unto my necessities, and to them that are with me ;"*—although he had power as an Apostle of demanding support and maintenance from the church, yet so far from doing this, we see he appeals to them—"*ye yourselves know, that these hands have ministered to my necessities, and to them that were with me. I have showed you all things, how that so laboring, ye ought to support the weak, and to remember the words of the Lord Jesus, how he said, it is more blessed to give than to receive.*" Acts xx. 31—35.

The Apostle here, you see, impresses on the elders the same principle which we have here in the epistle to the church, "LET HIM THAT STOLE, STEAL NO MORE ; BUT RATHER LET HIM LABOR, WORKING WITH HIS HANDS THE THING THAT IS GOOD, THAT HE MAY HAVE TO GIVE TO HIM THAT NEEDETH." You observe the difference then here, between "*the old man*" and "*the new man*," what we should put off, and what we should put on.

Again, the next principle is with reference to our conversation. The principle of the old man is, "CORRUPT COMMUNICATIONS OUT OF HIS MOUTH."

The principle of the new, "THAT WHICH IS GOOD, TO THE USE OF EDIFYING, THAT IT MAY MINISTER GRACE UNTO THE HEARERS."

The principle of the old man is, "CORRUPT COMMUNICATIONS OUT OF HIS MOUTH." Oh ! what a grievous state the world is in from that very sin,—"CORRUPT COMMUNICATIONS !" How awfully is that exhibited in the human character from the earliest period of life ! The Scripture, speaking of the ungodly, says, "*They go astray as soon as they be born, speaking lies*"—Psa. lviii. 3, meaning, that as soon as they come to the use of their tongue, that tongue is exercised in iniquity. So it is.—How painfully parents feel this ! how they continually hear the wicked words of their children ! how painfully we feel this in the education of our children ! we tremble to send our children to school from the "CORRUPT COMMUNICATIONS" to which they are subjected there. The sinful principles—the blasphemy—pride—obscenity—disobedience—wickedness of all kinds ; and that which is so readily imparted from the tongue of one is as eagerly received in the ears and hearts of others. "*Evil communications corrupt good manners.*" 1 Cor. xv. 33, there is no parent who has thought at all, even if they have not any true religion—there is no parent that has ever reflected, and who has felt as parents must feel, anxious for their children, who has not felt the pain of this.

Then again, how awful is the example that children often see in their relatives and even in their parents ! what "CORRUPT COMMUNICATIONS," what ungodly, wicked expressions ! perhaps Swearing ! Blasphemy ! Passion ! Rage ! Deceit ! Falsehood !—all the "CORRUPT COMMUNICATIONS" with which the world is full ! "*filthiness, foolish talking*," unseemly jests, which the Apostle speaks of in another passage, these are the fruits of the natural, corrupt heart of man ; "*Of the abundance of the heart the mouth speaketh.*" Mat. xii. 34. "*The heart is deceitful above all things, and desperately wicked,*" and the mouth speaks its deceits and desperate wickedness. Then he says, put these off, "LET NO CORRUPT COMMUNICATION PROCEED OUT OF YOUR MOUTH." That is "*the old man,*" put him off.

"BUT THAT WHICH IS GOOD, TO THE USE OF EDIFYING, THAT IT MAY MINISTER GRACE UNTO THE HEARERS." That is "*the new man*"—put him on.

You perceive, that it is to the source of the evil we must go. The unregenerate heart will speak its own unregenerate and wicked thoughts; the renewed mind, the renewed heart, will speak its renewed thoughts, but then you see, both these hearts are in the sinner, we have two hearts; as the poor negro woman said, "Ah! me feel me have two hearts, one heart to love my God, one heart to hate my God!"

This is the truth—we have "*The carnal mind, which is enmity against God,*" Rom. viii. 7,—and that new mind, which is the work of the Spirit, and which loves God always;—that heart which "*delights in the law of God after the inward man.*" Rom. vii. 22,—that heart—that spirit which would pray that it might never sin—which longs for holiness—loves to serve its God—pants to be delivered from the body of sin and death, that it may serve the Lord in holiness and righteousness forever,—and that corrupt and wicked principle which "*wars against the law of our minds, and brings us into captivity to the law of sin which is in our members;*" Rom. vii. 23,—therefore, we have to watch against the "CORRUPT COMMUNICATIONS" of the one, and we have to watch that we may be under the influence and be breathing forth the communications of the other. In our business—in our worldly occupations—in our intercourse with mankind—in society, yea, in all the relations of life, the natural heart is called forth; it is provoked, for instance, by neglect—by disobedience of children—by the conduct of servants; who again in their turn are stirred up to anger—children by the treatment of their parents, and servants by the conduct of their masters or mistresses. Relatives—neighbors—friends—are mutually irritated or offended by the conduct of each other; and therefore, in these circumstances, the natural mind, when it is excited, is ready to pour forth its displeasure—opposition—indignation—envy—revenge, or whatever feeling may be stirred up within it.

Here then it is the Christian's business to watch, to pray, that he may be kept in the midst of the world and in the midst of all or any of these various trials, from having his heart involved in them. Oh! let us be *in* the world, but let us not be *of* the world, let not our hearts be engrossed with its pleasures or its cares. Let us recollect that both alike choke the seed, "*The cares of this world, and the deceitfulness of riches, and the lusts of other things, entering in, choke the word, and it becometh unfruitful.*" Mark iv. 19.

If our hearts be engrossed with the things of the world, our feelings will be stirred up, and excited when these go wrong; wicked tempers, ungodly expressions, "CORRUPT COMMUNICATIONS" will be drawn out. Then "*Can a fountain send forth at the same place sweet water and bitter?*" "*Out of the same mouth proceedeth blessing and cursing.*" Jam. iii. 10, 11. You see how the Apostle James speaks of this subject in his 3d chapter. That chapter we ought to read with much attention. "*In many things we offend all. If any man offend not in word, the same is a perfect man, and able also to bridle the whole body.*" There is nothing in which we are more ready to offend than in word. What need have we then to pray with the Psalmist, "*Set a watch, O Lord, before my mouth, keep the door of my lips.*" Psa. cxli. 3. For what purpose do we set a watch on a door? To let no person go out, that ought not to go out of it. "*Keep the door of my lips.*" Oh, what a great and blessed mercy if the Spirit places a sentinel of sobriety, holiness, reflection, to mount guard, as we call it, on our lips, and before a word comes forth, to challenge it, as it were:—

"Who comes there?"

"Who are you that are coming forth?"

"For what are you going forth?"

"What business—what object have you in passing out of this mouth?"

"Do you come as a messenger of a wicked heart?"

"Are you going forth to provoke,—to excite,—to corrupt? Are you going forth to dishonor God? Are you going forth to injure your neighbor? Are you going forth in slander, in malice? Avaunt—begone:—back to your den,—to be smothered there forever."

Oh! what need have we, to have this watch set on our mouth, to "*keep the door of our lips!*" Oh! what need we have to pray for this!

Consider the description which the Apostle James gives of the tongue. "*Behold, we put bits in the horses' mouths, that they may obey us; and we turn about their whole body. Behold also the ships, which though they be so great, and are driven of fierce winds, yet are they turned about with a very small helm, whithersoever the governor listeth. Even so, the tongue is a little member, and boasteth great things; behold, how great a matter a little fire kindleth. And the tongue is a fire, a world of iniquity, so is the tongue among our members, that it defileth the whole body, and setteth on fire the course of nature, and it is set on fire of hell.*" Jam. iii. 3—6. There is nothing on earth so awful as a wicked tongue. And, though our tongue may not fall into the extreme of wickedness, yet, alas! how often sinful and wicked it is! How far from what it ought to be! Alas! what cause we have to be humbled for our sinful tongues! what innumerable causes we have to be ashamed! There is not one of us that has not reason to lie down in the dust before God, and cry to Him for mercy with shame and confusion of face for this very thing; for if there was not another member of our body that had sinned against our God, our tongues would cast us all into the depths of hell, where we would not have a drop of water to cool them! Nothing but the blood of Christ could wash the sins of our tongues as well as those of our hearts and lives. Dear brethren, let us think of this, and let us pray, that God may guard us in this respect!

So "*Put off the old man*,"—"LET NO CORRUPT COMMUNICATION PROCEED OUT OF YOUR MOUTH."

"*Put on the new man*," "BUT THAT WHICH IS GOOD, TO THE USE OF EDIFYING, THAT IT MAY MINISTER GRACE UNTO THE HEARERS." You see "*the new man*," what it means,—"THAT WHICH IS GOOD, TO THE USE OF EDIFYING, THAT IT MAY MINISTER GRACE UNTO THE HEARERS." How can that be, if we have not grace in our own hearts? How can we communicate that which we do not know? I cannot communicate a language or a science which I do not know, a secret with which I am not acquainted. I cannot communicate any knowledge which I do not possess myself,—and how can we communicate with our lips, or "MINISTER GRACE UNTO THE HEARERS," if we have not grace in our hearts! Oh, what a blessed thing it is, if the heart is renewed and instructed by the word and by the grace of God! so that "*out of the abundance of the heart the mouth may speak*," then indeed it will "MINISTER GRACE UNTO THE HEARERS," when it is filled with grace itself.

It is my privilege, I perceive, to address a number of females in this assembly. There is a sort of proverbial reproach on their sex for the use, or rather the abuse, of their tongue. I mean not to say how far this may in many instances be just or not. But Oh, how blessed the use of the tongue of the female may be! How sweet the tongue of the mother communicating instruction to her child, pouring into the infant ear the first accents of truth and love from the word of God—distilling upon the earliest thoughts that spring up and bud in the infant's breast, in "That sweet hour of prime," those "*doctrines that drop as the rain*," that "*speech that distils as the dew*," Deut. xxxii. 2,—of tender, faithful, holy instruction from the sacred volume of inspired truth. This is the greatest blessing that can be given to a child, to have a mother who will teach it faithfully.

So, next to a Christian Mother, I do not think there is a greater blessing in the world than a faithful Christian Instructress of the infant mind. What a wonderful blessing are these very Infant Schools.* The instruction that is conveyed to the children here, is given in their infant years, identified with all their first and earliest associations, when all their little thoughts and minds are just beginning to expand beneath the opening dawn of reason, these instructions will remain, even when those received at later periods are obliterated from their memories. I remember things I

* These Lectures were delivered in an Infant School.

learned when I was a little child with far greater clearness and intensity than I can recall those things which I have learned since. I remember thoughts received, and sentiments impressed, and lessons learned, when I was a child, while those of many a later date have been completely swept away from my recollection. What a blessing, I say, is the tongue of a tender Christian mother, or that of a tender Christian instructress, who trains the infant mind as his grandmother Lois or his mother Eunice, Timothy, that "*from a child they shall have learned the holy Scriptures, which are able to make them wise unto salvation, through faith which is in Christ Jesus.*" 2 Tim. iii. 15.

Then, the tongue of a sister, if she has grace in her heart, how sweet and blessed is its influence?—how she "MAY MINISTER GRACE" to her brother! how, by her kindness and affection she may allure him to his home, from evil company or from evil habits!

The tongue of the wife, who can estimate its value, if "*the law of kindness is upon her lips:*" Oh! how sweet, how winning is that charm! So the Apostle saith, "*If any obey not the word, they also may, without the word, be won by the chaste conversation of their wives, while they behold your chaste conversation coupled with fear.*" 1st Pet. iii. 1, 2.

How sweet the instruction, too, of the Christian mistress to her servants! When we compare this with the anger, the clamor, the scolding of an impatient unreasonable mistress—the ill-tempered and unruly tongue and spirit of a self-willed, ungovernable wife—the alternate caresses and corrections, alike ill-judged, excessive, and injurious, of a foolish, weak, indulgent, injudicious mother. When we compare too "*the ornament of a meek and quiet spirit, which is in the sight of God of great price,*" with the scandal, malice, gossip, tattling, slander—these curses, these pests of society which too often are to be met with in females,—when we look at the two characters, the character of a Christian female, and of an ungodly, worldly female,—the character of one who is going on her way to her Lord, and the character of one who is going on her way to death,—Oh! think of the solemn contrast! and pray, that you may be enabled to apply this practically. "LET NO CORRUPT COMMUNICATION PROCEED OUT OF YOUR MOUTH, BUT THAT WHICH IS GOOD, TO THE USE OF EDIFYING, THAT IT MAY MINISTER GRACE UNTO THE HEARERS,"—"*a word spoken in due season,*" saith Solomon, "*how good is it?*" Prov. xv. 23. And again "*a word fitly spoken is like apples of gold in pictures of silver.*" Prov. xxv. 11. Remember, how David blessed Abigail, when she came to arrest him, by her tender, kind, judicious, and well-timed expostulation—how she averted the heavy judgment that was about to be inflicted on her wicked husband Nabal, for his stinginess, hard-heartedness, and ingratitude—how she turned away the sword of David, which was to be unsheathed against all her husband's house—Recollect how David blessed her, and blessed God, that God had sent her to arrest his hand that day!

Then, there is another contrast between "*the old man*" and "*the new man.*" There is another work of "*the old man,*"—to grieve the Holy Spirit of God, to weary, to provoke the Lord to anger.

So the Prophet Isaiah says, "*Hear ye now, O house of David, is it a small thing for you to weary men, but will ye weary my God also.*" Isa. vii. 13.

And again by the same Prophet the Lord saith, "*Thou hast made me to serve with thy sins, thou hast wearied me with thine iniquities.*" Isa. xliii. 24.

And again, "*They rebelled and vexed his Holy Spirit; therefore he was turned to be their enemy, and he fought against them.*" Isa. xliii. 10.

And so the Lord saith, before he poured out the deluge on a guilty world, "*My Spirit shall not always strive with man, for that he also is flesh;*" Gen. vi. 3,—man, by rebelling against God, vexing and provoking, as it were, His Holy Spirit,—that is the natural character of man.

What can grieve a parent so much, as to see his child notwithstanding his kindness, his tenderness, and his love, always provoking him—always doing what he forbids—always neglecting to do what he desires—deceiving him—ever professing and promising, and ever violating his word;—what can wound or grieve a parent so much as that? What can so wound or irritate a man as to see a servant to whom he has been kind, indulgent, considerate, affectionate, to see that servant robbing him—plundering him; and instead of rendering him any service, serving the man who is his enemy? Yet this is a picture of man, a rebel against his God. This is the Lord's complaint of Israel, as a child, "*I have nourished and brought up children, and they have rebelled against me.*" Isa. i. 2. Such is man's treatment of God as a child. And as a servant, not serving his Master, but serving his enemy—serving the devil, instead of serving God—provoking Him in every way, returning His kindness, love, long-suffering, compassion, and mercy; with ingratitude, rebellion, and enmity against Him. So the Lord complaineth by another Prophet, "*A son honoreth his father, and a servant his master. If I be a father, where is mine honor? and if I be a master, where is my fear?*" Mal. i. 6.

Since this is the natural character of man, we need not wonder to meet this exhortation to the believer, "GRIEVE NOT THE HOLY SPIRIT OF GOD, WHEREBY YE ARE SEALED UNTO THE DAY OF REDEMPTION." Oh, think what that Spirit has done for you, if you are indeed a child of God! He has enlightened your eyes. He has opened your heart, to see and to embrace the glory of the love of God, he has taken you and bathed you in the blood of Jesus. Remember, that the whole work of Jesus is all in vain for man, unless the Holy Spirit of God takes of the things of Jesus, and shows them to the sinner's soul. There is no testimony in the Scripture of God's love—of the riches of His grace,—of the work that God has revealed as being wrought by His beloved Son,—or of all that

Christ hath wrought for the sinner, that could be of any use to man, more than to the beast that perisheth, unless the Holy Spirit awakens the sinner's heart, and writes on that heart the blessed testimony of God and of His Christ. It must be "*written not with ink, but with the Spirit of the living God: not in tables of stone, but in fleshly tables of the heart.*" 2 Cor. iii. 3.

Therefore, consider what the Spirit has done for your soul, if you are indeed brought to know and rest on Jesus. Well then the Apostle saith, "GRIEVE NOT THE HOLY SPIRIT OF GOD, WHEREBY YE ARE SEALED UNTO THE DAY OF REDEMPTION." Think what He hath done for you,—and grieve Him not. Remember what you owe Him,—grieve him not; He has sealed you to the day of redemption; He has set his seal on you—He has stamped you—you are His—the Spirit of God hath executed the covenant. It is an image taken from the sealing of a covenant, or an agreement, or bond, which when sealed, and the person who executes it says, that is my hand and seal, and I acknowledge that as my act and deed,—when he does that, it is executed, whatever it be. So the Holy Spirit of God, bringing to the sinner's heart the truth and the salvation of Jesus, seals him; he is sealed with the blood of the everlasting covenant; he is sealed by the Holy Spirit of God. It is a seal of consummation—of security—of finality. He who is sealed is made a member of that blessed covenant, brought into covenant relation to his God; no longer an outcast and alien. As we had, you recollect, "*You are no more strangers and foreigners, but fellow-citizens with the saints, and of the household of God, and are built upon the foundation of the apostles and prophets, Jesus Christ himself being the chief corner-stone. In whom all the building, fitly framed together, groweth unto an holy temple in the Lord. In whom ye also are builded together, for an habitation of God through the Spirit.*" This then is the Spirit's work.

Thus the Apostle saith here of the Spirit, "WHEREBY YE ARE SEALED UNTO THE DAY OF REDEMPTION." As surely as you are brought to the Lord Jesus Christ, and He is indeed the refuge of your soul, so surely "YE ARE SEALED UNTO THE DAY OF REDEMPTION." Are they not then redeemed already? Yes, of course,—certainly—they are redeemed by the blood of Jesus. But "THE DAY OF REDEMPTION" spoken of here, is that final day when the Lord's people shall be manifested, as redeemed both in body and soul; their soul redeemed from hell, as their body is redeemed from the dust, and soul and body together, in resurrection glory, rising to meet their Lord in the air. This is what he speaks of, as "THE DAY OF REDEMPTION," sealed for that glorious day, sealed for that glorious hope, set apart for that glorious triumph "*When the Lord shall come to be glorified in His saints, and to be admired in all them that believe.*" 2 Thes. i. 10.

Since then you are sealed to that day by the Holy Spirit;—therefore grieve not that Spirit,—grieve not Him who hath sealed you,—set you apart for such a glorious day; grieve not that

Spirit whereby you are brought into this blessed relation, and whereby all the glorious work of your adorable Redeemer is applied to your soul—grieve not that blessed Spirit who has sanctified you—set you apart as God's adopted children. Since "*because ye are sons, God hath sent forth the Spirit of His Son into your hearts, crying Abba, Father.*" Gal. iv. 6. "GRIEVE NOT THE HOLY SPIRIT OF GOD."

The Apostle proceeds to show how He may be grieved, "*The fruit of the Spirit is love, joy, peace, long-suffering, gentleness goodness, faith, meekness, temperance,*" Gal. v. 22. Therefore as the Spirit lusteth against the flesh—to bring forth the fruits of the flesh is to oppose and grieve the Spirit. So the Apostle presses these admonitions, "LET ALL BITTERNESS, AND WRATH, AND ANGER, AND CLAMOR, AND EVIL-SPEAKING, BE PUT AWAY FROM YOU, WITH ALL MALICE." Let all these, which are the works of the flesh—of "*the old man,*" "BE PUT AWAY FROM YOU;" and "*be renewed in the spirit of your mind, and put on the new man.*" "BE YE KIND ONE TO ANOTHER;" instead of "BITTERNESS, AND WRATH, AND ANGER, AND CLAMOR," "BE YE KIND ONE TO ANOTHER, TENDER-HEARTED, FORGIVING ONE ANOTHER."

The Apostle does not suppose—the word of God does not suppose, that there will not be in the believer, as there are, numerous faults. It is impossible that we can be together, it is impossible, that we can be united in any bonds, no matter what they be, in any relation whatever, however close or dear, as husbands, wives, parents, children, brothers, sisters, masters, servants—or in social relations, friends, neighbors, fellow-citizens, fellow-believers, fellow-communicants, associating together—it is impossible we can be united in any relations, and be much together in these relations, that we shall not see in each other's character and conduct something of what God sees, viz., that we are poor, helpless, weak, miserable, sinners. And just in proportion to the natural temperament of our respective characters, so, in proportion will there be evils developed in the conduct of one person that will offend, and grate upon the feelings of another: some person will be wounded or offended by some peculiarity in his relative, his connexion, his friend, or his neighbor, that another person would pass by, and with which he would not be offended at all. Hence it follows that we shall have mutual causes of forbearance with each other in all the varied relations of our existence. If a child must reverently forbear with many peculiarities in a parent—the parent will have perhaps more frequent cause to endure the provocations of the child. If the husband must treat with tenderness many of the evils of the wife—the wife will have equal cause to exercise forbearance with her husband. If the brother must have to bear some of the peculiarities of the sister—the sister will be frequently called on to forbear with those of her brother. If the master or mistress require to exercise patience with the servant—the servant will have no less need of patience with the master or mistress.

If one friend must pass over the singularities or failings of another —that other will have no less cause to exercise indulgence towards him. It is always the case. There is so much evil in all our characters, that we shall have great need of forbearance, patience, tenderness, kindness and indulgence towards each other; and so the Apostle saith, "BE YE KIND ONE TO ANOTHER, TENDER-HEARTED, FORGIVING ONE ANOTHER,"—as much as to say, "you have many things to forgive, and to bear with in each other." And so we have. And then why are they to be forgiven —what is the motive? "EVEN AS GOD, FOR CHRIST'S SAKE, HATH FORGIVEN YOU." This is the great principle that is to actuate the whole, you are forgiven by God, the Lord has blotted out your ten thousand talents, therefore learn to forbear and forgive the hundred pence of your fellow-servant. And this, as we have before observed, is a principle which the Lord puts, as a test, on His people, in that prayer which he hath taught us to use, "*forgive us our trespasses, as we forgive them that trespass against us.*" I need not again remind you that we cannot consider it as a condition of pardon, for that were to overturn the Gospel of Christ; but it is a test of sincerity and truth put upon the consciences of the children of God when they come to pray, that they may say, as it were, thus—

"Am I coming, with all my mighty debt, to my blessed Master for pardon? am I coming in sincerity and truth to my Lord for forgiveness for all my load of sin? and am I cherishing an angry, unforgiving temper or disposition to my poor fellow-sinners for their trifling offences against me? Such an one has provoked me; treated me badly—ungratefully—cruelly—but am I coming to the Lord for pardon for all my sins with a wicked temper, or an ungodly, revengeful spirit against my poor fellow-sinner?"

You see, the Lord puts it, as we have seen, as a test on the consciences of men; and we cannot come with sincerity, with our mighty debt—with all our sins, to our heavenly Master, that infinite love may blot them all out—if we are lifting up, as it were, one hand for mercy to the Lord, with the other on the throat of our fellow-servant for his offences against us.

You see, the motive is put by the word of God into the heart, "FORGIVING ONE ANOTHER, EVEN AS GOD, FOR CHRIST'S SAKE, HATH FORGIVEN YOU." What is this to awaken in the heart? Love. It is from love to Him who loved us, and hath blotted out our sins with His own blood, that our hearts are to be filled with love to Him. This is the true and only motive of love to God and our fellow-sinners. So we have it in the words of the hymn we have just been singing,

"Come, Holy Spirit, heavenly dove,
With all thy quickening powers;
Come, shed abroad the Saviour's love,
And that will kindle ours."

Think of this, and let us pray, beloved friends, that these blessed truths may be written on our hearts. Pray for me, that they may be written on my heart, that I may not be speaking of love, and preaching of love, and all the blessed fruits of the Spirit to others, but that I may have love in my heart and soul, engraven by the Spirit of God, as practical lessons, practical rules for my heart, my tongue, my life. Thus I trust I shall be enabled to pray for you, that we may be Christians, not in name merely, but in spirit and in truth, and that those who are connected with us may "*take knowledge of us that we have been with Jesus.*" Acts iv. 13—that we love our Lord and Master, and manifest that love by showing that it is a living principle in our hearts, developed in a life of love, both to God and our fellow-sinners.

THIRTY-SIXTH LECTURE.

EPHESIANS V.—1, 2, 3, 4, 5, 6.

"Be ye therefore followers of God, as dear children; And walk in love, as Christ also hath loved us, and hath given himself for us an offering and a sacrifice to God for a sweet-smelling savor. But fornication, and all uncleanness, or covetousness, let it not be once named among you, as becometh saints; Neither filthiness, nor foolish talking, nor jesting, which are not convenient: but rather giving of thanks. For this ye know, that no whoremonger, nor unclean person, nor covetous man, who is an idolater, hath any inheritance in the kingdom of Christ and of God. Let no man deceive you with vain words: for because of these things cometh the wrath of God upon the children of disobedience."

THE first verse of this chapter evidently shows, that it is taken in direct connection with the last verse of that which precedes it,—"BE YE THEREFORE FOLLOWERS OF GOD, AS DEAR CHILDREN." Wherefore? There must be a reason. Return to the last verse of the preceding chapter, "*Be ye kind one to another, tender hearted, forgiving one another, even as God for Christ's sake hath forgiven you.*" You are forgiven—your sins are blotted out—your iniquity is cancelled—you are reconciled to God—you are adopted into God's family—"*Because God, for Christ's sake, hath forgiven you.*" "BE YE THEREFORE FOLLOWERS OF GOD AS DEAR CHILDREN."

Now my dear brethren, to bring this single exhortation into practical experience in the sinner's heart, is the very sum and substance of all true religion and all true happiness,—to bring this, I say, so into practical experience, that the believer may be enabled to do as he is here commanded, that is—to be a follower of God as a dear child. I have had continual occasion to set before you, in Lectures on the Scriptures, the great difference, or rather, the entire opposition that there is between the natural ideas that men have on this subject, and the truth as it is in Jesus. The natural mind of men, even of those who are the most religious in any religion that is not that of the Gospel—I say the natural mind of the most religious persons always adopts this principle—that they shall endeavor to follow God, in order that they become God's children. Now, this is the very reverse of the truth, and of this text, because the truth is, that those who are really followers of God, are followers of God, *not that they may become his children*, but because *they are his children.* You see the total opposition there is between these two principles. To endeavor to serve God, in order that you may become his child. And to endeavor to serve God, or rather to serve Him willingly, because you are his child already.

The objection that is immediately presented to the natural mind on hearing this truth is, "Well then, if following God is not to make me His child, how am I to become His child? how is man to become a child of God, unless by following Him and serving Him?"

Here we come directly to the fundamental error of the natural mind, and as directly to the principles of the Gospel which are opposed to it. You are made a child of God, not by following Him, —not by serving Him,—not by doing anything for Him, to recommend yourself to His favor,—for you cannot do any thing to make yourself a child of God,—it is not in your power,—there is no means which you can possibly adopt by which to attain any righteousness that can commend you as a fallen sinner to God—there is no effort of your own by which you can possibly be made a child of God,—or brought in the least degree into his favor. You can only be a child of God by faith in Christ Jesus. This is the glory of the Gospel,—Christ Jesus hath wrought the work, Christ hath finished redemption,—Christ hath completed salvation,—"*Ye who were afar off, are made nigh by the blood of Christ;*"—"*Christ is all.*" Now mark again the last verse of the preceding chapter, "*Even as God, for Christ's sake, hath forgiven you.*" Mark, I say, these words, if it be "*for Christ's sake,*" it cannot be for any other cause. If that be the cause of your salvation, nothing else can be the cause of it: and if you know that that is the cause of your forgiveness, then here, and here alone, is rest for your soul,—"*Ye are all the children of God by faith in Christ Jesus.*" Gal. iii. 26. Trust in Christ, and all the salvation of Christ is yours; you are made a child of God by faith in Jesus. Therefore if there are any here who are not his children, Oh "*Repent, and believe the Gospel.*"

As long as your mind is in doubt and ignorance on this subject, so long you never can serve God freely or happily. You never can serve God freely—because you never can serve Him in His appointed way. You are in bondage under the law—you are forever laboring to perform a task which you feel you are wholly unable to accomplish. You never can serve God happily, because there is always a burden on your conscience,—your conscience is always afraid. There is always apprehension—fear—doubt—respecting the acceptance of your soul with God; and therefore, there is no freedom, no liberty, no love, no peace, no consolation, no true, genuine principle of solid, Christian obedience. If we are to obey God, there is, as I have often shown, but one principle that God admits as a principle of obedience, and that is—Love. But it is impossible that Love can exist in the heart, so long as the sinner is striving to make himself a child of God by his own righteousness—or to make peace with God by his own efforts, instead of coming boldly to God to obtain mercy, through faith in Christ Jesus. As long as the sinner expects that he is to come for acceptance to God in whole or in part through his own efforts or his own righteousness, so long the consciousness of sin must ever shut out all confidence in coming for acceptance to God. But when he comes through Christ, the consciousness of his sin and helplessness is the very ground on which he turns to his Saviour. Your being a sinner cannot hinder you from being a child of God through faith in Christ Jesus; for, if it could, no living mortal could be a child of God. Sin cannot come between the sinner and God, when the sinner comes to Jesus,—when feeling his lost condition, and that no virtue, no labor of his own, can do anything for his soul—he cries—"None but Christ"—"None but Christ." Sin cannot therefore shut you out from God, when you come to Christ; because when you come to Christ, your sins are cancelled: when you bring your sins to Jesus, they are cast into the fountain of his precious blood, and blotted out forever, "*their sins and iniquities will I remember no more.*" Heb. x. 17.

Therefore, let no terror of conscience prevent you from coming to Christ,—but come with your burden to Him, and cast that burden on Him without doubt or fear. Then shall you see "*The Sun of Righteousness arise with healing in his wings,*" Mal. iv. 2, on your soul. "*In him was life, and the life was the light of men.*" John i. 4. He saith—"*I am the light of the world: he that followeth me shall not walk in darkness, but shall have the light of life.*" John viii. 12, "*and if we walk in the light, as he is in the light, we shall have fellowship one with another, and the blood of Jesus Christ, his Son, cleanseth us from all sin.*" 1 John i. 7.

Here alone is Rest for your conscience—here alone Refuge for your soul. But it is a full, a perfect Refuge—and when you fly to this, then learn, that "*God, for Christ's sake, hath forgiven you.*" Every sinner that looks to Jesus, God through Christ has forgiven that sinner. If you are looking to Jesus—you are forgiven, it is a present salvation.

You are not to live here, as you naturally think, in a state of bondage to sin—of apprehension—and of guilty fear, till the day of judgment clears up the doubt, as you imagine; and then, it is to be known who is to be saved, and who is not. Instead of living in this unhappy state, your privilege, nay, your only true religion is, to live in present pardon, in the enjoyment of present forgiveness, peace, remission, complete remission of all your sins; for if you are indeed in Christ, they are completely cancelled; and you can look up, and come with confidence, and joy, and peace to your reconciled Father and your God as his child;—so "BE YE FOLLOWERS OF GOD AS DEAR CHILDREN."

Now let me intreat you, brethren, to ask your own consciences this question—"Is this a settled truth in my heart to-day—that I can come with confidence to my Lord, as a reconciled God and Father through the righteousness and blood of Jesus? Can I, come with confidence, with all my sins—all my iniquity—Can I come with confidence to my precious Saviour, and trust in Him for all that are cancelled in His blood? Can I lift up my eyes through Him with joy and peace to God?"

If you cannot do so, rest satisfied either that there is some great ignorance in your mind, of what the truth is, or, though you may know that such is the doctrine of the Scriptures, yet you are not living by faith in the Son of God, and trusting in Him as you ought to do. Either you do not know what the ground of a sinner's hope is; or else, if you know it, as a system of doctrine, you do not believe it as a solid truth. What is the use of your knowing that there is a refuge for the sinner in Christ, if you do not rest your soul on His salvation? or what is to hinder you from resting your soul on Christ? You will find that self-righteousness lies at the root of your unbelief. There is some pride of your own heart, that borrows the veil of humility, and imposes on you in that specious garb.

"Oh, I am not fit—I am too great a sinner to trust in Christ for pardon."

See what pride, self-righteousness, and unbelief is in that sentence. For what does it mean but this? "If I were but a little more fit—a little better—if I had a little more righteousness—then I might come to Christ." This seeming humility, is pride—this seeming self-condemnation, is really self-righteousness. You are thinking that some of your sins render you unfit to cast the remainder on Christ, and wishing for some righteousness to entitle you to do so! How easily are we blinded and deceived by some corruptions of which we are not aware! There is still some excuse for unbelief that Satan is ever suggesting to the soul. You are not simply taking God at His word, and going with all your sins, whatever they are, and your unbelief, which is one of the worst of them, bringing that along with the rest of your sins, and casting them all into the fountain of Immanuel's blood. Come, yea, come boldly to the Throne of Grace, and trust your Lord with confidence and hope, and joy and peace. Behold your sins as all done away in Christ, and when you feel sin, as you continually do, coming into your heart and conscience, bring it, as fast as it comes, to Christ. "*The life,*" saith the Apostle, "*that I now live in the flesh, I live by faith in the Son of God, who loved me, and gave himself for me.*" Gal. ii. 20. Faith is not an act of the mind that takes place, as it were, to-day, and then is done. Faith is a continual successive act—is a continual exercise of the heart on God's word, a continual turning of the conscience for cleansing to God's promises in Christ, producing in its due effect an habitual trusting of the heart and soul on God's testimony. "*Remember the word unto thy servant upon which thou hast caused me to hope*," saith David, Psalm cxix. 49. You have a constant necessity for the salvation revealed in the word, a perpetual need for trusting in it, so Faith, in its right exercise, is a continual going forth, as it were, of your heart on God's promises, and trusting in these promises of which you have need. You do not think of eating once, and saying, this satisfies me forever;—there is a continually-recurring feeling of weakness and hunger in your animal frame, and you are obliged to supply your necessities with food and drink,—so, there is a continual weakness—a continual sinking of the spiritual life—a fainting, a readiness to perish without spiritual sustenance, and therefore it wants continual revival and support with "*The Bread of Life*," Therefore, the Lord Jesus Christ is set up before us under the emblems of bread and wine; so we say, "*Feed on him in your heart by faith with thanksgiving*." "Feed on him."—You want continually the support of this food, and Jesus is "*The Bread of life*." "Feed on him." "*Drink this in remembrance that Christ's blood was shed for you, and be thankful*." Remember, that that precious blood was shed for you, and that it "*cleanseth us from all sin*." So saith our adorable Lord Himself, "*I am the bread of life, he that cometh to me shall never hunger, and he that believeth on me shall never thirst*." John vi. 35.

I know, that in one sense, the belief of the Gospel is an act done once for all in the heart of the sinner; so that, when the sinner does believe in the Lord Jesus Christ, he is "*justified from all things*," Acts xiii. 39, and there is no condemnation to him. But though that is the case in one sense—yet, he requires, in another sense, to have his soul continually going forth in the same exercise of faith and trust in his Lord, as if he had never believed before. He requires ever to hold fast that blessed hope. "*We are made partakers of Christ, if we hold the beginning of our confidence steadfast unto the end*." Heb. iii. 14. The truth that first gives us peace and comfort, we must hold fast—steadfast unto the end. Consider how important it is to have the truth settled in your mind. When we are exhorted to moral duties, we must have the principles on which they are inculcated established in the heart. I must continually press on you these principles, for I know how continually the heart forgets them.

Mark how they are implied in these first words, "BE YE THEREFORE FOLLOWERS OF GOD, AS DEAR CHILDREN." "*No more strangers and foreigners, but fellow-citizens with the saints, and of the household of God*," as we had in chapter ii. You are no more aliens, but children of God, and not only children, but "DEAR CHILDREN." As surely as you are a child, you are a dear child —then walk so. Let that point be settled in your consciences. Trust in your heavenly Father. Come to your heavenly Father —as a Father, and walk "AS DEAR CHILDREN"—in love, and in the full confidence of your Father's love. "*God commendeth his love toward us, in that, while we were yet sinners, Christ died for us.*" Rom. v. 8. Therefore walk in the confidence of your Father's love, and in the exercise of love to Him.

When you believe that God loves you—when you believe that God pardons you—that God bears with you—that God keeps you —when you believe that God watches over you—that He continually delivers you—when you believe He is your strength—your refuge—your salvation—your peace—your all—When you understand what He means when He says, "*I will be their God, and they shall be my people*"—when you believe, He is your God—your heavenly Father;—this it is, that draws out the affections of your heart, and teaches you to love your glorious Master. It is not the work of a slave, to serve the Lord—it is not the wretched, heartless, mournful obedience of a Pharisee—of an ascetic, who is continually denying himself almost the necessaries of life—mortifying and punishing himself—leading, what he calls a holy life, thinking he serves and pleases God by making himself miserable —No—it is our pleasure—our joy—our happiness—to serve the Lord, when we know that God is our Father. It is the true, the solid enjoyment and liberty of life to serve our Father. It is not mortification.

We are desired indeed to "*Mortify our members which are upon the earth, fornication, uncleanness, inordinate affection, evil concupiscence, and covetousness, which is idolatry;*" Col. iii. 5, but it is pleasure to do so; yea, the greatest pleasure that a believer can enjoy, is the subjugation of his evil propensities, for his Lord and Master. Travail is pain,—toil is pain,—weariness is pain;—but if travail, toil, and weariness are undertaken and endured for one we love, they cease to be pain;—they are turned into pleasure. It is a delight to undergo any labor, or any toil, for the person we love. The toil is forgotten, the pain is turned to enjoyment. Although it may be pain and toil considered in itself—it is no pain, no toil, considered in reference to our own hearts when we love the person for whom we undergo it. So, mortification of sin, self-mortification, is no mortification when we mortify sin for the love of our heavenly Father. Then it is a pleasure to deny ourselves anything for our Lord's glory and service—anything—however it would be for the gratification of the flesh. Therefore mortification ceases to be mortification—labor, labor—toil, toil—in that sense; because all is love. So, when the heart is set at liberty by the knowledge and love of Jesus, then it is at liberty indeed, set free from the bondage of the law and of fear, to serve its God; so the Psalmist saith, "*I will walk at liberty; for I seek thy precepts.*" "*I will run in the way of thy commandments, when thou shalt enlarge my heart.*" When the heart is set at liberty from the bondage of sin—of the dread of death and hell, then it is at liberty to serve its God. So saith the Apostle, "*But now, being made free from sin, and become servants to God, ye have your fruit unto holiness, and the end everlasting life.*" Rom. vi. 22. So saith our Lord, "*If the Son therefore shall make you free, ye shall be free indeed.*" John viii. 36.

"BE YE THEREFORE FOLLOWERS OF GOD AS DEAR CHILDREN." Walk not, and live not in slavery, in a slavish fear and apprehension of your judge; but "WALK IN LOVE," the love of your Father,—your reconciled Father,—your gracious Father,—your tender Father,—who hath so loved you—of your dear Lord who hath given Himself for you; "WALK IN LOVE, AS CHRIST ALSO HATH LOVED US, AND HATH GIVEN HIMSELF FOR US, AN OFFERING AND A SACRIFICE TO GOD FOR A SWEET SMELLING SAVOR." Therefore, you see, the great joy, the great privilege the believer possesses is this, that his sins being pardoned, being accepted with his God, being reconciled to his God, duty becomes pleasure, for His "*service is perfect freedom.*"

This it is that accounts for that, which is wholly unaccountable to the natural mind, namely the difference that exists between the pleasures of the believer and the pleasures of the world.

A worldly man or woman, when they see a person become religious, says, "Oh that person has given up the world, he has given up all the pleasures, the enjoyments of life."

And there are many persons whom I have known and heard, who say,

"I would not become religious—or I must give up all my pleasures, and all my enjoyments; surely there is no occasion for this."

So, they really think that persons give up enjoyment and happiness, because they do not go into the pursuits in which the world takes pleasure, as public amusements, balls, theatres, races, revellings of various kinds. I just mention these sort of things, because they are worldly amusements, and worldly men say, "If I were to become religious, I should give up all these—all my pleasures, company, enjoyments, and they actually think that a religious person undergoes great mortification and pain in giving up such things.

Now, it is totally the reverse. It is true indeed, persons who are religious do not enter into these things. But why? In the first place, they have really no pleasure in them, they could give them no enjoyment. It is not only that they know that such things are in opposition to God's will, and to God's word. But they know that, from such things, God is totally excluded, and therefore, they can have no pleasure in them. They do not give up pleasure, they do not renounce gratification, for these things would not really please them. Would it be enjoyment to you to be in a company where, if the name of the person who was dearest to you on earth was mentioned, it would be scoffed at, or thought not fit to be spoken of there? Now a believer can have no pleasure in a place, where, if he should mention the Lord Jesus Christ—the blessing of serving his Lord and Master—the glory of His salvation—it would be considered a perfect mockery of the person whom he addressed, of all the persons present, and of all that the people were doing. Suppose a man standing up on a race-course to ask God's blessing on a race!—or in a theatre, to invoke the blessing of God on a Tragedy—a Comedy—or a Farce!—Suppose, if you can, a man standing up in a ball-room to supplicate a blessing on a Quadrille—a Waltz—or a Polka! Would it not seem a mockery of God? Surely every one present would exclaim, "There is a time for everything"—"What business has religion here?" No business at all, certainly, and therefore the person who has any true religion has no business there—no happiness, no enjoyment there. Can a Christian be happy where the very name of his Lord were an intrusion?—where to ask His blessing were a mockery? If a person were to say to me, "Would you have me give up such an amusement—or such another pleasure?" I would answer, "Do you believe in your heart, that this amusement or this pleasure is consistent with your character as a servant of God? If not—then if it is a question with you, whether you are to give them up or not,—if your heart is in them, it is to be feared it is not right with God. It is to be feared you know nothing of Christ. But deal honestly with yourself. Let conscience do her office. Let me ask you one question—Can you conscientiously kneel down in your closet, and ask the Lord to accompany you there? Can you expect His presence and His blessing there? If He shall come, or summon you, can you be ready there? If not—then if you are a Christian, most certainly you can have no enjoyment there." As the flowers must droop and wither when placed where the sun cannot enter, so must the believer's heart where there is no place for Him who is his "*light and his salvation.*" Psal. xxvii. 1.

Therefore, to "WALK IN LOVE" rectifies all these things in the believer's heart and conscience. He sees and knows at once, by the test of love, what he is to do, and what he is not to do. Love is an instinctive judge of that which wounds its beloved, and thus, is really the test. "Shall I go here, into this society? Shall I go there, into that amusement? Is my Master there? Will my Lord be present? Can I look for His smile? Can I ask my Saviour's blessing in it? Can I lift up my eyes to Him without a blush, and say, 'Lord, here am I?' If I cannot, what pleasure can I have? what enjoyment can it be to me?" That one thought, that one single thought decides the matter.—If Jesus is not there—If I cannot expect His presence or implore His blessing—then what pleasure is there for my soul? What is the world to me?

Ask one who has inhabited and enjoyed the sunshine of a tropical clime, "Will you come and enjoy the pleasures of a Polar night?" "What!" he would say, "Is not the sun excluded there?—Is not the light of heaven shut out?—and do you bid me leave my happy glowing clime, where I am accustomed to bask in the light and heat of the sun, and seek for happiness in regions of eternal frost, of darkness, and the shadow of death?"

So might the believer ask, "Do you bid me seek for pleasure

where the Sun of Righteousness never shines?—where all the passing gleams of earthly pleasure and enjoyment are like the fitful flashings of the northern lights, that faintly flit along the sky, to supply the absence of the sun in the dreary polar night? How shall the children of light have pleasure or enjoyment in the place where darkness reigns?"

This test settles the case satisfactorily to the conscience of the believer, gives him at once a standard of judgment for his pleasures. This proves, that to become religious is not to give up happiness and true enjoyment. Religion was never designed to abridge, but to increase our happiness ten-fold; yea, ten hundred thousand fold. The believer has more true happiness in his darkest hour of trial and sorrow, that the unconverted sinner has, or ever had, in the greatest happiness he ever enjoyed, or can enjoy on earth. The believer, in the hours of trial, sorrow, and affliction, whatever they be, still has a refuge to which his soul can turn. It may be night with him, yea, even a dark and stormy night; but still, though "*heaviness may endure for a night, joy cometh in the morning*." Dark and gloomy though the vista may be, of the long and weary pilgrimage that is spread before him, there is a blessed gleam of light—there is a star that shoots its ray throughout its length,

> "With its long-levelled rule of streaming light—"

even the Star of Bethlehem that guides and cheers him on his way.

But the poor, blind, ignorant, unconverted sinner!—what has he to look to? What light to cheer him when his day is gone? His sun is about to set. The night is closing upon him. The valley of the shadow of death—the bar of judgment lie before him—where are all his pleasures and enjoyments then? His lamp is put out in death and outer darkness forever.

"BE YE THEREFORE FOLLOWERS OF GOD, AS DEAR CHILDREN; AND WALK IN LOVE, AS CHRIST ALSO HATH LOVED US, AND HATH GIVEN HIMSELF FOR US AN OFFERING AND A SACRIFICE TO GOD FOR A SWEET-SMELLING SAVOR." What a privilege to be able to walk, not in guilt and terror, but "IN LOVE" toward God. And not in malice and envy, but "IN LOVE" toward each other. "IN LOVE" toward God, for Christ is our Surety. "IN LOVE" toward each other, for Christ is our Example. "IN LOVE" toward God, "AS CHRIST ALSO HATH LOVED US, AND GIVEN HIMSELF FOR US, AN OFFERING AND A SACRIFICE TO GOD FOR A SWEET-SMELLING SAVOR." The work of our glorious Surety and Covenant-Head is accomplished. "*It is finished.*" John xix. 30—The offering is accepted.—Salvation is completed.—The sacrifice has ascended to God, and God receives it.—God is well pleased with it. "*This is my beloved Son, in whom I am well pleased.*" Mat. xvii. 5. This is pardon.—This is peace.—This is salvation.—Come to your reconciled Father, and "WALK IN LOVE."

We need not envy monarchs their crowns—their kingdoms—all that they enjoy, if thus we have peace, and can "WALK IN LOVE" with God through Christ Jesus. If we can enter into our closets, and shut to the door, and pray in the confidence of faith and love to our Father.—If we be thrown on beds of suffering and of sorrow, and can turn to our God as Hezekiah did on his bed of sickness—if we be afflicted—bereaved—despised and persecuted—yet, if we can come and pray to our God,—and walk in humble faith and love with Him, through our glorious Surety,—if we can do this, dear friends, we need not envy all the monarchs of the world. To walk in peace with God as a forgiven child—To walk in love with Him on this assured and everlasting foundation, that "CHRIST HATH LOVED US, AND GIVEN HIMSELF FOR US." This is joy and blessing for time and eternity.

But "WALK IN LOVE" not only toward God, but toward each other, "AS CHRIST ALSO HATH LOVED US AND GIVEN HIMSELF FOR US." Christ is not only our Surety, but our Example; and the example of His love in dying for us, is pressed on us as the motive of love even to death, for the brethren. See how it is enforced by the Apostle John, "*Hereby*," saith he, "*perceive we the love of God, because he laid down his life for us, and we ought to lay down our lives for the brethren. But whoso hath this world's goods, and seeth his brother have need, and shutteth up his bowels of compassion from him, how dwelleth the love of God in him? My little children, let us not love in word, neither in tongue, but in deed and in truth. And hereby we know that we are of the truth, and shall assure our hearts before him.*" 1 John iii. 16–19.

So here the Apostle Paul enforces the practical power and influence of love. "WALK IN LOVE." That is, let Love direct your steps. Let every movement be in the path of Love.

The Apostle then subjoins some of the proofs and testimonies that believers are to give in the purity of their life and conversation that they really walk in love. So he saith, "BUT FORNICATION AND ALL UNCLEANNESS, OR COVETOUSNESS, LET IT NOT BE ONCE NAMED AMONG YOU, AS BECOMETH SAINTS, NEITHER FILTHINESS, NOR FOOLISH TALKING, NOR JESTING, WHICH ARE NOT CONVENIENT, BUT RATHER GIVING OF THANKS; FOR THIS YE KNOW, THAT NO WHOREMONGER, OR UNCLEAN PERSON, OR COVETOUS MAN, WHO IS AN IDOLATER, HATH ANY INHERITANCE IN THE KINGDOM OF CHRIST AND OF GOD. LET NO MAN DECEIVE YOU WITH VAIN WORDS, FOR BECAUSE OF THESE THINGS, COMETH THE WRATH OF GOD UPON THE CHILDREN OF DISOBEDIENCE." verses 3—6. He shows that these things which constitute the prevailing sins, pursuits, and pleasures of the world in practice and conversation, are all to be excluded from the conversation and practice of the believer,—"FORNICATION, AND ALL UNCLEANNESS, OR COVETOUSNESS." We need not dwell on each of the vices that are here specified. The Apostle had thus described, as we saw in the preceding chapter, the state of all the nations,

"*Who being past feeling, have given themselves over unto lasciviousness, to work all uncleanness with greediness.*" iv. 19. The word there translated "*greediness*" with which, as it were, they coveted the indulgence of every evil passion, is here translated "COVETOUSNESS," and while some learned men have contended that it should here be used in a similar signification, I shall follow the simplicity of our translation, and take it just as it is, "COVETOUSNESS."

Now let us consider this sin. The whole world is occupied, more or less in every sphere of life, in contriving how they can gain, how they can best improve their condition, from the servant who leaves his place in hopes of getting a better—to the master, whatever be his rank, who is striving to obtain some increase of wealth, to enlarge his estates or his establishment—to aggrandize or to make a provision for his family, or something of that sort. Money is the God of this world; the human heart is worshipping it in every shape in which Satan chooses to mould it, no matter what that shape may be. The universal prevalence of the sin precludes it from observation, and in many cases from suspicion. Many persons say, "Such a man is not covetous, on the contrary he is a liberal man," meaning, that he gives perhaps his money very liberally. But the very man who does so may be as covetous as any miser on the earth. When our Lord saith, "*Take heed, and beware of covetousness,*" He does not illustrate the admonition by the parable of a miser, but of a rich and liberal man, "*I will pull down my barns, and build greater, and there will I bestow all my fruits and my goods.*" He was a man who spent his money, and employed many laborers. "*And I will say to my soul, soul, thou hast much goods laid up for many years, take thine ease, eat, drink, and be merry.*" Now he could not be merry alone; so, probably he had abundance of company. Yet he was a poor, covetous fool, see Luke xii. 15—20. Some men desire to get money to hoard it—some to spend it. One man to lock it up in his chest—another to squander it in pride, in vanity, or in ambition. One man will starve himself to death to save a farthing—another will squander thousands on his friends, neighbors, or dependants, to gratify or entertain them. It matters not which they do, the heart is covetous alike in both; whether it desire to possess, for display, for pride, for pomp, for vanity, or accumulation; it does not signify what it is,—the heart of the spendthrift is as covetous as the heart of the miser before God. The spendthrift who covets to spend, in whatever way he spends his money, desires to possess it to spend in that way. But the man who wishes to accumulate and hoard it up, accumulates it for his own lust of wealth, and hoards it for another to spend. How many hearts, yours and mine,—yea, our own vile hearts have been exercised with it! desiring sometimes one thing and sometimes another—thinking that if we were in such and such circumstances,—placed in such a situation, or had some certain means—how much happier, yea, perhaps, how much more religious we should be! This is our corrupt, vile, natural heart which is inclined to covetousness, as well as to countless other sins which we know by experience possess so much of our thoughts.

But the Apostle, speaking of these things, saith, "LET THEM NOT BE ONCE NAMED AMONG YOU, AS BECOMETH SAINTS." There is but one treasure you are permitted to covet,—"*The unsearchable riches of Christ*,"—one inheritance on which you are allowed to set your heart,—"*the inheritance incorruptible, undefiled, and that fadeth not away, reserved in heaven for you, who are kept by the power of God, through faith unto salvation.*" 1 Pet. i. 4. This Christ has purchased for you. This God is keeping for you, and as surely as your heart is set upon it, here is ample scope for the vast desires, the immense ambition of an immortal soul.

The Apostle continues, "NEITHER FILTHINESS, NOR FOOLISH TALKING, NOR JESTING, WHICH ARE NOT CONVENIENT." Who could ever suppose that offences like these require to be guarded against by a Christian? Yet, indeed there is deep necessity for such exhortation. When the propensities of the heart are wicked, the tongue when unrestrained is ready to give vent to them. The word translated "FILTHINESS" is the substantive of that used by the Apostle in the 12th verse—*shameful*, "*It is a shame even to speak of those things which are done of them in secret.*" What is shameful to do is shameful to speak of. But while, in the society of persons who are what is considered respectable, the exhortation may not be necessary: the other terms "FOOLISH TALKING AND JESTING, WHICH ARE NOT CONVENIENT," too constantly apply to them. For there are multitudes who call themselves Christians, who are continually guilty of offences such as these in their conversation. Indeed, purity of language, and purity of sentiment, require to be cultivated and guarded, even in that which ought to be the most refined and best society. For in these days, "*in this adulterous and sinful generation*," Mark viii. 38, it is, and has long been, very much the fashion to dress up ideas, in language of poetry for example, from which the mind and ear of modesty would revolt, if they were put into plain prose; and yet, they can be clothed in poetry—read—admired, and sung by persons who would be much displeased if their religion, or the purity and modesty of their conversation were called into question. Yet if their books, poems, and songs, were brought to the test of the holy Word of God, they would be cast into the fire as not fit to be admitted into society which bears the name of Christian.

The word here translated "JESTING," literally signifies an expression which can be easily turned, as it were, into another meaning, and which corresponds to that species of witticism called *double entendre*, in which, under the guise of one sentiment, another not fit to be plainly expressed, is conveyed. This is one of the commonest and most corrupting modes of giving vent to the wickedness of the heart, and is here enumerated amongst those which are "NOT CONVENIENT,"—that is most unbefitting, most unseemly And surely what can be more so, than that the profane jest—the indelicate insinuation—should be modulated in sounds of polished language, and spoken in the ear which never ought to hear, or pronounced by the tongue which never ought to speak them?

"LET IT NOT BE NAMED AMONG YOU, AS BECOMETH SAINTS" —is the Scriptural command. We may consider this to include all absurd, vain, foolish, trifling talking; and indeed we all, especially those of light and buoyant spirits and vivid imaginations, have need to watch against ourselves in this particular:—for as the Apostle James, speaking of the tongue, saith, "*In many things we offend all.*" chap. iii. 2.—The flippant remark—the sharp repartee—the satirical jest—all things that excite and wound the feelings of others, or turn them into ridicule, to which some of us are naturally so inclined, these and various other things that obtain so much in ordinary conversation, may be classed among those that are "NOT CONVENIENT," that is not suitable, not befitting the saint.

The Apostle adds, "BUT RATHER GIVING OF THANKS." The word translated "GIVING OF THANKS," as applied to conversation, may perhaps be considered to imply as a contradistinction, which the Apostle evidently means, to the evils which he had specified,—that *which tends to the praise and glory of God*—as the former tends to dishonor God—so let your conversation rather be such as tends to His praise and glory—expressive of gratitude to God rather than dishonor to Him.

He proceeds to the reason of this—"FOR THIS YE KNOW, THAT NO WHOREMONGER, NOR UNCLEAN PERSON, NOR COVETOUS MAN, WHO IS AN IDOLATER, HATH ANY INHERITANCE IN THE KINGDOM OF CHRIST OR OF GOD." He gives this as a reason against such conversation, justly implying, that men who are ready to speak of sins in their ordinary discourse, prove thereby, that they are inclined to commit them; and he argues from the effect to the cause; he shows when these things exist in the conversation and conduct, they are totally incompatible with the faith and love of the Lord Jesus Christ; and therefore, "THOSE WHO DO SUCH THINGS HAVE NO INHERITANCE IN THE KINGDOM OF CHRIST OR OF GOD."

And if any should be inclined (as no doubt many were then as well as now) to abuse the doctrines of grace, and to conclude against the Apostolic truth, that they might "*continue in sin that grace may abound.*" Rom. vi. 1. The Apostle is most clearly explicit on the subject against all such deceivers and perverters of the Gospel. "LET NO MAN DECEIVE YOU WITH VAIN WORDS, FOR BECAUSE OF THESE THINGS COMETH THE WRATH OF GOD ON THE CHILDREN OF DISOBEDIENCE." Let no man make light of sin;—"*Fools make a mock at sin.*" Prov. xiv. 9, let no man do so, and "LET NO MAN DECEIVE YOU WITH VAIN WORDS." For, all these sins and various others, are the causes why God's judgments are visited on the ungodly world; and therefore remember, that those who live in the practice of sins such as these in their life and conversation, can "HAVE NO INHERITANCE IN THE

KINGDOM OF CHRIST AND OF GOD." They are not God's children —they have the mark of their master the devil upon their foreheads—therefore, "*Know ye not that to whom ye yield yourselves servants to obey, his servants ye are to whom ye obey.*" Rom. vi. 16. "*The wages of sin is death.*" Rom. vi. 23, and if ye serve the Master, ye shall be sure to obtain the wages ye have earned.

Therefore, consider these things. Think, what evils we have to watch against in ourselves, and if we must watch against them in ourselves, how anxious should we be to guard against them in our associates. As we see the Apostle adds, "*Be not ye therefore partakers with them.*" That, which those who are ignorant of Christ, will pass over, and which will give them no offence in the society of the world, will be exceedingly painful and wounding to the ears and feelings of a Christian. Therefore, not only avoid these evils yourselves, but avoid all participation and association with those persons, whose conversation is such, as the Apostle here commands believers to watch and guard against. "*Be not deceived: evil communications corrupt good manners.*" 1 Cor. xv. 33. Avoid them.—Study the Word of God.—Cultivate the people of God.—Give yourself to secret prayer and communion with God,—Wait on the ordinances of God.—Pray that you may have your heart filled with the precious knowledge of His love, and with those principles and motives under the teaching of the Spirit, by which you may be enabled to guard against the evils here enumerated, and "LET NO MAN DECEIVE YOU WITH VAIN WORDS, FOR BECAUSE OF THESE THINGS COMETH THE WRATH OF GOD UPON THE CHILDREN OF DISOBEDIENCE."

You see, my dear friends, how the practical principles, are inseparably connected with the doctrinal truths of the Gospel. The idea, of taking out these rules of virtue and a holy life out of their place in the Bible—separating them from Christ—giving them to be a guide to men for their conduct,—preaching them to a congregation,—teaching them to children—pretending to set them up as the rule or standard for men to walk by!!!—You might just as well erect a manufactory in a church-yard, and call on the dead to arise and work it, as take the moral precepts of the Gospel, and give them as the rule of life, to those who are dead in trespasses and sins, and think they will or can put them into practice.

Hence mere moral books—moral precepts taken out of the Bible —the very holy Law of God itself, hung up in schools by way of teaching children to obey it, or the corrupt mutilation of God's Truth, selecting the moral parts of Scripture, and separating them from the great doctrines of the Gospel of Christ, as they stand identified with them in His blessed Word, by way of instructing the souls of children or grown persons, is all the mere blindness, ignorance, folly, and wickedness, of worms of the dust, assuming to be wiser than the Omniscient God.

We require all the power of the Gospel brought into our heart by the Holy Ghost, to bring the practical influence of the moral precepts of the Gospel into our lives. We require all the power of the Gospel by the Holy Ghost over our wills and affections, to regulate our conduct, and constrain us to live to Him who died for us. We must have the precepts of the Gospel and the principles of the Gospel, not only as God has incorporated them in His Word, but they must be incorporated by the power of the Spirit in our own hearts; otherwise they never can be manifested in our lives, and instead of being "FOLLOWERS OF GOD, AS DEAR CHILDREN," we shall be servants of Satan to the end of our existence.

May the Lord bring all these truths home to us, dear friends! May the Lord Jesus write them on our hearts by the power of His Spirit! make us "FOLLOWERS OF GOD, AS DEAR CHILDREN," and enable us to "WALK IN LOVE, AS CHRIST ALSO HATH LOVED US, AND GIVEN HIMSELF FOR US." Amen and Amen.

THIRTY-SEVENTH LECTURE.

EPHESIANS V.—7, 8, 9, 10, 11, 12.

"Be not ye therefore partakers with them. For ye were sometimes darkness, but now are ye light in the Lord: walk as children of light; (for the fruit of the Spirit is in all goodness, and righteousness, and truth;) proving what is acceptable unto the Lord. And have no fellowship with the unfruitful works of darkness, but rather reprove them. For it is a shame even to speak of those things which are done of them in secret."

IT is a truth ever to be reiterated, and ever to be remembered, that every practical duty of the Gospel of Christ, must be always enforced on the principles of the Gospel. It is wholly impossible that genuine Christian obedience can either ever be properly enforced by a minister of Christ, or ever be attained by his hearers unless on sound Christian principles. This is one reason why it has always been Satan's policy to undermine—to corrupt—and to depreciate the doctrines of the Gospel. This policy, the Prince of this world seems to have succeeded in embodying very generally, indeed, almost universally, into the public opinion of the present day; by what is denominated Liberalism—that is, that we are to be extremely liberal, as it is called, respecting the opinions that men may hold on religion; because it is not of much importance what doctrines men entertain on this subject. These are called mere opinions of theory—mere abstract sentiments—mere points of belief—mere matters of individual concernment—with which we have no right whatever to interfere; and therefore, which it is not our business at all to notice. But, as it is universally admitted, that the great end of the Christian religion in this world, is to produce, as far as man's social intercourse is concerned, good fruits, or good works; that all we have to attend to, is the practical part of religion—the morality of the Gospel—and that as to the doctrinal opinions, which men hold, it is entirely a matter of indifference what they are.

This, I say, is the policy of Satan—this is one of his favorite modes of sentiment, which he seems to have succeeded in diffusing so extensively into the minds of men, at the present day. The great mass of those who call themselves Christians, either hold or affect to hold these opinions.

Now this strikes at the very root of all true religion; for there is no such thing in any individual on earth, as Christian practice without Christian principle. Man must have the principle of the Gospel in his heart, before he can have the fruit of the Gospel in his life. You may think, I unnecessarily reiterate this assertion, but as often as men are called to act, so often, ought they to be called on to examine their principle of action. God admits but of one principle as the motive of moral action in man, and where that principle does not exist, there can be no such thing as genuine moral conduct. It is impossible. We may well require to have ever repeated in our ears, that which ought to be the habitual motive of our actions in the sight of God. These remarks, you perceive, are particularly applicable to the very point at which our Lecture this day commences. The Apostle, as you remember, had been warning believers against the ungodly practices—the ungodly principles—the ungodly conversation of the world, "*Fornication, and all uncleanness, or covetousness, let it not be once named among you, as becometh saints. Neither filthiness, nor foolish talking, nor jesting, which are not convenient, but rather giving of thanks. For this ye know, that no whoremonger, or unclean person, or covetous man who is an idolater, hath any inheritance in the kingdom of Christ and of God. Let no man deceive you with vain words, for because of these things cometh the wrath of God on the children of disobedience.*"

Then the Apostle proceeds—"BE NOT YE THEREFORE PARTAKERS WITH THEM." Why? What is the principle on which they are called, not to be partakers with such persons? "FOR YE WERE SOMETIMES DARKNESS, BUT NOW ARE YE LIGHT IN THE LORD, WALK AS CHILDREN OF LIGHT." Observe, how he commences the chapter, "*Be ye followers of God, as dear children.*" Observe the motive, to be His followers. "*And walk in love, as Christ also hath loved us.*" Then, having enumerated the different sins of practice and conversation which I have read, you see he brings forward again the same principle, "BE NOT YE THEREFORE PARTAKERS WITH THEM; FOR YE WERE SOMETIMES DARKNESS, BUT NOW ARE YE LIGHT IN THE LORD, WALK AS CHILDREN OF LIGHT." The principle on which he enforces these moral practical precepts is this, that they have been formerly in a state which he calls "DARKNESS," and that they are now in a state which he calls "LIGHT IN THE LORD." Therefore, I say, the principle on which Christian duty is here enforced, is this, that of a man being brought, by the Gospel, out of his natural darkness into the light of Christ's salvation, and he can no more walk in the light of truth, or in the ways of truth in his natural state of darkness, than a man can walk in the light of noon when it is midnight. Impossible.—He must have the principle in his heart, or he cannot have the practice in his life.

This is so important, that I must dwell on it for a moment.

Let me suppose a person here to ask, how do you prove that? Do you mean to say, that a man may perform—for example, an action, which you admit to be an act of Christian duty—of Christian kindness, or benevolence. Suppose—This person gives a large sum of money to benefit the poor—to feed the hungry—to clothe the naked—to heal the sick—to erect an hospital—something of that kind, which you yourself acknowledge to be an act of Christian benevolence; nay, that it is more than a man can be said to be bound to do, and that he does it voluntarily and liberally; and suppose he hopes that this will conduce to his salvation.

Another man, on what you call Christian principle, for the love of Christ, does the same. Do you mean to say, that one of these men who acts on what you call Christian principle, does really a good moral act, and that the same act performed by some man, who does not act on what you call Christian principle, is not a good act?

I mean to say exactly so.

The acts considered in themselves, or considered in their beneficial effects to the poor, are both the same; but considered in reference to the individuals who perform them, the one is an act of duty to God and to man—the act of a Christian, and accepted before God—the other is the act of an unconverted sinner, and the wrath of God, which abides on him by nature and practice, is not lessened in its weight or certainty a single iota, by that, or a thousand acts of the same kind. The motive of his act is false, it is an offering of ignorance and pride, and never can be accepted before God. Is that salvation which is the gift of God, which could be purchased from eternal justice, only by the blood of Jesus, to be bought with money to build hospitals or churches? A man's person (remember this) must be accepted, before his works can be accepted. His person must be accepted before God—his sins must be pardoned—he must be justified from his iniquity, by the righteousness and blood of Jesus—he must be in a state of peace and reconciliation with his God, before any act that he does can ever be received or accepted by Him. It is the acceptance of a sinner's person, through Christ, by faith in His salvation, that makes his works acceptable—and it is not his works being accepted through Christ, that leads to the acceptance of his person. This is a point of the very vital essence of Christianity. This is a fundamental principle of truth, if you do not understand this, you do not know the foundation of the Christian religion; and therefore, those principles on the subject of religion now so prevalent in the world, called liberal principles, which decry as bigotry, the assertion and maintenance of the distinctive doctrines of the Gospel, as if all those doctrines were mere speculative opinions, are all founded on falsehood—they strike a direct blow at the root of the Christian faith—they are propagated by the Prince of darkness, and their direct immediate tendency is to subvert the truth and the salvation of the living God. There is no such thing as Christian morality, but that which springs from Christian principle; it does not rise above the level of mere Pagan ethics; there is no such thing as one moral action accepted before God that proceeds from an unconverted sinner.

Does he bring forth no fruit? He does; but he brings forth fruit unto himself. So saith the Lord by the Prophet, "*Israel is an empty vine, he bringeth forth fruit unto himself.*" Hosea x. 1; every unconverted man brings forth fruit unto himself, not to God. Our blessed Lord is distinct and express on the point, "*As the branch cannot bear fruit of itself, except it abide in the vine, no more can ye except ye abide in me.*" No, "YE WERE SOMETIMES (or once) DARKNESS," saith the Apostle. But every unconverted man is here called "DARKNESS." Why?—If a man cannot see where he is going, he must be in darkness, so saith our Lord, "*He that walketh in darkness, knoweth not whither he goeth;*" John xii. 35. Either he is blind, or else, there is no light around him; if he cannot see where he is about to place his feet, he is in darkness. Now, every unconverted man is exactly so, he cannot see where he is going, death is before him—eternity is before him—the bar of God is before him—eternal judgment is before him—hell is before him—the wrath of God is upon him—the gulf of perdition yawns perhaps at his feet—his next step may be into it—but he cannot see it—he knoweth not whither he goeth; and if you tell him of it, if you warn him, he scoffs at your admonition—he does not see any spiritual truth—he does not know his own character in the sight of God—he does not see himself a sinner—God's law is not the rule of his conduct, nor the standard of his judgment—he is wholly ignorant of its spiritual character—he does not know the iniquity that defiles his best deeds—he is ignorant of the sins of his tongue—he never dreams of the deceit and desperate wickedness of his heart—on the contrary, you will see almost all unconverted men, console themselves for the sins of which they confess they are more or less practically guilty, on the principle of the goodness of their hearts. They mean thereby, that they have a certain intention of reforming and amending their lives at some future time, and they hope and intend that they will yet do right, and weighing these good intentions against their practical sins, they console themselves for their sins by the self-complacent conviction, that their heart is so good. Now a man in his natural state cannot see the evil of his heart;

he cannot believe that so far from being good, it is indeed the source of all his course of sin; he cannot see the natural corruption of his heart, life, and conduct; he knows nothing of the character of God; he has, as he thinks a confident hope in God's mercy; but tell him of his justice, holiness, and his certain determination to punish sin, he neither knows, nor believes, one tittle on the subject. "*He flattereth himself in his own eyes*," as David saith Ps. xxxvi. 27. He thinks himself so superior to multitudes around, that he secures himself by asking, "What will become of the world if he were to be cast away?" He infers, that this book which reveals his own character and God's character to him, is a dark, enigmatical, unintelligible book; and the reason why he finds such difficulties in the Bible is this—that the plain statements contained in that Word are in such flat contradiction to the natural opinions of the human mind, that, because man cannot reconcile the truth of the Bible with his own principles, he thinks there are enormous difficulties in the Bible. This is the fact. Whereas, although it is true, that the Bible contains depths of Divine Wisdom, wonders and mysteries, both of glories that are past, and of those that are to come, which the human intellect cannot now fathom—although the Bible is a book of such infinite wisdom, such infinite glory, that the more a man advances in the knowledge of it, the more does he feel that it is the book of God in the hands of a child—although this is the character of the Bible in many respects, yet the Bible is in many other things, the plainest Book on earth; in all things, I may say, that concern man's salvation and his conduct in this world. There is not in all Theology a single book written which contains in itself clearer, plainer, principles of truth, than those written in this blessed Word of God. But the difficulty of the Book consists, to the unregenerated man, not in its abstruse passages, but in its plain and obvious truths; because those truths come with such direct, explicit contradiction to the natural opinions—the natural corruptions and pride of the human heart; therefore, man in all things connected with his spiritual state—his present condition—his future prospects—his own character, and the character and attributes of God, in all these he is in darkness, he knows nothing of them; and until the grace of God shall have visited him, and until the light of God's eternal truth shall have shined into his heart, or as the Apostle says, until "*God who commanded the light to shine out of darkness shines into his heart, to give him the light of the knowledge of the glory of God in the face of Jesus Christ*"—he continues in that darkness. And then observe, there is the very process by which he is brought out of it, consider that text, 2 Cor. iv. 6; observe the same Almighty power that said when the world was in darkness, "*Let there be light, and there was light*," must say to every individual sinner's heart, "*Let there be light*" in that sinner's heart, and there shall be light. What is the light which God commanded to shine on the darkness of a created world? The Sun. What is the light that God commands to shine out of the moral darkness to lighten the sinner's heart? "*The Sun of Righteousness.*" Unto "*you that fear my name shall the Sun of Righteousness arise with healing in his wings;*" Mal. iv. 2. So, when "*God who commanded the light to shine out of darkness,*" shines into the sinner's heart, He gives "*The light of the knowledge of the glory of God in the face of Jesus Christ,*" he enables the sinner to see the glory of God in that blessed face—the glory of God's justice in punishing sin—the glory of God's mercy in pardoning sin, yea, the chief of sinners—the glory of God's faithfulness in fulfilling all His promises, which are all "*yea and amen in Christ Jesus.*" When "*the glory of God in the face of Jesus Christ*" shines into the sinner's heart, then he is "LIGHT IN THE LORD."—So the Apostle saith, "YE WERE SOMETIMES DARKNESS, BUT NOW YE ARE LIGHT IN THE LORD," this is ordinarily produced under the Divine blessing by the preaching of the Gospel of Christ, the light shines into the sinner's heart, through the belief of the testimony of the Gospel of Jesus, I trust it may shine into the hearts of some of my dear hearers to-day.

Yes—perhaps there may be some of you into whose hearts the light of this knowlege of Christ has not shined as yet, and I trust, that God may make use of His Word in my unworthy lips to-day, to shed that light into your hearts, even at this time.

Some of you may be saying within yourselves—"It is very true, I am going to death—I am going to judgment—to eternity—but know not whither I am going!—It is all uncertainty with me, like a man walking in darkness and not knowing where his foot is next to fall, so it is all uncertainty with my soul. I know not, if I were to die to-day where my foot is to rest, whether I should plant it on the Rock and enter into life, or whether I should step on the quicksands and sink into eternal death!"

Perhaps there are some of you here, who must come to this sad conclusion, of your own state. Alas! then, if so, you are in darkness; but now, by the preaching of the Gospel of Jesus—by the proclamation of pardon through the blood of the Lamb—of salvation through him who died for sinners—of the riches of God's pardoning grace in sending His Son to be the Saviour of the guilty—and the glory of Christ's grace in coming to die and "*bear our sins in his own body on the tree,*" 1st Pet. ii. 24. Perhaps, I say, through the preaching of this blessed truth, the light may break into your heart, and that you may be enabled to say, "Oh then, I see Christ is a Refuge for a sinner like me. If this be true, I may lean on Jesus, here is salvation for my soul in Christ—here is salvation for me in the blood of the Lamb." Well then, if this be so, if God shall teach you thus, then, though "YOU WERE SOMETIMES DARKNESS," even this morning—when you know and trust in Jesus, then you shall be "LIGHT IN THE LORD," even this very day.

There is no light—no salvation in any other. "*I am the light of the world,*" saith the Lord Jesus, "*He that followeth me shall not walk in darkness, but shall have the light of life,"* John viii. 12. Thus saith the Psalmist, looking to this light, "*The Lord is my light and my salvation, whom shall I fear, the Lord is the strength of my life, of whom shall I be afraid.*" Ps. xxvii. 1. This is what St. Peter says, speaking of the state of man by nature, and by grace, "*Ye are a chosen generation, a royal priesthood, an holy nation, a peculiar people, that ye should show forth the praises of him who hath called you out of darkness into his marvellous light.*" 1st Pet. ii. 9. You see the result of calling men into light is, that they should "WALK AS CHILDREN OF LIGHT," and manifest that they are of the light, so you observe what our Lord says to His disciples, when he tells them, "*Ye are the light of the world,*" He adds, "*Let your light so shine before men, that they may see your good works, and glorify your Father which is in heaven.*" Mat. v. 14—16.

Whose servant are you? What an important—what a momentous question! We cannot serve God and Mammon, and we must be servants of one or the other—of the "*Father of lights*"—or of the "*Prince of darkness.*"

One great use and blessing of light is that we should walk in the light; if you are a child of light, what is it for but that you should walk in the light. This is what the Apostle says, "YE WERE SOMETIMES DARKNESS, BUT NOW ARE YE LIGHT IN THE LORD, WALK AS CHILDREN OF LIGHT." This is an image repeatedly used in the Scriptures, as in 1st Thes. v. We have it there also practically applied, both to the present walk, and the future prospects of the Church at the coming of the Lord. Let us refer to the passage—"*But of the times and the seasons, brethren, ye have no need that I write unto you; for yourselves know perfectly, that the day of the Lord so cometh as a thief in the night.*" Look now at the state of those in darkness—"*For when they shall say peace and safety, then sudden destruction cometh upon them, as travail upon a woman with child, and they shall not escape.*" "*When they shall say, peace and safety,*" when the world is laughing at religion, mocking at those who are speaking of it, and calling their principles mere "religious opinions," "theoretical opinions," scoffing at them, "*Scoffers, walking after their own lusts, and saying, Where is the promise of his coming,*" 2nd Pet. iii. 3, 4. When they are saying this, and as our Lord describes those of old, "*They were eating and drinking, marrying and giving in marriage, until the day that Noe entered into the ark, and knew not until the flood came and took them all away; so shall also the coming of the Son of man be.*" Mat. xxiv. 38, 39.

"*As it was in the days of Noe, so shall it be in the days of the Son of man,*" Luke xvii. 26, "*when they shall say peace and safety, then sudden destruction cometh upon them, as travail upon a woman with child, and they shall not escape.*" 1st Thes. v. 3. Then shall their eyes be opened, and when their eyes are opened, what a fearful sight shall they behold! "*The Son of man coming in the clouds of heaven, with power and great glory.*"

Mat. xxiv. 30. Then comes that dreadful hour, when "*The kings of the earth, and the great men, and the rich men, and the chief captains, and the mighty men, and every bondman, and every freeman, shall hide themselves in the dens, and in the rocks of the mountains, and shall say to the mountains and rocks, Fall on us, and hide us from the face of him that sitteth on the throne, and from the wrath of the Lamb.*" Rev. vi. 15, 16. For these are they on whom "*When they shall say peace and safety, then sudden destruction cometh*"—these are they that are in darkness.

"*But ye brethren,*" adds the Apostle, "*are not in darkness, that that day should overtake you as a thief, ye are all the children of light, and the children of the day, we are not of the night, nor of darkness.*" Light consists in the knowledge of Him, through whom we are prepared for that time, so, in being prepared—ready for that day—in knowing that sin is blotted out—in knowing how, and through whom it is blotted out—in knowing that the very God who shall come in His glory to judge a guilty world, is the God of our salvation—our Refuge—our Hope—our Peace—that Saviour whom we have known so long as our only comfort, and to whom our heart has continually turned as all our Hope and all our Salvation.

These are they of whom the Prophet speaketh, when he saith, "*It shall be said in that day, Lo this is our God, we have waited for him, and he will save us: this is the Lord; we have waited for him, we will be glad, and rejoice in his salvation.*" Is. xxv. 9.

To these saith the Apostle, "*Ye are not in darkness, that that day should overtake you as a thief, ye are all the children of light, and the children of the day; we are not of the night, nor of darkness.*" 1st Thes. v. 4, 5.

But now mark the practical application of it—"*Therefore, let us not sleep as do others, but let us watch and be sober,*" verse 6; let us not give ourselves up to spiritual indolence, to sleep—to sloth—to apathy—to negligence, *But let us watch and be sober; for they that sleep, sleep in the night; and they that be drunken, are drunken in the night.*" These are the people that are in ignorance—in blindness—in darkness, "*But let us who are of the day be sober, putting on the breastplate of faith and love, and for an helmet the hope of salvation.*" We are engaged in a warfare, but it is in daylight—let us avail ourselves of the light to fight. We are in an enemy's country—surrounded with foes,—we have a constant battle to wage—but it is under the Captain of our salvation. Our enemies are without and within, the world, the flesh, and the devil—therefore, "*Let us who are of the day be sober, putting on the breastplate of faith and love, and for an helmet the hope of salvation.*" Why? "*For God hath not appointed us to wrath, but to obtain salvation through our Lord Jesus Christ.*" If we be believers, if we are looking to Christ, if Christ is our Refuge, let us remember that this is the testimony of God, "*For God hath not appointed us to wrath, but to obtain salvation through our Lord Jesus Christ, who died for us, that whether we wake or sleep, we should live together with him, wherefore comfort yourselves together, and edify one another, even as also ye do.*" 1 Thes. v. 9, 10. We see here the state of those who believe the Gospel of Jesus, we see what blessed privileges belong to them and their consequent duties; and you may perceive, that this is merely an expansion of the principle laid down here in this passage before us, where the Apostle tells them not to be partakers with the "*children of disobedience.*" The reason you see is, "FOR YE WERE SOMETIMES DARKNESS, BUT NOW ARE YE LIGHT IN THE LORD, WALK AS CHILDREN OF LIGHT; (FOR THE FRUIT OF THE SPIRIT IS IN ALL GOODNESS AND RIGHTEOUSNESS AND TRUTH.")

The fruit which the Spirit produces in the believer is "IN ALL GOODNESS AND RIGHTEOUSNESS AND TRUTH." The fruits of the Spirit, like those of the garden are produced and ripened in the light of day. This fruit is directly contrasted in Galatians v. 16, 17, with the works of the flesh, "*Walk in the Spirit, and ye shall not fulfil the lusts of the flesh; for the flesh lusteth against the Spirit, and the Spirit against the flesh, and these are contrary the one to the other, so that ye cannot do the things that ye would.*" That is—your natural disposition, your natural corrupt wicked heart is always lusting against the Spirit of God; "*The flesh lusteth against the Spirit, and the Spirit against the flesh.*" The Spirit of God is always in opposition to the natural inclinations and corruptions of man; "*And these are contrary the one to the other, so that ye cannot do the things that ye would.*" The believer "*Delights in the law of God after the inward man,*" Rom. vii. 22; the law is written on his heart by the Spirit. He would fulfil that law according to the dictates of that blessed Spirit, if his natural corruption allowed him, but he cannot. Let him do what he may, he feels that he never can do what he would—he never can pray, as he would—read the Word of God, as he would—meditate on it, as he would—believe, as he would—or do a single ordinary action, much less perform his best spiritual duties, as he would. So that the Apostle not only records the dictates of inspired truth, but the responsive experience of every servant of God,* when he says, "*Ye cannot do the things that ye would,*" ye know—ye feel that ye cannot. But he adds, "*If ye be led by the Spirit, ye are not under the law,*" ye are not condemned for these things; ye are under the covenant of grace and peace in Jesus. "*There is no condemnation to them that are in Christ Jesus,*" Rom. viii. 1; "*Ye are not under the law, but under grace.*"

* The experience of Bishop Beveridge furnishes a remarkable commentary on this in his "Private Thoughts," Art. IV., in which he says, "I do not only betray the inbred venom of my heart, by poisoning my common actions, but even my most religious performances also with sin. I cannot pray but I sin. I cannot hear or preach a sermon but I sin. I cannot give an alms or receive the Sacrament but I sin. Nay, I cannot so much as confess my sins, but my very confessions are still aggravations of them—my repentance needs to be repented of—my tears want washing, and the very washing of my tears needs still to be washed over again with the blood of my Redeemer."

Rom. vi. 14. "*Now the works of the flesh are manifest which are these, adultery, fornication, uncleanness, lasciviousness, idolatry, witchcraft, hatred, variance, emulations, wrath, strife, seditions, heresies, envyings, murders, drunkenness, revellings, and such like, of the which I tell you before, as I have also told you in times past, that they which do such things shall not inherit the kingdom of God.*" Gal. v. 19–21. They are manifestly walking after the flesh, and therefore are servants not of God, but of Satan.

Now observe, "*The fruit of the Spirit is love;*" that is the first, mark then the precept in the beginning of this chapter, "*Be ye therefore followers of God, as dear children, and walk in love.*" When we know what Christ has done for us, Christ must be precious to our souls. It is the chief office of the Spirit to testify of Christ to the soul, therefore "*The fruit of the Spirit, is love, joy, peace, long-suffering, gentleness, goodness, faith, meekness, temperance: against such there is no law. And they that are Christ's, have crucified the flesh with the affections and lusts.*" Gal. v. 22, 23. Therefore, we are walking at liberty, whenever we are brought truly to seek God's precepts, "*I will walk at liberty,*" saith the Psalmist, "*for I seek thy precepts,*" Ps. cxix. 45. Whenever the sinner is made willing to do the law of God, then he is not walking under constraint, against his inclinations, but walking at liberty, to do what he desires. A man is always at liberty when he can do what he likes, and when man likes to do what he ought to do, he is walking at liberty—he is no longer a slave—he is a freeman—he is set at liberty, why? because his heart is brought to know and love his Lord. He is not as a slave striving against his will to keep a law that he hates, and to obey the God whom he detests; laboring reluctantly to do what he does not wish to do, and abstaining as reluctantly from what he would desire to do. The best religion of the unconverted man is, labor to be religious; striving to deny himself what he would like to do, and laboring to do what he would wish to avoid. But the liberty of the believer, consists in this. He has been taught to love his Lord. He desires to serve his Heavenly Master. His lusts—his sins—these are the tyrants that he detests—he groans under their yoke. The service of his God is the liberty he loves —and he desires to walk in that liberty—he desires to walk in love. The natural corruptions of his heart, are, as it were fetters that bind his liberty; and he wishes if he could, to escape from these chains into the light and freedom of perfect holiness to the Lord. Therefore the walk of the children of light is a walk of love, and so the Apostle shows by the next words which are in a parenthesis, in which he intends, as it were, to remind them of what he means by walking as children of light, "WALK AS CHILDREN OF LIGHT, (FOR THE FRUIT OF THE SPIRIT IS IN ALL GOODNESS, AND RIGHTEOUSNESS, AND TRUTH)," as much as to say, "you know what I mean by this. You know how the children of light—those who are born of the Spirit, and called unto the glorious light of the Gospel—ought to walk." As he saith in another place, "*If we live in the Spirit, let us also walk in the Spirit*," Gal. v. 25, and if ye "WALK AS CHILDREN OF LIGHT"—that is, if you "*walk in the Spirit*," ye know that "THE FRUIT OF THE SPIRIT IS IN ALL GOODNESS AND RIGHTEOUSNESS AND TRUTH." Let your walk be one of universal obedience, not partial in some things, and careless or criminal in others—not like a tree with fruit on one bough and all the rest barren—but "IN ALL GOODNESS," in all "RIGHTEOUSNESS," and in all "TRUTH,"—the power of the Spirit pervading your heart, and the fruits of the Spirit manifested in your life—thus "WALK AS CHILDREN OF LIGHT,"—"PROVING WHAT IS ACCEPTABLE UNTO THE LORD." "PROVING," that is, manifesting—demonstrating it to others—to yourselves—to the Lord.

To others—so saith our blessed Master, "*Let your light so shine before men, that they may see your good works, and glorify your Father which is in heaven.*" Matt. v. 16. So saith the Apostle James, "*Show me thy faith without thy works, and I will show thee my faith by my works.*" James ii. 18. So the Apostle Peter, "*So is the will of God, that with well-doing ye put to silence the ignorance of foolish men.*" 1 Peter, ii. 15.

Proving it to yourselves—as saith the Apostle to the Romans, "*Know ye not, that to whom ye yield yourselves servants to obey, his servants ye are to whom ye obey; whether of sin unto death, or of obedience unto righteousness?*" Rom. vi. 16. So saith the Apostle John, "*Hereby we know that we are of the truth, and shall assure our hearts before him. For if our hearts condemn us, God is greater than our hearts, and knoweth all things. Beloved, if our heart condemn us not, then have we confidence toward God.*" 1 John iii. 19, 20, 21.

Proving it to the Lord as Peter, "*Lord, thou knowest all things; thou knowest that I love thee.*" John xxi. 17. This is to "*walk in the Spirit*"—to "*walk in love*"—to "WALK AS CHILDREN OF LIGHT."

But it is not only necessary in this world of sin and temptation to know what we ought to pursue, but what we ought to avoid. The children of light are surrounded by the children of darkness—the servants of Christ by the servants of the prince of darkness—therefore the Apostle instructs them in this too.

"AND HAVE NO FELLOWSHIP WITH THE UNFRUITFUL WORKS OF DARKNESS, BUT RATHER REPROVE THEM, FOR IT IS A SHAME EVEN TO SPEAK OF THOSE THINGS WHICH ARE DONE OF THEM IN SECRET."

We have here a double exhortation, and then a reason for it.—First to "HAVE NO FELLOWSHIP WITH THEM." He does not say do not practice them—but "HAVE NO FELLOWSHIP WITH THEM." It is a vulgar but an infallible adage, "Tell me your company and I'll tell you what you are." It is universally true that men love associates like themselves. The Apostle when he describes the various iniquities that defile the world—Rom. i. 29—31—giving a condensed catalogue of the vices, corruptions, and profligacies of mankind—adds this, as an universal characteristic of the human race, "*Who, knowing the judgment of God, that they which do such things are worthy of death, not only do the same, but have pleasure in them that do them.*" v. 32. There is a blessing, not only in avoiding evil conduct, but evil company. So the Psalmist, "*Blessed is the man that walketh not in the counsel of the ungodly, nor standeth in the way of sinners, nor sitteth in the seat of the scornful.*" Psalm i. 1. So, too, his son Solomon, "*Enter not into the path of the wicked, and go not in the way of evil men. Avoid it, pass not by it, turn from it, and pass away.*" Prov. iv. 14, 15.

So the Apostle here exhorts:—First, to "HAVE NO FELLOWSHIP WITH THEM"—but secondly, "RATHER REPROVE THEM." To reprove an offender is not only a sure way of avoiding his company, but the best way of insuring that he will be anxious to avoid yours. This exhortation, however, is more conditional than positive, there may be persons and circumstances where reproof to an offender could not be well administered by a servant of God. So the Apostle saith, but "RATHER REPROVE THEM"—"RATHER," than accept their invitation to do what is evil or follow their example, show your disapprobation by reproof, "FOR,"—the reason is—that "IT IS A SHAME EVEN TO SPEAK OF THOSE THINGS THAT ARE DONE OF THEM IN SECRET." And if a shame even to speak of them, how much more to do them—to join in them—or to have fellowship with them. Why should those who are enlisted in the service of the Lord of Glory—who have taken the name and profess to fight under the banners of the Great Captain of their Salvation—why should they give that which ought to be consecrated to Him, whose they are, and whom they ought to serve, to the servants or to the service of the Prince of darkness?

In the rebellion of 1798, the rebels took prisoner a little drummer of the king's troops, and they desired him to beat the drum for them. The little boy laid his drum on the ground and leaped into it, smashing the parchment into atoms—"God forbid," said he, "that the king's drum should ever be beat for rebels." The ruffians piked the little hero, but they could not obliterate the remembrance of a deed, worthy of a place in the noblest records of courage, loyalty, and fidelity—an example which, if it were imitated in a spiritual sense by the Christian, would best illustrate the fulfilment of the Apostle's exhortation here.

But now, my dear friends, the application of this to ourselves is the grand subject for consideration, and so the great question arises—to which class do you really belong?

Are you in darkness, or are you in the light? If you are in the light, you will perceive, that certainly a great change has taken place in your sentiments—views—opinions—feelings—and desires. If you really are brought out of your natural darkness, into the marvellous light of God's truth; it is not—it cannot be concealed from you. You must know that you are totally different, in many respects, from what you once were—though you feel you are very far from what you would aim at, and desire to be. "*If any man be in Christ, he is a new creature.*" 2nd Cor. v. 17. I know that the corruption and wickedness of their heart is a constant source of pain to believers. I know they often think and reason thus:—

"Alas! I cannot believe that I can be a child of God. I feel myself so vile, so guilty, how can I be called His child, or His servant?"

Well, that is a great change! For the time was, that you did not feel or reason thus—that you saw no sin, or but little, comparatively, in yourself—rather, probably, that you thought you were very good. This, then, is a great change. This appears to be a great symptom that the Lord has taught you to see yourselves in the light of His Holy Law. For, as the Apostle says, in the very next verse, "*Whatsoever doth make manifest is light.*" That which manifests your own sin and wickedness to yourselves, must be the light of God's Holy Law which hath shined into your heart. That is a great change! So it was exactly with the Apostle, as he tells us, in his own experience, "*For I was alive without the law once; but when the commandment came, sin revived, and I died.*" Rom. vii. 9.

Again, believers are not always conscious to themselves of being in a state of acceptance with God—they are often walking in darkness, and mourning over their sins and their unbelief. Therefore, although the knowledge and assurance of their acceptance with God, and the happy confidence of faith is their blessed privilege, and one, which they ought to aim continually to enjoy; yet it is not their privilege always to enjoy it. But whether you enjoy it or not, a great change has taken place, and you must be conscious of this in some particulars. You are perhaps, sad, afflicted, unhappy under a sense of your own sin; well, that is a great change. You may say, I do not enjoy the light of God's countenance, if it was so, if I was able to rejoice in Christ, I should be happy,—that is a great change too. Christ was of no value to you once—you did not regard the light of God's countenance, it was no regret—it was nothing to you whether He smiled or frowned, "*God was not in all your thoughts,*" Ps. x. 4. Your soul desires now to enjoy the light of your Redeemer's countenance. That is a great change! Christ is precious to your soul. We prize what we long for, as much as what we enjoy. The Apostle Peter gives this as the mark of a believer, "*To you that believe he is precious.*" 1st Pet. ii. 7. Who showed you that Christ was such a blessed object? Who showed you that the light of God's countenance was the light of life in which your soul desired to bask? None could show this to you, but the Holy Ghost. Therefore, though you may be often downcast and oppressed, take courage! It may be the "*day of small things*" with you, in comparison of the advanced experience of other believers. But if we speak of that experience, let it not be a subject of distress to any person who is "asking his way to Zion, with his face thitherward." God will not despise "*the day of small things.*" If there is one faint and feeble, but sincere desire in your heart to come to God—it must be by the power of His Spirit—there can be no such desire in the sinner's natural heart. Therefore, I say, take courage; and remember, the Lord says, "*Who hath despised the day of small things?*" Zech. iv. 10; as much as to say, "Certainly, I have not despised it;"—and, if the Lord does not despise it, then do not you despise it. Take courage—pray to the Lord—search His Word—"*Enter into thy closet; and, when thou hast shut thy door, pray to thy Father which is in secret; and thy Father, which seeth in secret, shall reward thee openly.*" Mat. vi. 6. Oh! think what a privilege it is, to have a God who sees and knows the weakest desire—who hears the faintest cry, from the poor sinner's heart! "*Because ye are sons, God hath sent forth the Spirit of his Son into your hearts, crying, Abba, Father.*" Gal. iv. 6.

It may be but a faint and feeble cry—but however weak—as the mother's ear is very quick, and she hears the cry of her little babe that does not see her, though she is watching over it—her eye—her ear are all alive to watch the slightest movement—and catch the feeblest cry;—yet not a thousandth part so quick, as the ear of the Lord to hear the cry of his poor children, how weak or faint soever it may be. "*The eyes of the Lord are over the righteous, and his ears are open unto their prayers.*" 1st Pet. iii. 12. The song of the redeemed around the throne in glory—"*The voice of many angels round about the throne*"—and of the "*ten thousand times ten thousand,*" Rev. v. 11, cannot intercept the feeblest cry that comes from the lips of him who calleth, "*Abba, Father.*"

We have a tender—gracious—compassionate Father! Let us come to Him; yea, and come boldly, for "*We have a great High Priest, who is passed into the heavens; Jesus, the Son of God.*" And, though we may have many doubts—fears—distractions—difficulties—many hard conflicts—and, though we may feel, that our prayer does not deserve the name of prayer, and that we are often unable to pray,—yet, if there is the least cry of sincerity in the heart, to God—that cry must have come from God, and that cry returns to Him. Think of this! And therefore let us pray to have all His truth engraven on our hearts. May the Lord write it there by His Spirit, for His name's sake! Amen!

THIRTY-EIGHTH LECTURE.

EPHESIANS V.—13, 14, 15, 16, 17.

"But all things that are reproved are made manifest by the light: for whatsoever doth make manifest is light. Wherefore he saith, Awake thou that sleepest, and arise from the dead, and Christ shall give thee light. See then that ye walk circumspectly, not as fools, but as wise, redeeming the time, because the days are evil."

THE Apostle was speaking, in the passage of Scripture which we considered on the last day, of the difference between man in a state of spiritual darkness, and man in a state of spiritual light, and of the duties of those who are in the light, "*Ye were sometimes darkness but now are ye light in the Lord, walk as children of light.*"

He had been warning his brethren against the works of darkness, "*Have no fellowship with the unfruitful works of darkness, but rather reprove them.*"

He had been contrasting these with the works of light; "*The fruit of the Spirit is in all goodness and righteousness and truth,*" and he exhorted his believing brethren, instead of having fellowship with the unfruitful works of darkness to reprove them; that so far from being associated with them practically, they should remember that even the very mention of them was a shame, "*It is a shame even to speak of those things which are done of them in secret.*"

He now shows what that is, which tests the works of darkness, and the works of light; and he says, that which reproves, and thereby brings them forth as it were into light, this makes them manifest, and it is this that tests them. "ALL THINGS THAT ARE REPROVED ARE MADE MANIFEST BY THE LIGHT: FOR WHATEVER DOTH MAKE MANIFEST IS LIGHT. WHEREFORE HE SAITH, AWAKE THOU THAT SLEEPEST, AND ARISE FROM THE DEAD, AND CHRIST SHLL GIVE THEE LIGHT." Those who had been in darkness, had been brought out of darkness into light—their darkness had been made manifest by the light; "FOR WHATEVER DOTH MAKE MANIFEST IS LIGHT." The change that takes place in the sinner's mind, when the light of divine truth shines into his heart, is like the change that takes place to the eye of a person when he has been in a dark room, where he has not seen anything within it—until the window is opened, and the light allowed to enter, and all its contents are exhibited to his view. And if, when the light broke into that dark and unseen chamber, he saw that he was surrounded with objects disgusting and appalling to his sight—how horrible would the scene appear!—how he would loathe!—how he would desire to fly from it! When the light of divine truth breaks in upon the sinner's heart, and shows him the corruptions and abominations that are there—not more horrible would the most disgusting natural objects appear to his eye, than the spectacle presented to his moral sense, when God gives him power to see it—when God sheds light upon it. We see ourselves full of sin and corruption—we see our hearts as He describes them, "*deceitful above all things, and desperately wicked.*" Jer. xvii. 9. We see we must be as loathsome in the eyes of a pure and holy God, as a corrupting carcase would be in our own. We are brought down to the dust under a sense of our own iniquity—we say with Job, "*I have heard of thee by the hearing of the ear; but now mine eye seeth thee: Wherefore I abhor myself, and repent in dust and ashes.*" Job, xlii. 5, 6. The light of God's truth shining into our hearts and consciences gives us to see the meaning of this text applied to ourselves as well as to others, "*all things that are reproved are made manifest by the light, for whatsoever doth make manifest is light.*" Now, God's Word and God's Spirit make manifest, to the enlightened conscience, that which God's judgment shall make manifest, when he shall bring every work into judgment. Yet sinners read and hear that word continually, without even deriving any light or knowledge of their own state from it. Persons will read over and over again, for example, God's testimony concerning their own hearts, that "*the carnal mind is enmity against God, for it is not subject to the law of God, neither indeed can be.*" Rom. viii. 7. After having read that statement, and heard it frequently, they have not the least light shed into their own hearts, concerning its truth as applied to their own state—they do not believe that their "*heart is enmity against God.*"

I have frequently quoted that text, and read it from the Scriptures, and asked persons, "Do you believe this is the state of your heart?" And they have answered, "No, I do not feel any enmity against God, I do not think that is the state of my heart." Now, the reason is, that those persons, when they hear the Word of God, have no light from the Spirit of God shed on their own heart or understanding, to make manifest, by the light of the Word, their own guilt and sin. They do not understand the nature of God's Holy Law, to which their heart is not subject; for when its full requirements are set before them, then they evince their enmity against its strictness and spirituality.

If a blind man were brought into a dark room, or into a light room, darkness and light would be the same to him, he wants the sense to see. Thousands, and tens of thousands, yea, multitudes of most learned men, in the midst of the light of Revelation, are as blind to the moral character of God and their own spiritual state, as any Pagan in the darkest regions of Heathen ignorance can be. The blind sinner, brought into the light of God's truth, sees nothing—his eyes must be opened—God's Word, when his eyes are opened, then makes manifest to him the truth, he sees it in the sacred pages as a person who had received sight sees objects clearly. A man in a dark room, with his eyes open, cannot see anything. The eyes are as necessary for the use of light, as light is for the use of the eyes. So man requires, not merely the power of the Spirit to give him sight, but the light of the Word, that he may see—not merely the sense to see—but the light to enable him to use that sense. The illumination of the Spirit, and the light of God's Word, are both alike indispensable. The Spirit is first given and enables him to attend—to think—to understand—to believe—to see—and derive from the Word, the knowledge of the corruption of his own heart. The Word of God makes manifest, and the Spirit of God makes manifest, truth concerning the sinner; and whenever the sinner is brought to see the corruption and evil in his own heart—he knows, and he understands, that God sees it too. The ungodly, as we read in Scripture, "*hath said in his heart, God hath forgotten: he hideth his face; he will never see it.*" Psalm, x. 11. The believer says, "*Thou hast set our iniquities before thee, our secret sins in the light of thy countenance,*" Psalm, xc. 8; or with the Apostle, "*All things are naked and opened unto the eyes of him with whom we have to do.*" Heb. iv. 13. When the sinner sees himself, and his sins in the light of God's countenance—and knows that God's bright face is shining upon him—and that the eye of God is looking upon all his guilt and sin—he sees that his sins must be blotted out by the "*Fountain opened for sin and uncleanness,*" Zech. xiii. 1, that his nakedness must be covered with "*white raiment,*" that will bear the light of God's countenance—or else, that he must be lost forever. This is what makes the righteousness of Christ precious to the sinner. This is the reason, why Christ saith to the Church in Laodicea, "*I counsel thee to buy of me gold tried in the fire, that thou mayest be rich; and white raiment, that thou mayest be clothed, and that the shame of thy nakedness do not appear; and anoint thine eyes with eye-salve, that thou mayest see.*" Rev. iii. 18.

"*That the shame of thy nakedness do not appear.*" How ashamed we should be, if our hearts were laid bare in the sight of man! You see men very anxious to avoid the inspection of their fellow-creatures—to conceal from their fellow-worms, what they really are. How carefully we conceal the thoughts of our hearts—the workings of our minds—our evil desires, propensities, and passions, from our fellow-creatures. But the moment the sinner is brought to see, and to feel, that though he may conceal these things from his fellow-creatures, they are naked and open to the eyes of God;—Oh! then he sees the blessedness of having a refuge to flee to—of having such a Saviour, who receives the poor and wretched—those whose consciences are taught to know that they are wholly lost, convicted and condemned—who receives those whose only fitness is, that they are sick and need a Physician—are lost, and have need of Him who "*came to seek and to save that which was lost*," Luke xix. 10—he sees the blessedness of having such a Saviour as this to fly to.

The judgment of God shall make manifest at last, to all, that truth which His Word makes manifest to His people now. So, the Apostle saith, "*Judge nothing before the time, until the Lord come, who both will bring to light the hidden things of darkness, and will make manifest the counsels of the hearts; and then shall every man have praise of God.*" 1st Cor. iv. 5. So our blessed Lord saith, "*Whatsoever ye have spoken in darkness shall be heard in the light; and that which ye have spoken in the ear in closets shall be proclaimed upon the house-tops*," Luke xii. 3. Therefore, when the sinner is brought really to know this—when he is brought to look for the judgment that shall reveal and make manifest his actions—his words, however secret—yea, the very thoughts of his heart—he knows, that there is nothing that can give him hope or rest, but to fly to that Saviour—in whom there is salvation—full and free salvation, for all. "WHEREFORE, HE SAITH, AWAKE THOU THAT SLEEPEST, AND ARISE FROM THE DEAD, AND CHRIST SHALL GIVE THEE LIGHT."

The light that makes manifest our danger would be a melancholy light indeed, unless it were to shine upon the refuge too. It would have been a melancholy thing, for a poor manslayer among the Jews, when the morning was beginning to rise, to behold the avenger of blood at his heels, with a weapon to slay him, unless the same blessed sun that revealed his pursuer to his eye, should have also showed him at the same time the way to the city of refuge. Therefore, the light that makes known to a sinner his spiritual state, were a melancholy light, if it did not make manifest to him the Refuge for his soul, and show him the way to the City, where he can find pardon for his iniquity, even in Christ—in Him, who is "*A refuge for the oppressed, a refuge in times of trouble*," Ps. ix. 9; then he is enabled to say, "*God is my refuge and strength, a very present help in trouble, therefore will I not fear, though the earth be removed, and though the mountains be carried into the midst of the sea, though the waters thereof roar and be troubled, and though the mountains shake with the swelling thereof*," Ps. xlvi. 2. Wherefore, O! thou guilty sinner, that art insensible on the brink of ruin, "AWAKE THOU THAT SLEEPEST, AND ARISE FROM THE DEAD, AND CHRIST SHALL GIVE THEE LIGHT."

Christ Himself is the light, because he gives life, "*In him was life and the life was the light of men.*" John i. 4; it is the pardon—the salvation—the life—that is in Christ, that gives light to the sinner's soul. So saith the Prophet, "*The people that walked in darkness have seen a great light, they that dwell in the land of the shadow of death, upon them hath the light shined.*" Isa. ix. 2: and so saith the Prophet Malachi, iv. 2, "*Unto you that fear my name, shall the Sun of Righteousness arise with healing in his wings.*" Jesus is the Sun of Righteousness, and his rising on the soul is said to bring healing and salvation; "WHEREFORE," he saith, "AWAKE THOU THAT SLEEPEST, AND ARISE FROM THE DEAD, AND CHRIST SHALL GIVE THEE LIGHT."

Now, if that which I am saying is not intelligible to you, as applied to your own case, and to your own circumstances, you are of those who are yet in darkness. If you do not see your own sin and misery, and if you do not see Christ as your Refuge, you are yet in darkness and in death, therefore, "AWAKE THOU THAT SLEEPEST AND ARISE FROM THE DEAD, AND CHRIST SHALL GIVE THEE LIGHT." It is in the preaching of the Gospel of Jesus, and in the command the Gospel gives to come to Christ, when accompanied by the Holy Ghost, that we have life; it is in the command, the power is conveyed. We know, that the sinner has no power in himself to awake—that a dead man has no power in himself to arise from the dead. Notwithstanding, Jesus said to the man with the withered hand, "*Stretch forth thine hand, and he stretched it forth, and it was restored whole as the other.*" Mat. xii. 13. Jesus said to the man who had been lying four days in his grave, "*Lazarus come forth. And he that was dead came forth.*" John xi. 43, 44. The man with the withered arm had no power to stretch it out; and Lazarus had no power to get up from his grave, but, in the command of God, power was conveyed to the withered hand, and life to the dead body. There is no power in man to do good or to awaken himself, but in the command from God to the sinner's heart, "AWAKE THOU THAT SLEEPEST," in that command, when accompanied by God's power, there is power to the weak, and life to the dead. The Lord's command to the Prophet is, "*Prophesy upon their bones and say unto them, O ye dry bones, hear the word of the Lord.*" Ezek. xxxvii. 4. Wherefore, we say, "AWAKE THOU THAT SLEEPEST AND ARISE FROM THE DEAD, AND CHRIST SHALL GIVE THEE LIGHT." Awake to the sense of your own guilt and wretchedness, your own lost condition, and your misery, and arise from the dead. You are in the world, that is, dead in trespasses and sins—surrounded by those, your fellow-creatures, who are dead in trespasses and sins—and if you are ignorant of Christ, you are dead, as the rest, yourselves. Come out then, with Lazarus—come forth from the grave, "AWAKE THOU THAT SLEEPEST AND ARISE FROM THE DEAD, AND CHRIST SHALL GIVE THEE LIGHT."

The pardon that is proclaimed to the sinner, in the blood of Jesus, conveys life to the soul. Again, remember the text, "*In him was life, and the life was the light of men.*" John i. 4. It is the life that comes from Jesus, that gives light to the soul. Just as when Lazarus came forth—when he received life from the Word of the Lord—his eye met his Redeemer—and he beheld once more the light of day—and he saw all those who stood around his grave. So when God grants to the sinner "*repentance to the acknowledgment of the truth,*"—when the sinner is taught by the Spirit to repent and believe the Gospel, the sinner receives life with light, and light with life—and he beholds and flies to the Lord Jesus, as a refuge for his soul, "WHEREFORE HE SAITH, AWAKE THOU THAT SLEEPEST, AND ARISE FROM THE DEAD, AND CHRIST SHALL GIVE THEE LIGHT."

Oh! my dear friends, what a blessing from God it is, for a sinner to be given the light of life in Christ Jesus! Alas! if any of you are walking in darkness, as "*he that walketh in darkness, knoweth not whither he goeth*,"—so the sinner that is walking without light in Christ, knows not, as we remarked the last day, whether the next step may not be over the precipice of eternal death! Oh, consider! then—reflect on this!

Then, what is the practical use of awaking from the dead, and receiving light from Christ?

What is the practical use of the sun, and of eyes to behold its light?—Is not one use,—that man may see where he is going—that he may direct his course by the light? So, this is the very use to which the Apostle applies it—this is the Spirit's practical application,—"SEE THEN, THAT YE WALK CIRCUMSPECTLY, NOT AS FOOLS BUT AS WISE, REDEEMING THE TIME BECAUSE THE DAYS ARE EVIL." The use of the light of day is to guide you in your course—the course wherein you ought to walk in all your daily occupations. So the use of the light of "*The Sun of Righteousness*" shining upon your soul, is to "*guide your footsteps into the way of peace.*" This is the very expression used in that beautiful passage, the Song of Zacharias; in which, addressing his son, John the Baptist, by the Holy Spirit, he saith, "*Thou, child, shalt be called the Prophet of the Highest: for thou shalt go before the face of the Lord to prepare his ways; To give knowledge of salvation unto his people by the remission of their sins, Through the tender mercy of our God; whereby the day-spring from on high hath visited us, To give light to them that sit in darkness and in the shadow of death, to guide our feet into the way of peace.*" Luke, i. 76—79.

And so, "*To give knowledge of salvation unto his people by the remission of their sins*"—that is the means, you perceive, by which "*the day-spring from on high*" visits the soul.

What a beautiful image of Christ! "*The day-spring from on high.*" A glorious light arising on a dark world. And recollect, that as the sun arises in the firmament of heaven upon this dark earth, the whole light of that orb arises on the sinner's eye that beholds him; so as the fulness of the glory of Jesus, rises in the firmament of revelation on a guilty world, to the sinner who is given eyes to see Him, the glorious "*Day-spring from on high*" rises on his sight and his soul too; he sees the glory of the Lord Jesus, just as if there was no other eye in the whole world to behold Him; just as the sinner who beholds the natural sun arising from the ocean, sees the fulness of his glory as much as if no other eye saw him. All the sun is his own, when he beholds him emerging from the waves—all Christ is his own, when he beholds Him rising on his dark soul. What a blessed truth! that all the fulness of Christ belongs to every individual sinner, as if there was no other sinner in the world; He is a full complete Saviour—an all-sufficient Saviour for the soul.

The Psalmist uses a somewhat similar expression, "*The entrance of thy word giveth light,*" Ps. cxix. 130. And so he says in that beautiful Psalm, in which he is comparing the light of the sun to the moral light of God's word, "*In them,*" (the heavens) "*hath he set a tabernacle for the sun, which is as a bridegroom coming out of his chamber, and rejoiceth as a strong man to run a race; his going forth is from the end of the heaven, and his circuit unto the ends of it, and there is nothing hid from the heat thereof.*" Then he applies the image to the word of God, "*The law of the Lord is perfect, converting the soul, the testimony of the Lord is sure, making wise the simple; the statutes of the Lord are right, rejoicing the heart; the commandment of the Lord is pure, enlightening the eyes.*" As the sun giveth light to the world, so do the beams of God's truth give light to the sinner's soul; and as the sun is to guide the feet of man, by the natural light that beams on his eye, so the "*Sun of Righteousness*" is to guide the feet into the way of peace by His heavenly light, that beams upon the soul.

So, if ye be "*Children of light,*" "SEE THEN, THAT YE WALK CIRCUMSPECTLY, NOT AS FOOLS BUT AS WISE, REDEEMING THE TIME, BECAUSE THE DAYS ARE EVIL." When you are walking in the light of the sun, you will not step into any place where you are likely to fall—you will not stand on ground that is likely to sink from under you—you will not stumble down a precipice—you will not run into any danger—you will avoid or fly from it. So, if you are walking in the light of God's countenance—in the light and life that is in Christ Jesus, what must be the effect of it? to hinder you from walking into temptation—to turn you away from the fatal precipices of passion, and of every evil lust—to warn you from the destructive paths of sin—from the snares of ambition, covetousness, pride, vanity, and folly—and to guide your feet into the way of peace; to teach you to walk with God—to walk in the fellowship of your Lord and Saviour, and in the true communion of His Spiritual flock. "*This then,*" saith the Apostle John, "*is the message which we have heard of him and declare unto you, that God is light, and in him is no darkness at all. If we say that we have fellowship with him, and walk in darkness, we lie and do not the truth. But if we walk in the light as he is in the light, we have fellowship one with another, and the blood of Jesus Christ his son cleanseth us from all sin.*" 1st John i. 5, 6, 7.

To walk in the light as "*children of light,*" is to walk in life and love—to walk in the ways of holiness, and happiness, and true wisdom, for "*Her ways are ways of pleasantness, aud all her paths are peace,*" Prov. iii. 17.

"SEE THEN THAT YE WALK CIRCUMSPECTLY, NOT AS FOOLS, BUT AS WISE." How do fools walk? how do those who are ignorant of God walk? In the ways of sin and ignorance with the ungodly world—on the "*broad way that leadeth to destruction,*" Mat. vii. 13. The sinner that is brought to the Lord Jesus Christ, is brought, that he may not walk as they do—that he may turn from the world—that he may walk in "*the narrow way that leadeth to eternal life.*"

What an awful thought it is, that sinners should console themselves, as they constantly do, with the safety—the security of their spiritual state, because they are walking as other people are!

"If we are lost, what is to become of the rest of the world?—we are not worse than our neighbors, and better than a great number," &c.

The very ground of their hope, our Lord marks as the pledge of their condemnation, for "*Wide is the gate, and broad is the way, that leadeth to destruction, and many there be which go in thereat: Because strait is the gate, and narrow is the way, which leadeth unto life, and few there be that find it.*" Matt. vii. 13, 14.

If you are walking with the multitude, you are walking to destruction. If you are walking with those with whom you have all your life been walking in your natural state, you are walking to destruction. There must be a difference between the walk of the ungodly, and the walk of the godly, because they are going in opposite directions. Those persons that are going together, you know must reach the same place;—if we go with the world, we must reach the place to which the world is tending. "*We know that we are of God,*" saith the Apostle John, "*and the whole world lieth in wickedness.*" 1st John v. 19.

If we go to the place to which the world is not tending, we must walk of course in the opposite direction. The world is in darkness, and knoweth not whither it goeth, "*Ye were sometimes darkness, but now are ye light in the Lord, walk as children of light.*"

"SEE THEN, THAT YE WALK CIRCUMSPECTLY, NOT AS FOOLS, BUT AS WISE." Scriptural wisdom and folly, and worldly wisdom and folly, are very distinct from each other. A man may be, in the estimation of the world, one of the wisest of its sons—and, in the estimation of God, he may be a fool. A man, in the estimation of the world may be a fool—but, in the sight of God, he may be wiser than the kings of the earth. Wherefore He saith, "*If any man among you seemeth to be wise in this world, let him become a fool, that he may be wise.*" 1st Cor. iii. 18.

But alas! my dear friends, what a melancholy thought it is, how continually persons seek for all other wisdom, but "*the wisdom that is from above.*" James iii. 17. How anxious do you see parents to educate their children in all kinds of learning—in languages—sciences—literature—accomplishments, &c., and how careless they are about the things that belong to their everlasting peace. And if their children make a proficiency in these things—if they are improved and accomplished in the learning of the world

—they are quite pleased and satisfied;—forgetting, that if they are ignorant of Jesus, "*It were better for them, that a millstone were hanged about their neck, and they were cast into the depths of the sea,*" Mat. xviii. 6. And so it is, alas! with those who are young themselves. Some are indolent and idle, and only think of indulging in amusement or sensuality. Some are very anxious to cultivate their minds—to improve themselves in all things, except in those that belong to their everlasting peace. But Oh! my dear young friends, remember that mighty question—apply all the powers of arithmetic to calculate that stupendous sum, "*What shall it profit a man, if he shall gain the whole world, and lose his own soul? or what shall a man give in exchange for his soul?*" Mark viii. 36. Oh! remember that it is written of man, "*His breath goeth forth, he returneth to his earth, in that very day his thoughts perish.*" Psalm cxlvi. 4.

The head of the ablest—the head of the most learned man—of the mightiest statesman—of the most powerful orator, who had guided the counsels of a nation—that head, whose

"Tongue had set the table in a roar,"

or commanded "the applause of listening senates," when its breath goeth forth, it is as mute—as empty—and as waste as the skull of a drivelling idiot. What then is genius? What is talent? What is all the wisdom that man can gain? What is all the learning that man can acquire, if he is not "*Wise unto salvation, through faith in Christ Jesus?*" Oh! think of this, and "SEE THEN THAT YE WALK CIRCUMSPECTLY, NOT AS FOOLS, BUT AS WISE."

If you walk as wise, in this sense, it must be as being "*wise unto salvation.*" You must have this wisdom—or you must walk as a fool! And where are you to find it? "*From a child,*" saith Paul to Timothy, "*thou hast known the holy Scriptures, which are able to make thee wise unto salvation, through faith, which is in Christ Jesus.*" 2nd Tim. iii. 15.

And here we may observe the awful system of ignorance that is set up amongst us now,* on high authority, by way of education for immortal beings, in our country. You hear men of high rank—men of great ability—men of great learning, and great power, who occupy a large space in the public eye—you hear these men standing up, and talking of the advantages of instruction for the nation. They will expatiate on the improvement of the people—the progress of knowledge—the "march of intellect"—"the spirit of the age," as they call it. We hear them talking of these things—setting up schools for national education; we hear, too, of different institutions for science, such as Mechanics' Institutes—of numerous publications—cheap magazines—cheap newspapers, to convey knowledge to the people! We hear long speeches, which some persons will say are full of learning, and wisdom, and talent—we see large sums of money voted in our senate, for the education of

* Irish National Board of Education, established 1832.

the country! But the Word of the eternal God—which alone can make an immortal being anything in the sight of God, beyond a fool—alone can deliver him from folly, sin, misery, death, and hell —that Blessed Word is dishonored, and forbidden to be made the standard of education for this unhappy nation. Yet man educated without the knowledge of God's Word—trained up without religion—must be trained up in the service of Satan. Men are always trained up in the service of Satan, when they are not trained up in the truth of God. It must be so! Every course—however specious and harmless it may seem—in which man can be trained on earth, is the way of Satan; when God's Word is excluded from his education. For if he is not trained up in the knowledge of that Book, all the sciences, and all the arts, and all the literature that could be conveyed into the human mind, cannot deliver man from the power of Satan! Nothing can deliver him from this, but the truth that is in Christ Jesus, as revealed in that Book. Therefore, when the Scriptures are not made a part of the education of men, they cannot but be educated in the worst ignorance. Men would say, a child could not be educated without Grammar, Arithmetic, History, or Geography—but count it no deficiency, to be educated without the Bible!!!

Take the wisest—the most learned man on earth—give him all the genius, all the talents, with which man was ever gifted—cultivate those with all the learning that ever was accumulated in one individual—and just ask one question:—

Is he "*wise unto salvation, through faith, which is in Christ Jesus?*" 2nd Tim. iii. 13.

If he is not—all his genius—all his talents—all his gifts—all his acquisitions,—the higher they exalt him, the deeper the plunge with which they precipitate him into perdition; because, the more he knows, the more he ought to have learned, that the God who gave him genius and talent—and the God who was the God of nature and science—and the God of all that can be worth knowing on earth, was the God whom he ought to have known and served—the God whom he ought to have worshipped—the God to whom he ought to be reconciled in Christ Jesus, as a guilty sinner! Therefore, there is not a principle that comes more directly from the Prince of darkness, than this:—that men can be improved by education, without the Bible. And all men who have any religion themselves, ought "*to set their face, like a flint,*" against such an infidel principle, as they fear their God, or love their fellow-creatures. Every man, every woman, in their department in life, minister and layman—master and mistress, father, mother, and children, ought to set their faces against it. And it proves awfully, the state of miserable apostacy from divine truth —from the standard of our pure and holy religion, into which the nation has fallen,—since such a principle can be entertained for a moment, much less carried into operation, in the country!—since it is not scouted out of the land, from north to south, from east to west!—that the nation is to be instructed, without the Word of the eternal God! Men are fools; and they must walk as fools, whatever be their rank or station—no matter who or what they are—they must be walking in ignorance and folly, if they are not walking in the wisdom of God's sacred truth! There is no wisdom on earth, that deserves the name, but that which comes from the God of truth. Oh, think of this—consider it for your own souls.

If you are not walking with God—if you are not walking wisely in the truth of God's Word—you cannot be walking happily in the light of God's countenance. If you are not, you have no wisdom—you are in darkness—you are a fool, if you were the Head of a University, or Prime Minister of the Empire. Then I say solemnly, consider this; because it is a matter of personal, practical religion, with every human being. We ought to consider, daily, hourly, momentarily, how we are to walk. "SEE THEN THAT YE WALK CIRCUMSPECTLY." If so, we must look where we are going. Let us remember, wheresoever we are walking in this world, that we are walking on the road to eternity.

If a friend met you in the street, or on the road, and asked you, "Where are you going?"—and that you replied, "Indeed, I do not know." Would not that be the answer of a fool? But when asked, as you hasten to eternity, "Where are you going?" and that you must answer, "I do not know,"—is that walking like a wise person, or like a fool? Are you walking without God—not in a state of peace with God—but at enmity with God? Alas, what a fool you must be! What a fool that man is, who is walking at enmity with God! Is he not the worst of fools? And every man is walking at enmity with God, who is not reconciled through Christ. Therefore, if you "WALK CIRCUMSPECTLY," you must both know where you are going, and look well how you are walking to your destination. And to see this, you must have the light of God's truth shining on your path—you must have "*the Sun of Righteousness*" arisen on your eyes, even Christ Jesus, the Lord!—or otherwise, you are walking in darkness; and walking not wisely, but as a fool. "SEE THEN, THAT YE WALK CIRCUMSPECTLY, NOT AS FOOLS, BUT AS WISE, REDEEMING THE TIME, BECAUSE THE DAYS ARE EVIL."

"REDEEMING THE TIME." Dear friends, how little we think of the importance of time! How criminally we waste our precious, irrevocable hours! We would think it a sin to throw away our gold—to squander our silver—we should say, that a man who did so, must be a fool. But let us remember, that all the gold in the world cannot buy back one moment of mis-spent time. It cannot recall—it cannot purchase back one moment you have given to Satan, or one moment you have taken from God. Remember, that all your time is due to Him, who gives it to you. You receive your hours, as if they were taken by the hand of God, and given to you—as if He said, "Here is another day bestowed on you, here is another hour granted to you." And will you take these hours and days from God, and spend them in the service of the Prince of darkness? Is it too much to say, that the time which we receive from God, should be redeemed for God? I do not know anything, in which a Christian has more cause to be ashamed of himself, and to feel more his sinfulness—his criminal forgetfulness of God—than in that one evil!—how little he values, how little he redeems his time. Alas! if the precious time that we have given to sin, to vanity, and folly, had been devoted to the service of God—to the study of His Word—to the practical discharge of the duties that He has enjoined on us—to the happiness of our fellow-sinners,—how different were the state of every one in this room, at this moment! What spiritual treasures had we gained! What spiritual advancement had we made! What spiritual comforts had we enjoyed! Alas! how we have squandered time! precious time!!

The wretched dying Infidel is reported to have said to his physician, "I will give you half my property, if you can give me another day." But all the world could not buy a moment. Kingdoms can be bought and sold, but all the kingdoms of the earth cannot buy one moment of time. Think of that—how precious it is! While time is yours, you have what kingdoms cannot buy—time squandered is throwing away what kingdoms could not purchase. "SEE THEN, THAT YE WALK CIRCUMSPECTLY, NOT AS FOOLS, BUT AS WISE, REDEEMING THE TIME, BECAUSE THE DAYS ARE EVIL."

Recollect, then on the whole, first, what it is that gives light—the Word of God.

Recollect, that the command of God goes forth to those who are asleep—to those who are "*dead in trespasses and sins*"—"AWAKE THOU THAT SLEEPEST AND ARISE FROM THE DEAD, AND CHRIST SHALL GIVE THEE LIGHT."

What a blessed mercy it is, that while the command of God might be justly addressed to you and to me, "*depart into everlasting darkness*," God says to us this day, "AWAKE THOU THAT SLEEPEST, AND ARISE FROM THE DEAD, AND CHRIST SHALL GIVE THEE LIGHT."

Then again consider, what is the use of light? That you may learn to "WALK CIRCUMSPECTLY, NOT AS FOOLS, BUT AS WISE, REDEEMING THE TIME, BECAUSE THE DAYS ARE EVIL."

Remember, that all wisdom without the Bible is folly and madness—all that the world calls wisdom, is comparatively ignorance and folly. How wisely some men walk to hell! how learnedly—how pompously they strut into perdition! Thus saith the Prophet, "*Therefore hell hath enlarged herself, and opened her mouth without measure: and their glory, and their multitude, and their pomp, and he that rejoiceth shall ascend into it.*" Is. v. 14—and what is the use of their wisdom when they get there! Every man that is ignorant of the Bible—of the way of peace and reconciliation with his God, with all his wisdom, he is going straight to everlasting death. Therefore consider—"SEE THEN, THAT YE WALK CIRCUMSPECTLY, NOT AS FOOLS, BUT AS WISE." Look before you—look around you—watch and walk in the light of God's truth, "REDEEMING THE TIME BECAUSE THE DAYS ARE EVIL." The Apostle might say so in his day, and surely we may say so in ours. Every servant of God may say so in all ages of the world, "THE DAYS ARE EVIL." But surely if ever there were days of evil—of sin—of wickedness, and of departure from God, they must be the days of a nation, bearing the name of Christian, yet refusing to have the Word of Christ as the standard of Education for their children.

May God, in His infinite mercy, not deal with this guilty Empire after its iniquities!

May the Lord give to us the light of His countenance! May He cause His face to shine upon us, and bring His blessed Word with power to our souls, that we may not walk in darkness, but in the smile of His favor and His love, through time to eternity. Amen!

THIRTY-NINTH LECTURE.

EPHESIANS V.—17, 18, 19, 20, 21.

"Wherefore be ye not unwise, but understanding what the will of the Lord is. And be not drunk with wine, wherein is excess; but be filled with the Spirit: speaking to yourselves in psalms, and hymns, and spiritual songs, singing and making melody in your heart to the Lord; giving thanks always for all things unto God and the Father in the name of our Lord Jesus Christ; submitting yourselves one to another in the fear of God."

A DIFFICULT and a dangerous way, in an enemy's land, requires vigilant attention and careful circumspection, in the soldier on his march, or the traveller on his journey. Therefore the Apostle, as we have seen, exhorts his brethren to "*walk circumspectly, not as fools, but as wise, redeeming the time, because the days are evil.*"

Evil days—evil circumstances—an evil world—an evil foe—evils within—evils without, are like the dangers—the difficulties—the ambuscades of a journey or march through an enemy's country. Therefore, the Christian must ever be on his guard—ever on the watch—must ever walk circumspectly. The days of his pilgrimage are few, and evil—therefore he must redeem the time, because those days are evil. "WHEREFORE," adds the Apostle, "BE YE NOT UNWISE, BUT UNDERSTANDING WHAT THE WILL OF THE LORD IS." In a strange country, a man gets a map, to direct his steps—in an unknown sea, a chart, to direct his voyage. God's Word is the chart and compass, whereby the believer is to steer his course—the map, by which he is to direct his journey, "*Wherewithal shall a young man cleanse his way? by taking heed thereto, according to thy word.*" Ps. cxix. 9

This keeps from sinning against God, "*Thy word have I hid in my heart, that I might not sin against thee.*" v. 11.

The study of this guides in the ways of God, "*I will meditate in thy precepts, and have respect unto thy ways.*" v. 15.

This gives happiness and solid counsel to the soul, "*Thy testimonies also are my delight and my counsellors.*" v. 24.

This strengthens and comforts the heart in distress, "*My soul melteth for heaviness: strengthen thou me according unto thy word.*" v. 28. "*This is my comfort in my affliction, for thy word hath quickened me,*" v. 50. "*I remembered thy judgments of old, O Lord; and have comforted myself,*" v. 52. "*Thy testimonies have I taken as an heritage forever: for they are the rejoicing of my heart.*" v. 111.

This gives true wisdom, and gives us really to understand, and be guided by the will of the Lord, "*Through thy precepts I get understanding: therefore I hate every false way.*" "*Thy word is a lamp unto my feet, and a light unto my path.*"

"*The entrance of thy word giveth light: it giveth understanding unto the simple. Thy word is true from the beginning: and every one of thy righteous judgments endureth forever,*" verses 104, 105, 130, 160.

"WHEREFORE, BE YE NOT UNWISE, BUT UNDERSTANDING WHAT THE WILL OF THE LORD IS." It is by the Lord's Word, alone, that we can understand the Lord's will; and by the understanding of His will, alone, that we are to direct our steps. Therefore, we must ever consult and study the Word of God, if we would not be unwise, but understand His will.

We have this sentiment expressed in different parts of Scripture; as for example, where the Apostle is exhorting his brethren in Thessalonica, in the same way, respecting their walk, he says, "*We beseech you, brethren, and exhort you by the Lord Jesus, that as ye have received of us how ye ought to walk and to please God, so ye would abound more and more.*" Observe, he saith, "*ye received of us how ye ought to walk and to please God,*" that is, we taught you true wisdom—we taught you His will.

"*For ye know what commandments we gave you by the Lord Jesus. For this is the will of God, even your sanctification.*" 1st Thess. iv. 1, 2, 3. The sanctification of His people—that is His will. If they understand "WHAT THE WILL OF THE LORD IS," they will understand this. Here the term, "*sanctification,*" is used in its secondary sense; that is, with respect to its practical application to the believer's life and conversation. It is here taken for the sanctifying power and influences of the Spirit; and this is what persons mean, if they speak scripturally, by progressive sanctification. Just exactly, as a man would seek to make progress in his journey, when he was going to his home. So we should make progress in our spiritual journey, on our way to that "*rest that remaineth for the people of God.*" Heb. iv. 9. So we should seek to make progress in the sanctifying power and influences of the Spirit of God. But you must ever bear in mind, that this is quite a distinct thing from that sanctification, of which we spoke at the beginning of this Epistle, when we considered the character of the saints of Christ; for all believers, as you recollect, I explained to you, are completely, in that sense, sanctified, and all alike sanctified in Christ Jesus. All who believe in Christ, are sanctified in Christ—set apart in Jesus—and evermore consecrated to God—members of His body—branches of the Vine. Such as the Head is, such are the members; such as the Tree is, such are the branches—all sanctified in Christ. Therefore, I again repeat, that the Lord Jesus is said to "*sanctify the people with his own blood.*" Heb. xiii. 12. Therefore, it is said of the will of God, "*by the which will we are sanctified, through the offering of the body of Jesus Christ, once for all.*" Heb. x. 10. In that sense, all believers are saints in Christ Jesus: that is, all are sanctified persons. Then to all such, their sanctification in life and conversation is the will of God. The will of their Heavenly Father is, that as they are saints, they should walk as saints, "*Be ye therefore followers of God, as dear children, and walk in love,*" verse 1. Therefore the will of God is, that they should be sanctified in their walk. So again, the Apostle tells the same church, "*In everything give thanks: for this is the will of God in Christ Jesus concerning you,*" 1 Thess. v. 18, and this appears to be the idea which the Apostle expresses in this passage before us.

"WHEREFORE BE YE NOT UNWISE, BUT UNDERSTANDING WHAT THE WILL OF THE LORD IS, AND BE NOT DRUNK WITH WINE, WHEREIN IS EXCESS, BUT BE FILLED WITH THE SPIRIT." They had been necessarily taught by the Spirit, they must have been so taught, or they could not have been brought to Jesus; "*For no man can say that Jesus is the Lord but by the Holy Ghost,*" 1st Cor. xii. 3; and "*Whosoever believeth that Jesus is the Christ, is born of God,*" 1st John v. 1. But then the Apostle is speaking here of the sanctifying power and influences of the Holy Spirit, contra-distinguishing, as it were, the effects produced by drinking the intoxicating poison of wine, from those produced by drinking from the "*wells of salvation,*" Is. xii. 3.

As we had before, "*They that sleep, sleep in the night; and they that be drunken, are drunken in the night; but let us who are of the day be sober,*" 1st Thes. v. 7, 8. So here, ye who are "*children of light,*" "BE NOT DRUNK WITH WINE WHEREIN IS EXCESS, BUT BE FILLED WITH THE SPIRIT."

The office of that blessed Spirit is to testify of Him, who saith, "*If any man thirst, let him come unto me, and drink,*" John vii. 37.

"*He that cometh to me shall never hunger, and he that believeth on me shall never thirst.*"

"*Whoso eateth my flesh and drinketh my blood, hath eternal life, and I will raise him up at the last day, for my flesh is meat indeed, and my blood is drink indeed,*" John vi. 35, 54, 55. Wherefore it is He who saith, "*Eat, O friends; drink, yea, drink abun dantly, O beloved.*" Cant. v. 1.

Wherefore then ye children of light, "BE NOT DRUNK WITH WINE WHEREIN IS EXCESS, BUT BE FILLED WITH THE SPIRIT," and so instead of the "*Song of the Drunkards,*" Ps. lxix. 12, ye shall be "SPEAKING TO YOURSELVES IN PSALMS AND HYMNS, AND SPIRITUAL SONGS, SINGING AND MAKING MELODY IN YOUR HEART TO THE LORD; GIVING THANKS ALWAYS, FOR ALL THINGS UNTO GOD AND THE FATHER, IN THE NAME OF THE LORD JESUS CHRIST, SUBMITTING YOURSELVES ONE TO ANOTHER IN THE FEAR OF GOD." So again, "*Rejoice evermore. Pray without ceasing. For this is the will of God in Christ Jesus concerning you,*" 1st Thes. v. 16, 17, 18. It is his will that His people shall be sanctified, that they should rejoice evermore in Him, "*Rejoice in the Lord alway, and again, I say, rejoice.*" Phil. iv. 4; It is his will, that they should "MAKE MELODY IN THEIR HEART TO THE LORD," and "*in everything give thanks,*" 1st Thes. v. 18. "GIVING THANKS ALWAYS FOR ALL THINGS UNTO GOD AND THE FATHER, IN THE NAME OF THE LORD JESUS CHRIST."

We need not dwell in any detail on the exhortation that is clear and explicit, and can require no commentary. "BE NOT DRUNK WITH WINE WHEREIN IS EXCESS." We may observe briefly on this, that it is very important that all Christian practice should be regulated on Christian principles. We hear now much of Temperance Societies, and I dare say they may have done some good, in reclaiming men outwardly from drunkenness, and may still do some good, in their way; but it seems a gross delusion, among those who call themselves Christians, that they are not founded on Christian principles. They ought to be so; and they ought to be so conducted, that people never could deceive themselves, by thinking that temperance, sobriety, or good conduct, is in any way the means of bringing a sinner to eternal life. If the sinner's soul is brought to Christ—sobriety, temperance, and all the fruits of a Christian life, are to be enforced as here by the Apostle, on Christian principle; but it is a very great mistake, if these things are ever substituted for the principles that ought to produce them, or for Christian holiness.

We see, there is no part of Christian conduct that is not marked out in God's eternal Word, "BE NOT DRUNK WITH WINE WHEREIN IS EXCESS." Persons indulge in intemperance frequently for the very purpose of exhilarating their spirits, trying, as they call it, to drown care. But Oh! how different are all the means that the unhappy sinner makes use of to banish care from his heart, from those prescribed in the Word of Life! All the expedients indeed to which the votaries of the world resort to amuse themselves, and to drown care in dissipation, are only another species of intoxication, another mode of trying to exhilarate their miserable spirits by the stimulants distilled from the alembic of this wretched world. But they awake as the inebriated man wakens from his drunken reverie to shame—to sorrow—to poverty—and to remorse.

"*As the crackling of thorns under a pot, so is the laughter of the fool.*" Eccles. vii. 6. It is a bright blaze, but very soon extinguished, and so, "*Even in laughter the heart is sorrowful and the end of that mirth is heaviness.*" Prov. xiv. 13. There are many persons who would pride themselves on their sobriety, and who are indeed, in one sense, in reference to wine, perfectly sober; but who live nevertheless in a state of as continual intoxication—as perpetual, as constant excitement, by the use of false stimulants to the intellect—to the imagination—to the feelings—and by a prostration of their intellectual and moral powers, with reference to all things that are really worth understanding—worth loving—and worth living for, as the man who is sunk in a habitual state of inebriety, and who drags on his existence, degraded to a level with the beast. The intoxication of pleasure—folly—vanity—dissipation—is in a spiritual sense, in no degree removed from the intoxication of the wretched drunkard that rolls or staggers through the streets. Consider, then, the means which the poor sinner takes of exhilarating his spirits; alas! how different they are from those prescribed in the Word of God. "BE FILLED WITH THE SPIRIT, SPEAKING TO YOURSELVES IN PSALMS AND HYMNS AND SPIRITUAL SONGS, SINGING AND MAKING MELODY IN YOUR HEART TO THE LORD." The singing of psalms and hymns—the praises of God—prayer and supplication to the Lord—these are counted by the worldling among the most gloomy occupations of man. "PSALMS AND HYMNS" are sad, depressing subjects to the natural heart of the sinner. The feast—the song—the dance—in these he expects to find exhilaration of his spirits. But "PSALMS AND HYMNS" he considers sombre, mournful, melancholy, to the last degree. He never voluntarily listens to such themes, unless it should be on Sunday, when perhaps he goes to Church, and endures to hear the praises of God, thinking that the good work, if not the penance and mortification of giving so much time to religion, must be doing something for the benefit of his soul. He may perhaps submit to listen to them, yea, enjoy them, if indeed the music is so sweet and harmonious, that it diverts him from the melancholy consideration of the words; on such occasions, at an oratorio, he may sit perhaps,

———————"Content to hear,
(O! wonderful effect of music's power!)
Messiah's eulogy———for Handel's sake."

Otherwise, the natural heart of the unhappy sinner cannot endure the praises of God, gloomy and melancholy is all their sound for him. How different it is in God's word as contradistinguished from the exhilaration of drunkenness. "BE NOT DRUNK WITH WINE WHEREIN IS EXCESS," "BUT," if you want to be cheered—to be comforted—to be exhilarated—to rejoice—"BE FILLED WITH THE SPIRIT, SPEAKING TO YOURSELVES IN PSALMS AND HYMNS AND SPIRITUAL SONGS, SINGING AND MAKING MELODY IN YOUR HEART TO THE LORD."

Ah! my dear friends, the poor creature that seeks for the exhilaration of his spirits in the world, feels that he must fly from himself. The drunkard must sit down with his companions, his head must reel amidst the jests that fly around, and he must try to forget his miseries and himself. The votary of pleasure that runs into the giddy crowd of company, folly, dissipation, does so, because he feels he must make an effort to fly from himself. The worst companion in the world, is a refuge from the misery of his own reflections. There are some men who at all times, and all unconverted men at some times, must fly from themselves, and from their thoughts, and forget them in the follies, the vanities, the masquerade of the world's amusements, in the hollow mockery of compliment of those that surround them, "*deceiving and being deceived.*" But the happiness the Word of God bestows on the sinner, is a happiness enjoyed in his own soul—a peace that the world cannot give—a joy that no man taketh from him. When you have embraced that blessed hope, which gives you to enjoy this pleasure, "SPEAKING TO YOURSELVES IN PSALMS AND HYMNS AND SPIRITUAL SONGS, SINGING AND MAKING MELODY IN YOUR HEART TO THE LORD;" you have not to fly from your own thoughts—nay—it is in your own thoughts of your Lord, derived from His Word that you are enabled to find peace. If you know the Gospel of Jesus, it is your privilege to say with the Psalmist, "*In the multitude of my thoughts within me thy comforts delight my soul.*" Psalm xciv. 19. "SPEAKING TO YOURSELVES IN PSALMS AND HYMNS AND SPIRITUAL SONGS, SINGING AND MAKING MELODY IN YOUR HEART TO THE LORD." Man flies from himself in his unconverted state, from thought, and from reflection, because he must fly from God. His spirit, when it reflects, is fearful of the presence of the Omniscient, Omnipresent Being, and that is a thought that he is unable to endure; therefore the reflections of his own spirit and his own heart are sad and melancholy, for God will intrude into them. Though we were walking through an earthly paradise in a fallen state, his conscience will hear the voice of God in the garden, in the cool of the day. It will say, "*Where art thou?*" Man like his fallen forefather must fly to hide himself. This is the true secret, why he cannot bear reflection—why he flies from himself and his own thoughts. It is, because, God will break in upon his heart. Eternity will force itself an unwelcome intruder on his thoughts, and therefore, he can only have peace in flying, from what he cannot otherwise escape, and what he is unable to endure.

But Oh! how different when the sinner is enabled to come to God as a reconciled God in Christ Jesus—when he is able to look up to Him as a God with whom he is at peace—a God who loves—who pardons him—a Saviour who washes him from all his offences—who has given Himself for him—his Blessed Saviour—his Heavenly Father. Then he is enabled "*to have rejoicing in himself, and not in another,*" he is enabled, in his own heart and conscience, to turn to God, and find peace with his

God through Jesus Christ. Then he understands this exhortation, "SPEAKING TO YOURSELVES IN PSALMS AND HYMNS AND SPIRITUAL SONGS, SINGING AND MAKING MELODY IN YOUR HEART TO THE LORD." He can have God for his companion, instead of sitting down to be "DRUNK WITH WINE," and to drown care and thought over a bottle, with wretched companions in sin and folly like himself: forgetting himself, or it may be, and often is, vainly trying to do so. O! what it is to be able to sit with your God! to retire with your God—to "*Commune with your own heart in your chamber, and be still*"—to "*Offer the sacrifices of righteousness, and put your trust in the Lord.*" Ps. iv. 4, 5. You recollect, David had the very same idea, in the next verse of that Psalm, "*There be many who say, who will show us any good.*" It is the inquiry of every poor sinner's heart, "*Who will show us any good?*" How shall I enjoy myself? Where shall I have profit, pleasure or amusement? How can I best indulge my own desires and propensities?—This is every man's natural inquiry. But do you remember what David adds, "*Lord, lift thou up the light of thy countenance upon us.*" Psalm iv. 5. Be Thou my happiness!—Thou my enjoyment!—Thou my good!—Thou my glory!—These are the ideas that Doddridge combines in his celebrated Epigram:—

> "Live while you live, the epicure will say,
> And take the pleasures of the passing day.
> Live while you live, the sacred preacher cries,
> And give to God each moment as it flies.—
> Lord, in my view let both united be,
> I live in pleasure when I live to thee."

"*Lord lift thou up the light of thy countenance upon us.*" That is the real goal of happiness;—when you are able to say this from the heart, then you can understand the exhortation before us, "SPEAKING TO YOURSELVES IN PSALMS AND HYMNS AND SPIRITUAL SONGS, SINGING AND MAKING MELODY IN YOUR HEART TO THE LORD," not flying from Him—not trembling at the thought of Him, but praising Him, rejoicing in Him, as this Apostle saith to the Philippians iv. 4, "*Rejoice in the Lord alway and again I say rejoice.*" For, saith he also to them, "*We are the circumcision which worship God in the spirit, and rejoice in Christ Jesus, and have no confidence in the flesh.*" Phil. iii. 3. Oh! dear friends, how different this is from the ignorant imagination of unconverted sinners, that religion is a gloomy subject! It is the only happiness in the world. There is no happiness whatever except in true religion. It is only false religion that makes men gloomy, true religion cannot but make all happy who understand and believe it. If you are not happy in religion, then the reason must be, that there is some ignorance or error in your mind, concerning the truth. You may rest satisfied, that there is some point of truth, which you do not understand or believe. You do not know the hope of the Gospel—the good tidings of great joy.

Perhaps you may say, "Alas! if this be so, I am afraid I am not a believer at all, for I am so unhappy. I often doubt, whether I can be a child of God, I feel so miserable."

Well—various may be the causes of spiritual unhappiness and dejection: for example, indulging in any known sin—allowing ourselves in the violation or neglect of known duty; these are incompatible with peace; for they are testimonies to the conscience, that we are not truly and sincerely trusting in our Father's love and mercy in Jesus. But, if you are indeed, sincerely looking for peace, and find it not; then you may rest satisfied though you may be a child of God; it is because you are not looking simply and believingly to the truth; there is some point of ignorance in your mind, you are looking into yourself for comfort, into your own heart—expecting to find it improved, and good; and disappointed, and unhappy, because you feel it is not so. If you are looking there for peace, you will never find it—never—as long as you live. The more you look to yourselves, the more cause you will have for sorrow, and not for joy—for humiliation, and not for comfort. You may rest satisfied, there is something wrong in your view, or belief of the truth, when you are not rejoicing in the Lord Jesus Christ; either you are not looking really and simply to the object of faith, or your faith is very weak; therefore, you are not living up to your privileges and rejoicing in the Lord Jesus Christ as you ought to do. Consider it well. It is your privilege, your duty to rejoice in your Lord and Saviour, to make melody in your heart to the Lord, "*This is the will of God in Christ Jesus, concerning you*," 1st Thes. v. 18; "*Rejoice in the Lord alway, again I say, rejoice*," Phil. iv. 4; it is His will you should do so, "SINGING AND MAKING MELODY IN YOUR HEART TO THE LORD." But oh! how different this is from the joy of the world!—the deceitful countenance of the worldling—how often it wears a sunny look, while the heart is sad! How often there is a delusive smile upon the cheek, while there is a pang of agony and anguish writhing in the bosom! In the words of the song—(even the writer of a song is sometimes constrained to express a solemn truth):—

"As a beam o'er the face of the waters may glow,
While the tide runs in darkness and coldness below—
So the cheek may be tinged with a warm sunny smile,
While the cold heart to ruin runs darkly the while."

It is so continually. The world smiles. Go into company, all is smile—all grace—all affability—all good humor and happiness. But if you could look into the hearts of those who compose that seemingly happy circle, Ah! there you would see sadness—sorrow—discontent—covetousness—ambition—consuming passions—envy—jealousy, all the evils that are enumerated in Scripture, as belonging to the natural heart of the unconverted sinner.

But it is not in making melody with a smile on your cheek, in outward show—it is not sitting down to sing for others, while your own dark miserable heart is full of sorrow, but "SINGING AND MAKING MELODY IN YOUR HEART, TO THE LORD." Oh! that is the thing, "*A merry heart maketh a cheerful countenance;*" It is not the hypocritical semblance of a cheerful countenance, when there is within a sad and heavy heart. There ought to be a merry heart, if you are looking to the Lord as you ought to look to Him. If you are going to the Lord Jesus, and rejoicing in your God and Saviour, you ought to be "SINGING AND MAKING MELODY IN YOUR HEART, TO THE LORD."

It is there we ought to make melody—there we ought to be at peace with God—resting on our dear Redeemer, and loving Him "*Who loved us, and gave himself up for us.*"

Well—but a believer may say, "It is easy to talk thus, still, there are so many things calculated to make us sad and gloomy here—so many things both within and without continually pressing on us that make us sorrowful—that afflict—that cast us down—distress—oppress—overwhelm us, that we may say, "*How can we sing the Lord's song in a strange land?*" How can you desire us to be cheerful and happy at all times, and under all circumstances?—Well, Does not the Lord know all this? Certainly he does, yet you see, He has provided for it too. Mark what he saith by the Apostle, not only "SINGING AND MAKING MELODY IN YOUR HEART, TO THE LORD," but moreover, "GIVING THANKS ALWAYS, FOR ALL THINGS UNTO GOD AND THE FATHER, IN THE NAME OF THE LORD JESUS CHRIST."

What! "GIVING THANKS ALWAYS?"

Yes, always!

What! "FOR ALL THINGS?"

Yes! for all things!

Does not the Lord know what He means, when He says, "GIVING THANKS ALWAYS FOR ALL THINGS?" When He says "ALL THINGS," does He not mean "ALL THINGS?"

How can that be? Because it is your privilege to do so, if you are looking to the Lord as you ought to do, because "*All things are yours,*" 1st Cor. iii. 21. "*All things are working together for good to them that love God, to them that are the called, according to his purpose,*" Rom. viii. 28.

When a wayward child is ill, and requires to have some medicine, perhaps very unpalatable, administered to it—when it receives the cup from the physician, you will see it very unwilling to take it, putting it away from its lips, crying, angry, rebellious at the idea of having to take such an unpleasant draught.

But you will see a person grown up, if he is a person of common understanding, knowing that he is ill, and requiring the aid of medical skill—when the physician comes—if he is one in whom he has perfect confidence—one who has come to him often, and who has as often administered medicine that was blessed to relieve him of his pain—when this Physician puts a cup into his hand, instead of putting it away from him, and acting like the child, he takes the cup, however unpalatable the medicine—he thanks the physician for it—and not only willingly, but gratefully takes it, and blesses God for it—and esteems it as a good—and as a mercy from His hand. So you may see many a silly child of God, (many of His children are babes and silly inexperienced creatures), not considering—not thinking of the skill of the Physician—the tenderness of the Father—the inveteracy of the disease—the necessity, and the efficacy of the medicine—when their Lord gives them a cup to drink, put it away from them—repine—murmur against the dispensation—and rebel when they are forced to drink it. But the believer, who is trained to maturity in the school of Christ—who is taught of God—who knows, as he ought to know, the skill—the power of the Physician—the love of his tender Father—the sure and certain blessing that is, and must be contained in the cup that is given to him by such Wisdom, and such Love—he receives it—he takes it—he finds balm and health in the prescription—and so, see what the Apostle says, "*And not only so, but we glory in tribulations also.*" Why? Is it because they are pleasant? No such thing, they are not, but mark the reason, "*Knowing that tribulation worketh patience, and patience experience, and experience hope, and hope maketh not ashamed, because the love of God is shed abroad in our hearts, by the Holy Ghost, which is given unto us,*" Rom. v. 5.

The Holy Ghost teaches the sinner the love of God, that lov—that rich, sovereign, and everlasting love, the Holy Spirit testifies of that to the believer's heart; and knowing that love, the knowledge of that love enables him to rejoice in tribulation; and although it is true, that "*no chastening for the present seemeth to be joyous, but grievous,*" Heb. xii. 11; yet there is no time, when the believer who is experienced in the School of Christ, sees more cause to bless his Father's hand, and to give thanks, than when that Father's hand is graciously pleased to chasten him in any way, by any trial, or any dispensation. Therefore, it is his privilege to "GIVE THANKS ALWAYS, FOR ALL THINGS, UNTO GOD AND THE FATHER, IN THE NAME OF OUR LORD JESUS CHRIST."

Hannah More tells a story, in one of her Tracts, of a poor collier, who was a faithful servant of God, and who had a habit of saying, "*Thank God,*" an all occasions. He used it as a kind of common expression, and was frequently laughed at by his profane companions, for this expression of thankfulness. One day, the men were sitting on the edge of a coal-pit, eating their dinner, which had been brought to them, and this poor man had laid his dinner beside him, and a dog ran away with it; his companions all laughed at him, and cried out, "Will you thank God for that?" He got up to pursue after the dog; before he returned, the time came when they were to go down into the coal-pit; when they did so, the chain gave way, and they were every one precipitated into eternity. By this circumstance, this poor man had his life saved. The writer relates the story to illustrate the Providence of God, watching over the poor soul who was enabled, in every thing to thank Him.

I think, I may appeal to the conscience and the recollection of any whom I address, and who know the Lord as their Refuge—I may appeal to them, for the truth of this, that in looking back on their lives they will admit, that the circumstances which they have thought most painful, disastrous, or bitter at the time—they have been afterwards taught to see as blessings, that they could not have anticipated, blessings that they had cause to be thankful for, and to praise the Lord for to this day. I am sure, if I were asked, "For what I think I have most reason to be thankful in all my life"? I should say, bitter trials, severe afflictions, visitations that have weighed heavily on my heart and soul. Therefore, we ought to know, that it is our privilege, "*In every thing to give thanks*," or, as here, to "GIVE THANKS ALWAYS FOR ALL THINGS UNTO GOD AND THE FATHER, IN THE NAME OF OUR LORD JESUS CHRIST."

How often is sickness a blessing to the children of God!

How often are they taught sober reflection, patient submission, and deep experience of their Father's love! How often faith, and confidence, and hope, that they could never have otherwise experienced or enjoyed, had they not been laid on beds of sickness!

How often have privation and poverty been made the means of turning the sinner's heart to seek for, and to find "*the unsearchable riches of Christ!*"

How often have bereavements been blessed to the sinner's soul, by the taking away of earthly props and idols, and teaching him to return and lean on the bosom of his God!

How often have many of the visitations, which the Lord has been pleased to send on us for our sins and follies—how often have they been made the means in His hand, of bringing us again to our right mind—healing our backslidings—lifting us up from our falls—and leading us again to sit, in faith, repentance, and humility—in grateful thankfulness and love, at our Master's feet! Therefore it is our privilege to "GIVE THANKS ALWAYS FOR ALL THINGS UNTO GOD AND THE FATHER IN THE NAME OF THE LORD JESUS CHRIST."

You see, it is "IN THE NAME OF THE LORD JESUS CHRIST," we are called on to give thanks. All our blessings come to us through Jesus. All our covenant mercies are given to us through Christ. He is the channel of every good to the sinner. He is himself the Great Dispenser of every blessing. "*All power is given to Him in heaven and in earth*," and "*He is head over all things to His church*;" as we had, chap. i. 22, "*He is the head over all things*" that are good, to give them their portion of blessings and mercies—"*He is the head over all things*" that seem to be evil, to cause them to work for good to His people, because it is in His covenant, "*All things are working together for good to them.*" Rom. viii. 28. It was this that supported Him Himself through all His trials. Do you not remember His words, when the cup of trembling was put into His blessed hands, do you not remember His expression upon that occasion? "*The cup which my Father hath given me, shall I not drink it?*" Oh! what a privilege, if the believer is able to say, "*The cup which my Father hath given me, shall I not drink it*"—how bitter soever it may be to the taste, when we remember it comes from the hand of a Father, it is sweet to the spiritual soul—to the enlightened conscience—to the subdued will. It is sweet to the sanctified affections of the heart, "*The cup which my Father hath given me, shall I not drink it;*" that sweet spirit of submission and thankfulness—not only the spirit of submission to God, but to one another—So the Apostle adds—

"SUBMITTING YOURSELVES, ONE TO ANOTHER, IN THE FEAR OF GOD." This is the reverse of the natural mind. The natural mind is—not submitting itself to another in the fear of God—but setting itself up above another, without either fear of God, or regard of man. The natural mind is, what we call—"holding our own," and we pride ourselves on that sort of disposition, that will hold its own. That is the principle on which the natural heart plumes itself. In other words, the natural pride, corruption, and wickedness of the heart, is completely opposed to the Spirit and will of God. This is his command, "SUBMITTING YOURSELVES, ONE TO ANOTHER, IN THE FEAR OF GOD."

"My dear friends, if we do not think ourselves inferior to any other fellow-sinner, we know there can be but one reason, and that is, because we do not know ourselves; for every individual, that knows himself, feels himself really more vile than any other. Paul saith, speaking of sinners, "*Of whom I am chief,*" 1st Tim. i. 15, the chief of sinners! Every believer who knows himself, knows himself to be the same thing; and the reason is clear.—It is this—because he sees in himself, what he cannot see in anybody else—that is, the working of a corrupt heart. He sees, in himself, more sin than he can see in all the world beside—he can only see the actions of others, or hear their words, but he can see the corruptions of his own vile heart, and therefore, he feels, from this knowledge of himself, and sees himself to be the chief of sinners.

This beats down the natural pride of the heart—where it is experimentally taught to us, by the Spirit of God. It gives us an humble spirit; and therefore, as Christians grow in grace, they grow in humility—that is the exhortation here, "SUBMITTING YOURSELVES, ONE TO ANOTHER, IN THE FEAR OF GOD."

Luther illustrates this, by a story of two goats, that he saw meeting together upon a narrow stick, placed like a bridge across a deep ravine, or chasm. The two goats were going in different directions along this stick, they met one another; they could not turn about, and they could not go down, for to fall was death, and he saw one of them lie down, to let the other go over him, and so they passed safely their respective ways along the stick. This story may illustrate this very text, "SUBMITTING YOURSELVES ONE TO ANOTHER IN THE FEAR OF GOD." If we have the spirit of one of these goats, we will lie down to let our fellow go by. If two men had been there, one probably would have endeavored to knock the other down. The goat lay down. "SUBMIT YOUR SELVES ONE TO ANOTHER IN THE FEAR OF GOD." Oh! the spirit of submission, of lowliness, is a rich blessing, "*In lowliness of mind, let each esteem other better than himself.*" Phil. ii. 3. And see what peace that gives, instead of the spirit of contention and jarring with each other, yielding submission, lowliness of mind, see how immediately it produces peace.

This is not meant, of course, to affect or interfere with the just exercise of authority and rule in those, in all relations of life, whose duty it is to command others, and to whom they are bound to submit. On the contrary, to all in subjection, this rule enjoins conscientious and religious submission, in the fear of God. And the Apostle proceeds from this general admonition, to the details of subjection, in the varied relations of life. But, I think, it is intended to enforce also, that lowliness and humility which may exhibit a Christian spirit in the highest station, which makes authority gentle, and obedience affectionate, and gives the spirit of the law of love, that is of the Law of God to both.

I remember hearing of a dear friend of mine, a minister in London, Mr. Howells; that he went once to visit two of his flock, husband and wife, they were contending in a bitter spirit, and they both complained to him. "Well," said he, "I advise you, let the innocent forgive the guilty, whoever is conscious, to themselves that they are innocent, let them pardon the other." It silenced both, of course.

Cultivate that spirit of forbearance; if we be in the right, instead of holding ourselves up, let us give way. If you think you are in the right, then, be humble—you will be still more in the right, if you give way, if you yield, if you submit. A spirit of tenderness—yielding—submission to each other—love to each other—Oh! with what a charm it allays all the contentions that disorder society, not to say domestic life.

Think of this—"SUBMITTING YOURSELVES, ONE TO ANOTHER IN THE FEAR OF GOD." But then, that never can be, as long as your eye is fixed on each other's faults. "This person wronged me, and that person wronged me, and I must do so to them." The only power that can subdue this is "THE FEAR OF GOD." When the Lord Jesus comes into the stormy heart—when He lifts up His head in the storm—when He says, "*Peace, be still,*" then, there is a great calm. Oh! how often the sinner has to say, when he sees and feels, what storms that raged within and without are allayed—how often he has to say, "*What manner of man is this, that even the winds and the sea obey Him?*" Oh! then, consider these things, and may the Lord give you understanding in all things! May the Lord apply His Word to our hearts, and bring it home practically to each of us, according to our manifold necessities, for His Name's sake. Amen.

FORTIETH LECTURE.

EPHESIANS V.—22, 23, 24.

"Wives, submit yourselves unto your own husbands, as unto the Lord. For the husband is the head of the wife, even as Christ is the head of the church; and He is the Saviour of the body. Therefore, as the church is subject unto Christ, so let the wives be to their own husbands in everything."

THE Gospel of Christ places all those who believe it, quite in a new position, both with respect to God and their fellow-creatures.

It places the believer in a new position *with respect to God.* From being an enemy—a condemned criminal, he becomes a child, a dear child; as the Apostle saith here, "*Be ye followers of God, as dear children,*"—delivered from all condemnation—his soul acquitted from all iniquity—washed in the precious blood of the Lamb, and presented, as we see in this portion of Scripture, a member of His Church, "*A glorious church, not having spot, or wrinkle, or any such thing.*" A church being composed of individuals, a spotted individual would make a spotted church, and therefore, when the Church is without "SPOT OR WRINKLE, OR ANY SUCH THING," every individual in the church must be so: therefore, every believer is placed in this condition, with respect to his God, he is presented to Him spotless and perfect, in Christ Jesus.

"*Whom we preach,*" as the Apostle saith in another place, "*warning every man, and teaching every man in all wisdom; that we may present every man perfect in Christ Jesus.*" Col. ii. 28. Therefore, the Gospel places the believer in a new and glorious position, with respect to his God; he is a spotless child of God—an heir of glory through his precious Lord and Redeemer, "*Who hath loved him and washed him from his sins in his own blood.*" Rev. i. 4.

So it places the believer also in a new position, with respect to all his fellow-creatures. Whenever the Gospel enters truly into the sinner's heart, it enters in its power into all the ramifications of his existence—into every relation of his life. The Gospel, like the mainspring of a watch, is to be the moving power that regulates and governs the Christian's heart, in every relation, whether as parent, child, husband, wife, brother, sister, relative in any degree—master, servant, friend, neighbor, sovereign or subject—governor or governed—high or low—rich or poor—in every imaginable position in which an individual can be placed—in every possible relation, in which he can stand to his fellow-creature, the Gospel of the Lord Jesus Christ ought to carry its influence—its power—and its motive into his heart, for the discharge of his duty, in that position, whatever that duty be. Therefore, the objections that the ungodly are continually raising against the Gospel, that the doctrine of salvation by faith in Christ, opens a door to licentiousness of conduct, arises, we reiterate again and again, from the ignorance of the individual who makes the objection. A person who speaks thus, can know no more of the Gospel of Christ than the beast that perisheth. "*The kingdom of God is not in word, but in power*," 1 Cor. iv. 20. Whenever the Gospel of Christ comes, it must come with power. That power, is indeed, greater or less in different individuals, and in the same individual at different times; yet it always comes with power—with constraining power—and that power is "*The love of Christ*," so saith the Apostle, "*The love of Christ constraineth us, because we thus judge*." (Now, observe, how the Apostle brings motive into operation,) "*The love of Christ constraineth us, because we thus judge, that if one died for all, then were all dead, and that he died for all, that they which live*," (that is—they who derive life from Him—who believe the Gospel—to whom the Gospel comes with power) "*should not henceforth live unto themselves, but unto him who died for them, and rose again*," 2 Cor. v. 14, 15. Therefore, it is very important, that you should always recollect, that which I must continually impress on you, that throughout the Apostolical epistles, you should ever view the individuals that are addressed in them, as believers. If you do not look at them so, you cannot understand the Scriptures at all. That is one of the many modes by which men deceive themselves. They will read religious books, the religion of which, is not the religion of Christ—books that teem with Scripture, and bring forward a great variety of passages out of the Apostolical Epistles. And they say, "This is the Word of God, here the Apostle desires us to do so and so." The Apostle desires you to do no such thing; the Apostle desires you to do so, only on the ground of your being a believer in the Gospel. Look at this chapter, how it commences, "*Be ye followers of God, as dear children*." All the Epistles of Paul are addressed to saints. This is addressed "*To the saints which are at Ephesus, and to the faithful in Christ Jesus*." How can persons be saints, if they do not believe the Gospel? How can they be "faithful in Christ Jesus," if they are not in Christ at all—if so far from being in Christ, they do not depend on the Lord Jesus as the Refuge for their soul?

"*Be ye therefore followers of God, as dear children*," because you are God's children, and because you are delivered from all your sins; follow your Heavenly Father—that is the language of the Gospel of Jesus. But what is the principle of falsely religious books, and falsely religious men? It is this—"Be ye followers of God, that you may be made the children of Christ Jesus."

The two things are as different as light and darkness.

The one is—"Because ye are the children of Christ, redeemed, delivered from all your sins—because ye are washed—because ye are presented without spot to God—Be ye followers of Him as such."

The other is—"Be ye followers of God, in order, that by your conduct, and by following God, ye may become such." Surely, two principles cannot be more directly opposed to each other, than these. In the one, the moral conduct is made to be the *cause* of being in Christ—of being saved. In the other case, the moral conduct is made to be the *effect* of being saved. The principles, therefore, are as different as cause and effect. Consider it well—for, if you do not thoroughly know this, you cannot understand the very fundamental principles of the Gospel of Jesus. "*Be ye followers of God, as dear children.*" Because you are children—because the Lord has loved you, and pardoned you—because He has washed you in the "*Fountain opened for sin and for uncleanness,*" therefore, be ye followers of the Lord. Think what a Father you have! What a Redeemer you have! What love your Father has manifested to you! and therefore, love Him: let your service to Him be a service of love—let your service be a service of joy—of peace—a service of glorious trust, and confidence, and hope, because your Lord has done all these things for you. Receive with grateful hearts, what He has done for you, and trust Him still for more. "*What shall I render unto the Lord for all his benefits toward me? I will take the cup of salvation, and call upon the name of the Lord.*" Ps. cxvi. 12, 13. Thus speaketh the man who holds the true principle.

But what is the language of him who holds the other? Let your service be a service of hesitating hope, and trembling fear, and anxious doubt—that is in truth, the service of a slave, who is trying to earn a reward, which he never can earn—which he tremblingly fears that he shall lose, and scarcely dares to hope he can gain.

Salvation on such terms, is not doubtful, it is impossible. It shuts out Christ from its plan. "*If righteousness come by the law, then Christ is dead in vain.*" Gal. ii. 21. "*Christ is become of no effect unto you, whosoever of you are justified by the law, ye are fallen from grace,*" Gal. v. 4.

This is not an abstract opinion, it is a principle that must come into every motive of the heart, every hope of the soul; it must be as intimately blended with every expectation of eternal life, and every single motive of the conduct, as the air that you respire is blended with your lungs, when it enters into and inflates them; it must be the moving principle that actuates the whole man, or else it is nothing at all.

We must always consider thus, all the practical duties of the Gospel. All the practical duties of the Christian's conduct, must be brought to the test of the true Scriptural motive, or they cannot be the genuine fruits of holiness, for, saith the Lord, "*As the branch cannot bear fruit of itself, except it abide in the vine, no more can ye, except ye abide in me,*" John xv. 4.

"WIVES, SUBMIT YOURSELVES UNTO YOUR OWN HUSBANDS AS UNTO THE LORD." You might just as well use that exhortation, in the Scriptural sense in which it is here applied, to an ungodly woman, as you might to a dead woman! You might as well go into a church-yard, and speak to a dead woman in her grave, as speak to an ungodly woman according to the motive of the Gospel of Christ. She cannot understand you. The wife may see that it is her duty to submit herself to her husband, and there are many wives that do so from a sense of duty, a mere moral sense of duty. Strict education—self-denying habits—proper discipline, without any true religion, may do much in the training of the female mind, as well as in the training of a man's mind; and I have known many individuals, in this sense, excellent wives, kind, amiable, benevolent, and indeed, fulfilling to all outward appearance, the letter of the Scripture precept on this subject—I have known them to do so, from what we may and do consider a naturally amiable disposition, and from being well-trained, and well brought up. If a mother brings up her daughter as she ought to do, she will, generally speaking, be more or less capable of discharging the duties of a faithful wife, but I have known them to do so without a particle of religion. One of the most naturally amiable women I ever knew, was one of the greatest opponents of the Gospel of Christ. In such characters the motive of love to the Lord, has no more to do in the regulation of their conduct, than it has in the guidance of the horse that is driven in their carriage. They have no principle of the Gospel, to inspire them with a motive. How is it possible they can, when they do not believe the Gospel? And you might address any unconverted woman—no matter if the wickedest woman in the world—you might as well address her on Gospel motives—as the most amiable woman in the world, if she does not believe the Gospel. She could not understand you. She might know and feel, that it was her duty to submit herself to her husband, and she might do so. But as to the sense in which it is here impressed on the Christian wife, and the argument drawn from Christ and His Church to enforce it—of that she has not the slightest notion. There is a certain sense, no doubt, of her duty to God, mingling with her duty to her husband, but it is as far from the principle laid down in Scripture, to a Christian female, as darkness is from light.

"WIVES, SUBMIT YOURSELVES UNTO YOUR OWN HUSBANDS AS UNTO THE LORD; FOR THE HUSBAND IS THE HEAD OF THE WIFE, EVEN AS CHRIST IS THE HEAD OF THE CHURCH, AND HE IS THE SAVIOUR OF THE BODY." Now, where a female is well educated, even in an ordinarily moral sense, and her mind well disciplined, and when she is naturally of an amiable temper, this may be, humanly speaking, an easy task. But if, as is generally the case with all of us, and certainly so with the vast majority, who are not under the direct influence of sound Gospel principles, if they be not well disciplined, and their tempers and wills not brought into proper subjection; if that be the case, then if this motive does not enter into the mind of the female, and regulate her deportment to her husband, she cannot, and will not pursue the line of conduct laid down, even outwardly—putting the principle out of the question—she will have no spirit of submission—she will have a will of her own; and if that will cross the will of her husband, it must be a source of trial, and grief, of pain and misery to both of them.

Therefore, recollect, this is addressed to a godly woman—to a converted woman—to a woman, who brings her duty to her husband, always into direct connection with her duty to the Lord her God. Her own will may be crossed—her own temper may be tried—she may be, as no doubt will be the case with all conditions of humanity, where we have to do with one another, vile, selfish sinners as we are—she may be tried in several ways; but she has her Lord to come to—she has her Redeemer to fly to—she has her Saviour as her "*strong hold whereunto she may continually resort*," she has her Lord always to direct—to guide—and to enable her, according to His blessed Word, thus to regulate her conduct.

Now a female must be placed in one of these two positions, as a Christian wife—either married to an ungodly or to a pious husband. If she be married to a pious man, and that they both have the Lord's Word, as the guide and rule of their conduct, then, that is indeed, a happy and blessed union; for it is God that maketh persons to be of one mind in an house; there is no union of spirit, of heart, so firm, so strong, so blessed, so indissoluble, as where hearts are one in Christ Jesus. Then both will keep their places to each other, in duty, and in love. The husband will keep his place, with the Lord's Word to regulate and govern him—the wife will also keep her place, they will walk together hand in hand to eternal life. This, is indeed, a blessed state for husbands and wives; and if there be any of you here, who are married, Oh! consider, what happiness—what peace—what comfort can you have in this poor world, if you love one another, and if the prospect at the end of it is, that you must be severed forever. Oh! think, the true happiness of the wife consists in this, with respect to her husband, that he is washed in the blood of the Lamb, and going on the path to eternal life. And the happiness of the husband must consist in the same, in reference to his wife; thus they ought to dwell with each other "*According to knowledge, as being heirs together of the grace of life*," 1st Pet. iii. 7.

But then, there is a very different position in which a female may be placed, she may be married to an ungodly husband. I have known many a pious woman married to an ungodly man. If a religious woman marries, from any motive, a man that is ignorant of the Gospel of Christ· she runs into a fatal snare! "*What communion hath light with darkness?*" 2 Cor. vi. 14. There is nothing more awful, than for a young person, man or woman, who knows the Gospel of the Lord Jesus Christ, to marry a person that is ignorant of that Gospel. It is, indeed, a fearful pitfall! that a man or woman, servants of God, should unite themselves with one who must be, as not being a servant of God, a servant of Satan !—what prospect of happiness can there be? It is often the case that one or the other is brought to the knowledge of the Gospel of Jesus, after they are married; one is taken, and another left. The Lord sometimes calls the wife, and leaves the husband, sometimes calls the husband and leaves the wife, "*It is not of him that willeth, or of him that runneth, but of God that showeth mercy.*" Rom. ix. 16. But suppose, from any circumstances, a pious wife is married to an ungodly husband, her duty is clear, "WIVES, SUBMIT YOURSELVES UNTO YOUR OWN HUSBANDS AS UNTO THE LORD." I have known some wives, making a profession of religion and married to ungodly men, and I have known them to make religion odious to their husbands, by the manner in which they conducted themselves towards them; thinking, that because they were religious, and their husbands not so, therefore, they should regulate, and govern and order everything in their own way. I have seen persons making a profession of religion, and acting thus, render it hateful, by such conduct. Let a woman remember that her husband's character, as being a believer or unbeliever, does not change her relation, nor consequently her duty to him. She should, if possible, be only the more scrupulous and careful in the discharge of that duty. It is a grievous evil, when the effect of religion is to lead persons who profess it, to exhibit neglect of duty, or unamiability of temper. I have known, on the contrary, a pious woman married to an irreligious man, so to adorn the doctrine of Christ, that she made religion sweet, even to those who knew it not—made them respect and honor the influence of true religion in her, though they did not honor it for its own sake. Such is the command of the Apostle, 1st Pet. iii. 1, 2, "*Likewise, ye wives, be in subjection to your own husbands; that if any obey not the word, they also may without the word, be won by the conversation of the wives, while they behold your chaste conversation coupled with fear.*" You see what a blessing is promised to a godly wife, even though she may be married to an irreligious husband, when even without the word, the husband may be won by her chaste and gentle deportment.

But nothing can carry her through this but the Lord. So you see she is referred here to her God, "BE SUBJECT UNTO YOUR OWN HUSBANDS, AS UNTO THE LORD." It does not mean that the wife is to put her husband upon an equality with God, for there is one plain rule to be observed here, as in all other cases of subjection, and it is this—whether wife or husband, child or parent, servant or master, subject or sovereign, there is one law to regulate obedience in all things, and that is this—That whenever the authority of man clashes with the authority of God, man's authority is to be postponed to that of God. If a husband should endeavor to make his wife do anything contrary to the plain commands of God, she is to be subject to God in this, and not to her husband; she must obey God rather than man. Therefore, if her husband were to turn her out of doors, she is to be turned out of doors rather than disobey God. So, if the child is commanded to do anything contrary to the will of God, the child is to refuse such a command. So, if the servant is commanded to do anything contrary to the will of God, his Master in heaven is to be prized before his master on earth. So, if the subject is desired to do anything contrary to the will of God, by the laws of his country, he is to set his face, like a flint against those laws, he must not obey the laws of his country in such a case—he is not to obey any power, if contrary to the will of God. Therefore, the Christian is to hold up God, and God's authority; and no law or authority of man, is to make him violate, in any relation of life, his duty to his God; that is the only standard, and that the only exception in all cases of subjection. In all other cases, obedience is a duty. But, when that clashes with God's authority—there, obedience to any human power, is to be conscientiously refused, and God alone is to be obeyed and honored. Therefore, this is the standard by which the conscience is to be regulated—"WIVES, SUBMIT YOURSELVES UNTO YOUR OWN HUSBANDS AS UNTO THE LORD." All authority that is delegated by God, is to be honored for God, and honored as God's appointment. God is the head of all authority, all power that is exercised on earth, in every station and sphere, ought to be exercised as it is derived—from God; and this is a great principle to be kept continually in view, in studying the practical parts of God's Word. This is a principle, against which, infidelity and anarchy are fiercely setting their faces, all through the world, at this moment. It is denied that God is the Source of power—that God is the Giver of authority. But in whatever way you consider it, whether in respect to the government of a country or a family —in respect to the government of a sovereign or a constitution—whether it be the rule of a father—husband—master—magistrate, or any government—Autocrat—Oligarchy, or Democracy—it does not signify in what point of view you look at government, you are not a Christian—or you do not know the Word of Christ—or you do not obey the Word of Christ, if you do not look at that authority as delegated by God, from whatever secondary source it may be immediately derived. And therefore, the principle that is now so much set up, namely—"That the people is the source of power," is a principle of the Prince of darkness, a principle which the devil sets up against the government and authority of Jehovah. For as God is the lawful Ruler of the world, there is no source of authority but God. All who exercise it, shall give account of their rule—and all over whom it is exercised, of their subjection. The representative of any body of electors, is as directly intrusted with his power by God, and shall give an account of his discharge of that solemn trust to God, just as much as an hereditary peer, or the heir of an hereditary throne. "*There is no power but of God; the powers that be, are ordained of God;*" Rom. xiii. 1, 2; and therefore, you see, religion is despised—God's Word and His authority are laid aside, or trodden under foot, in proportion, as men, not only adopt, but succumb to such a principle, or verge to it in any way. There is no verging to it without departing from God, there is no listening to it—no compromising with it at all. Jehovah—God over all, is the standard of all authority. His Word ordains its exercise, and His Word commands subjection to it. It is thus, He ordains that it should be carried into the heart of every servant of His—of every wife to her husband, as here. She should remember, that the authority of her husband is the authority of God, and she should carry her obedience to him always, as a matter of conscience unto the Lord—she should discharge it as a duty to her God. The Apostle gives this as the reason of his command. "FOR THE HUSBAND IS THE HEAD OF THE WIFE, EVEN AS CHRIST IS THE HEAD OF THE CHURCH, AND HE IS THE SAVIOUR OF THE BODY; THEREFORE, AS THE CHURCH IS SUBJECT TO CHRIST, SO LET THE WIVES BE TO THEIR OWN HUSBANDS IN EVERYTHING."

The Apostle, throughout this portion of his Epistle, which we shall have another day to consider, draws a parallel between the relation of the Lord Jesus Christ to His Church, and that of the husband to his wife—and when he brings that principle home to the heart of the believing wife, see how beautifully it is brought to bear on her conduct, by the reason assigned. "FOR THE HUSBAND IS THE HEAD OF THE WIFE, EVEN AS CHRIST IS THE HEAD OF THE CHURCH, AND HE IS THE SAVIOUR OF THE BODY." Now, since this relation between the husband and wife, is continually set forth as emblematical of the relation between Christ and His Church. Let us consider what it is—

When a man marries a woman, whatever the station of that woman may have been, however low, however mean compared with that of her husband; if, for example a king chooses to marry a beggar, as soon as the ceremony is performed, and he is united to her, instantly her own rank is totally merged, and she is raised to the rank of her husband. If I say, the king marries a beggar, she is as completely a queen, when his wife, as if she were the daughter of the greatest monarch in the world. See then, what an image this presents with respect to Christ and His Church. What is the difference between Christ and the sinner? Surely, the greatest monarch that ever sat on a throne, is not so far raised above the poorest beggar, that ever lived—or the best human being that ever breathed, above the vilest wretch that ever wore a human form, as the Lord of glory is raised above sinners—vile, guilty sinners, such as we are. Yet the moment the Lord Jesus Christ, washes a sinner in His precious blood, and clothes him with His righteousness, making him thus one with Himself; that moment, the sinner is delivered from all his guilt—that moment, the sinner is made righteous, as Christ is righteous—pure as Christ is pure—exalted as Christ is exalted—heir to the very kingdom of glory that Christ himself inherits. As the Apostle saith, "*Who hath delivered us from the power of darkness, and hath translated us into the kingdom of his dear Son.*" Col. i. 13. For saith he again, "*Ye are the children of God, by faith in Jesus*

Christ," Gal. iii. 26; "*And remember, if children, then heirs, heirs of God, and joint heirs with Christ,*" Rom. viii. 17; "*If a son, then an heir of God, through Christ,*" Gal. iv. 7. "*There is neither Jew, nor Greek, there is neither bond nor free, there is neither male nor female, but ye are all one in Christ Jesus,*" Gal. iii. 28, 29.

How beautifully the Lord Jesus Christ sets that forth in John xvii. 20, in His prayer, "*Neither pray I for these alone,*" (His disciples) "*but for them also, which shall believe on me through their word. That they all may be one, as thou, Father, art in me, and I in thee, that they also may be one in us, that the world may believe that thou hast sent me. And the glory which thou gavest me, I have given them, that they may be one even as we are one; I in them and thou in me; that they may be perfect in one, and that the world may know that thou hast sent me, and hast loved them as thou hast loved me.*" John xvii. 20—23. As then the wife becomes one with her husband—one, essentially in every sense, "*they twain shall be one flesh,*" raised to his station—enriched with his fortune—ennobled with his dignities—crowned with his honors—in all things identified with her husband. So it is with the church of Christ. And when a woman is enabled tc look to her Lord and Saviour, as being one with Him in spiritual life and union, how sweetly His commands come to her heart, to act in relation to her husband as unto the Lord.

One point more. Suppose a woman before her marriage overwhelmed in debt, suppose she is apprehensive that she may be taken and put into prison for her debts; (I have known such a case as I mention, an unmarried woman overwhelmed with debt,) the moment she is married, she does not owe a farthing—all her debts are transferred to her husband—he becomes responsible—no creditor can bring any demand against her—she cannot be put into prison for anything she owed—her husband must bear all the burthen—she is what is called in law, a *femme couverte*, a woman covered or sheltered beneath her husband; she is under the wings of her husband, he is the debtor—she is quite clear. Oh! what a blessed view is this of the Church of Christ! She is a *femme couverte*—she is under the shadow of the Immanuel's wings! The sinner, the moment he is brought to Christ, and united to Him by faith, is clear of all his debts—his mighty debt is paid—his ten thousand talents are cancelled—Christ has become answerable for all, as the Prophet says, "*It was exacted, and he answered;*" Is. liii. 7. (*Lowth*) so, "*He bare our sins in his own body on the tree,*" He paid our debts—He cancelled them all—they are all blotted out by the blood of Jesus. As the mute whom Charlotte Elizabeth mentions in her interesting little Tract, called "The Happy Mute." This little deaf and dumb child was brought to the knowledge of the Gospel, and the little boy, describing the pardon of his sins, says, "The Lord Jesus drew a pen, dipped in His own blood, across my debt, and scored it all out." Now, when a woman is able to look to the Lord Jesus Christ as her Refuge and Hope, when she can understand this, "*Thy Maker is thy husband, the Lord of hosts is his name;*" Is. liv. 5; then, she is happy indeed—then she can understand and bring the principle of love to Jesus, into her duties to her earthly husband. What a glorious image then, is the image of Christ, as one with His Church!

We must not forget that the husband becomes the protector, the guardian of his wife. An insult offered to her, is an insult to himself. Is she in danger, he will fly to protect her with his life—he watches over her—he takes care of her—he feels she is dependent on his guardianship. His feelings—his love—his honor—his character—his promise—his all are engaged to protect—to cherish—to maintain and support her. So it is with Christ and His Church, "*He that toucheth you, toucheth the apple of his eye;*" Zec. ii. 8. "*He is the head over all things to his Church,*" as we have in the 1st chap. 22. And in all her afflictions he is afflicted. As the husband is the head of his wife, so is Christ also the head of His Church—the Protector—Defender—Guide—Guardian of all His people. Every sinner that looks unto Him, may look to Him as a wife looks to her husband, as her guardian, protector, defender, her all.

Therefore, this is the Apostle's reason for the precept to wives, and for enforcing it as he does here, "FOR THE HUSBAND IS THE HEAD OF THE WIFE, EVEN AS CHRIST IS THE HEAD OF THE CHURCH, AND HE IS THE SAVIOUR OF THE BODY."

"THEREFORE, AS THE CHURCH IS SUBJECT UNTO CHRIST, SO LET THE WIVES BE TO THEIR OWN HUSBANDS IN EVERYTHING."

Let wives remember, that "AS CHRIST IS THE HEAD OF THE CHURCH, THE SAVIOUR OF THE BODY," and as therefore, in every point of view, it is her happy privilege to trust Him—to lean on Him—to repose in His faithfulness—to rest in His love—to cast herself into His protection—and to rejoice in His power, so that the Lord adopts the conjugal state, as an image and illustration of His own relation to His Church, and calls on every Christian wife, to remember, that she ought to glorify Him as a wife, in obeying her husband, as she ought to glorify Him as a Christian, in obeying Himself.

Consider, now, that this blessed relationship which is set forth between Christ and His Church, is a relationship, into which, if you have not already entered, you are invited to enter this very day. Christ sends His Gospel to call sinners, as Abraham sent his servant to get a wife for his son Isaac. That is a beautiful history of a servant, going in the fear of the Lord, to discharge his duty to his earthly master; Genesis xxiv. When he makes known his message, he says, "*And now if ye will deal kindly and truly with my master, tell me; and if not, tell me, that I may turn to the right hand or to the left,*" verse 49. Now, I may say, I am come with my Master's proposals, I invite you, in His Name, to come this day to be one with Christ, and now I say,

"*If ye will deal kindly and truly with my Master, tell me.*' Now, I say to you, that as Abraham's "*servant brought forth jewels of silver, and jewels of gold, and raiment, and gave them to Rebekah, and gave also to her mother, and to her brother, precious things,*" v. 53, so I have laid before you this day, some slight sketch of the riches of the glory of Christ, as the husband of His Church; that is, as the Saviour of lost and guilty sinners, and I come in my Master's name, with a proposal to all of you. Come, cast in your lot with "the Bride, the Lamb's wife!" Come to be one with the Lord Jesus Christ! Come to Him—come to be united to Him—to be a partaker of His love, and an heir of His glory! Come to have all your debts cancelled! Come to be raised up to the honor of your Lord and Master—"*To be raised up together, and made to sit together in heavenly places in Christ!*" chap. ii. 6. Come to be made partner of His kingdom! Come to be protected by Him—guided by Him—strengthened by Him, all your life through, that you may be one with Christ, as Christ is with the Father. "*And now, if ye will deal kindly and truly with my Master, tell me.*" Will you come to Christ? Oh! my dear fellow-sinners, will any of you say,

"No, go away, tell your Master I will not listen to His proposals, I will not give an ear to them—I will not come to the Lord Jesus."

Will any of you say so? Oh! consider! The Son of a King sends to demand your hand! Yea, the Son of the King of kings. Come to Him—He holds out his hand to you, and remember—the hand that Christ holds out to you, is the hand that was "*Wounded for your transgressions, and bruised for your iniquities.*" Oh! look unto Him, come, come to Jesus, come to Jesus! May the Lord teach you! May the Lord grant that we may all be found united to the Son of God, washed in His blood, clothed in His righteousness, and "*Kept by His power through faith, unto salvation.*" Amen, and Amen.

FORTY-FIRST LECTURE.

EPHESIANS V.—25, 26, 27.

"Husbands, love your wives, even as Christ also loved the church, and gave himself for it; that he might sanctify and cleanse it with the washing of water by the word; that he might present it to himself a glorious church, not having spot, or wrinkle, or any such thing; but that it should be holy, and without blemish."

WE cannot too frequently remember, and repeat, that it is the object of the Gospel of Jesus, that the principles of that Gospel should be called into operation in every act, word, and thought, of the child of God. It is only by this means, that the practical effects of Christianity, can be seen and felt in their influence by the world.

For, just exactly, as in making the tree good, the manure is intended to cherish and improve the sap that circulates through it, and imparts succulence, verdure, and fruitfulness to the plant—and, as thus a physical change and improvement is produced in that sap, that circulates through every ramification of the tree—so the principle of the Gospel of Jesus, which is to work effectually in the sinner's heart, "to bring forth fruit unto God," ought to diffuse itself throughout the whole of the sinner's spiritual life, through his heart—his affections—his understanding—his will—his principles—his motives—the Gospel of Jesus ought to pervade them all. Therefore, you observe, that in all the relations of life, in which the precepts of the Holy Scripture ought to be obeyed in the sinner's conduct—the truth ought to be brought home to the sinner's conscience, to work and fructify in his heart. All the power and influence of the Gospel of Jesus, ought to be identified with his motives, and embodied in them all.

As we saw this in our last Lecture, in the duties of the wife to her husband; so we have it here, in the duties of the husband to his wife. "HUSBANDS, LOVE YOUR WIVES." On what principle? It is not, that you may enjoy your life comfortably and happily. It is not, that all the blessings which flow from union of heart and spirit may be yours. These, indeed, will be likely to follow; but these are not the motives. No, but "AS CHRIST LOVED THE CHURCH"—that is the principle that is brought into the heart of the husband; just exactly, as we saw in the last Lecture, the principle that was brought into the heart of the wife was, that she should be subject to her husband, as the church is to Christ; so here we see, the husband is to love the wife, as Christ loved the church. Christ's love to His church, is to be the exemplar and the measure of the husband's love to his wife.

I need not remark to you, how utterly inapplicable all these precepts must be, to the mind of an unconverted sinner. Recollect, that the moral precepts of the Gospel of Jesus, are no more to be applied to the unconverted sinner, as commands that he is supposed to admit, and precepts that he is able to obey in his own strength—on his own motives—or his own principles—no more than they are to be addressed to dead men. The principle must be implanted in the heart, before the principle can be called into action in the life. How absurd, to expect to find grapes on a branch severed from the vine! Nor is it less so, to expect Christian principles and Christian fruits on those who are not in Christ. There can be no use in pressing a principle, which has no place in the heart. Our Lord asks, "*Do men gather grapes of thorns, or figs of thistles*"—and we have too, on the same Divine authority, that "*A good tree cannot bring forth evil fruit, neither can a corrupt tree bring forth good fruit.*" Mat. vii. 16—18.

I cannot go to a poor man and say—"Conduct yourself, as being heir of a throne"—the man is not the heir of a throne. I can go to the son of a king, and say—"Conduct yourself as the heir of a throne"—for he is the heir of a throne. I cannot say to an unconverted sinner—"Conduct yourself as a child of God"—because he is not a child of God, he is yet in his sins; I must first endeavor to show him his guilt and misery, and to lead him to the salvation of the Gospel of Jesus, and then, if the Lord leads him to himself, apply to such persons precepts like these—"*Walk as children of light*"—"*Be ye followers of God as dear children.*" Now recollect this—carry this principle into your consciences, or rather, pray, that the Spirit of God may carry it into your consciences—so that you must, in all things, come directly to Christ, to test your motives, and to prove your principles; you must look directly to Jesus, in the discharge of all your duties.

Remember, these are considerations that must devolve on us every day, through all our lives—through all the details of our existence. The duties of our several stations and relations, necessarily devolve on us; and therefore, the true principles, and approved motives of these duties, on which alone they can be acceptable to God, should always be present in our hearts. The true motive of love to Jesus, springing from faith in Him, sanctifies duty—yea, it makes duty a pleasure, even though it might be painful in itself. Duty is always pleasant when it is done in the name of the Lord Jesus; and when the affections of the heart are lifted up to Him. The service of the Lord is always light, when the heart is warmed with grateful love to its Lord and Saviour. Then, indeed, it is easy to do a thing heartily, as unto the Lord, and not unto men.

So, observe, through all this you see, how the principle brought before the heart of the husband is, the glorious work of Jesus—the glorious salvation of Jesus. "HUSBANDS, LOVE YOUR WIVES, EVEN AS CHRIST ALSO LOVED THE CHURCH, AND GAVE HIMSELF FOR IT; THAT HE MIGHT SANCTIFY AND CLEANSE IT WITH THE WASHING OF WATER BY THE WORD; THAT HE MIGHT PRESENT IT TO HIMSELF A GLORIOUS CHURCH, NOT HAVING SPOT OR WRINKLE OR ANY SUCH THING; BUT THAT IT SHOULD BE HOLY AND WITHOUT BLEMISH."

We considered, on the last day, the relation in which the wife was placed to her husband, by her union with him. That whatever her own previous rank had been, she was raised to the rank of her husband. However overwhelmed in debt, all her debts were immediately transferred to her husband, as soon as she was married. We considered these, and several other particulars, in the emblem of a wife; in reference to the blessed state of the sinner, when brought to Christ—raised up from his ignorance—darkness—guilt—and condemnation, to be united to his Lord and Saviour, Christ Jesus—immediately raised to the glorious rank of a child of the King of kings—immediately, all his debts cancelled, one with God, and with Christ Jesus.

Now, consider, there is a corresponding relation between husband and wife, "HUSBANDS, LOVE YOUR WIVES, EVEN AS CHRIST ALSO LOVED THE CHURCH, AND GAVE HIMSELF FOR IT." As the wife undertakes the duty of subjection to the husband, so he undertakes the regulation—the ordinance, and whole responsibility of all things connected with his wife. If he be on a throne, it is for the honor of his throne, and his own, that his wife be maintained in all the rank and dignity that is suitable to a queen. If his wife had contracted debts previous to her marriage, and they devolved on him, as they must, it is for his honor and dignity that these debts should be immediately discharged, so that no charge, no imputation of unpaid debt, can be brought against her—no reflection cast on one, who is the partner of his throne, and his bosom. If his wife, should be placed in any danger, it is the duty of her husband, and not only his duty, but it is for his honor, and not only his honor, but it is the instinctive feeling of his heart, that his very life should be forfeited, rather than, that his wife should perish or be in peril. All his friends—all his relations are placed in the same relation to her, in which they are placed to him; his father, is her father; his brother, her brother; his attendants, her attendants; his ministers, her ministers; they are all hers, as much as his. Whatever he considers suitable to his own rank, dignity, and honor—whatever he considers necessary for himself, to maintain himself in the exalted rank and station, in which he stands, considered as a king; then all that is necessary for his royal consort too. If it is fit, that he appear in royal robes, it is fit, that his wife should be dressed in royal attire, like her husband; everything that is necessary for, and appropriate to him, is also necessary for, and appropriate to her; and it is her husband's ambition, to take care, that she should have it all.

Oh! consider then, dear friends, what a wonderful subject this is! as it is applied here, the Apostle says, in verse 32, and well he may, "*This is a great mystery; but I speak concerning Christ and the church,*" to think, that God, in the riches of His grace and glory, should undertake to make Himself one with a vile sinner like you! For, recollect, that whatever is true of the whole church, collectively, is true of every member of that church, individually. Whatever is true of the state of the whole church of Christ—whatever view you take of her condition and glory, it is your privilege to take that view of your own self, as a poor, guilty sinner, if you are united by faith to the Lord Jesus Christ. Consider—that if the husband is to undertake all things for the wife, Christ has become responsible for all things, for the church.

"*For the husband is the head of the wife, even as Christ is the head of the church;*" and the most vigilant, tender, faithful, loving husband, with the best regulated family—the best regulated household that ever was, or ever could exist on this earth, never did, and never could, undertake to order everything for his wife's security—honor—dignity—comfort—and happiness, as the Lord Jesus Chris has undertaken to order, and does order everything for the good, and the glory of every sinner that is brought to look to Him. For it is His Covenant and His Word, "*We know*," saith the Apostle, "*that all things work together for good to them that love God, to them who are the called, according to his purpose*," Rom. viii. 28. He is not like the master of a family, whose knowledge and power are necessarily limited, and who is himself a weak, imperfect creature—many things escape his observation—many things are concealed from his knowledge—of many things, he sees not the evil or the danger—many things are beyond his power to remedy, and to many things he has not the wisdom, or the skill even to apply a remedy that is within his reach. But in all things, connected with every individual member of the Church of Christ, there is nothing that escapes the vigilance of His Omnipresent eye—nothing that eludes the skill of His Omniscient wisdom—nothing that can contravene the ordinance of His Almighty power and everlasting love—all His attributes are engaged for the everlasting blessedness of His church. Therefore, "*All things are working together for good to them that love God.*" Oh! my friends, if a sinner was able just to take this one blessed truth, to take it by faith, and apply it to all his circumstances—to repose his heart and conscience in the arms of everlasting faithfulness and love—on the bosom of his Saviour and his God! Oh! how unspeakably happy would he be! How blessed would it make him!

Just consider these words, "HUSBANDS, LOVE YOUR WIVES; EVEN AS CHRIST ALSO LOVED THE CHURCH, AND GAVE HIMSELF FOR IT." Suppose a wife tenderly attached to a husband; suppose her life in great and imminent danger, suppose the husband flies to her rescue—and suppose that in rescuing her, in defending her, he preserves her indeed, but at the expense of his own life—Imagine, you behold her hanging in anguish, over his dead body; and suppose, that as Jesus came to the grave of Lazarus, and said, "*Lazarus come forth*"—suppose, the Word of God, by the exercise of His mighty power, should revive that husband again, and give him back to her arms—how would all her tenderness, and all her affection be increased if possible, ten thousand fold! But "CHRIST LOVED THE CHURCH AND GAVE HIMSELF FOR IT;" He did not endanger—He did not venture His life—He "GAVE HIMSELF," and now "*He is alive for evermore, and has the keys of death and hell*," Rev. i. 18. Oh! when sinners are able to know, that Jesus has saved them by standing in their place, that Jesus has saved them, by giving his life for them, how it endears that Saviour to the heart! If a man flies to the rescue of a friend, who is dear to him, and who is in any danger, he still hopes and believes, that he will be preserved through it; and that in delivering his friend, he will also be delivered himself. But the Lord Jesus Christ knew, in His love, that there was no deliverance for him—He knew all that was before him—He knew all he was to encounter—He knew that the cup could not pass from him—and He gave His life—"HE LOVED THE CHURCH AND GAVE

HIMSELF FOR IT." Oh! when the sinner is able to see this—when he is able to know, that the love of Jesus Christ—of Him, who gave Himself for his sins—orders everything for his good, how it sanctifies all providences, trials, and dispensations of his life! How smoothly it makes the current of it glide along! My dear friends, if there be any of you who believe in the Lord Jesus Christ, and whose minds are troubled and bowed down, with either spiritual or temporal distress; your sins—your wants—your trials, or afflictions, whatever they may be—Depend on it, you are not realizing by faith, and resting as you ought, on the truth set before you in the everlasting Gospel, concerning the glorious offices of your Redeemer, and His covenant love to all His people. For all these things are working together for your good, the Lord Jesus Christ is watching over you. As surely as He has brought you to His feet—enabled you to look to Him—"*Opened your eyes, and turned you from darkness to light, from the power of Satan unto God*" brought you to Himself and washed you in His precious blood; so surely, every trial, everything concerning you, must be ordered for your good. Yea, even the very constant discovery of evil in your sinful heart, that makes you ashamed, and that distresses you, and under which you "*groan, being burthened*," the Lord Jesus Christ will overrule it for your good. He will humble you—He will prove you—He will make you know what is in your heart. Thus saith Moses to the Israelites, "*Thou shalt remember all the way which the Lord thy God led thee these forty years in the wilderness, to humble thee, and to prove thee to know what was in thine heart, whether thou wouldst keep his commandments or no.*" Deut. vii. 2. It was their hunger led them to prize the manna, and to learn their ingratitude after it was sent. It was their thirst taught them to prize the water from the smitten rock, when "*they drank of that Spiritual Rock that followed them, and that Rock was Christ*," 1st Cor. x. 4. He will bow you down in humiliation at his footstool. He will bring you hungry and thirsty to the Throne of Grace, and teach you, in the depth of your wants, to prize more and more the preciousness of the Saviour. He will bring you to Him, in all your necessities and sins. He will lead you to His precious blood, as unto a fresh open fountain continually for healing, and grace, and strength. Thus will he sanctify all his rods, and trials, and lead you to fly from sin, and to love and serve Him, who has loved you, and given himself for you.

Now, then, consider this—observe the end for which the Lord Jesus Christ gave Himself for the Church. "THAT HE MIGHT SANCTIFY AND CLEANSE IT BY THE WASHING OF WATER, BY THE WORD." Now, you see the end, and you see the means; He gave Himself for it, "THAT HE MIGHT SANCTIFY AND CLEANSE IT WITH THE WASHING OF WATER;" there is the *end*. The church is to be sanctified and to be cleansed with that washing, of which our Lord Himself appointed water as the sign and seal, even washing in the blessed Fountain opened for sin and uncleanness; and then you see the means, "BY THE WORD."

The church of Christ is a sanctified church—it is set apart to God. The wife is set apart to her husband, she is his alone, "*Keep thee only unto him, so long as ye both shall live.*" The church is sanctified, set apart to Christ, she is his alone. As He saith to his people, "*I will betroth thee unto me forever. Yea, I will betroth thee unto me in righteousness, and in judgment, and in loving-kindness, and in mercies; I will even betroth thee unto me in faithfulness, and thou shalt know that I am the Lord,*" Hos. ii. 20, 21. She is sanctified by the giving of the Lord Jesus Christ for her. The giving of the Lord Jesus Christ, and the shedding of His own precious blood, has sanctified all who believe in His name.

I have explained to you before, at large, this primary sense of the term sanctification, as we have it in Hebrews x., "*By the which will we are sanctified, through the offering of the body of Jesus Christ once for all;*" they are sanctified "*Through the offering of his body, once for all;*" they are washed, cleansed, purified, and thus set apart to God; and the instrument by which this is effected in the heart and conscience of the believer, is by the Word; they are brought by the Word to the fountain of Immanuel's blood. The Word of Christ opens to them the Gospel of Jesus. The Word of Christ explains to them their own misery—their own guilt, and the salvation wrought for them by the work of their Redeemer, and by that Word they are brought to Him; so saith the Apostle James, "*Of his own will begat he us through the word of truth,*" James v. 18; so the Apostle Peter, "*Being born again, not of corruptible seed, but of incorruptible, by the Word of God, which liveth and abideth forever,*" 1st Pet. i. 23. They are brought to Christ by the Word—that is, they are born again by the Word; for "*Whosoever believeth that Jesus is the Christ, is born of God,*" 1st John v. 1. Any of you who have been brought to the Lord Jesus Christ, have been surely brought by the blessed Word of God having been set before you by some means. It may be by a sermon—perhaps by a lecture—or by the Book itself—or by a Prayer-book, containing a portion of that Word—or it might be by a tract—yea, by a single text applied to you in conversation, by a friend—or even by a single text being brought to your remembrance by the Spirit. But by whatever means, it must be by the Word of God as the instrument. There is no other power by which a sinner can be brought to Christ, but by the Word of God. It is—it may be applied in a thousand different ways of Providence, or Grace by the Spirit, but there is no other means, no other channel, through which the sinner can receive a knowledge of God's salvation, but by the revelation of God's Eternal Word; and therefore, by that Word he is brought to the Lord Jesus Christ, and in the blood of Christ sanctified and cleansed.

You see, then, how important it is, that the Word of God

should be preached—that the Word of God should be read—that that Word should be diffused. Where the Word of God is shut up—there, there is a famine of the Bread of Life—there, there is an intercepting of the light of Heaven from the sinner's soul. Where the Word of God is open—has full course and is glorified—there, the people feed upon the Bread of Life—there, the light of God's Eternal Truth shines into the hearts of sinners. Who then, can duly appreciate the inestimable blessing, that the Word of God should be known to sinners, to bring them to Christ? But, this is what makes the study of the Bible precious to the soul of the believer. As it is by the Word we are brought first to Christ—so it is by the Word we are kept in Christ. The Holy Scriptures are not only the means of quickening, enlightening, regenerating, and converting the soul, but the sanctifying power of the Spirit acts through the Word. So, when the Lord prays for His disciples to His Father, you recollect His prayer, He says, "*Sanctify them through thy truth; thy word is truth,*" John xvii. 17. So it is His province to cleanse and purify the life and habits of the sinner with it. "*Wherewithal shall a young man cleanse his way? by taking heed thereto, according to thy word,*" Ps. cxix. 9. You will see this principle set forth, in the most encouraging and instructive manner in the whole Bible, in Psalm cxix. The blessing and power of the Word of God, as the means of calling—and keeping—strengthening—and directing—comforting—and building up the soul of the sinner. If there be any of you, therefore, who are ignorant of Christ and His salvation, and are, as you must be indeed, careless and negligent in the study of God's Word. Oh! consider, by what means can you ever be brought to know the truth, but by the Word of God! And, if you know the truth of God, and yet are, as too many are, careless in the study of the Bible—then you are proportionably uncomfortable, and barren in your own soul.

Recollect, the blessing of the man who avoids the ways of sin, and cultivates the study of the Scriptures. "*Blessed is the man that walketh not in the counsel of the ungodly, nor standeth in the way of sinners, nor sitteth in the seat of the scornful.*" Mark what he avoids.

Now see what he studies—"*But his delight is in the law of the Lord, and in his law doth he meditate day and night.*"

Now look to the result—"*And he shall be like a tree planted by the rivers of water, that bringeth forth his fruit in his season; his leaf also shall not wither, and whatsoever he doeth shall prosper,*" Psalm i. 1, 2, 3.

What wonder then, that if you neglect the study of the sacred Scriptures, your soul is not like a watered garden, and that you bring forth but little fruit in your life! How can the tree bring fruit to perfection, if it is but partially under the genial influence of the sun! This is one of the reasons why profession so far outstrips the practice of the present day. Persons acquire knowledge through the preaching of the Word of God—they acquire a knowledge of the doctrines of salvation, but there is an absence of the study of Scripture—a want of devotion to the Word of God, which leaves the souls of professors barren and unprofitable in their life and conversation. We cannot come fresh from the faithful study of God's Holy Word, and enter with a relish into the levities, and follies, and vanities, of an ungodly world. If we have, indeed, the Word of God in our hearts—of the abundance of the heart the mouth will speak, and the world will take knowledge of us, that we have been with Jesus—if indeed we have been with Jesus. The face of Moses shone brightly when he came down from the mount.

"*The soul of the sluggard desireth, and hath nothing, but the soul of the diligent shall be made fat.*" Prov. xiii. 4. If we study the Word of Life, we shall experience the blessing of this latter promise. But if not, then the soul of the sluggard shall be like the garden of the sluggard, overgrown with briars and thorns. What wonder that in such a neglected soil, "*The cares of this world, and the deceitfulness of riches, and the lusts of other things entering in, choke the word, and it becometh unfruitful.*" Mark iv. 19.

To return then more directly to the passage. Do not forget the means by which the church is cleansed. "CHRIST LOVED THE CHURCH AND GAVE HIMSELF FOR IT; THAT HE MIGHT SANCTIFY AND CLEANSE IT WITH THE WASHING OF WATER, BY THE WORD; THAT HE MIGHT PRESENT IT TO HIMSELF A GLORIOUS CHURCH, NOT HAVING SPOT OR WRINKLE, OR ANY SUCH THING, BUT THAT IT SHOULD BE HOLY AND WITHOUT BLEMISH." As an affectionate husband desires that his wife shall enjoy all the privileges, and all the blessings, that he himself feels and knows to be either suitable to his rank and dignity, or that he wills to have for himself, so, our Lord Jesus Christ wills that His church shall enjoy all those blessings—those privileges—and that glory which belongs to Himself. Hear His own words, "*And the glory which thou gavest me I have given them, that they also may be one, even as we are one,*" John xvii. 22. So here, "THAT HE MIGHT PRESENT IT TO HIMSELF A GLORIOUS CHURCH, NOT HAVING SPOT, OR WRINKLE, OR ANY SUCH THING, BUT THAT IT SHOULD BE HOLY AND WITHOUT BLEMISH." Well might the Apostle call it a great mystery—to think of a poor wretch, a vile sinner like one of us, being glorious.

If we are indeed taught of God, we cannot look at ourselves in the mirror of God's pure and holy law, without beholding ourselves all unclean, and feeling ourselves abashed, ashamed, and confounded, when we look within. As the Apostle saith, when he was ignorant of the spiritual nature of God's holy law, "*I was alive without the law once.*" Not certainly, without the letter, for he had been trained from his infancy in that; and while he only knew that, "*he was alive*"—that is, he thought so—he considered himself so—he thought he had spiritual life, and he had a good hope of gaining eternal life by his obedience to the law. "*But,*" he continues, "*When the commandment came, sin revived, and I* *died.*" Rom. vii. 9. When I knew the spiritual nature of the law, and how it was not merely a rule of outward conduct, but that it reached to the very thoughts, intents, and desires of the heart—that is, "*When the commandment came,*" with all its true spirituality and power, then "*sin revived and I died.*" I saw the full extent of my own sin and vileness, and that I was a lost and wretched criminal.* That it is our privilege to be really glorious in Christ Jesus—that, though we are in ourselves, as the Apostle describes himself, suffering under the consciousness of our inward corruption—that, though we feel in ourselves "*a law in our members, warring against the law of our mind, and bringing us into captivity to the law of sin that is in our members*" that, though we feel corruption working within—evil thoughts—wicked propensities—evil desires—evil passions, rising up, and continually corrupting and defiling the best we do—that, though we must always feel our uncleanness in the sight of God, yet, it is our privilege to look by faith out of self, to Jesus—and by faith to believe that all this body of sin and death is completely put off for ever—that we may—yea, that we are commanded to "*Reckon ourselves to be dead indeed unto sin, but alive unto God, through Jesus Christ our Lord,*" Rom. vi. 11; and that we stand before our God complete—washed from all our guilt in the precious blood—and clothed in the meritorious righteousness of our blessed Lord and Saviour, Jesus Christ—this—this is, indeed, a great and glorious mystery, which the angels may well "*desire to look into,*" 1st Pet. i. 12.

The Lord when speaking by the Prophet, of His bringing the church of His people Israel, from its natural state, describes it like that of a new-born child, cast out on a field to die. Imagine, a child just born, cast out and left on the open field! What must become of it? It must perish directly! Such is the state in which the Lord represents His church in Ezekiel, xvi. 5, 6, "*Thou wast cast out in the open field to the loathing of thy person, in the day that thou wast born; and when I passed by thee, and saw thee polluted in thine own blood, I said unto thee, when thou wast yet in thy blood, Live. Yea, I said unto thee when thou wast in thy blood, Live.*"

This is palpably applied to their spiritual state. Our spiritual state is just as hopeless—as helpless as that of a new-born child; we have as little power to save, or to do anything for ourselves, as

* Man comparing himself with the law, in his natural state, is like a blind deformed leper sitting before a mirror. The mirror is there, and he is there—he can touch it, and call it a mirror—but he does not see the loathsome image which it reflects—even himself. But give him his sight, and then he beholds his true picture at once, and revolts from the disgusting object. So is a self-righteous Pharisee or Moralist, when he talks of his virtues and his excellence, "*He is alive without the law*"—he is wholly ignorant of its spiritual nature. The mirror is before him—but he is blind, and cannot see that it reflects his inmost thoughts. But when God opens his eyes to see the truth, then he sees his real character—"*When the commandment comes, sin revives, and he dies*"—he beholds his real deformity in the sight of a Holy God, and in the mirror of His holy law—and confesses in spirit and truth, that he is a "*miserable sinner.*"

a child has to provide for itself, to get up and walk. We are vile—helpless—lost. And if we are brought out of that state, it is because God in His love, passes by and says unto us, "*Live.*"

If you read the beginning of that chapter, you will perceive, He gives a description of the Jewish people as in that state; and if true of the church collectively, it must be true of every individual of that church. What is true of a church, as in a state of sin, is true with respect to every individual of that church; what is true of a church, as in a state of grace, is true of every individual in that church. If the church is accepted, the sinner is accepted—if the church is righteous, it must be, that every sinner that belongs to that church is righteous; it could not be said of the whole church, that the church is "A GLORIOUS CHURCH, NOT HAVING SPOT, OR WRINKLE, OR ANY SUCH THING," if one unglorious, spotted, wrinkled sinner belonged to it; therefore, what is true of the whole church, is true of every believer in it.

If it is presented to God "A GLORIOUS CHURCH, NOT HAVING SPOT, OR WRINKLE, OR ANY SUCH THING," but "HOLY AND WITHOUT BLEMISH," then every poor sinner, who is indeed a spiritual member of that church, is presented a glorious believer to Christ, "NOT HAVING SPOT, OR WRINKLE, OR ANY SUCH THING, BUT HOLY AND WITHOUT BLEMISH." Though he is vile, and feels his own vileness, yet it is his privilege to look out of himself to Jesus, and then he beholds himself complete in Christ, as the Apostle says, Col. ii. 10, "*Ye are complete in him,*" and as it is said in this chapter, "*Then washed I thee with water, yea, I thoroughly washed away thy blood from thee, and I anointed thee with oil, I clothed thee also with broidered work, and shod thee with badger's skin, and I girded thee about with fine linen, and I covered thee with silk, I decked thee also with ornaments, and I put bracelets upon thine hand, and a chain on thy neck, and I put a jewel on thy forehead, and ear-rings in thine ears, and a beautiful crown upon thine head; thus wast thou decked with gold and silver, and thy raiment was of fine linen, and silk, and broidered work; thou didst eat fine flour, and honey, and oil, and thou wast exceeding beautiful, and thou didst prosper into a kingdom, and thy renown went forth among the heathen for thy beauty; for it was perfect through my comeliness which I had put upon thee, saith the Lord God,*" Ezek. xvi. 9, 14.

Under the image of a bride, He shows how He made Jerusalem to prosper and grow into such a glorious kingdom, and under the image of Jerusalem as a bride, he shows His love and grace to His church.

Their beauty was "*perfect through his comeliness,*" and so the beauty of His church is "*perfect through his comeliness.*" "*I am black, but comely,*" Cant. i. 5; black as the tents of Kedar—comely as the curtains of Solomon—polluted, yet spotless—unclean, yet clean—lost, yet saved—condemned, yet justified—sold under sin, yet delivered from all evil, and brought to glory.

The paradoxes of the Bible, how unintelligible they are to the unconverted sinner—how glorious to the believer! To feel what men are in themselves, and to know what they are in Christ Jesus, as here—"THAT HE MIGHT PRESENT IT TO HIMSELF A GLORIOUS CHURCH!" Now, what is the glory of the church? I think, I quoted a passage in our last Lecture, in reference to this subject, but it bears quotation again. That may well be quoted again and again, which shall be the theme of everlasting joy to the redeemed church of God throughout eternity. We should quote these texts over and over again, in our own hearts—we should cherish them—we should feed on Him, whom they set before us every day, and rejoice in Him as all our salvation. Now then, let us mark the Gospel of St. John, xvii. 22, it is a portion of the prayer of our Lord Jesus Christ, He saith, "*The glory which thou gavest me I have given them, that they all may be one, even as we are one.*"

What is the glory of the church of Christ?—the glory of Christ Himself. What is the glory of the wife?—the glory of her husband. What is the glory of the queen?—the glory of the king. What is the glory of Christ's church?—the glory of Christ Himself. "*The glory which thou gavest me, I have given them, that they be one, even as we are one.*"

Dear friends, is it not a wonderful thing to think, that a poor sinner, like you or me, can ever be really glorious! Our glory now is the glory we possess by faith; you see no glory in me, and I see no glory in you. We may be permitted to glorify God, if we are enabled to live to God, and devote ourselves to His service as we ought to do. If we "*let our light so shine before men, that they may see our good works, and glorify our Father who is in heaven.*" But there is no glory to be seen in us. But oh! let us think, that that which we now have by faith, if we are indeed of the church of Jesus, we shall soon have in reality, "*our citizenship,*" says the Apostle, "*is in heaven, from whence also we look for the Saviour, the Lord Jesus Christ.*"—and what then? "*Who shall change our vile body, that it may be fashioned like unto his glorious body, according to the working, whereby he is able even to subdue all things to himself.*" Phil. iii. 20, 21. That same glory which He possesses, shall then be the visible glory of every individual of His church—and so the Apostle John assures us "*Behold what manner of love the Father hath bestowed upon us, that we should be called the sons of God; therefore the world knoweth us not, because it knew him not.*" Christ's glory was veiled when He was on earth, the glory of His church is veiled too. "*Beloved, now are we the sons of God, and it doth not yet appear what we shall be, but we know that when he shall appear, we shall be like him, for we shall see him as he is.*" 1st John iii. 12.

"*We know*"—mark what the privilege of faith is—"*We know*" because our God has told it to us. "*We know*"—because "*He is faithful that promised.*" It must be true. "*We know that when he shall appear, we shall be like him, for we shall see him as he is.*" So, you have the same truth in 1st

Corinthians xv., where adverting to the resurrection glory—speaking of the resurrection of the body, the Apostle saith, "*There is one glory of the sun, and another glory of the moon, and another glory of the stars; for one star differeth from another star in glory, so also is the resurrection of the dead; it is sown in corruption, and raised in incorruption; it is sown in dishonor, it is raised in glory; it is sown in weakness, it is raised in power; it is sown a natural body, it is raised a spiritual body.*" 1st Cor. xv. 41, 42, 43. It is raised from the corruption—the dishonor—the weakness—the natural decay into the dust of death, to the incorruption—the glory—the power—the spirituality of a raised, renewed, regenerated resurrection body, even the glorious body that shall be given to the church, such as Christ Himself is clothed with.

We have the same glorious truth, given as a subject of consolation in 1st Thessalonians iv. 16—18, "*The Lord himself shall descend from heaven with a shout, with the voice of the archangel and the trump of God, and the dead in Christ shall rise first, then we which are alive and remain, shall be caught up together with them in the clouds, to meet the Lord in the air, and so shall we ever be with the Lord, wherefore, comfort one another with these words.*" So He presents His church to Himself, "A GLORIOUS CHURCH, NOT HAVING SPOT, OR WRINKLE, OR ANY SUCH THING, BUT HOLY AND WITHOUT BLEMISH." Go, look at that church-building which is in process of being built now in this neighborhood—you will see nothing on the spot but some stones of various shapes and sizes, scattered in disorder, lying here and there, and many are yet undrawn, many still unquarried. If you try to lay these stones in their intended order in the building, you could not attempt to do it—if you try to conceive the plan of that Church, you cannot even imagine it. The architect has it in his own eye—he sees, he knows the whole order, parts, proportions, plan, and elevation of it—it is all complete before him in his mind's eye, just as complete as it shall be when erected. So is it with the Church of Christ; the members of it are scattered, not only now throughout the earth, but the constituent parts of it are dispersed afar, through climes and ages past, and still to come: the eye of man cannot see, nor the heart of man conceive their glory in their union, and their elevation; but it is all complete in the eye of Jehovah—the Lord Jesus beholds it all—the Church is glorious in his eyes, and there shall not be a single stone wanting—not one that is to fill the smallest crevice, each one shall be there—each one fitted in its place, for shape, for strength, for stability, for beauty, honor, and glory, at the appearing of Jesus Christ. Then shall it be seen finished by the Mighty Architect, "A GLORIOUS CHURCH, NOT HAVING SPOT OR WRINKLE, OR ANY SUCH THING, BUT HOLY AND WITHOUT BLEMISH."

Surely, this is not now your case or mine; do we not feel that it is not? do we not feel that we are anything but glorious? do we not feel, that in ourselves we are spotted, wrinkled, and defiled—that we are poor, vile, miserable sinners; but it is the privilege of the Christian to look with the eye of faith, at what he is before God in Christ now, and what he shall be before the throne forever. "*Even as David also describeth the blessedness of the man to whom God imputed righteousness without works, saying—Blessed is he whose transgression is forgiven, and whose sin is covered—blessed is the man to whom the Lord will not impute sin.*" Rom. iv. 6, 7, 8.

Our blessedness consists then in a life of faith now, in taking all we have and all we are to the feet of Jesus, and looking unto Him, and casting ourselves on Him—taking His blood to bathe in —His righteousness to cover us—His power, faithfulness, and love, and all his precious promises, to sustain us—and living by faith on them, to look for and haste unto His coming.

We are struggling and conflicting with these bodies of sin and death, that we may be enabled to glorify our God, in mortifying them—crucifying them—during our stay here; looking for that glorious time, when we shall see Him face to face—when His servants shall serve Him without spot—and when we shall really be what now we hope to be, by faith. When we shall really be what we expect to be—yea! what we know we shall be, if we believe the glorious promises of our God.

This is what Christ then does for His Church—that "HE MAY PRESENT IT TO HIMSELF A GLORIOUS CHURCH; NOT HAVING SPOT OR WRINKLE, OR ANY SUCH THING, BUT THAT IT SHOULD BE HOLY, AND WITHOUT BLEMISH."

Remember, as the husband is bound to undertake everything for his wife, and to do everything for her, as he ought to do—so, Oh! wondrous truth! Christ is bound to His Church, in that same blessed relation. He is bound in an eternal covenant of love—He is bound by an eternal union—by the eternal promises; for all these promises in Him are yea, and in Him amen. What a blessing then it is, for a poor sinner to have such a Saviour to look to! Oh! that we may be enlightened to look thus to Him—and then, if we are enabled to carry this blessed faith into our different relations of life—it is thus, and thus alone, that we can be strengthened to discharge the duties of these stations. Therefore, you see they are brought home to His people continually, in all their circumstances. Parents, children, servants, masters, husbands, wives, all referred to Christ—all referred to the Lord Jesus Christ. Their principles and motives are all referred to Him, in whom alone they have spiritual existence; and from whom alone they can derive spiritual life or strength.

May the Lord our God bring His truth to our hearts; and enable us to know and rejoice in Him, and in the strength of His salvation, and in every relation of life to glorify Him with our bodies and spirits which are His.—Amen.

FORTY-SECOND LECTURE.

EPHESIANS V.—28, 29, 30, 31, 32, 33.

"So ought men to love their wives as their own bodies. He that loveth his wife loveth himself. For no man ever yet hated his own flesh; but nourisheth and cherisheth it, even as the Lord the church: For we are members of his body, of his flesh, and of his bones. For this cause shall a man leave his father and mother, and shall be joined unto his wife, and they two shall be one flesh. This is a great mystery: but I speak concerning Christ and the church. Nevertheless, let every one of you in particular so love his wife even as himself; and the wife see that she reverence her husband."

IN our last Lecture but one, we considered the relation in which the wife stands to her husband, as compared with that in which the Church stands to Christ.

In our last we considered the relation in which the husband stands to his wife, as compared with that in which Christ stands to His Church. And here we have the same subject continued in the last verses of this chapter. May the Lord enable us to understand the spiritual application of it to our souls! May He enable us to see the wonderful privileges here set before the Church of Christ—that we may learn to prize them for ourselves, and discover more and more of the riches of that glorious Redeemer, who is the Author and Finisher of this, and all covenant blessings to His people.

The Apostle pursuing the subject of the duty of husbands to their wives, presses it still farther from the intimate union, the absolute oneness that subsists between them. "SO OUGHT MEN TO LOVE THEIR WIVES AS THEIR OWN BODIES. HE THAT LOVETH HIS WIFE, LOVETH HIMSELF. FOR NO MAN EVER YET HATED HIS OWN FLESH; BUT NOURISHETH AND CHERISHETH IT, EVEN AS THE LORD THE CHURCH: FOR WE ARE MEMBERS OF HIS BODY, OF HIS FLESH, AND OF HIS BONES." He shows here, that the duty and affection of the husband to the wife is such, that it is actually identified with his love and duty to his own person; and that his affection should be founded exactly on the same principle on which he would love himself. "SO OUGHT MEN TO LOVE THEIR WIVES AS THEIR OWN BODIES. HE THAT LOVETH HIS WIFE LOVETH HIMSELF." And certainly, the husband stands, as we considered on the last day, actually identified with his wife in all circumstances, so that everything that brings reproach on her, brings reproach on him; and everything that tends to honor and exalt her, tends to honor and exalt him; so that if he would save himself from reproach, or exalt himself to honor—if he would deliver himself from evil—if he would promote his own good, or his own happiness, he is called on in the same proportion, and on the same principle, to save his wife, and deliver her from any evil, and promote her honor—her glory—her happiness, even as his own; "FOR NO MAN EVER YET HATED HIS OWN FLESH; BUT NOURISHETH AND CHERISHETH IT, EVEN AS THE LORD THE CHURCH: FOR WE ARE MEMBERS OF HIS BODY, OF HIS FLESH, AND OF HIS BONES."

Now the Apostle says, "THIS IS A GREAT MYSTERY." We can form a conception of this union, as applied to the relationship of husband and wife. But it is a marvellous mystery indeed, when we consider it as applied to the Lord Jesus Christ and the Church. To think, that sinners like you and me, can be taken and actually identified with the Lord of life and glory! That the Lord Jesus can take a vile sinner like any one of us—that He can take us and so identify us with Himself, and Himself with us, that actually His own dignity—His own honor—His own glory is promoted and established by all the blessing—all the dignity—all the honor—and all the glory that He can bestow on us!! Surely this is a great mystery!

The husband freely takes the wife, from his own love; he loves her, and he takes her because he loves her. There is this difference, however, between man and wife, and Christ and His Church:—that there is always something that either really is, or seems attractive—something that draws forth affection on the part of the husband to his wife; and he chooses her because he sees something in her that pleases him, or that is lovely in his estimation. But here indeed there is no parallel. For Christ sees nothing whatever in the sinner, to make him attractive in His sight. There can be nothing lovely whatever in the fallen, unholy creature, to attract the affection of the Lord Jesus Christ—nothing! The love of Christ to the sinner, without anything whatever to call it forth, springs spontaneously from the bosom of the Eternal God. Therefore, it is not a love that originates in time. The love of a man to his wife originates when he sees the individual, and beholds something in her that attracts him. But the love of Christ to His church does not originate in time—it is not awakened by the development of anything in the character, after the individual is born, that could be supposed to attract Christ. It is no such thing, "*I have loved thee with an everlasting love.*" Jer. xxxi. 3. It begins in eternity, as the Apostle says in this Epistle, "*God, who is rich in mercy, for his great love wherewith he loved us, even when we were dead in sins, hath quickened us together with Christ; (by grace ye are saved;) and hath raised us up together, and made us sit together in heavenly places in Christ Jesus: that in the ages to come he might show the exceeding riches of his grace, in his kindness towards us through Christ Jesus.*" chap. ii. 4, 5, 6, 7. So we are said to be chosen by the Father in Christ, before the world began. "*According as he hath chosen us in him, before the foundation of the* *world*." chap. i. 4.* And so the love of Christ commences from eternity—it flows from the fountain of eternal love, in the eternal bosom of Jehovah Himself. This is considered; and of course to any of you who do not know the Gospel of the Lord Jesus Christ, and who do not know yourselves, it must be considered a very strange doctrine. So are all the doctrines of grace. All the different truths of God are unintelligible to the natural, unenlightened heart of man. Perhaps they may be so to some of you. The eternal love of Jesus to His church, in all its purposes and all its developments, is the great subject matter of Divine Revelation. You may, perhaps, disbelieve—despise—disregard—or make light of this. But, surely, if you do, you do not know the Gospel. For if you knew the Gospel of the Lord Jesus—and if you knew yourselves—you would know that the fountain of your consolation is derived from the free and sovereign love of God. For if you do not know that truth—and if you consider that the love of Christ springs, as it were, from something of good foreseen or foreknown in the sinner—what is the result? Why it is that the love of God is exactly like earthly love, like the love of man. Men find themselves too often disappointed in the qualities that they imagined were possessed by the object of their affections. If they were attracted by personal beauty, they see that beauty fades like a drooping flower. The sparkling eye grows dim, and the love that it excited wanes and grows cold, when the sickly lamp that kindled it begins to flicker in the socket.

Thus if a sinner can believe that there is anything in himself that is considered to draw forth the love of God, when he is taught to feel that he is vile, and therefore the deserving object, not of God's love, but of his judgment, then, if he has that false view of the love of his Lord, that it depends on some good in his own character, or something to be approved in himself, he is driven to fear, to doubt, or to despair; because as he becomes better acquainted with himself, he sees, that so far from being an object of love to God, he should rather be an object of divine wrath and judgment. For thus every sinner that knows himself, feels and knows that such is his own character.

But when he has learned that the love of Christ is an everlasting love, not awakened by any qualities in himself, not deriving

* Some persons, who, unwilling to admit the utter corruption of man, and the freeness of God's election, and who are constrained to confess that the plain language of the Scripture must have some meaning; imagine that they reconcile the Scripture with their own schemes, by supposing that this election of sinners "before the foundation of the world" is dependent on the foreseen excellence and good conduct of the individuals. But surely they might see that this but removes the sovereignty of God, from the exercise of one act to the exercise of another. For, suppose this to be true—What sovereign power gives those imaginary qualities of excellence so worthy to be loved?—Who maketh one sinner to differ from another?—It merely shifts the difficulty. But indeed the experience of every servant of God denies and denounces such ignorance and folly—for he well knows, that while he finds nothing in himself that he must not be ashamed of, and condemn; there can be nothing which a holy God can admire and approve. As the old woman before cited well remarked, "I am sure, unless God saw something in me, to love, before I was born; He never saw anything in me since."

its origin from any traits of foreseen excellence in his own character; but just as I have said, springing purely—gratuitously from the fountain of God's own bosom of eternal love to His church, then no discovery of the evil of his own character leads him to doubt the faithful, everlasting love of his Redeemer and his God. He sees, that as there was nothing in him to attract in the first instance the love of his Redeemer, so the discovery of the evil in his own character will not cause that Redeemer to cast him away. There are no imaginary qualities in him in which Christ is disappointed, no beauty in him that fades away from before the eye of his Redeemer. God foreknew he would be a sinner—He knows he *has been* a sinner, and He knows he *is* a sinner, Jesus loved him *as a sinner*, before the foundations of the world were laid, called him *as a sinner*, in time, loves him *as a sinner* still, and will save him *as a sinner*. Therefore, the knowledge of his own character does not lead him to doubt the eternal faithfulness and love of his glorious Lord and Saviour. "*I have loved thee*," saith the Lord, "*with an everlasting love, therefore with loving-kindness have I drawn thee*," Jer. xxxi. 3, and "*having loved his own which were in the world, he loved them unto the end.*" John xiii. 1.

What was there in the character of Mary Magdalene, that drew forth the love of Jesus? Was it the seven devils that possessed her?

What was there in the character of Peter, that drew forth the love of Jesus? Was it that he denied his Master with an oath?

What was there in the character of Thomas? Was it that he said, "*Except I shall see in his hands the print of the nails, and put my finger into the print of the nails, and thrust my hand into his side, I will not believe?*" John xx. 25.

What was there in the character of any of the disciples? Was it that they "*all forsook him and fled?*"

What was there in the character of the thief on the cross? Was it that even when he was hanging on the cross, he joined the multitude and his fellow-thief in blaspheming Christ?

What was there in the character of Saul? Was it that he was "*breathing out threatenings and slaughter against the disciples of the Lord?*" was it this that drew forth the love of Jesus?

And now, let us leave them all, and come to ourselves. What is there in your character, what is there in my character, if indeed we are brought, through grace, to know Christ, what is there in us that has drawn Him to love us? Surely the more we know of ourselves, the more we learn the certain testimony of this truth, "*the heart is deceitful above all things, and desperately wicked, who can know it?*" Jer. xvii. 9. And that is our own heart and character, and therefore, so far from there being anything in us to draw Christ to us, there is everything in us to repel Him from us, and to banish us from his presence. Notwithstanding all, His grace aboundeth—His love is an everlasting love, and when in the riches of that grace and love, He hath taken the sinner, and brought his heart to Himself—when he hath said to his soul, "*Turn, O backsliding children, for I am married unto you, and I will take you one of a city, and two of a family, and I will bring you to Zion."*—Jer. iii. 14. Mark what does he say of the character of the very sinners to whom He gives this gracious invitation, "*They say, if a man put away his wife, and she go from him, and become another man's, shall he return unto her again, shall not the land be greatly polluted?*" But then see what he adds, "*But thou hast played the harlot with many lovers, yet return again unto me, saith the Lord.*" Jer. iii. 1.

Oh, my friends and fellow-sinners, this is love beyond all the love of an earthly husband. If the love of Jesus was not an unchanging and eternal love, what would become of sinners? what would become of you or me? we should have been in hell long ago;—so should all that have ever belonged to His church. If the love of Christ was not an everlasting love, there is not a sinner that ever descended from fallen Adam, that should enter the gates of glory. But His love is an everlasting love, "*I will never leave thee nor forsake thee,*" is His word. Heb. xiii. 5. He saith again of His sheep, "*I give unto them eternal life, and they shall never perish, neither shall any pluck them out of my hand. My Father who gave them me is greater than all, and no man is able to pluck them out of my Father's hand. I and my Father are one.*" John x. 28. Therefore, that is a most blessed doctrine, the doctrine of God's sovereign, unchangeable and everlasting love, while it is unintelligible to the natural mind. And while the sinner who is ignorant of God cannot approach to the understanding of it at all,—those, who are brought to the knowledge of Christ, and who understand clearly the doctrine of justification by faith in the righteousness and blood of a crucified Redeemer, know that it is their only refuge—that the eternal faithfulness and covenant love of God is the only security they see for their everlasting salvation.

Therefore, the love of Christ is totally contrary to anything that the unconverted world thinks, as that God foresaw something good in those persons who are saved, and so they deceive themselves, and flatter themselves with the hope that they are God's elect, because there is something good in them.

Alas! what total blindness, ignorance, and stupidity that is concerning the truth of God's word. You cannot explain it to such persons. But the fact is directly the reverse: it is because there is no good in them, nothing attractive, nothing excellent, they are altogether vile, and the salvation they receive from Christ is the salvation of free, full, glorious, covenant, and everlasting love.

It is indeed a "GREAT MYSTERY"—just consider it yourselves. Look into your own heart, and see is there anything good in you. Remember that all religion to be learned, must be personally and experimentally learned. Men are lost in reasoning on abstract theories of religion, and talking about third persons. If you want to learn truth, speak not of others, but of yourselves before God;—bring yourselves to God's word, apply God's truth to your own souls and to your own consciences, and that is the only way you can ever learn the truth. As long as persons give up their minds to abstract reasonings and theories about religion, they will never learn it. Religion is a solemn, personal, constant, experimental transaction between God and the sinner's own soul. Therefore, my dear friends, consider this, look into yourselves, and see, is there anything in you that you can think attractive in God's sight? anything that can attract the love of Christ? Let me put it to you in this point of view, just let me ask you this question, what would you take and let your heart, your real naked heart—your thoughts—imaginations—desires—be opened before the friend who loves you best in the world? what would you take and let these hidden monsters out? Do you think he could love you if he knew of you what you know of yourself? could he love you, if he could really see the workings of your heart within? your actual thoughts, imaginations, desires, feelings, passions? do you think the person who loves you most on earth, could love you if he saw you as you see yourself? Do you not live—do you not carry on your state of existence in society on this principle, that you conceal what you really are? If we would give vent to the thoughts of our hearts, to the thoughts that come into our minds, we would be intolerable;—the best of human beings would be insufferable, if they did not conceal the thoughts that come into their minds, their wicked desires—their wicked imaginations—is not that the truth? do you not know that it is true?

Well then, if we could not bear inspection—if the open exposure and development of our hearts would make us insufferable to our dearest friend, what must we be in the sight of a holy God? or what can there be in us to attract God to us? Surely nothing.

Well then, dear friends, consider, is it not a great blessing that the glorious Gospel of Jesus is just sent to us as sinners—as we are—that while there is nothing in us to attract God, but everything to repulse Him, there is no species of crime or wickedness in the poor, guilty sinner's heart, for which the Gospel of Jesus does not bring a remedy, fulness of salvation, pardon through the blood of Christ, "*For God so loved the world, that he gave his only-begotten Son, that whosoever believeth in him should not perish, but have everlasting life,*" John iii. 16, and "*the blood of Jesus Christ his Son cleanseth us from all sin.*" 1st John i. 7. Oh! behold then, what manner of love is the love of Christ to sinners! a full, free, finished salvation brought to us,—how? by his own precious blood. "*Unto him who hath loved us,*" is the language of the redeemed, "*Unto him who hath loved us, and washed us from our sins in his own blood, and made us kings and priests unto God and his Father, unto him be glory and dominion forever and ever. Amen.*" Rev. i. 5, 6. Here is hope for the sinful heart, for the guilty, conscious, self-convicted sinner.

You see how different this is, from the wretched condition of the miserable, unconverted sinner, who is trying to live in the same hypocrisy with God, as he does with his fellow-creature; to patch up the same hope from his own miserable righteousness, as he patches up a character for himself before man. If there be any of you here who do not know the Gospel of Christ, that is just what you are doing; you are trying to make yourselves something that God can approve of. But—"*Can the Ethiopian change his skin, or the leopard his spots? then may ye also do good, that are accustomed to do evil.*" Jer. xiii. 23.

I would just lay this thought on your consciences. Do your best—force yourselves as far as you can—"*Wash thee with nitre, and take thee much soap,*" as Job saith—make yourselves as clean as you can—and then refer to your own thoughts, enter into your own bosoms, and think thus, "Well, with all I do, what would become of me, if every one saw me as I really am, if every one could see as I see, my own naked heart?"

Then remember, you must say of God, with Moses, "*Thou hast set our iniquities before thee, our secret sins in the light of thy countenance,*" as we have in the "Prayer of Moses, the man of God," Psalm xc. 8. Remember, that thy heart is in the light of God's all-seeing eye. There it is—brought into the sunshine of that light that is far above the brightness of the sun; and there the Holy God is looking at you. What then are you doing? what will you be? what will you do in the end thereof? Shall it be found at the last that there was anything in you to attract the love of God? But, blessed be God, my dear friends and fellow-sinners,—we know this is not the Gospel—the Gospel takes your heart with all its vileness, all its guilt, all its abominations, and says, Come to Christ, how weary soever and heavy laden you may be—Come—because you are a sinner. Come—because you are guilty. Come—because you are vile. Come—because there is no good in you. "*If righteousness come by the law, then Christ is dead in vain.*" Gal. ii. 21. If you could save yourselves by anything in yourselves, "*Christ is dead in vain.*" He came to save sinners, that we poor sinners might come to Him, and as surely as He inclines our hearts to do so—as surely as our heart is awakened—yea, if the word I am now speaking shall awaken any true reflection never awakened there before—if you are even this day led to think thus—

"Ah! this is true, it is all true, I am vile! What shall I do, if God brings me into judgment? It is a great blessing that there is salvation and mercy for a poor sinner like me—it is a blessed thing that there is such a Saviour as Christ—O let my heart turn to Him, and lean on Him and trust Him, even now—"

I say, if these reflections, or such as these, are awakened truly in your hearts and consciences by God's blessed word and truth this very day, take courage—go on—pray that God may enable you to see more of yourselves, and to debate the case with your own consciences, spiritually and faithfully in the light of God's word,—and then, as surely as you are brought to do so, this glorious love of Christ is beginning to work in your soul, if you really are taught to feel yourselves sinners, and are led to look unto Jesus.

Oh consider what a great blessing that is! what a blessing is the breaking in of one beam of light into the poor, darkened sinner's mind! And if one beam of the true light thus breaks into the mind—if it even be but a beam—if it be true light, it is like a beam of the morning sun breaking in the grey dawn through the trembling, flying shades of night on the sinner's eye. As that is a sure harbinger that the sun himself is rising, so is a beam of heavenly light, that the Sun of Righteousness shall arise on the sinner's soul, with healing in His wings. Oh think of this, what a blessing the love of Christ is! that it is love to man, not as he seems, but as he is! and that it is an everlasting love; not originating in time, and therefore not to be destroyed by time; but flowing forth from eternity—and therefore flowing on to eternity. So the Psalmist saith in that beautiful contrast he draws, "*As for man, his days are as grass; as a flower of the field, so he flourisheth. For the wind passeth over it, and it is gone, and the place thereof shall know it no more. But the mercy of the Lord is from everlasting to everlasting, upon them that fear him, and his righteousness unto children's children, to such as keep his covenant, and to those that remember his commandments to do them.*" Psalm ciii. 15, 16, 17, 18.

"*To such as keep his covenant.*" Mark—that is the first thing. You cannot know the commandments of God, till you are brought first to keep His covenant. You must be brought into covenant relation to God before you can keep His commandments, or even know what they are in their spiritual sense, and what it is to keep them.

When we speak of the everlasting love of Christ to His Church, we must understand that that love is developed in time by its actings to the church. This is seen in the image used by the Apostle here. "NO MAN EVER YET HATED HIS OWN FLESH, BUT NOURISHETH AND CHERISHETH IT, EVEN AS THE LORD THE CHURCH." So in his character of Shepherd, Isaiah xl., "*He shall feed his flock like a shepherd; he shall gather the lambs with his arm, and carry them in his bosom, and shall gently lead those that are with young.*" Isa. xl. 11. This illustrates "NOURISHETH AND CHERISHETH IT, EVEN AS THE LORD THE CHURCH." And see, when the Lord, in sending Nathan the prophet to David, is describing the relationship in which Bathsheba stood to her husband, he says, there was "*a poor man who had nothing save one little ewe lamb which he had bought and nourished up: and it grew up together with him, and with his children; it did eat of his own meat, and drank of his own cup, and lay in his bosom, and was unto him as a daughter.*" 2nd Sam. xii. 3, thus he describes the relationship between the husband and the wife;—and here, the Apostle saith "HE NOURISHETH AND CHERISHETH IT, EVEN AS THE LORD THE CHURCH: FOR WE ARE MEMBERS OF HIS BODY, OF HIS FLESH, AND OF HIS BONES."

That is a wonderful character in which the Lord is represented in Scripture, as "*The head of the body, the church.*" Who are the members of Christ? If a man takes a member of his body if he looks at his own hand, or at his own limb and says, Is not this united to me? Is not this part of myself? Shall I hurt this? Shall I injure this? Shall I wound this? Shall I not keep it? Shall I not preserve it? Shall I not protect it? If I injure this, does it not give my head and all my body pain? do I not feel it in every other member? do I not feel pain in every single member of my frame, if I wound or injure this one member? Shall I not, therefore, preserve, protect, and keep it? "NO MAN EVER YET HATED HIS OWN FLESH; BUT NOURISHETH AND CHERISHETH IT, EVEN AS THE LORD THE CHURCH."

So, when a man thinks of his own members, he may say; "Thus Christ looks at every individual member of His church; thus He looks at every poor sinner that He has brought to Himself, and washed in His own precious blood, and clothed in His own righteousness, as a man would look at a member of his own body. So Christ saith, "*He that toucheth you, toucheth*"—not only a member, but the most sensitive member of the body, that member the very touch of which is pain, "*He that toucheth you, toucheth the apple of his eye.*" Zech. ii. 8.

"Well then," (the believer may say) "if this be so, how does it happen that I feel myself so wounded—so tired—so heavily afflicted in all the course of my pilgrimage? If I am so precious to Christ how is this the case?" This exercises the heart of every believer more or less. How heavily David was exercised with this trial we see in Psalm lxxiii., he says, he was so tried with this affliction that it almost shook him from his faith. He says, "*As for me, my feet were almost gone, my steps had well nigh slipped; for I was envious at the foolish, when I saw the prosperity of the wicked.*" verses 2, 3. He had even gone so far in his murmuring and discontent as to say, "*Verily, I have cleansed my heart in vain, and washed my hands in innocency. For all the day long have I been plagued, and chastened every morning.*"

But he adds—taught by the Spirit the experience of God's children. "*If I say I will speak thus, behold I should offend against the generation of thy children.*" verses 13, 14, 15. And it is so. Believers are often tempted to doubt the love of their Lord, when they feel themselves so tried, they think, "If I was loved by Christ—if all I hear is true concerning the love of Christ to His Church, and if I were indeed a member of that Church, how could I be so afflicted—tried—burthened—cast down as I am?"

Oh! my friends! Oh! for the eye of faith to see the covenant love of Christ, in, and above, and beyond every affliction! There is not a single trial you can meet with, not a single affliction you can endure—that is not a proof, (if you could only see it so), of the very love of Christ. It is the part of love to watch over and correct evil in those beloved. It is the part of a parent's love to his child, to watch over and to correct the evil of that child. It is the part of a husband's love to his wife to watch over and correct the evils of his wife. It is not the part of the husband, if he is married to a wayward wife, to give way to her temper; but it is his duty, if he can, to correct and repress it. Men may not be inclined to correct the evils of their fellow-sinners, their wives, their children, their servants, or any others. But it is a proof of the everlasting love of Jesus, that He will correct the evils of His children, it is a proof of His love to you or me, to correct and to conquer the evil that is in us.

Men may not be able to correct the evils of others—not so Christ, He is able to correct His Church—He is the Faithful Husband, the Faithful Father. He is able—and He will—and does correct.

There is also another difference—namely, that our corrections, even of those we love, proceed often from selfishness. "*We have had fathers of our flesh,*" saith the Apostle, "*which corrected us and we gave them reverence; shall we not much rather be in subjection unto the Father of spirits and live? For they verily for a few days chastened us, after their pleasure, but he for our profit that we might be partakers of his holiness.*" Heb. xii. 9, 10. Christ, when He corrects His Church, makes no mistake—there is no selfishness—there is no indulgence of any temper: it is not because He is wounded—not because His temper is excited—not because He is angry at some reproach brought on Himself by the conduct of His wife, the Church—but it is the faithful correction of infinite wisdom, and everlasting love; and therefore, in holy, righteous, gracious, tender faithfulness, the hand of the Lord Jesus is stretched out to correct every one of His children, or (to preserve the image), to correct His beloved wife, His Church, just because He loves her, and just because it is needful for His glory—for His honor—and for her everlasting happiness. Yes, and my dear friends, the Church shall see and confess this—you shall see it. Let me speak not of the Church collectively, but of every individual member. Let me say, that every individual member of the Church shall see and know this. Look back at your own experience—Oh! believer! you whom Christ hath loved, and whom Christ hath condescended to draw to Himself—to wash in His blood, and to clothe in His righteousness—to justify—to save—to keep—and bring to His feet. Look back to your own experience in all the days that are past. You have gone through many trials—you have endured many perplexities—you have encountered many difficulties—you have suffered many sorrows—you have wept over many bereavements—many a sigh has burst from your anxious heart—many a tear from your unsleeping eye—many a deep and bitter exercise of soul have you nearly sunk under in the solitude of your own chamber—in the exile of your own bosom, from the sympathies of all the world. But if they are passed, if they are gone, and if you can look back now at them without present suffering—without the cloud that came between you and the Sun of Righteousness now passing, as it were before your eye, and therefore hindering you from seeing the brightness of His glory—if it is all past—then, look back at it all, and say, is there one trial you ever suffered—one visitation that ever afflicted you—one perplexity—one difficulty—one sorrow—one bereavement—one sigh—one tear—one exercise of soul, however deep and bitter it may have been—is there one, of which you cannot say—of which you do not know and feel at this moment, "*He hath done all things well.*" "I needed it. It was necessary for me. My case required it. I know not what I should have done without it. I feel it was for my good. The cup was bitter—the medicine was unpalatable—but the love and skill of my Heavenly Physician mingled it, I know it was for my good. I recognize in it my Father's hand. The tender hand of love gave it to me. My blessed Redeemer, my precious Lord held it to my lips in love."

Oh! then, if even now you can say this, and whether you know it or not, it is as surely true as God is in heaven, and you on earth—if you know it now, what shall it be at the last?—Oh!

> "There is a secret in the ways of God
> With His own children, which none others know,
> That sweetens all He does. And if such peace,
> While under His afflicting hand we find,
> What shall it be to see Him as He is,
> And, past the reach of all that now disturbs
> The tranquil soul's repose—to contemplate
> In retrospect unclouded, all the means,
> By which His wisdom has prepared His saints,
> For the vast weight of glory that remains!"

Oh! yes, "WE ARE MEMBERS OF HIS BODY, OF HIS FLESH, AND OF HIS BONES," and the very trials that make us in our unbelief and folly doubt the Lord's love in our behalf, shall be manifested to be the proofs of that very love which they led us to doubt. "*Wherefore, lift up the hands that hang down, and the feeble knees,*" and be assured, that as surely as you are brought to know Christ as your Refuge and Hope—so surely the Lord Jesus loves and cherishes you, as one of the "MEMBERS OF HIS BODY, OF HIS FLESH, AND OF HIS BONES."

When Christ "*bowed his head and gave up the ghost,*" all His body, all His members were dead. So it is with His Church—all who believe in Him are dead with Christ, "*Buried with him by baptism unto death,*" Rom. vi. 4; all their sins cancelled—all their iniquity blotted out—dead—buried forever!

When the stone was rolled away from the supulchre, and when Christ came forth again into the light of heaven, all his members rose with Him. So it was with His spiritual mystical body—they rose with Christ—they are risen again with Him. Thus they are to believe—to reckon themselves. So saith the Apostle, "*Likewise reckon ye also yourselves, to be dead indeed unto sin, but alive unto God through Jesus Christ our Lord.*" Rom. vi. 11. As certainly as every one of His bodily members rose from the grave, so surely every mystical member rose in the councils of the Eternal Jehovah, and though they were not then born, or are not yet born—if millions of ages were yet to roll over the earth, all the unborn church of Christ rose in Christ, when Christ rose from the grave, all His members—one with Himself—His Church—His bride, rose when Christ rose, her life was bound up with the life of her glorious Lord, she "*is dead, and her life is hid with Christ in God. When Christ who is her life shall appear, then shall she also appear with him in glory,*" Col. iii. 3, 4.

"WE ARE MEMBERS OF HIS BODY, OF HIS FLESH, AND OF HIS BONES: FOR THIS CAUSE SHALL A MAN LEAVE HIS FATHER AND MOTHER, AND SHALL BE JOINED UNTO HIS WIFE, AND THEY TWO SHALL BE ONE FLESH." Christ is here represented as coming to take His church, to be united to His Church on this earth as His bride, as a man leaves his father and mother and is joined to his wife. Christ is represented as leaving His glory to come down to this earth, and take His Church as His bride, and that His bride is to be one with Him forever. Well may it be added indeed, "THIS IS A GREAT MYSTERY, BUT I SPEAK CONCERNING CHRIST AND THE CHURCH."

What a wonderful subject this is! after a person has lectured or preached on it—thought—meditated on it again and again, after all we must shut the Bible and say—"How little have I done! How ignorant I am! What need I have to know more of my precious Lord and Saviour! What need have I to receive more and more of the Spirit of God to teach and instruct me in His blessed Word! What need have I that my Heavenly Father should bless all the riches of His grace to me! What need have I to trust my glorious Redeemer, more and more—to lean on Him!" "*Who is this that cometh out of the wilderness leaning on her beloved?*" Cant. viii. 5. Is it not His Church? Is it not some poor weary heavy-laden soul like mine, that is taught to lean on Jesus as its Hope and Refuge? Come then—Come up out of the wilderness, leaning on your beloved! Look unto Jesus—think what blessed consolation there is in this subject, whatever point of view we take it in! See the blessed union that subsists between Him who died for sinners, and those sinners who look to Him! Oh! search the Scriptures—pray, that you may learn more and more of this most wondrous salvation.

And now, my dear friends, if there are any of you here who have never thought of these truths, or to whom they are foolishness, and who are just dragging on your existence without God in the world, ignorant of Christ, and who think—as many called Christians, think, that the subject on which I have been speaking is all mere rhapsody—fanaticism—enthusiasm or folly—this very fact, if it be so indeed, is a lamentable proof of your state as being lost, and blind, and "*dead in trespasses and sins,*" chap. ii. 1.

If the Gospel be foolishness, it is so to them that perish.

When "*Holy men of old spake as they were moved by the Holy Ghost,*" 2d Pet. i. 21; when it was not man who was speaking, but God in man—this is God's testimony concerning His preached Gospel, "*Who hath believed our report?*" saith the Prophet, Is. liii. 1. So saith the Apostle, "*the preaching of the cross is to them that perish foolishness,*" 1st Cor. i. 18; and again "*If our Gospel be hid, it is hid to them that are lost, in whom the god of this world hath blinded the minds of them that believe not, lest the light of the glorious Gospel of Christ, who is the image of God should shine unto them.*" 2d Cor. iv. 3, 4.

Therefore, if this is foolishness to you, and if you are still, as I have said, dragging on your existence without God in the world—you are vainly resting on your own imaginary moral character, expecting to qualify yourselves to gain salvation by your own righteousness, and flattering and deceiving yourselves that you are as well as the rest of the world. Alas! alas! my friends, what ignorance and folly! Yours is the mere natural religion, or rather irreligion of the human heart. If this be your case, "*What will you do in the end thereof?*" Jer. v. 31.

You are hastening to the judgment seat of Christ, you may be summoned ere an hour. Perhaps before you go home, you may lift up your eyes to the clouds of heaven and behold Him coming in His glory! How shall you meet your God? You must be aware, that if what we say upon this subject, be foolishness to you, it must be because this Word is foolishness to you. You cannot open your Bible and read for instance this chapter, and understand the meaning of its plain words—for the words are very plain, though the subject is "A GREAT MYSTERY."

Just take this passage which I have read, and spoken on. What is the meaning of this? What does God mean by this? You cannot understand it. It is foolishness to you. If you admit this to be God's revelation—if you know it to be His Word, and if when you go to read it, you find such and such passages all foolishness to you—that you cannot understand—that you cannot comprehend them; there must be some great blindness over your mind. God's Word must have a meaning—must be true. There must be in it, not merely wisdom, but infinite wisdom, and if it is foolishness to you, what must be your state? What must be your prospects? Again, I ask in the language of the Prophet, "*What will you do in the end thereof?*" Jer. v. 31.

Oh! let me entreat—let me beseech you to consider, "*To day while it is called to day,*" these things that belong unto your peace. Perhaps this subject which is brought before you to-day through God's mercy, is brought before you to make you feel and reason thus:

"Well, I must confess this is unintelligible to me. I know not what means this union with Christ, these privileges in Christ, this exaltation to the glory of Christ. This is indeed, not only a mystery, but all darkness to me. And if it is unintelligible to me, what must be my state? If I cannot understand God's Word, so as even to know what the mercies are, in which His servants seem to rejoice, then how shall I ever understand my own state before

Him? How shall I stand in judgment in His presence? How can those mercies belong to me?"

Oh! think of this! Pray, that you may know and understand the great truths that are revealed concerning the Lord Jesus Christ, and the great salvation of His Church—the great salvation He promises to poor sinners through His own precious blood and righteousness.

May the Lord bring it home with power to your hearts and to mine, that we may lift them up with joy and glory at His coming and His kingdom! Amen.

FORTY-THIRD LECTURE.

EPHESIANS VI.—1, 2, 3.

"Children, obey your parents in the Lord: for this is right. Honor thy father, and mother, (which is the first commandment with promise,) that it may be well with thee, and thou mayest live long on the earth."

THE Apostle continues in this chapter his practical exhortations to his Ephesian brethren; on the duties of their various relations of life. And let us recollect that the Gospel of the Lord Jesus Christ is intended, not only to bring eternal life to our souls, but to direct and guide us in all our circumstances and conduct in this world.

There is no greater abuse of Divine Truth, than to suppose that religion consists merely in the adoption of a particular creed. Where the truth is really believed, it must produce its fruits. Religion that is not practical is no religion—and therefore, the Apostle asks, "*What doth it profit, if a man say he hath faith and hath not works, can this faith save him?*" Jam. ii. 14. "*This faith,*" as it is in the original, that is, a faith that he merely says he has.

There are these two evils, between which Satan is continually endeavoring to mislead the church, and in which he holds his own servants for the most part captive in these nominally Christian lands. One, making the performance of religious duties the hope of their soul. The other, adopting the profession of a form of godliness, without its practical influence or power. He makes some to rest on their own works or merits before God. Others to make a mighty profession of believing the Gospel of the Lord Jesus Christ, while their lives and conversation prove that that Gospel has no influence whatever on their hearts; "*Having,*" as the Apostle saith, "*a form of godliness, but denying the power thereof,*" 2nd Tim. iii. 5.

I say, between these two evils, Satan is continually endeavoring to mislead the Church of Christ; and all who profess to belong to that Church, and do not really belong to it, are sunk in one or other of these abysses of evil. They are either like the great mass of professing Christians who are ignorant of the Gospel of Jesus, setting up their own merits, or some vain refuge of lies for the salvation of their souls; or else they are, as is too frequently the case where the Gospel has been long and faithfully preached, adopting the profession of the faith of Jesus nominally, so that they will be able clearly to discriminate between doctrines that are true and false, while their life and conversation manifest that the Gospel of Jesus is really not embraced in their hearts. For wherever there is genuine faith in the Gospel, that faith must work by love. Therefore, you see, the Apostles are not more clear in setting forth, fully and explicitly, the Gospel, and disentangling it from all sophistry and falsehood, that would turn the sinner's soul to any refuge but Christ, than they are in enforcing practically the various relative duties of life, on those who believe the Gospel, as the only test of the truth of their profession.

Therefore, you will recollect that the Apostle is addressing young persons who were professing the faith of the Gospel of Christ. He saith, "CHILDREN, OBEY YOUR PARENTS IN THE LORD: FOR THIS IS RIGHT. HONOR THY FATHER AND MOTHER, (WHICH IS THE FIRST COMMANDMENT WITH PROMISE), THAT IT MAY BE WELL WITH THEE, AND THOU MAYEST LIVE LONG ON THE EARTH."

Now, this law of God comes, like all other laws of God, to every sinner on earth, who hears it in two ways. It comes to them in an unconverted state, to their utter condemnation—to the ruin—to the destruction of their souls, as "*The ministration of death,*" 2nd Cor. iii. 7. Or it comes to them in their converted state, as the holy rule of their lives, according to which they are called upon to regulate their conduct, in liberty and love without fear. Now we shall consider it for a few moments in these two points of view.

It comes, I say, to unconverted sinners, as "*the ministration of death*" to destroy their souls. Now, I see several children here. Although we, a great number of us, have grown to a time of life when we cease to be called children, yet let us recollect, that that is a relation in which we all have stood or do stand; and the law of God, "HONOR THY FATHER AND THY MOTHER," comes to every one of us, if we be not brought to the knowledge of the Lord Jesus Christ to condemn us. There is not a single child now in this room, or a single one of us, whatever be our time of life, against whom that law has not, or does not write judgment and condemnation, if we were to be tried only on that ground before God, putting all our other sins out of the question. If tried before the bar of God only on that one ground—our duty to our parents—we should perish from the presence of God forever. Recollect that. And therefore, dear children, remember, when you learn that command, "HONOR THY FATHER AND THY MOTHER," ask your own souls, have I kept this commandment? Have I obeyed my parents? Do I obey my parents? Do I honor them? Your conscience answers, No! then the wrath of God abides upon you, if you are yet in your sins.

Remember, that God's laws, every one of them, are capital. This is a capital law—you are guilty. I mean by a capital law, a law that brings on the soul condemnation and death with its violation. You have violated that law—therefore you have incurred the sentence of death at the tribunal of God. Consider that. Now, then, as a child, if you are at a time of life that you can understand what I say—that you are a rational and accountable being, so that your father and mother punish you, and justly punish you for your offences, and that you feel and know the difference between right and wrong in your own conscience—if you are at that time of life, then remember, that the holy law of God which commands you—"HONOR THY FATHER AND MOTHER," brings the curse of God upon your soul for the violation of it. You have broken that law, you are a rebel against God. And remember, it is not your father's and mother's command alone that you violate when you disobey—remember, you are violating the command of God. It is God's law. It is not only your father or mother who desire you to do so, but God commands you to obey. There is only one exception—one single point in which you are not to pay implicit obedience to your parents. If your parents should command you to do anything contrary to God's law, to commit an act that you know to be contrary to His holy commandments, then you are bound to disobey them. There are some poor children taught to steal, and taught to tell lies—their parents teach them to do so. Now it would be an act of obedience to God in such a child to refuse to obey his parents. So, in any case in which the command of the parent is contrary to the holy will of God, there the child is bound to disobey. As I stated before to you—that is the rule of all government, public and private, that whenever a person is commanded to violate the law of God, there he is bound to disobey, and there only. All authority comes from God—and all authority is to be honored as from God. Recollect, then, that this commandment condemns your souls. If you had never committed another sin against God except the violation of that one law, there is not a single one of you who should not be cast into everlasting death on this one ground.

Here then, you have to observe the riches of the grace of the Gospel of Jesus. Here you have to mark the blessedness of that provision for man's salvation, which caused your glorious Redeemer to be born of a woman.

Christ might have been formed as Adam was formed, from the dust of the earth—Christ might have come down from heaven, and a human body might have been formed for him by the Lord as for Adam.

Or He might have come down from heaven in a human form,

and appeared on the earth as man; and He might have been a righteous man, a holy man—living as He did on the earth—and He might have died as He did. But if He had done thus, where would have been salvation for children? Observe, the Lord Jesus Christ, we are told, was "*Made of a woman, made under the law, to redeem them that were under the law, that we might receive the adoption of sons.*" Gal. iv. 4, 5. The Lord Jesus Christ was "*made of a woman, made under the law.*" A child owes obedience to God's law from the moment it can obey, from the moment that the dawn of reason comes to its heart, from the moment it becomes accountable to God. That is a moment which no one can presume to determine, we cannot say what that moment is, when the Judge of all the earth shall consider a child accountable to Him. But from that moment the child is responsible for obedience to God's laws.

Now a child knows, and that at a very early age, when it does wrong. Very early it is conscious of its sin. This is equally important to the old as to the young, but it is especially important to children. You know, my dear young friends, that when you offend against God—when you do what your parents or teachers tell you is wrong, you strive to hide it, to excuse yourselves. You will do a thing when your parents or your teacher are not present, which you would not dare to do if they were. What makes you do so? Your conscience tells you, you are wrong—that you are violating your duty—doing what you know is forbidden—and therefore, your conscience tells you, you are justly condemned. But reflect—If you are justly condemned in the judgment of your parents or your teacher, how much more must you acknowledge, that you are justly condemned before a Holy God!

But when you do not feel—when you do not fear condemnation before God for an offence, which you would tremble to commit before your parents—see what ignorance and blindness of understanding and heart that exhibits. It is as much as to say, "I do not care whether God sees me or not. If my father, or mother, or teacher do not see me—I do not care about God. When they do not see me, I will do so and so, and all I care for is that I shall not be detected."

See, how this shows the natural inbred wickedness of your heart. How this marks the truth of God's Eternal Word, "*The wicked are estranged from the womb: they go astray as soon as they be born, speaking lies;*" Ps. lviii. 3; and that is one of the first ways your wickedness manifests itself—your conscience accuses you of doing what you know to be wrong, and when you are detected and accused, you will deny it, if you think you can escape by your denial.

Now then, dear children, just consider what condemnation this ought to bring on your conscience; and Oh! how blind—how hardened—how rebellious does it exhibit our hearts to be, that children, as they grow up, through all the stages of their life, if they can conceal their sins from those who are placed over them, their conscience does not carry with it, as it ought, the sting of having violated God's law—or accuse them of sin committed in God's presence—nor have they any care or fear of God's righteous judgment abiding on them.

See, then, my dear children, what a state of sin is this! How inevitably it must bring guilt and condemnation on your soul. If you are saved, you can only be saved by this, that there is some person to stand in your place, to become responsible for you—to answer to God for your sins, and to fulfil as your Surety the law you have broken, and give you a righteousness which you have not of your own.

See then, the blessedness of having that glorious Saviour, who came on earth, to become a child to be "*made of a woman, made under the law.*" Gal. iv. 4. From the moment you were born, you owed obedience to the law, and the blessed Jesus was born that He might pay obedience to the law from the moment of His birth; so "*Jesus increased in wisdom and stature, and in favor with God and man.*" Luke ii. 52. He was "*the holy child Jesus,*" Acts iv. 27, 30—the spotless child Jesus. There is but one instance, in which the Lord Jesus Christ seems to have been chargeable with an act of neglect to His mother and His reputed father—that was this, when they went up with Him to Jerusalem, and He remained behind after their departure. When they returned, and were looking for Him, and they found him in the temple, and Mary said:—

"*Son, why hast thou thus dealt with us, behold thy father and I have sought thee sorrowing?*"

Do you recollect our Lord's answer? "*How is it*"—said He—"*that ye sought me, wist ye not that I must be about my father's business?*" Luke ii. 48, 49. "That I must be occupied in the service of my Father, you might have known that I could not be occupied in anything else, than in the service of my Father and my God." That was an appeal to His mother—an appeal to her knowledge of Him before God and man, that she had such constant and uniform experience of His obedience primarily to God, and subordinately to her, that she might have felt certain He could only be engaged in the business of His Heavenly Father.

Oh! What a blessed thing it is, that children have the child Jesus as their Surety to answer for them! that little children have the child Jesus to stand between them and God, through all the stages of their sins.

How old are you? However young you may be—remember, Jesus was the same age.

You are a sinner, in every stage of all your life. Jesus was righteous, from the manger to the cross. You are condemned—justly condemned as a sinner. Christ came to save, he is the Lord your Righteousness, as a child, as well as the Lord my Righteousness as a man. "*This is his name whereby he shall be called,* THE LORD OUR RIGHTEOUSNESS," Jer. xxiii. 6. In whatever stage of sin you are—at whatever time of life you are—

Christ must be your only righteousness before God, "*Who of God is made unto us Wisdom, and Righteousness, and Sanctification, and Redemption,*" 1st Cor. ii. 30.

What a blessed consolation that we have such a Saviour as this! Alas! dear children, if you are not looking to Christ—if you are not brought to the Lord Jesus Christ, as all your hope of salvation. Then, this command of God, "HONOR THY FATHER AND THY MOTHER," if there was no other commandment in the whole Bible, this one command must cast you into everlasting death; you are lost under this one law, if you are not looking to Jesus.

Think, what a blessed encouragement it is to you to look to Jesus, that He was "*made of a woman, made under the law,*" and that He was "*the holy child Jesus.*" We are told, "*In all things it behoved him to be made like unto his brethren, that he might be a merciful and faithful high-priest,*" Heb. ii. 17, and He was like His brethren as a child, as He was like them as a man. Remember, whatever you read of the holiness and purity and perfection of the Lord Jesus Christ—whatever you hear of Christ as a man, remember, he was the same as a little child—the holy, spotless Lamb of God. Oh! what a blessed thing it is for you to have such a Saviour!

Now then, my dear children, if you are really looking to that Saviour and Redeemer—when you feel disobedience to your parents in your own hearts—when you find your own will rebellious against their commands, much more if you are led to do any act contrary to those commands—then you will come to the Lord Jesus Christ, and pray to Him for the pardon of your sins—you will bring that rebellion of your heart—that wickedness of your will, by faith to the Lord Jesus, you will look to Him for salvation—for deliverance and pardon for your sin, and you will come to Him for strength, that you may be enabled to obey your parents—you will feel thankful, that your blessed Saviour has delivered you from the curse, and that the law shall not condemn you; though you feel and confess you break it, it shall not condemn you—Why? because Christ kept it for you—Christ fulfilled it for you—Christ obeyed it for you—and died for your sin—it shall not condemn you; "*For Christ is the end of the law for righteousness to every one that believeth.*" Rom. x. 4.

Now, my dear children, consider how very important this is, there are several of you, that can fully understand what I am saying. The time when children become responsible, so that they are condemned before God for their offences, unless they look unto Jesus, that time, I say, we cannot tell—we cannot tell how soon. I believe that all children that are called from this world, before they are held responsible and condemned for their own iniquity, are all washed in the precious blood of the Lamb of God who taketh away the sin of the world, and I believe that all such shall swell that countless multitude, and join in the everlasting song of "*Blessing, and honor, and glory, and power, be unto him that sitteth upon the throne, and unto the Lamb, forever and ever.*" Rev. v. 13.

But though we do not know, and dare not pretend to define, at what time children become accountable to God, and are condemned for their sins, if you read some histories of those who have been early brought to the knowledge of the Lord Jesus Christ, it would seem that they are early held accountable, and condemned both in conscience and in fact. For it is quite clear, that when children can see the salvation of the Gospel of Jesus, and fly to Him as the refuge for their souls—it is quite clear, that at that time they could not do so, unless they were conscious of their guilt and wickedness—unless they feel that their souls are justly condemned for their rebellion before God; and every rational being who knows, in this world, that his soul is justly condemned for his rebellion against God, must say amen to the sentence of that condemnation, which he shall hear pronounced from the mouth of the Judge of Heaven and earth.

Here too you see, the Apostle is addressing believing children, "CHILDREN, OBEY YOUR PARENTS IN THE LORD," in all things that they command you, according to the will and Word of God: "OBEY YOUR PARENTS IN THE LORD, FOR THIS IS RIGHT." There is one rule for all—all things that your parents command you to do, not contrary to God's law.

This, I think, might serve to supply to many young persons a standard of their conduct in many things about which they may be in doubt. There are many young persons, who, as they are growing up, are brought to the knowledge of the Gospel of Jesus, and whose parents are ignorant of the Gospel—there are many such cases, and these young persons are very often at a loss to know what they shall do, when their parents wish them to act in a way that is contrary to their conscience. They are desirous often, especially that their daughters should go into scenes, and to places of public entertainment, where they feel that a Christian ought not to go—where they feel that a servant of God is out of his place and character—where they feel they cannot consistently or in faith ask God's blessing or presence with them there; and they are very often in distress of conscience, "What shall I do? my parents wish me to do so and so, and it is quite contrary to my conscience, and to my sense of duty to God, and I feel quite miserable." I have known several young friends of my own—I do not know whether there are any here—who are in distress about this.

Well, the rule is clear: "OBEY YOUR PARENTS IN THE LORD." If your parents want you to do anything which your Bible teaches you, is contrary to God's will; then you must obey God, rather than man—that is your plain path of duty. And if children do so in a right spirit—do so as Christians—if children make their parents know and feel, that they do so, not setting themselves up against their authority—not because they wish to wound them—or to refuse obedience, not only to any command, but any wish of theirs—and that it is pain to them to be obliged to disobey them in anything—and if their parents see that they act thus, as a point of conscience before God—and if they speak with the respect and tenderness that they ought to do, on the subject, and show, on all other occasions, the alacrity of loving and dutiful obedience, as they ought—they will find, in all probability, from experience, that their difficulties will all vanish. For, if it be true even of an enemy, how much more of a parent? "*When a man's ways please the Lord, he maketh even his enemies to be at peace with him.*" Prov. xvi. 7.

Sometimes, it may not be so. I have a dear friend, who was turned out of her father's house, on the wide world, at eighteen years of age, because she would serve her God! She was left, with some small sum that was her own, to earn her bread. She went out, like him of old, from her kindred—she set up a school, and she kept her school as a servant of God; and the Lord blessed her, and the Lord brought many, under her teaching, to the knowledge of the Lord Jesus Christ. There are many who are in glory, who received the Gospel of Jesus through her; and there are many now alive who can stand up and call her blessed, and who know that they received the knowledge of the Lord Jesus, from her teaching. The Lord has blessed her, too, as to worldly things; she is at ease in the world—she has retired from her office, with a competence to support her declining years—and she now spends her time, as she can, in endeavoring to teach the children of the poor around her, and to bring them to the knowledge of the Gospel of Jesus. The Lord blessed her more than all, in allowing her to see both these parents who had turned her out, die in the faith of Christ. Whenever persons do, in the service of their Heavenly Master, what they ought to do, the Lord's blessing will rest upon them. Therefore "CHILDREN, OBEY YOUR PARENTS IN THE LORD: FOR THIS IS RIGHT. HONOR THY FATHER AND MOTHER; WHICH IS THE FIRST COMMANDMENT WITH PROMISE; THAT IT MAY BE WELL WITH THEE, AND THOU MAYEST LIVE LONG ON THE EARTH."

Now this passage, beside other important truths supplies a clear and conclusive answer to the very false ungodly principle, that abounds among many who make a high profession of the Gospel; and who say, that the Law is not the rule of life for believers. They say, "These ten commandments were commandments given to Moses; but the Moral Law is not the rule of life for believers; we are to take our rule of life, not from the Moral Law, but from the precepts of the Gospel." This principle is, in every tittle, absurd—as if there was any difference between the Moral Law and the precepts of the Gospel; or as if God gave one law, as a Moral Law, a law of duty to the Jews, and then, another law of duty to Christians—as if what was sin at one time, was not to be sin at another—as if the moral character, the government, the law of God, could ever vary. Our blessed Lord says, "*Till heaven and earth pass, one jot or one tittle shall in no wise pass from the law*," What law? He is speaking of the Moral Law, "*till all be fulfilled.*" Matt. v. 18.

But here we see the Apostle—that is, the Holy Spirit by the Apostle, quotes the Moral Law—quotes one of the commandments of the Decalogue, and thus asserts the Decalogue as the rule of life; and quotes this command, as a command to be observed, and the promise annexed to its observance.

Thus also in Romans, xiii. 9, we have the words of the Decalogue quoted, "*For this, Thou shalt not commit adultery, Thou shalt not kill, Thou shalt not steal, Thou shalt not bear false witness, Thou shalt not covet; and if there be any other commandment, it is briefly comprehended in this saying, namely, Thou shalt love thy neighbor as thyself.*" Here, the Decalogue is quoted, verbatim—and yet, these persons say—"The Law is not the rule of life!" What a gross perversion of Scripture it is! What an awful thing it is, for sinners to set up their own whims and fancies against the plain simple light and letter of God's blessed Word! It is because too many will not receive the kingdom of God as a little child—because they will not receive God's truth, in its plain simplicity. Men choose to be wise, not only above what is written, but even contrary to what is written. And therefore we hear so many novelties and absurdities started against the plain letter of God's eternal Word. We should pray to be kept from these evils—from all false refinements, and vain speculations—and to come to the Scriptures, with this prayer in our hearts, "*That which I know not, teach Thou me.*" I know persons, who hold this principle, whom I believe to be servants of God, who endeavor to walk in the precepts of the Gospel, which is in fact walking in the law. But although they may be kept, through God's mercy, from allowing their false principle to break out in sin in their own lives—they are, nevertheless, setting up a false principle, which may mislead, and does mislead others. Hence the doctrine of Antinomianism, which is a denial that the law of God is the rule of life for believers. And this, when it is acted on, carries out the principle that is objected to the Gospel, by gainsayers and blasphemers. "*Let us continue in sin, that grace may abound.*" Rom. vi. 1.

I have heard that system awfully maintained, by those who have made a profession of believing the Gospel of Christ. Oh! it is very needful for us, to pray that we may be kept walking steadily, according to the blessed light of God's Holy Truth. It is a great mercy, to be kept learning at the feet of Christ, and not seeking to refine away and speculate on God's Word. It is clear and simple, "*A lamp unto our feet, and a light unto our paths.*" Psalm cxix. 105.

Therefore, remember, that those who believe the Gospel are called to walk in the commandments of God. How plain are these words "CHILDREN, OBEY YOUR PARENTS IN THE LORD: FOR THIS IS RIGHT. HONOR THY FATHER AND MOTHER; WHICH IS THE FIRST COMMANDMENT WITH PROMISE; THAT IT MAY

BE WELL WITH THEE, AND THOU MAYEST LIVE LONG ON THE EARTH." I have not the least doubt that those who walk in the Lord's ways, will always find God's promises fulfilled. Now, there is a very remarkable instance of this in Scripture, Jeremiah xxxv. There you find the Lord saying to the Prophet, "*Go unto the house of the Rechabites, and speak unto them, and bring them into the house of the Lord, into one of the chambers, and give them wine to drink.*" Here, observe, the Lord commands His prophet to go to the Rechabites, and to bring them to the house of God, and give them wine to drink. Now, we should not suppose, there was anything wrong in that. So the prophet calls them, and brings them to the house of God—he does not command them to do anything wrong, he gives them wine to drink—he says, "*Then I took Jaazaniah the son of Jeremiah, the son of Habaziniah, and his brethren, and all his sons, and the whole house of the Rechabites; and I brought them into the house of the Lord, into the chamber of the sons of Hanan, the son of Igdaliah, a man of God, which was by the chamber of the princes, which was above the chamber of Maaseiah the son of Shallum, the keeper of the door: and I set before the sons of the house of the Rechabites pots full of wine, and cups; and I said unto them, Drink ye wine.*

"*But they said, We will drink no wine: for Jonadab the son of Rechab our father commanded us, saying, Ye shall drink no wine, neither ye, nor your sons forever: neither shall ye build house, nor sow seed, nor plant vineyard, nor have any: but all your days ye shall dwell in tents; that ye may live many days in the land where ye be strangers.*" Jer. xxxv. 2–7.

This Jonadab the son of Rechab, was a servant of God; for if you recollect, in the history of Jehu, when he was anointed king to fulfil the Lord's commands, he said to Jonadab the son of Rechab, "*Is thine heart right, as my heart is with thy heart? and Jehonadab answered, It is.*" Then Jehu asked him, "*Come with me, and see my zeal for the Lord.*" 2nd Kings, x. 15, 16. So he took him into his chariot, and he accompanied Jehu in executing the commands of God. Jonadab's heart was more right than Jehu's; he was a true servant of God, and he commands his children thus, and you see how they obeyed his voice. So they proceed.

"*Thus have we obeyed the voice of Jonadab the son of Rechab our father in all that he hath charged us, to drink no wine all our days, we, our wives, our sons, nor our daughters; nor to build houses for us to dwell in.*" Now this was about 277 years subsequent to the time that Jonadab accompanied Jehu, and they say, "*neither have we vineyard, nor field, nor seed: but we have dwelt in tents, and have obeyed, and done according to all that Jonadab our father commanded us. But it came to pass, that when Nebuchadnezzar king of Babylon came up into the land, that we said, come and let us go to Jerusalem for fear of the army of the Chaldeans, and for fear of the army of the Syrians. so we dwell at Jerusalem."* v. 8—11.

"*Then came the word of the Lord unto Jeremiah, saying, Thus saith the Lord of hosts, the God of Israel; Go and tell the men of Judah and the inhabitants of Jerusalem, will ye not receive instruction to hearken to my words? saith the Lord. The words of Jonadab the son of Rechab, that he commanded his sons not to drink wine, are performed; for unto this day they drink none, but obey their father's commandment. Notwithstanding I have spoken unto you, rising up early and speaking; but ye hearkened not unto me.*" 12—14.

The Lord commands the Rechabites to be brought into the Lord's house, that their example of obedience to their father may be exhibited to the whole house of Judah, and that the house of Judah may see, that while these men are obedient to the commands of their father, given nearly three hundred years previously—the whole house of Judah are disobedient to the command of God given even at that moment by the Prophet—hear then what the Lord saith to the Rechabites:—

"*Because ye have obeyed the commandment of Jonadab your father, and kept all his precepts, and done according to all that he commanded you: therefore thus saith the Lord of hosts, the God of Israel; Jonadab the son of Rechab shall not want a man to stand before me forever.*" 18, 19. This is before Christ about 607 years, and it is now 1837 years after Christ, and to this day, more than 2400 years, that promise of the Lord stands good. For Jonadab the son of Rechab, does not to this day, want a man to stand before the Lord.

In the journal of the Rev. Dr. Wolfe, he informs us that he has met the Rechabites. He tells us, that to this very day, they quote the words of the Prophet—they quote the promise of God to their fathers, "*Jonadab the son of Rechab shall not want a man to stand before God forever.*"—and to this day they obey the commandment of their father, to drink no wine. To this day, the Rechabites are living monuments of the truth of this promise; and the descendants of Jonadab shall stand as God's witnesses, when the descendants of that people to whom they were proposed as an example, the rebellious Jews, shall be brought back again, and when "*the earth shall be filled with the knowledge of the Lord, as the waters cover the sea.*" Isaiah xi. 9.

Then "HONOR THY FATHER AND THY MOTHER, THAT IT MAY BE WELL WITH THEE, AND THOU MAYEST LIVE LONG ON THE EARTH."

Here, I say, is a remarkable proof of the truth of God's Word, in this command. This instance of obedience to God's Holy Law, has been honored by God's gracious mercy and providence, fulfilling those promises to the descendants of Jonadab, the son of Rechab, to this day.

Well, I trust that this subject, of the obedience of children, has been profitable to us. I hope it is profitable to you, my dear children; and that you will attend to these things. Let us recollect it—let us always remember, in our relation of children, which we have passed through, that the oldest individual among us, as well as the youngest, has reason to bless the living God, that Jesus was a child—and that the righteousness of Jesus, as a child, is "*the end of the law for righteousness*," to every believing child. The righteousness of Jesus as a child, and the precious blood of Jesus, are just as needful to deliver our souls from hell, as children, as they can be our only salvation at any part of our lives.

FORTY-FOURTH LECTURE.

EPHESIANS VI.—4.

"And, ye fathers, provoke not your children to wrath: but bring them up in the nurture and admonition of the Lord."

HAVING enjoined on all children who belong to the Church of Christ, the duty of walking in the commandment of the Lord, in obedience to their parents. The Apostle proceeds to impress on all Christian parents, their correlative duty to their children.

Although there be but one verse in the chapter on this subject, it is yet a verse of the most ample and comprehensive meaning. Let us, therefore, consider to-day, this admonition of the Apostle to parents, in connection with his admonition to children.

"YE FATHERS, PROVOKE NOT YOUR CHILDREN TO WRATH: BUT BRING THEM UP IN THE NURTURE AND ADMONITION OF THE LORD." There are two points which are here insisted on by the Apostle, in his admonition to parents, (for we need scarcely remark, that both parents are included in it),—

First—What they are not to do, "PROVOKE NOT YOUR CHILDREN TO WRATH."

Secondly—What they are to do—"BUT BRING THEM UP IN THE NURTURE AND ADMONITION OF THE LORD."

First, "PROVOKE NOT YOUR CHILDREN TO WRATH." How does this admonition happen to be necessary for fathers? Because, when they undertake to instruct their children—to educate, and train them up—it is an evil into which they are too likely to fall, to irritate and provoke their children to wrath. We are vile creatures—very unwilling to render obedience, where obedience is due from ourselves to others—and very ready to exercise authority, and to exact obedience, where it is due from others to us. And thus there are these two faults—two extremes, into which parents are apt to run. One, neglecting the instruction of their children—not bringing them up with steady discipline, as they ought to do—suffering them to be idle and indolent—petting them, and giving way to their tempers—their wills—their follies—their sins. Another, when they do endeavor to teach and govern them; exercising authority so as to provoke their children to wrath, by correcting them, when they displease them on points that wound themselves, and on occasions that interfere with their own authority, and that excite their own feelings—and not with a calm and single eye to the good of their children, and with reference to their God.

Children easily see through the motive for correction. They easily see, why they are reproved or punished—they are very quick-sighted—they will instinctively observe, when their parents reprove or correct them, whether it is done in a sober, calm, tender, affectionate, faithful spirit—or rather in an angry one—an irritated temper—because their children have provoked and incensed them, by their misconduct; and that because they are provoked and incensed, therefore they correct and punish their offences. This, so far from producing a good effect on a child, rather stirs up its wicked temper against its parent, and excites it to wrath. And this appears to me, to be the evil against which the Apostle is warning parents, where he says, "PROVOKE NOT YOUR CHILDREN TO WRATH."

You will see this set forth, in Hebrews xii. where the Apostle, speaking of the chastening of parents, adverts to this evil. He says, verse 9, "*We have had fathers of our flesh which corrected us, and we gave them reverence: shall we not much rather be in subjection unto the Father of spirits, and live? For they verily for a few days chastened us after their own pleasure;*"—for their own objects—for their own views—perhaps their wills or tempers, as seemed good to them, "*but he for our profit, that we might be partakers of his holiness.*" You perceive the contrast, God has but one view in the correction of His children; but one aim, one object, and that is, "*our profit.*" Earthly parents have, too often, another view, and that is, the mere maintenance of their own authority in punishing their children, or avenging on them the wrong they have done.

I have known parents, who would indulge their children shamefully, and give way to their tempers and their fancies, or their caprices, and allow them to act in a way that was quite intolerable to others; and then, when those children would exhibit the temper which these parents had cultivated, towards themselves, and would do something to irritate—to provoke them—to put them out of their way—then, they would be exceedingly angry, and punish their children vindictively for this. This, so far from doing good, quite destroys the principles and tempers of children. And therefore, it is a very good plan, if a parent knows that his own temper is hasty, to defer reproof or chastisement to the children for some time after the fault is committed; then say to the child, "Now, you have said so and so, you have done so and so, you have acted in such a manner as you know provokes my displeasure extremely; but I shall not pronounce sentence of punishment upon you, for such a time—one, two, or three hours, to-morrow, perhaps—in order that you may see that I do not punish you, because you displease me, or because I am offended; but that I punish you, after grave and sober consideration, for your own sake, for your own misconduct." Now, that sort of punishment, deliberately inflicted in that way on a child, produces an efficient and lasting effect—the child sees and feels, this is for its good—the child sees and feels, that the parent does not punish it from excited temper, but with judgment—soberly, wisely, faithfully—this produces due effect on the mind of a child. "YE FATHERS, PROVOKE NOT YOUR CHILDREN TO WRATH."

Besides, exciting their tempers, precludes the right cultivation of their principles or their affections. The child will always respect and love the parent who wisely corrects it, far more than the parent who indulges it. The affections of a child will be more drawn out, as reason unfolds and judgment is formed—he will necessarily approve and love that parent more, because the love that proceeds from, and is united with respect, is always a feeling stronger, more durable, and more influential on the heart, than the love that proceeds merely from selfish gratitude for weak indulgence. Therefore, I say, children will love, their affections will be drawn out more to the parent who corrects them wisely, than to the parent who indulges them without correction. You will always see what is called a petted child, turn away with ill temper and disrespect, from the parent who has spoiled it.

But with the prohibition, "PROVOKE NOT YOUR CHILDREN TO WRATH," we see,

SECONDLY—the command, "BUT BRING THEM UP IN THE NURTURE AND ADMONITION OF THE LORD." They should be trained according to the Word of the Lord. Their feelings and affections should be drawn out towards God, by faithful Christian instruction in His Holy Word. Now, if you provoke their tempers, in your mode of treating them—you excite their feelings against that which it is your first duty to cultivate in their hearts; you do them thereby an incalculable injury. You should endeavor to draw out their affections to God, and therefore you should endeavor to make the instruction you give them, as little calculated to call forth any opposing feeling as possible. There is, alas! enough of natural enmity in the heart, to God, without cultivating it, by injudicious treatment. This is, however, a subject, in the detail of which, it is almost impossible for any preacher or lecturer to lay down general rules. It is a subject, in which every parent will find great difficulty. I have felt great difficulty in it, myself. It is extremely difficult to give to religious instruction, all the weight, all the importance, all the time you feel it requires; and, at the same time, not to give it so much as to injure your child's mind, and to excite disgust or dislike to the very truth which you wish to inculcate, and against which the natural mind is already opposed.

I do not know any subject, in which a parent requires more wisdom; and I could not pretend to instruct you, because I cannot instruct myself. I feel I want instruction from God; I feel I require continually to pray to God, for direction. If I were to lay down any rule on the subject, the circumstances of various persons might make adherence to that rule unwise and injudicious. Very difficult questions might arise for a parent to determine. No individual can lay down any general rule, even for himself, in his own family. Every regulation must be modified by the different circumstances both of parents and children. Conduct, wise and proper with respect to one child, would be injudicious and improper in the case of another; while one requires to be drawn out—encouraged—brought forward; another requires to be held back and repressed. So we may say, in this, as in all our duties, "*Who is sufficient for these things?*" We require to be taught of God.

And I would say to those children who are here, or to any young persons present, who may perhaps not be brought to the knowledge of the Gospel of Christ—I would say to you, my dear young friends, consider, if your parents know and love the Gospel of Jesus, and if you know in your own hearts that you are not religious, and do not embrace the truth—I say, consider, my dear young friends, the pain and difficulty which your parents or teachers must necessarily feel, in dealing with you. They feel, that everything else is utterly insignificant, compared to God's Word—all your learning—all your accomplishments—all that you could possibly acquire, is like the dust under your feet, compared with the knowledge of the Lord Jesus Christ. If you do not know him, you know nothing—if you shall not be brought to know Him, "*It were better that a millstone were hanged about your neck, and you were cast into the depths of the sea*"—it would be good for you, if you had never been born. If your parents know and feel the value of the Gospel, and you know and feel it not, your heart is pulling against them, and straining to follow the world. The world wears a very deceitful aspect in your eyes. You think it is all pleasant—all delightful—and that if you were in such and such circumstances, and like others who are enjoying it, you would be happy. Your parents know it is a delusion. You are anxious to go one way—they, another. Your temper is excited, you are displeased, when they do not give way to you. Now, consider the difficulties in which your parents are placed. Consider the great responsibility laid on them. Consider the deep, affectionate anxiety of their hearts, concerning you. If you had a pet lamb, or a favorite dog, and that you saw it endeavoring to go where you knew it would be devoured or torn—with what anxious efforts would you endeavor to prevent it; and shall not your parents feel, when they see the child of their love rushing into the jaws of him, who, "*as a roaring lion walketh about, seeking whom he may devour?*" 1st Pet. v. 8. Oh! what an awful responsibility is laid on young people, when they have instruction—when they have the means of knowing and learning the Gospel—when they have parents that are most anxious to "BRING THEM UP IN THE NURTURE AND ADMONITION OF THE LORD"—and when the language of their heart is, "*Depart from us, for we desire not the knowledge of thy ways.*" Oh! think, my young friends, if I address such, how awful the responsibilities that are daily accumulating on your heads, for the instruction you refuse to receive, and the admonitions you refuse to obey. How, when it is thus presented to you, can you answer to your own consciences? How shall you answer at the judgment seat of Christ? "*How shall you escape, if you neglect such great salvation?*" Heb. ii. 3.

The Apostle saith, in another place, "*Fathers, provoke not your children to anger, lest they be discouraged.*" Col. iii. 21. He gives, you perceive, the same admonition, and gives a reason for it, "*lest they be discouraged.*" The mode in which religion should be set before children, is, as it really is, the only means of true happiness. It should not be connected with unkind, painful concomitants of instruction—but set before them, as if it were equally your pleasure and your duty, to impart to them, that which constitutes your own real, solid happiness.

For observe, when you are commanded to "BRING THEM UP IN THE NURTURE AND ADMONITION OF THE LORD," there are two things you must consider. These are—First, the instruction you are to convey to your children. Secondly, the example you are to set before them. It is in vain, to tell your children that religion constitutes the real happiness of the sinner, if your children see that it does not constitute your happiness—if they see, that your heart really takes pleasure in the world, instead of the things that belong to your eternal peace. How can they believe you, when you tell them that true religion alone constitutes true happiness—if you set, by your example, a stumbling-block in the way of your precept? You cannot suppose, that your children will follow your precepts, and disregard your example; or, that you, can convince them, by setting before them what you say you believe, when their senses contradict your precept, by what they see you do. Recollect, that their hearts are all naturally inclined to follow the example that would lead them to the world, and disinclined to follow the precepts that would warn them from it; and if your example draws them in the opposite direction of your precepts, you cannot lead your children to God, by the one, when you practically lead them from Him, by the other. "BRING THEM UP IN THE NURTURE AND ADMONITION OF THE LORD." These two terms have a distinct meaning. "NURTURE," referring to the principles implanted in the mind—the truth in which they are to be instructed, as he saith to Timothy, "*Nourished up in the words of faith and of good doctrine.*" 1st Tim. iv. 6. "AND ADMONITION," reminding them continually to bring these principles and truths into practice.

Then observe, they are the principles and practice of Divine Truth. "THE NURTURE AND ADMONITION OF THE LORD." Surely if the proper end of man's existence is to be brought into the service of his God, the proper end of his education is, that he should be trained for that service.

Accordingly, there is scarcely any command in the Scriptures, that is more frequently insisted on by their Divine Author, than the instruction of children in "THE NURTURE AND ADMONITION OF THE LORD." We have it set before us, in Deuteronomy, where the Lord speaking by Moses to the children of Israel, saith, "*For what nation is there so great, that hath God so nigh unto them, as the Lord our God is in all things that we call upon him for? and what nation is there so great, that hath statutes and judgments so righteous as all this law which I set before you this day? Only take heed to thyself and keep thy soul diligently, lest thou forget the things which thine eyes have seen, and lest they depart from thy heart all the days of thy life, but teach them thy sons and thy son's sons.*" Deut. iv. 7, 8, 9.

It is utterly impossible we can be anxious to teach our children that which we disregard ourselves. A mother is exceedingly desirous that her child should excel in accomplishments—she places a high estimate on them. Accordingly, she will spend her time, her efforts, her labor, her money, in striving to have her child well instructed in these. Another parent is anxious that their child shall excel in languages and sciences, and they use every effort they can, to have their children instructed in these. Others again consider it of primary importance, that their children should excel in industry, and in providing for themselves in their profession, or their business, whatever it may be; and you see parents spend their anxieties, and all their energies, to instruct their children in these things. Why?—Because they are uppermost in their own thoughts, because they are the things they value most, on which their own hearts are set, in which their own time is occupied. The mother is anxious to set off her child to the best advantage, she wishes that she and her family should appear well in the eyes of the world. The father is very anxious that his son should be distinguished in literary attainments, and make great progress in the learned professions, therefore it is the desire of his heart to spend his thoughts, and time, and money, on these. The merchant—the shopkeeper—the tradesman, are very anxious that their children should excel in the business or trade to which he wishes to bring them up, and therefore he devotes his time and labor to this. But if the parent really feels that God and his Truth—His Word—His Law—His Gospel—His Salvation—His Service, are the first and most important things for his own soul; and that everything else is comparatively insignificant, as it is; he will impress the truth of God on the heart of his children, and his children will know from both his precept and example, that he does count it the most important thing for himself and for them, that it is the first desire of his soul to fulfil this precept, and to "BRING THEM UP IN THE NURTURE AND ADMONITION OF THE LORD."

Dear friends, what signify all the things of this world for our children? What would it profit if our children possessed all the accomplishments—beauty—learning—talents—wealth of the world—what are they all? I would rather see my child covered with sores, like Lazarus—carried from door to door—desiring to be fed with crumbs that fall from the tables of the rich—I would rather see my child thus, and enjoy the blessed hope that his soul was leaning on Jesus—than see him at the head of an empire, and have the misery of thinking that he was on the road to everlasting destruction. Oh! think of this, consider this. Alas! if you saw, as perhaps you may have seen or yet may see, your children laid on a dreary bed of illness, if you saw them lying cold in death before you—if conscience tells you, and bitter memory ratifies the accusing voice of conscience, that instead of endeavoring to bring your children to God, who has summoned them away, you trained them up for the world, which they have left to darkness, to despair, and to you—"*What will you do in the end thereof?*" What will your feelings be? When you think that your children through your criminal neglect, may have gone to everlasting death—that you neglected their souls; and that all your anxieties and cares, were expended in laboring for their progress and advancement in this wretched world. Alas! Alas! the bitterness, the anguish of the thought! my child, Alas! my child—my lost, neglected child!

But, it is in vain to talk of the education of children, if the hearts of the parents themselves are not impressed with true religion. Therefore the Lord saith again in Deuteronomy, "*These words which I command thee this day shall be in thine heart, and thou shalt teach them diligently unto thy children, and shalt talk of them when thou sittest in thine house; and when thou walkest by the way, and when thou liest down and when thou risest up, and thou shalt bind them for a sign upon thine hand, and they shall be as frontlets between thine eyes, and thou shalt write them upon the posts of thy house, and on thy gates.*" Deut. vi. 6—9.

You see, you must have the truth in your own heart, before you can impress that truth on the minds of your children. Dear friends, if your children are children of God, the Lord will take care of them. If my children are children of God, I have no anxiety about their temporal concerns; because I know they shall have the portion, not of my children, but the portion of the children of the King of kings—the Lord will give them the portion of His children—the Lord will take care of them—"JEHOVAH JIREH." The Lord will provide—is settled on them for an everlasting inheritance. All things are working for their good—everything is ordained for their happiness, because they are the children of God.

The Lord may be pleased to bring them low in the world, to bow them down, to afflict them with difficulties and trials; but if He does, that is the path in which He calls them to glorify Him, that is their inheritance. His eye—His hand—His heart—are over them, His power and love are engaged in their behalf; I do not care, it would not cost me a thought about their temporal concerns, let me but know that they are saints of the living God, members of the King's household. And if I commit my own cares, my own soul, all I value in time and eternity to the hands of my God, can I not commit my children to Him too? All the happiness I have for my own heart, I can have for my children, (I can have no happiness in the earth more than this) if I am able to look to the Lord Jesus Christ, as my Hope and Refuge. If I am, I know that the Lord will order all things for me. I may be encompassed with trials and perplexities, but they must all be good for me, "*We glory*," saith the Apostle, "*in tribulation also, knowing that tribulation worketh patience, and patience experience, and experience hope, and hope maketh not ashamed, because the love of God is shed abroad in our hearts, by the Holy Ghost, which is given unto us.*" Rom. v. 3, 4, 5.

This is the portion of the Lord's children, they are provided for in time and in eternity. Oh! what a load it lifts off Christian parents! what a mountain it rolls off our hearts! Indeed it does! And what a blessed illustration of the truth that "*Godliness is profitable for all things, having promise of the life that now is and that which is to come.*" 1st Tim. iv. 8.

And then, my dear young friends, consider this for yourselves. If you are brought to the knowledge of the Lord Jesus Christ, "*All things are yours.*" Your hearts may be delivered from all care about temporal concerns; if you have the one thing needful, the promise is express and direct, "*Seek ye first the kingdom of God and his righteousness, and all these things shall be added unto you.*" Matt. vi. 33.

If you are brought like Mary to sit at the feet of Jesus, and to choose that better portion, then, it "*Shall not be taken away from you.*" Luke x. 42. Oh! think of this, and what is the comparative value of anything else? Can you say of anything else in the world, it shall not be taken from you? What is it? Youth? Beauty? Accomplishments? Health? Wealth? Fame? Friends? Those that are dearest on earth? Life itself? Alas! all, all, are passing away, "And like the baseless fabric of a vision, leave not a wreck behind."

But if you are brought to the knowledge of the Lord Jesus Christ, if you are taught to choose that better portion, this, this shall not be taken from you forever; Christ does not decay, Christ does not fade away, Christ does not vanish like a shadow, like the things of time and sense, Oh! no—Jesus, the Lord of glory, is an everlasting treasure, "*Jesus Christ is the same yesterday, to-day and forever.*" Heb. xiii. 6. This—this is the portion for our sons, and our daughters, even "*The unsearchable riches of Christ.*" Then consider this my dear young friends, and "*Seek the Lord while he may be found, call ye upon him while he is near,*" Isa. lv. 6. This is His promise, and this is His testimony: "*I love them that love me; and those that seek me early shall find me. Riches and honor are with me; yea, durable riches and righteousness. My fruit is better than gold, yea, than fine gold; and my revenue than choice silver. I lead in the way of righteousness, in the midst of the paths of judgment: that I may cause those that love me to inherit substance; and I will fill their treasures.*" Prov. viii. 17, 18, 19, 20, 21.

The Lord shows, that the instruction of children is so important that He gives this as one of the reasons for His statutes and His ordinances, He says: "*And when thy son asketh thee in time to come, saying, what mean the testimonies, and the statutes, and the judgments, which the Lord our God hath commanded you.*" The Lord supposes the children of the Israelites, to see as they grow up, the daily sacrifices, the feast of the passover, and the different ordinances of the Lord, and to ask, "What is the meaning of this sacrifice? What is the meaning of that ordinance?" "*When thy son asketh thee in time to come, saying, what mean the testimonies, and the statutes, and the judgments, which the Lord our God hath commanded you? then thou shalt say unto thy son, we were Pharaoh's bond-men in Egypt: and the Lord brought us out of Egypt with a mighty hand: and the Lord showed signs and wonders, great and sore, upon Egypt, upon Pharaoh, and upon all his household, before our eyes: and he brought us out from thence, that He might bring us in, to give us the land which He sware unto our fathers.*" Deut. vi. 20, 21, 22, 23. They were to instruct their children, what were the origin, end, and object, of all these ordinances.

We see the same thing in Joshua, when the Lord commands a man of every tribe, to bring out twelve stones, a stone for every tribe, out of the midst of the river, and there erect these stones into a monument; He says, "*That this may be a sign among you, that when your children ask their fathers in time to come, saying, what mean you by these stones? Then ye shall answer them, that the waters of Jordan were cut off before the Ark of the covenant of the Lord; when it passed over Jordan, the waters of Jordan were cut off: and these stones shall be for a memorial unto the children of Israel forever.*" Josh. iv. 6, 7.

You see the ordinances that the Lord appointed, and this was one especial use of them, that they should be always a means of instructing children, and teaching the ways, the truth, and the dealings, of the Lord with his people. Thus there is nothing more strongly set forth throughout the word of God, nothing more strongly impressed, on the people of Israel than this, that they should teach and instruct their children, diligently in the ways of the Lord.

And as it belongs to the Father of lights to enlighten His people, and to impress on them the deep necessity there is for instructing their children in the things that belong to their peace; so it is one of the first aims of the prince of darkness, to intercept the light of truth from the young mind, and to prevent children from being brought up "IN THE NURTURE AND ADMONITION OF THE LORD." We have a melancholy example of this in our own country. Look at this miserable land—one of the heaviest blows, that Satan can aim at the existence of the Christian religion in a country, is to prevent the children from being taught in the knowledge of God. See how he has succeeded in this country at this moment, so as to set up a system of National Education—to shut out the light and authority of the Holy Scriptures, from the schools and cottages of the poor—to supersede in every National School, this very command of God; and to secure to parents under the Papal yoke, the pretended right to disobey; and that they shall not bring up their children "IN THE NURTURE AND ADMONITION OF THE LORD."

Now as it is God's work to bring up children, "IN THE NURTURE AND ADMONITION OF THE LORD," it is the work of the prince of darkness to prevent it; because if the youth of a Nation are brought up, "IN THE NURTURE AND ADMONITION OF THE LORD"—if children are educated in the knowledge of divine truth—if God's Holy Word is made the standard of their instruction, we may hope and expect under the Divine blessing, that true religion shall make a corresponding progress in the nation; and that the nation shall consequently derive a blessing, from God's sacred truth.

But if the Word of the Living God is shut out from the instruction of a nation, the necessary consequence must be, that the nation must grow up in ignorance of God and of true religion; and therefore, it is the policy of the enemy of souls by every means, to exclude the light of truth from the soul. Yet the cry is now, "Educate, educate the people, let knowledge be diffused and cultivated among the rising generation, to the utmost. But God's authority shall not be asserted—God's Word shall not be made an authoritative standard of instruction in any school—the law of the school shall be, that every child shall have a right to refuse subjection to the authority of God." That is in plain English, let Satan have unrestricted power to corrupt and pervert the minds of children, let God's government, and God's authority be shut out of their hearts. That is the plain state of the case.

To educate the human mind without the Word of God, is to cultivate man's intellect at the expense of his principles. To improve his reasoning faculties at the expense of his moral qualities, is to increase his power of indulging his natural evil propensities, to the exclusion of the only counteracting power of good.

We hear on every side the common cant:—"Surely, if men will not receive education in the Bible, it is better to give them the education they will receive, than to give them none at all. Better to educate them without the Bible, than to leave them in utter ignorance."

No principle can be more destitute of truth. Intellect cultivated without religion brings man nearer to the devil. It gives power and activity to evil. It would not be difficult to name men of this or of any age, exalted by their talents and destitute of religion, of whom it may truly be said, it were a blessing to themselves and their country if they had never learned to spell.

Many will, I know, consider this a barbarous sentiment; they will tell us that the refinement—the improvement—the very civilization of mankind must depend on education. I know it; but when religion is not the basis of that education, it but aggravates responsibility and guilt, to go intellectually and learnedly to perdition.

Unsanctified education—unsanctified refinement—the progress of ungodly men in arts and sciences; but gives to man increased capability and power of promoting evil and opposing good. So, it is seen at this very moment. Never was irreligion more rife in the British empire, than it is at this day. Whatever may be said of the increase of religion among individuals, never was the nation, as a nation, more awfully irreligious, than it is at this moment; and there can be no greater proof of it, than, not merely the toleration, but the progress of that one wicked, anti-christian principle—let men be educated without the Bible. The command of the mighty God to parents for their children is, "BRING THEM UP IN THE NURTURE AND ADMONITION OF THE LORD." The command of the prince of darkness is, bring them up without the nurture and admonition of the Lord.

God's command is, "Bring them up for me." The devil's command is, "bring them up for me"—and if they are brought up without religion, the devil is obeyed; they are brought up for the devil and not for God.

Think of this, my friends! No man considers the subject as he ought for himself, who does not consider it as anxiously for his country. And there is no greater proof of the want of pure, sound religion, among the Protestants of Ireland, than the passive apathy with which they have sat down under a system of National Education, that shuts out God's Eternal Word from the instruction of the children of their country. There is no man, who deserves the name of Christian, whose protest ought not to be loud—whose voice ought not to peal from north to south, and east and west of this island, against a system so dishonoring to God as this. Assuredly, it must end in the destruction, the utter desolation of a land which dares to say—Jehovah shall not exercise the authority of His Word, to instruct and rule the minds of the inhabitants of their country. Assuredly, a nation that casts off the authority of God, may well begin to tremble. Let not the Protestants of this nation, or this empire, flatter themselves that God will guard the establishments of their religion, when they abandon the foundation of that Eternal Word, on which alone, it is, or ought to be, established. Their laws—their institutions—their properties—their liberties—all that is, or can be dear to men, shall be like the driven stubble before the hurricane, when Jehovah shall lay His hand on them for their wickedness. O think! thus saith the Lord, "*Can thine heart endure, or can thine hands be strong, in the day that I shall deal with thee? I the Lord have spoken it. and will do it.*" Ezek. xxii. 14.*

* The Author's sentiments expressed in this Lecture in the year 1837, continue unchanged at the end of ten years, when they are now issued from the press. The

How men are to "BRING THEIR CHILDREN UP IN THE NURTURE AND ADMONITION OF THE LORD," the Scripture leaves us at no loss to determine. The Apostle fully instructs us in 2d Tim., and now observe what he says, he addresses his beloved Timothy thus:—"*Greatly desiring to see thee, being mindful of thy tears, that I may be filled with joy; when I call to remembrance the unfeigned faith that is in thee, which dwelt first in thy grandmother Lois, and thy mother Eunice; and I am persuaded that in thee also.*" What a blessed thing it is to have a pious grandmother and a pious mother! I lost my mother when two years old, and I was consigned to the care of a beloved grandmother, a servant of her God. She brought me up at her knee; taught me much of this blessed Word as the earliest lesson of my childhood. What a gracious mercy! A woman may be very old, very infirm, very feeble—she was very feeble and infirm; she was an invalid for thirty years; she could hardly move across the room without assistance; but she could teach me the Word of God—she could teach her grandchild to commit passages of the Holy Scripture to memory; and I bless those sainted lips that taught me lessons in infancy, which I remember to this day.

So you perceive the genuine spirit of faith, of which the Apostle speaks: "*Which dwelt first in thy grandmother Lois, and thy mother Eunice; and I am persuaded that in thee also.*" 2 Tim. i. 5.

Writer is convinced, that it is presumptuous in man to assume, that he can certainly specify any national sin, as being the direct cause of God's judgments being poured out on a nation. In truth, unless God were to reveal it, it can scarcely be said, with Scriptural propriety, that any one given sin is the cause of them.

The sins of nations, as of ungodly individuals, are not the mere occasional lapses of those who are servants of God, but the workings and evidences of growing wickedness, and increasing alienation from Him, which mark the character and constitution of the national mind, and of which, manifestations of greater or less magnitude appear from time to time, till they accumulate to fill the cup of a nation's guilt; and the Lord pours out His judgments when the measure of its iniquity is full. Herod slew James, and apprehended Peter with intent to slay him also: this murder and persecution of the Lord's disciples, might justly have been supposed to call down judgments on the murderer; but it was not, till the pride of his heart, which human eye never saw, appropriated to himself the glory due to God, for his gift of eloquence, that the measure of his iniquity was filled up, and the hand of God smote him with worms. Acts xii.

But it is most just and lawful for ministers of Christ, to mark out and specify acts of national guilt, which are calculated from their iniquity, to call down judgments on a nation, and to fill up the measure of her guilt, which have a necessary tendency to insult the Majesty of God, and to provoke the Divine vengeance.

Of such a nature, the Writer is conscientiously satisfied, is the Board of National Education in Ireland; and though it would be presumptuous, and he thinks untrue, to specify this, which is but one among a series of great and growing national crimes; yet he thinks, it is one of the many, which have provoked the Lord to stretch out His hand in judgment, and take away the stay of bread from the country.

It is to be remembered, that in that very year, when in defiance of all remonstrance, and all entreaties for Parliamentary aid, in promoting Scriptural Instruction for Ireland, not only was it peremptorily refused, but the System of National Education was incorporated in this country, which interdicts the authoritative distribution of the "Bread of Life" in every National School; and establishes a counter authority to interdict its reception by every child, on the pretence of a parental right to do so, but really to maintain the power of Apostate Rome.—It is to be remembered, that in that very year, God has taken away the means of support from the people, and made all the inhabitants of the land to feel the might of His arm, and the terror of His righteous visitation.

And how was Timothy instructed? We read in the third chapter: "*Continue thou in the things which thou hast learned, and hast been assured of, knowing of whom thou hast learned them; and that from a child thou hast known the holy scriptures, which are able to make thee wise unto salvation, through faith which is in Christ Jesus.*" 2 Tim. iii. 14, 15, 16. The doctrine of the prince of darkness is, that "experience teaches us that more evil than good, results from the unrestricted reading of the holy scriptures."* Hence the pretence that the Bible is a book too difficult for a child. Yea, hence from a pretended reverence for it, it is too holy to be tossed about, as a school book. Those who follow the precepts of the prince of darkness, and walk in his ways, they say the same things, and act on them too; but Jehovah saith, "BRING THEM UP IN THE NURTURE AND ADMONITION OF THE LORD," Jehovah teacheth how this is effected too, "*From a child thou hast known the holy scriptures, which are able to make thee wise unto salvation through faith which is in Christ Jesus.*" What matter what the world or the prince of this world—or all the rulers of the darkness of the world say, when God saith so? What is the answer? "*Let God be true, but every man a liar;*" Rom. iii. 4. He saith, His Holy Scripture is able to make children wise unto salvation, His Word is "THE NURTURE," His Word is the "ADMONITION OF THE LORD."

What a blessing it is for a mother to train up her child in the holy Scriptures; to nourish up her child in the word of the Living God. Oh! what a blessing is promised—and what a blessing rests upon her instruction!

What a blessing for a sister to teach her little brothers and sisters the Word of God! there is no way in which you learn more of the Scriptures yourselves, than by teaching them to others. God blesses you: "*He that watereth shall be watered also himself,*" Prov. xi. 25. That is His testimony, and His testimony is true, and you shall find it so, you shall find a blessing in teaching; for in teaching others, you shall be taught yourself of God, the Lord will be teaching you when you are teaching His precious Word. I never learned more of Scripture than in teaching young persons in a Sunday School; and you will find, by experience, that a blessing rests on it.

A parent or a teacher cannot teach a child the simplest text in the Bible, that they are not learning a lesson they require as much themselves. You have God's Word to encourage you, and dear friends, when we have the Lord's Word to lean on, with what confidence may we go on in anything! Let us have but the Lord's Word—the Lord's testimony—the Lord's assurance of anything on earth, and we may go on straight forward, without caring or thinking of what man says, or looking to the right hand or to the left. "*Thus saith the Lord,*" that is enough. On that we may venture all in time and all in eternity. Therefore O ye

* See Rule IV. of the Papal Index Lib. Prohib.

parents! "BRING THEM UP IN THE NURTURE AND ADMONITION OF THE LORD." This divine instruction is to the mind, as nourishment from the mother's bosom to the child, thus saith the Apostle: "*As new born babes desire the sincere milk of the word, that ye may grow thereby,*" 1 Pet. ii. 2, as a babe grows from the nourishment it draws from its mother's breast; so the soul grows from the nourishment it derives from God's Word—"*Desire the sincere*" (that is the pure, unadulterated) "*milk of the word that ye may grow thereby.*"*

Now the growth of a child—the strengthening of a child is gradual, continual, but imperceptible to the child; so the growth in spiritual strength and spiritual knowledge through the Word of God is gradual; it is imperceptible to the person who is receiving nourishment, but still it is certain, they are still growing. The child, at the end of a year, or two years, will be able to see and feel that it can walk, and can do many things—that it has strength, much greater than it had one or two years before, though on no one given day, could the child feel it had gained strength by the nourishment of that day. So, persons who feed on "*the sincere milk of the word,*" will be able to feel that they have derived power—strength—refreshment from its divine and life-giving nutriment, though they cannot feel its sensible increase on each successive day.

When you open your Bible, and read your allotted portions, you may not feel you have derived any spiritual strength or made any spiritual progress;—nay, you may feel directly the reverse—you may feel it has been a sealed book to your soul, and yet, if you are a child of God, you are making progress all the while.

How can that be? I will tell you how.

You open your Bible, as perhaps you often do, and you sit down to read—and you read—and you close your Bible, and you find—what? that you have not derived one particle of profit from a single word you have been reading—nay, that you have not been able to apply your mind to it, or to give it the least attention, that your heart has been wandering after some vanity, or folly, in which you really feel no interest—you awaken as it were from a wandering dream, and you feel but self-conviction and condemnation as all the profit that you have derived from reading your Bible.

* I cannot but record here, as I heard it from a brother Clergyman, a specimen o that struggle which the powers of darkness are carrying on in unhappy Irelan aided, I lament to say, as the National Board and the Endowment of Maynooth testify, by those who ought to be the last to patronize and promote the reign of ignorance and falsehood, through the instrumentality of spiritual taskmasters, against the poor Roman Catholics, who are longing for the light and liberty of God's blessed truth.

A Priest was threatening a poor Roman Catholic, who, he was informed, presumed to have a Bible in his possession, and told him amongst other reasons, why he had no right to have it, that, "He had no business with the Bible, for St. Peter said, it was not the Word, but the milk of the Word he ought to have"—and he confirmed his assertion by this text, 1st Pet. ii. 2. "I know that well, please your Reverence," replied the poor man, "but for fear the milk should be adulterated, I like to keep the cow that gives it with me in the house." Neither Popish Priests nor those who help them, can be able to keep such a people long in spiritual slavery, if those who are the servants of God, will be faithful to use the talents entrusted to them.

"Alas!" you say,—"What have I been thinking of? I cannot bring my mind to apply even to a single chapter of my Bible, my vacant eye has been floating over the page, while my heart has been wandering like the fool's eye to the ends of the earth. I have read my Bible only to condemn me, I have derived no benefit from this blessed word at all."

Such may be your exercise—such I know has often been my own.

Well now, can I truly say in this, I have derived no benefit from this painful exercise? no profit—no instruction from the Bible? nay, but on the contrary—much benefit—much experimental knowledge of the letter and spirit of the Bible.

How so? How can this be? Because that Bible tells you, "*the heart is deceitful above all things and desperately wicked, who can know it?*" Jer. xvii. 9. Now you have been learning the truth of this lesson of your own wicked vile heart, and you have been learning practically, from experience however painful, the truth of God's Word, as to the vileness of that heart; and even in that way, when you feel you have derived no profit from the Bible, you have derived great profit, because you have learned your own wickedness, and helplessness, and that you can do nothing, without the Spirit of God,—that you may read your Bible over and over, and at the end be as ignorant as when you began, if you are looking to your own wisdom and leaning on your own understanding. You have learned that the Word of God is a dead letter without the Spirit of God to teach you to know it—that you must look to God, Paul might preach to you the very words you read, but God must open your heart, as he did that of Lydia, to attend to them. All your strength must be derived from God, and you must learn, by experience, that the very Bible itself is a useless book unless God the Holy Ghost brings the truth of that Bible home to your heart and conscience. Therefore you are learning a great and important lesson when you learn the corruption—the ignorance—the impotence—the folly of your own sinful heart.

But to return, "BRING THEM UP IN THE NURTURE AND ADMONITION OF THE LORD." You, my dear friends, who may be discouraged in teaching your children, in sowing the seed; and who, often with an aching heart, shut your Bible, and sigh and say, "Alas! my dear child, I endeavor to teach him the word of God; but I see, I cannot make the least impression at all, he is just as far from God as ever, I am unhappy and miserable about his state."

Ah, my friend! you learn both from yourself and your child, that Paul may plant, and Apollos water; "*But God giveth the increase,*" 1st Cor. iii. 6, you learn the important lesson of your own unprofitableness for your children, as well as for yourself; and you learn, that you must come to God for every blessing for their souls, as for your own. But still go on in faith, and sow the seed. How often they that sow in tears, shall reap in joy.

As the root of the lily* sleeps in its bed of earth, through all the

* This image cannot but be familiar to those, who have read the beautiful lines, on the lily, by the author of Psyche.

winter; and while many a storm blows over it, and while it sleeps as dead, and never puts forth a bud till spring-time comes—yet then the silken leaf bursts forth, in vegetative life and beauty—then it unfolds its snowy petals, in the vernal sun; and He who clothes it testifies that "*Even Solomon in all his glory, was not arrayed like one of these.*" So, dark, unpromising, and cheerless, may be the wintry season, in which the seed a parent's care and love has sown, may lie to all appearance dead in the cold and sterile heart; but He who can alone give vegetative life and power, who clothes the lilies of the field, and causeth the earth to bring forth and bud, can in His own spring-time speak the word; and then the blessing shall be given—and then the fruit of all the care and love shall appear—and then though years may have elapsed—yea, though the parent may never live to see the blessing here, though they may not see it even, till the morning of the resurrection; yet then, even then, the blessed fruit of a parent's anxious care and trouble, shall burst to light and life; and the seed sown in tears in time, shall spring up into glory for eternity. Therefore, "BRING THEM UP IN THE NURTURE AND ADMONITION OF THE LORD."

I forget where I read the story of a pious minister, a faithful servant of God, who had three sons, and he had taken great pains with these three sons, and he saw no fruit whatever, no blessing attending his labors; and they were a grief to him as long as he lived. He died, and all his sons came to visit him on his death-bed. They saw their father die. It pleased God that he should die under a cloud, his mind was not at liberty, he was not able to rejoice in the Lord Jesus Christ, with any sort of sensible joy, he was rather sad and depressed, and expired in this unjoyous frame of mind. His sons saw this, and while they were sitting in the room where their father's corpse was lying, one said to the others,

"If our father—such a man—such a servant of God as he was—if he has died without joy, without sensible consolation, how shall we meet death, Oh! what will become of us?"

God blessed that one solemn reflection, to the hearts of these three sons; and that which all the instruction of their father could not convey to them in all his life, the cloud that was thus sent a messenger of mercy, at his death, brought home to their consciences; and they were brought to think, and brought to repent, and brought to Christ, by seeing their father die, without comfort in the prospect of death. So go on, "*In the morning sow thy seed, and in the evening withhold not thine hand: for thou knowest not whether shall prosper, either this or that.*" Eccles. xi. 6. Thou canst not tell, whether God will bless it morning or evening; for He alone can do so. "*Cast thy bread upon the waters: for thou shalt find it after many days.*" Eccles. xi. 1. Go on, instruct your children, "BRING THEM UP IN THE NURTURE AND ADMONITION OF THE LORD," instruct them diligently in the truth, and keep them continually in mind of it.

There are a great variety of important truths connected with this sacred duty, which, if time permitted, I might bring under your consideration, and I hope you do not think we have dwelt too long on the subject. It is exactly the same with ministers as with parents, and every person who teaches divine truth. We are nothing—we have nothing—we know nothing—we can do nothing; but if we are enabled, in simplicity, to learn, to think, to speak, and to walk according to God's truth; God, who can do all things, can bless our humble efforts. He can both enable us to teach His truth, and He can bring home the truth we teach to our congregations, and the truths they teach, home to the hearts of their children.

I trust the Lord will bless these remarks to those who hear this day, and enable us to endeavor to bring up our children, or those who stand towards any of us in any similar relation, whether we are parents, guardians, or teachers, "IN THE NURTURE AND ADMONITION OF THE LORD."

May the Lord teach and help us to do so, and impress on our hearts the solemn responsibility of having God's Word as the standard of all instruction for ourselves, our children, and for our country.—Amen.

FORTY-FIFTH LECTURE.

EPHESIANS VI.—5, 6, 7.

"Servants be obedient to them that are your masters according to the flesh, with fear and trembling, in singleness of your heart, as unto Christ; not with eye-service, as men-pleasers; but as the servants of Christ, doing the will of God from the heart; with good will doing service, as to the Lord, and not to men."

WE come next to consider, the duty of Christian servants. "SERVANTS, BE OBEDIENT TO THEM THAT ARE YOUR MASTERS ACCORDING TO THE FLESH, WITH FEAR AND TREMBLING, IN SINGLENESS OF YOUR HEART AS UNTO CHRIST."

"*Verily, Godliness is profitable for all things, having promise of the life that now is, and of that which is to come.*" 1 Tim. iv. 7. Consider here, that the persons addressed in this are believers—true Christian servants; for these exhortations could not be addressed to any who were not servants of Christ. These words: "IN SINGLENESS OF YOUR HEART AS UNTO CHRIST." these, can only be addressed to those who belong to Christ. "*The saints and faithful brethren at Ephesus,*" whether husbands or wives masters or servants, parents or children, these are the persons addressed through this Epistle. It is as vain to press on unchristian servants, the discharge of their duties, on Christian principles, as on children, parents or masters, who are not Christians. You cannot enforce moral precepts on unconverted sinners, from Christian motives; they do not understand them—they cannot put them into practice. This is one of the reasons, while we are continually upbraided for it, why we do not enforce moral duties indiscriminately on our flocks. We know that a great proportion of those who hear us are not competent to perform moral duties. Moral duties they ought to perform, obedience to God's law is necessary—the first duty of man. But how false to flatter his pride, and strengthen him in his natural presumption and ignorance, by telling him that as a fallen sinner who has violated it, he can possibly be able to recover himself by its observance; or to delude him with the hope that he may be able to do so. I must repeat, if it were the thousandth time, that the first lesson to teach him is, that he is condemned under the law for not fulfilling it; and until he is brought out of that state of condemnation, through Him who died for the guilty, into a state of peace with God, he cannot perform one acceptable duty. You might as well tell a dead body to discharge the functions of life, as tell a dead soul to discharge the duties of a Christian. Therefore, I say whatever duties are enjoined, or whoever be the persons, masters or servants—you must be Christians, before you can act on Christian principles, or discharge one duty acceptably to God. Education will not make you Christians, outward instructions—means—ordinances—sacraments will not make you Christians, nothing can make you so, but the power and Spirit of God, bringing home the truth as it is in Jesus to your souls; then, when born again, when born of the Spirit, made children of God through faith in Jesus Christ, then, and not till then, you are Christians in spirit and in truth.

If we teach not thus, we are not faithful ministers of Christ. Therefore, if you are not at peace with God, if you are not looking to Jesus, as the rest and refuge of your souls, do not deceive yourselves, with the vain imagination, that you can ever advance one step, in the way of salvation, by your efforts, to perform the moral precepts of the law of God; you cannot do it—it is a way in which thousands and tens of thousands blind themselves, and go on blindly to eternal death, salving their consciences with their efforts to perform their duties to God, while they are really dead in trespasses and sins, unpardoned—without peace—without hope—without God in the world.

Therefore as this precept refers to servants, remember it must be to servants as believers in the Gospel, they must be servants of Christ, so I say that "*Godliness is profitable unto all things, having the promise of the life that now is, and of that which is to come.*" And Oh! what a blessed thing it is, if a Christian master have Christian servants! What a comfort it is to have a servant, whom you have good reason to know to be a child of God, so that you can regard them, not as a servant, but as a brother in

Christ, or a sister in Christ! what a blessed privilege it is to have those, as members of your household, who are "*Fellow-citizens with the saints, and of the household of God*," chap. ii. 19, to whom you are bound, in the bonds of Christian fellowship, and Christian love, with whom you hope to pass an eternity of blessedness as fellow servants of the King of kings. Therefore to such persons—to such servants as these, you see the command of God to discharge their duties, comes as a privilege and blessing. "SERVANTS, BE OBEDIENT TO THEM THAT ARE YOUR MASTERS, ACCORDING TO THE FLESH, WITH FEAR AND TREMBLING, IN SINGLENESS OF YOUR HEART AS UNTO CHRIST." Now here is an important truth brought before us, that the Gospel of Jesus, while it brings men in all relations of life, into the closest bond of Christian and brotherly union and love, and places them in one sense completely on a level before God, does not in the slightest degree break in upon, or dissolve the bond of social order. The child that is a Christian child, is a brother with his parents, they are brethren, they are one, they are united as brethren together in Christ. But the bonds of duty—the parental authority—the filial subjection are not in the least degree weakened by this, but rather strengthened, the subjection of obedience is strengthened. It is true indeed, it flows from love. The authority of the Christian parent is the authority of love—the obedience of the Christian child, is the obedience of love—but still, the duty remains unbroken. So again, the Christian servant—the Christian master or mistress—are brethren, they are sisters, they love one another, in the bonds of Christian fellowship. So the Apostle very beautifully sets before us in his Epistle to Philemon, where he speaks of Onesimus, his slave, who had run away, and whom the Apostle Paul sends to his master with this most beautiful Epistle, no longer now as a Pagan slave, but as a Christian brother, "*For perhaps, he therefore departed for a season, that thou shouldest receive him forever.*" How beautifully this shows that the very sins, into which the poor sinner falls, the Lord can make them, in His own wondrous providence, the means of bringing that sinner into his fold forever. His offence in running away as a fugitive slave from his master, by which, under the Roman law, he had forfeited his life, and deserved to be crucified—that very offence was overruled by God, as the means of bringing him within the reach of the Gospel of Christ, proclaimed to him by the Apostle Paul; and he sent him immediately back to his master, Philemon. See the effects of the Gospel; he had been a blind idolatrous Pagan—a fugitive slave—he hears the Gospel—God enlightens him to believe it—and then the first act of his life, is to discharge his duty to God and to his master, he sees his error—he acknowledges his sin; and the immediate effect of the Gospel, is to lead him to come directly back to his master, and to return to the discharge of his duty. Back he comes: but, Oh! what a change the Gospel has wrought in the relation between him and his master; so the Apostle saith, "*Perhaps he departed for a season, that thou shouldest receive him forever; not now as a servant, but above a servant, a brother beloved, specially to me, but how much more unto thee, both in the flesh and in the Lord,*" Philemon, 15, 16; especially beloved of me as my own child—my own son in the faith, but how much more of thee as his master so long, and now as his brother.

With what exquisite taste, if we may use the expression as applied to words of inspiration, does the Apostle write here to Philemon. There is not I will affirm within the whole compass of human language, a more perfect specimen of exquisitely eloquent and finished taste, than this Epistle of Paul. See how he embodies all the power of the love of the Gospel, in the sentiment in which he commends Onesimus to Philemon. "*Not now as a servant, but above a servant, a brother beloved, specially to me, but how much more unto thee, both in the flesh and in the Lord.*" You see then the Gospel does not dissolve the bonds of duty: therefore he saith to servants, "BE OBEDIENT TO THEM THAT ARE YOUR MASTERS, ACCORDING TO THE FLESH, WITH FEAR AND TREMBLING." He does not mean that they should be in a state of fear and trembling, or unhappiness in the service of their masters; but that they should have a respectful and humble fear, of both doing their duty, and offending against their master. For you see it is, "IN SINGLENESS OF HEART AS UNTO CHRIST." Which shows that as brotherhood does not dissolve the bonds of order and obedience, so that obedience does not dissolve the bonds of Christian love. The Christian love that necessarily springs up between master and servant, from their union in Christ does not dissolve nor relax the bond of subjection in the one, or authority in the other. So the Gospel does not, in any degree, tend to weaken the bonds of social order. This is a very great mistake, and much to be guarded against, when those in the humbler classes of life, think they may presume on their Christian fellowship, so as to forget the station which the Lord has been pleased to allot them. Or when those in the higher ranks of life, think that they should leave the duty of their appointed sphere, so as to abandon the position in which it has pleased God to place them. Such principles are in flat contradiction to the whole course and tenor of the Scriptures, both in the Old and New Testament. God is the Author of order, and not of confusion. Society is held together by order. Government—both in public and domestic authority, and subjection in all stations of life, the Gospel does not dissolve, but strengthens and establishes in them all; and as in this passage, in all the relative duties, makes the discharge of those duties, both in authority and subjection, a test and evidence of the conduct and character of a Christian, to his Heavenly Master.

Whenever there is a departure from this, there is a departure from the Word of God. Therefore you see, when Satan sets up a system of irreligion, and when you see a contempt of religion in the world, you see also that contempt of religion, accompanied with a contempt of order—of discipline—of authority and subjec tion. So you see, at this moment, that is the very principle that is threatening to dissolve the framework of society, striking at the very root of all social order; and tending to bring on that time, which I believe is nearer than we think: of which our Lord tells us, such a time was not since the world was, and never shall be. You see a tendency to the confusion, the awful confusion, the tremendous anarchy that shall precede the outpouring of God's judgments, throughout the world at this very moment, in that very principle, that authority is to be despised and trampled on—men are, as they call it, to govern themselves—the government of man, as the institution of God, is to be abolished—and the government and authority of Jehovah's Word is to be made light of, and abandoned.

You see, in every part of Scripture, that principle is completely opposed by the authority of God. Here, in families, when you see individuals brought together, masters and servants, in the common bond of Christian love—you perceive they are especially commanded, to discharge their duties to each other, as Christian brethren, and you see that order, subjection and authority are to be carefully preserved—the servant's duty is to preserve his subjection; as the master's duty is to preserve his authority, but both as unto Christ, "BE OBEDIENT UNTO YOUR MASTERS, IN SINGLENESS OF YOUR HEART, AS UNTO CHRIST."

Now you see what a principle of obedience is here given, and let us recollect that in all our relations in life we are to be in subjection. Every one is in subjection—we must be so. Children are in subjection to their parents—servants are in subjection to their masters—masters and families are also in subjection to all the constituted authorities, and therefore, the principle of obedience is to be the same in all. It is to be in all "IN SINGLENESS OF HEART AS UNTO CHRIST."

There is one single principle that should regulate and govern the sinner's heart, and that is this, that he should discharge his duty to his fellow man as unto his God. It is not because he desires to please man, it is not because he desires to flatter or gratify man, but because he desires to serve and please his God in singleness of heart. There should not be any mixture of motives. A mixture of motives generally leads to expediency. If servants wish to please their masters, to court their favor, then "*the fear of man bringeth a snare*," and if their masters or mistresses be persons who have not the fear of God before their eyes, to please them, would be perhaps to displease God; therefore that would lead a servant to shuffling in his duty to God, it would lead him to a sort of compromise in which he would not have a single eye to his Heavenly but to his earthly master. It is a system of pleasing man that leads men in all stations of life to accord with ungodly and unchristian policy, they have not a single eye, a single heart, they do not desire to serve God, Jehovah's service is not the object at which they aim, but pleasing men, therefore, "*the fear of man bringeth a snare*,' and also bringeth a curse:

for the result is, that God is thrown off, and man is set up as the ruler of the heart, and the being to be pleased. Whenever that is the case, contempt and misery must follow, in all stations in life, from a family to an empire.

"IN SINGLENESS OF HEART AS UNTO CHRIST," that is the standard for every one, by which to regulate their duties, in all situations. I have known Christian servants, who did their duty "IN SINGLENESS OF HEART AS UNTO CHRIST."

I have known Christian servants, to deal faithfully with their masters; and refuse to do what was contrary to the will of God, I have known them to set a faithful example to their masters, because they could not please them, without disobeying the will of God. I had a servant once myself, whom God was pleased to bring to the knowledge of His Gospel, in my service, with whom circumstances obliged me very reluctantly to part. He hired afterwards into the family of an English gentleman of property, and lost an excellent situation, as far as emolument was concerned; because, when his master went to London, he peremptorily refused to say, that he or his mistress were not at home, when he knew they were. They foolishly lost a servant who did his duty to them as unto God. And what a blessed thing it is when a servant has that principle in his heart! So if we have that singleness of heart, if we desire to please God, our object, our heart's desire will be to serve Him and to serve any authority under which we are placed, in singleness of heart as unto Christ.

Then you see what a blessing the Gospel brings to servants in the discharge of their duties, "NOT WITH EYE SERVICE AS MEN PLEASERS," not merely when your master's or mistress's eye is over you, but as unto God. A child or a servant that is merely a man-pleaser will do what they think they ought to do, if the eye of the parent or master is over them; but as soon as that eye is withdrawn, there is no influence to make them do their duty, they idle, they will not do what they ought to do. But where God is set up in the heart, when they are brought to believe the Gospel, and are become children of God through faith in Jesus Christ, then it is "NOT WITH EYE SERVICE AS MEN PLEASERS," it is not because their parent's eye or their master's eye is over them—but they will do their duty, "AS THE SERVANTS OF CHRIST WITH GOOD WILL, DOING THE WILL OF GOD FROM THE HEART."

That is the promise of the Lord, Psalm xxxii., where he saith, "*I will guide thee with mine eye.*" When the believer cometh to Christ and saith, "*Thou art my hiding place, thou shalt preserve me from trouble, thou shalt compass me about with songs of deliverance;*" Psalm xxxii. 7. Then as much as to say, "Dost thou come unto me?—Then thou shalt not come in vain"—The Lord answereth, "*I will instruct thee and teach thee in the way wherein thou shalt go, I will guide thee with mine eye,*" Psalm xxxii. 8; or, as the margin reads it, "*I will counsel thee, mine eye shall be upon thee.*" A servant, who is a man-pleaser, will do his service for his master; or a child, who is a man-pleaser, will obey the command of his parent, just when the eye of the master or parent is upon them. But when the believer remembers that promise, "*I will guide thee with mine eye*," or, "mine eye shall be upon thee," that is, "Thou shalt remember that thy Lord is looking on thee, thou shalt remember thou art pleasing me, serving me,"—then this leads him to serve, "IN SINGLENESS OF HEART AS UNTO CHRIST,"—this leads him to "DO THE WILL OF GOD FROM THE HEART." For he remembers that the eye that looks on him, was closed in death for him—that blessed head was bowed in death for his salvation—that glorious Lord, to whom he runs, as to a hiding place, is the same who hath loved him, and given Himself for him. So the eye that guides, is the eye of his Redeemer. He is not his own—he is bought with a price, and that price was that Redeemer's precious blood.

Therefore, Oh! believer, remember thy Lord's eye is over thee, thy Redeemer's eye is following thee, thy Shepherd's eye is watching thee, and then thou shalt go on, not with eye service, as pleasing man, but heartily as unto God even as the servants of Christ.

You see what security this gives for obedience, universal obedience, and willing obedience.

For universal obedience.—Because wherever the sinner is, when he is enabled to remember that his Lord is near, there he remembers the principle of his duty.—What is that principle?—Love.

Therefore his obedience is a willing obedience.—If a parent or master is loved, they will be willingly obeyed, but then mere earthly affection is fleeting, fickle, selfish, and therefore, that love is at best very unequal and inoperative; for although a child may love a parent, or a servant a master, they love themselves more, the selfish love of the heart is stronger than their love to others. But where "*the love of God is shed abroad in our hearts by the Holy Ghost, which is given unto us*," Rom. v. 5, this draws out the sinner's love to his Lord, then there is "GOOD WILL, DOING SERVICE, AS TO THE LORD, AND NOT TO MEN." There is universal obedience, for the Lord is everywhere—and willing obedience, for it is the obedience of love—and that, not to man but unto God.

What a blessing then it is, to cultivate our privileges! God is graciously pleased to make the correlative duties of this life, and the discharge of those duties, a blessing to us. And thus the Lord makes the exertion of a Christian master or mistress, who faithfully labors for the salvation and enlightening of their servants, the means of conferring important blessings upon themselves! Not that this is a Christian's motive—it is no part of the motive—but I only say, that the Lord does make the correlative duties of life a blessing, to those who faithfully discharge them.

There are not many here, in the situation of servants; but I address masters and mistresses. Now I ask you, do you take pains, to instruct your servants in the things that belong to their eternal peace, so that the principles of their obedience may be Christian principles? Do you endeavor to instruct your family in the Word of God? Have you family prayer? Have you the worship of God in your household? If you have, do you merely go through it as a sort of duty? Do you call your servants into prayer—and having so done, and having certain duties performed, morning and evening, do you then think no more about it? Or do you really endeavor to impress the Word of God upon the hearts of those who are members of your household?

Consider, you have a most solemn duty to discharge. You have a great responsibility laid upon you. Why are you in the situation of master or mistress? Why has God been pleased to place you in a sphere of life, in which you can have persons to serve you, instead of being yourselves servants? Who hath made the difference between you and the servant of your household?—between you and the beggar in the street? "*Who maketh thee to differ from another*," in temporal things as well as spiritual? Why were you born in a sphere of life in which you can employ others, instead of being put into a sphere of life in which you should labor for your bread? God has placed you there, and God has given you means, opportunities, and talents, and you are responsible to Him for them. He has given you additional talents, and additional responsibilities, if you know the Gospel of Christ. You know there is a heavy responsibility laid on your soul, that you should endeavor to instruct those who are placed under your care—that you should endeavor to lead them to the knowledge of Christ. Has He led you to the knowledge of Himself that you should be careless of others?—that you should be careless of the eternal salvation of your fellow-sinners, even of those who are placed in your household? Oh! consider this! How shall you answer to God, if you neglect your duty? How can you expect others to discharge their duty to you, when you neglect your duty to them? Are you occupying the sphere in which God has placed you, if you leave those around you uninstructed, untaught in His holy Word?

What wonder is it, that those who call themselves Christians—Protestants—are in such a wretched miserable state as they are, when there is such a total failure in the discharge of their duty to God, and their duties to their fellow-men!

There are many persons—many of our poor fellow-sinners, Roman Catholics, who think it is a dangerous thing to read the Bible without the interpretation of their church—it is a sealed book to them. But, alas! what multitudes there are who speak of the Bible—who boast that it is their rule of faith—who vaunt that it is their privilege, as Protestants, to read the Sacred Volume, and that it is the standard of their Church, and so on. But, alas! it is neither the standard of their faith and hope, nor of their lives and practice. It is not the standard of the instruction they wish to receive themselves, nor to convey to others. What use are their boasted privileges to them? They are nothing but an increase of judgment, an accumulating weight of guilt and condemnation on their heads.

An awful responsibility is laid on those, who make a profession of the true religion, in this country. I firmly believe, if God does not pour out a spirit of repentance, and of a deep sense of our great responsibility upon us—if we do not make an effort to discharge our duty faithfully before our God—I do believe, the awful retributive sentence for our neglect, will be poured out in judgment on the head of this country; and on none more than on the masters and mistresses, who bear the name of Protestants, who neglect to instruct those around them, and dependent on them, tenderly, faithfully, sincerely, and affectionately, in the word of God. Think what a blessing it is, if we are brought to know the privilege of masters and servants being Christians—being all servants of God. If we knew the value of the principles of the Gospel for our own souls, we would surely be desirous to communicate that Gospel to our fellow-sinners. We must be so. Think then, Oh! think of your privileges—your responsibilities—and your duties—lay them to heart. If there be any of you whose conscience testifies that you neglect them, consider what I have been saying to you to-day; your conscience tells you it is true. Begin now, make it a subject of prayer. Do you know the value of Christ, for your own soul? Then if so, endeavor to communicate the knowledge of the Lord Jesus Christ to all your household—to your children—to your servants—to all your poor dependants. Reflect what opportunities you have, and, consider what a blessing, what a glorious privilege it is, to be instrumental in leading one sinner, to the Lord Jesus Christ. See how Paul rejoices over Philemon, and over Onesimus his runaway slave. When Paul was a prisoner, the Lord brought this poor slave to him, by His gracious providence, and brought him by the Apostle's instrumentality to himself; and the Holy Ghost inspired and preserves on record this letter to Philemon, this blessed letter, about this poor slave in this book; and shall we profess to call ourselves Christians, and say we have no regard for the souls of our servants?

If I address any servants here, what a blessed privilege you have, if you be indeed Christians, to be exhorted thus to your duty, "NOT WITH EYE SERVICE AS MEN PLEASERS; BUT AS THE SERVANTS OF CHRIST." Oh! think what a privilege it is, to be the servant of Christ! a servant of the King of kings! Persons may be poor and humble servants—in a poor and humble station; but then if they are servants of the Living God—Oh! what a glorious privilege it is!—How often are servants anxious "to better themselves" as their phrase is, and to think if they could get out of their present master's service, and get into a higher place, with more wages, they would be better, and that the higher they get, the better they are. How sadly disappointed do they often find themselves. But Oh! if a servant is a servant of the King of kings, and Lord of lords, this is indeed the highest privilege to be attained; to be a servant of Christ, is to be higher than the kings of the earth—a servant of Christ, is in His glorious time to be a king—to have a crown of glory "incorruptible, undefiled, and that fadeth not away."

Whose servant are you? Oh! if the person is able to answer, "I trust I am a servant of the Living God." Or who is your master? If he can say the Lord—the Lord of lords—what state, what throne on earth, is equal to a station such as this—what dominion in the compass of the world is equal to that blessed privilege, to be "SERVANTS OF CHRIST, DOING THE WILL OF GOD FROM THE HEART."

Then, what a burden it takes off our heart, when we are enabled to serve God—when, whatever we do, we desire to do it to the Lord; we do not care whether this person or another person is looking on us—we care not, we regard not the inspection of man. Our Heavenly Master who saith, "*I will guide thee with mine eye*," is watching over us, and it is therefore our desire to do our duty to our God. If this be so, our duty will be done—joyfully done. The child will not say,—"My parent's eye is over me"—the servant will not say,—"My master is watching me." It is enough to say—"My Lord's eye is over me—I am desiring to serve my God, my Heavenly Master." When this is the case, what a burden then, I say, it takes off the heart. We care not to please men—but simply desire in singleness of heart to serve our Lord and Master. How this relieves our heart from irksome toil! Duty is no longer a burden, it is our privilege, our pleasure. The service of God constitutes our happiness.

This is what David says,—"*I will walk at liberty*"—do you remember the reason he gives? "*For I seek thy precepts*," Psalm cxix. 43. "*I will walk at liberty, for I seek thy precepts.*" I desire to do thy will, and therefore I walk at liberty. "*He that committeth sin is the servant of sin;*" when we have a task that we do not like to perform, but desire to do something else, and yet are obliged to do that task—that is the greatest slavery in the world. But when the task is one we lay out for ourselves to do, that we wish to do—that we delight to do—then it is no more a task, it is a pleasure—we are free—we freely do what we wish to do—and when what we wish to do is our duty, the obligation to duty is freedom. The coincidence of will and duty is the highest happiness and liberty of man.

That man is always free, who desires to serve the Lord. Oh! what a blessed privilege it is! Think of this, and your hearts will be set at liberty when you are brought to serve your God. You will obey in every station of subjection, "NOT WITH EYE SERVICE AS MEN PLEASERS, BUT AS THE SERVANTS OF CHRIST, DOING THE WILL OF GOD FROM THE HEART."

And now, dear friends, though we may not be servants, there are many relations in which we may seek to discharge our duties, striving to please others, and so far as this is according to the Lord's will, it is well to do so; but in whatever sphere of life we are, if we have "SINGLENESS OF HEART AS UNTO CHRIST," then our duty becomes our privilege, and it is the truest enjoyment of our lives.

Then what a blessing it is, in all our different relations—in our different spheres of life—if, instead of seeking to change or alter them—we remember, we are just in the sphere in which God has placed us. The natural mind is forever saying, like a discontented servant, "If I was in other circumstances—in a different condition from that in which I am—then I would discharge my duty better." This, as we considered on a former occasion, is a delusion of the enemy of our souls—he wishes to make us murmur. We are in the sphere, in which the Lord has placed us. Let us remember this, if we be His children, then in singleness of heart, let us serve our God. Depend on it, it is in His service, and not in any peculiar station of life, that true happiness is to be found. I trust you see, there is an important lesson to be derived by all, from these instructions to servants, because you perceive that the same principle is carried out into every situation, "WITH GOOD WILL, DOING SERVICE AS UNTO THE LORD, AND NOT UNTO MEN, KNOWING THAT WHATSOEVER GOOD THING ANY MAN DOTH, THE SAME SHALL HE RECEIVE OF THE LORD, WHETHER HE BE BOND OR FREE." We shall have to consider more on this subject, and refer more to the duties of masters and servants.

May the Lord apply what has been said to all our hearts, that we may be enabled in every situation of life, in all our stations, whether of subjection or authority, to have a single eye to the Lord's glory, to please all who are placed in authority over us, so far as our service may consist with the service of our God! that is the scope and boundary of all human obedience, and of the happiness of man!

FORTY-SIXTH LECTURE.

EPHESIANS VI.—7, 8, 9, 10.

"With good will doing service, as to the Lord, and not to men: knowing that whatsoever good thing any man doeth, the same shall he receive of the Lord, whether he be bond or free. And, ye masters, do the same things unto them, forbearing threatening: knowing that your Master also is in heaven; neither is there respect of persons with him. Finally, my brethren, be strong in the Lord, and in the power of his might."

WE resume in the 7th verse the subject of the Apostle's exhortation to servants, "WITH GOOD WILL DOING SERVICE, AS TO THE LORD, AND NOT TO MEN." How different true religion is, from every form of that which is false! not more different in the principles which it inculcates; than in the doctrine it teaches—not more different, in the motives it implants, than in the opposition that there is between the Gospel, which proclaims salvation freely to sinners, through the "*Redemption that is in Christ Jesus*," and all the various religions of man, which under every shape and form, set up the false and wicked principle, that man is to be saved by something which he is to do for his own soul. True religion, is not more different as opposed to all false systems, in any other point, than it is in this; that the practical principles of genuine obedience to God, are brought by it into the heart and conduct of man, in every relation of life. Every unconverted sinner takes up his religion, at certain stated times, whether he be, for example, Protestant or Roman Catholic. When the time comes, for going to his place of worship, then, that is his time for his religion—he will go there. When the time comes, for going to the sacrament —he will go there. When the time comes for going to any stated public ordinance, he will go there. Perhaps, if he carries his religion a little farther than some persons, he may have stated times for family prayer. Every true servant of God ought to have family worship; but several have family worship, who are not servants of God; but all such individuals, as soon as their religious exercise whatever it be, is over—as soon as they quit their church —their stated public ordinance—their stated form, for the time—then their religion is over, then they go back to the world again. While he is in the world, he is of the world. While he is at his religion, he is religious. When he is serving God, as he calls it—then that is his time for serving God, that is the time for this occupation—Then, when this is over, the rest of his time is for business—pleasure—enjoyment, there is a time for everything, he says, whatever it be, and quotes the book of Ecclesiastes, to support him. While engaged in the duties of religion—that is the time for religion; but when engaged in his business or amusement, religion is not to intrude there, that is not the place for religion, religion would be gloomy there.

If you speak to a man who is ignorant of the Gospel, he will say, "Oh, surely, one cannot be always thinking of these things, we must be doing our business sometimes. I really have not time to be always talking of religion." Another person will say, "Oh, this is no time for such solemn subjects, there is a time for everything, everything in its proper place." This is the language of the unregenerate heart.

Now, true religion is not more different from this ignorance, in principle, than in practice; because it brings its principles into all times, circumstances, occupations, and relations of life. Wherever a man is, if he is indeed a servant of God, his religion is with him. Whatever he is occupied about, whatever time he is engaged in other services, that is the time for his religion too. He has no business with anything, where he cannot have his God with him. He has no business in the discharge of any duty in which the service of his God, is not the principle on which that duty is to be discharged. There is not a more certain truth than this, that a man who is not truly religious at all times, is never truly religious at any time. Religion is an inseparable part of the character of the believer. It is an occasional part of the occupation of an unregenerate sinner. The religion of such a man is like the assumed loyalty of a rebel, he acts the part at certain stated times, and for certain purposes, and when the performance of the part is over, he returns to his natural character: a man who is really loyal, will have his loyalty in his heart, in his own home, as much as in the palace of his sovereign.

Now, my dear friends, consider this. See how religion is brought in this chapter, into all the relations of life, the husband—the wife—the parent—the child—the master—the servant.—On what principles are all the relative duties to be performed? On the principle of love to their God. God is to regulate the duties, between husband and wife—between parents and children—between masters and servants—between friend and friend—between neighbor and neighbor. God is to be the Regulator of all their conduct in all religious, political, social, and domestic relations.

When this is really the principle of the heart, there you see true religion; so that as for instance, in the relation of which we are speaking to-day, whatever the servant is doing, no matter what it is, no matter how he is occupied, if he is employed in the most trivial or menial occupation, whatever it be, he is to remember this principle: "WITH GOOD WILL DOING SERVICE AS TO THE LORD, AND NOT TO MEN." This is the word of Him who "*Took upon Him the form of a servant*," Phil. ii. 7, for our sakes—this is the word of Him, in whom there was no sin, who says, "*I have set the Lord always before me: because He is at my right hand, I shall not be moved.*" Psalm xvi. 8. Mark then, how impossible, how utterly impossible it is to bring this principle into operation in any heart, except the heart of a genuine Christian. When we are afraid that God is angry with us—when we are at enmity with God—when we are striving and working like slaves, to save our souls—when we blindly imagine, that the good which we think we do on one occasion, atones for the sins and omissions of another, or makes us acceptable with God—when therefore we hate God, because our conscience tells us, we have not done enough even to satisfy our own convictions—when this is our religion, and this is the religion of every unconverted man, how can we bring this principle into practice? Impossible! totally impossible! This is the reason why, when an unconverted man has done with the business of religion, he has done with God for the day. Therefore, love to God is never brought as a practical principle or motive, into his life. Christ must first be in our heart, and dwell in our heart. "*The love of Christ constraineth us*," saith the Apostle, 2nd Cor. v. 14, we must have "*Peace with God, through our Lord Jesus Christ*," Rom. v. 1. We must be able to look to God, as a reconciled God and Father in Christ; and then the service of God is easy; "*Take my yoke upon you*," saith Christ, "*my yoke is easy, and my burden is light,*" Mat. xi. 29, 30. Why is it easy? Because it is a yoke of love. A yoke of love is always light. We can bear any burden, when we are harnessed to it, so to speak, with a yoke of love. So Christ saith, in those verses, "*Take my yoke upon you and learn of me, for I am meek and lowly in heart; and ye shall find rest unto your souls, for my yoke is easy and my burden is light.*" Therefore, when we love Christ, we can have Him in our hearts, our thoughts, and whatever our service be, to our fellow men, we know and feel the principle: "WITH GOOD WILL DOING SERVICE, AS UNTO THE LORD AND NOT UNTO MEN," and the Apostle gives a general principle, as a reason, "KNOWING, THAT WHATSOEVER GOOD THING ANY MAN DOETH, THE SAME SHALL HE RECEIVE OF THE LORD, WHETHER HE BE BOND OR FREE."

Now, we have here a principle brought before us, which is important for us to consider. "KNOWING THAT WHATSOEVER GOOD THING ANY MAN DOETH, THE SAME SHALL HE RECEIVE OF THE LORD, WHETHER HE BE BOND OR FREE."

Now, an objection arises immediately, in the mind of the unenlightened sinner. "Do not you see here," he says, "we are to receive for every good thing we do, and if we are to receive for every good thing we do, how can you say, that the good things we do are not essential to our salvation? Are not these the words—" WHATSOEVER GOOD THING ANY MAN DOETH, THE SAME SHALL HE RECEIVE OF THE LORD, WHETHER HE BE BOND OR FREE?"

This brings us again to the principle which I so often endeavor to impress upon your mind, that you must consider to whom this is addressed. Do you mean to draw a conclusion from this, that the Apostle is here speaking to unconverted men; and that therefore, whatsoever good thing unconverted men do, they shall receive of God? I answer to that, there is no such thing in the Bible, as an unconverted man doing any good thing, for it is written of the whole race: "*There is none that doeth good, no not one.*" Psalm xiv. 3. It is expressly declared, "*They that are in the flesh, cannot please God.*" Rom. viii. 8. "*Without me*" saith Christ, "*ye can do nothing.*" John xv. 5. And that is one of the means, whereby sinners blind themselves continually, in reading the Scripture, they do not consider to whom the various parts of Scripture are addressed. Look again at this Epistle. To whom is it addressed? "*To the saints which are at Ephesus, and to the faithful in Christ Jesus.*" Chap. i. Read again what we have gone over as to their spiritual state. "*Blessed be the God and Father of our Lord Jesus Christ, who hath blessed us with all spiritual blessings, in heavenly places in Christ, according as he hath chosen us in Him, before the foundation of the world, that we should be holy and without blame before Him in love, having predestinated us unto the adoption of children by Jesus Christ to himself, according to the good pleasure of His will, to the praise of the glory of His grace, wherein He hath made us accepted in the beloved, in whom we have redemption through His blood, the forgiveness of sins according to the riches of His grace.*" Chap. i. 3—7. Such was their state—now look at their faith. "*In whom ye also trusted, after that ye heard the word of truth, the Gospel of your salvation, in whom also after that ye believed, ye were sealed with the Holy Spirit of promise.*" Chap. i. 13. Again see their former and present state: "*God who is rich in mercy, for His great love wherewith He loved us, even when we were dead in sins, hath quickened us together with Christ, by grace ye are saved, and hath raised us up together, and made us sit together in heavenly places in Christ, that in the ages to come He might show the exceeding riches of His grace, in His kindness to us by Christ Jesus. For by grace are ye saved through faith, and that not of yourselves, it is the gift of God, not of works, lest any man should boast.*" Chap. ii. 4—9.

Look through all the Epistle, see what characters these persons were: and here is all the difference, between the moral duties impressed on him who is a servant of God; and the vain ideas that men who are not His servants conceive of their own powers. How can another man's servant do the work of your house? no more can he who is a servant of Satan, do the work of God. Our Lord is explicit on this point: "*No man can serve two masters, for either he will hate the one, and love the other, or else he will hold to the one, and despise the other, ye cannot serve God and mammon.*" Matt. vi. 24.

Works are throughout the Scripture, declared to be the test of man's salvation, "*We must all appear before the judgment seat of Christ, that every one may receive the things done in the body, according to that he hath done, whether it be good or bad.*" This is the universal testimony of the Scripture. Works are declared to be the test of man's salvation, before God and before man. But works that men call good, or that are comparatively so, no more can purchase man's salvation, than those that confessedly are wicked. Let us come to facts, and examine the principle. Who for example, will deny, that honesty is better than theft—truth than falsehood—sobriety than drunkenness—liberality than covetousness? But these virtues can no more save, or help to save the soul, than the vices that are opposed to them; because the man who is most honest, most true, most sober, and most liberal on earth, is still a sinner before God—he can no more stand the test of God's law, than the man whose character is most opposite to his own, the best he can do must condemn him, if God were to enter into judgment with him. He must fly to the Blood of his Redeemer, as his ransom; and to the righteousness of his Redeemer, as his only merit.

But here is the point. The believer, accepted—justified—acquitted—"accounted righteous before God, only for the merits of our Lord Jesus Christ, by faith, and not for his own works or deservings"—Art. x., washed from all his sins, by the precious blood, and clothed in the full merit of the spotless righteousness of Christ —standing complete in Christ—pure and accepted in Him—

"*Without spot or wrinkle, or any such thing*" is brought into the glorious relationship of acceptance, adoption and sonship, with his God. Then the works of that man are done entirely on a new principle—the whole of his morals are transported to a new foundation—not one act is done to save his soul, he never performs a work with the hope that it can save him, or deliver him from hell, he never does an act to appease the wrath of God; his whole hope, all his joy, and all his salvation is this, that Christ has wrought salvation for him. What then is his principle of action? Love to his Lord. He loves his Lord, and therefore he serves him. Hence his works are necessarily taken, as the test of judgment of his soul—as the genuine proof of his being a servant of God. This is the motive given to His disciples, by the Lord Jesus Christ: "*If you love me, keep my commandments,*" John xiv. 15. Hence too he saith, "*Whosoever shall give you a cup of water to drink, because ye belong to Christ, verily I say unto you, he shall not lose his reward.*" Mark ix. 41.

Now, mark this. There is not an unconverted sinner on earth, that ever did, or ever will give, as much as a cup of cold water, to another fellow-sinner, because he belongs to Christ. A man that does not believe the Gospel, has not the slightest notion of any such relationship, as that of belonging to Christ, nor of any such principle of conduct. Such men may give food, raiment, money, to their fellow-creatures; and many of them do so largely, liberally, abundantly. But why? Some of them do it, that it may help to obtain salvation, in their ignorant perversion of the text that "*Charity covereth a multitude of sins,*" because they think they are to be rewarded for it. Some because they are of a liberal, generous disposition. Some from feelings of compassion, to relieve the wants of the poor—there are various motives. But to give it to a fellow-sinner, a fellow-disciple, "*because they belong to Christ,*" and from love to Christ, such a principle never entered their head—they could not do it—they have no idea, not the slightest conception of that bond of union, that unites the disciples of Jesus to each other, and to all their fellow-sinners. "*Because they belong to Christ!*"—nay, that is very often the reason why a man, ignorant of the Gospel, would turn such a person away from his door; they would perhaps call them, or at least consider them methodists, canters, hypocrites, yea, even those who were generous and kind to worthless characters, who would give charity to others abundantly, would do so. I remember well when such were my own feelings—I hated what I thought a hypocritical affectation, of being more religious than others. All men who are ignorant of the Gospel, dislike the religion of Christ. They cannot endure to hear it asserted that all their charity, and all their gifts, and all they can possibly bestow, can do nothing for their salvation, that "*all their righteousnesses are as filthy rags*" before God, unable to cover the nakedness of their poor souls; and that they can afford them no ground of hope, before the bar of Christ. Their real opinion and principle is, that their works are to be adduced, for the justification of their persons, instead of the proof of their faith, as being justified by the Lord Jesus. They do not like, nay, they hate that doctrine.* They do not like to be told, much less do they know, that they "*are wretched, and miserable, and poor, and blind, and naked,*" Rev. iii. 17. They will not hear Christ's counsel, "*I counsel thee to buy of me gold tried in the fire, that thou mayest be rich; and white raiment, that thou mayest be clothed, and that the shame of thy nakedness do not appear.*" Rev. iii. 18. They know not, alas! that the only hope of their acceptance must be, the righteousness and blood of the crucified and risen Saviour. Therefore, all such persons so far from gaining a reward for all their morality and all their religion, are merely whitewashing the sepulchre of a blind, unrenewed, proud, ignorant, self-righteous heart. Such were all the works of the Pharisees in our Lord's day; and such are the works of every Pharisee, from the day of our Lord to the present moment. But such works can never stand the test of God's judgment, because the whole principle on which they are done is false. Love to Christ is no part of their motive—they know not for what to love Him—they are afraid of Him, and tremble at the very thought of His coming. And such works, so far from being adduced as a test of their faith, the very motive of their performance is a proof of their unbelief. They do not prove the soul to be in a state of salvation, but they prove it to be in a state of condemnation; to be alienated from God and in utter ignorance of Him.

But not so, the believer, "KNOWING, THAT WHATSOEVER GOOD THING ANY MAN DOETH, THE SAME SHALL HE RECEIVE OF THE LORD, WHETHER HE BE BOND OR FREE." There is not a single act done by such a servant of God; there is not a single work done from love to his Master, however small it be, that the Lord does not receive, accept and reward; and therefore eternal life is spoken of in that sense as a reward. "*God is not unrighteous to forget your work and labor of love, which you have showed for his name sake, in that ye have ministered to the Saints, and yet do minister.*" Heb. vi. 10. But observe this, that in order to make it a work of this character, the principle of the work is, that so far from thinking it good, the believer considers it defiled and worthless, and not fit to be named in the presence of God; the best thing he could do, he brings to be washed in the blood of the Lamb. Therefore, whatever he does, whatever labor he goes through, whatever alms he bestows, whatever he does for his fellow-creatures, or for his God, in his own estimation of it, it is, as indeed in itself it is, vile and worthless, and not fit to be presented in the presence of his God. He feels that he must cast it all into the fountain

* This is the very vital essence of Popery, their whole religion is built on the antichristian principle; that man is to be justified by his works, moral, ceremonial, sacramental, penitential, &c. Hence, the whole system is antichristian; whether the word is taken as implying that which is opposed to Christ, or put in the place of Christ; and this is the foundation of the whole Tractarian heresy—hatred of the fundamental principle of the Gospel, that a sinner is justified only and fully, by the righteousness and blood of our glorious, and ever blessed Redeemer.

opened for sin and uncleanness, and that it must be washed in the blood of his Redeemer. This is the principle of the believer for all his works.

We see this clearly illustrated in Matthew xxv., where our blessed Lord brings forward all the nations as arrayed on His right hand and on His left, on the day when He shall come in judgment, "*When the Son of man shall come in his glory, and all the Holy Angels with him; then shall he sit upon the throne of his glory, and before him shall be gathered all nations, and he shall separate them one from another, as a shepherd divideth the sheep from the goats, and he shall set the sheep on his right hand but the goats on the left. Then shall the King say unto them on his right hand, come ye blessed of my Father, inherit the kingdom prepared for you from the foundation of the world.*" Now mark, he makes their works the test and proof of their salvation,—"*For I was an hungered, and ye gave me meat: I was thirsty, and ye gave me drink: I was a stranger, and ye took me in: naked, and ye clothed me: I was in prison, and ye came unto me.*"

Now, observe the answer of the righteous: "*Then shall the righteous answer him saying, Lord, when saw we thee an hungered, and fed thee? or thirsty, and gave thee drink? when saw we thee a stranger, and took thee in? naked, and clothed thee? or when saw we thee sick, or in prison, and came unto thee?*" So far from bringing forward anything that they have done as the ground of their hope; they are not conscious that they have done anything for their Lord; and they ask, "When did we do so?" Our Lord replies, "*Verily I say unto you, Inasmuch as you have done it unto one of the least of these my brethren, ye have done it unto me.*" You have evinced your love to me in your love to the least of these my brethren. So far from having the slightest hope, the slightest confidence in anything that they have done, they think they have done nothing; but the Lord himself brings forward their works as the manifestation of their character as His servants, and adduces their love of Him evinced in their conduct to the humblest of his disciples, as a test and proof of the sinner's acceptance before God; because it is a test of his love to his Lord and Master, and therefore of that "*Faith which worketh by love,*" Gal. v. 6. Therefore, the Apostle says, "*If any man love not the Lord Jesus Christ, let him be Anathema Maran-atha,*" 1st Cor. xvi. 22. Now, no man can love the Lord Jesus Christ, but the sinner that knows Him as the Refuge and Salvation of his soul. You see every portion of divine truth brings us back to the simple, "*Truth as it is in Jesus.*" We must resolve all pure light of doctrinal and moral truth into the glorious effulgence of the Sun of Righteousness; as all the light that illuminates and vivifies the earth, converges to the glorious orb of day.

If our views are clear on the simple principles of Divine truth, the Bible is an unsealed and open book to us; and if we are blind and ignorant of these, it is all shut; it is a sealed book to us. We are all confused and dark in every point of doctrine and every principle of morals. Therefore, how important it is in reading the Apostolical Epistles, and perceiving works enforced on the hearts and consciences of Christians—How important it is to keep in view, that persons there so addressed are Christians in spirit and truth.

Do not say, "Oh! we are all Christians."

None of you are so, if you are not brought to Christ: you have a name to live, but you are dead—you are not Christians in spirit and in truth, if you are not really looking unto Jesus. If you are not washed in the blood and clothed in the righteousness of the Lord Jesus Christ. If you are looking to yourselves—to your own righteousness, you are yet in your sins—you "*have neither part nor lot in this matter*," Acts viii. 21.

Consider this, Oh! consider it diligently—meditate on it—examine it—pray over it—lay it to heart. May the Lord enable us all to do so! May we consider these great truths—for these are the only truths to live by, and to die by, "*Looking unto Jesus.*" And if we are indeed looking unto Him, then let us know, "THAT WHATSOEVER GOOD THING ANY MAN DOETH, THE SAME SHALL HE RECEIVE OF THE LORD, WHETHER HE BE BOND OR FREE." It is stated, that for every good thing any man doeth, he shall receive a reward. But you see, that the object of receiving the reward, is not the motive for his action; it is his privilege to know that when he is indeed "*Looking unto Jesus,*" the Lord forgets nothing that he does—He neither forgets his sins to blot them out, nor his humblest services to reward them; so that the believer may rejoice in thinking, that if it be but a cup of cold water given to a disciple in the name of the Lord, it shall in no wise lose its reward.

Therefore, let no one, if he is ever so humble or poor say, alas! I can do but little. Remember, that the poorest believer in the world, laboring in the humblest sphere, is as highly esteemed in the eye of God, if he really is serving him in spirit and truth, as the person who is laboring most conspicuously in His service. The humblest member of any congregation is just serving his Lord and Master, if he is a faithful servant, as much as perhaps the Minister who is spending his life in laboring among that flock. Each of them is living and laboring in that sphere in which his blessed Lord has placed him, and if serving faithfully, is serving acceptably. The humblest work, if it be but a cup of cold water, is just as much accepted before the Lord, and just as much rewarded when done on the principle of love to the Lord Jesus, as the greatest labor that man can do; for we can do nothing but as the Lord gives us power, according to our different gifts and talents; we can do nothing for Him but just what He bestows on us, "*If there be first a willing mind, it is accepted according to that a man hath, and not according to that he hath not.*" 2nd Cor. viii. 12. When the Lord was pleased to give a widow but two mites, and gave her a heart to cast it into the treasury; she cast more into it in the Lord's estimation, than all the rich men who had cast in of their abundance.

Therefore, you see what a blessing that principle is that is laid down here for the Christian servant, "WITH GOOD WILL DOING SERVICE AS UNTO THE LORD AND NOT UNTO MEN; KNOWING THAT WHATSOEVER GOOD THING ANY MAN DOETH, THE SAME SHALL HE RECEIVE OF THE LORD, WHETHER HE BE BOND OR FREE." Whatever he is occupied about—whatever service he is doing for his master, when he is doing it faithfully, earnestly, anxiously wishing to do it, not with eye service, as pleasing men, but as unto the Lord; the Lord accepts it and rewards it as much as any service of his master—it is equally regarded "WHETHER HE BE BOND OR FREE."

When he gives himself heartily to his master's service, because he desires to serve the Lord—he gives himself in his sphere to the Lord, and whatever he does on that principle—whatever the discharge of duty to his master be, as unto the Lord; the poorest, humblest service he renders for his Heavenly Master's sake, and for his Heavenly Master's glory, is as much accepted before the Lord as the labor of that master, if he were the greatest monarch in the world. Think of this—what a privilege it is—think with what confidence the humblest creature in the world may look to his Heavenly Father, and be satisfied, that whatever he does for His sake is graciously accepted, because Jesus has died for sinners, and he is looking to Jesus as the hope and refuge of his soul.

"THE SAME SHALL HE RECEIVE OF THE LORD, WHETHER HE BE BOND OR FREE."—So the Apostle saith in the Epistle to the Galatians, "*Ye are all the children of God by faith in Christ Jesus; for as many of you as have been baptised into Christ, have put on Christ,—there is neither Jew nor Greek, there is neither bond nor free, there is neither male nor female: for ye are all one in Christ Jesus,*" Gal. iii. 27, 28. "*All one,*"—The master—it is his privilege to look on his servant as a brother, when they are brethren in Christ. The servant—it is his privilege to look on his master as a brother, when they are brethren in Christ. And as we remarked before, while they are brought into this relationship to God and to each other; so far from dissolving the tie that subsists between them, or deranging the order of society; it establishes social order, on the only principle on which it can be firmly established—the service of God, as a God of order, authority, and obedience, as both derived from his ordinance, and to be exercised for his glory.

"AND YE MASTERS DO THE SAME THINGS UNTO THEM," that is, they are called on to discharge their duty to you, "*in singleness of heart as unto Christ,*"—"DO THE SAME THINGS UNTO THEM"—discharge your duty to them "*in singleness of heart as unto Christ.*" They are desired to do their duty to you, "*not with eye service as men pleasers;*" therefore you are to do your duty to them, "*not with eye service as men pleasers,*"—not as if men were looking on you and thinking well of you—not as if your servants were looking at you and gratified with your conduct; but do your duty to them as remembering that your God is looking upon you. If they are to do service to you as "DOING THE WILL OF GOD FROM THE HEART, WITH GOOD WILL DOING SERVICE AS TO THE LORD AND NOT TO MEN." You are with good will to exercise authority over them as to the Lord and not to men.

"DO THE SAME THINGS UNTO THEM."—As they are called upon to discharge their duty in reference to God, exercise your authority to them in reference to God.

"FORBEARING THREATENING, KNOWING THAT YOUR MASTER ALSO IS IN HEAVEN."—Authority, in any circumstance, is a dangerous thing to entrust to a poor sinner. Men too generally misuse their power. Few are fit to be entrusted with authority in any way. Man almost always abuses his power at some times and in some ways, in every relation of life. The only security against the abuse of his power, is the continual remembrance that he holds that power from God, and the deep conviction that it is his duty to discharge the office with which he is entrusted as unto God.

For example,—the power of a parent over his child, he is warned in this portion of Scripture against the abuse of that: "*Ye fathers provoke not your children to wrath.*" As much as to say, you will be inclined to misuse your power over them—to exercise your authority, not with a single eye to the good of your children, but to indulge your own temper and provoke your children to wrath, instead of doing them good.

Just so, in the case of the power of masters—they are warned here against the abuse of that power—as much as to say, that instead of "FORBEARING THREATENING," and remembering "THAT YOUR MASTER ALSO IS IN HEAVEN," and dealing with your servants as brethren; you will be inclined to exercise your authority tyrannically—to threaten them—to exercise your power harshly and severely over them—that is the natural disposition of your heart, and you ought to watch against it.

"FORBEARING THREATENING."—Do you not feel naturally inclined to speak and act toward your servants in a manner that you ought not to do, when they provoke you, as no doubt they will provoke you with their disobedience, their neglect, their misconduct, their lies, their drunkenness, the various other evils into which too many of your servants fall? Are you not inclined to exercise authority over them too harshly?

The Apostle here supposes the relation of a Christian master and Christian servant; but we are called on continually—unfortunately—alas, to exercise, as masters, authority over servants that are not Christians. See, how God is pleased to make the acts of men's own wickedness fall on their own heads! If the Protestants—the educated Protestants of the Protestant Church were Christians in spirit and truth as they ought to be, if they served their God according to their privileges as they ought to do, if the Rulers of this Empire in the Church and Government—the Statesmen—the Bishops—the Clergy—the Protestant Landlords of this country had been faithful servants of their God, as they ought to be, the poor of this country, both Roman Catholics and Protestants, would not be, the one—so ignorant and ungodly in a true Church, nor the other—so wicked and buried in the superstitions and idolatries of a false Church, as they are. The country would not be as it is, if men in their respective spheres did their duty to their God as they ought to have done, and if we were Christians as we ought to be.* There is nothing to be expected in individuals, families, nations, nothing to be looked for, or hoped for of good, unless men are brought, individually and collectively, to be servants of the living God.

But then, consider, in your relation and in your duty to your servants as masters and mistresses—consider, how this principle is forced on you; you are to remember, that "YOUR MASTER ALSO IS IN HEAVEN,"—that you are to deal with your servants as before God; and let me again advert to a point, which I endeavored to impress on you before—if that was your principle, how should you act towards your servants? What should be the first thing that would occupy your mind with respect to them? Certainly this, that you should endeavor to bring your servants to the knowledge of their Lord and Saviour. If you know the value of Christ for your own souls, you cannot neglect your servants—you cannot neglect them any more than your children—you cannot neglect those who are placed in subjection under you; and you can have no better test of your own practical disregard of God and His truth than this, that you disregard the souls of your servants. Depend upon it, if there be any of you here who are disregarding the souls of your servants, you are neglecting your own soul. Depend upon it, your own soul is in an awful state before God—you are not thinking of your Lord and Master, as the Refuge for your own soul, if you are neglecting the souls of your household. How is it possible, you can be a servant of Christ at all? Think of this,—if there be any among you to whose conscience this comes home, who have neglected the salvation of your servants, let me beseech you for God's sake, remember, "YOUR MASTER ALSO IS IN HEAVEN, NEITHER IS THERE RESPECT OF PERSONS WITH HIM." If you profess yourselves, as you do, to be servants of the King of kings, then beware that you deal with your servants, not

* The Author anticipates that perhaps much offence may be taken at these sentiments, and many may be inclined to reprove him for what they may term "*unjust charges*"—"*presumptuous assertions*"—"*audacious reproofs*," &c. &c. But these sentiments were uttered before God, in the discharge, as he believed, of his solemn duty as a minister of Christ. And when committing them to the Press, at the long interval of ten years afterwards, he soberly considers that every year establishes their truth. The only question for him to determine, is not "*Who will be pleased?*" or "*Who will be offended?*" but "WHAT IS TRUTH IN THE SIGHT OF GOD?" and therefore, the Author dares not to cancel what he believes to be solemn truth. And he fears, that while many are inclined to attribute the judgments of God on this land exclusively to Popery—he thinks the guilty neglect of duty—the abandonment in theory and practice of the principles to which they are pledged on the part of Protestants, both in the Church and State, is calculated even more than the crimes of Popery, to provoke the displeasure of Almighty God. Those who call themselves Protestants, have been the instruments of carrying out, and carrying on the worst evils, and the worst systems, that defile the country and disgrace the British Empire.

as unto man, but as unto God; that you endeavor to instruct them as you value your own salvation. Be assured, you shall find a blessing to yourselves, in endeavoring to convey the knowledge of the truth to them.

What vast responsibility is laid upon you! Alas! alas! when one thinks of masters and servants—parents and children in Hell, reproaching one another—drawing forth the bitterness of everlasting remorse from the abyss of fell recriminating recollections!!!

"I was so long in your house—I was so long in your service, or still more awful, I was your child and you told me nothing, and taught me nothing about God—you found me in ignorance and sin—you brought me forth in sin—you brought me up in sin—you kept me—you trained me—you left me in ignorance and sin—here you are, and here I am."

Oh! if one could give scope to the horrors of imagination, and suppose parents and children, masters and servants, husbands and wives, who had lived and died, serving the Devil in this world, with the Bible within their reach—the Bible unopened in their houses—a throne of grace to come to—a Saviour inviting them—Ministers entreating them to look unto Jesus;—But no, they will despise all—they will serve the Devil in time, and they are cast away to serve him and to suffer with him for eternity!

Oh! think, what an awful thing it is for sinners to be living without God in the world, in whatever relation of life they are! What will signify all your occupations, your successes, your enjoyments, your gains, your being at ease in the world—what matters it, that you have your comforts, your houses, your servants; that you have everything in neatness and in order around you—that you have children, relations, friends, more than all that your heart can wish, while you are living without God in the world.—Christ is not in your heart, or in your houses—among yourselves, your children, your family, your servants,—in your drawing-room, in your closet, your kitchen,—"*What will you do in the end thereof?*"—Alas! alas! "*what shall it profit a man, to gain the whole world and lose his own soul; or what shall a man give in exchange for his soul?*"

Hear the word of God:—"YE MASTERS DO THE SAME THINGS TO THEM, FORBEARING THREATENING, KNOWING THAT YOUR MASTER ALSO IS IN HEAVEN,"—this is addressed to Christian masters;—"YOUR MASTER ALSO IS IN HEAVEN, NEITHER IS THERE RESPECT OF PERSONS WITH HIM." What a solemn thought!—This is one of the many things we cannot realize at all,—or that we find it so difficult to realize, that "*God is no respecter of persons.*" Respect of persons, we are so justly, in a certain sense, and so continually imbued with, from our infancy, that we cannot think, that the sovereign on a throne, and the beggar on a dunghill, are just exactly the same before the Holy God; and that they shall just appear the same before the judgment seat of Christ, stripped alike of their robes of office and their rags, exactly in one character, sinners:—the Kings, Queens, Princes, Lords, all the great men—and the mighty men—and all beggars on the earth, all the same!—no respect of persons;—the only difference between them shall be:—the ornaments, the respectability, the rank, education, power, learning, opportunities, all the gifts that God gives to men to exalt them in this world; these shall press with accumulated weight of responsibility on their souls. The only difference between them shall be, that a heavier judgment shall fall on the head of those who have been great in all the various gradations of life; with all the talents committed to them; and who have trampled upon and neglected all the means of usefulness, and all the gifts and opportunities that God had blessed them with on earth. It is very difficult to realize, "NEITHER IS THERE ANY RESPECT OF PERSONS WITH HIM," very difficult, but it is true—there is not a truth more clearly laid down in His Holy Word.—Every individual stands on a level with his fellow man—*Sinner*, is the name of each, and *Rebel*, is his rank. Then, the only—the mighty—the everlasting difference is this: whether or not, he is among the redeemed of the Lord—brought to the feet of Jesus—washed in the precious blood—and clothed in the righteousness of the Son of God.

I shall just read, and only read the 10th verse in conclusion, because the Apostle refers us in it to the only ground on which it is possible for us to discharge any duty, to embrace any truth, to trust on any promise, or to expect any blessing. "FINALLY, MY BRETHREN, BE STRONG IN THE LORD, AND IN THE POWER OF HIS MIGHT,"—as much as to say, you are all weakness—you have nothing, and are nothing in yourselves, when these duties are pressed on you; all your strength can be derived alone from God. "BE STRONG IN THE LORD,"—you must be "IN THE LORD," before you can "BE STRONG IN THE LORD,"—you must be *in Christ*, before you are *strong in Christ*—you must be looking unto Jesus—you must be found in Jesus, before you can be strong in him. Therefore, to believers alone, can it be said, "BE STRONG IN THE LORD, AND IN THE POWER OF HIS MIGHT." Well, dear brethren! so we can be strong if we are looking to Jesus.—"*I can do all things through Christ, which strengtheneth me*," Phil. iv. 13, saith the Apostle.

May the Lord apply this to our hearts, and enable us to consider the means by which the sinner alone can "BE STRONG IN THE LORD," even by putting on *the whole armor of God*. May the Lord engrave this truth on our hearts, and seal instruction on our souls, for Christ's sake. Amen.

FORTY-SEVENTH LECTURE.

EPHESIANS VI.—10, 11.

"Finally, my brethren, be strong in the Lord, and in the power of his might. Put on the whole armor of God, that ye may be able to stand against the wiles of the devil."

WE merely cursorily touched on the 10th verse, in our last Lecture. And we are to observe, that with this verse begins the conclusion of this address from the Apostle to the church at Ephesus, where he comes to the close of all his exhortations to them, as he does in this chapter.

"FINALLY, MY BRETHREN"—That is, in conclusion—after all I have written to you, "FINALLY, MY BRETHEN, BE STRONG IN THE LORD, AND IN THE POWER OF HIS MIGHT." As much as to say,—

"My brethren, I have now entered fully into the glorious subject of the Gospel—the redeeming love of our Lord and Saviour Jesus Christ. I have gone back to the everlasting love of Jehovah to His Church. I have shown you the completeness of that Church as redeemed in Jesus. "*Chosen in him before the foundation of the world*," chap i. 4. I have gone back to the commencement of your own spiritual life. I have shown you how you "*were dead in trespasses and sins*"—"*how God who is rich in mercy, for his great love wherewith he loved you, even when you were dead in sins, hath quickened you together with Christ; (by grace are ye saved) and hath raised you up together, and made you sit together in heavenly places in Christ Jesus*," chap. ii. 1—6. I have shown you, "*How in Christ Jesus, ye who sometimes were afar off, are made nigh by the blood of Christ.*" I have shown you the glorious privileges to which you are raised—"*No more strangers and foreigners, but fellow-citizens with the saints, and of the household of God*"—the glorious foundation on which you are built, even "*the foundation of the Apostles and Prophets, Jesus Christ, himself, being the chief corner-stone.*" I have shown you, how you have been hewn out, and brought as living stones to this foundation, and built up in Him, "*In whom all the building fitly framed together groweth unto an holy temple in the Lord*," chap. xiii. 19—21. I have shown you the glorious mystery, "*Which in other ages was not made known unto the sons of men, as it is now revealed unto his holy Apostles and Prophets by the Spirit, that (you) the Gentiles should be fellow-heirs, and of the same body, and partakers of his promise in Christ, by the Gospel.*"

chap. iii. 5, 6. I have prayed for you, "*That he would grant you according to the riches of his glory, to be strengthened with might, by his Spirit, in the inner man, that Christ may dwell in your hearts by faith; that ye, being rooted and grounded in love, may be able to comprehend, with all saints, what is the breadth and length, and depth and height, and to know the love of Christ which passeth knowledge, that ye might be filled with all the fulness of God,*" chap. iii. 16—19. Having shown you all your wondrous privileges, and prayed for all these blessings upon you, I have exhorted you to "*Walk worthy of the vocation wherewith ye are called, with all lowliness and meekness, with long-suffering, forbearing one another in love.*" I have exhorted you to "*Endeavor to keep the unity of the Spirit in the bond of peace,*" chap. iv. 1—3. I have shown you the glorious privileges that belong to each of you, as members, different members of the body of Christ, and that in all your several places, whatever place God has appointed you in that body, you are all to keep your places, and "*Grow up unto him in all things, which is the head even Christ.*" I have exhorted you, how you ought to walk and to please God—how you ought to "*Put off, concerning your former conversation, the old man which is corrupt, according to the deceitful lusts, and to be renewed in the spirit of your minds,*" chap. iv. 22, 23—to put off all your sins, and vanities, and deceitfulness in which ye walked as Gentiles. I have called you to holiness. I have called you to put away every evil deed, and every evil word—to "*Let no corrupt communication proceed out of your mouth, but that which is good to the use of edifying, that it may minister grace unto thine hearers.*" I have exhorted you "*Not to grieve the Holy Spirit of God, whereby you are sealed unto the day of redemption,*" chap. iv. 29, 30. I have exhorted you to "*Be followers of God as dear children,*" and "*Walk in love, as Christ also hath loved us, and given himself for us,*" chap. v. 1, 2. I have called you to remember that you should avoid every sin, every unclean act, in deed, word, and thought, and that you should "*Let no man deceive you with vain words,*" as that ye might walk in these, and still be of Christ's body; for that "*Because of these things, the wrath of God cometh on the children of disobedience.*" And shall the members of Christ have license to commit the sins that condemn His enemies?

"I have exhorted you, in all your several relations of life, as Husbands, Wives, Parents, Children, Masters, Servants, in all your various circumstances and positions; I have exhorted you, and delivered to you how you ought to walk, to serve and glorify your Lord and Master: but after having done all these things, I come to the close of all my testimony, and all my admonitions to you, and now remember, that in all these things you are weak—nay, utterly impotent in yourselves; unable to understand any principle—to comprehend any mystery—to believe any truth—to embrace any hope—to enjoy any promise—to perform any duty that I have laid before you—and that all your strength must be derived from the Lord. Therefore, "FINALLY, MY BRETHREN, BE STRONG IN THE LORD, AND IN THE POWER OF HIS MIGHT."

Oh! what an important exhortation is this, with which to close this inspired Epistle. I say, what an important exhortation it is!—an exhortation commended to the experience of every Child of God, who has ever read, or understood a syllable of its sacred truth. For there is one lesson we are continually learning, as long as we are being trained in the school of Christ; and that lesson is this, our own continual weakness; our utter inability to do, say, or think anything for our God, as of ourselves; we are learning the lesson which the Apostle speaks of, when he says, "*Not that we are sufficient of ourselves to think anything as of ourselves, but our sufficiency is of God.*" 2nd Cor. iii. 5. He does not merely say, *to do*, or *to speak*—but "*to think anything as of ourselves.*" And if such was the experience of the Apostle, surely such must be yours and mine! I do believe, if a Christian watches himself, that there is not one night he lies down on his bed, if he reflects on his actions, words, and thoughts, during the day, that he will not have to feel, that in every single instance he was perfectly weak in himself, and incompetent to any good; that in fact he could do nothing—that whenever he was able to do anything—to think of anything aright; he must know, and feel more and more daily, that it could come alone from God. Therefore, "FINALLY, MY BRETHREN, BE STRONG IN THE LORD AND IN THE POWER OF HIS MIGHT."

There are two points to be considered here: first—our own weakness; our inability to do anything of ourselves,—this is a subject of self-examination, of self-abasement, leading to humiliation and to prayer. The second thing is—our strength, the strength of the believer in Christ. "BE STRONG IN THE LORD, AND IN THE POWER OF HIS MIGHT."—This is a subject of rejoicing. Here we are to look out of self—to lift our eyes above self—to look beyond self—and look up to our glorious covenant God.—"BE STRONG IN THE LORD,"—as much as to say, when you are weakest—remember, strength is provided—your help is laid on one that is mighty,—so saith the Lord, "*I have laid help on one that is mighty.*" Psalm lxxxix. 19. Mighty to succor, and mighty to save. God has laid our help on Christ; therefore when he saith, "BE STRONG IN THE LORD," think, what a consolatory reflection that is to the poor believer—that it is his privilege to be so—that his Divine Master's strength is provided for him, so that he is never to be discouraged under any sense of his own weakness; because there is such glorious encouragement for him continually, and strength in the power of his Lord; as much as to say,—remember! Oh! believer, your own weakness—but Oh! remember, the strength that is laid up for you—remember, what is provided for you; you are weak indeed, but Christ is strong, though you are weak. And remember, that the strength that is provided for you in all these things, is the strength of omnipotence. Therefore, "BE STRONG IN THE LORD." Ah! dear brethren, this is a very difficult lesson for us to learn; but, the Lord teaches it to us, by many a hard experience; for we are never content to derive our strength from God; we are always ready to lean more or less on our own; and if we find we have any spiritual strength, we are just as apt to be proud of it, as strong men are of their muscular power, they are proud of their strength, and they call it their own—we are proud of our spiritual strength, and call it our own; and therefore, one of the many ways we are often taught our own weakness, is by letting us feel it—leaving us to ourselves. There is no way in which a sinner is more immediately taught his own weakness, than when he is left to himself. We are like children just beginning to walk—the parent holds the child by the hand, and then the child, confident in its fancied strength, supported by its parent, thinking it is supporting itself, and proud of its own imaginary power, desires to walk alone—it is left to make the effort for a moment—it falls, and cries to its parent, to lift it up again. This is exactly the state of a self righteous—weak—self confident believer; his whole strength is derived from the support of the hand of his God, who holds and keeps him by his power. Then he thinks he is able to walk alone—sometimes he is left to try the experiment, he does so—then he learns his weakness, by many a heavy fall—many a severe wound, of which, perhaps, the world knows nothing, but which he deeply feels within. Does he not?—Oh believer! have you not felt it thus? Have you not had many a severe fall, that no one ever knew, but that has wounded your own conscience? Oh yes! your own experience testifies what grievous falls you have suffered—what deep—what heavy falls—wounding your conscience—bowing down, perhaps your head like a bulrush—making you cry with the Psalmist, "*My wounds stink and are corrupt through my foolishness.—I am troubled—I am bowed down greatly; I go mourning all the day long.*" Psalm xxxviii. 5, 6. The world may never know anything about it; but you and your God have known it. The cause is your own pride—your fancying yourself strong in your own strength. Do you recollect how the Apostle Paul was taught and trained in this school of trial?—Do you recollect, where he speaks of the spiritual revelations vouchsafed to him, and the danger of spiritual pride resulting from these? He says, "*Lest I should be exalted above measure, through the abundance of the revelations, there was given to me a thorn in the flesh, the messenger of Satan to buffet me, lest I should be exalted above measure.*" 2nd Cor. xii. 7.

Some persons consider, that this was some bodily affliction; but they who say so, seem, I think, to know but very little of the spiritual experience of the believer. "*A thorn in the flesh!*"—"*The messenger of Satan!*"—It is much more probable, it was some deep temptation—some hard spiritual trial—some sin—some strong besetting sin, under the power of which he groaned, being burthened. This is often the case. When we are not at all aware of the existence of some particular sin in our hearts—some temptation brings it out at once; and Satan sends a messenger to stir it up—to stir up as in a muddy pool, the sin that lies at the bottom of the heart.

Some men, for example, may think their tempers very much subdued. But an irritation—a provocation they did not expect, or anticipate, shows them, in a moment, how easily they may be excited, and what a vile temper and spirit they are of, if the Lord would leave them to themselves.

Some persons imagine, that their minds are abstracted from the world, and that they have got rid of covetousness, or of ambition; a temptation is thrown in their way, they run greedily after gain—they tremble for something they are afraid to lose—they are disappointed in something that they expected to attain, and then, their heart is brought to see how worldly, and how full of covetousness or ambition it is.

Some think that they are very honest—they are tempted and overtaken in a snare.

Some flatter themselves, that they are very pure and chaste—they are tempted, and are taught to feel how unclean they are, and that there is no health in them.

Some think they are resigned to the will of God; they are soon taught how full of murmuring and rebellion their heart is. Thus, by some temptation—some thorn in the flesh—some fall, they are brought to discover, and to feel their vileness, their wickedness, their weakness, their utter impotence to stand in their own strength, or to do anything that is good.

Then, they desire to get rid of this—they desire to conquer it—they hope to subdue it. So did Paul, "*For this thing*," he says "*I besought the Lord thrice that it might depart from me*,"—this trial,—this temptation—this thorn whatever it was; and this is what the believer does—he wants to get rid of the thorn.—"Oh!" saith he, "if I could get this sin out of my heart—this accursed sin—if I could conquer it—if I could get my heart delivered from it—free from it, what relief, what a mercy it would be to me!" Perhaps he prays for this like Paul, that it may depart from him. But no! he must learn a lesson—he must learn the lesson that Paul learned;—the Lord's answer to his prayer for deliverance, was this, "*He said unto me, my grace is sufficient for thee.*" That is, it is not in the departing of this thorn in the flesh that you are to take comfort; it is not in this that you are to find rest; you must find it in my grace—you must bring the evil to my grace—you must come to the blood of Jesus—you must come humbled, bowed down, wounded, as a helpless sinner; it is in my grace alone, you can find rest and salvation, and not in your conscious deliverance from your own trials, and your own corruptions.

Yes, and that grace is the only means by which corruption can be conquered; it is in the sufficiency of grace alone, that we can find the power to conquer sin; for it is there we learn to be strong in the Lord.—"*Thou therefore, my son, be strong in the grace that is in Christ Jesus*," 2nd Tim. ii. 1. So the Apostle saith,

"*Grow in grace, and in the knowledge of our Lord and Saviour Jesus Christ.*" 2nd Pet. iii. 18.

If this thorn had departed from Paul, he would have thought he was strong in himself; and if we were enabled to get rid sensibly of the corruptions that are in ourselves—to conquer our own sins, and to banish our own iniquities, we should imagine we were strong in ourselves, and we should be proud of our own strength; but we must learn, that it is in the grace of our Lord alone, that we can find power to conquer; that is, in the humiliating prostration of ourselves at the feet of Jesus, as sinners. To live in pardon of sin, is to live in victory over sin. We are thus learning more deep, humiliating lessons of our own vileness, nothingness, weakness, and learning to live out of self, and in Christ—"*The life which I now live in the flesh,*" saith Paul, "*I live by the faith of the Son of God who loved me, and gave himself for me.*" Gal. ii. 20.

These are lessons, dear friends, which we are brought to learn through many deep and humbling trials, and experiences of our own evil hearts. The more we learn of ourselves—our own weakness, helplessness and sin, the more we learn that which our Bible teaches us:—"*The heart is deceitful above all things, and desperately wicked, who can know it?*" Jer. xvii. 9. We think we have fathomed our hearts to-day, and to-morrow we find depths of sin within them, beyond the line of all our former knowledge; so the Apostle learns the lesson most gladly; "*My grace is sufficient for thee, my strength is made perfect in weakness.*" If we had any strength of our own, we would call it our own strength—we would glory in it, as in our own strength. But God teaches us our weakness, that we must learn to glory in His strength—in His grace, to rejoice, not in ourselves, but in our God. "*We are the circumcision which worship God in the Spirit; and rejoice in Christ Jesus, and have no confidence in the flesh.*" Phil. iii. 3. Learn to be strong not in yourselves, but in your Lord. "FINALLY, MY BRETHREN, BE STRONG IN THE LORD,"—and so the Apostle saith, "*Most gladly, therefore, will I rather glory in my infirmities, that the power of Christ may rest upon me.*" 2nd Cor. xii. 9.

Oh! that is a wonderful lesson for a sinner to learn—to be able to feel his own infirmities—his own sins—his own corruptions—his own wants;—and to be able to go out of them all, into the righteousness and blood—the strength and power of Christ! to be nothing, and take Christ for his all. It is then he is taught to understand experimentally this exhortation: "FINALLY, MY BRETHREN, BE STRONG IN THE LORD, AND IN THE POWER OF HIS MIGHT."

Consider, then, these two points: your own weakness, and the strength of the Lord; and consider, what a glorious privilege it is for the believer to know, that that strength is free—full—all-sufficient for him—complete—perfect.—"*My strength is made perfect in weakness.*" Alas! how much we live by sense!—how little we live by faith!—how continually we are apprehensive of ourselves; dreading—distrusting—doubting—falling—because we are leaning on our own will and understanding, and confiding in our own strength. But if we are brought to know and feel our own weakness experimentally, and to learn to lean on the strength of Jesus—dear friends, that is the real life of faith. Live on the strength and fulness of the Lord Jesus Christ; that is the faith that gives love—that is the love that gives power—that is the power that moves and actuates the man; so that the whole of a believer's life; all his spiritual life, and all his practical life, is derived from the strength of his Lord; and living in that strength, he is "STRONG IN THE LORD, AND IN THE POWER OF HIS MIGHT." Therefore, the Apostle saith, "*I can do all things*."—How? "*Through Christ which strengtheneth me*." Phil. iv. 13. If we are really able to come to Christ for strength, we shall be able to do all things that we ought to do; and we may rest satisfied, that if we find ourselves unable to do what we ought to do; it is because we are not coming to our Lord for strength. Therefore, the Apostle shows in detail, how we are to be strong for our warfare. "BE STRONG IN THE LORD, AND IN THE POWER OF HIS MIGHT; PUT ON THE WHOLE ARMOR OF GOD, THAT YE MAY BE ABLE TO STAND AGAINST THE WILES OF THE DEVIL."

The Apostle then commences to speak of the power of the enemy, with whom we have to contend, and he says, "PUT ON THE WHOLE ARMOR OF GOD, THAT YE MAY BE ABLE TO STAND AGAINST THE WILES OF THE DEVIL." He here represents the life of faith in Christ Jesus, under the image of Christian Armor. No doubt, you have often seen representations in pictures, or statues, of the armor, or perhaps, you have seen the armor itself, with which warriors, in ancient times were covered from head to foot, when they went out to battle. The Apostle says, "PUT ON THE WHOLE ARMOR OF GOD." Not only the armor, but "THE WHOLE ARMOR;" we must be armed—we have need of armor in every part for the battle in which we are engaged. The ancient warriors would have considered that they were totally deficient in preparation for the field, if they went out without any part of their armor. If they went out without their helmet, their head would be unprotected—if without their breastplate, their breast would be unguarded—if without their shield, of course they would be altogether exposed to the foe—if without their greaves, their legs and feet would be vulnerable. Whatever part of their armor they left behind, they would be so far unprepared and unfit to go into combat with their enemies; therefore he saith, "PUT ON THE WHOLE ARMOR OF GOD."

The armor of God is complete, there is nothing wanting. It furnishes the warrior from head to foot. It covers him altogether. In that armor there is no imperfection, no weak part, as there was in the armor of the ancient warriors. You remember the "*Man who drew a bow at a venture, and smote the King of Israel between the joints of the harness*." 1st Kings xxii. 34.—There are no joints in the armor of God. It is complete armor. If you put it on, you are invulnerable to all the weapons and power of your enemies. We shall see this I trust, if we are spared to examine the different parts of the armor which the Apostle enumerates in the rest of the chapter. But let us mark the necessity of the exhortation,—he saith, "PUT ON THE WHOLE ARMOR OF GOD, THAT YOU MAY BE ABLE TO STAND AGAINST THE WILES OF THE DEVIL." He here sets before the church the enemies with whom they have to contend, "THAT YE MAY BE ABLE TO STAND AGAINST THE WILES OF THE DEVIL." Dear friends, the greatest dangers that accrue from the temptations of the devil, are his wiles.—"*Surely, in vain the net is spread in the sight of any bird:*" Prov. i. 17. The man who goes out to trap game or birds, what does he do? He covers and hides his trap, so that the animals that are to be caught may not see it; he covers it over in such an artful way, that the animal does not suspect any trap or snare is laid for him there. If the animal were to see the trap, he would never be caught, he would flee from it; therefore, "*Surely, in vain the net is spread in the sight of any bird.*" The devil knows this,—he knows how to catch us, better than the game keeper knows how to trap his birds; and therefore, he lays his snares so that we cannot see them. If we could see the evil of the sin into which we are led—if we could see the abomination of that sin in the sight of God, to which the devil tempts us—if we could see how from one sin we are gradually led on to another;—how one false step tends to involve us in a precipitous course of evil; and if we could see hell yawning at the end of that course, then no one would be led into sin. If we could see the reality of the spiritual evil, and the spiritual judgments that are annexed to that evil by God, we would no more run into sin, than we would run into a fiery furnace; but the devil deceives us—he does not allow us to see that—he does not allow us to see, either the real nature or the end of sin; he says it is not evil—he calls it good. The delusions that Satan practises on us, he covers over, so that we cannot see them; we cannot see the end—the issue;—we cannot see whither we are going,—he completely blinds and deceives us; and just exactly as a lure or bait is placed on a trap by the person who wishes to deceive his prey, so Satan always has some lure to present to our hearts, that he knows is peculiarly tempting to us. There is not a single one of us here, for whom the devil has not some particular lure or temptation, which he knows is most especially suited to each of our tastes. He will supply a temptation that will gratify the vanity of one person—the pride of another—the palate of another—the ambition of another, and so on. He will set his snares—his allurements exactly to what he knows to be their peculiar inclination. These are the wiles with which the devil ensnares us. That which would be a temptation to you would be none to me. That, which would be a great snare to me might be none to you. One person will feel inclined to run into a sin, for which another has not any inclination. No person is prone to all sins. Perhaps, the best man in the world may be inclined to some sort of excess, from which the very vilest of the human race is entirely exempt. All have their peculiar inclinations—their besetting sins, and for all these, the devil has temptations exactly suited to their taste. These are some of the wiles of the devil.

But there is no way in which the devil succeeds more effectually with mankind, than by tempting them to the disbelief of his own existence and his power. Unbelief, with reference to the devil, is just as prominent an evil in the human heart as unbelief with reference to God. The same word of eternal truth proposes to our belief the facts concerning the devil, that proposes to our belief the facts concerning God. We learn the devil's character—power—wiles—temptations—and success with the human race, on the same authority that we learn everything connected with God the Father, God the Son, and God the Holy Ghost. And the rejection of revealed truth, in reference to the devil, is, I repeat, as marked a proof of the unbelief of the heart, as the rejection of revealed truth concerning God. Both alike, are a rejection of God's testimony—both a rejection of the truth of His written word. Therefore, all unenlightened men who know not the Gospel, are just as unbelieving respecting the devil, as they are respecting God. They speak of Satan as a sort of imaginary being. All those who believe the Gospel, on the contrary, have their belief in the existence, agency, and power of the devil, increased in direct proportion as their faith in Christ is increased:—we grow in faith, in all that God reveals to us of the devil, as we grow in faith in all that He reveals to us of Christ; we grow in the knowledge, faith, and experience of the devil's wickedness—of his power—of his devices—and his wiles—and of all the attributes of his character and nature, as we grow in the knowledge and faith of our blessed Lord and Master, in the experience of his power and of his love. And therefore, while to speak experimentally of the temptations and snares of the devil, is considered by the ungodly just as enthusiastical or fanatical, as to speak experimentally of the grace and love of the Lord Jesus Christ—the knowledge of these things—the knowledge of the devil, is just as experimental, as practical and true in the believer, as the knowledge of his Lord and Master.

The influences and power of the devil are felt—they are known to the believer as experimentally as the influences and power of the Spirit of God;—they are known thus.—You cannot perhaps, speak of some particular operation in your own mind, as contradistinguished from your own natural corruption, and say—"This is the devil;" just as you cannot speak of some particular operation in your own mind, to the exclusion of your own will, and faculties, and power, and say—"This is the Spirit of God." The spirit and power of the devil, and the Spirit and power of the Lord are discernible more in their effects, than in their immediate operations upon us. Thus, our Lord saith,—"*The wind bloweth where it listeth, and thou hearest the sound thereof, but canst not tell whence it cometh, and whither it goeth: so is every one that is born of the Spirit.*" John iii. 8. The processes of spiritual influences and operations on our minds, either of good or of evil, are as unknown to us as the beginnings and terminations of the course of the wind; but the effects are discernible as those of a storm or a calm. We know and feel the influence and the power of sin—we feel, that it is often not only involuntary, but against our will. We feel, that "*when we would do good, evil is present with us.*" Rom. vii. 21. There is a power—a potent influence—counteracting the motions of good within us. So saith the Apostle also: "*To will is present with me; but how to perform that which is good I find not.*" Rom. vii. 18. We find, thus, when we kneel down to pray, distracting thoughts are brought to our memory—diverting illusions before our imaginations, over which we feel we have no possible control, but which quite intercept and interrupt the capability of prayer. We find vividly, brought back to our recollections, some scenes, follies, vanities, absurdities of days gone by, that we were not dreaming of when we knelt down to pray; brought too, with a power to our minds that we cannot possibly account for, when it is against our will and our prayer. We find some foolish, vain, absurd, ridiculous ideas suggested to us,—we feel our heart going forth after some sinful lust—some silly day-dream, perhaps of imaginary happiness or misery. Our fancy, building, (as we say) some "castle in the air." We feel these presented to our minds, like the shifting of scenes in a theatre—and especially, when we would pray, or engage in any spiritual exercise, we feel this to be so. I will venture to say, that there is no believer present, who has not felt it to be so. Alas! how often have I found myself rising from my knees, and saying to myself—"Where am I? Where have my thoughts been wandering? Where have I been straying from my God? I knelt down to call upon my Heavenly Father, and my mind has been running after some foolish train of thought, that turns me away with a thousand trifles. My heart has been wandering, 'like the fool's eye to the end of the earth.'"

Now, without at all extenuating our sin, or palliating our impiety and corruption, I say, this is the power of the devil. This is mingled with the agency and influence of an unseen spiritual power, that is more or less at intervals, working on the mind; and especially so, at the very time, and under the very circumstances when the mind would most desire to devote itself to God. I venture to say, that you have never felt the power of Satan in this particular, more exerted on you than at that very time when you would most wish to be delivered from it. When you would go to prayer—when you would sit down to read your Bible—when you would desire to profit by a sermon, or a lecture—perhaps, some word spoken even by the minister, by whose instructions you wish to profit, might suggest to you some train or association of ideas. Nay, it may be the case with some here, at this very moment, and when you next turn to listen to the subject, you find you had lost everything that he was saying in the intermediate time—you find your attention has been turned after some other vain pursuit, and that the subject has been obliterated from your thoughts.

This is the Lord's testimony concerning the preaching of the word. Do you remember what He saith in the parable of the sower,—"*Some fell by the way-side; and it was trodden down, and the fowls of the air devoured it.*" And then He explains it,—"*Those by the way-side are they that hear; then cometh the devil, and taketh away the word out of their hearts, lest they should believe and be saved.*" Luke viii. 5, 12. Now I say, the very same testimony that teaches you to believe that the person who spoke these words was the Lord Jesus Christ, the Lord of life and glory, should lead you to believe the word He spoke; and that the word He spoke was the word of truth concerning Satan, as well as what He saith concerning Himself. And when He saith, "the devil cometh, and taketh away the word out of their heart," we must believe that the devil does come and take the word out of the heart.

Now to illustrate this, perhaps some of you may have come here, as no doubt you have, not thinking or caring about the power of the devil, or not believing in his influence over the human mind.—Now if you go away, and continue to disregard and disbelieve it—if you say, "Oh! these things about the agency of the devil, cannot be really as they are represented, I do not believe that the devil has any power over my mind, I should be sorry to think the devil had any power or influence over me." If you say or think this, I say then, it is the devil that leads you to think so. He does not allow you to receive the word of Christ into your heart—he takes it away like the seed on the wayside. This is one of his wiles,—he does not allow you to see or believe his power, as the man who attends a decoy, does not allow the wildfowl to see him. The "strong man armed keepeth his palace, and his goods are in peace." He has quiet and peaceable possession of your soul, he has peaceable possession of your conscience, and there can be no surer proof than the fact, that you do not know or fear or understand his power, at least to a certain extent, for none of us understand it, or fear or guard against it, as we ought to do. If we did, we would walk through the world as men would walk near an Indian jungle, or an African forest, watching, lest a tiger or a lion should spring out on them, we would be always on our guard, so saith the Apostle Peter, "*Be sober, be vigilant, because your adversary the devil, as a roaring lion walketh about, seeking whom he may devour.*" 1 Pet. v. 8. "*Be sober, be vigilant.*" If you heard there was a lion, prowling about the fields in this vicinity, if you went out to take a walk in the fields, and that it was impressed on your minds he might be near you, you would walk very cautiously, if indeed you walked at all, you would keep your eyes very carefully about you. Now, there is a lion worse than the fiercest monster in the deserts of Africa, that "*goeth about, seeking whom he may devour.*" The Lord commands you "*be sober, be vigilant,*" for that very reason. There he is represented as a roaring lion, going about, and ready to spring upon his prey. Here he is represented in another character. We read here of "THE WILES OF THE DEVIL;" here he is a wily antagonist and look at the power ascribed to him, and the fearful odds against us—"WE WRESTLE NOT AGAINST FLESH AND BLOOD, BUT AGAINST PRINCIPALITIES, AGAINST POWERS," not one,—his name is Legion, they are many; "AGAINST THE RULERS OF THE DARKNESS OF THIS WORLD." The rulers of darkness, they rule in darkness, and they rule by darkness,—"AGAINST THE RULERS OF THE DARKNESS OF THIS WORLD, AGAINST SPIRITUAL WICKEDNESS IN HIGH PLACES," or heavenly places "against spiritual wickedness in the heavenlies." Satan is called in another place, as you recollect, we had it before in chap ii. 2, "*the prince of the power of the air, the spirit that now worketh in the children of disobedience.*" This name implies his subtlety and power, he is called, "*the Prince of the power of the air,*" from his all-pervading subtlety; that, as there is no place in which you can be, which can exclude the intrusion of the air; so there is no place, that in the same way, can be able to keep out Satan, there is no crevice in your room that the air will not penetrate; and there is no crevice in your room—there is no crevice in your heart, that the devil will not get through—no moral chemistry can seal you up hermetically from the devil. As he is called "*the Prince of the power of the air,*" in the 2d chapter, so here he is called the "*spiritual wickedness in heavenly places,*" meaning in the regions of the atmosphere, the regions of the air above your head. Have you ever seen a hawk or kite hovering in the air—resting on the wing—looking down with his piercing eye on all the fields beneath him—watching every hedge till his eye fixes on his prey, and then like lightning he pounces on it? Well, his eye is not half so quick, or his wing half so swift, or his stoop half so rapid, as the eye and wing and power of the devil; and remember, this is just exactly how Satan rules in the heavenly places, in the regions of the air, watching as it were with his legions of fiends over the human race. And Oh! how often he darts upon us! and if it was not for the mighty hand that sustains and shields us—for the mighty hand that keeps the people of God, we never should escape the strength and subtlety of Satan. But our God will keep us. And therefore for this reason, "BE STRONG IN THE LORD, AND IN THE POWER OF HIS MIGHT;" "FOR" he saith "WE WRESTLE NOT AGAINST FLESH AND BLOOD, BUT AGAINST PRINCIPALITIES, AGAINST POWERS, AGAINST THE RULERS OF THE DARKNESS OF THIS WORLD, AGAINST SPIRITUAL WICKEDNESS IN THE HEAVENLIES," as if there was a continual warfare, a continual conflict going on between the soul and Satan, as there is between the soul of the believer and sin.

Now, consider this—consider the enemy with whom you have to contend—think of him—consider, and pray over these verses.—Pray that you may learn to believe the truth concerning the devil—that is, pray that you may believe God's testimony concerning the power—the malice—the wickedness—the wiles of your enemy.

Pray that you may learn to believe in God—that is—Pray for faith in all that is revealed of His Divine nature—character and attributes—His justice—His holiness—His mercy—His love—His power—His truth—His great salvation. Pray for faith in all that is revealed of the character of God; and pray for faith in all that is revealed of the character of Satan,—that as you may know in the one, whom you have to avoid or to resist—you may know in the Other, whom you have to fly to and to trust; that as you may know in the one who is the enemy of your souls, you may know in the Other, who is the Refuge and the Friend of sinners. The more you examine—the more you reflect on yourselves—the more you consider God's Word—His Divine testimonies of the character and power of Satan—the more you will see what need you have for sobriety, vigilance, and faith. And the more you know of the power of Satan, the more will you learn to feel your need of the armor of God—to prize the grace of Christ, and the riches of the glory of Him who has come to destroy the works of the devil. Remember! that "*For this purpose the Son of God was manifested, that he might destroy the works of the devil.*" 1st John iii. 8. And therefore, our belief in the very work of Christ, includes our belief in the workings of that foe, that Christ was manifested to destroy.

May the Lord enable you and me to know—to understand—to believe—to watch and pray—and to stand, as we have such need to do "AGAINST THE WILES OF THE DEVIL," through our glorious Redeemer.—Amen.

FORTY-EIGHTH LECTURE.

EPHESIANS VI.—12, 13, 14.

"For we wrestle not against flesh and blood, but against principalities, against powers, against the rulers of the darkness of this world, against spiritual wickedness in high places. Wherefore take unto you the whole armor of God, that ye may be able to withstand in the evil day, and having done all, to stand. Stand therefore, having your loins girt about with truth, and having on the breastplate of righteousness."

BEFORE I commence the passage on which I have to speak to-day, I wish to make a few observations on some expressions in my last lecture, which I hear were misconceived by some who were present. It has been represented as very extraordinary doctrine, to teach, as they say, faith in the devil. If any persons have made this remark, I take it for granted, that they misunderstood the subject. Though I do not write my addresses to you, I hope and trust, that I do not speak unadvisedly,—I desire to use "*sound speech that cannot be condemned.*" And I might have concluded, that I had failed in this, and that I had not sufficiently explained myself, if I had not the means of ascertaining exactly what I said.

But I have received from the reporter who attends here, an exact transcript of my words, and on the most careful consideration of them, I must say, that I see nothing that I could alter in the subject. On the contrary, I am glad that it has fastened on the minds of any, in order that you may be led more soberly and attentively to consider it.

I endeavored to impress on your minds, that we can know nothing of the character of Satan, unless what God has revealed to us. Everything we learn of our enemy, we learn on the authority of God. Therefore, to believe all that God tells us of that enemy, against whom we are to watch; and of whom the apostle is expressly speaking here, and instructing us, that those who believe in Christ, are to take "THE WHOLE ARMOR OF GOD" for the especial purpose of being "ABLE TO STAND AGAINST THE WILES OF THE DEVIL." To believe—I say, in Satan—that is, in all that God reveals of him, is to believe God's word,—God's testimony,—God's truth. Now I am glad, that you should think of this. There is no subject of which we have more occasion to think. Even now while we are speaking of it—while we are reading in God's word about it, the enemy is busy with our souls, as he is at all times. This formidable enemy—this "*Prince of the power of the air*"—this "RULER OF THE DARKNESS OF THIS WORLD," is always on the watch,—not only to keep those fast who are his servants, but to pluck, if he were able, those who believe the Gospel of Christ out of the hand of their Shepherd. Therefore I am glad, that we should dwell on the subject; we have great reason to do so.

We are ignorant of the devices of Satan, by nature, just as we are ignorant of the character of God and of Christ. The natural man disbelieves the character of Satan, just as much as he disbelieves the character of God the Father, and of Christ; and I repeat what I told you before, that we grow in the knowledge of the wiles and power of the devil, just as we grow in the knowledge of the grace and power of our Lord; and I have no doubt, the experience of every true child of God practically bears out this assertion. I told you, there is no way in which the devil succeeds more effectually against the human race, than by tempting them to the unbelief of himself. Unbelief with respect to the devil is just a similar evil in the human heart, as unbelief with respect to God, because it is the same word of eternal truth, that proposes to our belief the facts concerning the devil, that proposes to our belief, the facts concerning God.—Is it not so? We learn the devil's character—his power—his wiles—his temptations—and success with the human race, on the same authority that we learn everything connected with God the Father, God the Son, and God the Holy Ghost; and the unbelief of the heart in reference to the devil, just as the unbelief of the heart in reference to the character of God, exhibits an evil heart of unbelief, as in both instances we reject God's own testimony.

How could we possibly receive the divine revelation concerning fallen spirits, or the fall of man?—How the various testimonies in all the Old and the New Testaments?—The trials of Job?—The temptations of David?—The lying spirit of the false prophets?—The temptations and miracles of our blessed Lord?—All the predictions concerning Satan, as to his association with the man of sin?—The mystery of iniquity?—The nature and power of Antichrist—papal, and infidel, or both?—The snares and temptations of believers, against which they are now called to watch and pray, and against which, as developed in the character of Satan, they are called on as here, to contend in the whole armor of God?—How could we understand the promised blessings of future glory in this world, one part of which will consist in the binding of the enemy of mankind, that he will not deceive man as he does now?—In short, how can we either understand or believe the Bible?—How can we believe God, if we do not believe in the devil?—We might just as well say, a general or a soldier is not called to understand and believe all that he can learn of the character, positions, plots, and machinations of the foe, against whom he has to contend for his life; as that the Christian is not called on to understand, and to know, and to have implicit faith in every word of God, concerning the existence, character, nature, power, plots, and malice of the devil. Therefore, my beloved friends, I hold it a minister's bounden duty to teach his flock to pray that they may believe in the foe, as well as in the Friend of their souls, for their security, and their salvation.

I trust that there is not one here who does not agree with this statement; and I should rejoice that any expression was misconceived, if the explanation and enforcement shall lead you more deeply to think on the subject, and that it may be brought home more effectually to your understandings, your hearts and consciences. It was my earnest wish that it should so rest on your minds, that you might ask yourselves, "Do I believe in Satan as God has revealed him? Do I really believe what God says?" I think, my dear friends, that we have the deepest need, every moment, to pray that God, by his Spirit and word, should give us light on this subject; for Oh! what an enemy we have to deal with!! You recollect, I quoted to you our Lord's own expression on the subject, in the parable of the sower, where He expressly tells us, that Satan and his emissaries are continually occupied to blind sinners, and especially in the preaching of His word. Every sinner who goes away from hearing the truth of the Gospel, and that that word produces no effect on his mind,—the Lord Jesus Christ expressly tells you, that, "*Then cometh the devil and taketh away the word out of their hearts, lest they should believe and be saved.*" Luke viii. 12. And the same truth is most emphatically reiterated by the Apostle, thus,

"*If our Gospel be hid, it is hid to them that are lost: in whom the god of this world hath blinded the minds of them that believe not, lest the light of the glorious Gospel of Christ, who is the image of God, should shine unto them.*" 2nd Cor. iv. 3, 4. So that you see inspired testimony demonstrates the powerful agency of Satan in every unbeliever who rejects the word of life.

And if he has the power of preventing the effect of God's word at all on the hearts of those that hear it—he has the power, and a tremendous power too, in tempting, deceiving, and drawing aside from God, those who are God's children; and those who know most of their own hearts, and the power of sin, know most of the awful power that Satan can exercise over them. Therefore, I hope, as in many other instances, that Satan has overreached himself as he continually does, in leading any of us to have misconceived anything on the subject; so that we shall only be led to think more of it to-day, and that so far from being able to produce any error or any difference among us, we shall only learn the more vigilantly to watch against our fearful foe, and be led more to pray—to study God's blessed word, and to "PUT ON THE WHOLE ARMOR OF GOD THAT WE MAY BE ABLE TO STAND AGAINST THE WILES OF THE DEVIL."

And let us remember most constantly, the reason; "FOR WE WRESTLE NOT AGAINST FLESH AND BLOOD, BUT AGAINST PRINCIPALITIES, AGAINST POWERS, AGAINST THE RULERS OF THE DARKNESS OF THIS WORLD, AGAINST SPIRITUAL WICKEDNESS IN HIGH PLACES," or in the heavenly places.

I endeavored to illustrate this by the image of a bird of prey. The eagle will soar into the air far above the reach of human eye; though the human eye cannot see the eagle there, the eagle can see the smallest object of his prey on earth, and he will dart down from his lofty flight like a flash of lightning and pounce on the object on which his eye is fixed. So, with the enemy of our souls, he soars in the region around us—all the earth is beneath him. So, the Lord testifies concerning our foe, in order that we may be on the watch against him. Wherefore, you see this is the reason, because we have such a foe, because we have such a vigilant and powerful enemy, because this enemy is in the high places, as "*the prince of the power of the air*," sometimes going about like a roaring lion among us, sometimes exalted over our heads, watching us, ready to dart on us and destroy us, "WHEREFORE, TAKE UNTO YOU THE WHOLE ARMOR OF GOD, THAT YE MAY BE ABLE TO WITHSTAND IN THE EVIL DAY, AND HAVING DONE ALL TO STAND." "THE WHOLE ARMOR OF GOD"—all that God has given to sinners for their protection, in the conflict that they have with their spiritual foe.

Consider, dear friends; the time when a man becomes really a Christian in spirit and truth—when he is brought to know and believe the Gospel—then begins, for the first time, that which is called in Scripture, his warfare—the conflict between the flesh and the spirit. There is no warfare in the natural mind; there are sometimes compunctious visitings of conscience—there are sometimes secret whispers, or it may be, more than whispers—sometimes, a voice of thunder within the breast of the sinner, that will make him tremble before God. When Paul was reasoning of "*Righteousness, temperance, and judgment to come, Felix trembled*"—there was a voice within the breast of that hardened Pagan sinner—a voice that God had placed there as a witness that echoed the language of the holy Apostle, and made him tremble at its sound; but that was "*like the morning cloud, or like the early dew, that passeth away.*" Felix, though he trembled then, continued the unenlightened, hardened Pagan still; and he sent for Paul afterwards, not to hear his words and receive instruction—but, as the Divine testimony tells us, making a pretext of holding conversation with him, but really expecting, that the Apostle would give him money to release him. Herod, we know, "*heard John gladly, and did many things*" under his instruction, but beheaded him at the last. So there may be such workings in the sinner's heart, though he may remain hardened and unconverted. But there is a conscience within the breast, that when the sinner comes before the tribunal of the living God, will be summoned and stand forth as a swift witness against him; so that he will be compelled, by that very testimony which he is forced to give against himself, to say, "Amen," when God shall pronounce the sentence of eternal judgment on his soul. But, that is very different from the warfare of the Christian. All the visitations and compunctions—all the stings and the terrors of conscience that may, and often do, harass or overwhelm the bosom of the unconverted sinner, are totally different from the warfare which is commenced and carried on in a believer's heart.

In the first place—the workings of an unenlightened sinner's conscience, generally take place in reference to outward acts of sin. A man's conscience reproaches him for certain deeds of evil, which perhaps may have entailed punishment or disgrace in their train, for which he, probably, may have lost, or may fear to lose, his character. Remorse of conscience, in such persons, is often rather regret for the consequences of sin, than contrition for the evil of sin.

Sometimes, there are terrible agonies and horrors of conscience even in the mind of the ungodly—as in the case of murder, where the murderer, although he has escaped detection, has come forward to acknowledge his crime, and surrendered himself up to justice. In such a case as this, the terrors of conscience have made life a burthen to the sinner.

Sometimes, there are fearful agonies of conscience, under certain awful visitations of Providence—for instance, in a thunder storm—in a hurricane—in a storm at sea. Sometimes it is seen on beds of sickness—beds of death; there, there are sometimes terrible compunctions of conscience; the sinner is alarmed, when he is shaken, as it were, over the pit of hell! He trembles to think, how he shall meet the judgment of his God!

But again, very often, the unconverted sinner dies without any terror oı fear. I have seen men die without the least apprehension on their minds, while their language in their lives never gave the slightest hope of their salvation. But so saith the Psalmist, "*There are no bands in their death*," Psalm lxxiii. 4, speaking of unconverted men. They had no fear of God before their eyes in life, and they have none in death as the children of God have. But all these states of the natural conscience are totally different from either the warfare, or the peace in the sinner's heart when brought to God; for then, it is not merely the visitings of conscience for certain acts of sin, but his conscience, now enlightened by the spirituality of God's holy law, testifies against his acts, words, and thoughts—against his holy things, as well as against his sins; his conscience testifies against the workings of his natural heart, at all times—against the continual iniquity and continual corruption that he feels within; for then his conscience, illuminated by that holy word which is a "*lantern to our feet and a light unto our path*," takes the lamp of divine truth, as it were, into the depths of his heart, and holds it, as you would hold up a lantern to survey a cavern, and turns his eye within, to the dark recesses of sin that are concealed within his soul, and he shrinks back with horror at the sight of himself. So Paul saith, "*when the commandment came, sin revived and I died*."

There is no converted sinner on earth, that does not recoil with disgust from the sight of his own vileness, his own corruption. He feels, indeed, that the language expressive of his own experience is beautifully and scripturally put into his mouth in our admirable Liturgy, when it teaches him to confess on his knees—"*We have erred and strayed from thy ways like lost sheep; we have followed too much the devices and desires of our own hearts; we have offended against thy holy laws; we have left undone those things which we ought to have done, and we have done those things which we ought not to have done, and there is no health in us*."—"*No health*," no spiritual health in us. The believer feels that, therefore, there is a continual conflict between the Spirit and the flesh, between the spiritual corruptions of which he now is conscious, and the holy law, which he desires, through the Spirit, to fulfil. This is accurately described by the Apostle Paul, "*the flesh lusteth against the spirit, and the spirit against the flesh, and these are contrary, the one to the other, so that ye cannot do the things that ye would*." Gal. v. 17.

Now, the devil always takes part with the world and the flesh, against the Spirit, and he uses them as weapons in the conflict. He has thus always this advantage against us, that he finds a traitor in the camp, in our heart within, against the Spirit; therefore he is brought before us here not only as our spiritual foe, but as one against whom nothing but God's armor can enable us to stand, and against whom we have this warfare continually to carry on. And now, my friends, if there be any of you who do not feel this conflict within, you may depend on it that you are in darkness and ignorance concerning your real state before God.

The testimony of God in his word concerning man is, that "*every imagination of the thoughts of his heart is only evil continually.*" Gen. vi. 5.

That "*the heart is deceitful above all things and desperately wicked, who can know it?*" Jer. xvii. 9.

That "*the carnal mind is enmity against God, for it is not subject to the law of God, neither indeed can be.*" Rom. viii. 7.

This is his testimony in all his word by Moses, Prophets, and Apostles. Now if you do not know this to be true—if you do not feel it to be true—then you are blind and ignorant as to your own natural state. For you may depend on this, that God does not make a statement respecting your heart in His holy Word, that he will not demonstrate to be true at the last day. His testimony of your heart is true, as He Himself is true, and if you do not know it to be so—it is not that God's word is in error, but it is that you are ignorant and blind. It is not that God is wrong, but that the guilt, the unbelief and darkness of your heart is proved, in your not knowing Him to be right.

This is only one lesson that the believer is continually learning, and it is one of the means whereby he sets to his seal that God is true, in all his testimony concerning him. He is constantly learning that he cannot fathom the depths of his own sin, not only that "*his heart is deceitful above all things and desperately wicked.*" But he understands the force of the question, "*Who can know it?*" The language of the believer's experience is, "My God, I feel I cannot know it." Oh yes! for alas! when perhaps we think that we have conquered some sin—when we think we have subdued some iniquity—we shall find another break forth that we did not even suppose existed in ourselves—we shall find that iniquity drawn forth, so that we shall be constrained to say, "Alas! I little thought my heart was so vile and wicked as I feel it." Perhaps the very sin that we thought had been subdued within us, Satan will bring some fresh temptation to blow on it, like the blast of a furnace on half-smothered embers, and out it bursts again in all its power within, so as to overwhelm us with shame and confusion of face under the sense of our own iniquity. I appeal to the experience of your own hearts, if indeed you see them in the light of truth whether these things are not true. Therefore, what need we have to hear the Apostle's admonition, to "TAKE UNTO US THE WHOLE ARMOR OF GOD, THAT WE MAY BE ABLE TO WITHSTAND IN THE EVIL DAY, AND HAVING DONE ALL TO STAND."

"IN THE EVIL DAY."—What day is that? The day of conflict and the day of peace.—The day of affliction, and the day of ease. The day of temptation, and the day of rest from it.—The day of the power of sin and Satan, and the day of fancied victory and triumph.—The day of tribulation, and the day of prosperity.—The day of persecution, and the day of conquest over our enemies.—The day of health, and the day of sickness. The day of life, and the day of death.—Every day we live, and to the very hour we die, we have need to "TAKE UNTO US THE WHOLE

ARMOR OF GOD, THAT WE MAY BE ABLE TO WITHSTAND IN THE EVIL DAY, AND HAVING DONE ALL, TO STAND."

We can never put off our armor as long as we are in this world. We are in an enemy's country, as long as we are in the body. We are surrounded with foes—we are like soldiers campaigning in a foreign land where we have subtle, powerful, mighty foes surrounding us; and where there are snares—pitfalls—ambuscades—hidden enemies ready to dart on us and attack us every moment. We know not where to turn that we can be safe from the assaults of our foe, we are not safe from them any moment—under any circumstances—or in any place.

Retire into your closet, shut to your door, take your Bible, and go on your knees,—Satan will enter there.

Assemble your family to prayer—Satan will try to impede the blessing.

Come to any public means of grace—come sit down as here to listen to lectures on the word of God—go to Church—join in the public worship—hear the Gospel, if Paul himself were the preacher—go to the Lord's table, if the Apostles administered the ordinance—Satan is there. You find him, wherever you go, always trying to counteract the blessed influences of the Spirit, and to oppose the will, the word, and the ordinances of God. You cannot escape from your subtle and mighty foe, he will attack you in every place, and most of all when and where you are most anxious to serve your God. But you are promised this blessed armor of God; you are told to "*resist him, and he will flee from you.*" James iv. 8. He will meet and attack you, but if you resist him, he will flee from you. Let us proceed to examine the parts of the armor we are called to put on.

"STAND THEREFORE, HAVING YOUR LOINS GIRT ABOUT WITH TRUTH." Now, if you examine this armor as we go through it, you will find that every portion of it represents Him in whom alone the sinner stands complete before God; you will see, that every portion of the spiritual armor represents our glorious Lord and Master Jesus Christ. "STAND, THEREFORE, HAVING YOUR LOINS GIRT ABOUT WITH TRUTH." That is, as men going to run a race, to go out to battle, or to enter into any active exercise, would gird up their robe that it should not entangle or incommode them, so he says having your loins, "GIRT ABOUT WITH TRUTH," and in another place the Apostle Peter, "*gird up the loins of your mind,*" 1 Pet. i. 13, as your body is girt in going into battle, which implies preparedness, watchfulness, readiness for the encounter; so your minds must be girt in entering on your spiritual warfare, "HAVING YOUR LOINS GIRT ABOUT WITH TRUTH." You might apply this term to all God's word, that is, that you are to take all the truth, all God's truth, as a means whereby you are to be prepared to enter into your spiritual conflict. But there is One of whom it is said by Himself, "*I am the truth!*" The Lord Jesus Christ, and the Apostle says in another place, "*put ye on the Lord Jesus Christ,*" Rom. xiii. 14. If you go to resist the power of Satan and his allies, that is the world, the flesh, and the Devil, you must take Him who saith, "*I am the truth,*" as the girdle of your loins, you must "*put on the Lord Jesus Christ.*" It is he of whom David saith "*thou hast girded me with strength unto the battle, thou hast subdued under me those that rose up against me,*" Psalm xviii. 39. "*Blessed be the Lord my strength,*" saith he again, "*who teacheth my hands to war, and my fingers to fight;*" Psalm cxliv. 1. It is only as you have Christ, as it were, girt about you, that you can be safe from the assaults of Satan, or be able to discharge any active duty in the service of God, so the Psalmist again, "*he that trusteth in the Lord, mercy shall compass him about.*" Psalm xxxii. 10. You cannot serve God, till you have taken Christ, as the refuge and salvation of your souls, you must be brought into a capacity to serve, before you can serve him; you are not in a capacity to serve him, till you are reconciled to God in Christ, you can make no resistance to Satan whatever, or be able to serve your God, unless you are found in Christ.

There are none, perhaps, here, who have arrived at any maturity of understanding, who may not be able practically to admit and feel the truth of this. Even those who know not the Gospel of Christ. I would appeal to those, I care not who they be, suppose any individuals here, however careless, thoughtless, or ignorant they may be of divine truth, I would appeal thus to their consciences. You have often felt compunctions for sins from which you have desired to refrain in future. I am sure there is not even a child who has not felt the same;—you have felt that speaking falsehood, disobedience to parents, giving way to wicked tempers, and many other sins have brought you into disgrace and affliction, so that you would desire to refrain from them afterwards, and I say with confidence to each of you, you have often promised to do so,—you have often inwardly resolved—you have sincerely determined in your own minds to do so. I am sure I can say for myself, before I knew anything of the Gospel of Christ, I have felt sin a severe burden to my conscience, and often resolved,—resolved, with what I thought a most irrefragable resolution, that I would not commit such or such a sin that had oppressed and afflicted me again.

But let me ask, have you been able to keep your resolutions? Have you been able to carry your most sincere intentions into effect? I appeal to all who hear, and I feel confident that every one who hears will answer, No—those, who know the Gospel have most felt their own weakness and their own impotence, Oh, how often! Now, when the sinner is brought to know Christ, to lean on Christ, for pardon and salvation—when the sinner is enabled to cast his burden on his blessed Saviour, he finds that he is girded with strength unto the battle. Have you not found in yourselves, power and strength not only to resist certain sins, but that those very sins to which you felt most inclined were peculiarly hateful to you? Have you not felt strength to watch against your besetting sins? I know, O believer, you have on many occasions. It is true, they will return again, and again—you will feel the corruption rise with power within you.—The enemy of your souls will attack you in various ways, and present fresh temptations to call it forth, but still, whenever you gain a conquest over any sin, it is the very same victory of which we are told in the book of Revelation, and which the servants of Christ achieve over their foe.—All their victory is through Christ;—"*I heard a loud voice saying in heaven, Now is come salvation and strength, and the Kingdom of our God, and the power of his Christ; for the accuser of our brethren is cast down which accuseth them before our God, day and night; and they overcame him by the blood of the Lamb, and by the word of their testimony.*" Rev. xii. 10, 11. Look at the power of Satan there spoken of! The continual accuser before God of his people; always tempting and trying to lead them into sin, and always accusing them like a traitor who tempts men to a crime, and then informs against them. Always accusing them of the sins to which he tempts them. "*But they overcame him.*" How? "*By the blood of the Lamb, and by the word of their testimony.*" There is no conquest recorded of God's people over Satan, but through the salvation of the Lord Jesus. The testimony of the revealed truth of God, for all God's children, is this,—that "*they overcame him by the blood of the Lamb.*" Therefore, if you have been able to overcome sin and Satan, it is by the love and power of the Lord Jesus Christ, and through faith in his blood. If you have been girded with strength, it is because you have been girded with truth—if you have been girded with truth, it is only as you have been girded with Christ—for in Him alone we have victory; as saith the Apostle, of all the hardest conflicts, in which we can be engaged,—"*Nay in all these things we are more than conquerors, through him that loved us.*" Rom. viii. 37.

Again the next part of the armor enumerated by the Apostle is the breastplate.—"HAVING ON THE BREASTPLATE OF RIGHTEOUSNESS."

What righteousness?

Is it our own righteousness? Is our righteousness a breastplate which will defend us from the assaults of Satan? Observe—One of the attacks of Satan is accusation—one of the means whereby Satan keeps possession of the soul is accusation. He brings a charge against the sinner's conscience, and this is one means whereby he keeps the sinner from Christ. Sinners think, in their natural ignorance, that there is something which they must do in order to prepare and fit themselves to come to Christ, and that they cannot avail themselves of the privileges and blessings of the Gospel, till they are,—what they call, fit to do so. Now Satan charges them with sin, whenever Christ is presented to them. The Gospel is preached,—salvation proclaimed.—Satan says, "Oh, you are too guilty a sinner,—you are not fit to come to Christ;—you have neither humility enough,—nor contrition—nor penitence,—nor do you feel the burthen of sin enough—nor have you any love to God. You love such and such a sin—you must be a very different man before you are fit to come to Christ." Such is his language.

See, how he turns away men from the Lord's table in the same way! He persuades them, that they are not only, not fit to come to Christ, but not fit to partake of the emblems and memorials of our blessed Redeemer's sufferings—they hope they will be fit sometime before they die.

This beyond all doubt is the work of the Devil. He tells sinners they are not fit to come to Christ—he accuses them of sin, and at the very same time, he flatters them with the vain hope and expectation of their self-righteousness. He deludes the Pharisee.—"Oh! now you are fit to come—you have abstained so long from sin—you are so good—you have prepared yourself—now you are fit. You have performed such and such things—you have prayed so much—you have refrained so long from indulgences in the world—you have gone through a whole 'week's preparation'—you have been so charitable—have done so much good—you must be fit to come to Christ." He thus accuses some, and builds up others, (perhaps the same persons again,) in self-righteousness.

So you recollect when our blessed Lord dined with Simon the Pharisee, when the poor woman came behind Him and poured out her tears like rain on his feet, as the original so beautifully conveys it, and wiped them with the hairs of her head; the Pharisee said "*within himself*,"—(he did not venture to say it aloud,) "*This man, if he were a Prophet would have known who and what manner of woman this is that toucheth him, for she is a sinner.*" Luke vii. 39. Now, what was the meaning of that? That was as much as to say,—"It is very fit He should come into my company—come and dine with me,—but it is not fit, that that woman should even pour out her tears on his feet—nay, if He were a Prophet, He would have known what a vile creature she is, and he would not allow her even to touch him. There you have the self-righteousness of this Pharisee. A counterpart of the language of another of his brethren, in another parable:—"*God, I thank thee, that I am not as other men are, extortioners, unjust, adulterers, or even as this publican,*" or this vile woman. Luke xviii. 11.

Now, the breastplate of the Pharisaical heart, is self-righteousness; and let me ask, is this righteousness fit to guard us against the assaults of Satan? When Satan accuses of sin, is our righteousness such as that we can challenge Satan, and can say, we are not sinners? When Satan builds us up in self-righteousness, is our righteousness such, that we can believe Satan, and take that righteousness as clear, and challenge God, to try it at his bar when we appear before him? No,—a man might as well take a breastplate made, (to use the Prophet's expression,) of old rags, to protect him in battle! What does he say of our righteousness? "*All our righteousnesses are as filthy rags.*" Isaiah lxiv. 6. It is not this righteousness we can wear as a breastplate, in conflict with our spiritual foe. But there is a righteousness with which a sinner can cover himself, as with a breastplate, and meet the assaults of Satan,—even the righteousness of Him, of whom it is said, "*This is his name whereby he shall be called, the Lord our righteousness.*" Jer. xxiii. 6. That righteousness of which the Apostle speaks, when he saith, "*Even the righteousness of God, which is by faith of Jesus Christ, unto all, and upon all them that believe,*" Rom. iii. 22.—That righteousness of which he speaks, when he says, "*Yea doubtless, and I count all things but loss for the excellency of the knowledge of Christ Jesus my Lord: for whom I have suffered the loss of all things, and do count them but dung, that I may win Christ, and be found in him, not having mine own righteousness which is of the law, but that which is through the faith of Christ, the righteousness which is of God by faith.*" That is the righteousness which he here exhorts believers to put on as a breastplate.

Satan charges a believer with sin.

"You have no righteousness before God—you are a vile sinner—you are not fit to come to Christ."

What is the answer?

"I am a vile sinner—I know it well—I know I have no righteousness, but I am fit to come to Christ; for it is written,—'*This is a faithful saying and worthy of all acceptation, that Christ Jesus came into the world to save sinners.*' 1st Tim. i. 15. And therefore you may tell me I have no righteousness—you may tell me, I am ever so vile—you may bring against me all the corruptions of my vile heart, but you cannot tell me half, how vile it is. You speak truth in this, though you are "*the father of lies;*" but you speak it for a lying purpose, when you speak to keep me from Christ. For, just because I have no righteousness—just because I am guilty—just because I am vile. I come to Him, who is "*the end of the law for righteousness to every one that believeth.*" Rom. x. 4. To him who "*receiveth sinners.*" Luke xv. 2—who saith, "*Him that cometh to me, I will in no wise cast out.*" John vi. 37.

So when Satan endeavors to build up a sinner in his own self-righteousness, the believer saith, "Do not talk to me of my own righteousness, of what I have done, or can do, as a ground of trust for my soul. I cast it all off. I bring all the filthy rags of my righteousness to the blood of Christ. I cast my righteousness and my sins, all I have, and all I am, I cast them, into that blood of the Lamb—that blessed fountain open for sin and uncleanness; and I take the righteousness of my Lord and Saviour to cover the sins of my vile heart. That is the righteousness in which alone I can stand before God, and in which alone, as I do now, I can answer the devil."

That is the way to stand against the wiles of the devil. This is to "HAVE YOUR LOINS GIRT ABOUT WITH TRUTH, AND TO HAVE ON THE BREASTPLATE OF RIGHTEOUSNESS." Oh! that is an impenetrable breastplate; all the darts of Satan cannot pierce through it.

No charge can get at the conscience, when the conscience is covered with the breastplate of Christ's righteousness. No—and no argument of Satan can persuade the believer to take his own righteousness to cover him, when he can have the righteousness of Christ to fly to. He will not listen to the counsel of Satan, to take his own righteousness, when he has the glorious counsel of his Lord to take His. "*I counsel thee to buy of me gold tried in the fire, that thou mayest be rich; and white raiment that thou mayest be clothed, and that the shame of thy nakedness do not appear.*" Rev. iii. 18.—"*Their righteousness is of me saith the Lord.*" Isaiah liv. 17. He will not plead his own merits or works before God, when he has the finished righteousness of his Lord and Saviour to plead. Now, consider these things, dear friends, think of them; and I hope and trust that the Lord will enable us all to think of them—to know them—to feel them—to value and do them—that we may be "*doers of the word and not hearers only, deceiving our own selves.*" James i. 22. Let us pray over this passage of Scripture—let us pray, that we may be able to take this whole armor of God, to meet and to conquer our foe. And let us be assured, that we never can know enough of the danger that surrounds us, and the power of that deadly enemy with whom we have to contend. But blessed be our God—greater is He who is for us than all who are against us, as we shall see, in considering the remaining part of this armor; if the Lord permits us to go through it, we shall see the blessed salvation in which it is the privilege of the believer to rejoice, who takes Christ as the Alpha and the Omega of his hope—in whom, all who believe, are covered with a glorious panoply, in which, when they contend against their foe—they are more than conquerors—their victory is secured forever and ever.

FORTY-NINTH LECTURE.

EPHESIANS VI.—15, 16.

"And your feet shod with the preparation of the gospel of peace; above all, taking the shield of faith, wherewith ye shall be able to quench all the fiery darts of the wicked."

THE Apostle, pursuing the image of the Christian armor, in the 15th verse, exhorts his brethren to stand not only "*having their loins girt about with truth, and having on the breastplate of righteousness,*" but he adds, "AND YOUR FEET SHOD WITH THE PREPARATION OF THE GOSPEL OF PEACE." That is, that we should not be impeded, entangled, ensnared or misled in our walk,—that we should be enabled to go in the right way, and that we should walk in that way as we ought to walk in it, steadily, uprightly, and perseveringly, unto the end.

If you were going to a place, through an enemy's land, three things are necessary.

First,—that you should be on the right road,—Secondly, that you should have a faithful guide—and Thirdly, that you should walk on in the way guardedly and circumspectly, and steadily pursue it, to your journey's end. Now so exactly is it with reference to the believer's pilgrimage.—He must be satisfied first that he is on the right path to eternal life; secondly, that he follows a faithful guide;—and thirdly, that he is walking along it to his journey's end,—vigilantly, and guardedly in his way.—For this purpose, you must have "YOUR FEET SHOD WITH THE PREPARATION OF THE GOSPEL OF PEACE." That is that you should be in the path of the Gospel, and walking as guided and guarded by it in your way.

Our blessed Redeemer, you perceive, is typified under every part of this armor. He is "*The truth*" as the girdle of the loins, He is "*the Lord our righteousness*" as a breastplate, so He "*is the way*" and "*he is our peace*" as the preparation for our feet. The meaning of this figure is, that you should walk in the salvation of that blessed Redeemer, as he is revealed in the Gospel of peace. That Gospel is your guide under the teaching of the Holy Spirit. "*Thy word is a lamp unto my feet and a light unto my path.*" Psalm. cxix. 10. That Gospel brings you to Christ who is the only way. It reveals this to you as his own authority—"*I am the way, the truth, and the life; no man cometh unto the Father, but by me.*" John xiv. 6. It teaches you too, that in your warfare and your dangers, in Him alone you can have peace. It tells you, this was the announcement of His birth.—"*On earth peace, good will toward men.*" Luke ii. 14. That through Him is given "*the knowledge of salvation unto his people by the remission of their sins, through the tender mercy of our God; whereby the day-spring from on high hath visited us, to give light to them that sit in darkness and in the shadow of death, to guide our feet into the way of peace.*" Luke i. 77, 78, 79.

It tells you that "*he is our peace.*" Eph. ii. 14. That He hath "*made peace through the blood of his cross.*" Col. i. 20.

It gives you His own consolatory commentary on His last conversation with His disciples, before He suffered, "*these things have I spoken unto you, that in me ye might have peace,*" He warns them of the trials of their warfare, "*in the world ye shall have tribulation:*" but He encourages them to confidence in Him, "*but be of good cheer; I have overcome the world.*" John xvi. 33.

So the Gospel of peace is the preparation for your feet: it shows you the way in which you are to walk—the peace in which you are to walk—the confidence with which you are to walk,—and so it encourages you to persevere unto the end, "*as ye have therefore received Christ Jesus the Lord, so walk ye in him: rooted and built up in him, and stablished in the faith, as ye have been taught, abounding therein with thanksgiving.*" Col. ii. 6, 7. So it enables you in all your warfare to say, and to feel, "*Though I walk in the midst of trouble, thou wilt revive me: thou shalt stretch forth thine hand against the wrath of mine enemies, and thy right hand shall save me.*" Psalm cxxxviii. 7. And so it carries you on to the end—"*Yea, though I walk through the valley of the shadow of death, I will fear no evil: for thou art with me; thy rod and thy staff they comfort me.*" Psalm xxiii. 4.

This is that path, in which none can ever walk but those whose feet are "SHOD WITH THE PREPARATION OF THE GOSPEL OF PEACE." Too many flatter themselves that they are in the right way, but they only prove the truth of the passage—"*There is a way which seemeth right unto a man, but the end thereof are the ways of death.*" Prov. xiv. 12. Unconverted persons generally consider, the right way is their profession of religion, whatever it may be. The Roman Catholic will tell you, the Romish Church is the way. The unconverted member of the Church of England will tell you, the Protestant Church is the way. An unconverted Dissenter will tell you, his form of worship is the way. All unconverted sinners imagine, that by some outward form of worship, they are to be led, or to be kept, in the right way to eternal life,—but Jesus saith, "*I am the way, the truth, and the life; no man cometh to the Father but by me.*" If you are not in Christ, you cannot be in the way to eternal life; therefore, when the Apostle in Heb. x. has set forth the fulness and completeness of the salvation finished by the Lord Jesus Christ on the Cross; he uses the image of Christ, as a way, he says, "*Having therefore, brethren, boldness to enter into the holiest by the blood of Jesus, by a new and living way, which he hath consecrated for us, through the vail, that is to say, his flesh; and having an High Priest over the house of God; let us draw near with a true heart in full assurance of faith, having our hearts sprinkled from an evil conscience, and our bodies washed with pure water.*" Heb. x. 19—22. If you are in Him you are in the right way, if you are in Jesus you are not only in the right way, but in a holy way, "*a highway shall be there,*" saith the Lord, speaking of the way of approach to his glorious Church, "*a high way shall be there, and it shall be called the way of holiness.*" You know, we testify always in the strongest, most emphatic manner, that although holiness never can purchase, in whole or in part, a sinner's salvation,—nor can help him on to his salvation,—that his whole salvation is Jesus,—that he is "*the Alpha and Omega, the first and the last,*" yet the Scripture expressly tells us, "*without holiness, no man shall see the Lord.*" Heb. xii. 14. Why? Because without holiness, we are not in Jesus as the way. Sin is hateful to the renewed mind of an enlightened sinner. If the love of Jesus is in the heart, sin will be hated, and that is the reason why a believer is brought to hate and loathe himself, because he feels the burden of his own sin. He feels sin, which is always hateful, continually working within him; hence arises the continual conflict, the constant warfare which he has within himself, which makes this armor necessary against the foe, who attacks him within and without. He has the new principle, the principle of the Spirit of God given to him, which lusteth against the flesh, and he has also that flesh continually lusting against the Spirit of God. "*The flesh lusteth against the Spirit, and the Spirit against the flesh: and these are contrary the one to the other: so that ye cannot do the things that ye would.*" Gal. v. 17. Therefore, although the way of the believer never can be a way of perfect holiness, so that he never can be walking in a way in which he does not feel deeply defiled with sin, yet the way of walking to eternal life, and the Christian walk, is a way of holiness;—that is, —The believer in Christ is set apart in Him and holy unto the Lord,—he is totally different from his former self, and totally different from the unconverted world, and his holiness consists rather in a continual conflict with sin, than in a fulfilment of righteousness, for to this he feels he never can attain, "*ye cannot do the things that ye would.*" Gal. v. 17.

But Oh my friends! believers ought to be particularly watchful. There seems to be, (I know not how it is,) such a profession of religion now, that the world is ready, in some things, to conform to the profession of a Christian life. It serves the cause of the devil, to assume a degree of conformity to religion—his object in this is to draw believers into the world; and he seems to have succeeded, to a great extent, by infusing such a mixture of worldliness into the profession of Christianity, that those who profess the Gospel of Jesus seem to be grievously drawn into conformity to the world. Some of them seem to think, that they may go a certain length with the world; and in doing so, they flatter themselves, that it is an adoption of the Apostolic maxim, a sort of "*becoming all things to all men, that they may by all means save some.*" But this is a disastrous mistake. The Christian never gains by compromise of principle, in action, word, or thought. He never gains for himself, or his Master; he always loses for both.—Always. He loses for himself. "*Be not deceived: evil communications corrupt good manners.*" 1st Cor. xv. 33. He loses for his Master's cause. The world never respects a Christian for condescending to its conduct—its conversation, its maxims, or its motives; on the contrary, it uniformly despises him. The Christian never can hold his standard too high for *himself*. This standard is perfection. It cannot be a lower standard than perfection, for it is the law of God. His attainments are, therefore, always imperfect. He not only frequently violates his rule of right in that which is positively evil, but he always falls short in his best things, according to the language of the Apostle—"*The good that I would I do not: but the evil which I would not, that I do.*" Rom. vii 19. But his standard does not fall in his conscience to the level of his conduct, no more than a rule can vary with that which it measures. His standard is always perfection. so the Lord saith: "*I will put my laws into their hearts, and in their minds will I write them.*" Heb. x. 16. And therefore the believer has the standard of God's law as his only acknowledged standard of good, although his conduct he feels to be ever transgressing, or ever falling short of it. Therefore, he always feels himself a sinner—always deserving of condemnation. But when he knows that Jesus is "*the way,*" and comes to Jesus, then his feet are "SHOD WITH THE PREPARATION OF THE GOSPEL OF PEACE." Oh! my friends, let us always endeavor to hold in that way, and to walk in that way; and thus, and thus alone shall our "FEET BE SHOD WITH THE PREPARATION OF THE GOSPEL OF PEACE." Thus, we shall be walking in Christ; and thus our walk shall be a walk becoming the Gospel of Christ. We shall "*be followers of them who through faith and patience inherit the promises.*" Heb. vi. 12. We shall be followers of the Lamb. "*Because Christ also suffered for us, leaving us an example, that we should follow his steps.*" 1st Pet. ii. 21. As the Apostle saith in this Epistle, chap. v., "*Be ye therefore followers of God, as dear children, and walk in love;*" and in another place,—"*I beseech you therefore, brethren, by the mercies of God, that ye present your bodies a living sacrifice, holy, acceptable unto God, which is your reasonable service. And be not conformed to this world: but be ye transformed by the renewing of your mind, that ye may prove what is that good, and acceptable, and perfect will of God.*" Rom. xii. 1, 2.

You see the walk is a walk of peace, and a walk of love. The Lord gives us motives to enforce His command. His command is —love.—"*The end of the commandment is love.*" 1st Tim. i. 5. And the motive which God gives to His children to walk in His commandments is love; so that the motive and command become one and the same in the heart of the believer. That is one of the most wonderful dispensations of God, by which, in His very method of taking away sin—of pardoning the greatest breaches of His commandments—He opens a way for the keeping of those commandments. It is by His own wondrous love in Christ Jesus, He takes away the sins of the vilest sinner, and it is by that very means He draws the heart of that sinner in love to Himself. His love draws our hearts to love,—therefore, "*Walk in love;*" and that your foe may not hinder you—walk "HAVING YOUR FEET SHOD WITH THE PREPARATION OF THE GOSPEL OF PEACE."

"THE GOSPEL OF PEACE!"—Then it should be a peaceful walk, and a happy walk. A believing walk is a peaceful walk; and a believing walk, and a peaceful walk, is a holy walk, and therefore, always a happy walk; and an unbelieving walk, or an unholy walk, or an uncircumspect walk, is always an unhappy walk; and against these, how constantly ought the believer to watch and pray. We say nothing of the unbeliever—the misery of a creature walking in ignorance and unbelief of the Gospel of

Jesus. But when believers allow themselves in any sin, when they are not zealously watchful against sin; it is because of their unbelief—because they have not gone forth with "THEIR FEET SHOD WITH THE PREPARATION OF THE GOSPEL OF PEACE;" and they are walking proportionably, always unhappily. Allowed sin, necessarily throws a doubt on the truth of their profession, in their own mind. "*If our heart condemn us, God is greater than our heart, and knoweth all things.*" 1st John iii. 20. It necessarily makes them question their own sincerity, and their own state before God; their walk must be uncertain and unhappy.—Thus the Apostle saith, "*I therefore so run, not as uncertainly; so fight I, not as one that beateth the air: but I keep under my body, and bring it into subjection;*" 1 Cor. ix. 26, 27. Therefore, my beloved friends, though our walk is never the least ground of the hope of salvation, because all our salvation, I say again, and again, is in Christ, and in Him alone, yet, "*in keeping of his commandments there is great reward;*" there is no reward *for* keeping them, but there is great reward *in* keeping them; there is blessedness and happiness in keeping them, and you will always see that the happiest Christian is the holiest Christian; and there is not one of you who believes the Gospel of Jesus, whose own experience does not testify that your own sins—your own carelessness, your own want of watchfulness, have brought you into many snares—many griefs—many doubts—much sorrow. Is it not so? Oh then, dear friends, let us watch and pray. Let us have "OUR FEET SHOD WITH THE PREPARATION OF THE GOSPEL OF PEACE," be sure that walking in Christ, is the only holy walk, and the only happy walk; and it is happy even in the midst of trials. So in the book of Habakkuk, you have a beautiful exposition of "THE FEET SHOD WITH THE PREPARATION OF THE GOSPEL OF PEACE," the faith and conquest which is connected with it; "*Although the fig tree shall not blossom, neither shall fruit be in the vines, the labor of the olives shall fail, and the fields shall yield no meat, the flocks shall be cut off from the fold, and there shall be no herd in the stalls, yet I will rejoice in the Lord, I will joy in the God of my salvation.*" Hab. iii. 17, 18. Though there be heavy trials, deep privations, bleak bereavements of all comfort, yet in spite of all, "*I will rejoice in the Lord, I will joy in the God of my salvation.*" Well, what follows? "*The Lord God is my strength, and he will make my feet like hinds' feet, and he will make me to walk upon my high places.*" v. 19. When we are walking in happy, holy confidence in the Lord—holy trust in the blessed Jesus, in spite of all difficulties and trials, He will make the feet of his people like hinds' feet. It is to this that the Song alludes; —"*How beautiful are thy feet with shoes, O Prince's daughter,*" Cant. vii. 1.—That is, "YOUR FEET SHOD WITH THE PREPARATION OF THE GOSPEL OF PEACE," Isaiah, so speaking of the messengers of the Gospel,—"*how beautiful upon the mountains are the feet of him that bringeth good tidings, that publisheth peace, that bringeth good tidings of good, that publisheth salvation, that saith unto Zion, thy God reigneth,*" Isaiah lii. 7. The feet of those who preach the Gospel of peace, are beautiful, and so are the feet of those who are shod with the Gospel they preach.

Now, if our feet are "SHOD WITH THE PREPARATION OF THE GOSPEL OF PEACE," wherever we go, we shall be sure to carry the Gospel always with us. It is a bad thing to profess—to seem to have the Gospel, as is too much the case in any place, and not to have it in every place.

Some persons profess to have the Gospel at home, but they seem as if they had forgotten it whenever they go abroad—and some, on the contrary, profess to have it when they go abroad, but appear as if they had lost it, by the time they return home. A form of religion in the family and an absence of its influence in all our business in the world, or a profession of religion in the world, without any influence or power of it in the temper, habits, and conversation when at home, savors very little of the genuine servant of God.

One sees this in the intercourse of persons professing to be religious, their conversation degenerates into a mere worldly gossip, or, it may be religious gossip, as is very much the case. Religious things and persons are spoken about by way of religion. Religious men—preachers or missionaries—religious books—religious societies—and subjects such as these, form a part or often the whole of what is called religious conversation, and frequently comparing and setting up one above another. Now remember, none of these things are Christ, none of them bring peace to the soul. These are not the Gospel. Preachers are not Christ. And when these are set up as they generally are, one above another, according to the tastes and opinions of men, it generally leads to divisions. See how Paul treats this in the Church at Corinth in his day.—"*Every one of you saith, I am of Paul, and I of Apollos, and I of Cephas, and I of Christ. Is Christ divided? Was Paul crucified for you, or were you baptized in the name of Paul?* 1 Cor. i. 12, 13. And again, "*Who then is Paul, or who is Apollos, but ministers by whom ye believed, even as the Lord gave to every man? I have planted, Apollos watered; but God gave the increase. So then neither is he that planteth anything, neither he that watereth; but God that giveth the increase.*" 1 Cor. iii. 5—7. So, remember, ministers are not Christ. Religious societies are not Christ. Religious books are not Christ. And yet, allow me to ask, many of those who hear me, and who believe the Gospel, as I trust many of you do, is not conversation of this sort a continual substitute for the Gospel of Christ? My dear friends, let us remember that "*out of the abundance of the heart the mouth speaketh,*" Mat. xii. 34, and the application of these various parts of armor to the person, is but an image to imply the power and efficacy of the truth as influencing, directing, and regulating the heart—and, therefore, the whole life. The having the "FEET SHOD WITH THE PREPARATION OF THE GOSPEL OF PEACE," expresses the power of the Gospel in the heart in directing our walk. So to "*walk by faith*," 2 Cor. v. 7, to "*walk in love*," Eph. v. 2, to "*walk in Him*," (Christ) Col. ii. 6, to "*walk in the light*," 1 John, i. 7, to "*walk in the Spirit*," Gal. v. 16, to "*walk honestly*," Rom. xiii. 13, "*walk worthy of the vocation wherewith we are called*," Eph. iv. 1, to "*walk worthy of the Lord unto all pleasing*," Col. i. 10, are all so many expressions indicating the power of the Gospel in the heart, and evincing in our walk and our warfare—for our walk is a warfare, that our feet are "SHOD WITH THE PREPARATION OF THE GOSPEL OF PEACE." Thus wherever we go, the Gospel should go along with us, we should walk in the Gospel—carry it in our hearts—it should direct our steps and regulate our conversation, so shall we glorify our God, and strengthen, help, and edify one another.

One cause of the divisions and dissensions among Christians, is this. The two grand principles of the Gospel, the pillars of all truth for our salvation, for our walk,—Faith in our glorious Lord, and Love to that Lord, and love to one another—these two great principles are swamped, if I may use the expression, in the sea of disputations and divisions about ordinances and Churches, and forms, and ceremonies, and governments, and men. Man's traditions and authorities, beggarly elements, which whatever be their use in their own place, have nothing to say to the great and glorious principles of faith and love. It strikes me as very singular to hear men who seem to be sound in doctrine, talking as they very often do, about certain "*questions that gender strife*," causing divisions on these, and forgetting, that in that very thing, they are violating the great principle, the very chief command of Jesus, that "*we should love one another*." There is nothing on earth for which these two great principles, faith and love, are to be sacrificed.—We cannot wander far from the path of Christian duty, if we walk in these two great principles. If our heart is filled with faith and hope in our blessed Lord, with love to him and love to our brethren, we cannot far diverge from the straight path. There are many points in which our knowledge and attainments will of course be very deficient and different from one another, and we shall have our various besetting sins to conflict with, our several prejudices, and our ignorances, to combat; we shall all have these. But if those who profess the Gospel held up these great principles in their hearts, lives and conversation, we should be walking in a blessed, happy state of unity, and not in a wretched state of disunion, discontent and division. The evils of this are best known to those who have had most experience of them. Oh! if the feet of all who profess to know Christ were "SHOD WITH THE PREPARATION OF THE GOSPEL OF PEACE," they would stand in one united phalanx against the common foe, instead of affording him the advantage of dissensions and divisions in the hosts of the Lord. Then indeed the Church of Christ would "*look forth as the morning, fair as the moon, clear as the sun, and terrible as an army with banners*." Cant. vi. 10.

The next part of the armor the Apostle speaks of is, "THE

SHIELD OF FAITH." "ABOVE ALL, TAKING THE SHIELD OF FAITH, WHEREWITH YE SHALL BE ABLE TO QUENCH ALL THE FIERY DARTS OF THE WICKED."

A shield was an instrument of defence of various dimensions. It was generally of a circular form, made of strong brass or sometimes of hides of oxen, from three to five or six feet or more in diameter. It was carried by the warrior on his left arm:—there were two fixed rings in the inner part of it, through one of which he passed his arm, and the other he grasped with his hand, and so he had a firm hold of this shield, and could move it in every direction, whether to intercept the arrows, darts, or javelins that were hurled at him from a distance, or the blows aimed at him in close combat with the foe. The shield was therefore a moveable part of his armor, the other parts were fixed—the helmet fixed on the head, the girdle on the loins, the breastplate on the breast, the greaves on the feet, but the shield and the sword were two moveable pieces of armor. The sword in the right hand to fight with, the shield on the left arm to protect the soldier in the battle.

Now you observe wherever the blow was aimed, there the shield was opposed to it. If the blow was aimed at the head, the shield was raised to protect the head; if at the heart, the shield was placed to guard the heart; wherever the blow was aimed, there the shield was opposed to it. Now this is the image the Apostle uses to express what he considers the most important part of the armor. "ABOVE ALL, TAKING THE SHIELD OF FAITH, WHEREWITH YE SHALL BE ABLE TO QUENCH ALL THE FIERY DARTS OF THE WICKED." Now we have an enemy to contend with, who is always aiming his blows at every part which he thinks most vulnerable, where he thinks he can strike us best. Of course any skilful opponent engaged in conflict always does so. If a man were fighting, he would aim his blow wherever he thought he could hit, wherever he thought his blow would tell, where he hoped the shield could not save his adversary. So it is with Satan, the enemy of our souls; wherever he thinks he can wound us, there he is sure to aim his blow. He aims it at the head—the heart—the feet—at every part where he thinks we are most vulnerable, and that he can most successfully strike us. Now what is the meaning of this? How can Satan be said to strike a blow at the head? He strikes at the understanding of man. He hopes to overthrow his faith, by blinding and deceiving his reason.—Hence, all the sophistries of superstition and infidelity—the casuistry of Popery—the subtleties of Neology, Deism, Arianism, Socinianism, and all the questions that are raised by Satan and his agents, to puzzle and mislead the intellect of man, and through these means to draw men away from God, if he can. For this he sends his emissaries to make them doubt about the truth of divine revelation, and turns every subject on which the human mind can be exercised, into an instrument for its seduction from true religion. Of this we see many examples in the present day. He endeavors to press every science into the service, and to pervert the very phenomena of creation into arguments, against the Revelation of Him who formed it. Geology furnishes a very wide field for the suggestions of speculative infidelity. Phrenology too—nay, even Astronomy itself, is perverted by the ingenuity and malice of the devil, to oppose the truth and glory of Jehovah. Why should we place a limit to the just, legitimate investigation of the works of God—of all the things that His hands have formed—in the heavens above or in the earth beneath—in the waters under the earth—in the human form, or in all His wondrous works—all—all are worthy of investigation, all declare His glory, and show forth His handy work. But the devil takes occasion by these means, to suggest infidel doubts and infidel ideas into the minds of men. When any then are puzzled, perplexed, and drawn aside by these objections against Divine truth, Satan succeeds and hits them a blow on the head. Well, how are we to meet him, "ABOVE ALL, TAKING THE SHIELD OF FAITH, WHEREWITH YE SHALL BE ABLE TO QUENCH ALL THE FIERY DARTS OF THE WICKED." It does not signify what principle a false philosopher writes in a book, or what principle he lays down in a lecture, or what speculative notion he suggests to the human mind, if it is opposed to the plain revelation of God—the believer, if he just simply sees this—if he knows that it is contrary to God's revealed truth, then he justly and directly concludes without further trouble that it must be a lie. It is of no consequence to him how clever the lie is, or how well argued the lie is, or how many learned men support the lie, if it is against God's revealed word, he knows it must be a lie, it must come from the father of lies. Now, that settles the question in the believer's mind at once, he opposes "THE SHIELD OF FAITH," to this blow aimed by Satan at his understanding, what God has said must be true, "*let God be true and every man a liar.*" That is enough for him. Therefore, every suggestion of Satan that tends to puzzle the understanding, if the mind is only satisfied of this, that it is contrary to God's revealed truth—that is enough. Then it is a lie. This satisfies the mind, this quenches the fiery dart of the enemy—in a moment.—This was our blessed Lord's mode of dealing with Satan "*It is written.*" "*It is written again.*" This should be ours too—this is using "THE SHIELD OF FAITH." It is thus we learn to silence infidel objections against all things connected with Creation,—"*through faith we understand, that the worlds were framed by the word of God, so that things which are seen were not made of things that do appear.*" Heb. xi. 3. So against the Lord Jesus, as the Creator, "*For by him were all things created that are in heaven and that are in earth, visible and invisible, whether they be thrones or dominions, or principalities, or powers, all things were created by him and for him;*" Col. i. 16. Now that one text, is enough completely to overturn all the sophisms and lies of all those who impugn the divinity of our glorious Lord and Master—the believer may simply repeat that text—or he may say, "*In the beginning was the Word, and the Word was with God, and the Word was God. The same was in the beginning with God. All things were made by him; and without him was not anything made that was made. And the Word was made flesh, and dwelt among us, and we beheld his glory, the glory as of the only begotten of the Father, full of grace and truth."* John i. 1, 2, 3, 14. These are simple texts—a child can understand them—know them as matters of fact, know them as God's word. Therefore, all cavils, all sophistries, all falsehoods, are most completely met, by simple faith in God's word, God saith so—Jehovah saith so—and that is enough. This is to oppose "THE SHIELD OF FAITH," to Satan's blows aimed at the head.

But the devil aims most chiefly, most continually, at the heart of man. For one blow he aims at our head, he aims a thousand at our heart, at our affections, our desires, our wills, to draw them away from God, and this by a thousand ways. Sometimes he excites us to murmur and rebel against the Lord's dispensations, stirring us up to desire things that the Lord has not given to us, as well as to murmur at things He has given us, exciting us to turn to the creature, and to place those affections on the creature that are due to the Lord alone, drawing us into that sin of which the Lord speaks, when he saith, "*My people have committed two evils; they have forsaken me the fountain of living waters, and hewed them out cisterns, broken cisterns, that can hold no water.*" Jer. ii. 13. This is that to which the natural mind is always inclined, therefore, Satan's great effort is to draw the heart from God.

God's claim is on the heart of man. This is His divine law, He hath a legal right and title to it, "*Thou shalt love the Lord thy God with all thy heart.*"

The devil's object is to keep the heart from God. "*My son give me thine heart,*" saith the Lord. Prov. xxxii. 26. Nay, "give me thine heart," saith the devil, or "give the creature thine heart," or "give anything thine heart but God." It is of no consequence to what Satan can draw the heart, provided he can draw it from God. If the heart is not God's, it is no matter to what sort of idol it is given. It does not signify whether we bow down to an image of wood or stone, or whether our hearts are fixed on worldly things; as our Lord saith, "*take heed and beware of covetousness;*" Luke xii. 15; which the Apostle tells us "*is idolatry,*" Col. iii. 5. When our hearts are fixed on the creature, whatever the creature be, they are withdrawn from God; and if the heart is turned away from God, the object of Satan is effected, therefore he aims his blows continually at our hearts. Now, how is he to be met? Only by the armor of God. "ABOVE ALL, TAKING THE SHIELD OF FAITH, WHEREWITH YE SHALL BE ABLE TO QUENCH ALL THE FIERY DARTS OF THE WICKED." The means by which the heart is protected from being turned aside from God, is by having the heart filled with faith in Christ. This draws it to its proper object "*faith worketh by love,*" love is produced by the belief of the love of Christ to sinners. Therefore, faith in Christ must produce love to Christ; it cannot be otherwise, and therefore, when you want to produce love, the way to cultivate love is to cultivate faith. Love is the result of faith. Both are the fruits of the Spirit. We cannot love the Lord, till we believe on Him. When we believe in Him, we cannot but love Him. Therefore, the way to have the affections kept fixed on Christ is to have the heart fixed on Christ by faith, it will be necessarily drawn to Him by love, if it be fixed on Him by faith. Why? Because faith is the belief of His love—the belief of His work—the belief of His salvation—of His great and everlasting salvation. This necessarily brings happiness and peace to the soul—necessarily draws the heart's affections to Himself. "*We love him, because he first loved us.*" 1 John iv. 19. He gains our heart because He gives us His heart. He "*gave his back to the smiters, and his cheeks to them that plucked off the hair: He hid not His face from shame and spitting.*" Isaiah l. 6. He gave his hands to the nails, He gave His heart to the spear for sinners, and He says to every soul who trusts in His redeeming love—"*My son, give me thine heart.*" When we are able to believe on Him—to receive the gracious pardon—to look for the glorious inheritance purchased for us, by His precious blood—then we learn to love Him—to trust Him as the conqueror of sin and Satan—death and hell. It is this faith and love of Christ that guards the heart from Satan. Stand therefore, "TAKING THE SHIELD OF FAITH, WHEREWITH YE SHALL BE ABLE TO QUENCH ALL THE FIERY DARTS OF THE WICKED."

Thus, and only thus, can you guard your hearts and your affections from the fiery darts of Satan.

But Satan aims those darts too, at the conscience of the sinner,—He aims many fiery darts against the conscience as well as the heart.

Perhaps he is aiming at the consciences of some of my hearers here to-day, and it is well to consider how he wages his warfare.

One mode of his attack is—he tells you—"you are not fit to come to Christ, you are too bad." Perhaps he avails himself of your besetting sin to tempt you to some evils, or perhaps, he injects some corrupt imaginations, passions, lusts into your heart, and then makes use of these as arguments, to keep you from Christ. He says "how can you be fit to come to Christ? or how can such a sinner as you be a child of God?" He tells you that "Whatever others may be, there are in your case certain aggravations, with which he now charges your conscience, that both preclude you from the hope of having ever been a believer in Christ, and utterly unfit you to come to Christ. Now, you must be delivered from the power of such and such a sin—you must conquer such and such a propensity—you must totally abandon such and such a lust and become a new creature, before you can have any trust or confidence in coming to Christ, and before you can possibly conclude that you can be a believer." This is a fiery dart of Satan, aimed at the conscience to keep the poor sinner from Christ, to wound him so deeply,—to fasten that dart in his conscience, as a barbed arrow that cannot be drawn, to hinder him from looking to Jesus—to make him think, that the blood of Jesus cannot pardon the guilt and heal the wound. How now are we to meet such an assault or quench such a dart as this? "TAKE THE SHIELD OF FAITH." Acknowledge your sins. When Satan marshals and parades your sins before your conscience, and numbers the host that are against you—when he upbraids you with their number and extent—when he endeavors to fasten the stings of guilt in your conscience—to make you think yourself too bad to come to Christ, that Christ cannot receive so vile a sinner,—Then "TAKE THE SHIELD OF FAITH,"—acknowledge your sin—tell Satan you know it all and more too—tell him you are viler than even he can represent you to be—tell him that, liar as he is, he cannot exaggerate your sin—that it is as great or greater than he can make it. But tell him "*This is a faithful saying and worthy of all acceptation, that Christ Jesus came into the world to save sinners.*" Tim. i. 15. Tell him, God declares that "*The blood of Jesus Christ His Son cleanseth us from sin.*" 1 John i. 7. Tell him that the Lord, who inspired that word, knew the extent—the nature—number and depth of all the sins that ever should defile the human race, when He said "*Him that cometh to me I will in no wise cast out.*" John vi. 37. When He said, "*Come unto me all ye that labor, and are heavy laden and I will give you rest.*" Matt. xi. 28. When He said, "*I have blotted out as a thick cloud, thy transgressions, and, as a cloud, thy sins.*" Isaiah xliv. 22. When He inspired the Prophet to say, "*Thou wilt cast all their sins into the depths of the sea.*" Mic. vii. 19. And if Satan could bring any sin on this side hell, too great to be forgiven—too great for the blood of Christ to cleanse—he must falsify all the truth of God—he must dry up the Fountain opened for sin and uncleanness,—he must be able to prevent "*the Lamb of God from taking away the sin of the world,*"—he must pluck the sheep of Christ out of his hand—he must hurl God the Father from His throne of grace, and God the Son from His throne of glory. Therefore, tell Satan that the Lord is your Sun, and the Lord is your Shield, and that he must overcome the Lord of life before he can conquer you, or pluck you out of His hand. This is to use the shield of faith, and thus "*We are more than conquerors through Him that loved us.*" Rom. viii. 37.

If the devil tries to turn the heart to vain hopes and to refuges of lies—leads it to look to other means of salvation besides Christ —if that single text, "*The blood of Jesus Christ His Son cleanseth us from all sin,*" 1st John i. 7, is brought home by the Spirit to the heart, all other refuges vanish like the shades of night before the rising sun. I remember a dear young friend of mine, a Roman Catholic, who was often listening to the Gospel, to whom I had constant opportunities of speaking on the subject, and I set before him constantly the blessings of the Gospel, and he listened and read his Bible. One day a clergyman, a friend of mine, came to see me, and he was talking to this young lad. Amongst other things—he said to him, "*The blood of Jesus Christ cleanseth us from all sin.*"

"What!" said the other, "is that in the Bible?"

"Yes," said the clergyman, "it is."

"Where?" he inquired.

My friend found the text and gave it to him.

He read the passage, "*The blood of Jesus Christ His Son cleanseth us from all sin.*" "Then," said he, "if that be so, everything else must be vain. Every other hope and refuge must be false!"

The Lord brought the light of that text to his heart—and therefore his heart fled to Jesus, rested on Jesus. Popery was gone. He saw that every other refuge was false. The prejudices, ignorances, and superstitions, in which his mind had till then been trained, vanished from before him, all other refuges were renounced, when the Gospel proclaimed Jesus to him, and he beheld "*The Lamb of God who taketh away the sins of the world.*" He believed that the blood of Jesus cleanseth from all sin, and the next Lord's day he received the Communion, the commemoration of the finished work of Christ, in the congregation of the Church of England. If your consciences are, like his, delivered from fear through the belief of the Gospel—If you are like him enabled to come to Christ, and to cast your souls on Him, without doubt or fear—If you are resting simply on the Lord Jesus Christ and his glorious work for all your salvation, and for the security of an inheritance of glory—If you are able to rest on that one truth, "*the blood of Jesus Christ cleanseth from all sin,*" what is the consequence? Your language ought to be, "*Return then unto thy rest, O my soul; for the Lord hath dealt bountifully with thee. For thou hast delivered my soul from death, mine eyes from tears, and my feet from falling.*" Psalm cxvi. 7, 8. "*What shall I render unto the Lord for all his benefits toward me? I will take the cup of salvation, and call upon the name of the Lord.*"—"*I will take the cup of salvation,*" I will receive the blessed, glorious testimony of his everlasting Gospel; I will look to "*the Lamb of God who taketh away the sins of the world.*" I will rejoice in the light of the Sun of righteousness, I will take the Lord as my Sun and the Lord as my Shield.—This is "THE SHIELD OF FAITH WHEREWITH I SHALL BE ABLE TO QUENCH ALL THE FIERY DARTS OF THE WICKED."

Again, there is no time that Satan aims such volleys of fiery darts at a poor sinner, as when he catches him backsliding. Satan will endeavor to deceive him, to make light of sin, that it is only a small thing—a small deviation—a little compromise with the world—a trifling concession on his part—it will not do him any harm. He will say, "Don't be uneasy—don't be afraid," until by suggestions such as these, he gradually draws on the sinner, till he finds he has backslidden and fallen away from God. Then he turns on him, and reproaches him bitterly with his fall. He says, "Now you are gone—you have brought reproach on the

Gospel—you have trodden under foot the Son of God—you have fallen from grace, and there is no hope for you.

Well—Is there no armor against this fiery dart? Is there no shield to take hold of, or oppose to this accusation of Satan? It is written, "*Return, ye backsliding children, and I will heal your backslidings.*" Jer. iii. 22. We often fall when none see us fall but God, ourselves, and the devil; we often fall, when our own conscience is the only earthly witness; we feel our own fall, and Satan aims volleys of fiery darts—of fierce accusations—bitter reproaches—blasted hopes, and unbelieving terrors, and all to frighten us from Christ. But then, as at all times, gird your armor close. "TAKE THE SHIELD OF FAITH, WHEREWITH YE SHALL BE ABLE TO QUENCH ALL THE FIERY DARTS OF THE WICKED." Tell him, "True, I have fallen, yes alas! I have fallen deeply," but it is written, "*Return, ye backsliding children, and I will heal your backslidings.*" Tell him, what a glorious image the Lord uses there, to show the riches of His grace in healing backsliders! "*They say, if a man put away his wife, and she go from him, and become another man's, shall he return unto her again? shall not that land be greatly polluted? But thou hast played the harlot with many lovers, yet return again to me, saith the Lord.*" Jer. iii. 1. And will He put you away? Oh! no, after all your ingratitude! "*Yet, return again to me, saith the Lord.*" Oh! what love! What mercy! Christ is the only Husband that would say to such a wife—"*Yet, return again to me, saith the Lord.*"

Tell Satan this, and shout unto him in the language of the Prophet, "*Rejoice not against me, O mine enemy: when I fall, I shall arise; when I sit in darkness, the Lord shall be a light unto me. I will bear the indignation of the Lord, because I have sinned against him, until he plead my cause, and execute judgment for me: he will bring me forth to the light, and I shall behold his righteousness.*" Micah vii. 8, 9. Shout this, I say, in the very face of Satan.

Understand then, what it is to take the shield of faith! It is to take God's Word—to take God's promises—to take God's truth, and to answer the objections of sin, Satan, the world, death and hell, with the salvation of Jesus. This is to "TAKE THE SHIELD OF FAITH." Thus shall you "QUENCH ALL THE FIERY DARTS OF THE WICKED;" and whether they are aimed at the head, to wound it with difficulties, doubts, and evil counsels—or at the heart, to fill it with distractions, terrors, lusts, evil passions and imaginations—at the conscience, to frighten it with sin—with all the evils of the head—the heart—the life. No matter at what vital part, or at what member of the body the fiery darts of Satan may be aimed, guarded with all the armor of God in every part, "ABOVE ALL TAKE THE SHIELD OF FAITH," wherewith you shall be able to intercept and quench them all. That is, in plain, unfigurative language, bring Christ, by faith, against Satan; bring Christ, His Word—His work—His righteousness—His blood—His promises—His love—His power—His faithfulness and truth, against all the power and malice of the devil, and you shall be "*More than conqueror, through him that loved you.*" This is that which the Apostle says, "*Whatsoever is born of God overcometh the world, and this is the victory that overcometh the world.*" What? Not our resolutions—nor our strength—nor our moral principles—nor our religious education—nor our privileges—nor our Church—nor ordinances—nor prayers—nor anything we have or are, but it is this—"*Even our faith. Who is he that overcometh the world, but he that believeth that Jesus is the Son of God.*" 1 John v. 4, 5. He that believeth in Jesus—in all His revealed character—His Word—His work—His offices; He it is, and He alone, that overcomes, and can overcome the world, the flesh, or the devil. Therefore, "ABOVE ALL TAKING THE SHIELD OF FAITH, WHEREWITH YE SHALL BE ABLE TO QUENCH ALL THE FIERY DARTS OF THE WICKED."

Blessed, then, be our God! He sends us this armor to buckle on us; and Oh! what need we have of it! Every moment our enemy is on the alert—always active—always watchful—always full of malice; we have need continually, then, of an Almighty power, and an Almighty protector. "*We wrestle not against flesh and blood, but against principalities and powers.*" So David saith, "*There be many that fight against me, O thou Most High.*" Ps. lvi. 2. And you see, it is under the image of armor that Christ is given to us, as our all in all—our Alpha and Omega. For you observe, in all parts of the armor, every one of them is but an image of Christ; so that we may say with the Psalmist, "*Our soul waiteth for the Lord, he is our help and our shield,*" Ps. xxxiii. 20; again, "*Behold, O God, our shield,*" and again, "*the Lord is a sun and shield,*" Psalm lxxxiv. 9, 11. "*The Lord is my light and my salvation, whom shall I fear? the Lord is the strength of my life, of whom shall I be afraid? When the wicked, even mine enemies and my foes came upon me to eat up my flesh, they stumbled and fell. Though an host should encamp against me, my heart shall not fear; though war should rise against me, in this will I be confident.*" Ps. xxvii. 1—4. All these passages in these Psalms—all that can give trust and confidence in our God, may serve to illustrate being clothed with the armor of God, for in Him is all our strength, and all our salvation. "*He is a shield to them that put their trust in him.*" Prov. xxx. 5. Therefore, we may "*Be strong in the Lord, and in the power of his might,*" so shall we be "*more than conquerors, through him that loved us.*"

"*Now unto him that is able to do exceeding abundantly above all that we ask or think, according to the power that worketh in us. Unto him be glory in the Church, by Christ Jesus, throughout all ages, world without end, Amen.*" Chap. iii. 20, 21.

FIFTIETH LECTURE.

EPHESIANS VI.—17, 18.

"And take the hemlet of salvation, and the sword of the Spirit, which is the word of God: praying always with all prayer and supplication in the Spirit, and watching thereunto with all perseverance and supplication for all saints."

HAVING shown, I trust in some faint degree, the figurative meaning and spiritual use of "*the shield of faith, wherewith we shall be able to quench all the fiery darts of the wicked*," we come to consider in the 17th verse, the other parts of the Christian armor, added by the Apostle—"AND TAKE THE HELMET OF SALVATION, AND THE SWORD OF THE SPIRIT, WHICH IS THE WORD OF GOD." With these, to complete his armor, the Christian is equipped for his warfare. He is armed here from head to foot. His "*loins are girt about with truth.*" He has on "*the breastplate of righteousness.*" He has his "*feet shod with the preparation of the Gospel of peace.*" He has "*the shield of faith*" upon his left arm, to guard every part of his body which the enemy can assault. And now his head covered with "THE HELMET OF SALVATION, AND THE SWORD OF THE SPIRIT, WHICH IS THE WORD OF GOD," in his right hand, with which, in turn, he is to strike and vanquish his foe.

What does he mean by the "HELMET OF SALVATION?" The expression occurs again twice in the Sacred Volume; once as applied to the Mighty Conqueror Himself, the Lord Jesus, Isaiah lix. 17; and again, as applied to His followers, 1 Thess. v. 8, "*Let us who are of the day be sober, putting on the breastplate of faith and love, and for an helmet, the hope of salvation.*"

It is here called "*the hope of salvation.*" We considered on the last day, these two great principles of the Christian, faith and love; and here we have another joined with them, Hope.

"Hope springs eternal in the human breast,
Man never is, but always to be blest,"

said a Poet, who did not know, poor fellow! in what the hope that really could alone support the soul of man consists. The principle is true. It is the necessary condition of a rational, immortal being, in a finite stage of his existence, that he should live on hope.

Man is formed to live on hope, and he does live on hope, every human being lives on hope; and that last stage of mental anguish, which our language supplies us with a word to describe, is that of despair, which is derived from the very words which signify, being cast down from hope. It is from the Latin words, *de* and *spero*, as it were, *de spe dejectus*, that is, cast down from hope, in despair, having no more hope.

From the moment that the mind of a child can form to itself the anticipation of any enjoyment, which it can attain on this earth, from that moment hope springs up in his breast. When the child sees a thing and likes it, he hopes to possess it; he stretches out his little hand—he hopes and tries to gain it. And so it is, when he grows up through every stage of childhood, boyhood, youth, manhood, even to the last extremity of age. Hope is the moving principle of the human heart. But, alas! it appears that man in this, as in all other things, is fallen—and fallen from his God. He has lost the only true and solid source of happiness, and therefore, he has lost the true and solid object of hope. We have found, every one of us, that our hopes, as far as they have been confined to this world, have universally ended in disappointment. We have hoped, and we have often been disappointed in attaining our hopes, but, perhaps, man is never more disappointed in losing the object of his hope, than he is in gaining it; for if he is disappointed in losing the thing he hopes for, he is much more disappointed in finding, that when he has attained it, it was, at best, but a delusion; and there is no man more unhappy than the man who knows not God—whose hopes of happiness are fixed on earth, and who has it in his power to indulge himself in his vain pursuit of that happiness, by gaining the successive objects of his restless desires.

The man who can most easily gain the object he is continually seeking for on this earth, as far as money and power can attain it, is, generally speaking, the most unhappy man; just exactly as the child whose parents most indulge, and most desire to gratify all its whims, and to procure for it whatever it wishes, is always the most unhappy child in the world. And so a man—an indulged man, if I may use the expression, a man that can indulge himself in the things he desires, is, generally, the most unhappy sinner.

Therefore, the hope of the natural heart, resting, as it does, on earthly objects, while it is the spring of human endeavor, is, at the same time, the continual source of disappointment; and never, until man is restored to the right object of his hope—never until his hope is fixed on that which does not disappoint, but satisfies the soul—never till then, is he enabled to enjoy the happiness of solid hope.

When man, then, is brought through the riches of the grace of Christ, to believe the everlasting Gospel—when the glorious hope of salvation is given to his heart—when he knows how that hope is secured to him through the blood of the everlasting Covenant—then, indeed, it is a hope in which he is enabled to rejoice—a hope in which he never can be disappointed—a hope in which the joy of fruition outstrips the eagerness of expectation. If we have that hope, we may place it as an impenetrable helmet on our head, and stand without a fear in the thickest of the hottest conflict.

The devil is continually holding out false hopes to men. It is one of his innumerable wiles that he holds out false deceptive hopes—and fills the head with vain delusive dreams and schemes of happiness. Do you not know something of this? Do you not know what it is to build castles in the air? Have you never built them? I am sure I have, very often. The devil seeks to employ us in building these as much as he can. To delude—to deceive, and to divert from sober truth, is Satan's constant aim. He deceived our first parents by holding out delusive hopes of imaginary good, and preventing them from the belief of the real evil that was before them. As he led them to hope, that God would not fulfil His word. God is not so severe as He says. God will not execute such a severe threat on you "*Thou shalt not surely die.*" So he deceived them, by leading them to hope foolishly for happiness, thus he added, "*For God doth know, that in the day ye eat thereof, ye shall be as gods, knowing good and evil.*" Gen. iii. 4, 5.

Now, the excitement of false delusive hope, with which the devil deceived our first parents, in this instance, is just an example of the very same efforts that he is always making, to produce similar delusions in the mind of all their posterity; and the very same disappointment of their hopes which they experienced, is an emblem of the universal disappointment ever attending the hopes of earthly happiness, with which he is continually deluding the imaginations of men. They did know good and evil; the devil told them the truth, and he often tells truth in that way, but he tells truth for a lying object; the end of the devil's truth is a lie, they did know good and evil, but they knew good and evil only to be involved in one, and excluded from the other—to be involved in sin, and to be shut out from Paradise. They knew good, the tree of life was shut out from them, the light of God's countenance, the blessing of His favor was turned from them, they knew evil, they were driven out from Eden to condemnation, toil and death, sentence of death was passed upon their body and their soul.

So it is with us when all our hopes of happiness are fixed on earth, disappointment, misery, eternal death succeed. Now, I say, the devil fills the head of men with vain delusive hopes,—with vain abortive projects, of happiness and peace on earth. And so when the Lord would make His people conquerors, in their conflict with their spiritual foe, He gives them one great and glorious hope with which as it were to crown their heads, he commands them to "TAKE THE HELMET OF SALVATION." Let all your schemes, plans, objects, tend to that one glorious end, that blessed hope, in which you shall not be disappointed. There is a hope secure and solid, sealed by the blood, and ratified by the covenant, and by the oath of God.

Oh! consider, what the blessed object of that hope is—eternal happiness—eternal joy—eternal glory—an eternal inheritance in the presence of our Covenant God at his coming—an "*Inheritance incorruptible, undefiled, and that fadeth not away.*" 1st Peter, i. 4. "*They shall hunger no more, neither thirst any more; neither shall the sun light on them, nor any heat; for the Lamb which is in the midst of the throne, shall feed them, and shall lead them unto living fountains of waters: and God shall wipe away all tears from their eyes.*" Rev. vii. 16, 17. Oh blessed hope!—This is that hope that is spoken of by the Apostle, when he saith, "*Looking for that blessed hope, and the glorious appearing of the great God and our Saviour Jesus Christ.*" Tit. ii. 13. Then consider, how that hope is ratified. We have it set before us in Heb. vi. The Apostle, in that chapter is reminding believers of the covenant promises that God made to Abraham. At the 11th verse he says, "*We desire that every one of you do show the same diligence, to the full assurance of hope unto the end.*" Mark those words: "*The full assurance of hope.*" It ought not to be a vague hope—not a vain hope—but a confident—assured—solid hope. "*The full assurance of hope,*" that is a solid assurance that your hope shall not be disappointed.

It is quite necessary for the comfort of hope, that we have a confident expectation that it shall not be frustrated. Therefore, persons, before they allow themselves to entertain the hope of anything, ought to know on what grounds they cherish it. I must be a fool to hope, if I have not solid ground on which that hope is founded. And if we have solid ground for hope, in proportion as we have, so we should indulge, enjoy and cherish it—so he saith, "*We desire that every one of you do show the same diligence, to the full assurance of hope unto the end.*" You see the glorious hope of the Gospel is one of which we may have full assurance; and then, as much as if the believer should say, what ground have I for this! What ground is there for this full assurance? The Apostle explains and enforces his meaning:—"*That ye be not slothful, but followers of them, who through faith and patience inherit the promises.*" Heb. vi. 12. Hope is founded on faith; the hope that the believer has of eternal life, is founded on his belief of the promises of God, by which that hope is secured; so he says, "*That ye be not slothful, but followers of them, who through faith and patience inherit the promises.*" That which is promised is the thing we hope for. The ground on which we hope for the thing promised, is the confidence we have in the person who promises it. So the promises of God are the security for our hope, and our belief of the promises—our confidence in the faithfulness and truth of God, is that, on which our hope is built. When we know, that when God has promised, He cannot lie; therefore we trust in His promises, and hope for that which He promised us. Hence faith produces diligence—leads us to hope, and to act on our hope, and here is the solid ground for them both.

"*For when God made promise to Abraham, because he could swear by no greater, he sware by himself, saying, Surely, blessing*

I will bless thee, and multiplying I will multiply thee. And so after he had patiently endured, he obtained the promise." Heb. vi. 13—15. God had promised him that seed, in whom "*all the nations of the earth should be blessed;*" and after he had patiently endured throughout the time that elapsed between the giving and the fulfilling of the promise, during the progressive age of himself and his wife Sarai, see what cause of faith and patience Abraham had; and so he says, "*After he had patiently endured, he obtained the promise.*"—Now observe! "*For men verily swear by the greater: and an oath for confirmation is to them an end of all strife. Wherein God willing more abundantly to show unto the heirs of promise the immutability of his counsel, confirmed it by an oath.*" Heb. vi. 16, 17. He sware by Himself, He gave His covenant promise, and He sware by Himself, that that promise should be kept, saying, "*Surely,*" that is, "as surely as I exist"—"*that by two immutable things in which it was impossible for God to lie,*" namely, God's covenant promise, and the oath by which that promise was confirmed,—"*We might have a strong consolation, who have fled for refuge to lay hold upon the hope set before us: which hope we have as an anchor of the soul, both sure and stedfast, and which entereth into that within the veil.*" Heb. vi. 18, 19. Our hope is within the veil—it is in the presence of our God—we are "*Kept by the power of God through faith unto salvation.*" 1st Peter i. 5. We depend on the covenant promise of God; and therefore, in depending on that, we have the full assurance of that hope which is ratified by God's covenant promise and God's oath; and it is here called the anchor of the soul—"*which hope we have as an anchor of the soul, both sure and stedfast, and which entereth into that within the veil.*" The anchor is cast into the deep—it is out of sight—we cast it forth, and where the anchor gets its firm hold, and where the cable that moors the vessel to the anchor is sure, the vessel will outride any storm. The winds may blow, the sea may rage—but while the anchor holds its grip, and the cable the anchor, there the vessel rides in security. So when the believer has his hope cast within the veil, there it is out of sight—there it is fixed—fixed, fast as the covenant promise, oath and power of a faithful and omnipotent God can hold it, so we may say, "*If God be for us, who can be against us?*"—"*Who shall separate us from the love of Christ.*" Rom. viii. 34, 35. The winds may rage, the storm may howl, the billows may foam, but it is the believer's privilege to outride every storm, because God is his salvation, so he trusts and need not be afraid. Hope is "*the anchor of his soul, both sure and stedfast, which entereth into that within the veil.*"

It is this glorious hope of salvation, which is here called "THE HELMET OF SALVATION." It is placed as it were, on the head, for this reason, I suppose, because the hopes of men are always derived from the vain projects, and imaginations of their brain, and their own schemes of earthly good. All these are now to be cast aside, and there is to be but one scheme—one project—one hope of sure and solid happiness that is to fill the head—and it is this, the glorious hope that is secured by the covenant promise and oath of God in that which is to come. Therefore, the Apostle has a beautiful prayer to this effect, in his Epistle to the Romans where God is called "the God of hope." "*Now the God of hope fill you with all joy and peace, in believing, that you may abound in hope through the power of the Holy Ghost.*" Rom. xv. 13.

He is called the God of hope, because He is the God whose promises alone can give all true, all solid hope, and in whose faithfulness alone our hope can be confidently fixed, and whose power secures the performance of His promises for his people. He is the God who gives it, and the God who secures it; whose grace cherishes and keeps alive that hope in the heart,—who shall never disappoint, but shall fulfil it to the day of everlasting glory. So it is the Holy Ghost who inspired the prayer which He will Himself fulfil. "*The God of hope fill you with all joy and peace in believing, that ye may abound in hope through the power of the Holy Ghost;*" "*fill you with all joy and peace in believing;*" therefore, not only with hope, but with a sure, solid, abiding, yea, and an abounding hope, ratified by the covenant promise and oath of God. Therefore, you see, as long as a person is ignorant of the Gospel of Jesus, he can have no hope; he can have no peace nor joy in believing; and so, when the Lord describes in his Word, the miserable state of the ungodly, as we have it in this very Epistle, ii. 11, 12. He saith, "*Remember, that ye being in time past Gentiles in the flesh, who are called uncircumcision by that which is called the circumcision in the flesh made by hands; that at that time ye were without Christ, being aliens from the commonwealth of Israel, and strangers from the covenant of promise, having no hope, and without God in the world.*" Chap. ii. 11, 12.

Observe their state, "at that time," they had "*no hope,*" and were "*without God in the world.*" Then, what gave them hope? "*But now in Christ Jesus, ye who sometimes were afar off, are made nigh by the blood of Christ.*" Chap. ii. 13.

When you have Christ to depend on, you have the glorious hope that these promises ratify and confirm. You are warranted to enjoy the full assurance of hope—you can put on "THE HELMET OF SALVATION," then you can say with the Prophet—"*behold, God is my salvation; I will trust, and not be afraid; for the Lord Jehovah is my strength and my song; He also is become my salvation.*" Isaiah xii. 2. You can say with the Psalmist, "*O God the Lord, the strength of my salvation, thou hast covered my head in the day of battle.*" Psalm cxl. 7.

Now then, dear friends, let me ask you this question—Have you this helmet on your head? Is the one grand project of happiness that fills your thoughts, that your soul should enjoy the eternal blessings that are promised to you in the glorious Gospel? Is Christ your hope? Is Christ all your salvation? Are you looking for the glorious appearing of the Lord Jesus, "*who shall change our vile body, that it may be fashioned like unto His glorious body*," when that earthly tabernacle, that so soon shall be in the dust, shall arise again from its grave, a glorious body, reunited to your spirit, and so you shall be ever with the Lord? Is that the hope of happiness which you lay out for yourself? Or are you putting away all these things from your consideration, and is your happiness resting on something for which you are looking in this world? Oh! my dear friends, if your happiness is resting on this world, how vain is your hope! How miserable are your prospects! How wretched is your condition! How naked and unarmed you are! How defenceless is your head in the midst of your foes, a prey to them all—world, flesh, and devil!

Oh! what a blessed privilege it is, to have a religious hope. When the head is covered with "THE HELMET OF SALVATION," we are more than conquerors over sin and death and hell!

See how soon a person may be cut off! Youth, health and strength are no securities from death. My dear friend and brother—my young brother in the ministry, for whose afflicted family we have been praying:—Mr. S. was cut off in a moment; fever came and swept him away, just when commencing the exercise of his ministry; just at the moment of entering on a post of usefulness, where he was calculated in every respect, to be a blessing to those around him! In a moment he was cut off! But he had "THE HELMET OF SALVATION" on his head—Christ the hope of glory. He was taken from the evil to come; he was ready to go. Though his mind was wandering much under the influence of fever, yet it did not seem in the least to wander from his Lord. This sometimes happens to believers. But it was not so with him—"I am happy," his last words were, "I am thine and thou art mine." What a blessed joyful hope!—A hope that maketh not ashamed!

Alas! my friends, if we are destitute of this hope when we are well and strong, to what are we to look when death shall come upon us? A time of fever, or of acute disease, is a bad time to begin to learn the hope of our salvation. Of what use can a minister of Christ be to a sinner who cannot understand him? Of what use is the Bible when he can neither read, hear, or listen to it? Of what use is prayer, when he can neither attend or join in it?' Now is the time to ask, have you that blessed hope?—that blessed hope that is spoken of here—that glorious "HELMET OF SALVATION,"—Christ the hope of glory? Oh! dear friends, "*to-day, while it is called to-day*," "TAKE THE HELMET OF SALVATION"—put it upon your head. "THE HELMET OF SALVATION!" Think of that—no weapon can pierce through it.—"THE HELMET OF SALVATION" is impenetrable—it is cast in the armory of God—it is complete—perfect—it can neither be perforated, cleft, nor broken. Salvation is a finished work—a perfect work—nothing can be added to it—nothing can be taken from it—Salvation is complete as the Lord of Glory can make it. "IT IS FINISHED," was his own glorious testimony. "THE HELMET OF SALVATION!"—Oh, that you and I may have it on our heads! We need not fear any battle or any conflict, if we go with our heads armed with the "HELMET OF SALVATION," then may we boldly say, "*The Lord is my light, and my salvation; whom shall I fear? the Lord is the strength of my life; of whom shall I be afraid?* Psalm xxvii. 1.

This is the last part of our defensive armor; but the warrior is not to act, merely, on the defensive: he is to attack and conquer his foe—He requires, therefore, weapons as well as armor—but he is fully provided in the armory of God. So the Apostle adds, "AND THE SWORD OF THE SPIRIT, WHICH IS THE WORD OF GOD;" that is the weapon of our warfare. We must be engaged in constant warfare, and "THE SWORD OF THE SPIRIT" is the weapon with which we are to carry on all our battles.

What is the meaning of that? What is meant by having "THE SWORD OF THE SPIRIT, WHICH IS THE WORD OF GOD?" The sword is an instrument, both of attack and defence; it is an instrument with which the combatant not only attacks his foe, but parries the thrusts that are aimed at him by his opponent. So the Word of the living God is not only that weapon by which we are to attack our enemies; but that with which we are to parry the thrusts they make at us. Some blows and darts are to be intercepted by the shield—some are to be warded off, and parried by the sword. He knows but half the use of his blade, who cannot guard as well as thrust with it. Some false principles are suggested to us: How are they to be met? By the word of God. Many temptations are presented to us. How are they resisted? By the word of God. We see The Mighty Warrior using this weapon in a deadly conflict—a conflict on which the salvation of a world depended; even the Captain of our salvation, we see him using "THE SWORD OF THE SPIRIT, WHICH IS THE WORD OF GOD." When Satan came upon our blessed Lord, and found him suffering under all the weakness of human necessity, of want, and hunger:—He attacks our Divine Master, and takes advantage of his sufferings as man to tempt his majesty as God; "*If thou be the Son of God, command that these stones be made bread.*" Now, he came into the world to manifest that He was the Son of God; He came into the world to manifest his mighty power as the Son of God, to save, to show that he was the promised Christ—the anointed Messiah, who was to "*come to seek and to save that which was lost.*" The devil puts Him here upon the proof of His person and office as it were—he puts it upon Him, either to manifest His power, or to confess his inability to do so—"*If thou be the Son of God, command that these stones be made bread.*" Mat. iv. 3; as much as to say—"If you cannot command that these stones be made bread, you must acknowledge you are not the Son of God. If you comply, then I compel you to act at my order—if you refuse, I force you to forego your power as the Son of God." He places our Lord, as he supposed, in a dilemma, and thought, that let Him do what He would, he must have the advantage over Him. Look at the cunning, the malice, the audacity of the prince of darkness, daring the Omnipotent to show forth His power—

daring the majesty of the Son of God to show forth the truth of His claim to the title—so that it would seem as if His honor and glory demanded, that He should comply with the suggestion of the devil.

But how does the Lord meet him? He answered and said, "*It is written, man shall not live by bread alone, but by every word that proceedeth out of the mouth of God.*" Mat. iv. 4. The devil tempted Him, you see, as God,—"*If thou be the Son of God;*" he dared His omnipotence. Jesus teaches the devil a lesson. He shows him, that he was also man. His answer was as much as to say, "You dare me as God, but I am here as man, I am God, but I am also man; I am God manifested in the flesh—I am Jehovah revealed in humanity, I have taken upon myself the responsibility of man—I have taken upon me to fulfil the laws of God for man—God's word is therefore my standard—God's word is my weapon. The time shall come soon enough when you shall know and feel that I am the Son of God, but I am now to make you know and feel that I am a righteous man, and '*man shall not live by bread alone, but by every word that proceedeth out of the mouth of God.*'" How glorious it is to see the Lord Jesus Christ putting forth the full actings of His nature as man—to see His holiness as man—His sinless righteousness—His obedience as man—His devotedness to God, His heavenly Father, as man—showing, that it was His meat and His drink, to do the will of Him that sent Him, and to finish His work. Here you see the mighty Conqueror, the "Captain of our salvation" with "THE SWORD OF THE SPIRIT," parrying the attack of the devil. Satan is foiled—his taunt against Jehovah manifest in the flesh, falls powerless, and is retorted on his head, by the man, Christ Jesus. He had not another word to say—he was silenced. It is a great blessing to see the power of "THE SWORD OF THE SPIRIT!" To see it wielded thus by our Divine Master, falling with one blow on the head of Satan, that needs no second stroke to crush him! There is no argument that man can use, let it be ever so beautifully composed—ever so logically arranged, and so exquisitely expressed that can silence an adversary, no matter who he is, half so powerfully as one text of Scripture.

I recollect an eminent minister telling me, he had been thrown into company with an infidel. He was bringing forth the objections of infidelity against Christianity. Instead of entering into any of his arguments, "I answered him," said he, "by quoting text after text from God's word. Unable to answer the Scriptures, and irritated at his own incompetence, he said,"

"But how do you prove that this is the Word of God?"

"Why," said I "when I use a sword and pierce my adversary, and see him fall powerless at my feet, is it not absurd to ask me 'how do you prove this is a sword?' I see, and you feel that it is 'THE SWORD OF THE SPIRIT WHICH IS THE WORD OF GOD.'"

But observe, how our Lord wields this Divine weapon again. "*Then the devil taketh him up into the holy city, and setteth him on a pinnacle of the temple, and saith unto him, if thou be the Son of God, cast thyself down."*

Now mark—The devil, in the first place, tempted Christ from His suffering—from His bodily suffering, and weakness. He was weak with hunger, and he took occasion from that, to tempt him as God to prove His omnipotence as Jehovah. Our Lord answered him, by proving His faith, and His obedience as man, and quotes the Scripture to silence him. Here the devil retorts on our Lord with his own weapon, he tempts now our Lord's faith in God's power and providence as man. He tempts Him with the authority of Scripture, and puts His faith in God's promise to the test, "*If thou be the Son of God, cast thyself down.*" That is to say, "If you have faith in the word of God, then here is a promise, '*For it is written, he shall give his angels charge concerning thee, and in their hands they shall bear thee up, lest at any time thou dash thy foot against a stone.*' Mat. iv. 5, 6. If therefore you believe the promises of God, here you are as a man; now if you believe the word of God,—if you depend on the truth of God,—if you have faith in the power of God,—if you are, as you profess, such a righteous, faithful man—and if you shall live '*by every word that proceedeth out of the mouth of God,*' now I put your faith and obedience to the test; '*Cast thyself down,*' here is a '*Word that proceedeth out of the mouth of God,*' to protect you."

Mark now, our Lord's next blow with the "SWORD OF THE SPIRIT:" "*Jesus said unto him, it is written again, thou shalt not tempt the Lord thy God.*" Mat. iv. 7. That is to say, "If I, as a man, throw myself down from the pinnacle of the temple, I tempt God. I do what is irrational, wicked, wrong in every respect for any man to do. Therefore I tempt God—I violate God's laws —I do that which any man doing, would commit an act of suicide. God's word is to be trusted by man in the path of duty. To affect to trust it to guard man in a violation of duty, is not to trust, but to tempt Jehovah. Now, '*it is written, thou shalt not tempt the Lord thy God.*'" Therefore, the Lord Jesus Christ brings His duty, as commanded by the word of God, to parry the thrust of Satan who tempts Him to violate it in reliance on the promise of God; placing our blessed Lord in this dilemma, that if He refused, it would prove His want of faith in the promise—and, if He complied, it would be an act of sin.

Mark how the answer of our blessed Lord dissolved his sophistry and condemned his malice! How important this use of the Scripture is! If false principles ever appear to be sanctioned by an appeal to Scripture, a counter-appeal to Scriptural truth and Scriptural duty, is the only way to expose them. You will find books that have the name of religious books, abounding with false principles; and abounding with false applications of Scripture, which seem to support them; and you require to have your minds furnished from the armory of heaven with "THE SWORD OF THE SPIRIT WHICH IS THE WORD OF GOD," to keep you faithful and steady in the path of duty—to regulate your conduct by the standard of truth—and to resist false principles by its power, which Satan often tries to make it seem to sanction.

Observe our Lord again in the next temptation. "*The devil taketh him up into an exceeding high mountain and showeth him all the kingdoms of the world, and the glory of them, and saith unto him, all these things will I give thee if thou wilt fall down and worship me.*" Mat. iv. 8, 9. There—the usurper, the prince of darkness, tempts the God of glory, and tempts him by what? by the promise of ceding to Him His own rightful dominions—those dominions that are secured to Him, as His own inheritance, of whom it is written, "*I will give thee the heathen for thine inheritance, and the utmost parts of the earth for thy possession.*" Psalm ii. 8. The devil says, "They are now mine—I now rule over them, but I will give them all to Thee, if Thou wilt fall down and worship me." He had tempted him as God. He had tempted him as man. Now he tempts the Lord as both—as the God-Man who is the Ruler and Inheritor of all the kingdoms of the earth. He affects to claim as his own rightful property that glory which is Christ's own—His power—His authority—His rightful dominion over the earth—and to bestow on Him the kingdoms of the world; to give them to Him, without that humiliation and suffering by which they were to be bought. He was to buy the kingdom, he was to purchase, with his precious blood, that people who should inherit it,—he was to purchase the travail of his soul, by dying on the cross; and Satan taunted Him to take His kingdom of glory without this ordeal of suffering. And surely both the glory of God, and all the best and purest feelings of a holy man would have demanded, as one should think, that Christ should not have waited a moment longer, but have vindicated His own glorious majesty, and dashed the fiend into the fathomless abyss, who dared to call on Him, the Lord of heaven and earth, to do homage to him for His own dominions. But how then should the Scriptures be fulfilled?—It was through death that Jesus was to "*destroy him that hath the power of death,*" and He was first to triumph in his own sufferings over Satan, sin, death and hell; and soon the time shall come, when He shall crush the head of this Prince of darkness, and all his principalities and powers, and wrest all the nations of the earth from his grasp, when "*the kingdoms of this world are become the kingdoms of our Lord and of his Christ. And he shall reign forever and ever.*" Rev. xi. 15.

How then does our blessed Lord answer him? "*Get thee hence, Satan, for it is written, thou shalt worship the Lord thy God, and him only shalt thou serve.*" He does not condescend to notice his blasphemous audacity in insulting the majesty of His God—He does not upbraid him with his guilt and wickedness.—He does not deign to tell him of the glory with which He shall rend this earth from his power, and cast him into the bottomless pit—but as men bow down to Satan, and worship him for the things of earth—He answers him, as a man with "THE SWORD OF THE SPIRIT, WHICH IS THE WORD OF GOD;" "*It is written, thou shalt worship the Lord thy God, and him only shalt thou serve.*"

Here we see how the Captain of our Salvation wields "THE SWORD OF THE SPIRIT," leaving us an example how we ought to wield it, and both to strike our foe, and to defend ourselves against the attacks and assaults of Satan. And thus it is to be wielded against all false principles, and all wicked companions. Oh! how little is this mighty and invincible weapon taken and used in the conflict as it ought to be, either individually by believers, or by the Church as an army!

If, when your friends or your companions would lead you into that which is wrong, your mind were stored with Holy Scripture as it ought to be; and if you would say—"No, this is contrary to the Word of God—God commands me to do so and so—I cannot disobey His Word." That is the right use to make of "THE SWORD OF THE SPIRIT" as a defensive weapon—and thus, all our enemies within, our own corruptions—our own evil propensities, desires, passions, all the iniquity that we feel within us, and all the evil that is without us, should be met by "THE SWORD OF THE SPIRIT, WHICH IS THE WORD OF GOD." It is by that alone we can attack and conquer. The promises—the faithful covenant promises of our God to which the soul flies in all her distress, and all her wants, these are the weapons with which she is made more than conqueror.

The fears of hell, how are they conquered? By the promises of God.

Our doubts, how are they dispelled? By the promises and Word of God.

Our conduct, how regulated? By the holy law—the precepts of God. Thus "THE SWORD OF THE SPIRIT, WHICH IS THE WORD OF GOD," is the great weapon which we are continually to use. It is in our hands. Oh! that it may be in our hearts! "*The weapons of our warfare are not carnal but mighty, through God, to the pulling down of strongholds.*" 2 Cor. x. 4.

Oh! if that one weapon, "THE SWORD OF THE SPIRIT," were but wielded as it ought in our land, what mighty conquests would it not achieve! And where "THE SWORD OF THE SPIRIT" is left, as it were, to rust in the scabbard, there is no hope, no prospect of peace or happiness, either individually or nationally. The neglect of wielding this weapon aright, has been the great guilt of the Protestant Church in this country. The Protestant Church has not wielded "THE SWORD OF THE SPIRIT WHICH IS THE WORD OF GOD." She has used her laws—her power—the power of her Protestant King—her Protestant Lords—her Protestant Commons—her Protestant possessions. She has used this power to secure her Protestant interests—her Protestant ascendancy. She has not taken the armor of God—she has not wielded "THE SWORD OF THE SPIRIT," against the Apostacy that surrounds her, and therefore the heavy visitation of God has lighted on her. If she will not awaken it shall be more than a visitation—I fear it will be ruin and desolation. If she had taken "THE SWORD OF THE SPIRIT"—if she had maintained the eternal truth of God, as the one ground on which she was to stand—if that had been the standard of her kings—her parliaments—her bishops—her clergy—her laity—in all their dealings with our poor benighted countrymen around us—"THE SWORD OF THE SPIRIT" had long since felled the dark Apostacy, and laid the superstitions of Popery prostrate in the dust. We should have been, long since, united in heart and hand with our poor countrymen, instead of being, as we are now, in a state of division, distraction, and misery, and exposed continually to the sword of intestine war, that is generally, as it were, suspended by a thread over our heads.

Oh! that there was the power of the Holy Ghost, to awaken those who profess the faith of Christ in the land, to use the "SWORD OF THE SPIRIT!" That is a mighty—an invincible weapon. If that weapon were wielded as it ought to be, wickedness, ungodliness, superstition, idolatry, perjury, murder, and other crimes, would not defile and blacken the face of the land, and call down the judgment of God on our heads—they would fall before the power of "THE SWORD OF THE SPIRIT, WHICH IS THE WORD OF GOD."*

May the Lord put it into our hearts and hands individually, and into the heart and hand of our Church! May we learn to put on "*The whole armor of God!*" May we be clothed and cased in that armor, that we may "*be able to withstand in the evil day, and having done all, to stand.*" Amen and Amen.

* The Writer has so often, and in so many ways, set forth his convictions, that the only remedy for the miseries of this unhappy country, is to be found in the faithful labors of Missionary preaching, and fearless exposure of the awful evils of Popery, in a spirit of Christian faithfulness and love to the Roman Catholics, that he only reiterates it in this note, to record it in a Work, which, he trusts, may survive the passing controversies of the day. It is now ten years since this Lecture was delivered, and every intervening hour only confirms and ratifies his judgment on the subject. The prevalence of Popery that has been the curse and ruin of this country, is, through the ignorance, the apathy, and the want of sound principle and sound truth amongst Protestants, spreading its influence into the heart of the British Empire and Constitution; gradually breaking down the barriers that protected our Institutions and corrupting and undermining the laws and liberties of the realm. God has sent scourge after scourge on the Church of Ireland, to awaken her to a sense of her duty. He has now sent famine and pestilence to chastise the whole nation—and if for all this, instead of being awakened to a sense of duty, Protestants go on compromising with the Apostacy, and with the Prince of darkness, either God must change His dealings with men, from those recorded in His Holy Word—or judgments must overtake the Church and Nation of this Protestant Empire, that will serve as a lesson to other lands, as their desolation and ruin ought to be a warning to us.—1847.

FIFTY-FIRST LECTURE.

EPHESIANS VI.—18—20.

"Praying always with all prayer and supplication in the Spirit, and watching thereunto with all perseverance and supplication for all Saints; and for me, that utterance may be given unto me, that I may open my mouth boldly, to make known the mystery of the Gospel, for which I am an ambassador in bonds: that therein I may speak boldly, as I ought to speak."

OUR last lecture concluded the several items of the Christian armor, which the Apostle exhorted his brethren at Ephesus to put on. But there is no use in a warrior clothing himself with armor, if it were the best that ever was produced by the hands of the armorer, unless he has strength and skill to use his weapons. If he has no power to use a shield or a sword, he might as well be without them. Now, the whole strength and power of the Christian to use his spiritual armor, can be derived alone from God. "*The girdle of truth—the breastplate of righteousness—the preparation of the Gospel of peace—the shield of faith—the helmet of salvation, and the sword of the Spirit, which is the word of God,*" might just as well be proposed to the sinner to put on, whose heart is unwakened, unquickened, unenlightened by the power of the Holy Ghost, as the various parts of the armor of a warrior might be laid before a dead body. You might just as well try to clothe a corpse in armor and expect the dead man to use it, as set all the blessings of the salvation of Jesus before the sinner whose heart is dead in trespasses and sins, till the Spirit quickens him. A man must have spiritual life and strength to use the heavenly armor, as well as animal life and power to use carnal weapons. Life must be given and sustained by the Holy Spirit—the soul of man must not only be quickened into life, but supported by continual supplies of strength from God. The manna gathered in the wilderness, if the Israelites attempted to put it by, corrupted, and was unfit to use the next day—so, all divine truth laid up in the heart would necessarily, as it were, decay there, unless the Holy Spirit of God was continually renewing the soul—renewing the spiritual life and powers of man to profit by it, to use it, and rejoice in it, to live on it, and to live to God.

Now God has appointed, that the communications of His Blessed Spirit with power to the sinner's heart, should be given in answer to prayer:—"*I will yet for this be inquired of by the house of Israel, to do it for them, saith the Lord.*" Ezekiel xxxvi. 37. Therefore, you see, often in the first instance, the blessing of salvation communicated to the sinner, in answer to the inquiring cry of distress and want. "*What must I do to be saved?*" Acts xvi. 30, was the cry of the Philippian jailor. "*Men and brethren, what shall we do?*" Acts ii. 37, was the exclamation of those assembled on the day of Pentecost. When the Lord was pleased to send Ananias to lead Saul of Tarsus to the knowledge of the Gospel, He saith, "*Go into the street which is called Straight, and inquire in the house of Judas for one called Saul, of Tarsus: for behold he prayeth.*" Acts ix. 11. Peter was sent to Cornelius in answer to prayer. The Lord is pleased frequently, to send His sovereign grace and His word to the sinner's heart, in a hardened, rebellious, prayerless, thoughtless state—to the sinner who is not thinking of God—who is not looking to God.—"*I was found of them that sought me not; I was made manifest unto them that asked not after me.*" Isaiah lxv. 1, saith the Prophet, and the Apostle re-echoes it, Romans x. 20. God is pleased to send His word to the sinner's heart and to awaken him—to enlighten him—and bring him to His feet—but when He does, He always pours on the awakened sinner a spirit of prayer. In fact, the Spirit teaches him his want, and teaches him to cry. Therefore, prayer is called the breath of the new-born soul; that, as when a person is born into the world, he begins to breathe; so when the sinner is born of God, he begins to pray; he begins, for the first time in his life, to cry unto God; and there is no such thing as genuine spiritual prayer to God, until the sinner is really touched by the Spirit of God, and taught to pray. In our natural state, we "*will not come to him, that we may have life.*" John v. 40.—"*No man,*" saith Christ, "*can come to me, except the Father which hath sent me draw him.*" John vi. 44. But he adds, "*Every man therefore, that hath heard and hath learned of the Father, cometh unto me.*" John vi. 45. Therefore, the Apostle, when he exhorts his brethren to put on the whole armor of God, closes his exhortation on this subject in the 18th verse, in these words,—"PRAYING ALWAYS WITH ALL PRAYER AND SUPPLICATION IN THE SPIRIT, AND WATCHING THEREUNTO WITH ALL PERSEVERANCE AND SUPPLICATION FOR ALL SAINTS."

We perceive two exhortations given in this verse: an exhortation to prayer, and an exhortation to watchfulness. "PRAYING ALWAYS"—at all times—under all circumstances. When you hear the Gospel, pray. Now, at this time, when you hear your poor fellow sinner, with the word of God in his hand, endeavoring to set before you the truths of that blessed word, your hearts should be lifted up in prayer—you should pray thus:—

"Lord enable me to profit by this Holy Word—let all that is according to thy blessed truth—all that is spoken according to the mind of the Holy Ghost, let it come with light and power to my heart."

So I ought to pray, that the things I speak to you should be brought home by the Spirit of God to my own heart; that while I endeavor to feed you with the Bread of Life, the Lord would feed my own soul. Unless the Lord feeds us all with the "*Bread that cometh down from heaven and giveth life unto the world,*" we must all starve, we must all perish. Therefore, I say, when you hear the Gospel of Christ, you should pray—whatever you feel your spiritual need of, you should pray for it.

Your heart is hard, you should pray that it might be softened.

Your faith is weak, you should pray that it might be strengthened.

Your understanding is dark in many points, you should pray that it may be enlightened.

Your will is rebellious, you should pray that it may be conformed to the will of God.

Your affections are "*earthly, sensual, devilish;*" you should pray that they may be lifted up continually to the Lord, that you may be able to set them "*on things above, not on things on the earth.*"

Your path in life, whatever it be, is, no doubt, encompassed with difficulties. There is no human being on earth who does not feel, more or less, that they are in a wilderness, and that their path is perplexed and difficult; you should pray that the Lord may make His way plain before your face. There is no servant of God who does not feel it for themselves. And then, if their relations in life are multiplied, if they have husbands, wives, children, families—there is not one who does not feel what multiplied need they have of direction from God; not only for themselves, but for all who are dear to them. And therefore, in all these circumstances, what are we to do but to pray?

Then again, we are in danger,—we should pray for preservation, every day we arise, we should pray to God to keep us through that day in our bodies and our souls. "*Who can tell what a day may bring forth?*" How little my dear Christian friend and brother, whom we have remembered in our prayer, anticipated when going to take a walk with his little children, the awful visitation with which he was to be afflicted!* How little any one can tell, what a day or an hour may bring forth! There is not a day that passes, in which numbers are not involved in difficulty and danger from which there is no escaping. What have we to do, then, but to pray that God may keep us, and as we are every moment pensioners on His mercies, to pray that His grace may prepare us for all the dispensations of His providence.

Then again there is nothing certain as to this life, but death. Then what is there that we can have to comfort and cheer us in "*the valley of the shadow of death*" unless our God is with us. Then how ought we to pray, that we may be enabled to say, "*Though I walk through the valley of the shadow of death, I will fear no evil: for thou art with me; thy rod and thy staff*

* This alluded to a truly pious servant of God, who with his children had been attacked and severely lacerated by an infuriated dog which was supposed to have been mad a few days before this lecture was delivered, but he was kept calm and in perfect peace, and it pleased God that it was but a trial of his faith; the dog proved not to have been mad, and he and his children were graciously preserved.

they comfort me." Psalm xxiii. 4. Every moment we need afresh the application of the blood of Christ to our souls to pardon our sins, and to "*purge our conscience from dead works to serve the living God.*" Heb. ix. 14. How are we to obtain these blessings? —By prayer.

But it is in vain that I should endeavor to enumerate all the various circumstances in which we are called to pray. Let me rather ask you—Tell me any circumstance in which we can be placed at any moment of our life in which we do not need prayer. If you tell me any moment that we need not God's pardoning grace and mercy—His support and power—His love—and faithfulness—and truth, to guard—and help—and bless us—to preserve us from the assaults of Satan, then I will tell you a moment when you do not need prayer; but if you want these every moment, then every moment we need this exhortation, though clad in "*the whole armor of God,*" "PRAYING ALWAYS WITH ALL PRAYER AND SUPPLICATION IN THE SPIRIT, AND WATCHING THEREUNTO WITH ALL PERSEVERANCE." This is that which really delivers the heart from care and burden. So the Apostle saith to the Philippians, "*The Lord is at hand, be careful for nothing.*" How can that be? How can it be that we who have so many cares can be careful for nothing? He tells us, "*But in everything by prayer and supplication with thanksgiving let your requests be made known unto God,*" and see then the blessed result— "*And the peace of God, which passeth all understanding, shall keep your hearts and minds, through Christ Jesus.*" Phil. iv. 6, 7.

And so saith the Apostle Peter, "*Casting all your care upon Him; for He careth for you;*"—"*Casting,*" you see, in the present tense, it is an habitual work, a daily, hourly, momentary operation, "*Casting all your care upon him.*" And so here, it is in the present tense, "PRAYING ALWAYS WITH ALL PRAYER AND SUPPLICATION IN THE SPIRIT, AND WATCHING THEREUNTO WITH ALL PERSEVERANCE AND SUPPLICATION FOR ALL SAINTS."

Here the natural heart in its blindness and ignorance asks— "What! Are we to be always praying?—always on our knees? How are we to carry on the business of life if we are to be always praying?" The heart of man in its natural blindness, has no idea of spiritual religion in any sense, it knows nothing but mere form. The believer can pray everywhere, in all occupations—at all times and under all circumstances. A word—a look—a thought—can carry a prayer to the Throne of Grace, that can bring down a blessing on the soul—"*Lord, if thou wilt, thou canst make me clean,*" Mat. viii. 2, delivered the leper from his leprosy. "*Lord, save me.*" Mat. xiv. 30, rescued Peter from the depths of the sea. A prayer quick as thought, and but in thought, in the interval between a question from his Sovereign and the answer, brought to Nehemiah, directions and wisdom from God, in a case in which the interests of a whole nation were involved: Nehem. ii. 4. The mind can be in a spirit of prayerful dependence every moment, for everything, though not a word escapes the lips on the subject.

The necessity of our continually praying to God, continually waiting upon Him in prayer and supplication, looking to Him for all things, is the first point that is brought before us in this verse. But let us remember always that there is but one way of access to the throne of God.—" *No man cometh to the Father, but by me,* is the testimony of Christ. It is only in the way in which God's righteous government can be administered, His holy law fulfilled—His holy attributes vindicated—His eternal justice satisfied—and His glorious mercy opened in its tide of love to sinners, it is only in that way, that God can hear or answer the prayer of the sinner; —therefore, the sinner who prays must come in God's appointed way, through the Lord Jesus Christ.

We all close our prayers with these words "*through Jesus Christ our Lord.*" Did you ever consider the reason of that? Did you ever think that it is impossible that your prayer could find access to God, unless you come in Christ's Name? The Apostle, I need not observe, addresses this to those who believe, to whom, indeed alone, these exhortations could apply. None but those who come through Christ can pray "IN THE SPIRIT." And it is the Spirit alone who can teach us to come through Christ. We must have the Spirit to teach us the truth, through whom we are to pray; and the Spirit to help us when we believe that truth, that we pray.

Now it is the office of the blessed Spirit, to take of the things of Jesus, and show them to our souls. And therefore, when our Lord speaks of prayer, in that passage, in which he gives such delightful encouragement, to the sinner to pray, he speaks of the Spirit of God, as the precious gift that is given in answer to prayer. I allude to Luke, chap. xi., in which His disciples asked him, "*Lord teach us to pray,*" Luke, xi. 1. And then He teaches them the Lord's prayer. Then, if you look from the 5th to 13th verse, I do not know any passage in the whole Scripture, that is so encouraging to the weak and helpless sinner, to pray to God. I do not know what we could wish to add to it. If you were given that passage and desired to mention anything, which you could wish the Lord to have added to it to encourage your own soul, I know not what addition you could make.

Our Lord saith "*Which of you shall have a friend, and shall go unto him at midnight, and say unto him, friend, lend me three loaves: for a friend of mine in his journey is come to me, and I have nothing to set before him? And he from within shall answer and say, trouble me not: the door is now shut, and my children are with me in bed; I cannot rise and give thee. I say unto you, though he will not rise and give him, because he is his friend, yet because of his importunity he will rise and give him as many as he needeth. And I say unto you, ask, and it shall be given you; seek, and ye shall find; knock, and it shall be opened unto you.*" Luke xi. 5—9. Now, you see, what encouragement there is given here by our blessed Lord; not only for prayer, but for importunity in prayer. It is as much as to say —"As a man would not be put off, who was in want at midnight, by a friend, to whom he came in his distress—as he would insist on his request, and use every importunity, that his friend, however reluctant, should get up and give him what he needs;—so, do you come with earnestness—with repetition—with importunity in prayer to God; if you are not answered, go again—and again—and again—and again—do not leave the throne of grace till you receive what you ask for." Surely, here is encouragement, not only to prayer, but to importunity in supplication. Now, look at the character that is given of God (10th verse); It is an express declaration of the God of truth: "*For every one that asketh, receiveth; and he that seeketh, findeth; and to him that knocketh, it shall be opened.*" This is He, who hath the keys of Heaven, and the keys of death and hell; the Lord of life and glory—He saith, "*It shall be opened.*" What can you add to that? Can you add any more to strengthen you in confidence?—to encourage you to importunity? Look at the gracious character of God drawn in the next verses:—"*If a son shall ask bread of any of you that is a father, will he give him a stone? or if he ask a fish, will he for a fish give him a serpent? or if he shall ask an egg, will he offer him a scorpion? If ye then, being evil, know how to give good gifts unto your children; how much more shall your Heavenly Father give the Holy Spirit to them that ask him?*" verses 11—13.

Now, see the appeal that Christ makes here to the feelings of a child and of a father. There is not a child in the world, and there is not a parent in the world, whose heart must not respond to that appeal. There are several little children here.

Little children, do you think, if you were to go to your father and ask him for bread, would he give you a stone? Or, for an egg, would he offer you a scorpion? Would he give you a poisonous reptile instead of an egg? You even smile at the thought, because you know it is impossible. You know he could not do so. You know, that if you went to your father or mother and asked them for bread; if they were hungry themselves, they would rather first supply your wants. See how your Heavenly Father encourages you to come to Him. Then again, the feelings of a father's heart, or a mother's heart respond to this in a moment. My children come to me for bread, could I give them a stone?—Could I refuse to a word, or even a look, that expressed the necessity of hunger? If it was the last morsel I had in the world, would I not give it to my hungry children? Now the Lord Jesus appeals to our own heart, whether as children or as parents in putting the character of God before us: "*If ye, being evil, know how to give good gifts unto your children, how much more shall your Heavenly Father give the Holy Spirit to them that ask him.*"

Now think, children, of what God says to you! Think, what an encouragement it is to you to pray to God!—Call on him in your own rooms, and you will prevail—call on God in prayer, and he tells you in his word expressly, that if your parents would give you bread if you were hungry, "*how much more shall your Heavenly Father give the Holy Spirit to them that ask him.*" Here is God's heart, as it were, set before us, with more than the tenderness of a father's heart; even, as our Heavenly Father is higher than an earthly father.

Then think, what an encouragement this is to parents. How can you answer to God, if you live without prayer? Without calling on him? What can you say? Can you say, I was afraid —I did not think you would hear me, or answer me? The Lord would say, 'Did not I appeal to your own affections? Did I not tell you, that I was more ready to receive—to bless—to answer—to give you all you could ask, than your own hearts could be to give bread to your own hungry children—yet you disregarded?" "*You would not come to me, that you might have life.*" Oh! how shall the prayerless sinner be able to answer to God? Now, I defy you to add encouragement to this passage of Scripture. Sit down, and think of any one image that you can use—any metaphor—any expression, that you can possibly invent, to encourage your own heart to pray to God. I defy you to add to what our adorable Lord has spoken in that passage of Scripture in the way of encouragement. Then, as there is encouragement to pray, see what is to be given in answer, "*How much more shall your Heavenly Father give the Holy Spirit to them that ask him!*" This is what they want—the Spirit of God—so Christ hath promised to send Him to his people: "*If I depart, I will send him unto you.*" John xvi. 7, to teach them all things—to instruct them—to guide them into all truth—to reveal Christ—to glorify him—to comfort them—to direct them—to help their infirmities in prayer—in their walk—in their warfare—in all things—and this is the answer promised to prayer, by Him whose office it is to baptize with the Holy Ghost.

We are taught in this passage of Ephesians, that our prayer and supplication must be "IN THE SPIRIT." This implies, of course, our need of the Spirit. See how our Lord hath given the promise of the Spirit. And then the help of the Spirit is set before us in the Epistle to the Romans, on which we dwelt at large, Romans viii. 26, "*Likewise the Spirit also helpeth our infirmities; for we know not what we should pray for as we ought, but the Spirit itself maketh intercession for us with groanings that cannot be uttered, and he that searcheth the heart knoweth what is the mind of the Spirit, because he maketh intercession for the saints, according to the will of God.*" The Spirit of God, poured into the heart of the sinner, crieth in prayer to God from the sinner's heart. If we utter or breathe one spiritual prayer acceptable to God, it must be from the Spirit of God.

Then, I hope, my beloved friends, you will consider from these words your need of prayer at all times—your great encouragement to pray in all things—your incapacity to pray of yourselves, and the exceeding great and precious promises that are given to you, of the Spirit of God to help you, and teach you to pray—to teach you to call on the Lord for all you can want, "PRAYING ALWAYS, WITH ALL PRAYER AND SUPPLICATION IN THE SPIRIT." And then, there is another most important addition—"AND WATCHING THEREUNTO WITH ALL PERSEVERANCE, AND SUPPLICATION FOR ALL SAINTS."

Now, this is a characteristic of the unconverted sinner, which invariably attends him—that let him pray as often as he will, (for unconverted sinners do certainly pray in their own way,) let him pray as often as he will, he never watches, never looks for an answer to his prayer. Never! There is no such thing as an unconverted man praying for, or expecting, an answer from God to his prayer. He does not believe in God's answering prayer; on the contrary, I never knew an unconverted sinner that did not laugh at the idea as enthusiastic and fanatical, to think that God would answer prayer. They pray as a matter of duty. That it is a duty is very true, but still, the duty of prayer arises from this—the necessity of the sinner, and the need of his receiving supplies from God. Therefore, to pray without expecting an answer, to pray without looking for or expecting these supplies, the need of which makes prayer necessary, is, in itself, a gross absurdity, and shows, even in this one feature, the blindness of the natural, unconverted heart. The unconverted sinner may pray—he does not in spirit and in truth pray, but still he prays in his own way; but his prayer is merely going through a form of duty, in which, he thinks, he is actually rendering a service to God, and that because he prays; God must be, as it were, indebted to him. Now, there is no such thing as real genuine prayer, without watching for an answer to that prayer. There is no such thing as real spiritual calling upon God, without really thinking that God will hear and answer that prayer. True religion is the most rational thing in the world; false religion is the most absurd and irrational. Now applying this rule to prayer, you will find how irrational and absurd the prayer of the unconverted sinner is. What would you think of a man who went with a petition to his sovereign, for instance, and who sent in his petition for something which he professed to say was of importance, and turned away, and never again thought of inquiring whether his petition was heard or answered? What would you think of any beggar that asked you for alms, and then, before you had time to answer him, turned his back on you, and went away? Would you not think the person was mocking you? Suppose a poor man sent a petition to your house, and you should ask, "where is the petitioner?" and you were told, that the moment he gave the petition he turned about and went away, you would say, "What did he mean? He came with a petition here, and the moment he gave it to my servant, he turned and went away; he could not be serious—he could not have wanted what he asks. He says, he is in great need—in great poverty—very miserable, and entreats I will relieve him, and yet he went away the moment he left his petition at the door! Why the man cannot want it at all!" You would naturally—necessarily say so.

What are your forms of prayer? What do you say when you go to church? How do you cry to God for mercy, as a miserable sinner? How earnestly do you supplicate God to hear you? Read your prayer-book—consider what you say! Then look at your hearts when you go to public worship and utter these petitions;—Do you expect that God will hear your prayers, or answer them? When you go to your rooms, you are, perhaps, in the habit of *saying* your prayers, as you call it; you kneel down and *say* your prayers, morning and evening, and you get up, and think the work is done, and there is no more about it. As surely as you exist, this is your natural state, and your conscience must confess that it is.

You see, then, that false religion is the most irrational thing in the world. You would think it so contrary to all common sense for a fellow-creature to send you a petition and not to wait for the answer, and yet you are so absurd and foolish, that you send up petitions, most importunately worded, to the God of heaven, and you neither expect, nor think, of His hearing or answering you. Are such petitions true prayers? Or, do you mean anything you say? Dear friends, consider these things—calmly, deliberately reflect on them! If you call on God, in spirit and in truth, for anything, then watch, that your prayer is heard and answered. If you seek for faith really, and are taught by the Spirit to do so, you will not be content till your heart is enabled to trust in Jesus. If you really seek for spiritual instruction, you will use God's appointed means for receiving that instruction, namely, the study and the hearing of His blessed Word. If you pray for spiritual comfort and strength, you will wait on the Lord. If you pray in earnest against any besetting sin, you will wait and watch for strength against that sin, and against the temptations that lead you to it. In fact, if you are sincere in prayer to God, watchfulness must be part of the character of true prayer, so he says, "PRAYING ALWAYS WITH ALL PRAYER AND SUPPLICATION IN THE SPIRIT, AND WATCHING THEREUNTO WITH ALL PERSEVERANCE AND SUPPLICATION FOR ALL SAINTS."

It is only this, my dear friends, that can enable us to enjoy the truth in our own souls. We may have a clear knowledge of the doctrines of the Gospel, but if these doctrines are not spiritually applied to the comfort and edification of our own spirits, to our own personal direction and government, and holy life and conversation, if they are not so applied, they are nothing. They cannot be so applied but by the Spirit of the living God, bringing them home with power to our hearts. This is to be received in God's appointed means by waiting on the Lord in prayer, see how encouragingly that is set forth by the Prophet, "*Even the youths shall faint and be weary, and the young men shall utterly fail; but they that wait upon the Lord shall renew their strength, they shall mount up with wings as eagles, they shall run and not be weary, and they shall walk and not faint."* Isaiah xl. 30, 31.

Now see what encouragement there is in "PRAYING ALWAYS WITH ALL PRAYER AND SUPPLICATION IN THE SPIRIT, AND WATCHING THEREUNTO WITH ALL PERSEVERANCE AND SUPPLICATION FOR ALL SAINTS," not merely for ourselves but for others, for all the Church of Christ, it is our privilege and our duty to carry them all in our hearts to our God. It is his will, you are commanded to do so, and in this, is one of the most blessed privileges of the Communion of Saints—Communion in faith, hope, love, in our glorious covenant God, and our mutual and everlasting glory in Him, and with Him, forever.

And now, I would remark, that there seems a great defect among the servants of God, in this particular. They will pray for the conversion of sinners, and of those whom they love; but they seem to think, that when they are converted, everything is done.

"Oh! now they are converted—brought to Christ—now we may be satisfied."

But, my dear friends, the very time that sinners most of all require continual support from God, is when they are brought to the knowledge of the truth as it is in Jesus. If it could be possible, that man wants help from God, more at one time than another—he wants it more after his conversion than before. It is not indeed a proper expression to use, because man is always alike dependent on his God. But if we could use the expression, it might be specially applied to his converted state; for it is then first, his conflict begins. Till then, he is dead in trespasses and sins. Satan, "*the strong man armed, keepeth his palace, and his goods are in peace.*" But the moment he is brought to the knowledge of Christ, then begins his warfare within and without; his warfare against his enemies, the world, the flesh, and the devil. Then Satan who flattered him, and soothed him, and kept him in peace before, turns round to exhibit his enmity against him. Then he plies him with temptations—spreads his nets for his feet—endeavors, if possible, by every suggestion within, and temptation without, to draw him away from his God. When does a soldier need his armor most? When need most watchfulness?—most energy?—most activity?—the eye of his commanding officer to be peculiarly over him—directing him? Surely, it is in the battle. And when does the Christian soldier require it most? Surely, it is when he enlists in his Heavenly Master's service, and begins his warfare here below. He is in an enemy's land, surrounded by foes—foes within, and foes without. Therefore he is called on to buckle on his armor, and never put it off till he lays down his body of sin and death; till his spirit returns to his Lord and Saviour; then, when his warfare is past, it may be said, "*Blessed are the dead which die in the Lord from henceforth: yea, saith the Spirit, that they may rest from their labors.*" Rev. xiv. 13.

As the feeling of the necessity of prayer for ourselves, should lead us instinctively, to see and feel the necessity of prayer for those we love,—therefore, the Apostle joins intercessory prayer with prayer for own souls—"SUPPLICATION FOR ALL SAINTS,"—all the children of Christ.

The Apostle shows, how great is the necessity for prayer for all the saints of God, when he especially names himself,—"AND FOR ME, THAT UTTERANCE MAY BE GIVEN UNTO ME, THAT I MAY OPEN MY MOUTH BOLDLY, TO MAKE KNOWN THE MYSTERY OF THE GOSPEL." This great and eminent Apostle, called by such a special and marvellous revelation of God—set apart by God, to be his witness and his minister among the Gentiles; speaking under the inspiration of the Spirit of the living God—this great Apostle, calls upon his Christian brethren, in praying for all the Saints of Christ, to pray, especially for himself—"AND FOR ME." And now, what does he call upon them to pray for? He brings forward that very thing, for which, if we were to express our opinion on the character of the Apostle Paul, we should say, he was most peculiarly eminent, and most peculiarly inspired and gifted by God. He calls upon them to pray, especially, for boldness—"AND FOR ME, THAT UTTERANCE MAY BE GIVEN UNTO ME, THAT I MAY OPEN MY MOUTH BOLDLY, TO MAKE KNOWN THE MYSTERY OF THE GOSPEL, FOR WHICH I AM AN AMBASSADOR IN BONDS: THAT THEREIN I MAY SPEAK BOLDLY, AS I OUGHT TO SPEAK." Surely, if ever there was a man on the face of the earth that "OPENED HIS MOUTH BOLDLY TO MAKE KNOWN THE MYSTERY OF THE GOSPEL," that man was the Apostle Paul. We know how at Damascus, after his conversion, "*straightway he preached Christ in the synagogues*," Acts ix. 20, immediately and boldly testifying against all his friends—all his prejudices—all his former habits—all the Jews. And we know the outcrying wrath of those who were all now turned into enemies against him, "*but he increased the more in strength, and confounded the Jews which dwelt at Damascus, proving that this is very Christ.*" Acts ix. 22. We know his testimony to the Elders of this very church in Ephesus, at Miletus, though "*the Holy Ghost testified that in every city bonds and afflictions abided him*," yet saith he, "*none of these things move me, neither count I my life dear unto myself, so that I might finish my course with joy, and the ministry, which I have received of the Lord Jesus, to testify of the Gospel of the grace of God.*" Acts xx. 24. Yet he calls upon them to pray for him even in that very particular in which he had borne such a testimony by his profession and life; as much as to say, even in these things in which we are strongest—in which we appear to others to be most safe, most secure, yea, most eminently gifted by the Lord, even there we entreat your prayers and supplications. Oh! consider, if this eminent Apostle required that his brethren should bear him on their hearts even for this, what sinner on earth does not require prayer and supplication, from the heart of faith and love, to the throne of grace in his behalf?

We may remark on this, that that, for which the Apostle especially entreated their prayers, was, that he might be strengthened in the service of his Master. It was not for any individual, personal want of his own, but that he might be eminently strengthened for the glory of his God, and the salvation of his fellow-creatures, and that is, and ought to be, the first prayer of every Christian.

I think, that this is another point, my dear friends, in which we are, in general, exceedingly negligent. When we are brought to the knowledge of the Gospel of Jesus, self still predominates too much in our very religion, and we, ourselves, are chiefly, if not solely, the subject of our prayers; our own wants—our own fears, trials, difficulties, interests, unbelief—all these, are the chief, if not the only subjects of our prayers. This is all right to a certain extent; all our wants of body and soul are legitimate subjects of prayer, and we ought to feel, deeply feel, our need of prayer and supplication on these subjects, and on all things in which we are entirely dependent on our God. But our own wants ought not to be the first subject of a Christian's prayer. The first subject of a believer's prayer ought to be the glory and kingdom of his Lord and Master. I speak on the highest authority, on the authority of our blessed Lord Himself. For, observe, the prayer which is given to us as our pattern and model of prayer by our blessed Lord, when His Apostles asked Him, "*Lord teach us to pray.*" Look at the Lord's prayer, and observe the order of the petitions as they occur in that prayer. What is the first subject that man is taught to pray for? "*Our Father, which art in heaven, hallowed be thy name, thy kingdom come, thy will be done in earth, as it is in heaven.*" The glory of his God—the hallowing of His Name—the coming of His kingdom—the doing of His will on earth as it is in heaven; these are the first petitions put into the lips of God's servants when they are taught to pray scripturally, and that, before the supply of their daily wants, or pardon for their sins. For then come the petitions, "*Give us this day our daily bread, and forgive us our trespasses as we forgive them that trespass against us.*" Now, if this were the general spirit of prayer in the Church, I firmly believe, religion would wear a different aspect from that which it wears at present in the world. I believe, that all the genuine servants of God, would stand out more clearly and separately from the world—they would appear more in their true character—they would be more manifest as servants of God—their hearts too, would be set more at liberty—they would have less occasion to pray for their own individual and personal necessities, because they would feel them less—their spiritual state would not be so sickly as it is, if they were to pray more for their Lord's kingdom, and to stand up faithfully and boldly for the service and glory of their Master. I firmly believe, if we were to give ourselves more to speak of, and pray for, and labor for the kingdom and glory of our blessed Lord and Saviour, and for the salvation of our fellow men, we should not feel these doubtings and misgivings, that arise from our own selfishness, and continually moping over our own character, and poring over our own hearts; we should feel them, I say, far less, and have much more liberty in the Gospel of Jesus—much more love to the brethren—much clearer manifestations of the genuine character of the servants of the Lord Jesus Christ. His Church, would exhibit a far clearer light of His truth, and His salvation to the world. We do not find the Apostle Paul asking those to whom he wrote, to pray for him that he should be delivered from suffering. No doubt, he did suffer—we know he did deeply, as every poor sinner must suffer from corruption within, but we do not find, that this is the subject for which he entreats their prayers, but the glory of the Lord's kingdom. He does not say to them, "Pray for me, that I may be enjoying peace—that I may be enjoying tranquillity of mind—that I may feel comfortable in the views of my own acceptance with God—that I may be satisfied that my faith is strong—that I may be enabled to enjoy so and so, and to feel so and so.' He does not say, pray for these. No—but "THAT I MAY OPEN MY MOUTH BOLDLY, TO MAKE KNOWN THE MYSTERY OF THE GOSPEL." Pray, that I may stand out for my Master's cause—for my Master's glory—that though I am "AN AMBASSADOR IN BONDS," in the midst of Nero's court—in spite of bonds, and in spite of men, Pagans, idols, and devils, "THAT I MAY OPEN MY MOUTH BOLDLY, TO MAKE KNOWN THE MYSTERY OF THE GOSPEL, THAT THEREIN I MAY SPEAK BOLDLY, AS I OUGHT TO SPEAK."

See, what an example this is for us! See, what an example for the servants of Christ in this country! If we were more employed in the work of our Master, we should be thinking less of ourselves, and doubting less of our own character than we are when we are sitting down and doing nothing, moping about our own concerns, whatever they are, and saying, "I do not know whether I am a Christian or not, or whether I am a servant of God at all." No wonder men doubt so much about themselves and their own spiritual state, when they are not engaged in the service of their Master! Surely, it becomes the servants of a Heavenly Master, to be employed in doing their Heavenly Master's work. This was the desire of the Apostle's heart, and the object of his life, and therefore, he entreats their prayers that he may be enabled "TO OPEN HIS MOUTH BOLDLY, TO MAKE KNOWN THE MYSTERY OF THE GOSPEL."

It requires boldness to do so—Why? because the Gospel of the Lord Jesus Christ, stands in eternal opposition to the natural corruptions, ignorance and wickedness of man. Wherever the Gospel of Christ is proclaimed, wherever the Gospel is to be proclaimed, it has to encounter rebellion, opposition, hatred, contempt in the heart of fallen sinners; and therefore, the Gospel of Christ, is an eternal controversy against man. There is no such favorite principle of the devil as peace. Peace is the favorite watch-word of the devil; another is Liberality, and Charity is a third, all these are favorite watch-words of Satan. "Let us have peace—let us have no controversy. Peace, and liberality, and charity, towards one another! do not let us find fault with each other, "*Judge not that ye be not judged*," for that is a favorite text of the devil, he has many favorite texts in the Scriptures. "Let every man follow his own way, we all agree that religion should lead us to avoid contention—let us all avoid contention—let us quietly pursue our own religion, and as to what other men think, say, or believe, let that be a subject of peace,—let us have no difference about that, no controversy." This is the favorite doctrine of the devil on religion, he is a great preacher of this sort of charity. It is thus that, "*the strong man armed, keepeth his palace and his goods are in peace*," and the peace he wants is, to let him alone, and not disturb or awaken the world. But God's word must disturb the world! God, has a controversy with the world! "*The whole world lieth in wickedness*," 1 John v. 19, or as it might be translated "*in the wicked one*," asleep as it were in the arms of the devil. And it is the business of the servants of the living God to testify against the wickedness of the world—to testify, that the wrath of God, abideth on the world—to proclaim to sinners the glorious salvation that there is in Jesus, and to call on them thus to turn to Jesus, that they may have life and peace. Therefore, the Gospel is an eternal controversy with the ungodliness of a wicked world! so the Apostle calls on them to pray, "THAT THEREIN HE MAY SPEAK BOLDLY, AS HE OUGHT TO SPEAK." If Paul was alive in these days, he would be scoffed at, treated as beside himself, a fellow that "*turneth the world upside down*," a disturber of the peace, just as he was before. And wherever the Gospel of Christ is faithfully carried forth against the ignorance, the wickedness, and the false religion of man—there the same principle in the corrupt heart of man will always give the same reception to the glorious Gospel of Christ. And therefore, whenever there is fidelity to the cause of Christ, there must be an eternal controversy, with an ungodly world. The Christian ought to be always tolerant, most tolerant, most kind, as to persons in whatever error they may be sunk, but the Christian ought to know no toleration for false principles, however specious—or for wicked principles, however popular—for any principles opposed to the Gospel of Christ. True Christianity is utterly intolerant of falsehood—it will not bear it. God's truth, God's word, Christ's salvation, His cause—His honor—His glory—that is the object of the man, that knows and loves, and serves his God. It ought to be the object of every one. There is indeed a proper, wise, discriminating, sound judgment always to be exercised in things that are not essential to salvation, in things that do not oppose the vital truth of God, in things that God has left at large, or indifferent things that men may hold, or may not hold, without opposing God, or dishonoring His word, or His Gospel; and with respect to these things, we are called on to be patient, kind, forbearing, "*endeavoring to keep the unity of the spirit in the bond of peace*,' that is the duty of those who are the servants of God, and herein they are to exercise a sound scriptural judgment. But, with respect to all the great principles of God's eternal truth, the great principles of the Gospel of Jesus—the righteous authority of His holy word—the integrity and perfection of His sacred volume, as the standard of man's salvation—the instructor of His youth, and the guide of His age—the man who surrenders one tittle of these principles, surrenders his religion, his God, everything that ought to be most dear to an immortal being. This is a specimen of Satan's peace, crying "*peace, peace, where there is no peace.*" But the servants of God can make no peace with Satan, they must open their mouths boldly, "*though briers and thorns be with them, and though they dwell in the midst of Scorpions,*" Ezek. ii. 6, yet must they set their face like a flint, and lift up their voice like a trumpet, so for this, the Apostle entreats them to pray for him, "THAT UTTERANCE MAY BE GIVEN UNTO HIM, THAT HE MAY OPEN HIS MOUTH BOLDLY, TO MAKE KNOWN THE MYSTERY OF THE GOSPEL, THAT THEREIN HE MAY SPEAK BOLDLY, AS HE OUGHT TO SPEAK."

This was always the case with all the servants of God. If you look through the prophecies, look through the history of their lives—their doctrines, and their fate, you will see that the Prophets and Apostles, so far from being men of peace, (men of peace, indeed, in one sense they were, and they ought to be men of peace,) but you will see, that in fact they were men of contention. So the Prophet Jeremiah saith, "*Woe is me, my mother, that thou hast borne me a man of strife and a man of contention to the whole earth.*" Jer. xv. 10. They, as well as the Apostles, were obliged to contend; and it is an Apostolic legacy to the Church of Christ, to "*Earnestly contend for the faith which was once delivered unto the Saints.*" Jude 3. God's severest judgments were, we see, denounced against the false Prophets who deceived the people with the false principles of hollow charity and lying peace—saying "*Peace when there was no peace.*" Hear His words by the mouth of the Prophet Ezekiel:—"*Because, even because they have seduced my people, saying, peace, and there was no peace; and one built up a wall, and, lo, others daubed it with untempered mortar.*"—That is, with false principles—false doctrines—skinning over the wounds of the consciences of sinners—plastering them over with lying flatteries, and deceitful hopes and vain delusions, like a stone wall built and plastered over with untempered mortar, which cannot endure the pressure of the storm. "*Say unto them,*" saith the Lord, "*Say unto them which daub it with untempered mortar, that it shall fall: there shall be an overflowing shower; and ye, O great hailstones, shall fall; and a stormy wind shall rend it. Lo, when the wall is fallen, shall it not be said unto you, where is the daubing wherewith ye have daubed it?*" Where are your lying principles?—Where, your false peace?—Where, your mock charity?—Where, your hollow liberalism, when the eternal truth of the living God—the authority of Jehovah's despised and neglected word, and the judgment of the great day, shall fall like a tempest on your head?" "*Therefore thus saith the Lord God; I will even rend it with a stormy wind in my fury; and there shall be an overflowing shower in mine anger, and great hailstones in my fury to consume it. So will I break down the wall that ye have daubed with untempered mortar, and bring it down to the ground, so that the foundation thereof shall be discovered, and it shall fall, and ye shall be consumed in the midst thereof: and ye shall know that I am the Lord.*" Ezekiel xiii. 13, 14.

Oh consider this!—mark, how false is the peace which false teachers speak to an ungodly world, and how certain the opposition that must exist between that world and the testimony of God's eternal truth! So the Lord said to this Prophet: "*Behold, I have made thy face strong against their faces, and thy forehead strong against their foreheads. As an adamant harder than flint have I made thy forehead: fear them not, neither be dismayed at their looks, though they be a rebellious house.*" Ezekiel iii. 8, 9. What wonder, then, that the Lord Jesus was rejected and crucified! What wonder, that the Apostle felt his need of the prayer of the Church! Whenever the faithful testimony of the Lord is borne in an ungodly world, there must be an eternal opposition between that ungodly world and that truth. There can be no peace between God and the devil. The truth of God cannot make peace with the falsehoods of Satan. And Satan's falsehoods cannot make peace with the truth of God. Therefore, well might the Apostle call on his brethren, when he was in bonds for the truth of the Gospel, to pray for him, that he might be enabled "TO OPEN HIS MOUTH BOLDLY, TO MAKE KNOWN THE MYSTERY OF THE GOSPEL, FOR WHICH HE WAS AN AMBASSADOR IN BONDS: THAT THEREIN HE MIGHT SPEAK BOLDLY, AS HE OUGHT TO SPEAK."

It is most important for us to know, and to attend to these principles, because, really, in the present day it seems, as it were, to be the perfection of charity to have no religion—to prove that men have no sense of the value or importance of any religion for themselves, by the avowal, that they consider it of no consequence, what is the religion of any of their fellow-creatures.

Charity, falsely so called, is the sheep's clothing of the wolf, that preys on the Church and Nation at this day, which, with the cloak of kindness and tenderness to men's consciences—in keeping peace with man, and having no disturbance on account of religion, would trample upon truth and the Bible, in the land. But we must go to our Bibles, we must remember it is written, "*Let God be true, but every man a liar.*" Jehovah's word must stand. Let man think, or say, or do what he pleases. Let us remember, that God's Word must have a controversy with man, and so must all those who are servants of Jehovah. Men do not put on armor in time of peace—we are called to put on Christian armor, because Christianity is war—war against Satan—war against sin—war not against sinners, but against sin, and the hardest battle of all is to be fought in our own bosoms.

"*The weapons of our warfare are not carnal, but mighty through God to the pulling down of strong holds.*" 2 Cor. x. 4. Men may wage war for earthly objects, and with carnal weapons, but the weapons of the warfare of the Christian, are God's truth, God's Holy Word. Oh! that we may be given to be clothed with His armor, and armed with His weapons, and that we may be enabled at the last, to say with the Apostle, "*I have fought a good fight, I have finished my course, I have kept the faith: Henceforth there is laid up for me a crown of righteousness, which the Lord, the righteous Judge, shall give me at that day: and not to me only, but unto all them also that love his appearing.*" 2 Tim. iv. 7, 8. Amen and Amen.

FIFTY-SECOND LECTURE.

EPHESIANS VI.—21—24.

"But that ye also may know my affairs, and how I do, Tychicus, a beloved brother and faithful minister in the Lord, shall make known to you all things: whom I have sent unto you for the same purpose, that ye might know our affairs, and that he might comfort your hearts. Peace be to the brethren, and love with faith, from God the Father and the Lord Jesus Christ. Grace be with all them that love our Lord Jesus Christ in sincerity. Amen."

THE boldness of the Gospel of Christ, in those who are really eminent saints and servants of God, is, or at least, ought to be, always tempered with gentleness, tenderness, and sympathy towards our fellow-sinners. As the man who is the most truly brave is always the most truly humane and benevolent; so this ought to be peculiarly exemplified in the spiritual mind of the Christian. It was eminently so, in the character of the Apostle Paul. For we see, while he entreats his brethren to pray, that he might "*Open his mouth boldly, to make known the mystery of the Gospel,*" so that neither the bonds he endured, nor the city of idolaters in which he suffered, nor the cruelty of a Nero, should make him shrink from his duty to his Lord and Master. Yet he exhibits the greatest kindness and tenderness of heart. So he saith, "BUT THAT YE ALSO MAY KNOW MY AFFAIRS, AND HOW I DO, TYCHICUS, A BELOVED BROTHER AND FAITHFUL MINISTER IN THE LORD, SHALL MAKE KNOWN TO YOU ALL THINGS: WHOM I HAVE SENT UNTO YOU FOR THE SAME PURPOSE, THAT YE MIGHT KNOW OUR AFFAIRS, AND THAT HE MIGHT COMFORT YOUR HEARTS." The Apostle knew how anxious his dear brethren were to know everything about him.

"Our dear and faithful Paul! Our beloved Paul! Our beloved Minister! Our blessed Apostle, who was so long with us, and so labored amongst us! We wonder how he is! We wonder how he is enabled to stand! Is his life in danger? How does he get on in the Heathen Emperor's court? Who supplies his wants? Who attends to them? Has he any that would be glad to minister to him as we would?"

All these anxious inquiries he knew were in the heart of his Ephesian brethren, therefore, he says, "THAT YE MAY KNOW MY AFFAIRS, AND HOW I DO, TYCHICUS, A BELOVED BROTHER AND FAITHFUL MINISTER IN THE LORD, SHALL MAKE KNOWN TO YOU ALL THINGS." How sweet and delightful these touches are throughout the whole of God's Word, in which we see such tender, affectionate sympathies that come home to our own hearts! We know how much we feel ourselves, for those we love when in danger. We know how beloved flocks feel when their pastor is removed from them—and see, how the Lord knows we feel this. These great servants and saints of God were men "*of like passions with ourselves*," we see they were. And observe, how the Lord is so gracious even in these things, that do not seem intended to instruct us—that do not profess to teach us points of doctrine, yet how beautiful they are, and how illustrative they are of the true character of genuine Christianity, tender, faithful, sympathetic, affectionate, loving. Such was this mission of Tychicus, by the Apostle, "WHOM I HAVE SENT UNTO YOU," he says, "FOR THIS SAME PURPOSE, THAT YE MIGHT KNOW OUR AFFAIRS, AND THAT HE MIGHT COMFORT YOUR HEARTS." There were many circumstances, no doubt, which the Apostle would not, and could not commit to writing, which Tychicus could easily communicate, and much to refresh their hearts, with respect both to himself and the cause of Christ, in the court of Nero, which it would have been wrong to embody in a letter. But the Apostle sent Tychicus, both to tell them all things and to comfort their hearts, building them up in the Lord Jesus Christ, and enabling them to see, that though in bonds at Rome, yet "*That the things which happened unto him, had fallen out rather unto the furtherance of the Gospel.*" As he saith to the Philippians, "*So that,*" saith he, "*my bonds in Christ are manifest in all the palace, and in all other places.*" Phil. i. 12, 13—all the distress and difficulty through which I have passed, in the end have been made the means of making known the Gospel of the Lord Jesus Christ to others; so that, though in bonds, though a prisoner, yet I rejoice in the Gospel of Jesus myself, and I have been through that very circumstance, made the instrument of making known the Gospel, even to those who are of Cæsar's household—even in the midst of the Pagan court of the cruel Nero!

What a privilege then—what a duty is intercessory prayer! What a blessing it is, to ourselves and others! We see how this great Apostle, entreated the prayers of all his brethren at Ephesus, and if he did, what need have we of prayer! What need have we poor vile sinners! and above all, what need has every minister to entreat the prayers of his Christian brethren! If those in private spheres of life have need continually of the prayers of their brethren, how much more do those who are engaged in spheres of public duty, difficulty and trial, how much more do they need continually, the prayers and supplications, of all those to whom they are known, as brethren and ministers of Christ! I am sure, if I may ask a favor, a kindness, from you, my beloved brethren, it is that you will remember me in your prayers, at the throne of Grace, praying the Lord Jesus, according to the riches of His grace, and my deep necessities, to pour His Spirit into my heart, and O! what a blessed thought it is, that we have such an High Priest, "*who ever liveth to make intercession for all that come unto God by him.*" I trust we shall be enabled to bear one another, in our hearts to the throne of His grace.

The Apostle concludes, as he began, with a benediction.

The beginnings and conclusions of the Apostolical Epistles are like the beginnings and conclusions of the life of grace in the soul of the sinner. They begin, as we have seen, with the benediction of "*Grace and peace from God the Father, and the Lord Jesus Christ,*" as in this Epistle, "*Grace be to you, and peace, from God our Father, and from the Lord Jesus Christ,*" chap. i. 2, and they close, as we see here, "PEACE BE TO THE BRETHREN, AND LOVE WITH FAITH, FROM GOD THE FATHER AND THE LORD JESUS CHRIST. GRACE BE WITH ALL THEM THAT LOVE OUR LORD JESUS CHRIST IN SINCERITY, AMEN."

So it is, my dear friends, with the life of a believer. His spiritual life begins from grace, grace commences the work. His spiritual life is carried on by grace, grace continues the work. His spiritual life is closed by grace, grace consummates the work. When the top-stone of the spiritual temple shall be laid, it shall be with shoutings, crying, "*Grace, Grace unto it,*" Zech. iv. 7.

Grace brings peace to the soul, and so peace comes from God the Father and from the Lord Jesus Christ. The entrance of the Gospel into the sinner's soul imparts to him the knowledge of peace, from his God. The sinner is at war with God by nature, and he thinks that God is at war with him; his conscience tells him, that he has provoked his God, that God has reason to be angry with him, he would long to hide from Him—he is afraid of His presence, and therefore he trembles to meet His Heavenly Judge. But when his eyes are opened to see the glory of the Gospel of Jesus, he sees it is a message of love from God, proclaiming to him pardon and peace. Whenever the Gospel does really come to the sinner's heart, this is the truth, the great truth—the light that breaks in upon his soul. "Can this be true?" he asks—"Is there, indeed, peace for a sinful wretch like me? Is there peace—is there pardon from my God? Is it indeed my blessed privilege to look up to my Heavenly Father as a reconciled God? Can I come to Jesus as my friend? Can I pour out my heart before him? Can I tell Him what I would not dare to tell my dearest earthly friend? Can I lay bare my iniquity before Him, and be assured that He will not cast me out, but will cover me with His righteousness, and wash me in His blood, and save me, and take me, and bring me to Sion? Can I be assured of this? Is this the Gospel? Oh good news!—Glad tidings of great joy!—Oh blessed peace!" It is then the sinner begins to understand the sacred Scriptures, when they speak the language of peace to his soul. He comprehends something of our blessed Lord's conversation with His disciples in the 14th, 15th, and 16th chapters of St. John, which he closes with these memorable words:—"*These things I have spoken unto you that in me ye might have peace. In the world ye shall have tribulation: but be of good cheer; I have overcome the world.*" John xvi. 33. He begins to comprehend that passage on which we dwelt so long, in the 2nd chapter of this Epistle:—"*But now in Christ Jesus ye who sometimes were far off are made nigh by the blood of Christ. For he is our peace, who hath made both one, and hath broken down the middle wall of partition between us; having abolished in his flesh the enmity, even the law of commandments contained in ordinances; for to make in himself of twain one new man, so making peace; and that he might reconcile both unto God in one body by the cross, having slain the enmity thereby: and came and preached peace to you which were afar off, and to them that were nigh.*" Chap. ii. 13—17. Peace is the language of the Gospel as addressed to the believer's soul. So the Apostle saith here,—"PEACE BE TO THE BRETHREN, AND LOVE WITH FAITH, FROM GOD THE FATHER AND THE LORD JESUS CHRIST." The beginning of preaching is to bring peace. The end of preaching is to bring peace. Not as if the end of God's glory was to be found in the heart of the sinner. But the end of God's glory is to bring up the sinner's heart to God—to bring the sinner's affections to God—the sinner's will to God—the sinner's body and soul to God—to bring him into the service and love of his Heavenly Master. And how is this achieved? By peace with love and faith; so he saith, "PEACE BE TO THE BRETHREN, AND LOVE WITH FAITH, FROM GOD THE FATHER AND THE LORD JESUS CHRIST. GRACE BE WITH ALL THEM THAT LOVE OUR LORD JESUS CHRIST IN SINCERITY." PEACE be to them FROM GOD THE FATHER, AND THE LORD JESUS CHRIST. LOVE be to them from God the Father, and the Lord Jesus Christ. FAITH be to them "FROM GOD THE FATHER, AND THE LORD JESUS CHRIST." These are all his gifts, and they are all spoken of with reference to their own peculiar ends or operations. Peace be to the sinner's soul—a proclamation of pardoning mercy, and peace from God, through Christ. Love be to the sinner's soul, the testimony of God's love—the proclamation of God's love, as the Apostle saith, "*Hope maketh not ashamed; because the love of God is shed abroad in our hearts by the Holy Ghost which is given unto us.*" Romans v. 5. The Holy Ghost testifies of the love of God to the sinner's soul—commends—proves that love to him, in that "*while we were yet sinners, Christ died for us,*" Rom. v. 8. That love from God produces love in the sinner's heart; we have a common phrase, "Love begets love," and it is a very true one. If our fellow-sinners love us, and manifest their love to us, it will necessarily produce in our hearts love to them—we cannot but love them. How much more, when "*the love of God is shed abroad in our hearts by the Holy Ghost which is given unto us.*" When the Holy Spirit testifies of the love, the exceeding riches of the love of Christ, in pardoning our guilt—in bearing "*our sins in his own body on the tree,*"—taking us out of the midst of our iniquity —washing us in his precious blood—keeping us by his power— and bringing us to Sion. When the Spirit testifies of such love to the sinner, it necessarily produces in the heart love to God. Love, then, produces the fruits of love, that is, holy obedience—a desire to love; for we feel our love, alas! so cold, and our best obedience so defiled, compared with what it ought to be, that we can scarcely feel it amounts to more than a desire to glorify Him, and to manifest that we are his, as we ought to do. Therefore, we have ever need to pray to Him, as in that beautiful thanksgiving of our Church, that he will "give us such a due sense of his mercies, that our hearts may be unfeignedly thankful, and that we may show forth His praise, not only with our lips but in our lives; by giving up ourselves to His service, and by walking before Him in holiness and righteousness all our days." There is—there can be no such thing as godly practice, but that which springs from godly principles. There can be no such thing as obedience to God, but the obedience that comes *from* God. There is no such thing as love to God, but that love which He imparts to the heart, from the knowledge of sin blotted out by the blood of the Lamb. The notion men have of loving God, from the loveliness of God's nature—the amiability and goodness of God's character, which is a favorite principle of the Church of Rome; and as we hear of, in what is called natural religion, is all a mere delusion of Satan—a well-dressed lie, coming from the father of lies. There is not a shadow of truth in it. "*The world by wisdom knew not God.*" 1 Cor. i. 21. And man cannot love a Being of whom he is totally ignorant. The natural man cannot appreciate or understand God's character! on the contrary, when God's character is set before him, he hates the Divine Being. He loves a god of his imagination—he loves the God of beautiful flowers, and waving harvests, and sunny days, and moonlight nights—he loves the God of the calm sea—of the lovely heavens and a smiling earth. He loves the God of all these things, but he does not love the God of earthquakes, darkness, whirlwinds, hurricanes, famines, and pestilences—the God that shall rend the heaven and the earth, to sit in judgment upon a guilty world, and "*take vengeance on them that know not God, and obey not the Gospel.*" Set forth God in the holiness and justice of his character as a God that "*will by no means clear the guilty,*"—he cannot bear that God. He loves a God of what he calls mercy—a god who will not punish sin; who will extenuate his failings, and make allowance for his faults —who will allow for the religious amiabilities of his character, and be satisfied with his efforts to please Him at some times, as an atonement for his sin at others; or who will be propitiated with his self-inflicted penances and prayers for his sin—he likes a god of that kind:—but he hates the righteous, just, holy God, who declares, "*Whosoever shall keep the whole law, and yet offend in one point, he is guilty of all.*"—"Who denounces a curse on every one that continueth not in all things that are written in the book of the law, to do them." He abhors that God. Therefore, when you set the real character of God, as revealed in His Holy Word, before the sinner in his natural state, he hates the God of the Bible as much as he was pleased with the god of his imagination. The notion of loving God from the contemplation of God's character, is a dream—a delusive dream of lying superstition, or infidel philosophy; it has neither truth nor Scripture to support it. The only way in which a sinner can be brought to love his God is by the knowledge of God's eternal word; the knowledge of God's truth bringing peace to his soul—by pardon for all his guilt; and that not on the false assumption of ignorance, that God will not punish sin, but on the tremendous terms—the awful purchase of the blood of our blessed and adorable Redeemer, "*who bore our sins in his own body on the tree.*"

When this conveys to the sinner's soul, the peace that flows from the pardon of sin through the blood of Jesus, then indeed there is love of God's character; he can then behold Him, in the most tremendous exercises of His attribute of justice; and the very justice of God, endears and exalts his character to the conscience of the vilest sinner, because he sees he can "*be just and the justifier of him that believeth in Jesus;*" he sees that glorious Redeemer, in whom mercy and truth meet together, in whom the righteousness of Jehovah's character, and still, peace to the vilest sinner, have kissed each other; then he understands the Apostle's word in this place, "PEACE BE TO THE BRETHREN, AND LOVE WITH FAITH." By God's love to you, your love is kindled and your heart is drawn to your God, that you may know, and love, and serve Him. It is this that makes religion not a mere nominal profession; but, a vital principle, a genuine living principle in the heart, "*We love Him, because He first loved us,*" 1 John iv. 19 we love Him "*Who hath loved us and given himself for us.*" v. 2. Then death—death so horrible to nature—even death loses its sting, because you know that He will walk with you, through the valley of its shadow. And then the coming of your glorious Master, the coming of that blessed Lord, to which the unconverted sinner looks with horror, that is your season of true anticipated joy—that is your harvest time of hope and glory, for "*to them that look for Him shall he appear the second time without sin unto salvation.*" Heb. x. 28. Then your body, raised up in the glory of the resurrection, shall be reunited to your glorified spirit and then you shall be with your Lord forever. Then peace, and love, shall last for evermore.

Peace and love, can never come but with faith—through faith alone we can receive the blessing of peace, it is "*being justified by faith, that we have peace with God through our Lord Jesus Christ.*" Rom. v. 1. It is by faith alone we can apprehend the love of our blessed Lord, which thus makes faith work by love in our hearts, faith can apprehend these now in a degree, but then it shall be lost in everlasting joy and glory.

Therefore what a blessed benediction with which to close this Epistle, "PEACE BE WITH THE BRETHREN AND LOVE WITH FAITH, FROM GOD THE FATHER AND THE LORD JESUS CHRIST." Then shall the power of divine truth, the power of the glorious Gospel be really manifested to your soul, and really draw your heart from sin and Satan, the world, the flesh, and the devil, into the love and service of your Heavenly Master.

Perhaps, some one here may complain, as all are, more or less, constrained to do. "Oh! that I could but feel the power of love within! Jesus is my only Refuge—He is all my hope, and all my Salvation—but, alas! I feel so cold and dead, I never feel I love Him as I ought to do."

My dear friends, you never can love the Lord Jesus Christ as you desire to love Him; but the very feeling, that you do not love Him as you ought to do, proves that you do love the Lord Jesus. Mourning for the absence of a person, proves our love to him, as much as rejoicing in his presence. The soul that is cast down under a sense of not loving the Lord, shows that it loves the Lord as much as when it rejoices in the light of His countenance. Therefore, be not discouraged when you look within, and when you find yourselves full of sin, and pride, and deadness, and misery, but lift up your eyes and look to your glorious Saviour. See, what a blessed ground you have, for loving and trusting your Lord and Master! You will find in the heart of Jesus, a Refuge from the deadness, and coldness, and baseness, and ingratitude of your own. Oh! look to Christ! What a precious Saviour He is to poor, helpless, guilty sinners like us! Oh! "*look unto him and be ye saved!*" "PEACE BE TO THE BRETHREN, AND LOVE WITH FAITH, FROM GOD THE FATHER AND THE LORD JESUS CHRIST."

See, again here, what a blessed thought the unity of the Godhead is to the soul of the sinner! You cannot look to God the Father as an angry God; and to God the Son as your Peace. God the Father, and God the Son, are One in essence, in glory, in will, and in all the covenant of Salvation, "*I and my Father are one,*" saith Christ, John x. 20. All the blessings that are proclaimed to you in Scripture through Jesus, come to you from God the Father, and the Lord Jesus Christ. Our blessed Lord sets this forth most conclusively, where He shows that the Church of His people, are the Father's gift to Him, that in their salvation He fulfils His Father's will, "*All that the Father giveth me shall come to me, and him that cometh to me, I will in no wise cast out; for I came down from heaven, not to do mine own will, but the will of him that sent me. And this is the Father's will that hath sent me, that of all which he hath given me, I should lose nothing, but should raise it up again at the last day.*" John vi. 37—39. See, the love of God the Father is but manifested in the love and salvation of Christ Jesus to the sinner, in his salvation from first to last! So the Apostle but sets forth the glorious covenant of the ever-blessed Trinity, when he saith, "PEACE BE TO THE BRETHREN, AND LOVE WITH FAITH, FROM GOD THE FATHER AND THE LORD JESUS CHRIST." What God the Father giveth, the Lord Jesus giveth—what God the Son giveth, God the Father giveth. Oh! what a blessed love is that to the poor sinner! All his salvation secure in the eternal covenant of God the Father, Son, and Holy Ghost.

Then, it is remarkable, he says, "PEACE BE TO THE BRETHREN." But he had just been exhorting them, as we have seen in the preceding part of this chapter, to put on the armor of war—that they were in the midst of war, and to prepare for battle. Yet, though he tells them they are in the midst of war and conflict, he says, "PEACE BE TO THE BRETHREN."

Well, and so there is peace in the midst of war—peace in conflict—peace in battles—peace in the midst of enemies—peace, while all the powers of darkness, earth, and hell are raging around the sinner who is brought to trust in his Redeemer. There is peace in the midst of all. Not peace with his own body of sin and death—not peace with sin—not peace with the enemies of God—not peace with the devil—but peace with God, in the midst of war with them all. Oh! if we have peace with God, it is no matter through what conflicts we have to go—and if we have not peace with God, poor and wretched is the miserable peace that sinners can enjoy with the world, the flesh, and the devil. "*When he giveth quietness who then can make trouble?*" Job xxxiv. 29. And when the sinner has not peace with God—when he is at war with his God, what matter with whom he can be at peace!

"*When the strong man armed keepeth his palace, his goods are at peace;*" but that is a terrible peace, for the end of that peace shall be eternal war with God. But when the sinner has peace with God, through Jesus Christ our Lord, then, all his conflicts shall soon be past, and then, eternal peace and "*everlasting joy shall be upon his head.*" Oh! my beloved friends, I trust the Lord will give us all that peace "PEACE FROM GOD THE FATHER AND THE LORD JESUS CHRIST."

He then concludes with a prayer for all the children of God "GRACE BE WITH ALL THEM THAT LOVE OUR LORD JESUS CHRIST IN SINCERITY. AMEN." This is the great bond of union between God's people. It is not an outward unity of form. An outward form presents a very slender bond of union indeed, between those who bear the name of Christ. Many men, we see, are united in outward form, whose hearts and principles are totally and diametrically opposite. They know not, and cling not to the Lord Jesus Christ. No form can graft men into The Living Vine. And where there is no vital union with the stem, there cannot be a vital union between the branches. The great bond of union is this—love to Jesus. "GRACE BE WITH ALL THEM THAT LOVE OUR LORD JESUS CHRIST IN SINCERITY." Now, observe, he saith, "GRACE BE WITH THEM." Remember, that those who most love and serve Christ, have just as much need of grace at the last, as at the first. We cannot live for a moment without the sovereign grace of God, freely pardoning our sins. We want pardon continually—we want grace to pardon us, and mercy to keep us every day and every hour. We must, as we have often said, begin, continue, and end with grace. Therefore, he says, "GRACE BE WITH ALL THEM THAT LOVE OUR LORD JESUS CHRIST IN SINCERITY." And, my dear friends, that is given to the sinner's heart through the knowledge of the Gospel of Jesus.

It is love to Christ and love to His servants, which proves and tests the genuine conversion of a sinner to God, this is the love of those who love their Redeemer, "*We know*," saith the Apostle John, "*that we have passed from death unto life, because we love the brethren*," 1 John iii. 14, and that is as we have seen, the grand principle, which is declared to us by the Lord Jesus Christ, to be the test of man's salvation, in the day of His coming. "*I was an hungered and ye gave me meat, I was thirsty, and ye gave me drink, naked and ye clothed me, sick and in prison, and ye visited me*," and then He illustrates His meaning, and the application of His principle, "*In as much as ye have done it unto one of the least of these my brethren, ye have done it unto me.*" Matt. xxv. 40, as He declareth in another place to His disciples, "*Whosoever shall give you a cup of water to drink in my name, because you belong to Christ, verily I say unto you, he shall not lose his reward.*" Mark ix. 41, but, no person can give to their fellow men, even a cup of water, because they belong to Christ, unless that person belongs to Christ, himself. Then this is his language, "Here is my brother, or my sister, who loves my Lord, and Master—who "LOVES THE LORD JESUS CHRIST IN SINCERITY," therefore my heart saith, "GRACE BE WITH THEM." They are the children of my Father. They are one with my Lord and Master, and one I trust with me for eternity. Shall I not give to them because they belong to Christ? This is the principle—the true principle of love. Hence how could the Apostle more appositely conclude an Epistle, that breathes of grace and love, than with these words, "GRACE BE WITH ALL THEM THAT LOVE OUR LORD JESUS CHRIST IN SINCERITY." This is the principle that ought to animate the heart of all God's people. If we belong to Him, we shall surely love "ALL THEM THAT LOVE OUR LORD JESUS CHRIST IN SINCERITY."*

* Those who may remember the delivery of these Lectures, will perhaps observe omitted here a dissertation, on the value and importance of Infant Schools, as early

And now my beloved friends, I must bring my lectures to a close I cannot do so without expressing my gratitude to Almighty God, for the privilege of having been permitted, when shut out of any sphere of more active service in His Church, through a visitation of His own Almighty hand, to minister, however humbly, in His Holy Word, now for so long a time among you. I trust through His grace, these plain and unpretending efforts, to set forth in simplicity the truth of His everlasting Gospel, may have been blest to awaken—to help—to strengthen—to comfort and refresh the souls of many among you, on your way to Zion; and that so His glorious Word may have been made a blessing to your souls. I am sure it has often been a blessing to my own, to set before you that truth which is all my own salvation; and so far from counting it a trouble to come here, be assured, my dear friends, I have considered it a happy privilege. But having now, as you know, other duties imposed on me, having undertaken a task which I have not been able to attempt for many years,* I do not think I could, under any circumstances, have been able to continue my lectures among you; and therefore, I trust, we shall all see and feel, that as they were commenced through the Lord's providence, so they are by His gracious dispensation, providentially brought to a close. I have to express my sincere sense of gratitude to your Rector, for his kindness in permitting me to conclude these lectures on the Epistle to the Ephesians.

And now, my beloved friends, I speak to you who know the Blessed Gospel of the Lord Jesus Christ; when we cease our ministrations in any way, or when the Lord is pleased to close the door of them by any of His dispensations—by removal, by death—or by any other means, we ought to speak of it with thankfulness, for the blessings we have enjoyed in any means of grace which He has afforded to us.

When we meet at the right hand of the Lamb, before our glorious and adorable Redeemer, we shall look back with gratitude and praise, at all the means we have enjoyed, whether domestic means—or sermons in Churches—or lectures in School-houses, or in any other way which His mercy has afforded us. We shall be enabled to remember and recall all the means by which the Lord has been pleased to strengthen and help us, and build us up in our most holy faith—teaching us to look for and haste unto the coming of the Lord Jesus Christ. One means whereby the Lord very often builds up his people is, by teaching them not to lean on an arm of flesh—on broken cisterns. Dear friends, it is a blessing—a comfort—a ground of joy, to those who are permitted in any way to minister among the people, and to be of any use to them, that

instilling into the breast of childhood, the principles of the knowledge and love of the Lord Jesus Christ, and an appeal to the inhabitants of Bray, to support that one in which these Lectures were delivered. The Lecturer trusts they do not forget the subject of that appeal, but, it would be irrelevant to retain it in this publication.

* The Author was just at this time appointed to the Church at Harold's Cross, in 1838; having been for many years unable, from inflammatory attacks in the trachea, to undertake any stated service in the Church.

there should be a bond of union and affection between them, as I think there is between us, and shall be, I hope, for eternity. But like every other blessing, this one is often greatly abused. We are alas! too apt to lean on an arm of flesh, and to think of poor instruments more highly than we ought to think. What are we? Nothing, but poor, wretched, miserable earthen vessels; the best of us is nothing but a broken cistern. If we have the excellency of the treasure of God's word within us, it is, that "*the excellency of the power may be of God and not of us.*" And indeed, dear friends, if we have taken sweet counsel together with our teachers at any time, or in any way; and enjoyed the blessing of the Gospel in their ministrations, we are too prone to depend on them, and to think of them above what is written. And therefore, it is often a great blessing, that the Lord is pleased to break these bonds, and to teach us, that "*neither is he that planteth anything, neither he that watereth; but God that giveth the increase,*" 1 Cor. iii. 7, to teach us that all are broken cisterns, that can hold no water; and therefore to make us turn to "*The Fountain of living waters.*" So dear friends, I hope we shall learn to drink more deeply of that Blessed Fountain. That Ministry alone is truly blest which teaches us to prize the Lord Jesus Christ more and more, to grow in grace—to study our Bibles—to pray to God more earnestly, and more diligently to seek Him in His Holy Word. If you had Paul to plant, and Apollos to water, God alone could give the increase. No matter from what earthly source we may receive instruction, we can receive no profitable instruction but from God. None. Therefore, let me earnestly entreat you, as a parting admonition, to study your Bibles—to search the Scriptures, in the length and the breadth of them—to bring all human instruction "*To the law and to the testimony*"—to pray earnestly and devotedly to your Lord for yourselves—for your families—for all whom you are bound to bear on your hearts to the footstool of the Throne of Grace. If you are enabled to rest on the Lord, and to drink at the "*Fountain of living waters,*" you will learn more and more that broken cisterns are nothing—you will learn more, to "*Cease from man, whose breath is in his nostrils, for wherein is he to be accounted of?*" Isaiah ii. 22.

I have to return you my grateful thanks, (I have waited till now to do so,) for the beautiful Bible with which you have been so kind as to present me. I trust, I shall keep it as the most acceptable proof of your love—and as the most grateful token of your affection. I trust I shall keep it with an affection, at least, proportionate to the love with which I know it has been bestowed. I have only one favor to ask, and that is,—I would most humbly and earnestly entreat of you all, that I may have an interest in your prayers, and be remembered at the Throne of Grace.

My dear friends, every poor sinner needs the prayers and supplications both of himself and his fellow-sinners; but of all persons, ministers need it most. We had in our last lecture, St. Paul entreating the prayers of his Ephesian brethren; and if an inspired Apostle felt it needful to solicit the prayers of his Christian brethren, how much more may a poor unworthy sinner, such as I am! Therefore, dear friends, I would most earnestly entreat your prayers to the Throne of Grace, for my own soul, and for my ministry, especially, as you know, I am much engaged on subjects of controversy, I would earnestly entreat your prayers in my behalf. Controversy is a trial to the spirit of a Christian; we are so very apt to engage in it in our own strength, and we are so very apt to forget even the highest and most important interests of truth, unless our gracious God keeps us by His Spirit and His power. We are too often, alas! ready to forget them, and perhaps to contend for argument, and self, and victory rather than for truth—for the glory of our God, and the salvation of our fellow-men. This is a great evil in us; but it does not make controversy, for the cause of Christ, a less important duty. It is a most solemn duty —it is a most awful duty—imperative on every Christian in this country, and I hope the Lord God will raise up men to a sense of their duty, till our poor fellow-countrymen are brought to the knowledge of the Lord Jesus. But all who are engaged in it need the prayers of their brethren, for their own souls—for the success of their work and labor, which ought to be a labor of love, (and I trust I can say I desire it to be so, as far as I can engage in it,) for the souls of their poor fellow-sinners. And I would earnestly call on you to pray, too, for our poor Roman Catholic countrymen, that God would send out His blessed Word amongst them, and bring them out of darkness into His marvellous light, and out of the Apostacy of Rome into the bosom of the Christian Church.

And now, my beloved friends, let me speak a word to those of you who know the Lord Jesus, as the whole salvation of your souls, and who "*have fled for refuge to lay hold on the hope set before you.*" Heb. vi. 18.

How sweet is the consolation of the Gospel to the heart of the believer; how does it temper with love and mercy all the dispensations of God to his soul. If we part from those we love, but to whom we are united in the bonds of Christian affection, how is the trial tempered with the joyful hope, that it is but for a season, that when we part from each other we have a blessed prospect of being soon reunited, that "*When Christ, who is our life, shall appear, then shall we also appear with Him in Glory,*" Col. iii. 4, when we "*shall be ever with the Lord,*" when we "*shall go no more out,*" but dwell in the mansions of our Father's royal house, which is our home and our rest, forever and ever. Therefore, the very trial of parting from friends, with whom we have taken sweet counsel, serves but to enhance the consolations of the everlasting Gospel, as the miseries we endure on a journey, or a voyage, but give a double relish to the sweet prospect before us of arriving at our journey's end, and at our happy home, wherefore, let us "*comfort one another with these words.*" 1 Thess. iv. 18.

But, let me now say a few words to those among my hearers, if there are, as I fear there may be, some who have been in the habit of attending my humble ministrations, but who are still without Christ, and without any hope or consolation in the Gospel.

It is now five years since I have had the privilege of carrying on these Lectures; and we have carefully considered two of the fullest portions of the inspired instructions of the Apostle Paul—his Epistles to the Romans and Ephesians. I trust I can say, I have endeavored faithfully, however humbly, to set before you the Gospel of Jesus; faithfully to warn you of the guilt and danger of remaining in an ignorant and unconverted state, and of rejecting that glorious message of mercy and salvation, which is proclaimed to you through the righteousness and blood of a crucified, risen, and ascended Saviour. And now, alas! my friends, is it, indeed, the case, that you still continue to "*neglect such great salvation?*" Is it, alas! too true, that the glorious mercy proclaimed in your ears, is but "*A savor of death unto death*" to your souls! O! consider, my dear fellow-sinners, "*What will ye do in the end thereof?*" Must I part from you under the awful impression, that my humble efforts to instruct you in the Gospel of Jesus, shall be but a fearful witness against you—that instead of hoping to meet you through grace at the right hand of the Lamb, if I am brought there through mercy, I shall be but a swift witness against you at the bar of God! O! think—think, my dear friends and fellow-sinners, while it is called to-day, think of what it is to have the very mercies of God but as barbed arrows of fire, rankling in the conscience through an unchangeable eternity! Oh! think, that other weeks, and months, and years, perhaps, may pass away—other opportunities may be neglected—other ministrations and means of grace and mercy disregarded—and all, all still but rise in awful judgment against your souls—and all that the world, to which you are enslaved, shall leave to you, will be but agonizing recollections of remorse, and anticipations of despair. The summons must come, and ye shall cry, "*The harvest is past, the summer is ended, and we are not saved.*" Jer. viii. 20.

Oh! then, "*to-day,*" this very day, "*if you will hear his voice, harden not your hearts.*" This day, let my last word be to your souls, a proclamation of pardon, through the blood of the covenant—a message of mercy—a proclamation of salvation, through Jesus, the only refuge—the only salvation of the lost. Come to Him even at the eleventh hour—come to him while it is called to-day.

"*The Spirit and the bride say, Come. And let him that heareth say, Come. And let him that is athirst come. And whosoever will, let him take the water of life freely.*" Rev. xxii. 17. Come! it is Christ who died, yea rather, who is risen again, who sends you once again, an invitation of His glorious love and mercy—"*Jesus Christ, the same yesterday, to-day, and forever.*" Heb

xiii. 8. May God bless His Glorious Word to us all, according to our wants. "PEACE BE TO THE BRETHREN, AND LOVE WITH FAITH, FROM GOD THE FATHER AND THE LORD JESUS CHRIST. GRACE BE WITH ALL THEM THAT LOVE OUR LORD JESUS CHRIST IN SINCERITY. AMEN, AMEN."

THE END

Booth, Abraham.
THE REIGN OF GRACE, ... $ 60

Borrow, George.
THE BIBLE AND GYPSIES OF SPAIN, . 1 00

Boston, Rev. Thomas.
SELECT WORKS. 8vo, ... 2 00
FOURFOLD STATE, ... 50
THE CROOK IN THE LOT. 18mo, . . 30

Brett, Rev. W. H.
THE INDIAN TRIBES OF GUIANA, . . . 50

Brewster, Sir David.
MORE WORLDS THAN ONE, ... 60

Bridgeman, Eliza J. G.
THE DAUGHTERS OF CHINA. 18mo, . 50

Bridges, Charles, A.M.
THE CHRISTIAN MINISTRY. 8vo, . . 1 50
AN EXPOSITION OF THE PROVERBS, . 2 00
EXPOSITION OF PSALM CXIX, . . 1 00
MEMOIR OF MISS M. J. GRAHAM, . . 1 00

Broken Bud, The;
Or, REMINISCENCES OF A BEREAVED MOTHER, ... 75

Brother and Sister;
Or, THE WAY OF PEACE. 18mo, . . 50

Brown, John, of Haddington.
EXPLIC. OF ASSEM. CATECHISM. 12mo, 60
" " " 18mo, 10
CATECHISM. 32mo, per hundred, . . 1 25
CONCORDANCE. Gilt, 30; plain, . . 20

Brown, John, D.D.
DISCOURSES AND SAYINGS OF OUR LORD JESUS CHRIST, illustrated in a series of Expositions. 2 vols. 8vo, . . 4 00
LECTURES ON FIRST PETER. 8vo, . 2 50
SUFFERINGS AND GLORIES OF CHRIST, . 1 50
THE DEAD IN CHRIST, ... 50
COMMENTARY ON ROMANS. 8vo, . .

Brown, Rev. David.
ON THE SECOND ADVENT, . . . 1 25

Buchanan, James, D.D.
COMFORT IN AFFLICTION, . . . 40
ON THE HOLY SPIRIT. 18mo, . . 50

Bunbury, Miss Selina.
GLORY, GLORY, GLORY, ... 25

Bunyan, John.
THE PILGRIM'S PROGRESS. Large type, 1 00
THE PILGRIM'S PROGRESS. Close type, 50
THE JERUSALEM SINNER SAVED. 18mo, 50
THE GREATNESS OF THE SOUL, etc., . 50

Butler, Joseph, D.C.L.
COMPLETE WORKS. 1 vol. 8vo, . $1 50
SERMONS ALONE. 8vo, ... 1 00
ANALOGY ALONE. 8vo. 75
And WILSON'S ANALOGY. 1 vol., . 1 25

Caird, Rev. John.
RELIGION IN COMMON LIFE. A Sermon preached before the Queen. 18mo, . 25

Calvin, John.
THE LIFE OF JOHN CALVIN, the Reformer, by Professor Henry, of Berlin, translated by Stebbings. 8vo, . 2 00

Cameron, Mrs.
THE FARMER'S DAUGHTER. 18mo, . 30

Cave, William, D.D.
LIVES OF THE APOSTLES AND EVANGELISTS. 2 vols., ... 1 50
PRIMITIVE CHRISTIANITY; or, The Religion of the Ancient Christians in the First Ages of the Gospel. 2 vols., 1 50

Cecil, Rev. Richard.
COMPLETE WORKS. 3 vols., 12mo, . 3 00
SERMONS, separate, ... 1 00
MISCELLANIES AND REMAINS, separate, 1 00
ORIGINAL THOUGHTS ON SCRIPTURE, . 1 00

Cecil, Catherine.
MEMOIR OF MRS. HAWKES. 12mo, . 1 00

Chalmers.
SERMONS. 2 vols. 8vo. With Portrait, 3 00
LECTURES ON ROMANS. Portrait. 8vo, 1 50
MISCELLANIES, ESSAYS, REVIEWS. 8vo, 1 50
SELECT WORKS. 4 vols., 8vo, . . 6 00
EVIDENCES OF CHRISTIAN REV. 2 vols., 1 25
NATURAL THEOLOGY. 2 vols., . . 1 25
MORAL PHILOSOPHY, ... 60
COMMERCIAL DISCOURSES, ... 60
ASTRONOMICAL DISCOURSES, ... 60

Charles Roussell;
Or, INDUSTRY AND HONESTY. 18mo, . 40

Charnock, Stephen, B.D.
ON THE ATTRIBUTES. 2 vols., 8vo, . 2 50
CHOICE WORKS. 18mo, . . .

Cheever, Rev. George, D.D.
POWERS OF THE WORLD TO COME. 12mo, 1 00
LECTURES ON THE PILGRIM'S PROGRESS, 1 00
BIBLE IN THE COMMON SCHOOLS, . . 75
LECTURES ON COWPER, ... 1 00

Child's Own Story Book.
Illustrated. Square, ... 50

Christian Retirement.
12mo, ... 75

Clara Stanley.
By the author of "FLORENCE EGERTON." 18mo, ... 50

Claremont (The) Tales.

Illustrations of the Beatitudes, $ 50

Clark, John A., D.D.

A Walk about Zion. 12mo, . . 75
Gathered Fragments, . . . 1 00
The Young Disciple, ... 88
The Pastor's Testimony, . . . 75
Awake, Thou Sleeper. 12mo, . . 75

Clarke, Samuel, D.D.

Daily Scripture Promises, . . 25

Colquhoun, Lady.

The World's Religion, . . . 30

Commandment with Promise, The.

By the author of the "Week," . . 40

Cowper, William.

The Task. With sixty superb illustrations, from designs by Birket Foster. Cloth, gilt, $4 50; morocco, 6 00
Complete Poetical Works, . .

Cumming, John, D.D.

A Message from God, ... 30
Christ Receiving Sinners, . . 30

Cunningham, Rev. J. W.

A World without Souls, . . . 30

Cuyler, Rev. T. L.

Stray Arrows. 18mo, . . . 40

Daily Commentary.

By 180 Scottish Clergymen. 8vo, cloth, 3 00

D'Aubigne, J. H. Merle, D.D.

Hist. of the Reformation. 5 vols., . 2 50
" " In 1 8vo vol., 1 50
Life of Oliver Cromwell, . . . 50
Germany, England, and Scotland, . 75
Luther and Calvin. 18mo, . . 25
The Authority of God, etc. 16mo, . 75

Davies, Rev. Samuel, A.M.

Sermons on Imp. Subjects. 3 vols., . 2 00

David's Psalms

In metre. 12mo. Embossed, 75c.; gilt, $1; Turkey morocco, $2. 18mo, sheep, 38c. 48mo, sheep, 20c.; mor., 25c.; morocco, gilt, 31c.; tucks, 50c.
With Brown's Notes, 18mo, sheep, . 50

Davidson, Dr. D.

Connection of Sacred and Profane History. 12mo, ... 1 00

Dick, Thomas, LL.D.

The Christian Philosopher. New edition, re-written and enlarged by the author, with 170 Illustrations, .

Dick, John, D.D.

Lectures on Theology. 2 vols. in 1, 8vo, cloth, $2 50; in sheep, $3; 2 vols., cloth, ... $3 00
Lectures on the Acts. 8vo, . . 1 50

Doddridge, Philip, D.D.

*The Family Expositor; or, a Paraphrase and Version of the New Testament, with Critical Notes, and a Practical Improvement of each Section. Royal octavo, sheep, . . 3 00
The Rise and Progress, . . . 40
Life of Colonel Gardiner, . . 30

Drummond, Rev. T. D. K.

On the Parables. 8vo, . . . 1 50

Drummond, Mrs.

Emily Vernon. 18mo, . . . 50

Duncan, Rev. Henry.

Sacred Philosophy of the Seasons, . 2 50
Tales of the Scottish Peasantry, . 50
The Cottage Fireside. 18mo, . . 40

Duncan, G. J. C.

Life of Dr. Duncan, ... 75

Duncan, Mrs. M. G. L.

Memoir of Mary L. Duncan, . . 50
Memoir of George A. Lundie, . . 50
Children of the Manse, . . . 50
America as I Found It, . . . 1 00
The Waking Dream, etc., . . . 25

Duncan, Mrs. Mary L.

Rhymes for My Children, . . . 25

Eadie, Rev. Dr.

*Commentary on the Colossians, . 2 00

Edward Clifford;

Or, Memories of Childhood. 18mo, . 50

Edwards, Jonathan.

Charity and its Fruits, . . . 50

English Pulpit, The.

A Collection of Discourses by the most eminent English divines, . . 1 50

Erskine, Ralph.

Gospel Sonnets. 18mo, . . . 50

Evening Hours with My Children.

Illustrated with 12 quarto plates, . . 75

Evidences of Christianity.

Lectures Delivered at the University of Virginia. 8vo, . . . 2 50

Fanny and Her Mamma.

Illustrated. Square, ... 50

Family Worship;
A Series of Prayers for every Morning and Evening throughout the Year. Adapted to Domestic Worship. By 180 clergymen of Scotland. 8vo. Cloth, ... 3 00

Fisk, Rev. George.
The Holy Land, ... 1 00
An Orphan Tale, ... 25

Flavel's Catechism.
18mo, ...

Fleetwood, John, D.D.
History of the Bible. 8vo, . . 2 00

Florence Egerton.
Illustrated. 18mo, ... 50

Follow Jesus.
By the author of "Come to Jesus," . 25

Ford, Rev. D. E.
Decapolis, ... 25

Foster, John.
Essays; On Decision of Character, 75
On Popular Ignorance, . . . 75

Fox, John.
The Acts and Monuments of the Church; containing the History and Sufferings of the Martyrs. New edition. Edited by M. Hobart Seymour. Royal 8vo. Illustrated, . 4 00

Frank Harrison.
18mo, ... 30

Frank Netherton;
Or, The Talisman. Illustrated, . . 40

Fritz Harold;
Or, The Temptation. 18mo, . . . 40

Fry, Caroline.
Christ our Example. 16mo, . . 75
The Listener. Illustrated. 16mo, . 1 00
Christ our Law. 16mo, . . . 60
The Scripture Reader's Guide, . 30
Sabbath Musings. 18mo, . . . 40

Geldart, Mrs. Thomas.
May Dundas. 18mo, ... 50

Giant Killer, The;
Or, The Battle that All must Fight. By the author of the "Claremont Tales." 18mo, ... 30

Gilfillan, George.
The Martyrs, Heroes, and Bards of the Scottish Covenant, ... 60

Goode, Rev. F.
The Better Covenant, . . . $ 60

Goodrich, C. A.
*A Geography of the Bible, . . . 25

Gosse, Philip Henry.
Life in its Lower, Intermediate, and Higher Forms; or, Manifestations of Divine Wisdom in the Natural History of Animals. Illustr. 12mo, 1 00

Guthrie, Thomas, D.D.
The Gospel in Ezekiel. A Series of Discourses. 12mo, ... 1 00

Guthrie, William.
Christian's Great Interest, . . 50

Grahame, James.
*The Sabbath, and other Poems. Illustrated by Birket Foster. 8vo. Cloth, $2 50; morocco, . . . 3 50

Gray, Thomas.
Elegy Written in a Country Church-yard, and other Poems. Illustrated by Gilbert. Small 8vo. Cloth, $1; full gilt, $1 50; Turkey morocco, ... 3 00

Haldane, Robert.
Exposition of the Romans, . . . 2 50

Haldane, Alexander.
Memoirs of R. and J. A. Haldane, . 2 00

Hall, Joseph, D.D.
Treatises, Devotional and Practical. 16mo, ... 75

Hamilton, James, D.D.
Life in Earnest. 18mo, . . . 30
The Mount of Olives. 18mo, . . 30
Harp on the Willows, . . . 30
Thankfulness. 18mo, . . . 30
Happy Home. Illustrated, . . . 50
Life of Lady Colquhoun, . . . 75
The Royal Preacher, . . . 85
The Lamp and the Lantern, . . 40
Memoir of Richard Williams, . . 75
Emblems from Eden, ... 30
Lessons from the Great Biography,

Hawker, Robert.
The Poor Man's Morning and Evening Portion. In 1 vol., . . . 1 00
Zion's Pilgrim. 18mo, . . . 30

Henry, Philip.
Life. 18mo, ... 50

Henry, Matthew.

*AN EXPOSITION OF THE OLD AND NEW TESTAMENTS. Illustrated with Practical Remarks and Observations. With a Life of the Author by Palmer, and Introductions by Rev. Dr. Alexander and Rev. E. Bickersteth. 5 vols., quarto, sheep, . . . $15 00
MISCELLANEOUS WORKS. 2 vols., . 4 00
A METHOD FOR PRAYER. 18mo, . . 40
THE COMMUNICANT'S COMPANION, . 40
DAILY COMMUNION WITH GOD, . . 30
PLEASANTNESS OF A RELIGIOUS LIFE, . 30

Hervey, Rev. James.

MEDITATIONS AND CONTEMPLATIONS, . 40

Hetherington, Rev. William M.

HISTORY OF THE CHURCH OF SCOTLAND, 1 50
HISTORY OF THE WESTMINSTER ASSEM., 75
THE MINISTER'S FAMILY. A Tale, . 75

Hewitson, Rev. W. H.

MEMOIR OF. By the Rev. J. Baillie, . 85

Hill, George.

LECTURES ON DIVINITY. 8vo, . . 2 00

Historic Doubts

REGARDING NAPOLEON BONAPARTE, . 50

Hodge, Charles, D.D.

EXPOSITION OF THE EPHESIANS, 8vo, . 2 00
*ON FIRST CORINTHIANS. 12mo, . .
ESSAYS AND REVIEWS. 8vo, . . 2 50

Hooker, Rev. H.

THE PHILOSOPHY OF UNBELIEF, . . 75
THE USES OF ADVERSITY. 18mo, . 30

Howard, John;

Or, THE PRISON WORLD OF EUROPE, . 75

Horne, Thomas H.

*AN INTRODUCTION TO THE CRITICAL STUDY AND KNOWLEDGE OF THE HOLY SCRIPTURES. 2 vols., royal 8vo. Half cloth, $3 50; cloth, $4; library style, $5; in 1 vol., sheep, . 4 00

Horne, Bishop.

A COMMENT. ON THE BOOK OF PSALMS, 1 50

Howe, John.

THE REDEEMER'S TEARS, . . . 50

Howell, Rev. J. W.

PERFECT PEACE. 18mo, . . . 30

Howie, John.

THE SCOTS WORTHIES. 8vo, . . 1 50

Huss.

MEMOIR OF JOHN HUSS, . . . 25

Infant's Progress.

Illustrated. 18mo, ... 50

Jacobus, Melancthon W., D.D.

NOTES ON THE NEW TESTAMENT, Critical and Explanatory. And incorporating, with the Notes, on a new plan, the most approved harmony of the four Gospels. With Illustrations.
Vol. I.—MATTHEW. 12mo, . . $ 75
Vol. II.—MARK AND LUKE. 12mo, . 75
Vol. III.—JOHN. 12mo, . . . 75
Vol. IV.—ACTS. (Preparing), . .
*CATECHETICAL QUESTION-BOOKS ON THE ABOVE:
Vol. I.—MATTHEW, per dozen, . . 1 50
Vol. II.—MARK. " . . 1 50
Vol. III.—LUKE, " . . 1 50
Vol. IV.—JOHN, " . . 1 50

James, Rev. John Angel.

THE YOUNG WOMAN'S FRIEND, . . 75
THE YOUNG MAN'S FRIEND, . . . 75
CHRISTIAN DUTY, ... 75
THE COURSE OF FAITH, ... 75
CHRISTIAN PROFESSOR. 16mo, . . 75
THE CHRISTIAN FATHER'S PRESENT, . 75
THE ANXIOUS INQUIRER, . . . 30
CHRISTIAN PROGRESS, ... 30
THE TRUE CHRISTIAN, ... 30
THE WIDOW DIRECTED, . . . 30
YOUNG MAN FROM HOME. 18mo, . 30

Jamie Gordon.

Illustrated. 18mo, ... 50

Janeway, James.

HEAVEN UPON EARTH, ... 50
A TOKEN FOR CHILDREN, . . . 30

Jay, Rev. William.

MORNING AND EVENING EXERCISES, for every day in the year. New and elegant edition, on large type and fine paper. In 4 thick vols., royal 12mo, ... 4 00
MORNING EXERCISES. Common edit., 75
EVENING EXERCISES. Common edition, 75
FEM. SCRIPTURE CHARACTERS. 12mo, 1 00
AUTOBIOGRAPHY AND REMINISCENCES, 1 25
THE CHRISTIAN CONTEMPLATED. 18mo, 40

Jeanie Morrison.

Illustrated. 18mo, ... 50

By the same Author:

KATE KILBORN. Illustrated. 18mo, . 50
THE PASTOR'S FAMILY. 18mo, . . 25

Job, The Book of.

*THE BOOK OF JOB. Illustrated with fifty Engravings, from drawings by John Gilbert. 8vo, cloth, gilt, $; Turkey morocco, ...

Johnson, Dr. Samuel.

RASSELAS, ... 50

Kennedy, Grace.
- ANNA ROSS, ... $ 30
- PHILIP COLVILLE, ... 30
- FATHER CLEMENT, ... 30
- PROFESSION IS NOT PRINCIPLE, . . 30
- JESSY ALLAN, THE LAME GIRL, . . 25
- DECISION, ... 25

Key, F. S.
- POEMS, including the "Star-Spangled Banner." 16mo, ... 75

Key
- TO ASSEMBLY'S SHORTER CATECHISM, . 20

King, David, LL.D.
- THE RULING ELDERSHIP, . . . 50

Kitto, John.
- DAILY BIBLE ILLUSTRATIONS. 8 vols., 8 00
- THE LOST SENSES. 12mo, . . . 1 00
- LIFE. By Ryland. 2 vols., 12mo, . 2 00

Krummacher, F. W., D.D.
- THE MARTYR LAMB, ... 40
- THE LAST DAYS OF ELISHA, . . . 50

Lectures to Young Men.
- Delivered in London. Per vol., . . 1 00

Leighton, Bishop.
- ON THE CREED, LORD'S PRAYER, etc., . 75

Lee, William.
- *THE INSPIRATION OF HOLY SCRIPTURE, 2 50

Lighted Valley, The.
- MEMOIR OF MISS BOLTON. 16mo, . 75

Little Annie's First Book.
- With 70 cuts, ... 35

Little Annie's Second Book.
- Illustrated. Square, ... 40

Little Lessons for Little Children.
- Colored plates, ... 50

Living to Christ.
- 18mo, ... 40

Locke, John.
- THE REASONABLENESS OF CHRISTIANITY, 75

Loftus, William K.
- TRAVELS AND RESEARCHES IN CHALDEA AND SUSIANA. 8vo. Illustrated, . 2 00

Luther, Martin.
- A COMMENTARY ON GALATIANS, . . 1 50

Lyman, Henry.
- THE MARTYR OF SUMATRA. 12mo, . 1 00

Mackay, Mrs. Colonel.
- THE FAMILY AT HEATHERDALE, . . 50

Mamma's Bible Stories.
- Square. Plates, ... $ 50
- SEQUEL TO THE SAME. Plates, . . 50

Marshall, Walter.
- ON SANCTIFICATION, ... 50

Mason, Jno. M., D.D.,
- *MEMOIR OF, ... 2 00

Martyrs and Covenanters.
- 18mo, ... 40

McCheyne, Rev. R. M.,
- WORKS OF. 2 vols., 8vo, . . . 3 00
- LIFE AND LETTERS, separate, . . 1 50
- SERMONS, separate, ... 2 00

McCosh, James, D.D.
- ON THE DIVINE GOVERNMENT. 8vo, . 2 00
- TYPICAL FORMS AND SPECIAL ENDS, . 2 00

McCrindell, Miss R.
- THE CONVENT, ... 50
- THE SCHOOL-GIRL IN FRANCE, . . 50

McGhee, Rev. Robert J.
- LECTURES ON EPHESIANS, . . . 2 00

McIlvaine, Rt. Rev. C. P.
- THE TRUTH AND LIFE. 8vo, . . 2 00

Meikle, James.
- SOLITUDE SWEETENED, ... 60

Michael Kemp.
- Illustrated. 18mo, ... 40

Missionary of Kilmany, The.
- BEING A MEMOIR OF ALEX. PATERSON, 40

Missions.
- *THE ORIGIN AND HISTORY OF MISSIONS, 3 50

Morning and Night Watches.
- 16mo, ... 60

By the same Author:
- THE FOOTSTEPS OF ST. PAUL, . . 1 00
- THE WORDS OF JESUS. 16mo, . . 40
- THE MIND OF JESUS. 16mo, . . 40
- MIND AND WORDS OF JESUS, in 1 vol., . 60
- FAMILY PRAYERS. 16mo, . . . 75
- THE WOODCUTTER OF LEBANON, etc., . 50
- THE GREAT JOURNEY, ... 30
- EVENING INCENSE. 16mo, . . . 40
- MEMORIES OF BETHANY. 16mo, . . 60
- FAITHFUL PROMISER & ALTAR STONES, 25

Moore, Rev. T. V.
- A COMMENTARY ON HAGGAI, ZECHARIAH, AND MALACHI. 8vo, . . 2 00

More, Hannah.
- PRIVATE DEVOTIONS. In a handsome 18mo, 50c.; in 32mo, 20c.; gilt, . . 30

Morell, J. D.
History of Modern Philosophy, $3 00

Newton, Rev. John,
The Works of, ... 2 00

Newton, Miss A. L.,
Memoirs of. By Rev. J. Baillie, . 75

Opie, Amelia.
Tales; or, Illustrations of Lying, . 40

Owen, John, D.D.
*On the Hebrews. 8 vols., 8vo, . 12 00
On Spiritual Mindedness, . . . 60

Paley, William.
Evidences of Christianity. 12mo, . 1 25
Horæ Paulinæ. 8vo, ... 75

Pascal, Blaise.
The Provincial Letters, ... 1 00

Paterson, A. S.
On the Shorter Catechism, . . . 50

Pearson, Rev. Thomas.
On Infidelity. 8vo, ... 1 00

Peep of Day.
18mo, ... 30

By the same Author:
Line upon Line, ... 30
Precept upon Precept, ... 30
Scripture Facts. 32mo, ... 50
Near Home, ... 50
Far Off, ... 50

Philip, Rev. Robert.
Devotional Guides. 2 vols., . . 1 50

Pollok, Robert.
The Course of Time. 16mo, cloth, . 75
Tales of the Covenanters, . . 50
Helen of the Glen. 18mo, . . 25
The Persecuted Family. 18mo, . 25
Ralph Gemmell. 18mo, . . . 25

Poole, Matthew.
*Annotations on the Bible. 3 vols., 10 00

Quarles, Francis.
Emblems, Divine and Moral, . . 75

Ray of Light, A.
By the author of "A Trap to Catch a Sunbeam," 35

Richmond, Legh.
Annals of the Poor, ... 40
Domestic Portraiture, ... 75

Ridgely, Thomas, D.D.
A Body of Divinity. 2 vols., 8vo, . 4 00

Romaine, Rev. William.
Life, Walk, and Triumph of Faith, $ 60
Letters on Important Subjects, . 60

Ryle, Rev. J. C.
Living or Dead? 18mo, ... 50
Wheat or Chaff? 18mo, ... 50
Startling Questions. 18mo, . . 50
Rich and Poor, ... 50
Priest, Puritan, and Preacher, . 50
Expository Thoughts on the Gospels:
Matthew. 12mo, ...
Mark and Luke, ...
John, ...

Rutherford, Samuel.
Letters of Rev. Samuel Rutherford, 1 50

Sampson, F. S., D.D.
*A Critical Comment. on Hebrews, 2 50

Schmeid, C. Von.
A Hundred Short Tales, ... 50

Scotia's Bards.
Illustrated. Cloth, $2; cloth, gilt, . 2 50

Sermons on Retirement, etc.
By Hall, Taylor, Leighton, Barrow, South, and others. 16mo, . . . 75

Seymour, Rev. M. H.
Evenings with the Romanists. 12mo, 1 00

Sigourney, Mrs. L. H.
Water Drops, ... 75
Letters to my Pupils. 18mo, . . 50
Olive Leaves. Illustrated. 18mo, . 50
The Faded Hope. 18mo, . . . 50
The Boy's Book. 18mo, . . . 40
The Girl's Book. 18mo, . . . 40
The Child's Book. Square, . . 35

Sinclair, Catherine.
Modern Accomplishments, . . . 75
Modern Society, ... 75
Charlie Seymour, ... 30
Holiday House, ... 50

Sprague, Rev. W. B., D.D.
*Annals of the American Pulpit.
Vols. I. & II.—Congregationalists, 5 00
Vols. III. & IV.—Presbyterians, .

Stevenson, Rev. John.
Christ on the Cross. 12mo, . . 75
The Lord our Shepherd, . . . 60
Gratitude, ... 75

Storrs, R. S., D.D.
On the Human Soul. 8vo, . . 1 75

Symington, Rev. Wm., D.D.
On the Atonement, ... 75

Tales from English History.
Illustrated. 18mo, ... 50

Tales from Travellers.
By Maria Hack. 16mo, . . . $ 75

Tales from History of Sweden
AND THE NORSEMEN. 16mo, . . . 75

Taylor, Jeremy, D.D.
THE SERMONS OF JEREMY TAYLOR, . 1 50
LIFE OF CHRIST, 3 vols., ... 2 25
LIBERTY OF PROPHESYING, . . . 75
GOLDEN GROVE, ... 75

Taylor, Isaac.
LOYOLA, ... 75
NATURAL HISTORY OF ENTHUSIASM, . 75

Taylor, Jane.
LIMED TWIGS, ... 50
HYMNS FOR INFANT MINDS, ... 40
LIFE AND CORRESPONDENCE, . . 40
DISPLAY, a Tale. 18mo, . . . 30
ORIGINAL POEMS, ... 40
RHYMES FOR THE NURSERY, . . . 50
CONTRIBUTIONS OF Q. Q. 18mo, . . 50

The Way Home.
18mo, ... 50

Theological Sketch-Book;
Or, SKETCHES OF SERMONS. 2 vols., 8vo, 3 00

Thornwell, J. H., D.D.
DISCOURSES ON TRUTH, ... 1 00

Three Months under the Snow.
18mo, ... 30

True Heroism.
18mo, ... 25

Tucker, Miss E.
THE RAINBOW IN THE NORTH, . . 50
ABBEOKUTTA, ... 50
SOUTHERN CROSS & SOUTHERN CROWN, 50

Tulloch, Rev. Dr.
THEISM, ... 1 00

Turnbull, Rev. R.
THE GENIUS OF SCOTLAND. 12mo, . 1 00

Tyng, S. H., D.D.
LAW AND THE GOSPEL, ... 1 00
THE ISRAEL OF GOD, ... 1 00
CHRIST IS ALL, ... 1 00
THE RICH KINSMAN. 16mo, . . 1 00
RECOLLECTIONS OF ENGLAND. 12mo, . 1 00
CHRISTIAN TITLES. 16mo, . . . 75

Tyng, Rev. Dudley A.
THE CHILDREN OF THE KINGDOM. 16mo,

Vara;
Or, THE CHILD OF ADOPTION, . . 1 00
By the same Author:
NELLIE OF TRURO. 12mo, . . . 1 00

Very Little Tales.
2 vols., ... 75

Vicars, Captain Hedley.
MEMOIRS OF. 18mo, ... 40

Victory Won.
By the same author. 18mo, . . 25

Walter Binning;
ILLUSTRATIONS OF THE LORD'S PRAYER, 25

Wardlaw, Rev. Ralph, D.D.
ON MIRACLES. 12mo, ... 75

Watson, Thomas.
BODY OF DIVINITY. 8vo, . . . 2 00

Watts, Isaac.
HORÆ LYRICÆ. 16mo, ... 75
DIVINE AND MORAL SONGS, . . . 40

Week, The.
18mo, ... 50

Whately, Richard, D.D.
THE KINGDOM OF CHRIST DELINEATED, 75

Whitecross, John.
ANECDOTES ON THE CATECHISM, . . 30

White, Rev. Hugh.
MEDITATIONS ON PRAYER, . . . 40
THE BELIEVER, ... 40
ON THE SECOND ADVENT, . . . 40
WORKS OF HENRY KIRKE WHITE, . 1 00

Wilberforce, William.
A MEMOIR OF WILLIAM WILBERFORCE, 50
A PRACTICAL VIEW. 12mo, . . 1 00

Wilson, John.
LIGHTS AND SHADOWS OF SCOT. LIFE, . 75

Willison, John.
SACRAMENTAL MEDITATIONS, . . 50
COMMUNICANT'S CATECHISM. Per doz., 75

Winslow, Octavius.
MIDNIGHT HARMONIES, ... 60
PERSONAL DECLENSION AND REVIVAL, 60

Wings and Stings.
18mo, ... 25

Young, Edward.
NIGHT THOUGHTS. 16mo, . . . 75
Small edition. Close type. 18mo, . 40

Young, John, M.A.
THE CHRIST OF HISTORY. 12mo, . . 75